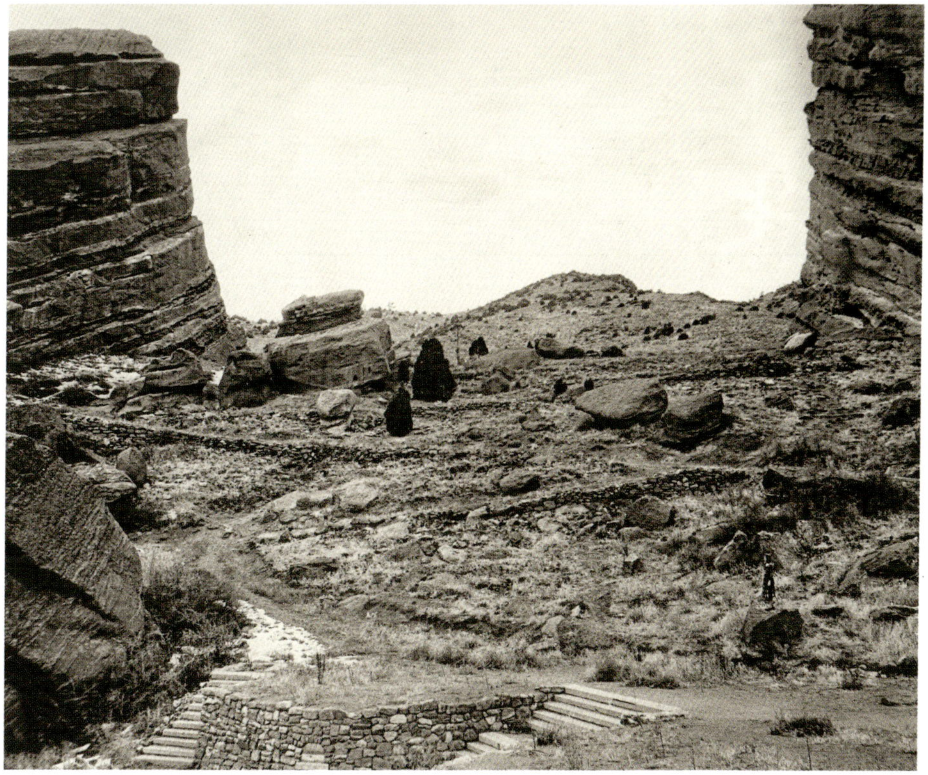

Garden of the Titans, c. 1920

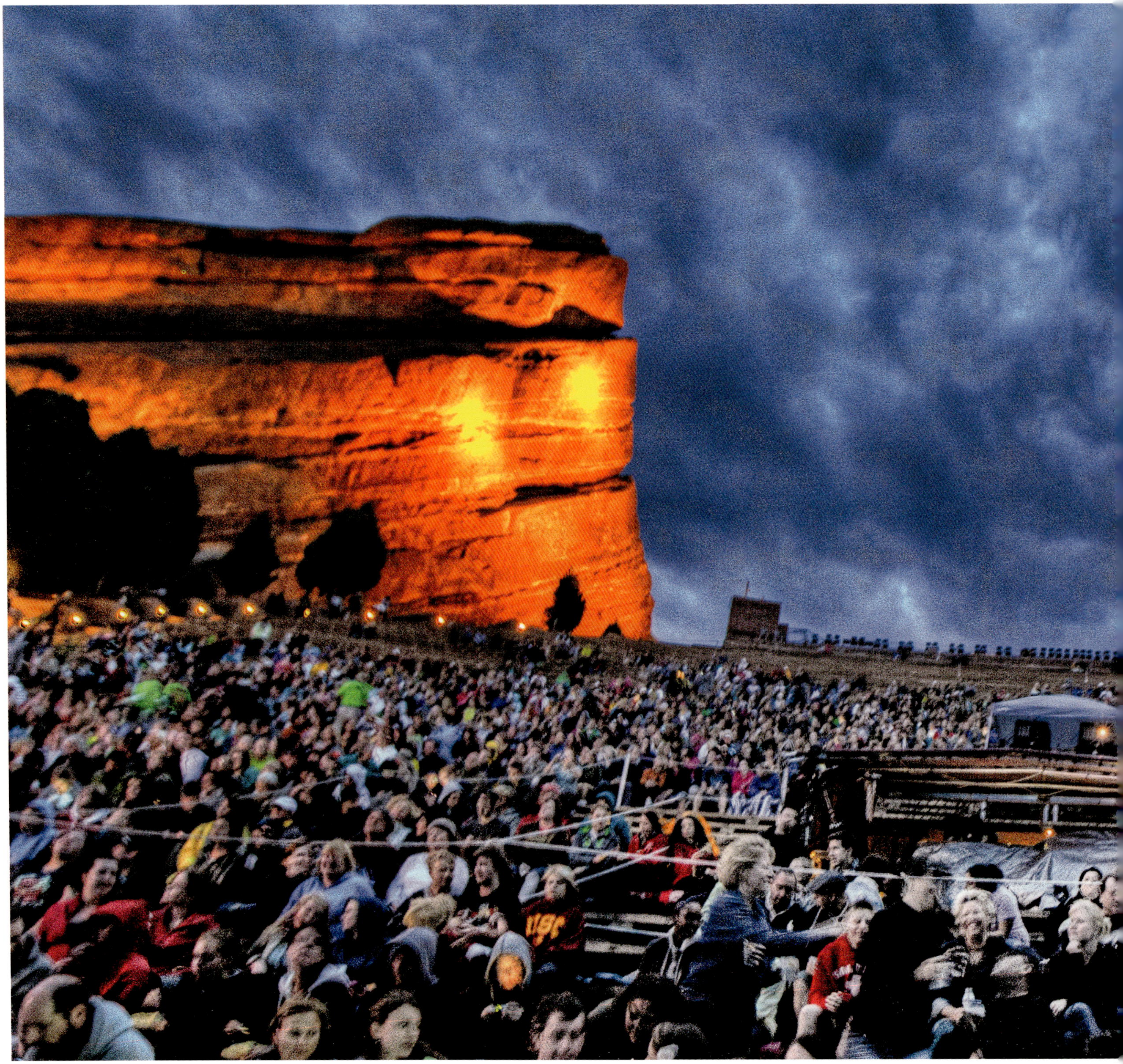

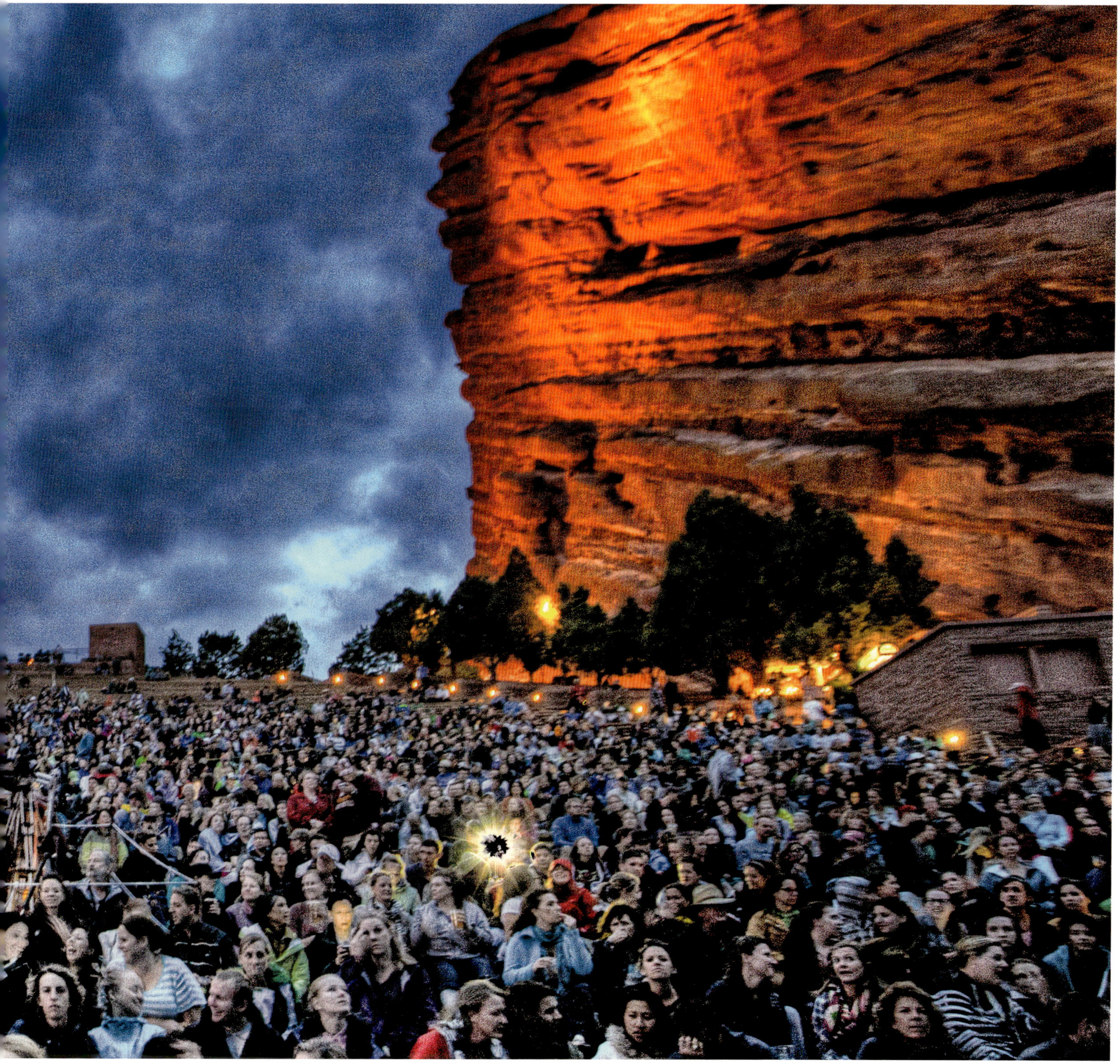

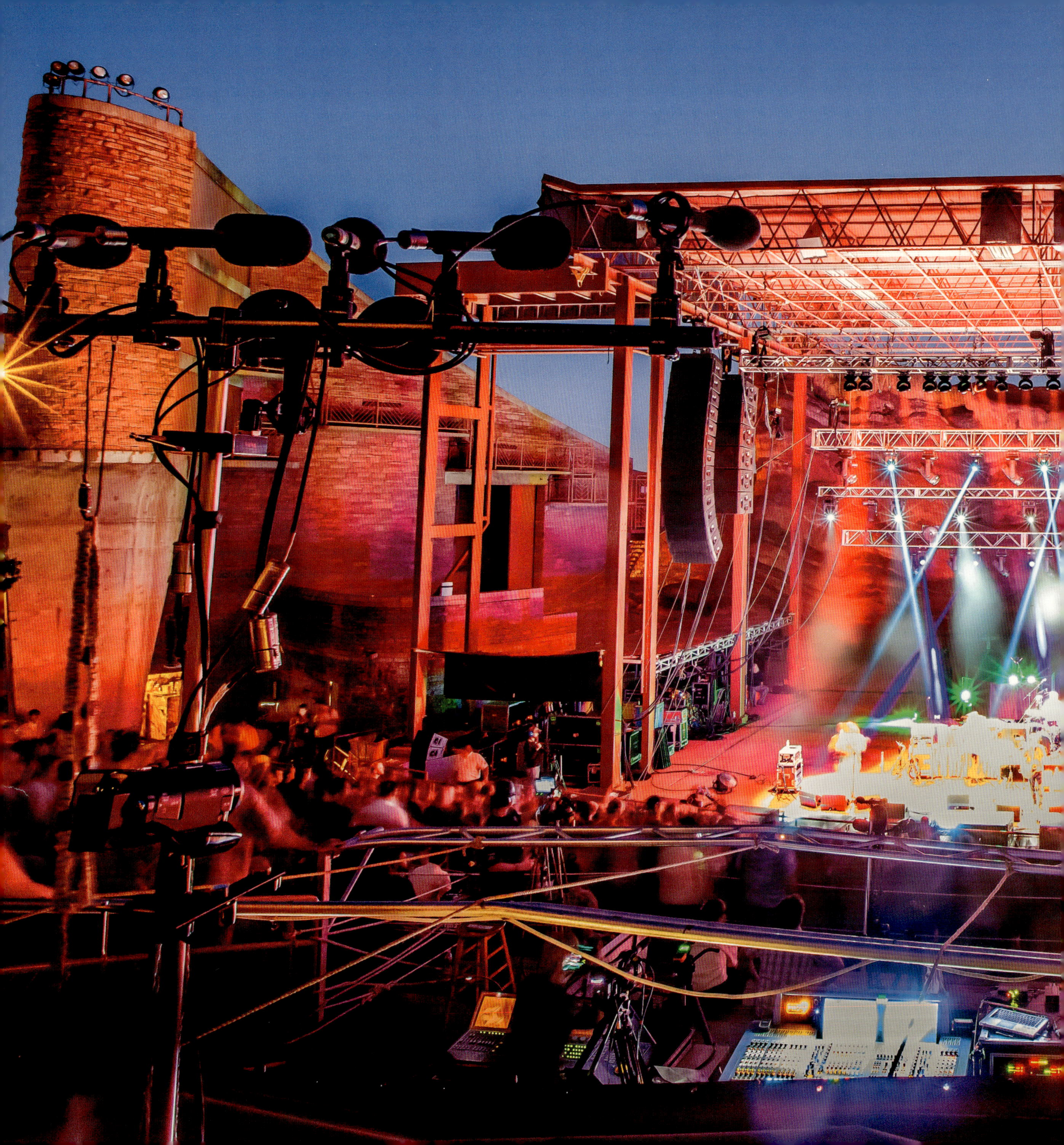

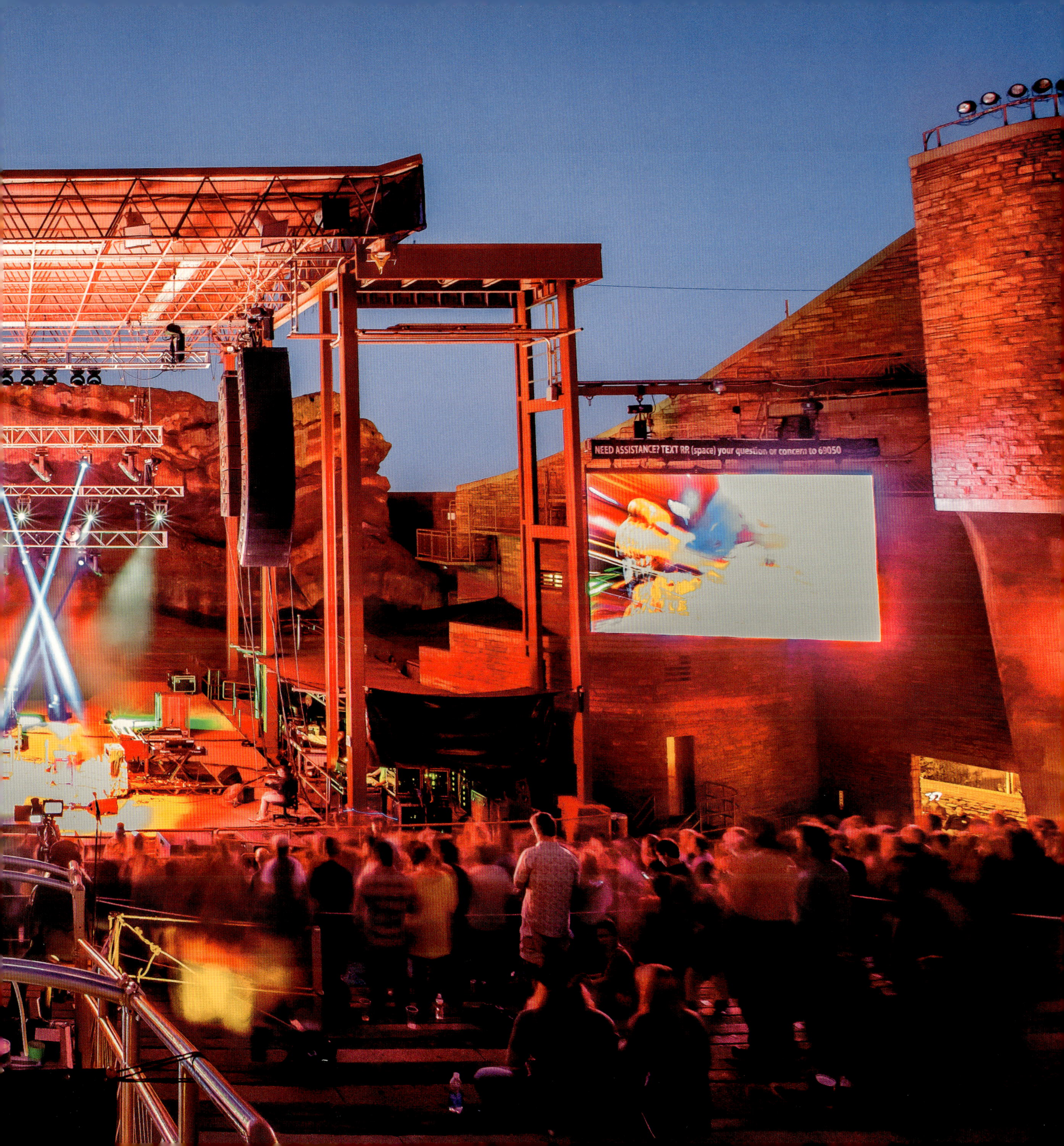
NEED ASSISTANCE? TEXT RR (space) your question or concern to 69050

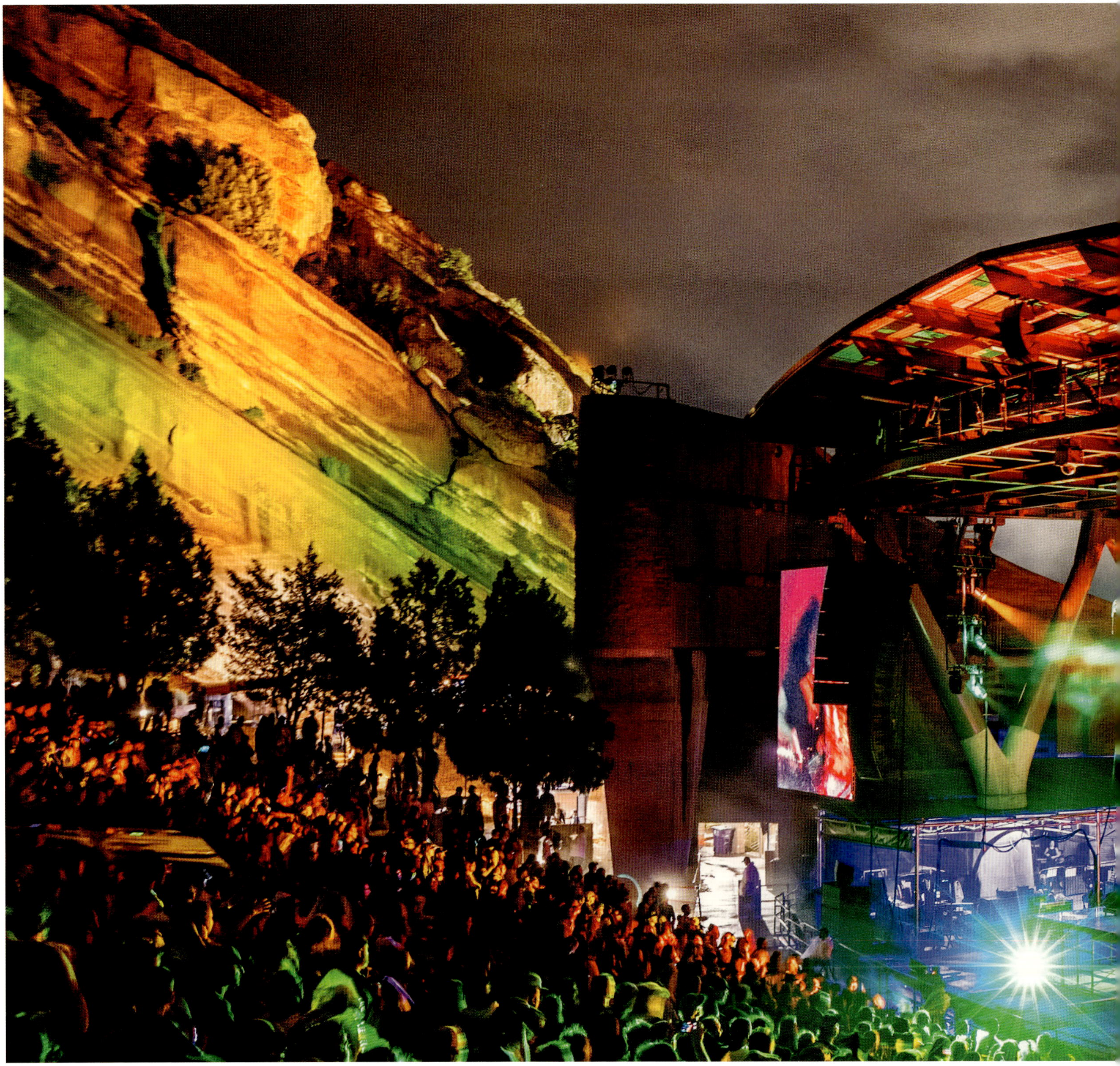

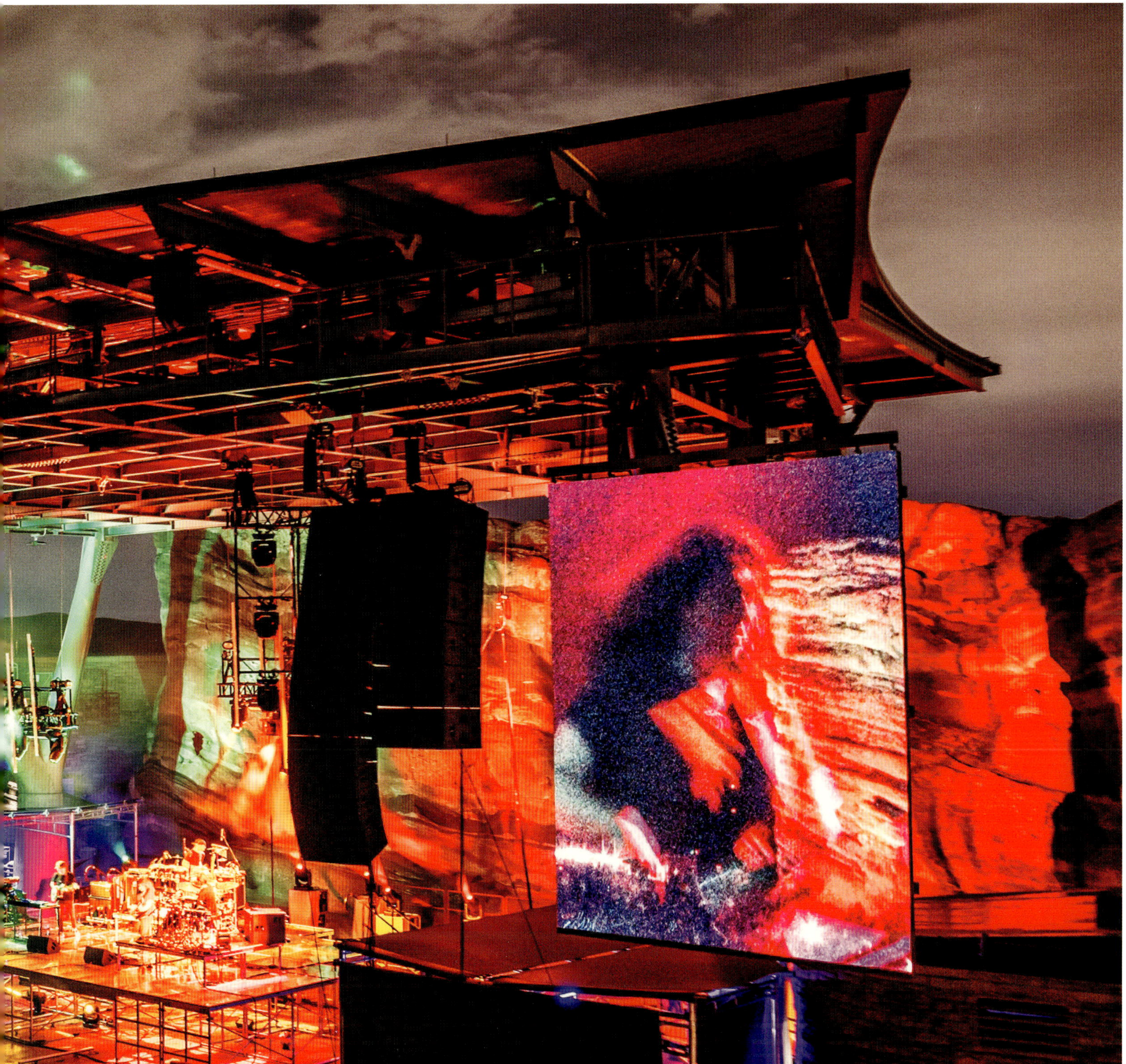

Previous spreads
Pages 2-3: c. 2012
Pages 4-5: c. 2012
Pages 6-7: Sound Tribe Sector Nine, 2021

Facing page: Red Rocks Park, 1938
Following spread: Billy & the Kids, 2015

EDITOR | **JON RIZZI**
ART DIRECTOR | **KATE GLASSNER BRAINERD**

ISBN: 978-0-9915668-7-7
Printed in China through Asia Pacific Offset

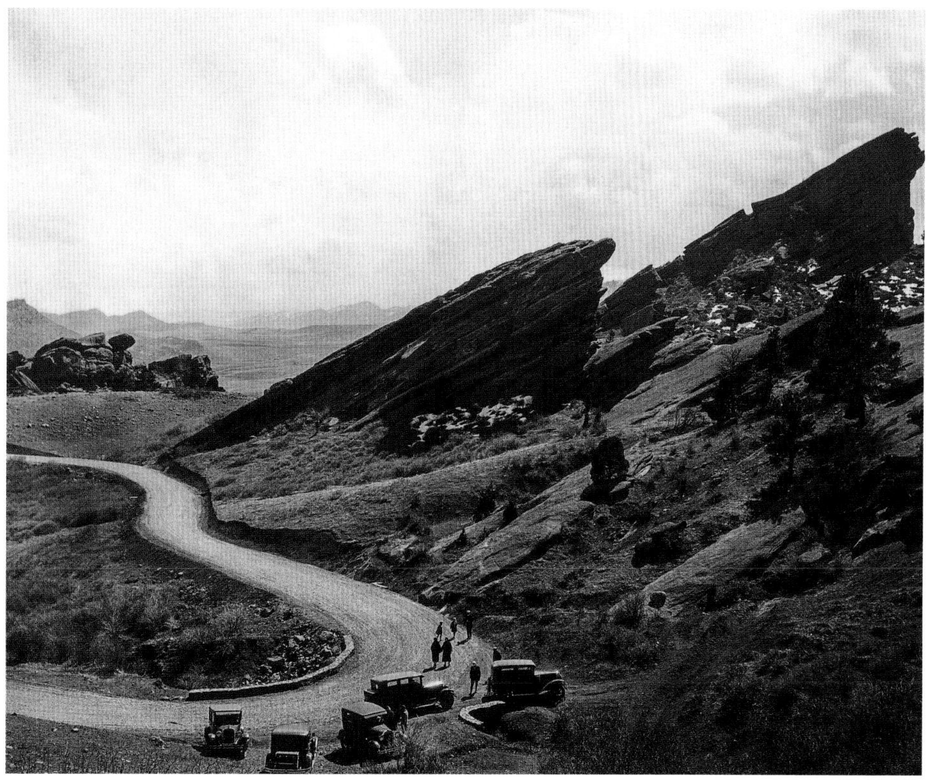

Garden of the Titans, c. 1920

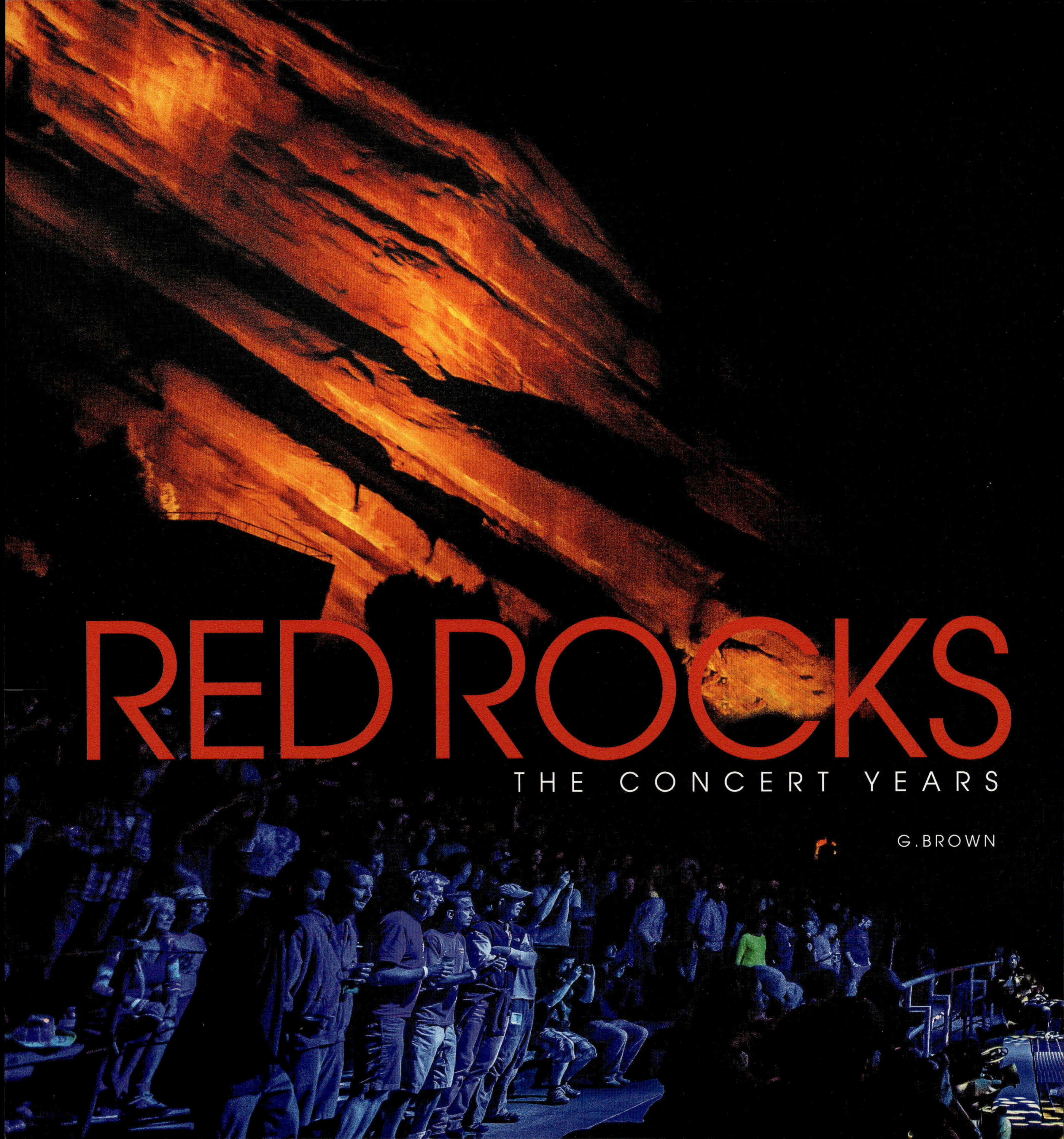

RED ROCKS

THE CONCERT YEARS

G.BROWN

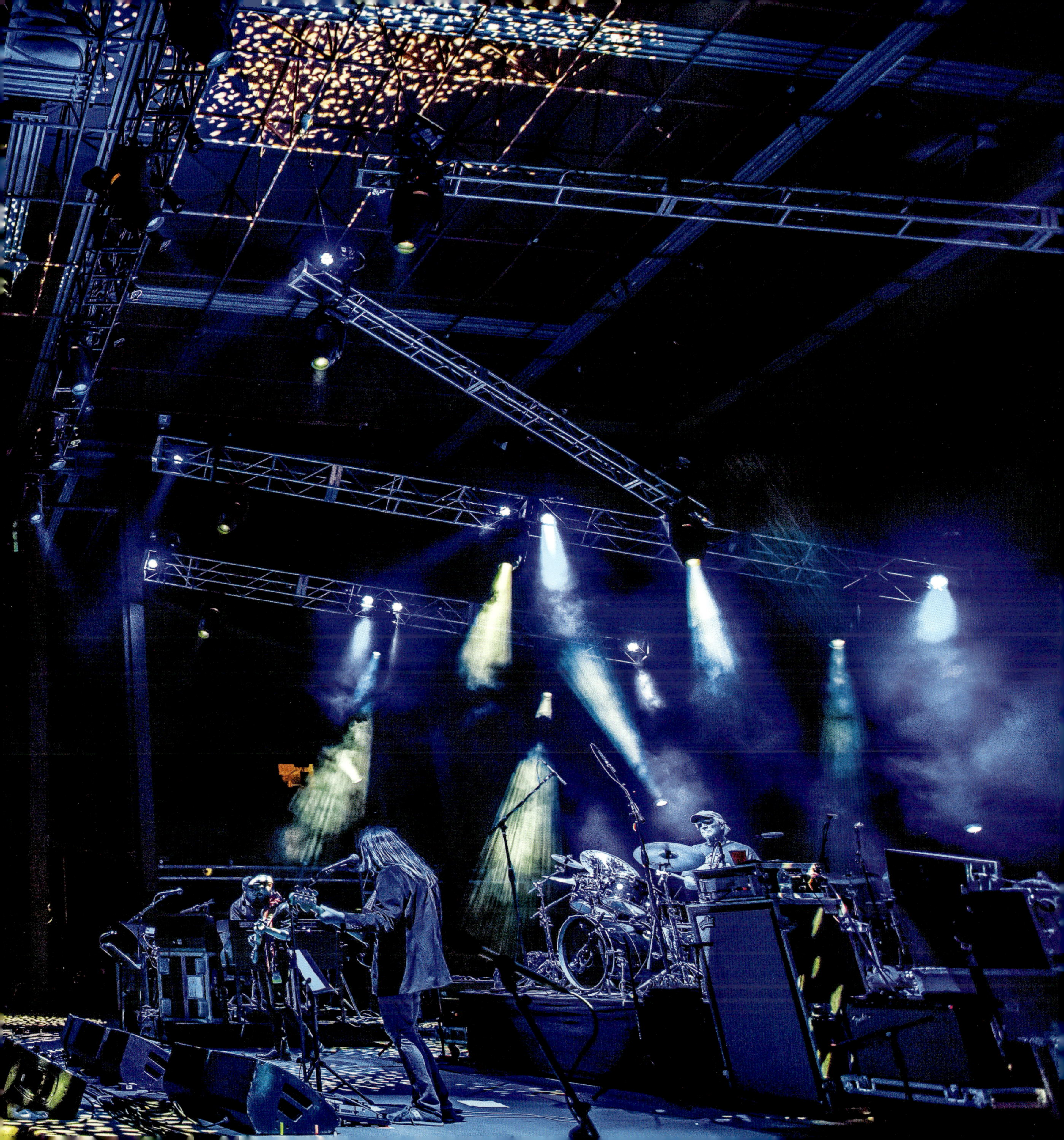

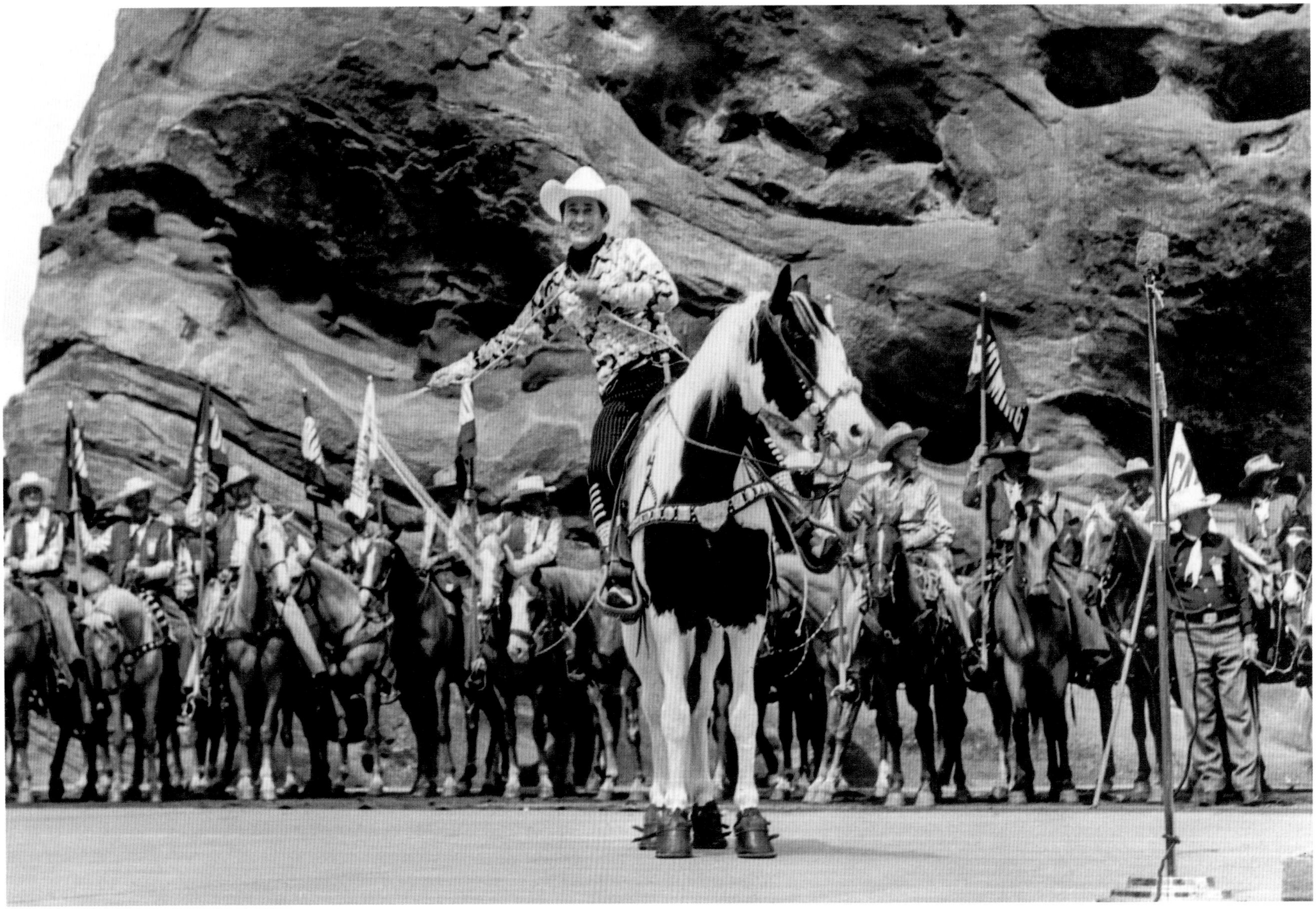

Montie Montana with the Roundup Riders of the Rockies, 1952

CONTENTS

GALLERIES

FOREWORD CARLOS SANTANA

RED ROCKS is not just dirt and stones and sky. It's a temple, a shrine. It's the same setting that that the Greeks performed in at the beginning of civilization, and it definitely has the sacred American Indian spirit—you can feel the vibe. There is nothing like playing at Red Rocks under a full moon. Anything can happen!

I first performed at Red Rocks in 1979. It was very special that nature sculpted this venue for musicians to engage with the audience. You're totally connected and close to each person there. You get to see and feel everything. All you have to do is take a deep breath, go inside and be soulful, sincere and honest with the music you're offering. That's the best thing that any musician can do, no matter who you are. And at a place like Red Rocks, it's almost natural, because you can't hide. You can't lip-synch there. If you suck, you're going to suck. If you're supreme with excellence, you're going to be supreme with excellence.

There's a vortex of energy in Red Rocks. It takes the music to another level, especially if the musicians who will manifest the music are sensitive—then something else takes over. When I'm backstage and I see the pictures of so many people who have played there, I feel wonderment. It's a shame that the pictures don't have a CD or video counterpart. In fact, I would suggest that Red Rocks should sell its own CDs—Stevie Ray Vaughan live at Red Rocks, the Beatles at Red Rocks, Santana or Robert Randolph—all representing the magic from this venue.

The erratic weather enhances this magic. For a period of about four or five years, every time we played at Red Rocks, it rained, and I mean really rained. So I was thinking we should just charge people extra because we're going to bring rain with us. If you have a drought, call us—we'll end it!

Seeing concerts at Red Rocks, you can put aside your everyday worries. When musicians who can really, really play bombard your molecules, it makes your spirits even stronger. I always feel very grateful and honored that I'm able to bring our music in. The whole experience is still very impressive, because the venue continues to do new things to be even more accommodating to people. I'm happy to put it this way: God is a good architect. ■

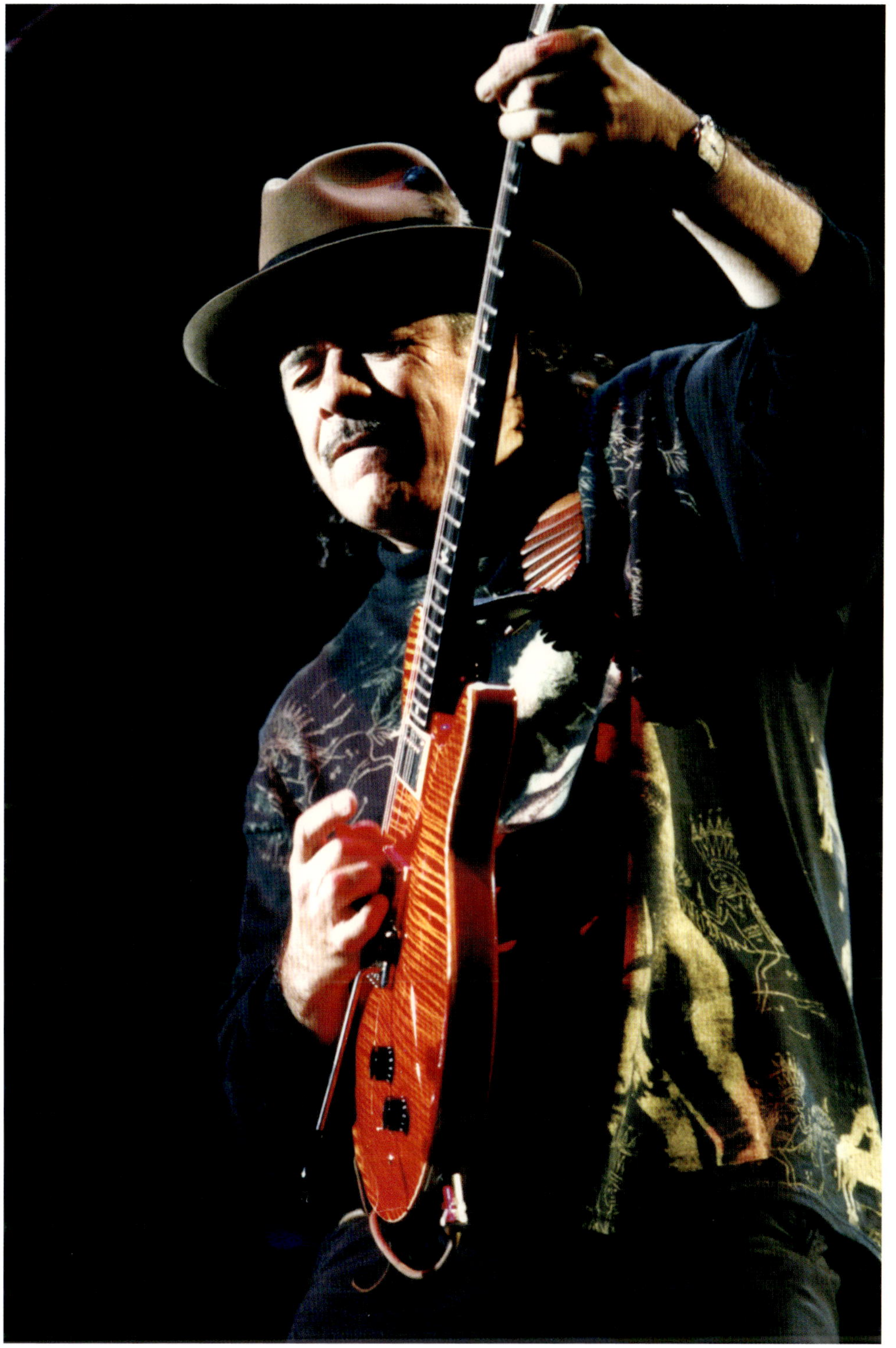

Santana, 1999

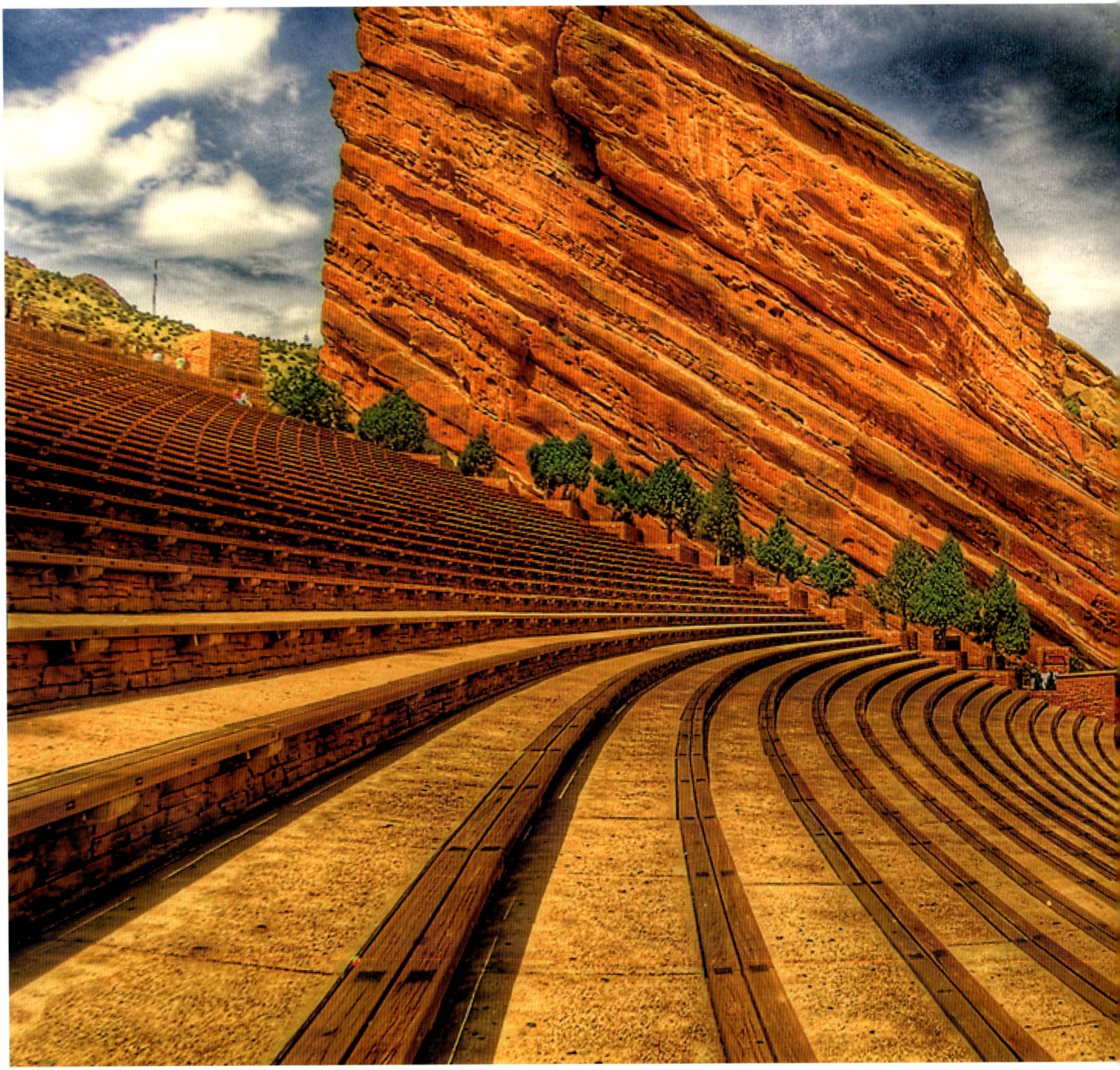

c. 2009

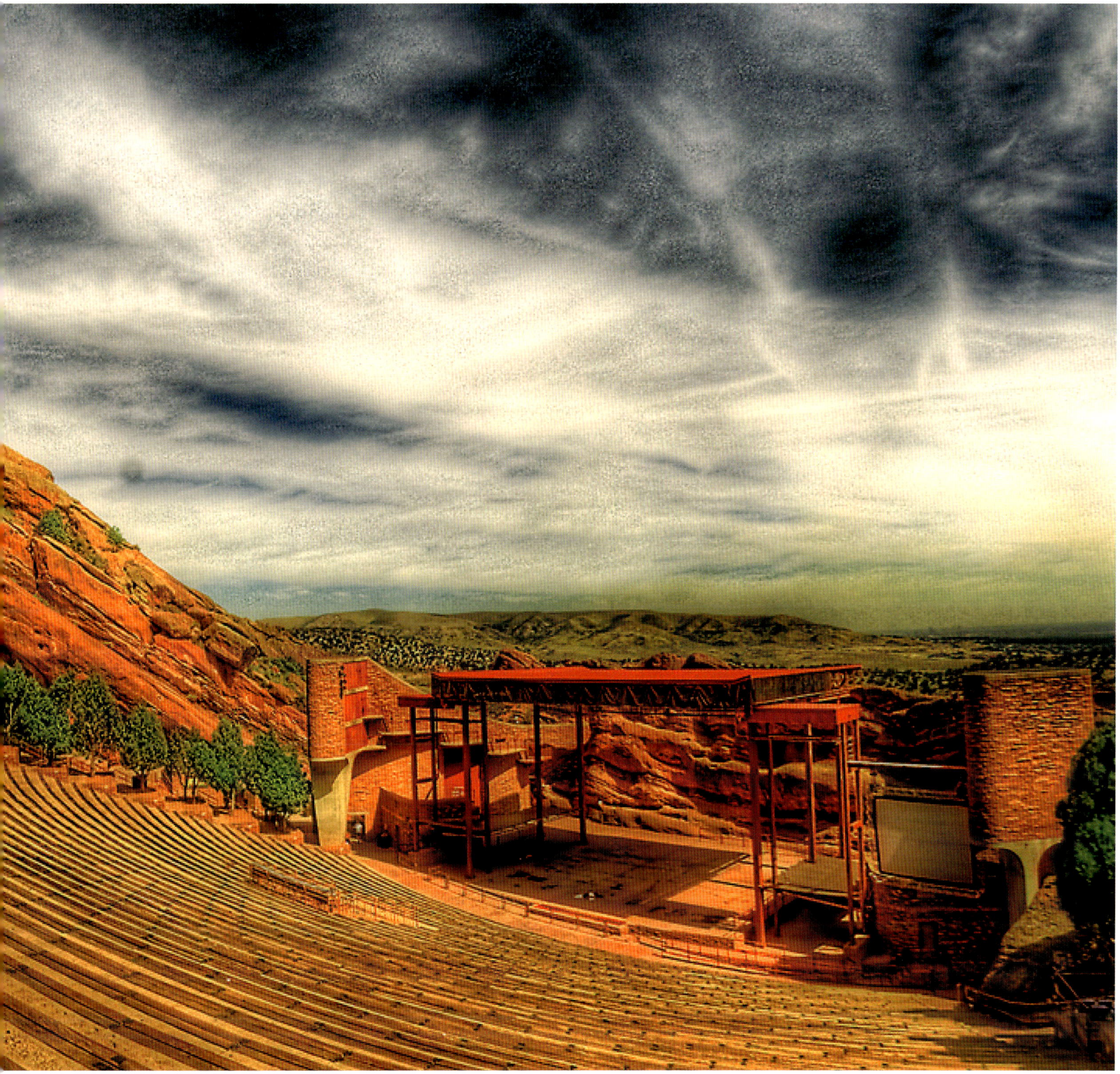

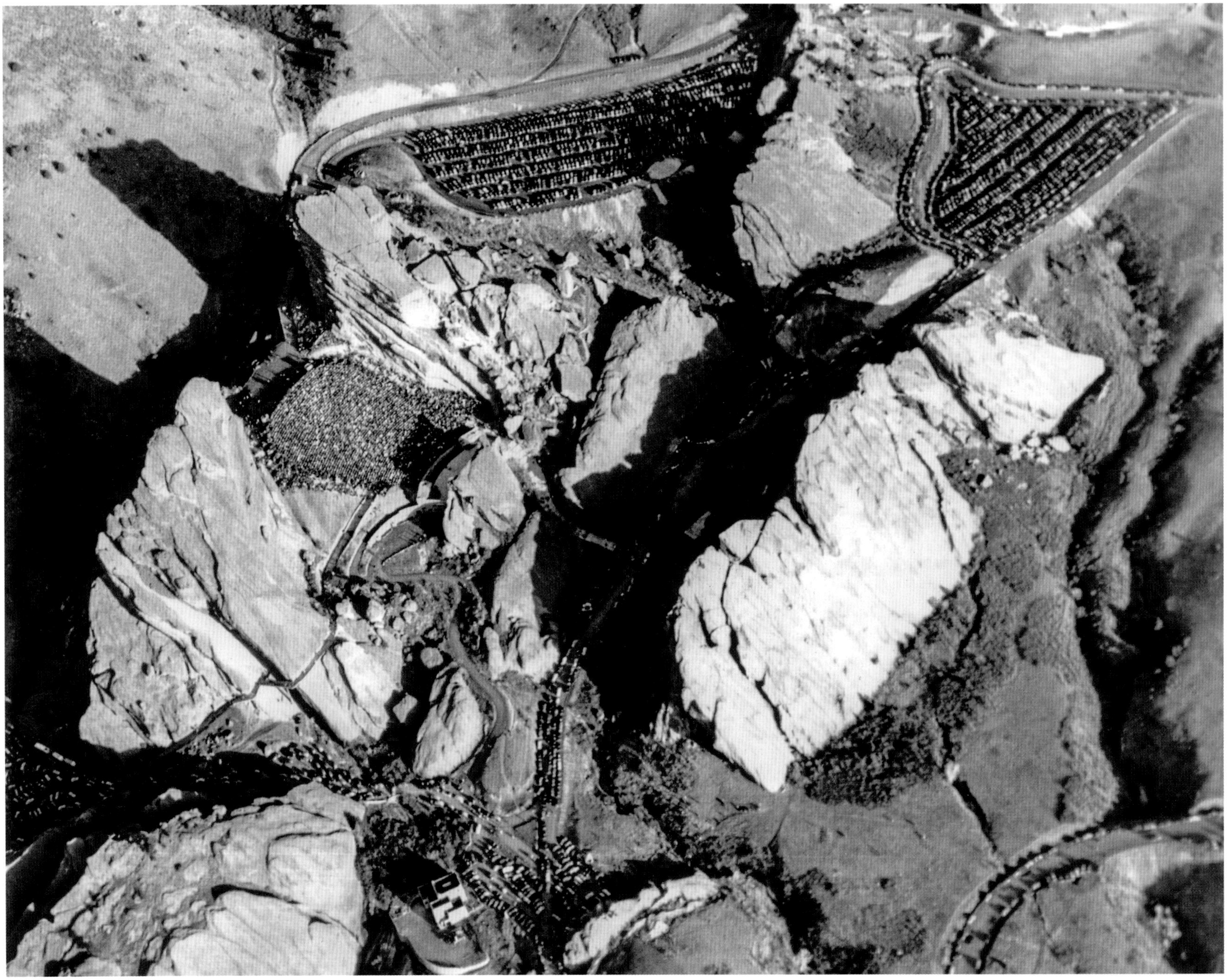

c. 1957

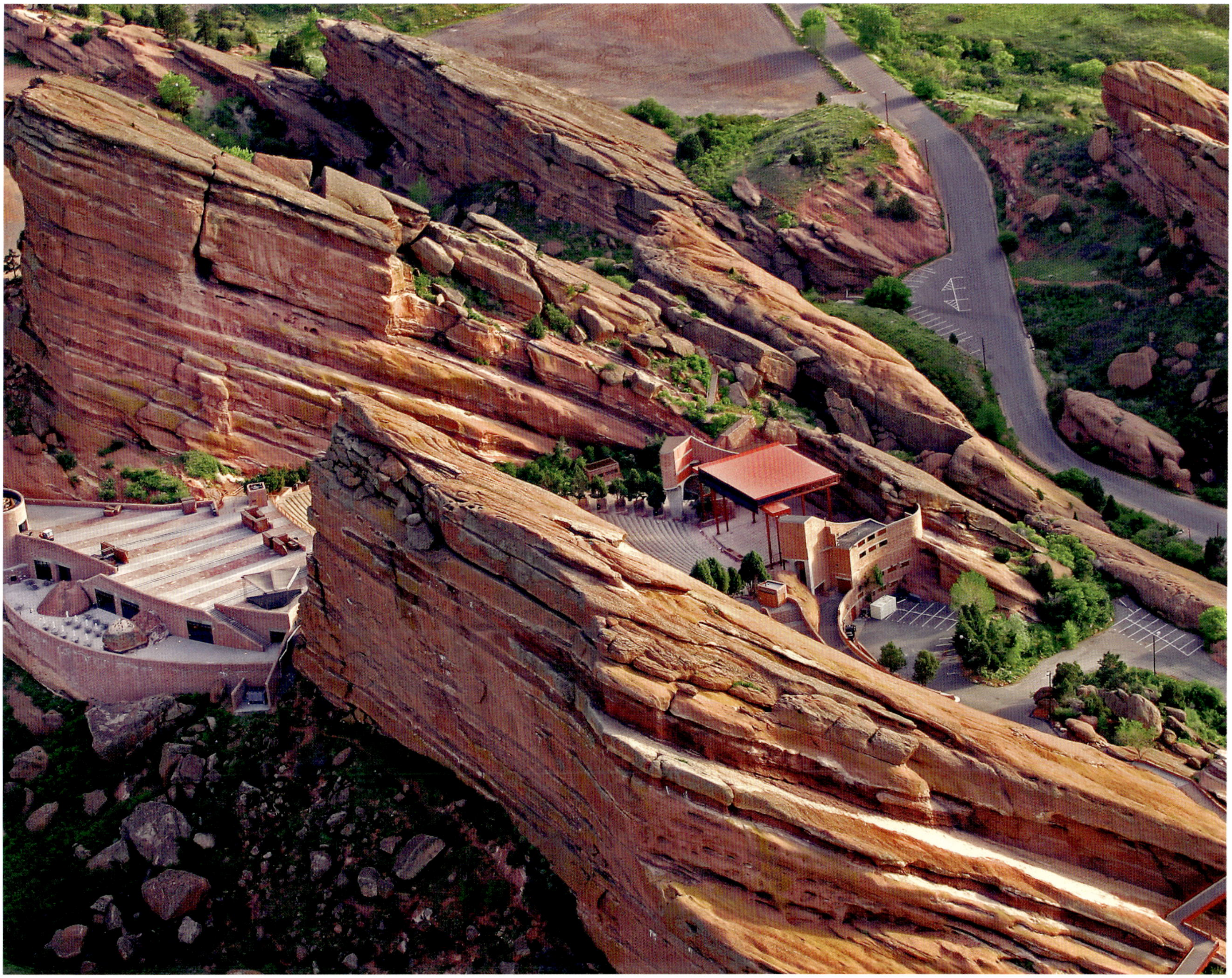

c. 2003

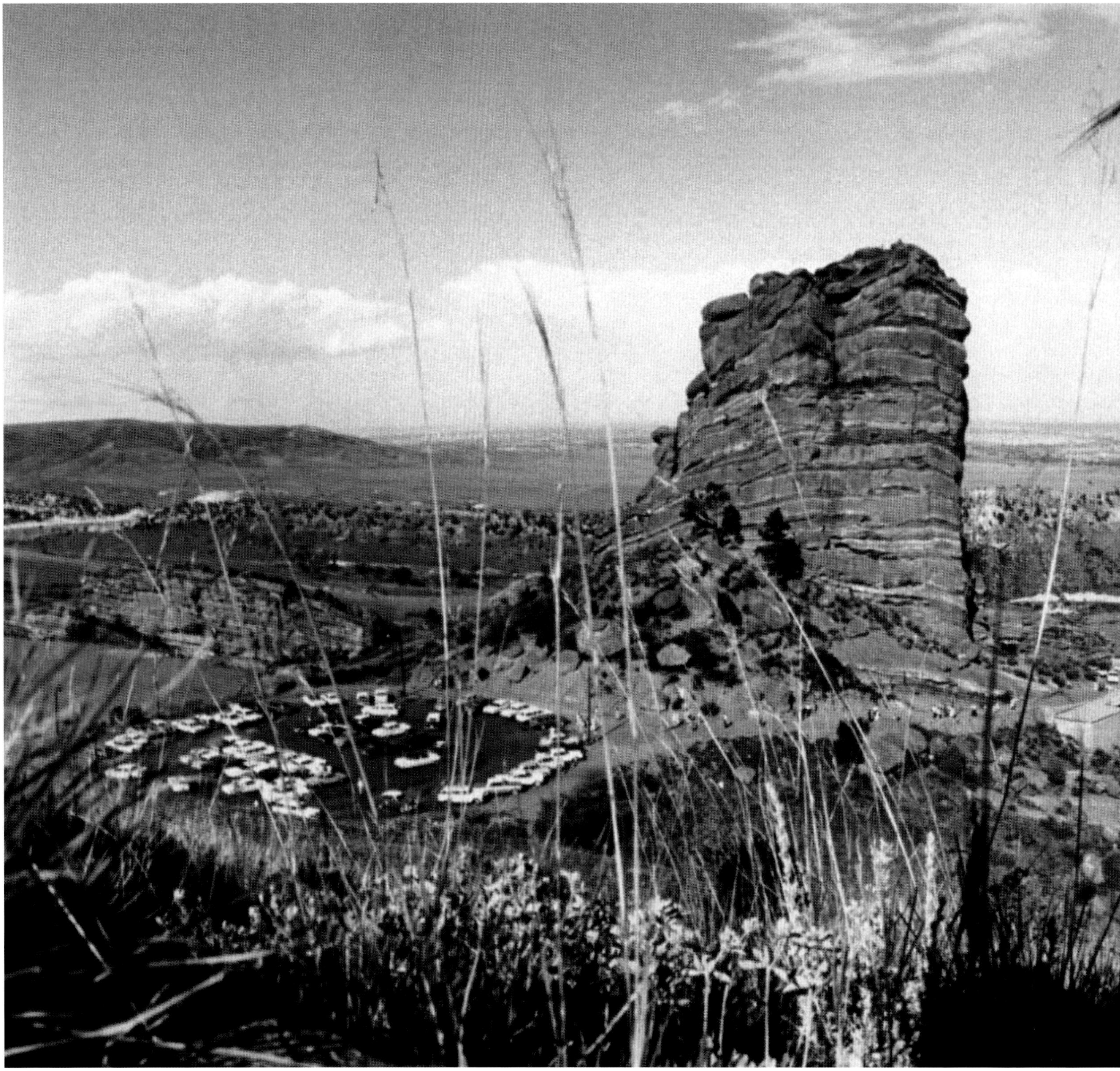

c. 1962

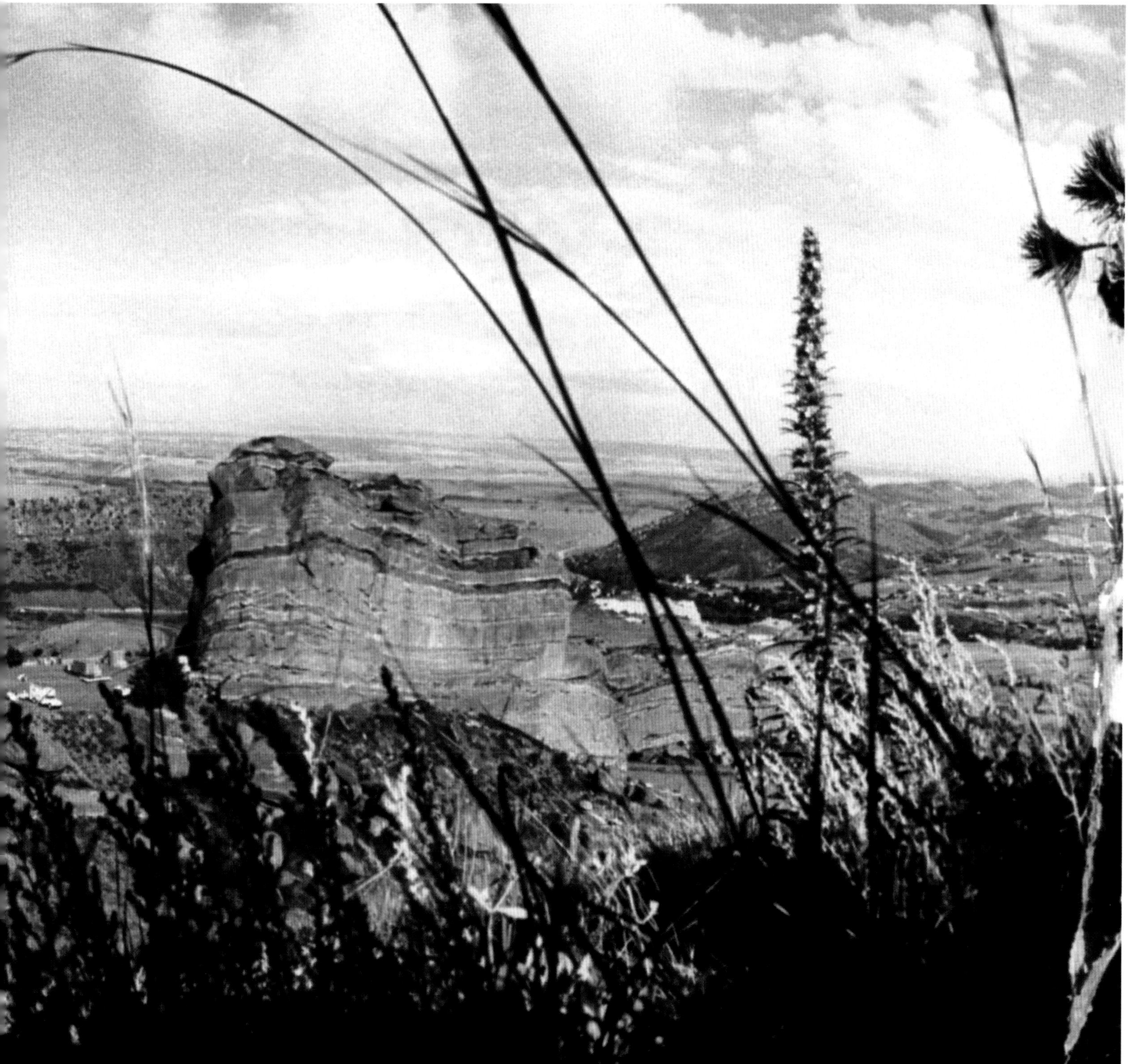

DEEP IN the foothills of Morrison, Colorado, twenty minutes from downtown Denver, sits an undeniably magical, spiritual and emotional place. One of the planet's most legendary outdoor music venues, Red Rocks Amphitheatre is an acoustically perfect sounding board and a visual marvel of natural rock formations.

This is not just some steel-and-mortar edifice with martini bars, glassed-in restaurants and comfy fixed seats. The majestic, open-air amphitheatre was at one time considered one of the Natural Wonders of the World, included with the Hanging Gardens of Babylon and the Pyramids. After eleven years of being named *Pollstar*'s best small music venue, Red Rocks became the namesake of the award.

Red Rocks is unlike any other place in the world. Two enormous slabs of stone—Ship Rock on the south (forming what boosters used to call "the Gateway of Heaven and Earth") and sharp-angled Creation Rock on the north (towering 500 feet from its base)—flank the amphitheatre's 9,450 seats. The aptly named Stage Rock backs the performance space; beyond it sprawl hogbacks leading toward the skyline of Denver and distant panorama of Colorado's Eastern Plains.

Red Rocks' seating configuration—bench seating on four-foot treads—contributes to the experience. People stand and dance two to three deep; the steep rake of the seating ensures nobody's view is blocked. Patrons come to revel in the unique splendor, but its incredible beauty also blows away performers. Watching the sun set as the city lights sparkle in the distance, hearing the riff of a tune carried on a soft mountain breeze—it doesn't matter who's on stage. Red Rocks is the star.

Nature's prehistoric uplift started the construction job some 70 to 40 million years ago with the Laramide orogeny—the elevation of the landscape that led to the creation of the Rocky Mountains. Weathering flattened and eroded those areas, with the next big folding of the land referred to as the Neogene uplift. Around six million years ago, volcanic disturbances pushed up the thick sedimentary beds of sandstone, formed in the floor of an ancient sea covering the Midwestern plains. Frost, heat, wind and strong water currents have since worked their erosive magic, giving the rocks irregular shapes and a variety of coloring.

Over the centuries, the pageant of human life has passed beneath the jagged cliffs of Red Rocks—from primitive man to Indians, Spanish Conquistadors to French trappers, American explorers to gold seekers. The miracle of Red Rocks is that a city government actually thought of a use for such an incredible, dazzling geological phenomenon—and proceeded to implement it without diminishing the grand setting.

1870-1912

TENDING THE GARDEN

On the Fourth of July in 1870, a group of pioneer settlers nestled in Bear Creek Canyon undertook a "Champagne March" to the ruddy sandstone monoliths. Upon arriving, Jefferson County Judge Martin Van Buren Luther delivered a patriotic address, christening the rocks as the Garden of the Angels. He also placed a curse on anyone attempting to change the name; his pronouncement had no great effect. From that day forward, people called the expanse the Park of the Red Rocks.

The first recorded owner was Marion Burts, who in turn sold to Col. Leonard H. Eicholtz. In May 1905, the *Denver Republican* reported that Eicholtz had sold 4,000 acres of land to *Cosmopolitan Magazine* editor and industrialist John Brisben Walker, who envisioned a great outdoor theater in the red rock formations. He had a firm belief in the future of tourism in Colorado and could see the need to preserve large expanses of fragile foothills land, but Denver's Chamber of Commerce turned a cold shoulder to his suggestion for mountain parks outside Denver.

Walker began hyping the park, which he labeled Garden of the Titans to compete with the Garden of the Gods near Colorado Springs, using names from Greek mythology for the rocks. Roads were scraped at the location, and the first recorded concert took place on Decoration Day (now Memorial Day), May 30, 1906. The event featured Pietro Satriano, one of Denver's most popular bandleaders, with a brass ensemble of 25 pieces. They performed on a crude wooden platform constructed at the western face of Stage Rock. There were no seats for the audience, only a boulder-strewn field. The Colorado & Southern Railway ran five trains from Denver to Morrison, carrying some 1,600 people. About 1,000 more traveled by wagon, tally-ho carriage, foot and horseback. A few even arrived via automobile.

Walker said it was only the beginning. He soon built trails and a teahouse and an observation deck on Creation Rock. He also designed and had constructed a funicular railway to ferry passengers west from Creation Rock up the 2,000 feet to the top of Mount Morrison. It opened in 1909, with a gauge of five feet four inches and cars capable of handling 100 passengers per trip.

In 1910, Walker announced an August 7 concert by Francesco Ferullo's 50-piece band (on loan from Lakeside Amusement Park). Round trip tickets to Morrison on the Colorado & Southern Railroad cost 60 cents and included admission to the park. Encouraged by the success of the Ferullo concert, Walker pursued the goal of staging vocal concerts among the huge rocks that flanked the site. The key, he was convinced, would be the enthusiastic testimony of a big star—Mary Garden of the Chicago Opera Company.

Walker made sure that Garden's outing to his "open-air auditorium" on May 12, 1911 received coverage in all the Denver papers. Accounts had the singer riding to the park by way of everything from a burro to a carriage, but an enthusiastic story in the next day's *Denver Times* pointed

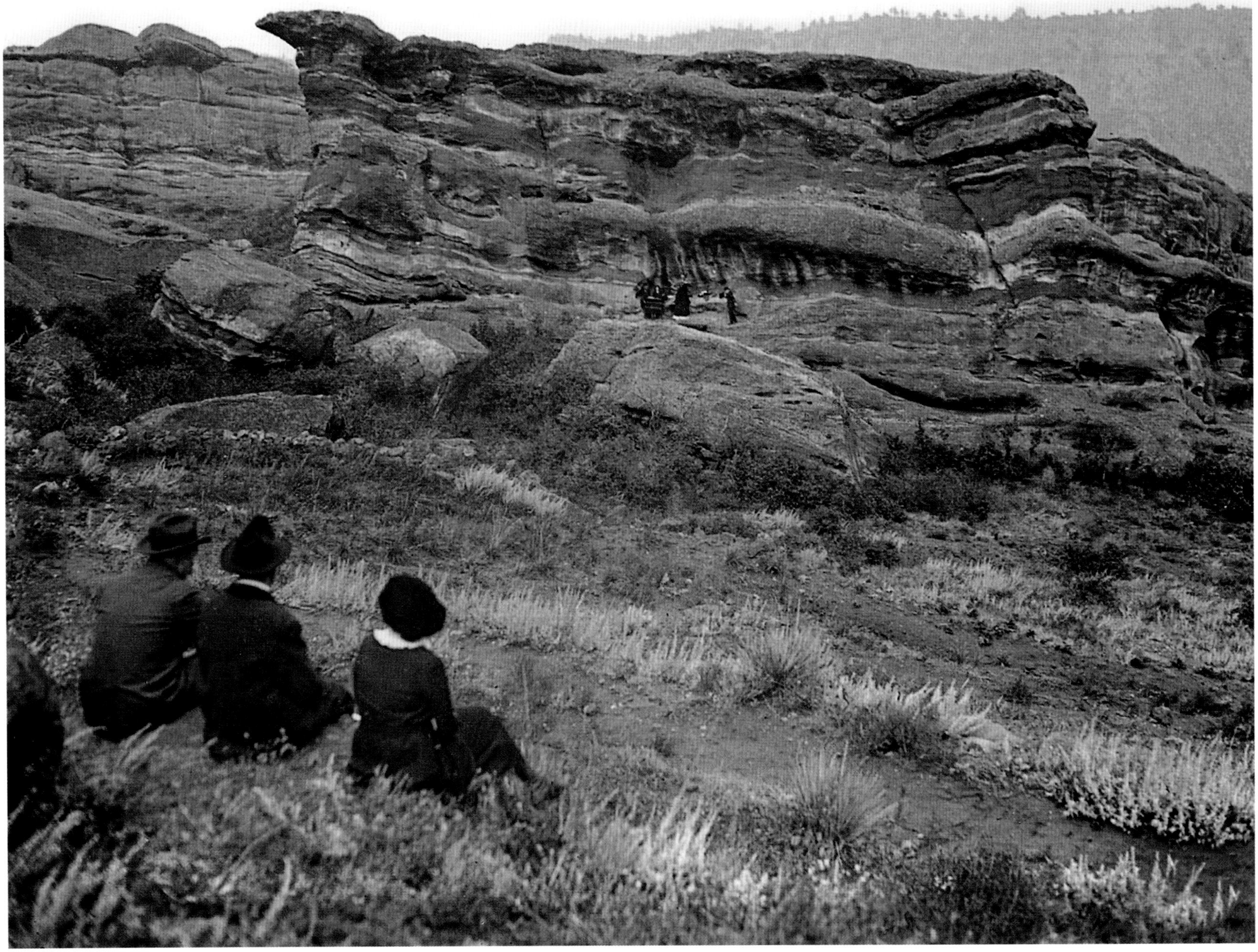

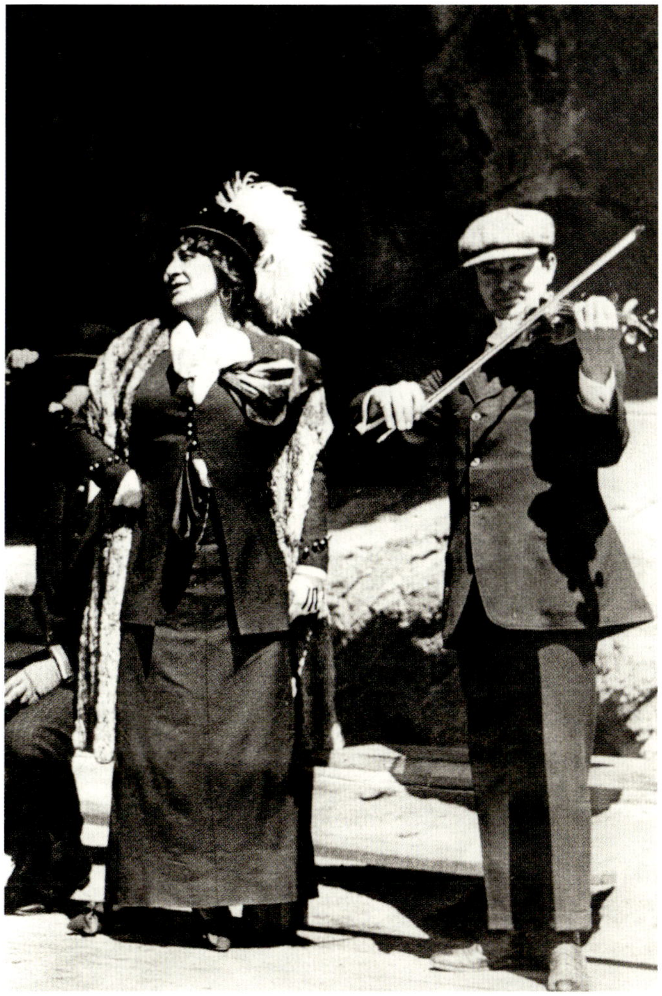

Acoustics test, c. 1906 (left); Mary Garden, c. 1911

out how the sales manager and the president of the McDuffee Motor company had driven Garden's party in two Chalmers motor cars. Several Morrison schoolchildren formed the audience; they sat on rocks spread over the expanse. Walker placed Garden at the base of Creation Rock for an informal 20-minute show, where she sang in normal tone—and realized her voice had carried to the highest portion of the theater.

Over the six-hour period Garden spent roaming the hills, Walker asked if singing in the open air had strained her vocal organs. She replied, "Oh, no…the rock here protects one just as a stage would and there is no strain whatsoever."

She then exclaimed, "It is the most wonderful thing I ever saw. The scenery is so inspiring. And every note is so clear. It is wonderful! Wonderful! Whenever you complete this place, I want you to invite me to sing here…nothing could make me more happy."

Garden lived past 90, but she never returned to the park.

1913-1934
UP AND ON THE ROCKS

In 1913, Walker published a promotional folder advertising the Red Rocks area as a tourist attraction. He was also mulling over extensive development plans. A focal point was to be a castle on the summit of Mount Falcon, 2,000 feet above Bear Creek, a massive structure with turrets and towers, bridges and underground passages that he proposed as a summer White House for U.S. Presidents.

Despite his enthusiasm and a decade of optimistic growth, Walker's fortunes declined. His other commercial operations faltered. The city and state would not finance his summer White House, and efforts to arrange his own financing failed. By the early 1920s, his Garden had fallen into disrepair. The funicular railway had stopped operating and was finally sold for scrap, leaving only a gash straight up the north side of Creation Rock. The observation deck on Creation Rock also closed, and a fire had consumed his Mount Morrison Dance Pavilion. The land remained crisscrossed by cow-paths and blanketed in wild buffalo grass; there was no easy way to access the park's features.

Giving up on his personal vision, Walker offered to sell the 2,700-acre tract to the City of Denver for $100,000. City accountants balked, advising Mayor Ben Stapleton that the price was too high; the park was too far away and no one would ever come to it. Ultimately, once the price had dropped to $54,133, Stapleton decided that purchasing the park would be a good investment, and the deed to Red Rocks fell

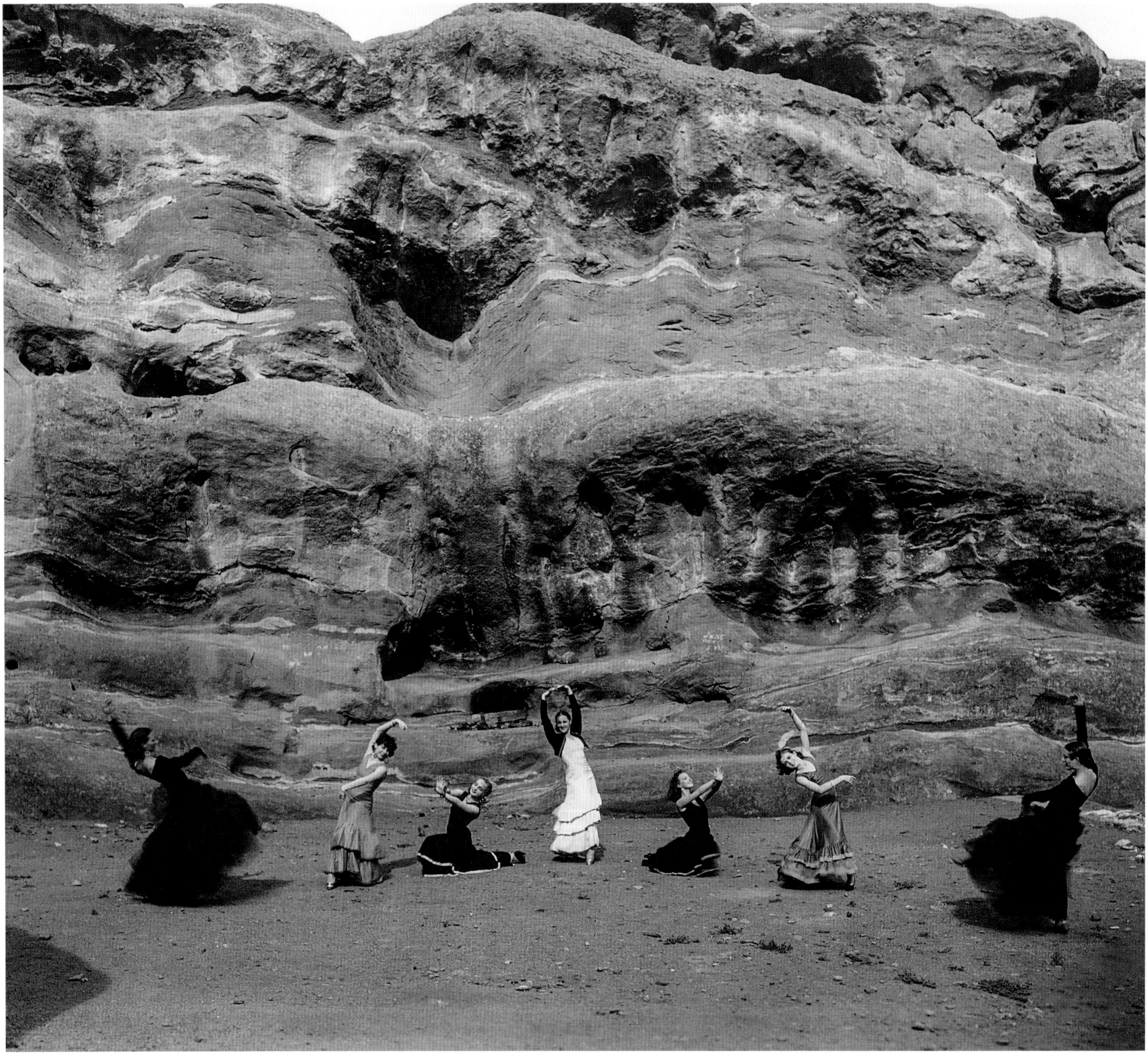

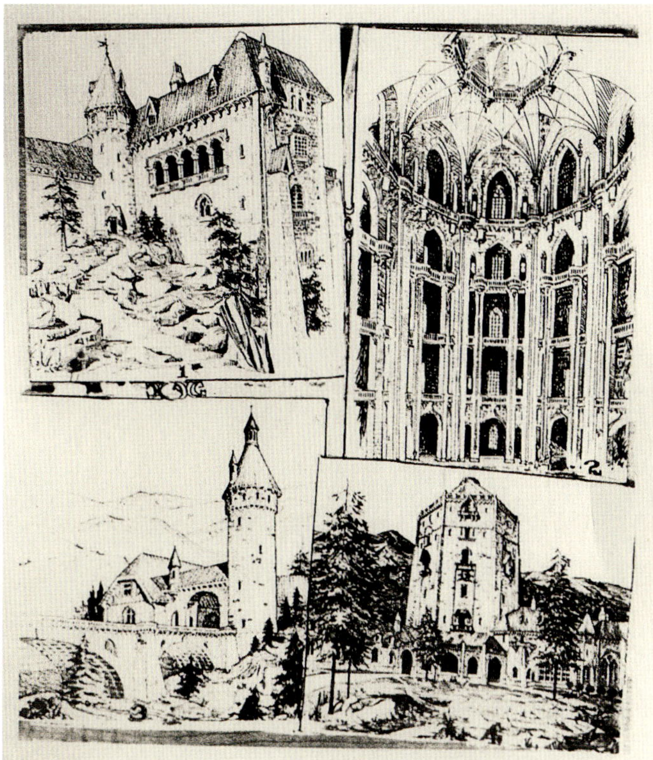

Lillian Cushing School of Dance at Sounding Rock, 1933 (left); Summer White House drawings, 1913

into the city's possession on June 3, 1927, with 1,100 acres purchased as being fit for use.

Two years later, crews armed with dynamite began blasting roads into the rock to make Stapleton's "rock garden" more accessible to the residents of Denver. Walker died in 1931, the year that the pueblo-style Indian Trading Post opened on the original site of his Mount Morrison Dance Pavilion, serving as a visitor center for those wishing to buy souvenirs and snacks. Red Rocks became a place for Denverites to relax and enjoy Colorado's mountain beauty without venturing too far from the city. Musical programs included a May 1932 benefit for the unemployed, an event billed in The Denver Post as "the formal dedication of the Natural Theatre of the Red Rocks" (for 25 cents, attendees were entertained by the Denver Municipal Band); the Denver A Cappella Choir conducted by John C. Wilcox; and the Lillian Cushing School of Dance (in a performance of Spanish dance).

1935-1940

A DYNAMITE IDEA

Denver native George Cranmer had a bigger vision for Red Rocks than a rock garden. During a 1902 high school field trip to the site, he'd noticed its excellent acoustics. Twenty-five years later, while traveling in the Mediterranean with his wife and children, Cranmer saw the ancient Greek outdoor theater at Taormina in Sicily, built by the Greeks several centuries before Christ, and decided to make Red Rocks the greatest open-air theater in the world. A retired stockbroker, Cranmer had time on his hands. He went to Stapleton, once again a mayoral candidate in 1935 (he had served two terms from 1923 to 1931), and became his campaign manager. When Stapleton was elected, he appointed Cranmer Manager of Improvements and Parks.

One of Cranmer's responsibilities was to find labor for the thousands still left unemployed by the Great Depression. Full of plans for Red Rocks, Cranmer saw in the New Deal programs of the Civilian Conservation Corps (CCC) and Works Progress Administration (WPA) an opportunity both to provide employment and to keep down the costs of building a theater.

Cranmer took photos of the location and sent them to Washington. He followed up with a personal call on the Secretary of the Interior. The result was permission to use CCC youths to build the theater and WPA to create access roads, parking facilities and connecting roads.

Burnham Hoyt, a young Denver architect who had helped map out

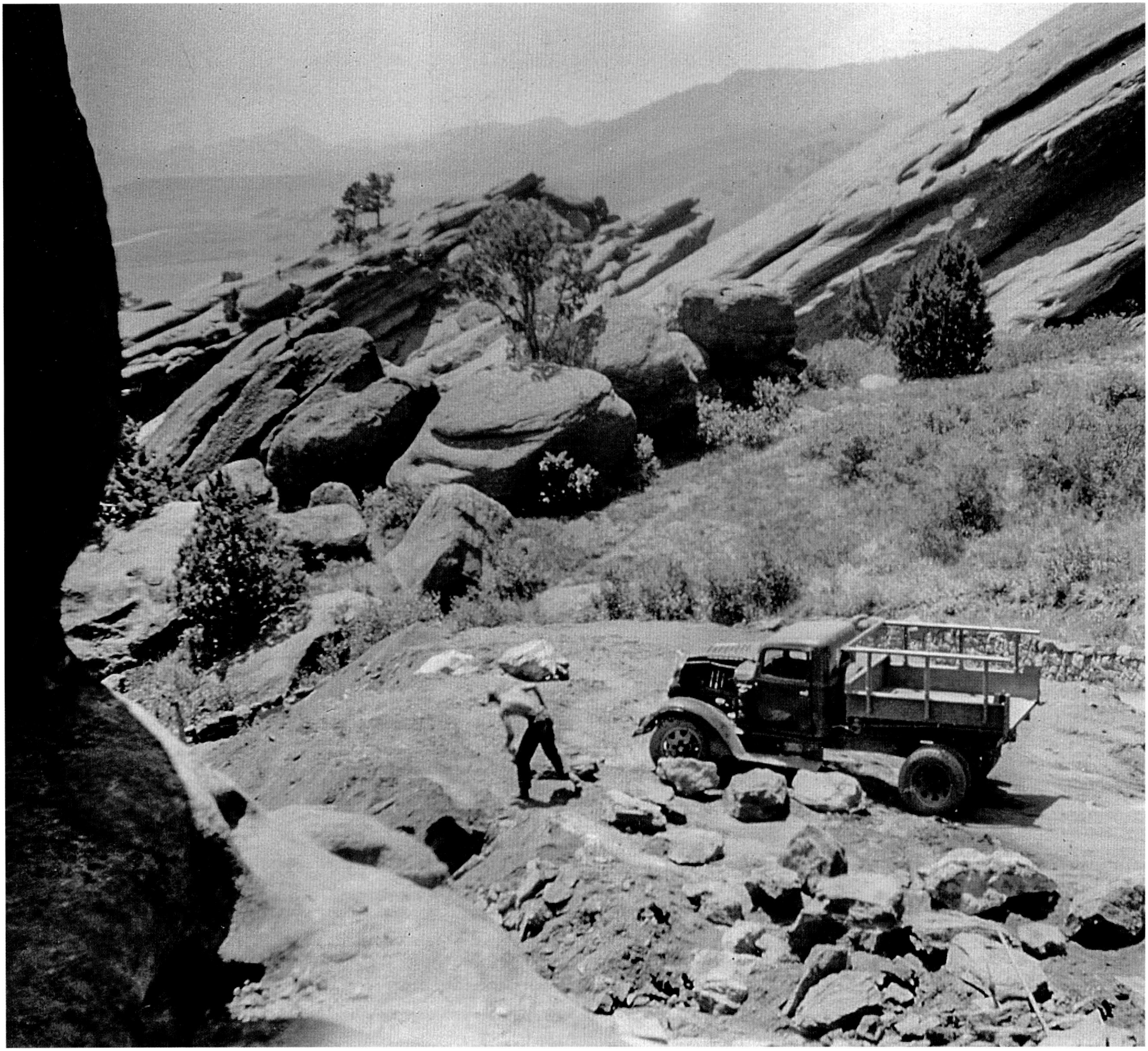

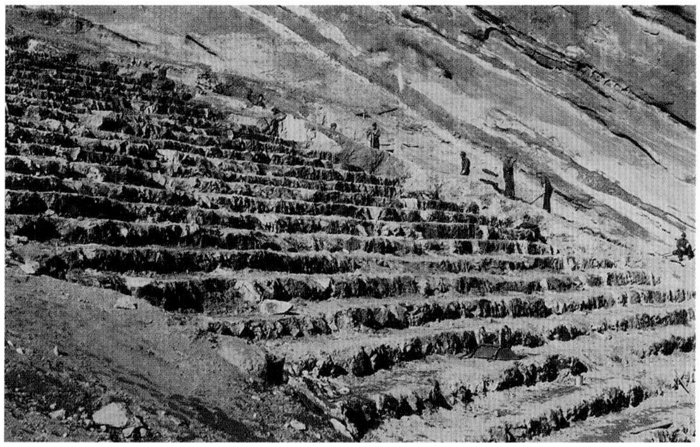

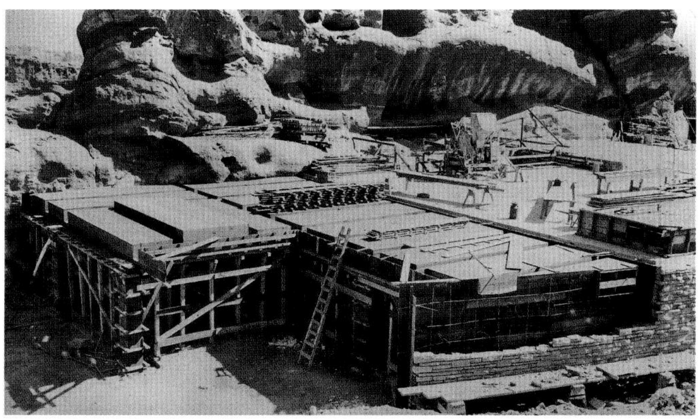

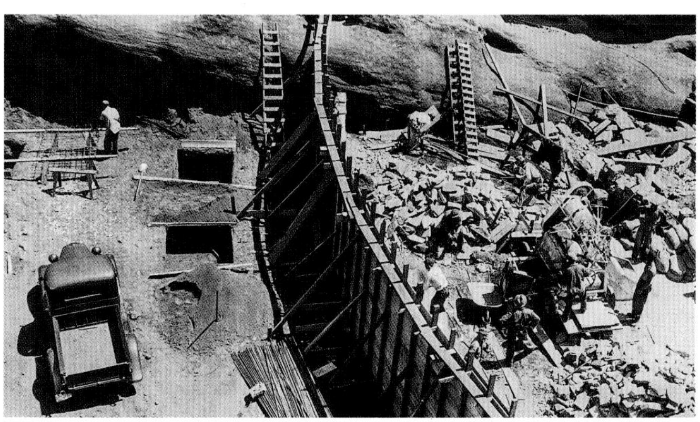

Clearing the hillside (opposite); seating (top); dressing room deck (middle); south wall forms, 1936 (bottom)

New York's Radio City Music Hall, was employed to lay out a feasible seating plan for the Park of the Red Rocks. Devoted to enhancing the unique natural setting, Hoyt designed the venue to be tucked between the massive rocks.

CCC company No. 1848 came to Morrison in 1935 and first built a base of operations, obtaining the required cooperation of the National Park Service. On May 11, 1936, work started the project, which was hazardous and expensive—a rough estimate of the total cost of labor and materials came in at well over $300,000 according to Edward Teyssier, superintendent of the job.

The first problem was clearing the hillside of boulders, many of them so large they could not be removed without breaking them up. Stapleton, who still visualized Red Rocks as a rock garden, was very fond of the boulders. Cranmer pointed out to the foreman that the job all had to be done at once; otherwise an executive or council order could stop the project.

Cranmer arranged with the foreman to demolish all the boulders between Ship Rock and Creation Rock in one huge dynamite blast, so Stapleton couldn't complain. On the day it was done, when the mayor came looking for him, Cranmer made it a point not to be in his office.

The main task then began, to cut a proper stage with 69 rows of wooden benches for seating out of the sloping red rock. Hoyt attempted to blend the walkways and dressing rooms into the rocks as unobtrusively as possible. In front of the stage was an orchestra pit built of stone; behind it, in full view of the audience, the lights of Denver would mark the horizon.

Day in and day out, the CCC veterans, stone masons and carpenters blew up the rocks, dug out the dirt, embedded the steel and then reshaped stone and concrete over it. For the parking lots alone, Teyssier estimated, they moved more than 300,000 yards of dirt; excavation for the theater meant moving 60,000 yards more.

The difficulty of getting trucks and machinery up the winding and perilous roads made the work unavoidably slow. Muffled charges of dynamite and other blasting powder boomed through the valley daily.

The project went smoothly, sometimes to the accompaniment of a cappella grand opera, as Cranmer brought a steady stream of artists to the park to test and retest the acoustics—violin virtuosos Mischa Elman and Albert Spalding, conductor Jerzy Bojanowski and tenor Ladis Kiepura (both of Poland), and opera singers Rose Bampton, Jennie Tourel, Igor Gorin and Lily Pons. In November, 1937, in what was termed an informal "christening of the outdoor Red Rocks Theatre," mezzo-soprano Gladys Swarthout of the Metropolitan Opera Company

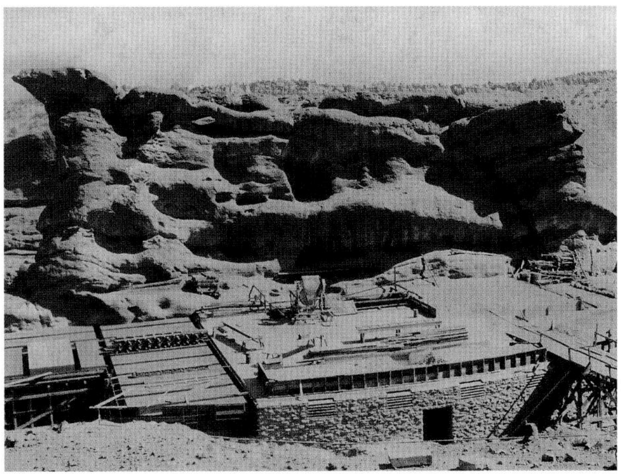

Construction, 1936; aerial view, 1941 (right)

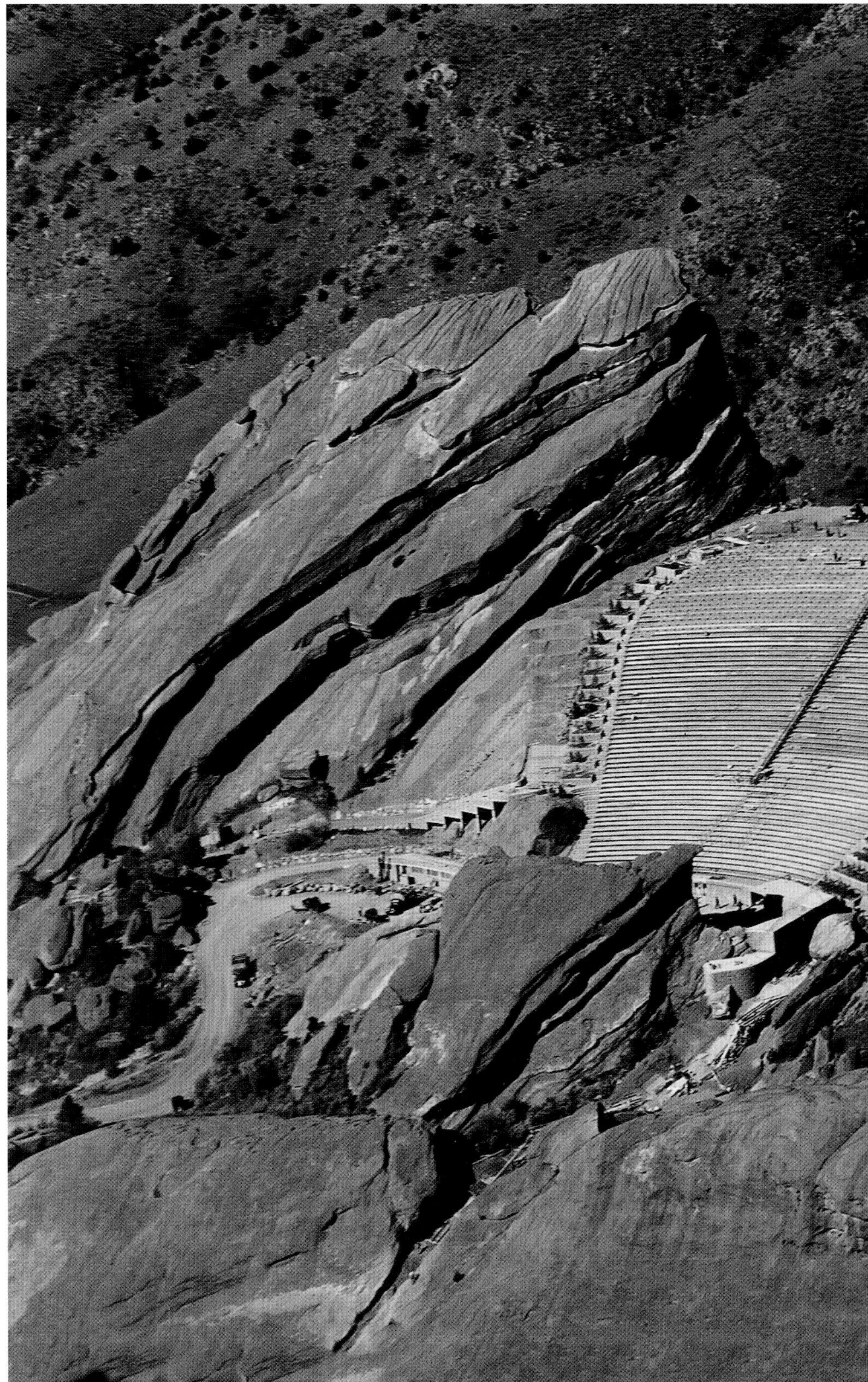

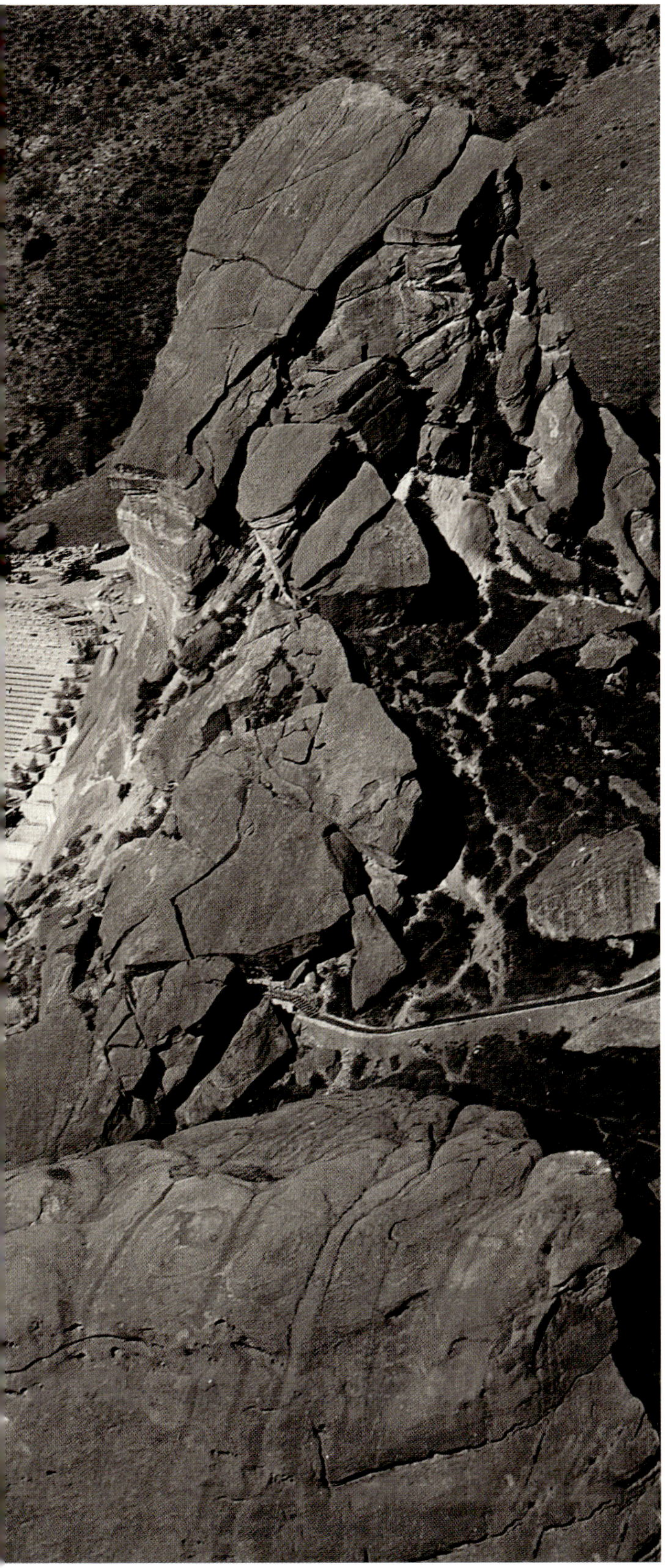

and her pianist Lester Hodges gave an illustrious performance.

Elogene Pierson was a music student at the University of Denver and the studio and rehearsal pianist for the Lillian Cushing School of Ballet. "It had been said that the sound made by dropping a dime in the natural bowl could be heard all the way to the top," she remembered. "I think George Cranmer was also curious to see how a performing group would appear on the new stage."

So up to Red Rocks they went, in the summer of 1939. "Only minimal structures existed then at right and stage left," Pierson said. "Someone with a pickup truck brought an upright piano for my use. They also placed a plywood cover on the stage to level it out. It was rough, not made for ballet dancers. With me at the piano, Miss Cushing's top dancers and ten to twelve girls performed some numbers we had practiced from the productions for the Cheesman Park Opera and the Central City Opera.

"Everyone seemed pleased with the results—and the dime test was also successful!"

1941-1961
FAME COMES TO RED ROCKS

The new venue debuted June 8, 1941, with entertainment supplied by the 80-piece Denver Junior Symphony and a 100-voice chorus directed by John C. Kendel. Cranmer acted as master of ceremonies, praising Burnham Hoyt, the WPA, the CCC and the National Park Service for the actual creation of the park. The formal dedication took place the following Sunday, June 15, and was paired with the convention of Rotary International, an event that brought people from more than 30 countries to Denver—a growing metropolis of more than 300,000 eager to show the world that they didn't comprise a philistine cow town.

Helen Jepson, the Metropolitan Opera soprano, was the featured attraction. She provided a gracious initiation, saying, "One doesn't have to sing here, the music just rolls out. Those big rocks just seem to pick up every little pianissimo tone and make it live." Part of the performance was picked up for international radio transmission by the Columbia Broadcast System (CBS). The event was a sold-out success.

Other events filled that summer, but use of Red Rocks as an entertainment facility was sporadic during World War II, though it was a popular place for picnics. After the war, in 1946, the Koshare Club of La Junta, Colorado, the world's largest group devoted to the study of Indian lore, danced at the Red Rocks rededication (the club had taken

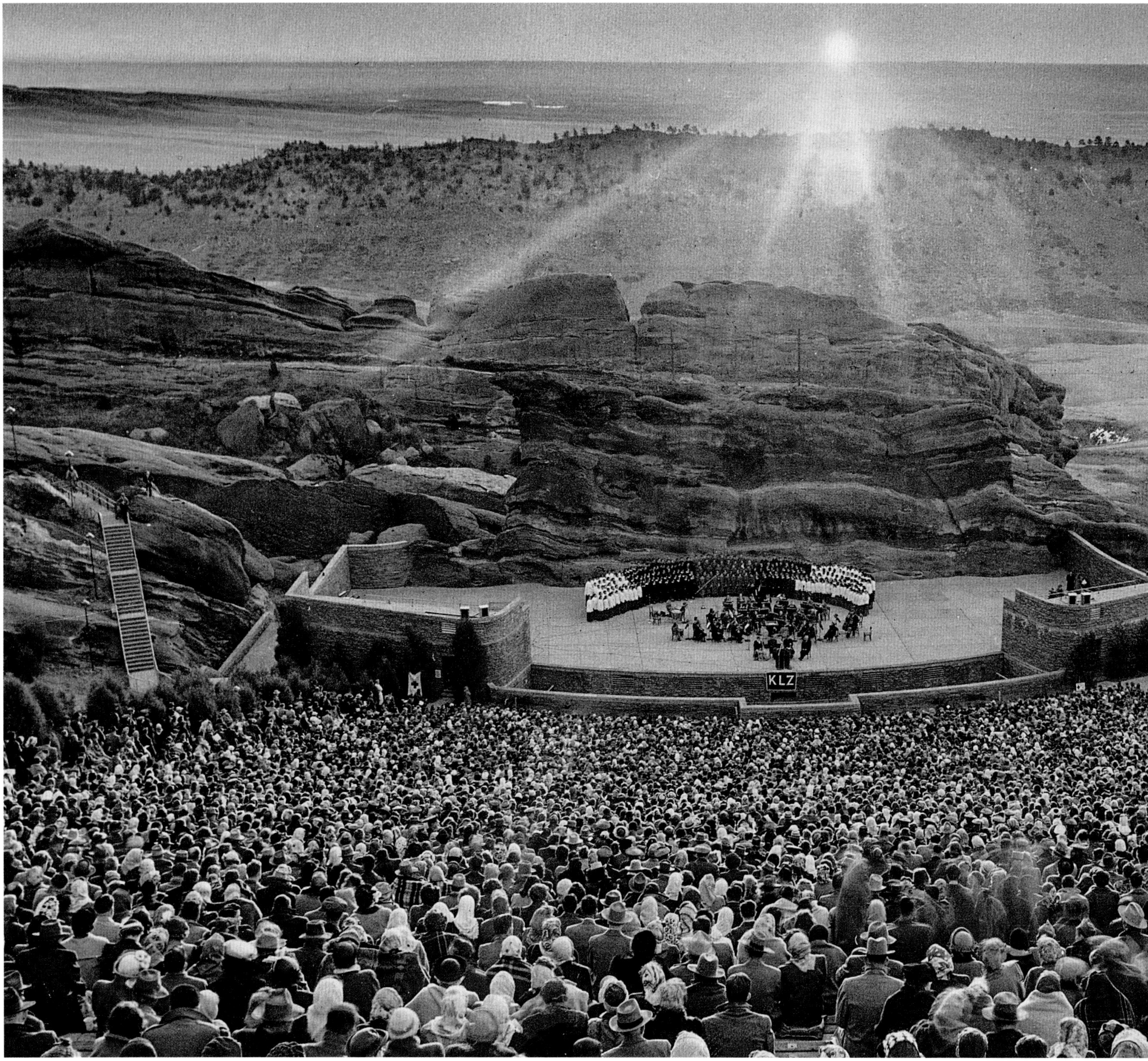

Easter Sunrise Service, 1949

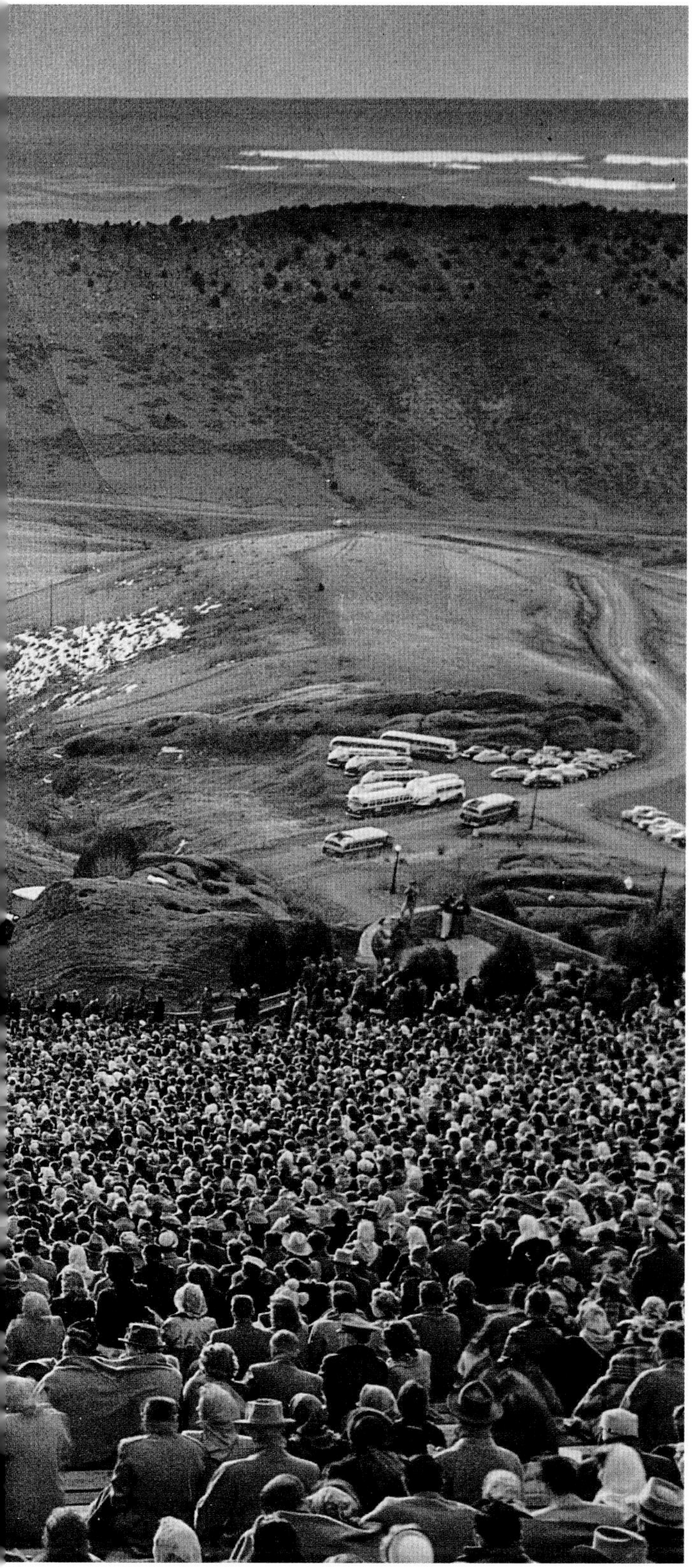

part in the 1941 opening and would perform numerous other times). But Denver's newspapers expressed a mounting displeasure with the lack of world-class events at "Cranmer's white elephant." Red Rocks appeared dirty and ill-kept, and people booed Cranmer at a salute to Buffalo Bill Cody because of the oily grounds that passed for parking lots.

The first event of 1947 was the genesis of a cherished tradition—the first Easter Sunrise Service held in the park. Few expected the huge turnout. Fifteen thousand people reportedly rose before dawn and jammed the area to ponder the great theme of the Resurrection, with perhaps double that number in cars unable to move along Alameda and the other two-lane roads to the park. With no multi-lane highway and insufficient parking, many gave up attending, while others simply abandoned their vehicles and walked. Many hours after the service, cars remained snarled in a huge traffic jam.

The same year, a series of Festival Concerts was booked on the rocks, beginning with pianist Leonard Pennario and ending with singer Regina Resnick, who called for the "match trick"—at her count of three, every man in the audience struck a match. Thousands of tiny pinpoints of flame leaped out of the darkness and flickered in union.

The series proved successful enough for Mayor Quigg Newton to approve the creation of a non-profit organization to present future festivals at Red Rocks, chaired by Gen. John F. Curry. Between 1948 and 1961 the Saul Caston-conducted Denver Symphony Orchestra took over the presentation of a yearly concert series with manager Helen Black becoming the de facto booking agent. With little or no staff, she set about attracting big names such as Eugene List, famed conductor Igor Stravinsky, Helen Traubel and the Ballet Russe de Monte Carlo—a tribute to her salesmanship and daring.

Those using Red Rocks for the first time often had trials by fire; even figuring out the best place to put players in the orchestra was a learning process for all involved. The weather did not always cooperate. Violent crosswinds and sudden cloudbursts caused havoc on the uncovered stage, blowing away orchestra scores and other unattached items.

During the second season, in 1948, Stravinsky and his pianist son Soulima thrilled the Red Rocks crowd. Their performance was followed by composer Morton Gould doubling as guest conductor and pianist of music by George Gershwin and Aaron Copeland. Traffic presented an enormous problem at the last concert of the season, as an estimated 11,000 people turned out to hear Helen Traubel, the superstar soprano with the Metropolitan Opera.

Season tickets for the 1949 season were available for $6 at outlets such as the Red Rocks box office at 16th and Champa; individual shows cost

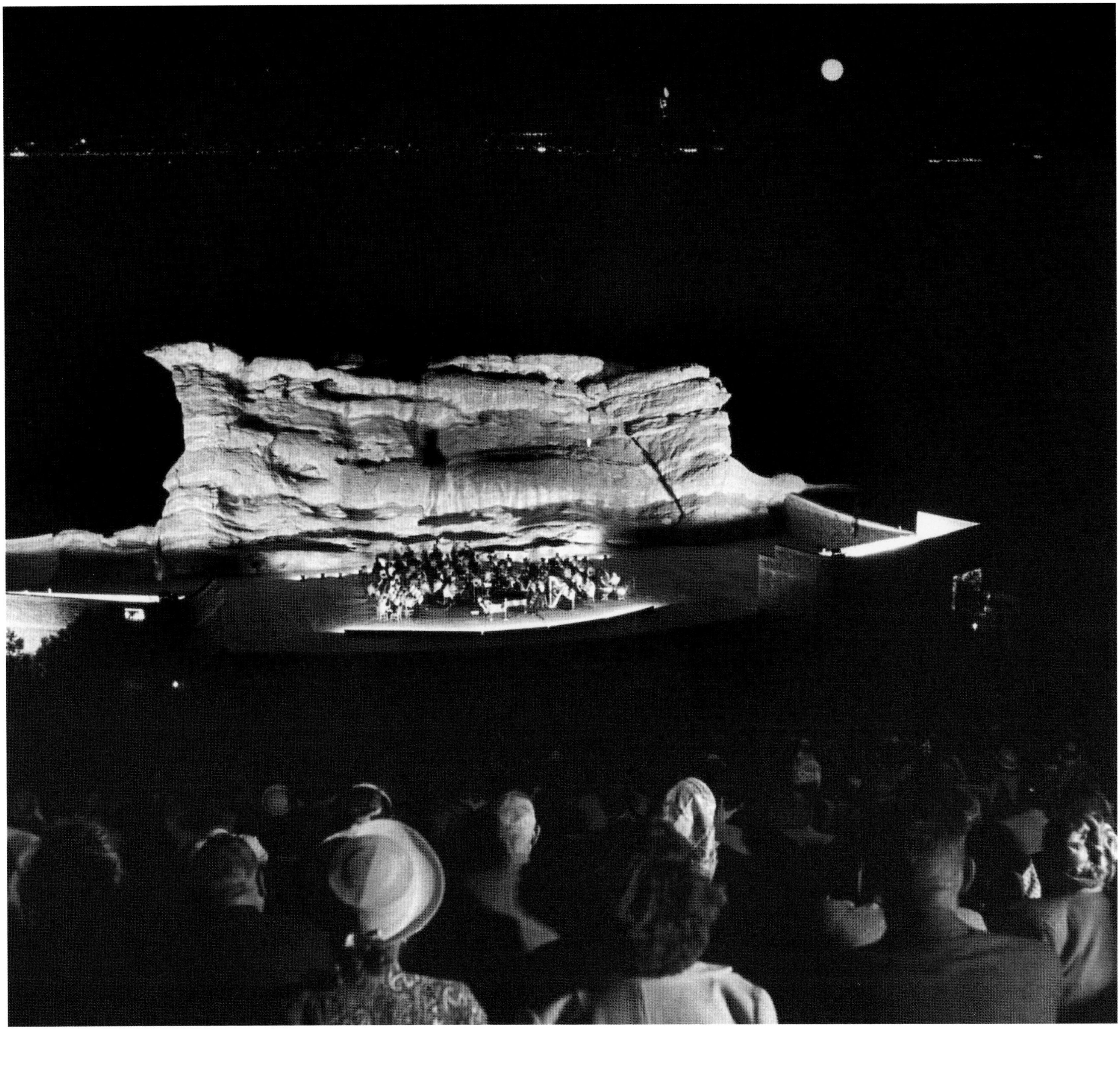

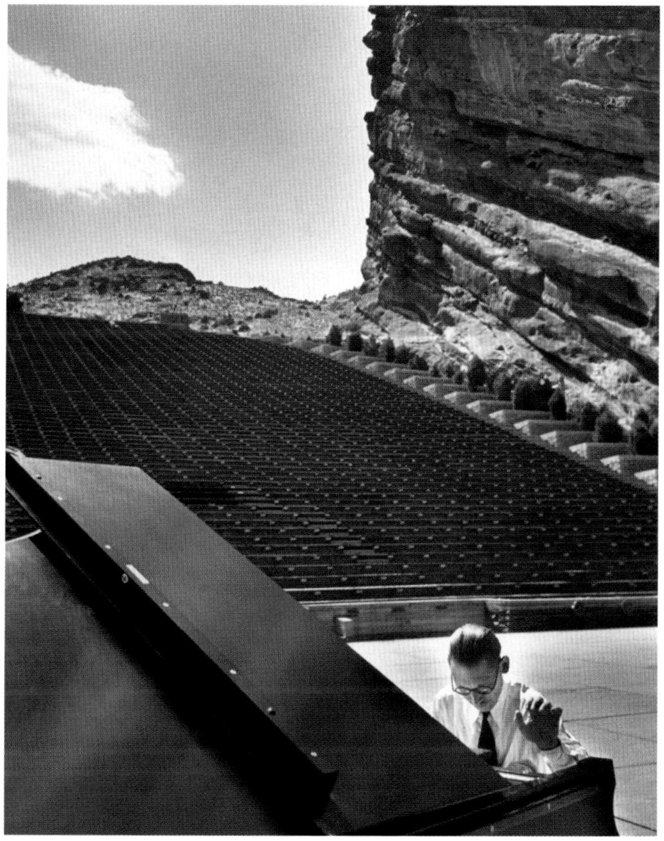

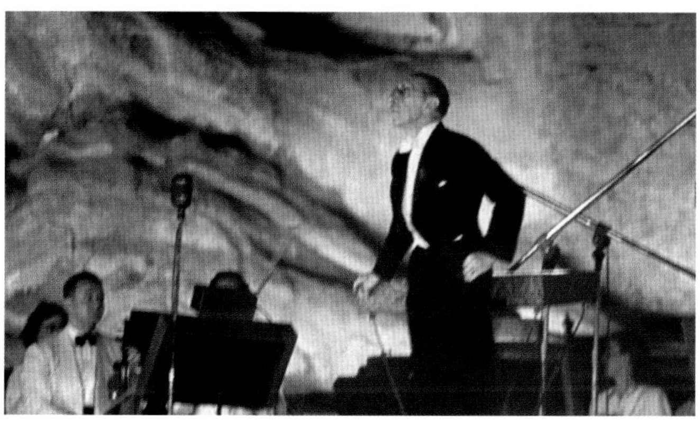

Igor & Soulima Stravinsky performance , 1948 (left); Soulima Stravinsky rehearsal (top); Igor Stravinsky conducting *The Fairy's Kiss* (bottom)

$1.75 for adults and 75 cents for kids 12 and younger. In addition to the concert series, there was square dancing every Saturday evening with bus service provided to and from the park.

The first show of 1949, featuring pianist José Iturbi, was the biggest yet. People who didn't have tickets decided to drive up to Red Rocks up to three hours early and park in the lots, displacing those who had ducats to the sold-out event. Iturbi nearly missed the performance, as police barricaded the roads leading to the park 15 minutes before Caston hit the stage; a police cruiser escorted Iturbi through the mobs of cars. Curry pledged that it would not happen again; for the remainder of the summer, no vehicles were admitted to the parking lots unless occupants had concert tickets.

For the 1950 season, the Ballet Russe de Monte Carlo performance featured some trickery by Helen Black, who locked the ballet company's managers backstage when they voiced the possibility of canceling the show due to bad weather.

At the final show of the Red Rocks Music Festival that year, August rains forced an early intermission for a performance by Metropolitan Opera baritone Robert Merrill. Future president Dwight Eisenhower, who was in the audience, was prevailed upon to give a short speech to the rain-soaked souls who gave him (as well as Merrill) a resounding round of applause.

Plenty of orchestras took advantage of Red Rocks' superior acoustics, and by the 1950s, solo artists began to appear with more regularity as well. Red Rocks grew in stature with star turns by Benny Goodman and Jeanette MacDonald. Helen Black sensed a great publicity opportunity when coloratura soprano Lily Pons of the Met came to Red Rocks the day before Independence Day in 1952. Birds would often fly out of the rocks during shows, and Black reckoned it would make a great photo op if they would fly around Pons, whose singing was described as "the voice of a happy bird." To make sure the feathered friends didn't take the night off, Black and her assistant Dolores Plested rounded up some pigeons from a local lab and drove them up to Red Rocks. They were released at the proper time, and the resulting picture accompanied an article in the July 14, 1952 issue of *Time* magazine.

The City Center Ballet, generally recognized as America's finest and largest ballet company, opened the Festival's seventh season in 1953. In the 1954 season, conductor Andre Kostelanetz had a good grasp of weather on the rocks when he picked the song "Cloudburst" from Ferde Grofe's *Grand Canyon Suite* since, Kostelanetz said, "it could have been written specially for Red Rocks." The year also saw the return to Denver of native son Paul Whiteman, the proclaimed "King of Jazz"

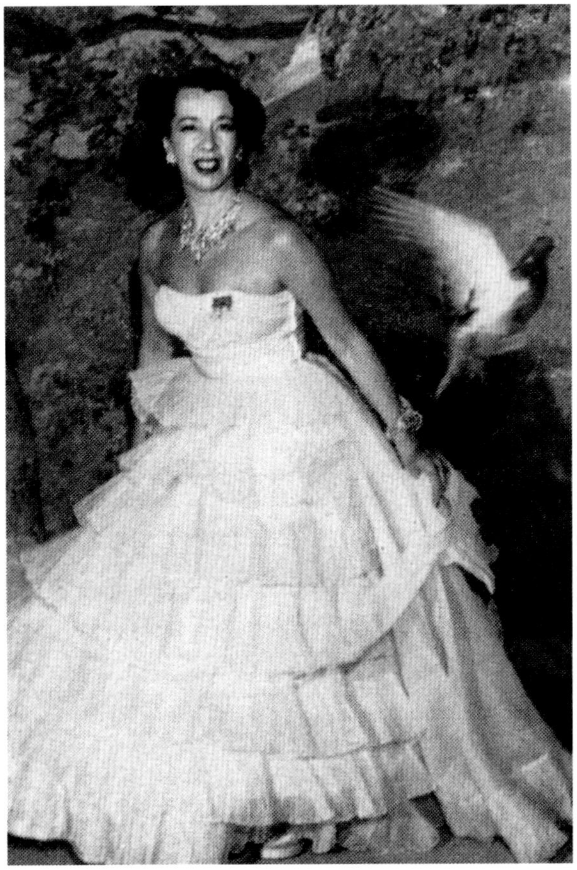

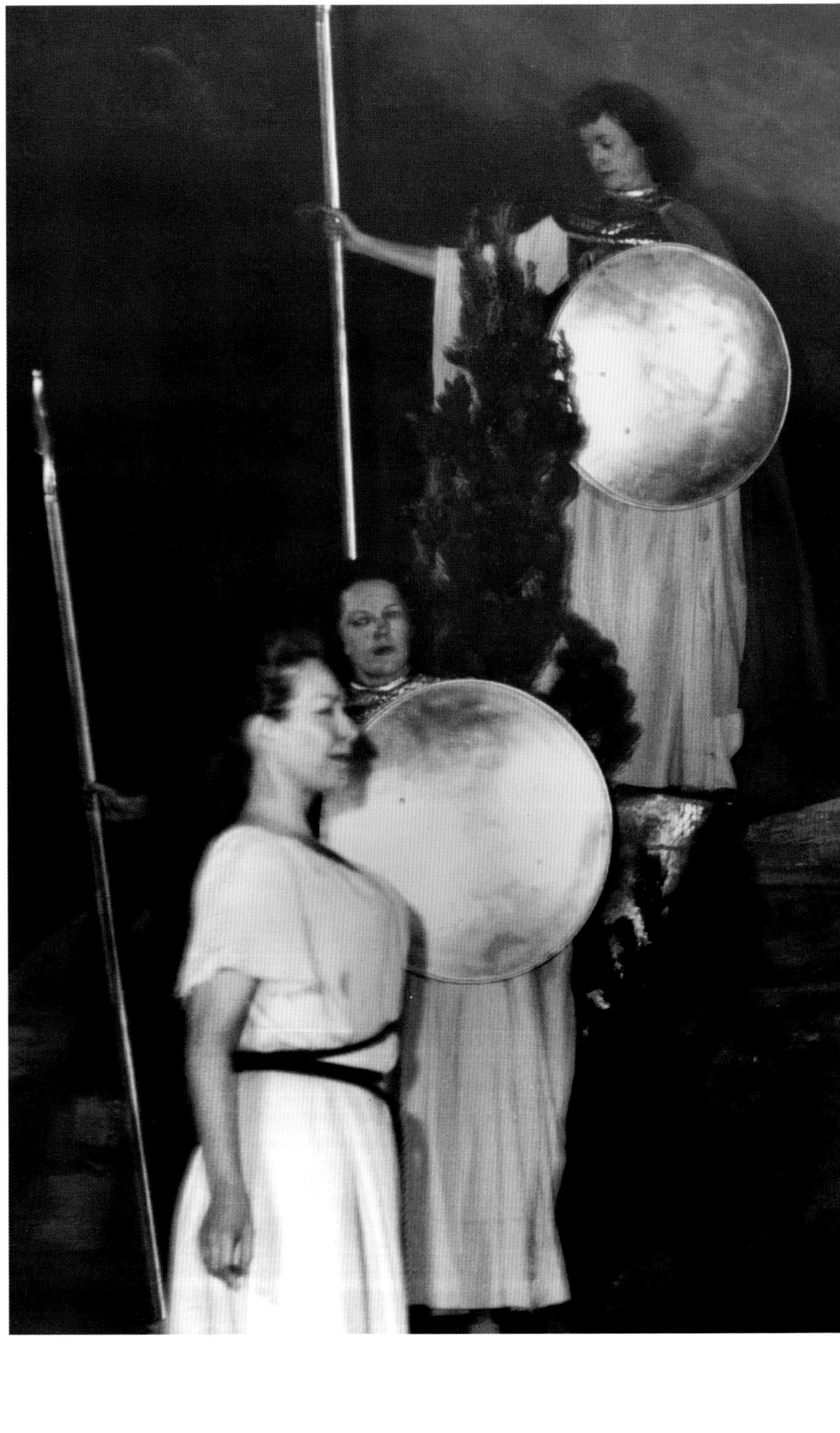

Lily Pons, 1952 (above); *Die Walküre*, 1958 (right)

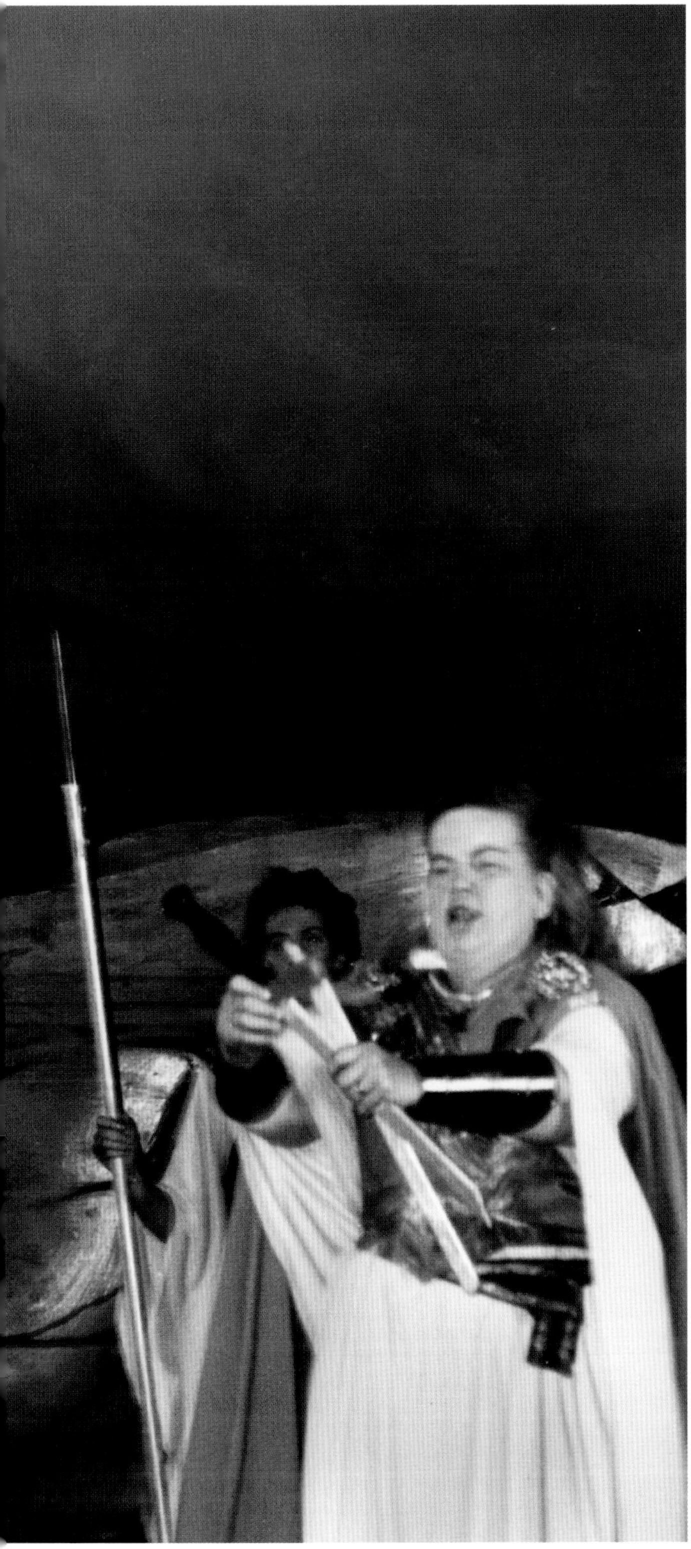

who had sold millions of records. Joseph Silverstein presented a chamber music show in a different area of the park, outside of the amphitheatre.

A highlight of the Red Rocks Music Festival's 1955 season was Dorothy Maynor's show; candles were passed out for the last number, "Amazing Grace," and the audience held them aloft and sang with the star. The year 1956 marked the most ambitious season yet. The event schedule tripled, including a visit from Salt Lake City's world-famous Mormon Tabernacle Choir in the first three-day booking in the Festival's short history. Some 460 choristers and friends took a special Rio Grande Railroad train to Denver, with most housed by the small local Mormon community. In a Red Rocks first, a pipe organ was brought in from Los Angeles free of charge from the California Organ Company.

The first television broadcast from Red Rocks—and the attendant organizational ordeal—came that year when NBC telecast a portion of a free concert by the Denver Symphony Orchestra coast-to-coast on the program *Wide Wide World*. Using television and electronic gear from Colorado and Wyoming, the network telecast the orchestra's performance as well as an unprecedented glimpse of Denver's spectacular mountains and plains.

Rock 'n' roll was starting to invade the consciousness of old, square America, but that music didn't immediately translate to Red Rocks. For Denver's cultural elite, Red Rocks was the place to be for the July 1957 presentation of Wagner's *Die Walküre* featuring Metropolitan Opera star Margaret Harshaw as Brünnhilde and James Pease as Wotan. The show ran for three nights with an encore performance of two nights in 1958. Helen Black had climbers from the Colorado Mountain Club to assist ladies playing the Valkyries on the rocks above the amphitheatre. She also cajoled the Army into supplying napalm for *Die Walküre*, as well as a cannon for a stirring performance of Tchaikovsky's *1812 Overture*.

With Jerry Lewis, Lawrence Welk, Nat King Cole and Van Cliburn booked for the 1958 season, the Red Rocks staging areas and acoustics underwent numerous improvements. An adjustable rain shield was designed for the orchestra pit to protect both players and instruments, and more dressing rooms were added to the upper stage. Raising the height of the north and south walls helped cut down the wind that swept the stage; it also gave performers a place to hide behind before entering the stage (the Forest Service had previously cut down trees and placed them on either side of the stage to keep dancers out of sight).

During 1959's "Rush to the Rockies" celebration of Colorado's territorial centennial, major productions included the Puccini opera *Girl of the Golden West*; a University of Colorado production of *Guys and Dolls*; a performance by José and Amparo Iturbi; Haydn's *The Creation*;

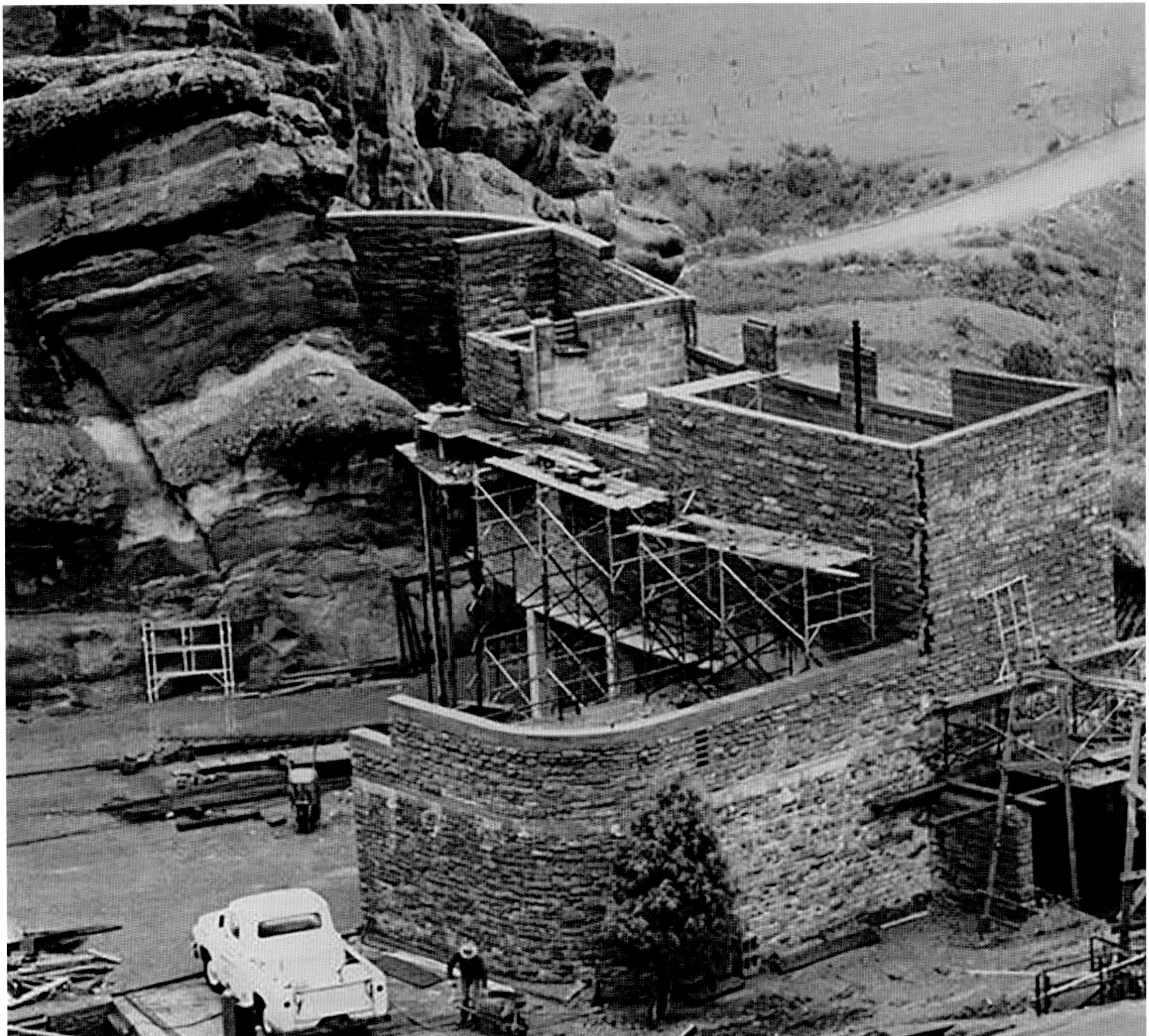

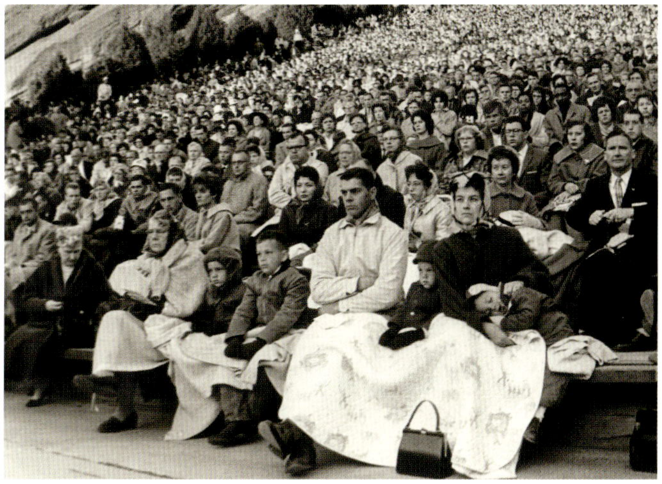

Easter Service, 1963 (above); *Guys and Dolls* orchestra pit, 1959 (right); *Brigadoon*, 1963 (below); c. 1958 (left)

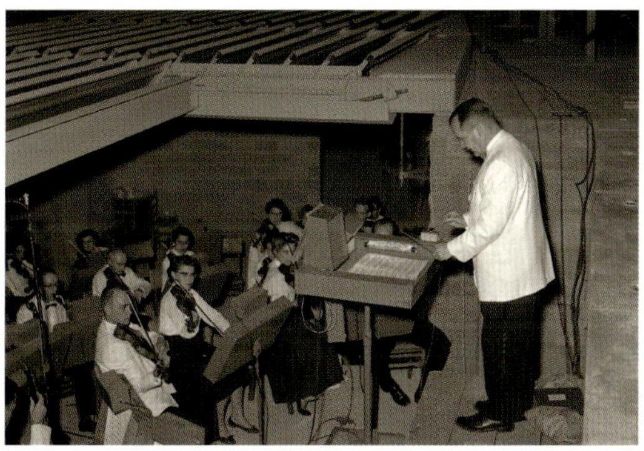

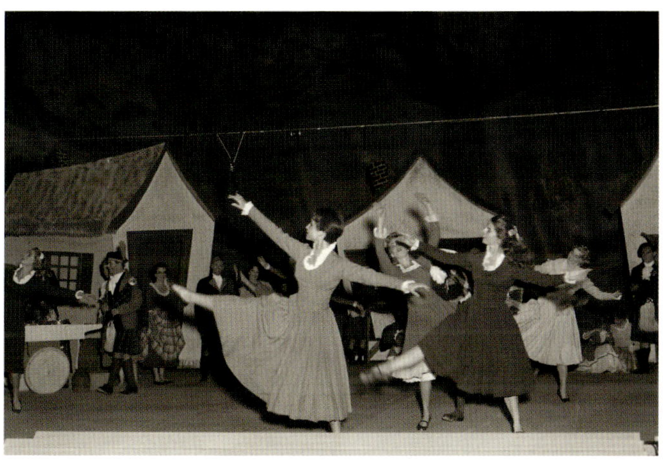

a musical pageant titled "Colorado Story"; and an appearance of the New York Philharmonic Orchestra with Leonard Bernstein conducting.

But such events, while they added to Colorado's prestige, were not bringing out enough fans. The one show that would have—the first attempt at booking rock 'n' roll at Red Rocks—was rained out; Ricky Nelson's act had to be moved to the Denver Coliseum.

Cranmer, a fan of highbrow entertainment, ascertained the changing musical climate at his beloved creation. The 1960 season's first show was the popular folk group the Kingston Trio; sex-kitten chanteuse Eartha Kitt played later that summer. In August, a sold-out audience for the Bernstein-conducted New York Philharmonic Orchestra could clearly see one of the Soviet Union's Sputnik satellites circling overhead.

The 1961 season saw entertainer Danny Kaye sing, dance, mimic, pantomime and joke for his performance at Red Rocks. Arthur Fielder teamed up with the Denver Symphony Orchestra, but the DSO had struggled to pay the rental fees for the use of Red Rocks, and just before the expected symphony month of July came the announcement that the orchestra would no longer present an annual musical festival at the amphitheatre.

1962-1969
THE TUNES THEY ARE A-CHANGIN'

The union of youth culture and popular music became an increasing presence at Red Rocks—the 1962 season included a capacity crowd for the Kingston Trio's return engagement on July 20—and the adult community was unhappy. Parents who had sat quietly amidst symphonic lullabies watched helplessly as their hordes of offspring, willing to spend their allowances on entertainment and fueled by alcohol and testosterone, wrote the first ugly chapter of Red Rocks history.

In the early years of the rock 'n' roll era, Denver's untapped concert promotion business was small, informal, and up for grabs. The ill-fated August 21, 1962 Ray Charles date at Red Rocks featured a performer who had the No. 1 song in the country with "I Can't Stop Loving You" from his groundbreaking album *Modern Sounds in Country and Western Music*. The year before, "Hit the Road Jack" had also topped the charts.

The concert deteriorated into a debacle. According to Joe Salankey, director of theaters and arenas for the city, the trouble started when a few spectators began throwing beer cans at a teen who stood waving his arms while the Ray Charles Orchestra was playing. Some musicians

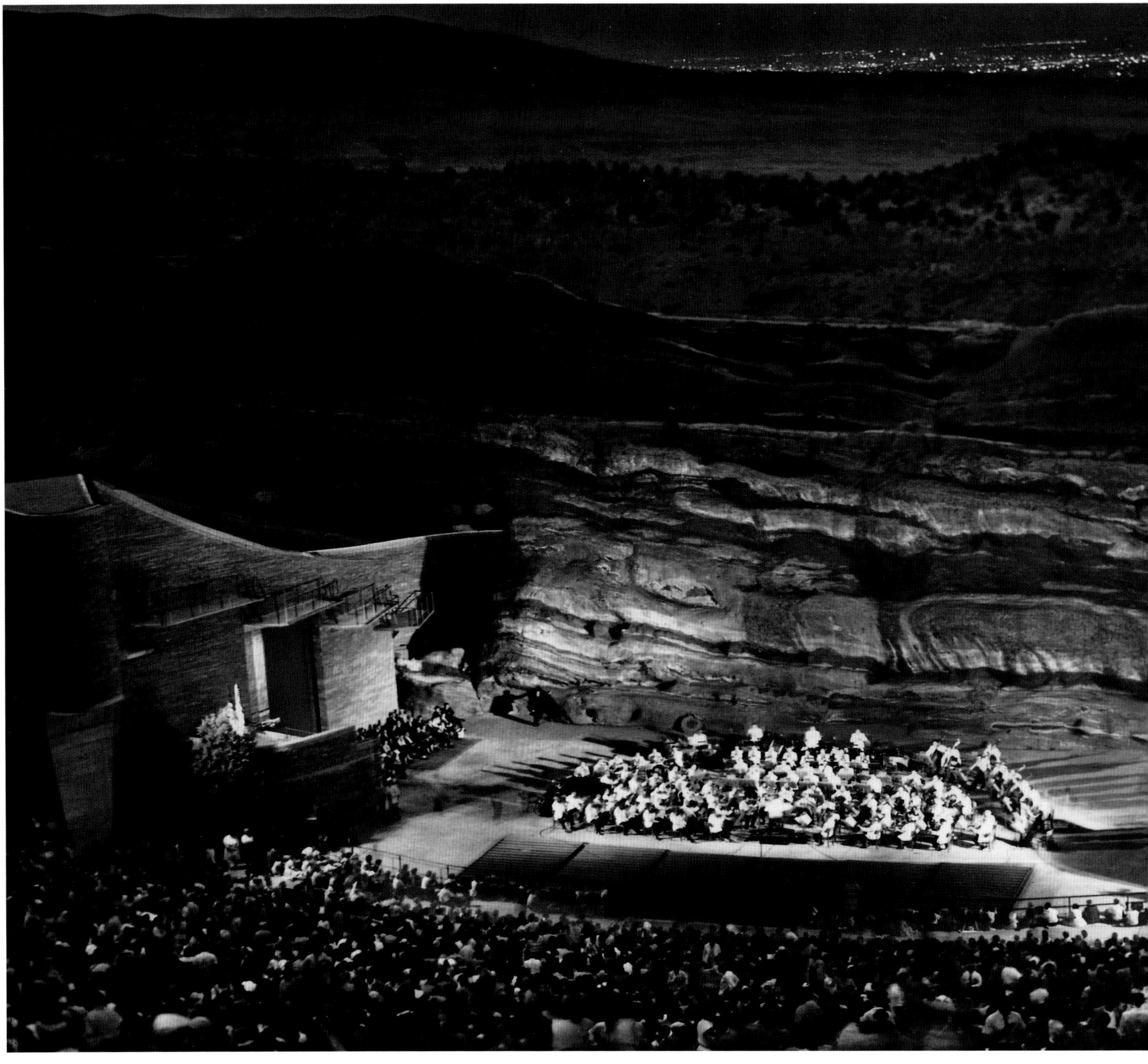

New York Philharmonic Orchestra, 1960

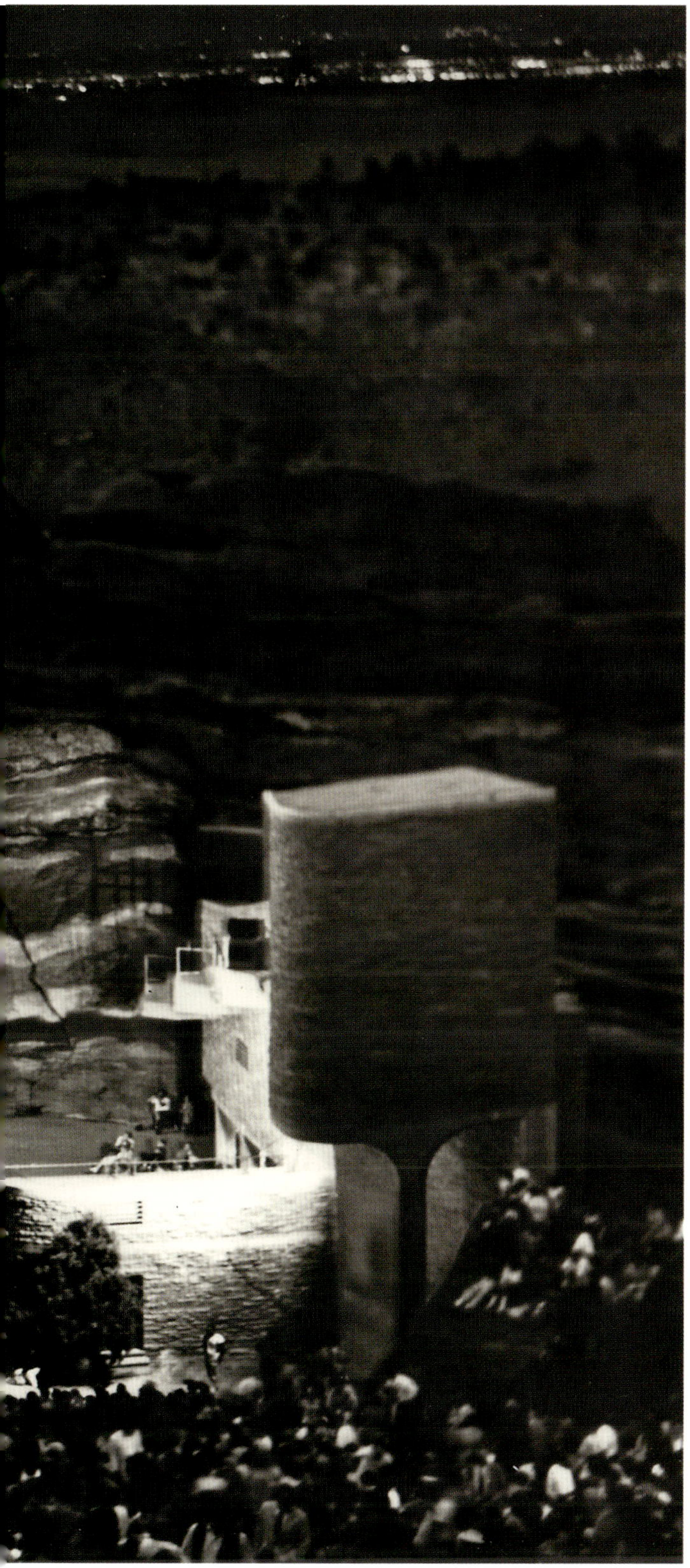

became alarmed and got off the stage. The emcee, disc jockey Pogo Poge of Denver's Top 40 radio station KIMN, demanded that the crowd display better comportment or the show would be canceled.

Charles arrived late and didn't wish to go on, but was prevailed upon by Charles Sullivan, West Coast promoter for Hugh Hooks Entertainment. Following chants of "We want Ray!" Charles performed for 45 minutes, then ducked out. The beer cans flew once more, from high up in the amphitheatre with great velocity on the unsuspecting fans below. Charles' piano was overturned. A show of force might have caused more trouble, so Sgt. George Eberle and eight other policemen hustled the drunken crowd from the theater. Eighteen people were treated for injuries.

Charles later said, "I didn't feel I could ask the musicians to risk being exposed alone for 45 minutes. The emcee didn't help things any. He tried to make it look like the band was responsible. What he said was wrong. It just made it worse."

The 1963 season satisfied the emerging appetite for folk music with the New Christy Minstrels, the Brothers Four and Denver native daughter Judy Collins in her first appearance at the park. Headlining the first annual Red Rocks Jazz Festival, Ella Fitzgerald and Dave Brubeck acknowledged a long, loud ovation.

In July 1964, Mexican-American singer Trini Lopez appeared at Red Rocks, as well as actor/folk singer Theodore Bikel and comedian Woody Allen; Judy Collins and the New Christy Minstrels both returned. The Smothers Brothers played to a capacity crowd that the local scribes described as "well-behaved." But Peter, Paul & Mary had to deal with a thrown beer can.

"In order to get up the mountain trail that leads to the rocks, the kids started coming early," Peter Yarrow said. "Well, they had a lot of time on their hands and they were drinking beer. It was the first drunk crowd we'd ever played for. And in the middle of the concert, a beer can came sailing at the stage and missed Mary (Travers) by a few inches. Mary burst into tears and left the stage. I got furious and really bawled them out. When I stopped, the whole audience applauded. They were really behind us. No more beer cans, and Mary came back."

The "beer can bomber" incident and general rowdiness preoccupied everyone as the biggest group in the world—the Beatles—was booked to appear in August. The legislature passed an ordinance banning alcoholic beverages, cans and bottles in the park. The security force was also increased—estimates ranged from 137 to 250 Denver policemen—and auxiliary recruits received briefings on "Beatle Invasion" strategies and were assigned to "mop-top" duty.

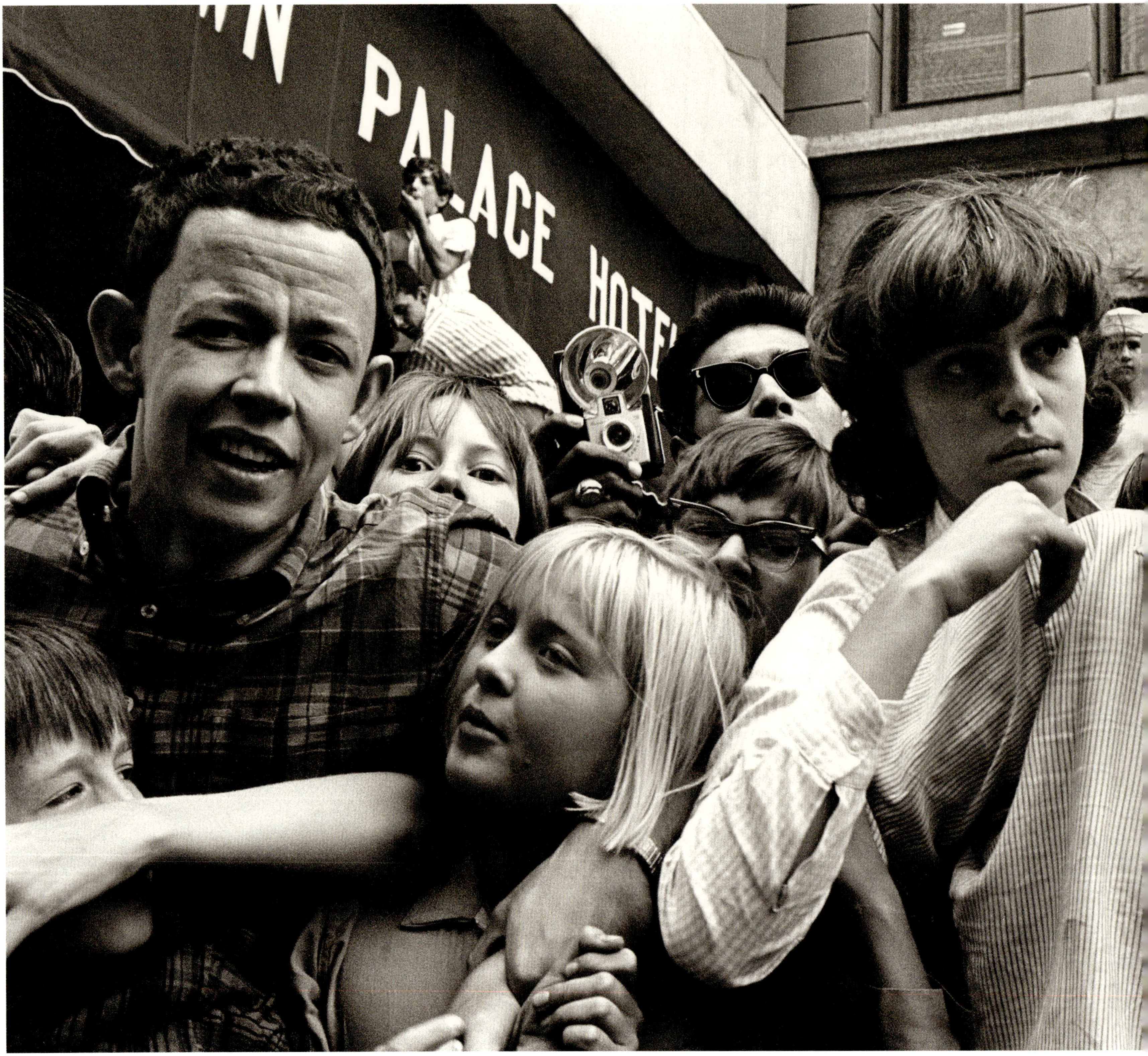

Beatles fans, 1964

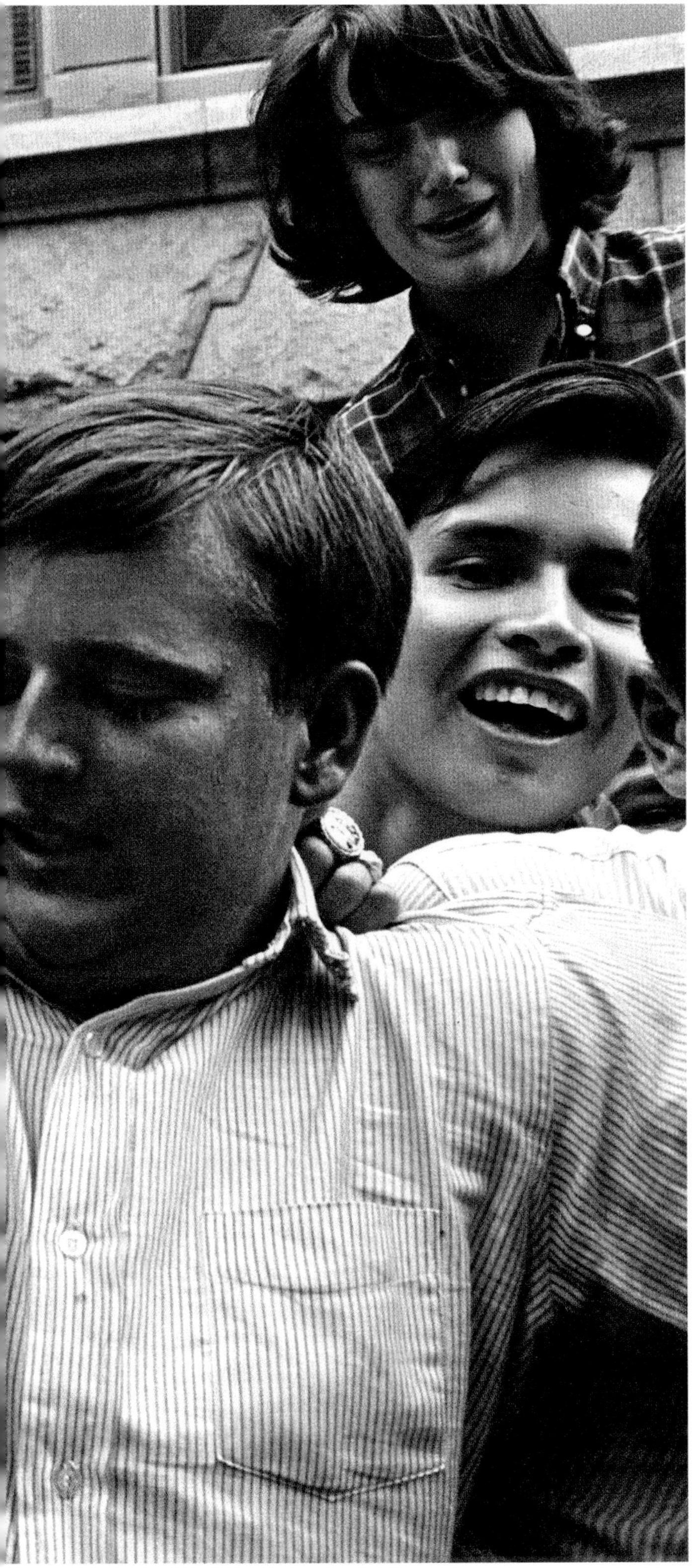

Nevertheless, Denver, like the rest of the country, succumbed to Beatlemania. The Beatles had appeared on *The Ed Sullivan Show* in February, and the first wave of the British Invasion, as it came to be called, was so swift that in the first week of April, the band held the top five positions on *Billboard*'s Hot 100 singles chart, a feat no other band or artist has ever accomplished. The Beatles' 32-day visit on their first American tour was the longest concert swing they ever shouldered. The sixth stop was a performance at Red Rocks.

For all of its seeming magnitude, the concert almost didn't happen. The expense of bringing the band to Colorado was viewed as prohibitive, and the booking nearly fell through several times. Verne Byers' Lookout Mountain Attractions promoted the show, although Byers said he didn't know the Beatles particularly well, noting they used their bowl-shaped haircuts as a "gimmick" to separate themselves from Peter & Gordon, the Beach Boys and similar acts that were touring that summer.

On the Wednesday morning of August 26, some six hours before the Beatles plane touched down, hundreds of kids bearing "I Love the Beatles" signs, Beatles hats and Beatles pins were already waiting at Stapleton Airport. By noon, nearly 10,000 had blanketed a fenced area on an adjoining boulevard. Huge numbers of sobbing and fainting teens mobbed the front entrance of the venerable Brown Palace Hotel on Broadway, where the group stayed before the show. Six girls and one harried policeman (who had been bitten on the wrist trying to hold back the hysterical mob) were treated at Denver General Hospital.

Nearly a thousand Beatlemaniacs also crowded the road leading to Red Rocks, waiting for the gates to open at 3 p.m. Seating was general admission. Weather predictions called for rain, and emergency plans were made to transfer the show to the Denver Coliseum if necessary.

Later, the Beatles arrived at Red Rocks and held a backstage press conference. Members of the Colorado Jaycees committee presented the four with official vests (called "boleros") with the band members' first names on them—John, Paul, George and Ringo.

Fans politely sat through Jackie DeShannon, the Righteous Brothers, the Exciters and the Bill Black Combo, the opening acts on the bill. Then, at 9:30 p.m., the audience erupted into 35 minutes of nonstop screams when the Beatles finally took the stage and opened with "Twist and Shout." The piercing teenaged shrieks drowned out whatever music might have been audible on the primitive sound system. The band, dressed in black suits, white shirts and skinny black ties, speedily performed its repertoire of hits, bowed to the audience, and left the stage without so much as an encore.

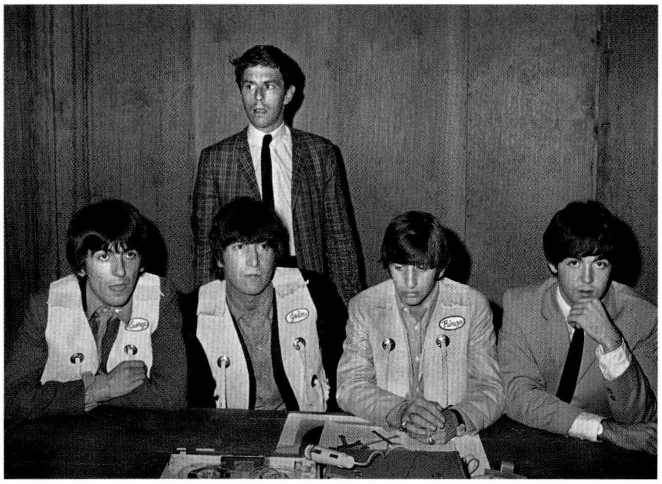

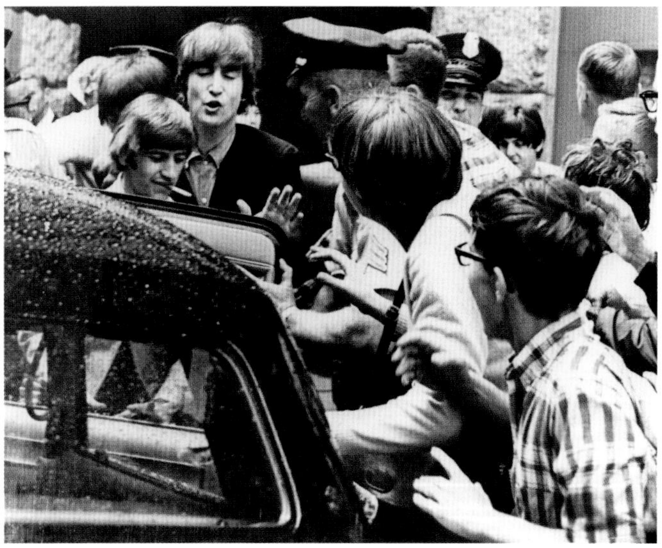

Press conference, (top); Beatlemania (above); the Beatles, 1964 (right)

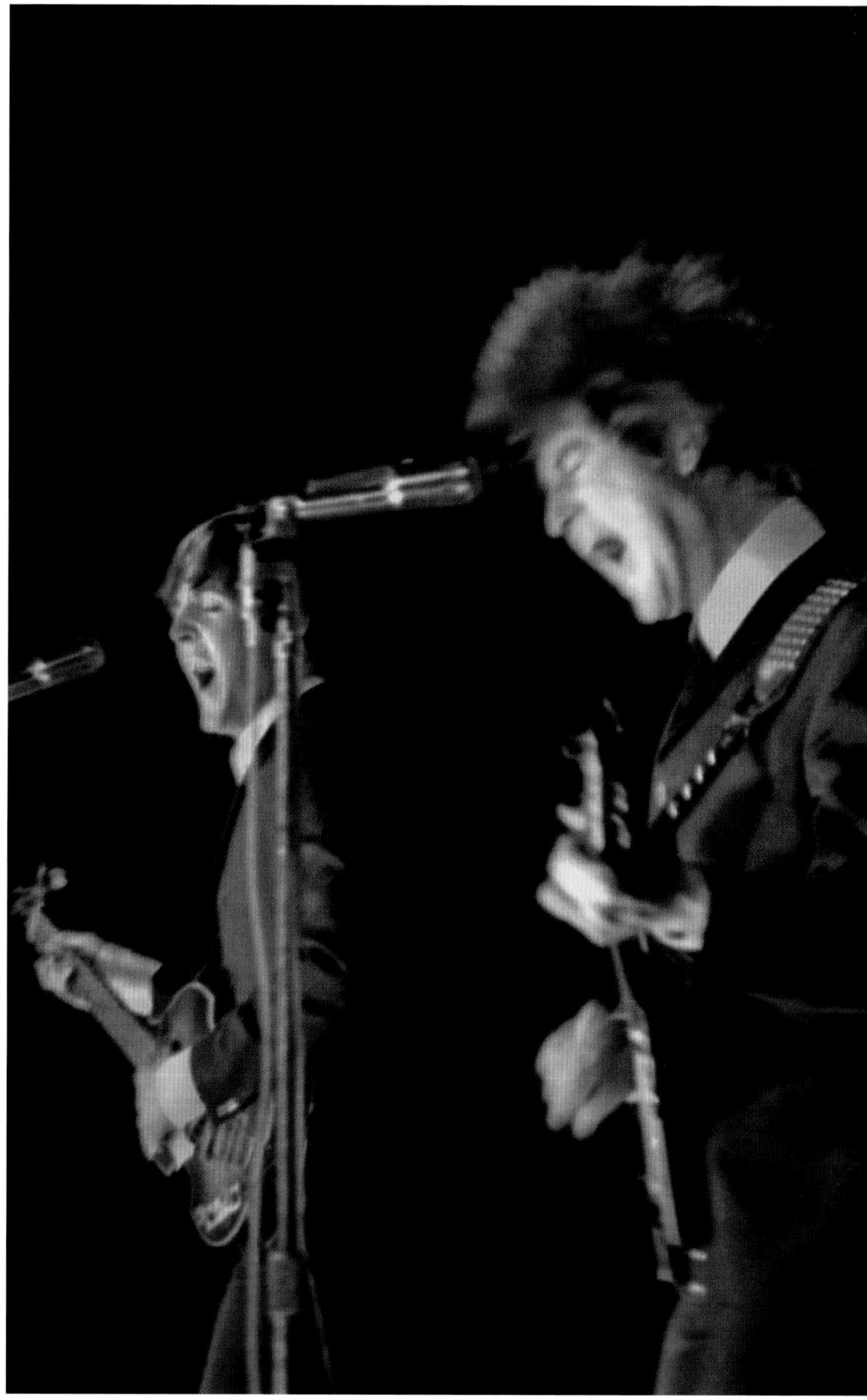

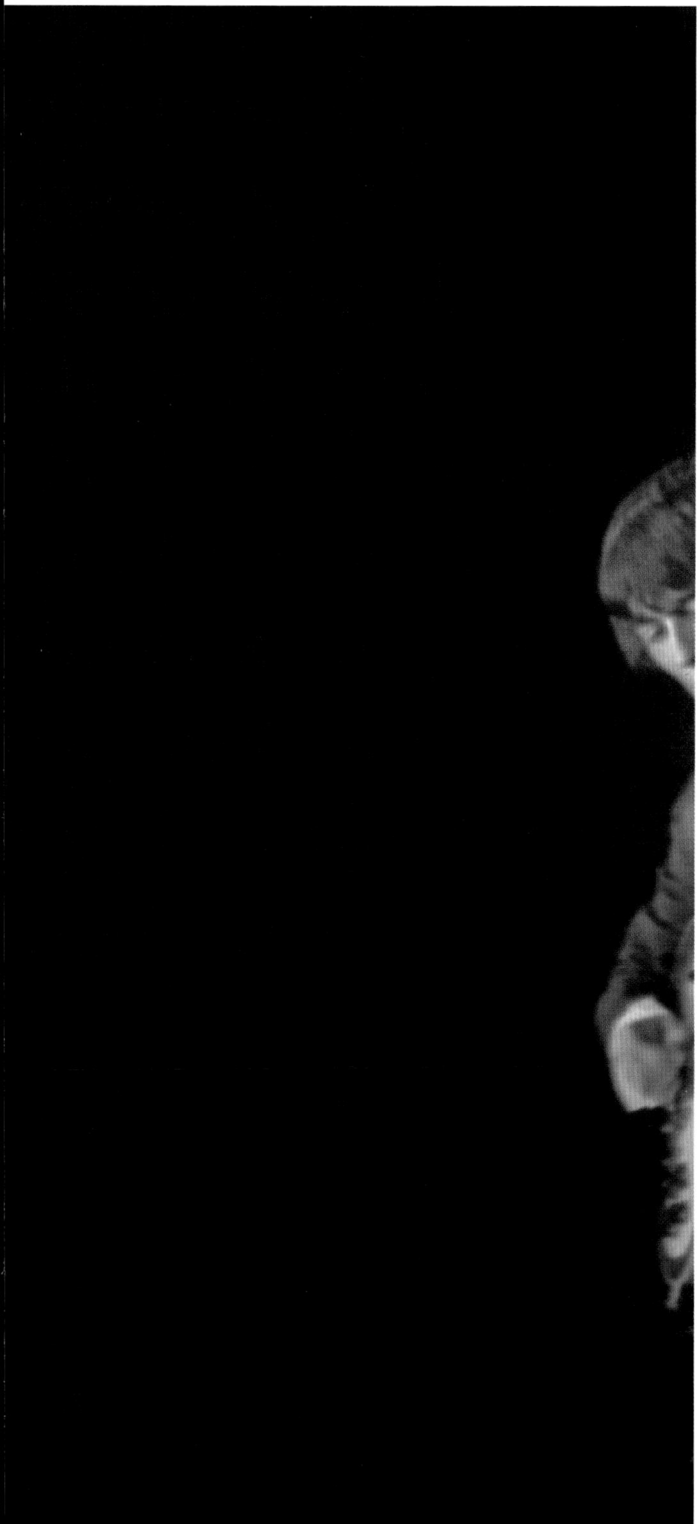

The altitude proved the only troublesome factor during the Beatles' performance—halfway through the first song, they were gasping. The members wound up using strategically placed oxygen canisters.

"We were all told it was high above sea water, altitude. We thought, 'Well, so? What's the difference?' We got there, and we started finding it a little hard to breathe," Paul McCartney said. "I remember singing 'Long Tall Sally' and thinking, 'Hey, this is great, hyperventilation of the highest order! Well, Long Tall Sally, *wheeze, wheeze...*' I was sweating, but I got through it. It was an interesting experience, physically. It was a lovely arena, beautiful at night."

Fans did pelt the Beatles—with handfuls of jelly beans (reportedly their favorite candy), not beer cans. Police officers stationed themselves across the front of the stage, and the wall held. Men on horseback, on foot and in jeeps along with mountain climbers cleared the rocks of kids who wanted a better view of the band, but many determined fans scaled the rocks and snuck in.

Red Rocks was the only date on the Beatles' 1964 tour that did not sell out—at least officially. Only 7,000 fans bought general admission tickets to see the show in the 9,000-plus capacity venue. Press accounts blamed the unsold tickets on the "out of the way" location, coupled with no public transportation for teens.

But photographs and news clips showed a well over-capacity crowd and no empty seats. At $6.60, tickets were nearly $3 more than those for a recent performance by Igor Stravinsky, who was considered the world's greatest living composer. Although the cost paralleled prices across the country, many fans suffered from Fab Four sticker shock and plotted alternate ways to get into Red Rocks—which many still viewed as a mountain park rather than a musical venue. It was common knowledge among Denver-area high school students that Red Rocks had hardly any gates, ticket takers or bouncers, and a few thousand enthusiasts managed to sneak into the event.

After the show, John, Paul, George and Ringo were whisked back to Suite 840 at the Brown Palace, and visited for a while with Joan Baez, who would perform at the amphitheatre two nights later. The predicted rain finally arrived as the Beatles headed for the airport the following day. An estimated 3,500 people waited at Stapleton. Shortly after noon, the group left Denver for Cincinnati, never again to return as a band.

Reportedly, the $48,000 gate netted the city $2,000 in rent, but with crowd control costing nearly $3,000, the city lost money on the Beatles.

Baez's performance at Red Rocks resulted from her friendship with Harry Tuft of the Denver Folklore Center. Because of his connections

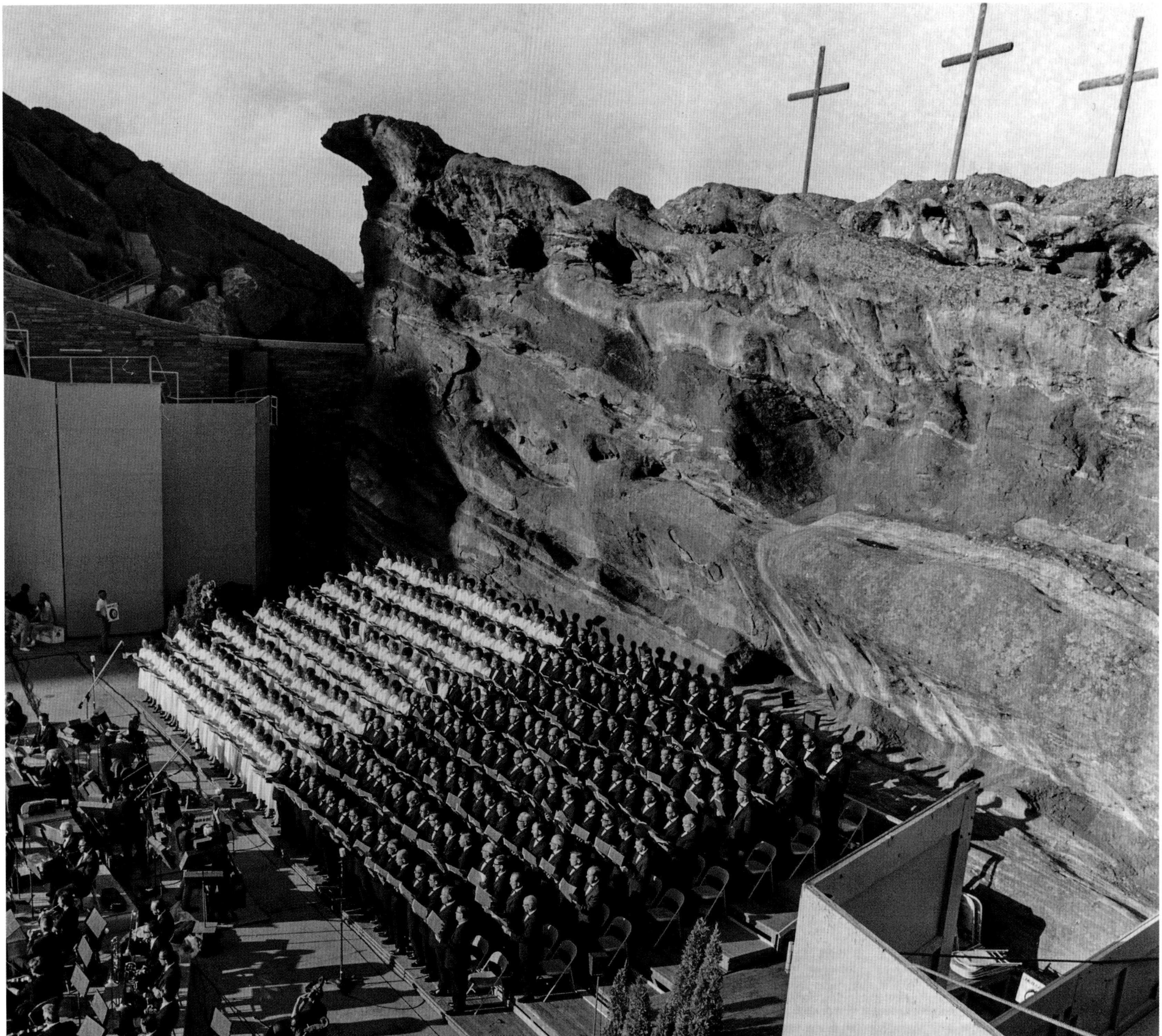

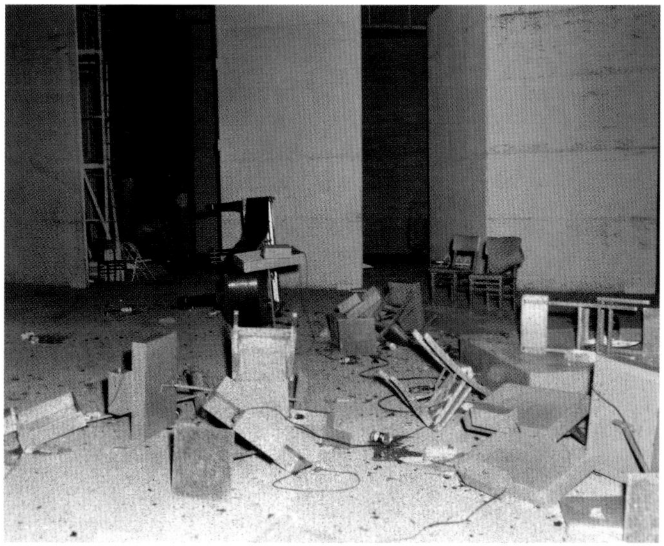

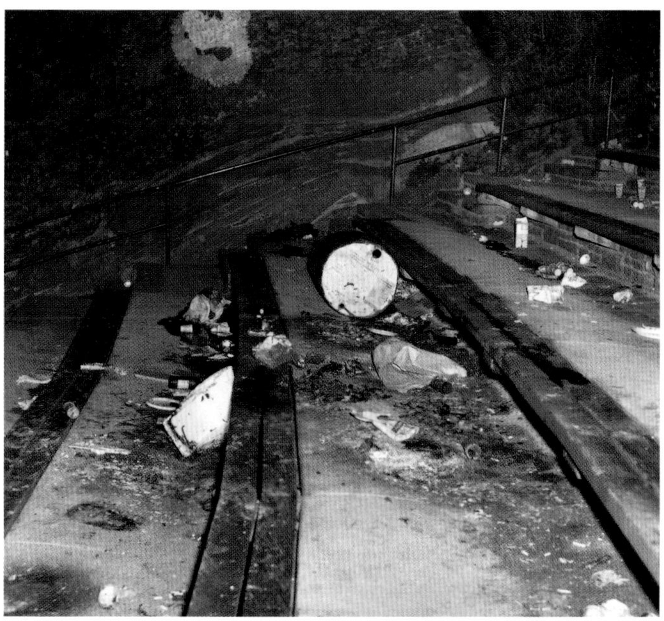

Mormon Tabernacle Choir with the Bell Telephone Orchestra, 1966 (left); Aretha Franklin concert riot, 1968 (top, bottom)

with many leading performers in New York and Philadelphia, and given Denver's convenient location on the way to and from the West Coast, Tuft had begun to promote shows at Red Rocks.

After quietly urging Baez to perform there, he took her to the empty amphitheatre and they performed an impromptu drama on the stage. Seeing the place convinced Baez it would work. Her visit with the Beatles then cemented the deal. On August 28, to an enthusiastic crowd of 3,000, Baez spoke of Bob Dylan, presidential candidate Barry Goldwater—and the Beatles.

The following year, fans heard country music at Red Rocks for the first time with an August 1965 appearance by Johnny Cash with Tex Ritter, the Statler Brothers and the future Mrs. Cash, June Carter. In 1966, the Mormon Tabernacle Choir combined talents with the Bell Telephone Orchestra to record Handel's *Messiah*, recorded by NBC at Red Rocks for a national broadcast the following Easter. For several years, shows went smoothly at Red Rocks, with such acts as Bill Cosby, Herb Alpert & the Tijuana Brass and Peter, Paul & Mary providing light-hearted entertainment.

But the vibe changed in August 1968, when a planned appearance by Aretha Franklin got nasty.

Tickets were $6; crowd estimates ranged from 1,800 to more than 3,000. The contract called for Franklin's entire fee of $20,000 to be paid in cash prior to the performance. Promoter Carl Robinson said he had lost money on the show and couldn't come up with the remainder of the purse until the following morning. Franklin refused to sing—and went onstage to announce her decision.

Most people left peacefully, but a few angry fans went on a 20-minute rampage, breaking up chairs, music stands, a grand piano and footlights; some protesters set fire to trees, bushes and trash piles around the park until the police could clear them out. Bottles and rocks rained onto the stage and metal trash barrels rolled down the grandstand. Three people were arrested for attempting to steal microphones and speakers.

An upset Franklin went back to her Denver Hilton Hotel suite and cried. "I had full intentions of performing," she stated. "I transported a 23-man troupe 2,100 miles to perform with me. I did this because I felt that the promoter would honor the contract that he signed."

The counterculture's idea of rock music—as opposed to the latest Top 40 hit—started to dominate in Denver. The city's general objection to rock at Red Rocks wasn't good news for a fledgling promoter whose career would span four decades—Barry Fey.

Fey founded his promotions firm, Feyline, in 1967. By the following year he had grown ambitious enough to book Red Rocks—his first

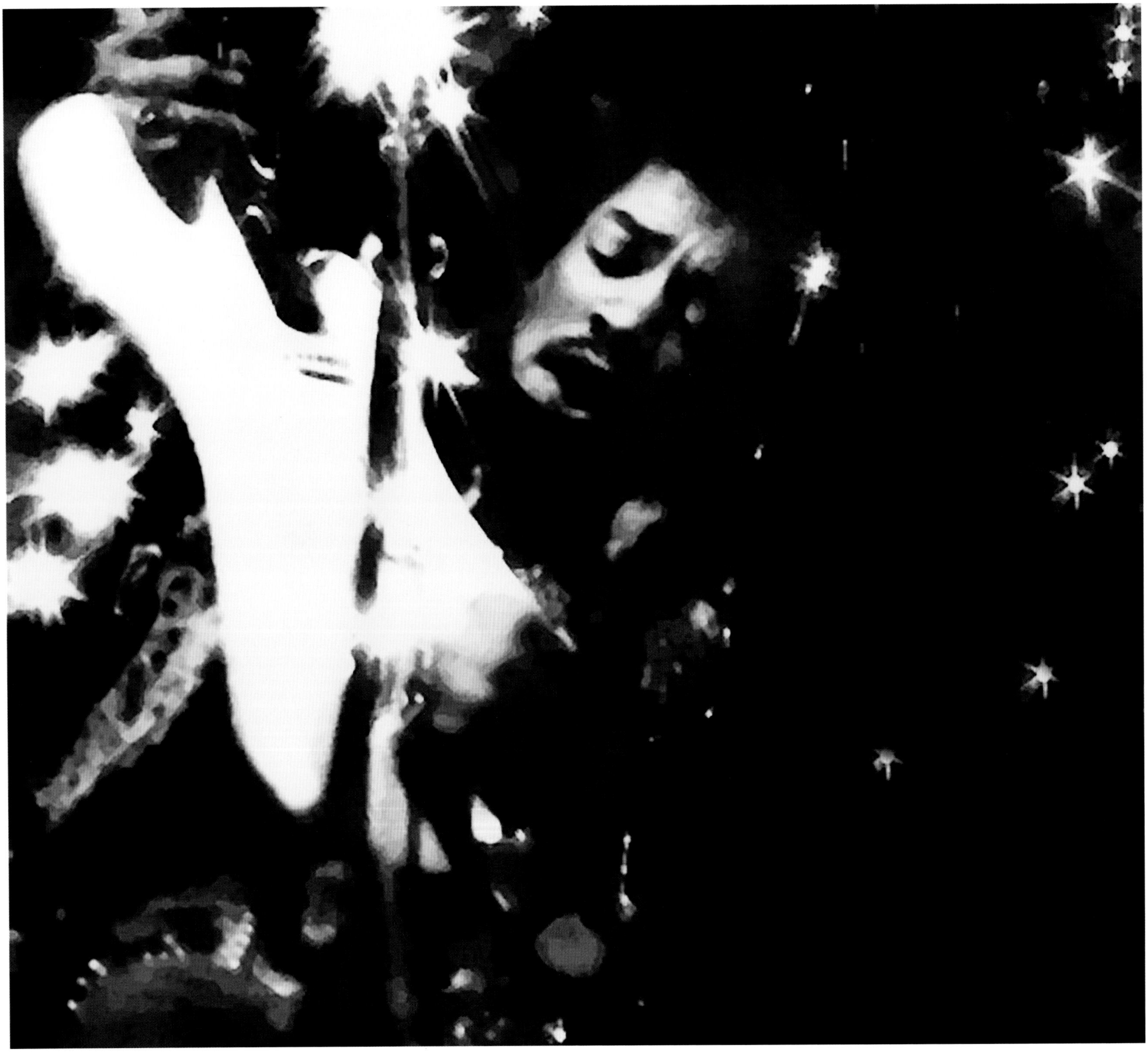

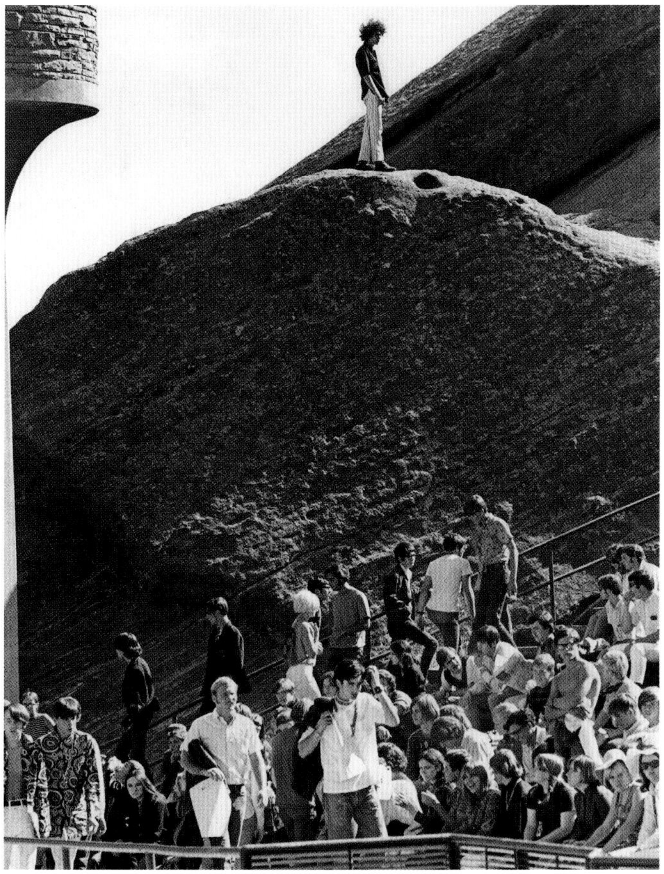

The Jimi Hendrix Experience (left), Jimi Hendrix fans (above), 1968

concert using a city facility—to close the season. Tickets to the Vanilla Fudge/Jimi Hendrix Experience/Soft Machine billing cost $4.50. Some audience members staked out front-row seats more than twelve hours before the beginning of the concert.

An airline bungle delayed the arrival of Vanilla Fudge by 45 minutes; the trucks carrying the band's equipment also got there late, as did Hendrix's flight. All the while, stage announcements urged those people who had climbed into every nook and cranny of the rocks above the seating and stage areas not to try and "fly"—an act attempted by a recent concertgoer on LSD. Anyone having difficulty was reminded to stay put until Rocky Mountain Rescue could help them down. Harry Tuft, the emcee, tried to keep the audience's spirits up during the long delays.

Hendrix finally took the stage, walked to the mike and said, 'For those of you up in the rocks...if you think you can fly, maybe we can help you along!'"

Then one of Hendrix's Marshall amplifiers blew. He stopped playing while roadies replaced tubes in the back of the amp; when that didn't work, they swapped it out altogether. "I'm really sorry," an upset Hendrix apologized. "I don't know what the hell we are trying to do up here."

By all accounts, Hendrix didn't stack up to the competition at Red Rocks. He later said, "I had a lot of fun at Red Rocks. That was groovy and nice, 'cause people are on top of you there, or at least they can hear something. That's where it should be, natural-theater type things."

Noel Redding, bass player for the Jimi Hendrix Experience, said, "Unfortunately, Jimi didn't play very well that night, and afterwards Denver had nothing to offer in after-gig entertainment. Or even daytime entertainment, for there was nothing to do the next day either, so we all took acid and went into the mountains."

Something positive did ultimately result from Hendrix's sole appearance at Red Rocks. After the gig, he returned to his Cosmopolitan hotel room in downtown Denver and wrote the liner notes to his *Electric Ladyland* album.

Another Fey production became the biggest Red Rocks show of 1969. Despite rain showers and heavy winds, Diana Ross & the Supremes treated a packed amphitheatre to their signature Motown sound. That August, Tuft brought Joan Baez, the first lady of the antiwar movement, back to Red Rocks. Her concert tour was being filmed as a documentary, the 1970 film *Carry It On*.

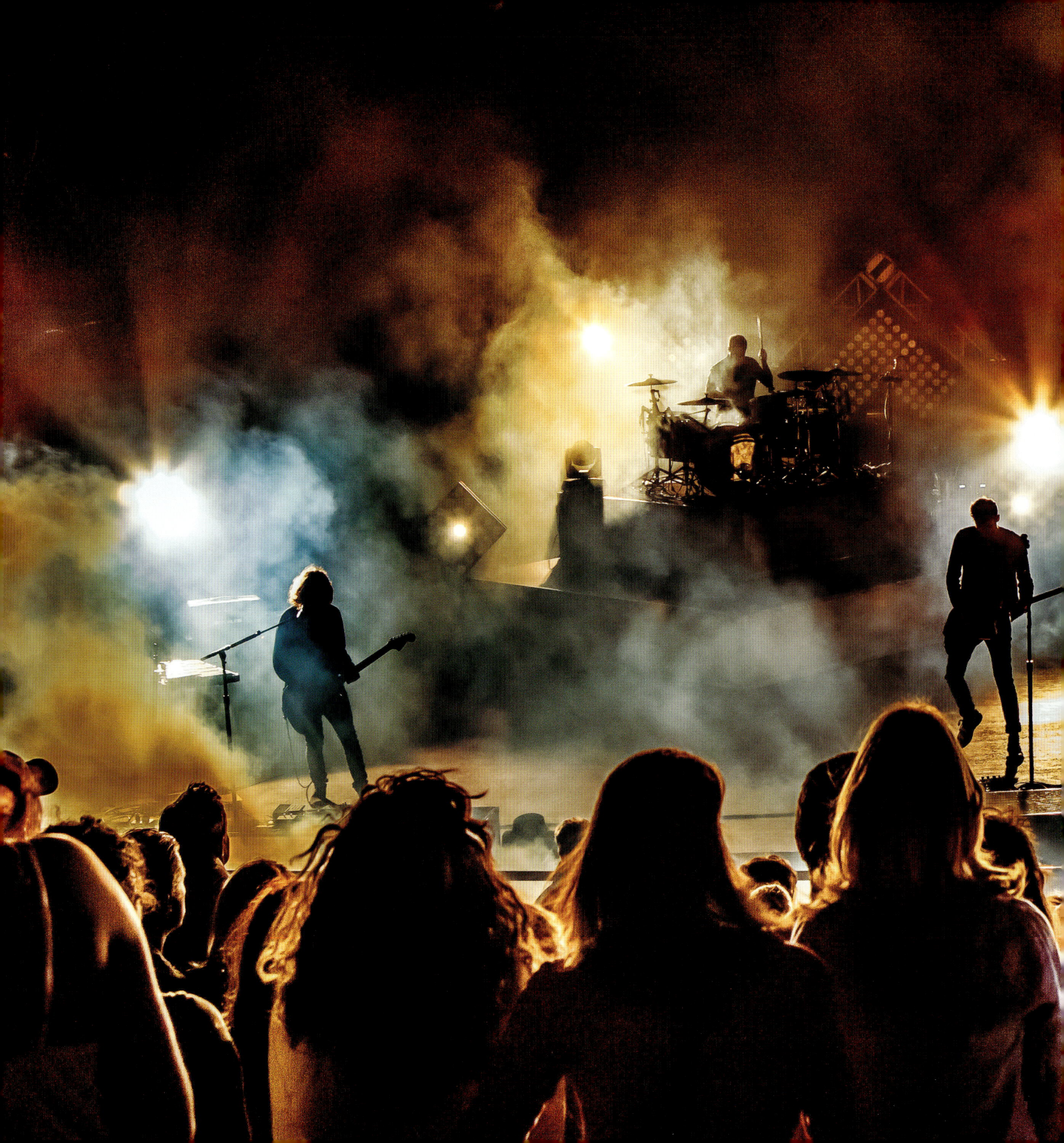

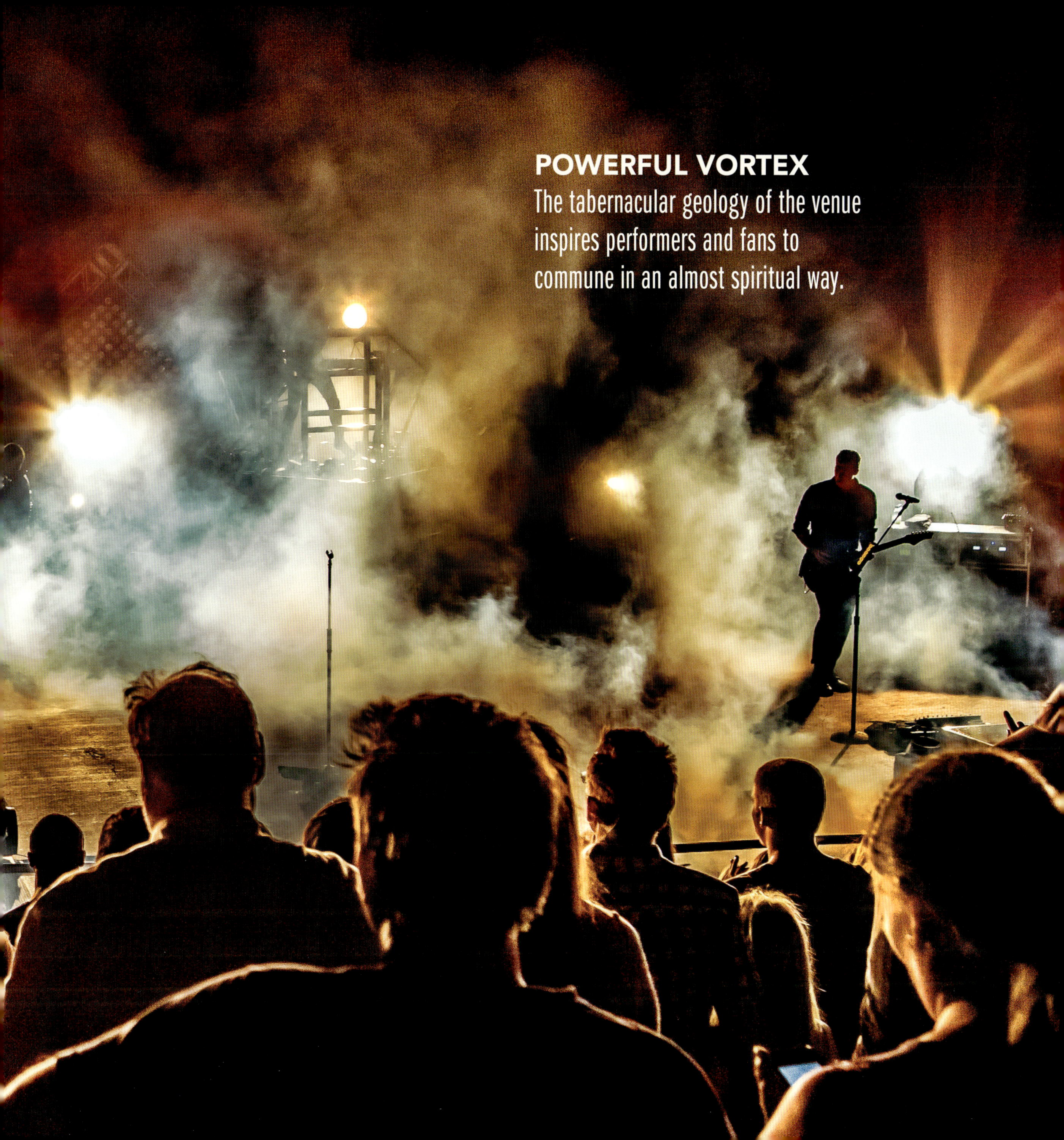

POWERFUL VORTEX
The tabernacular geology of the venue inspires performers and fans to commune in an almost spiritual way.

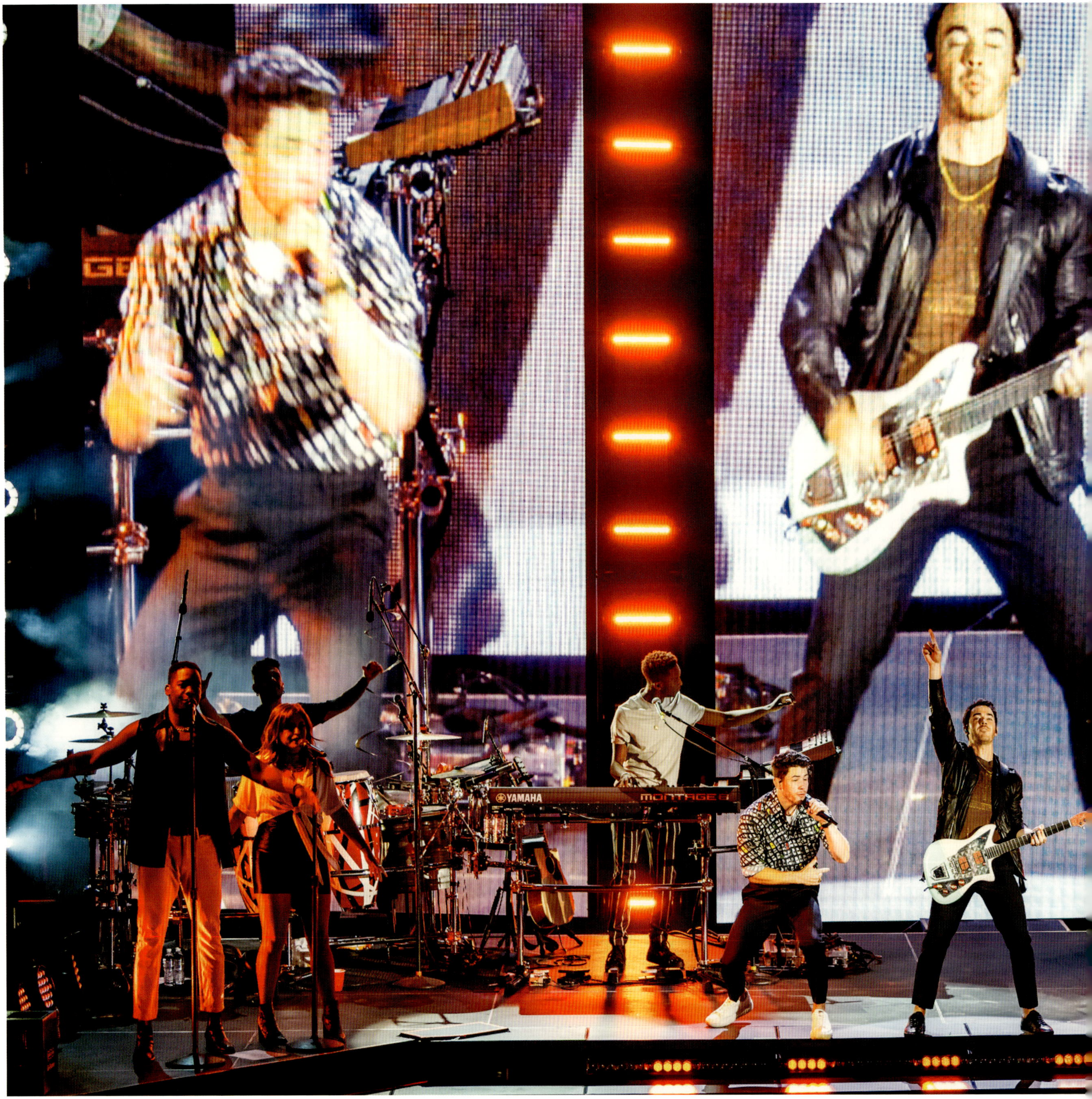
YAMAHA
MONTAGE 8

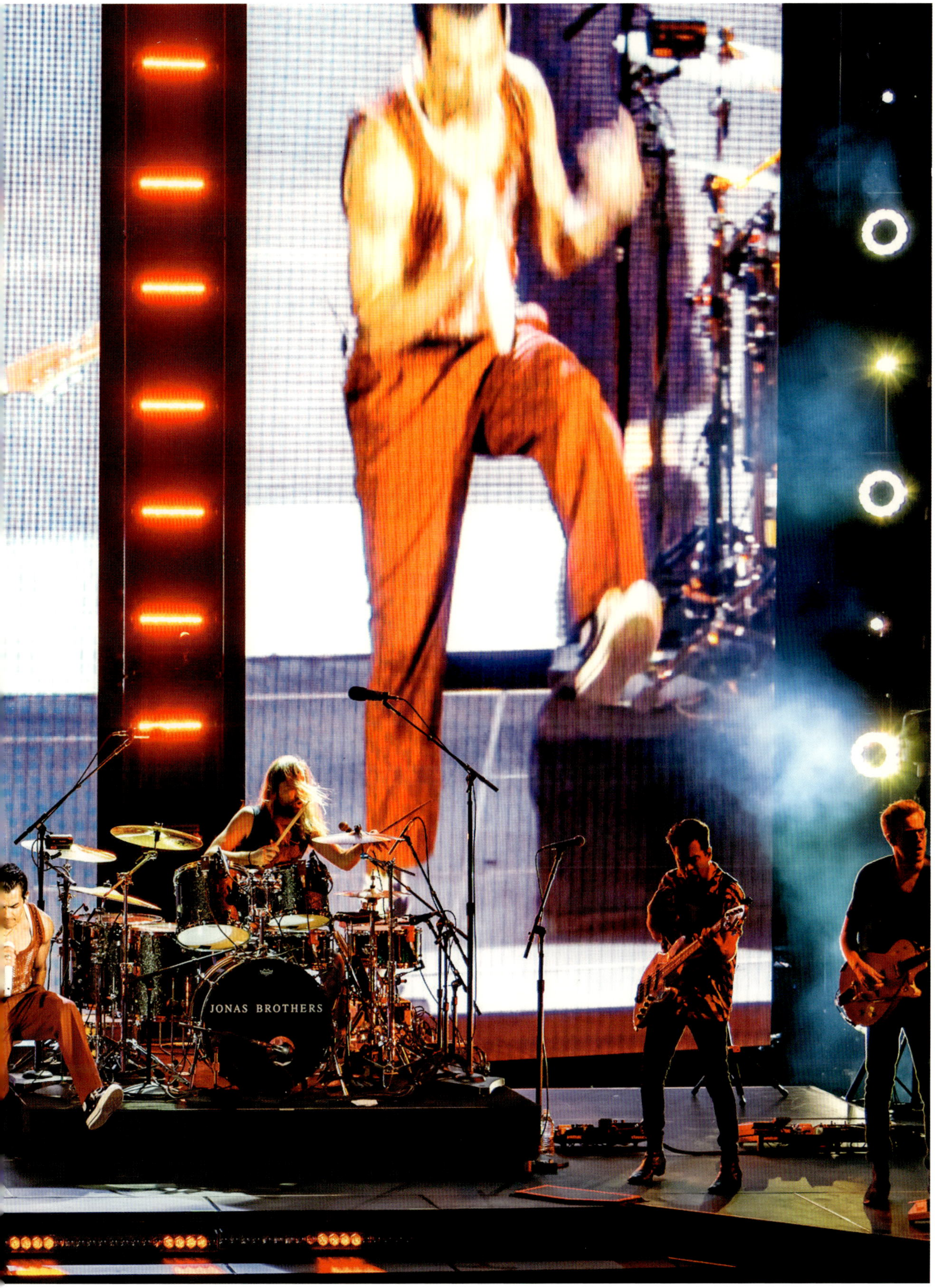

Jonas Brothers, 2021

Previous spread: OneRepublic, 2014

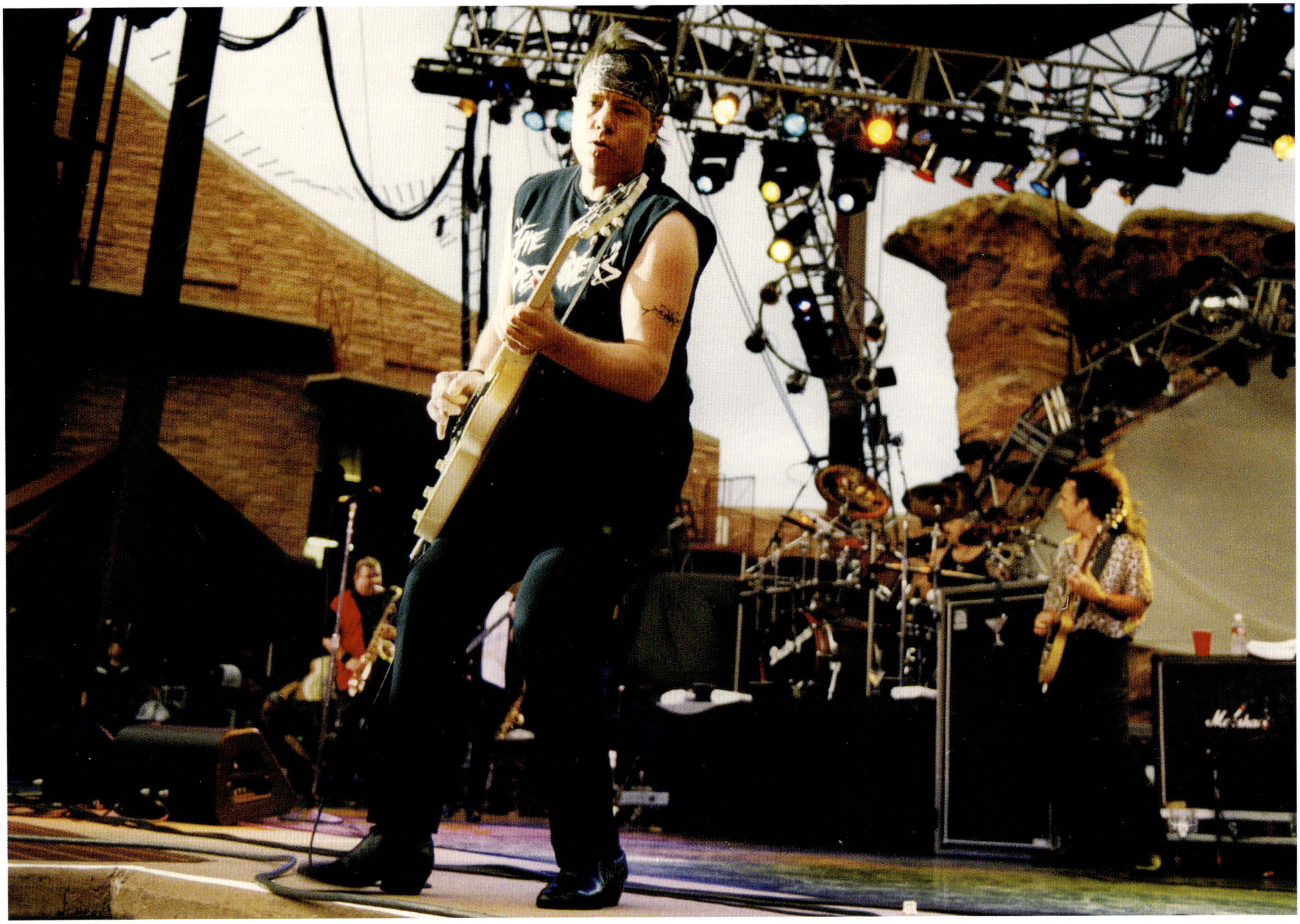

George Thorogood & the Destroyers, 1990; John Butler Trio, 2011 (right)

Following spreads
Page 56-57: Mötley Crüe, 2005
Page 58-59: Illenium, 2018

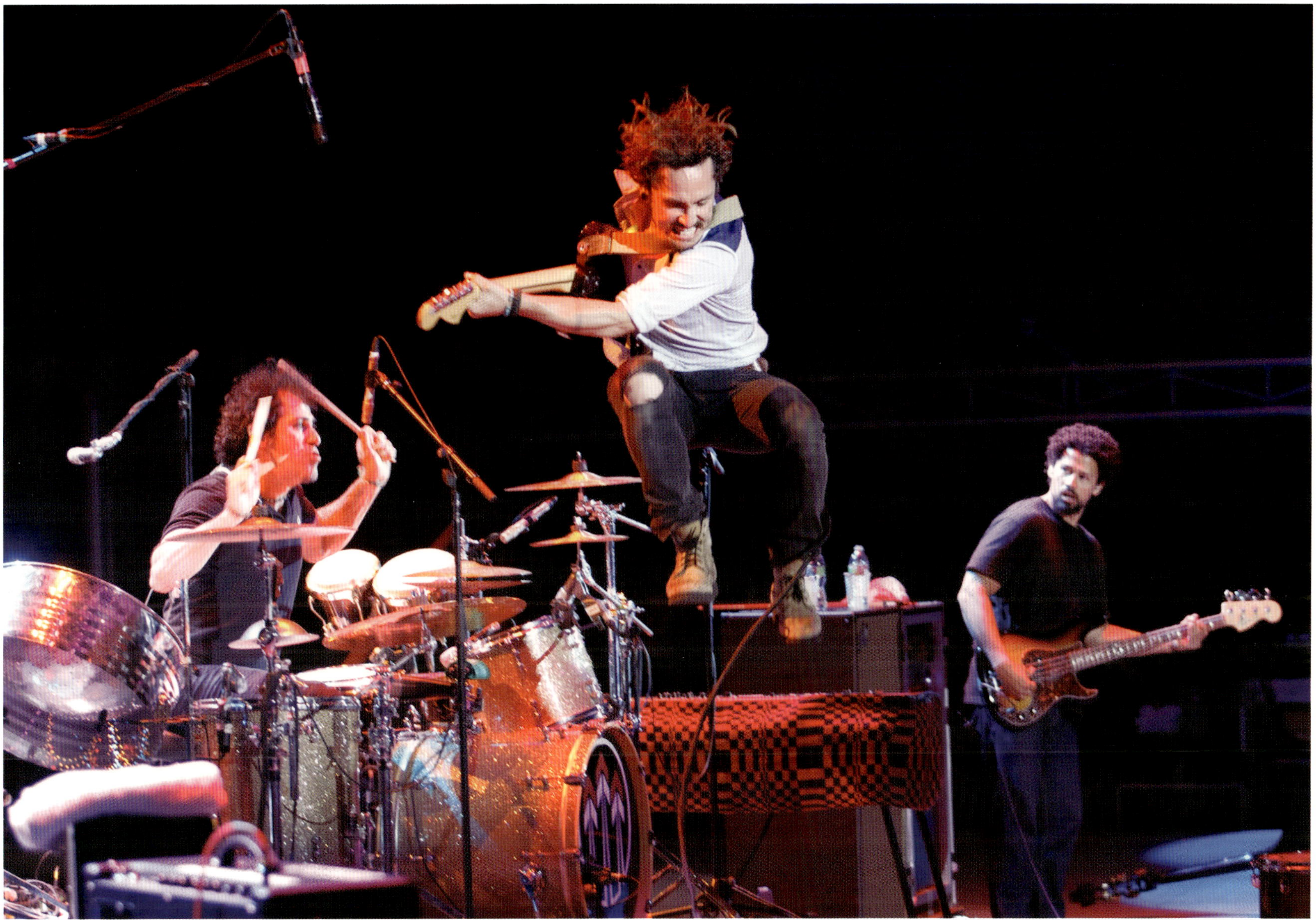

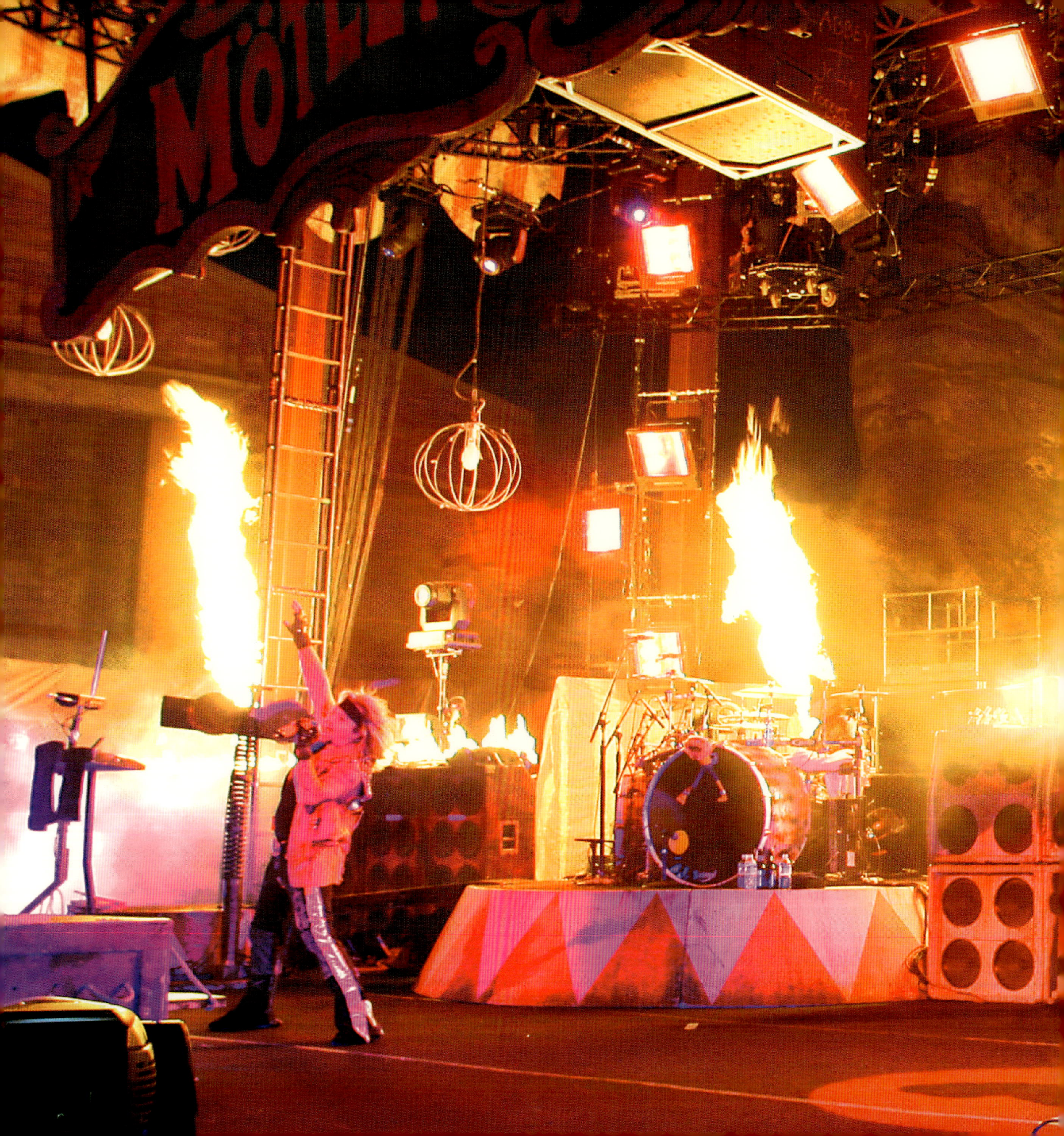

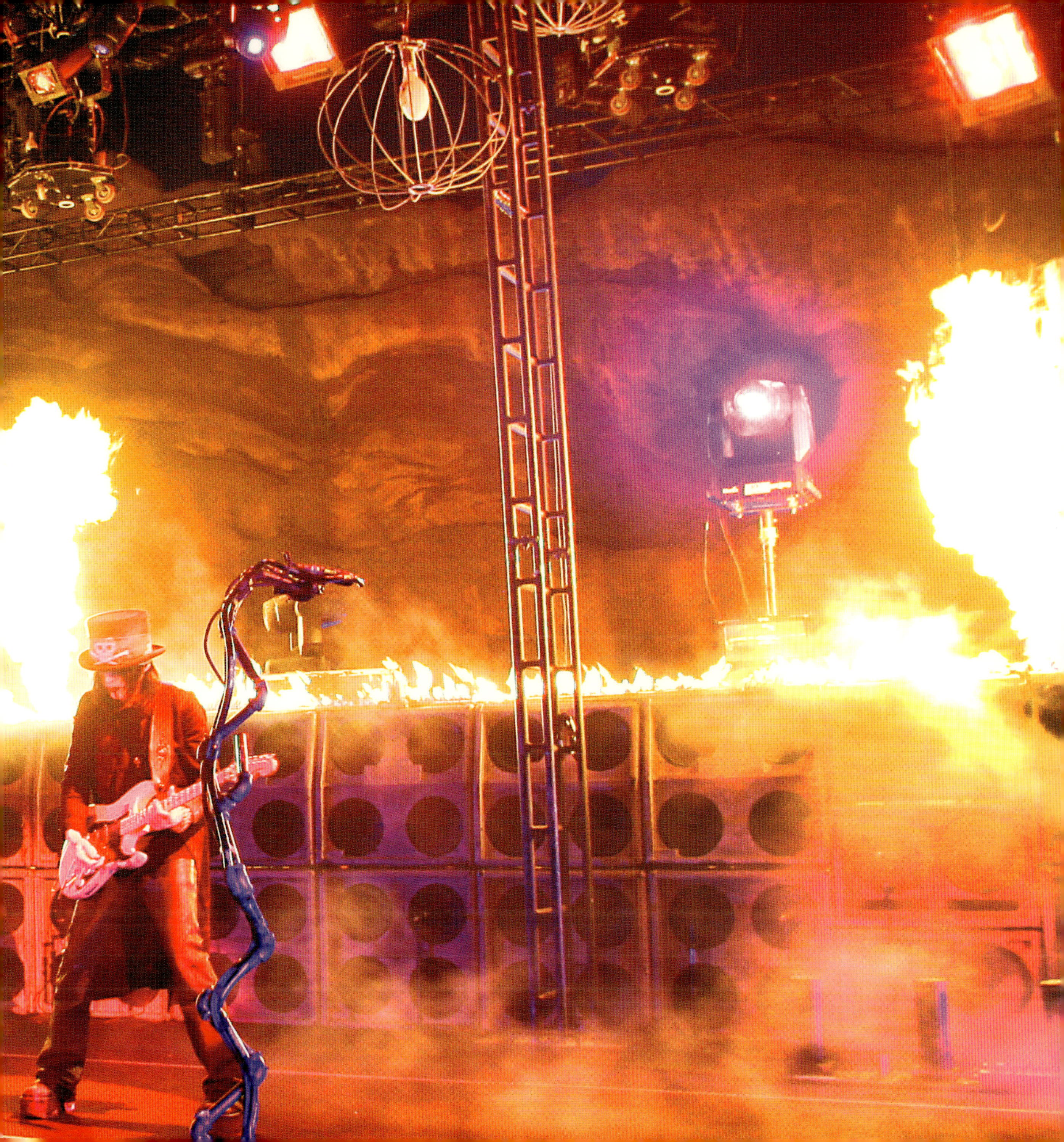

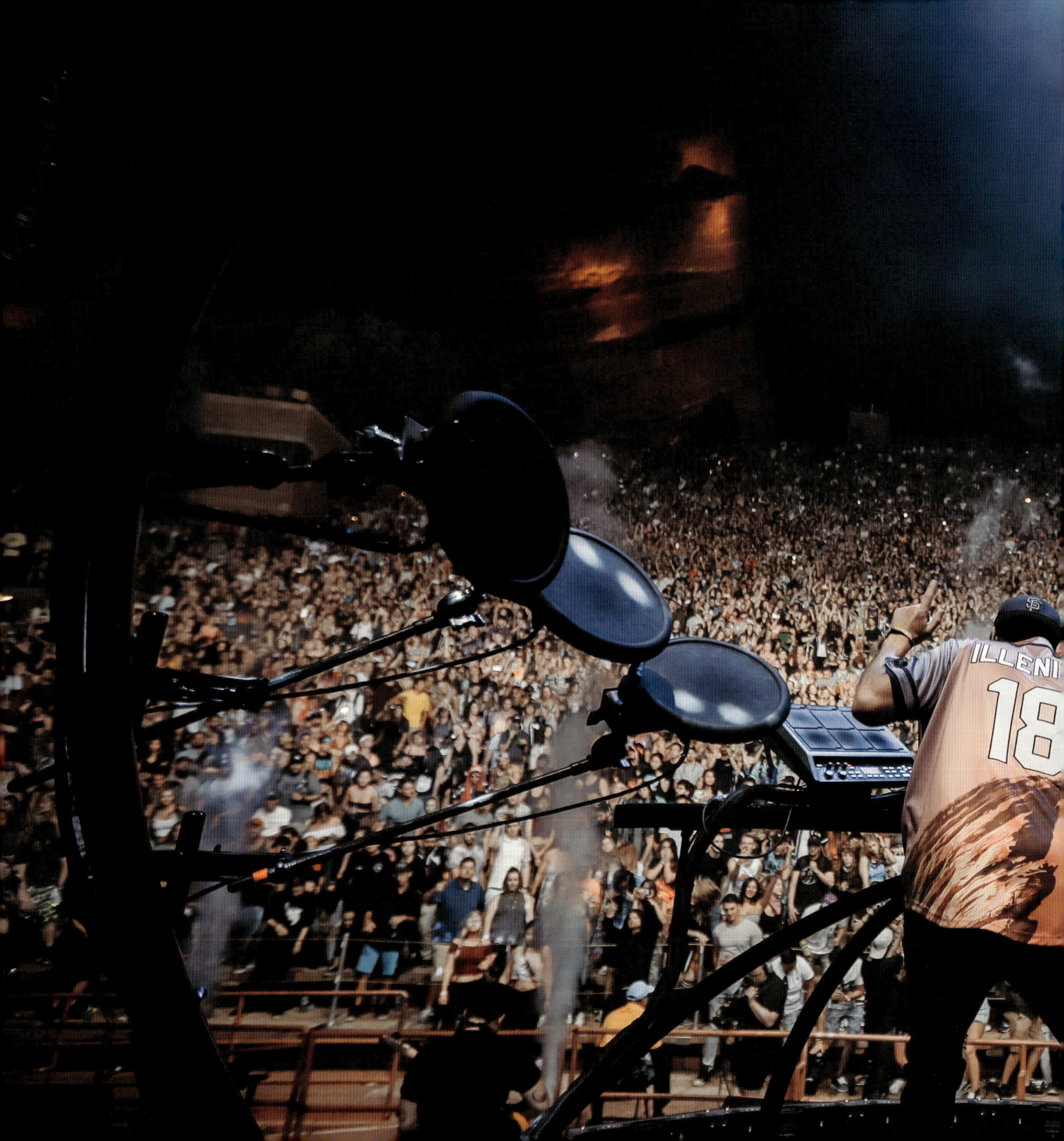
ILLENI
18

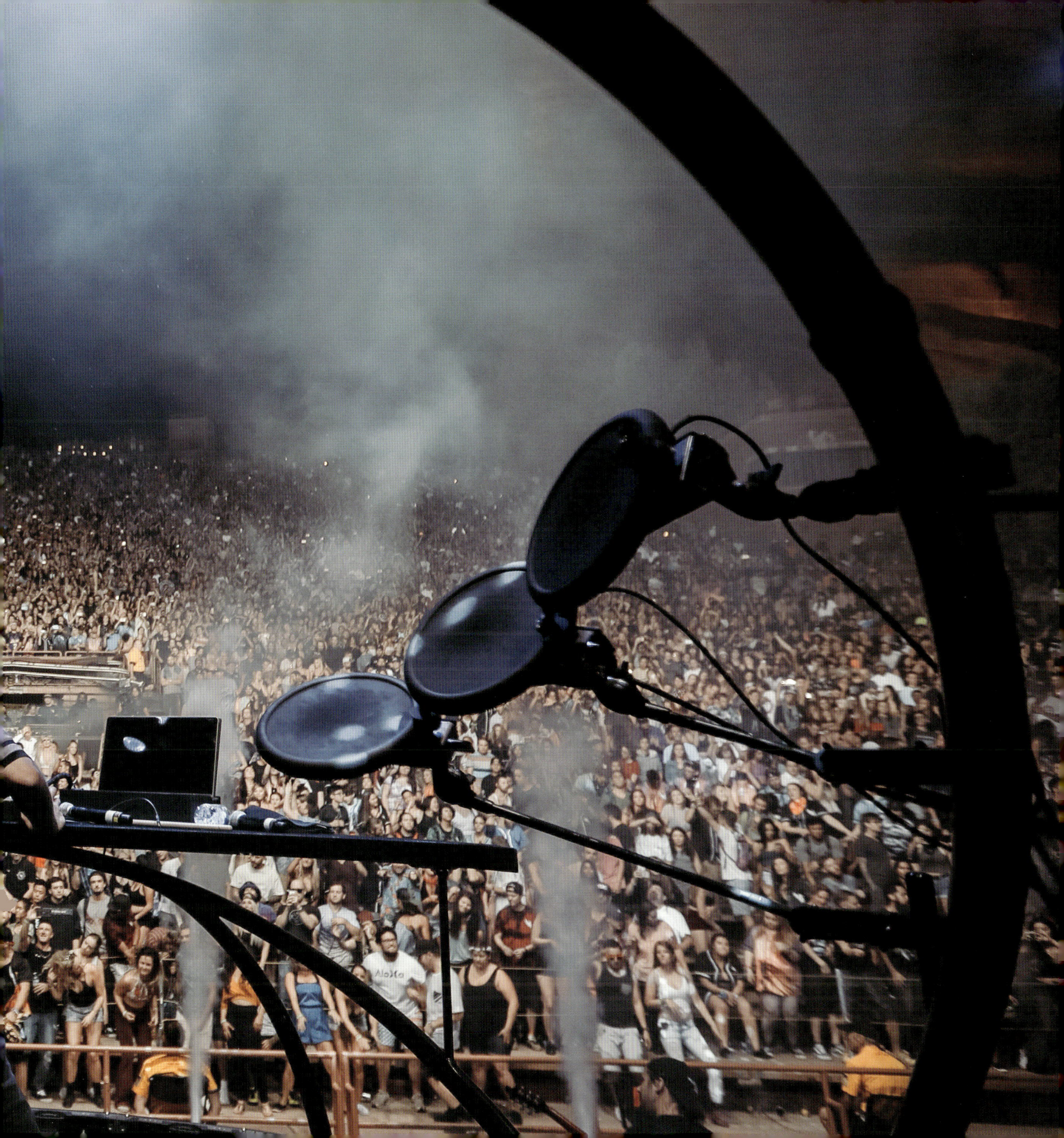

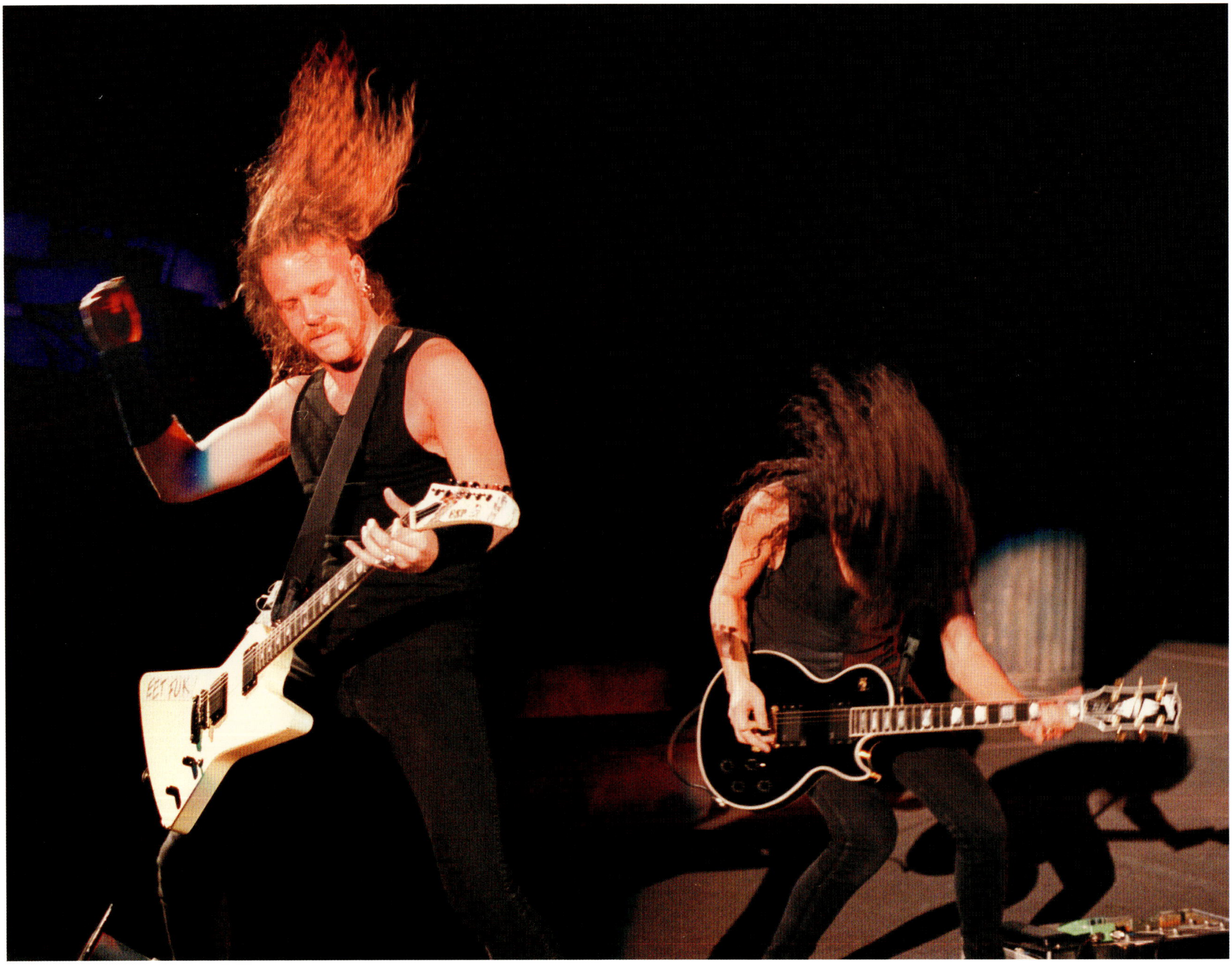

Metallica, 1989; Red Hot Chili Peppers, 1990 (right)

Following spread: Dermot Kennedy, 2021

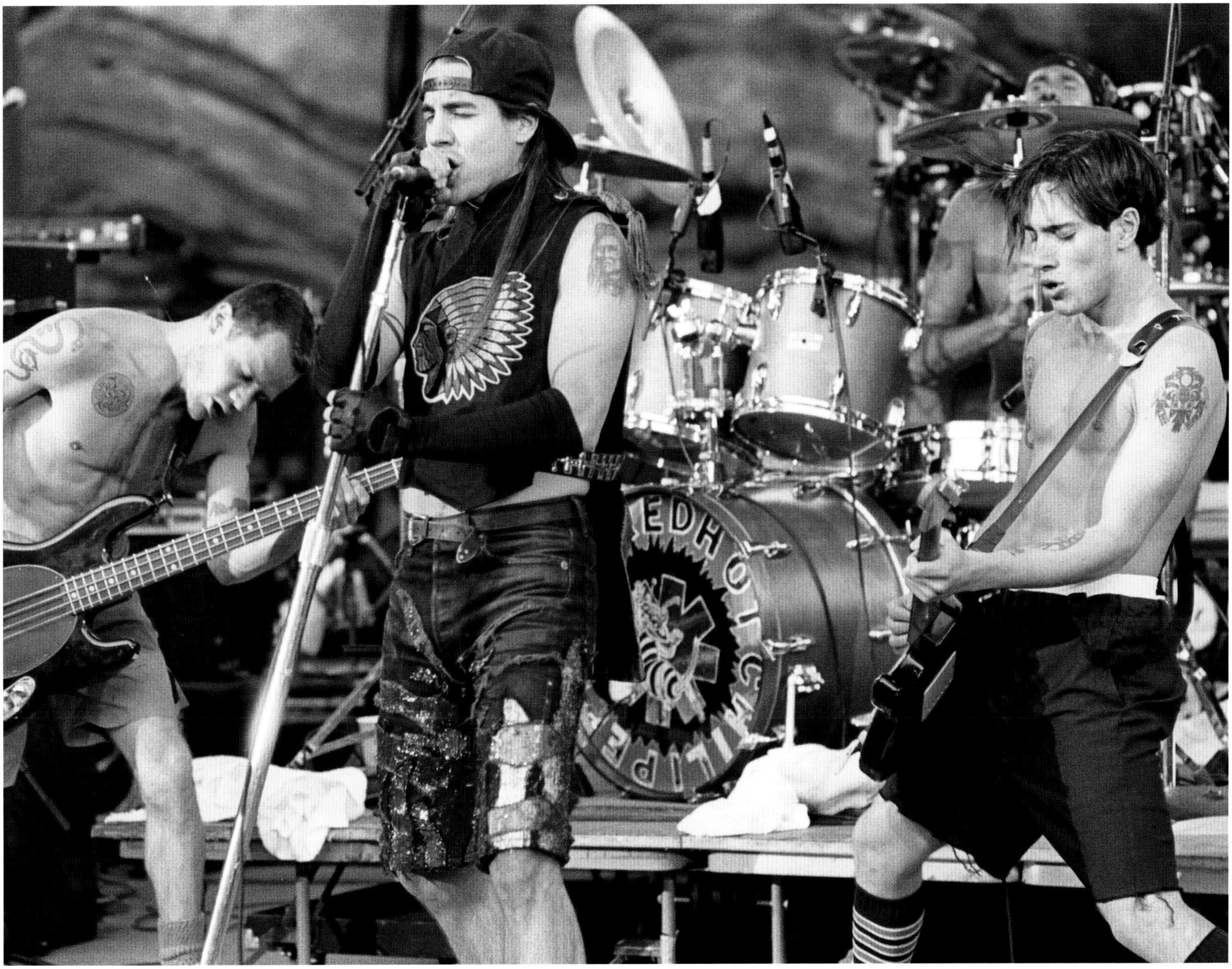

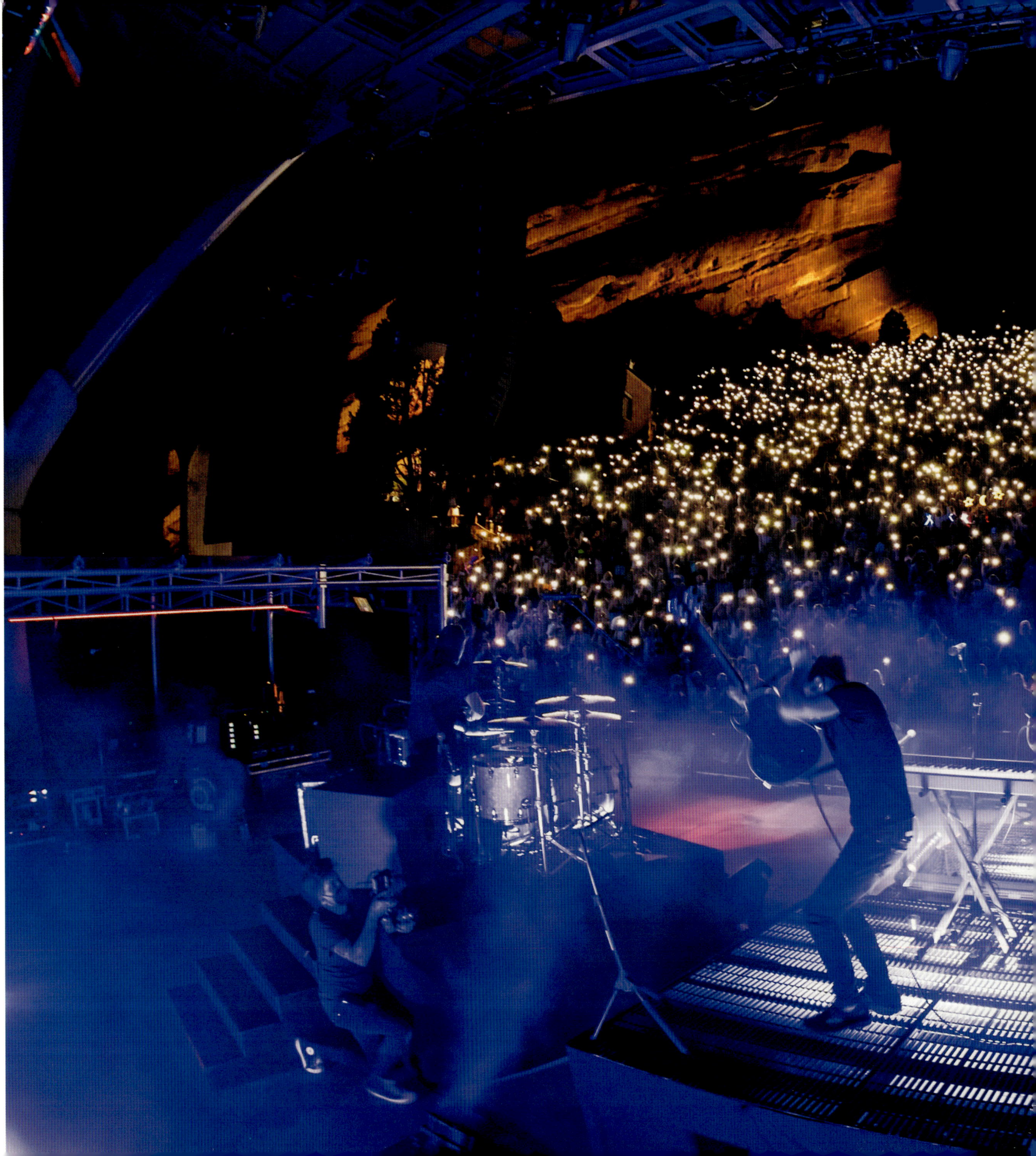

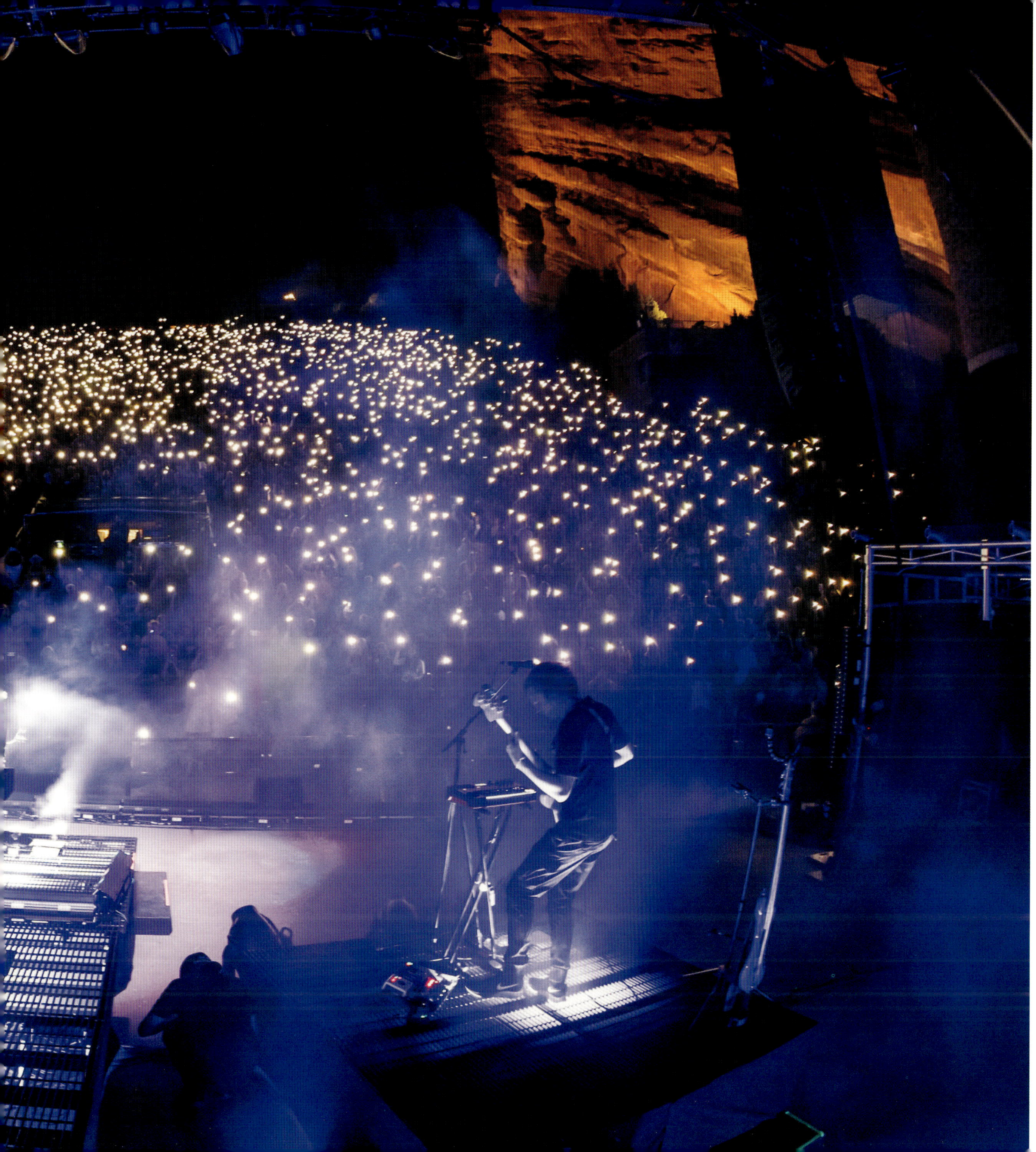

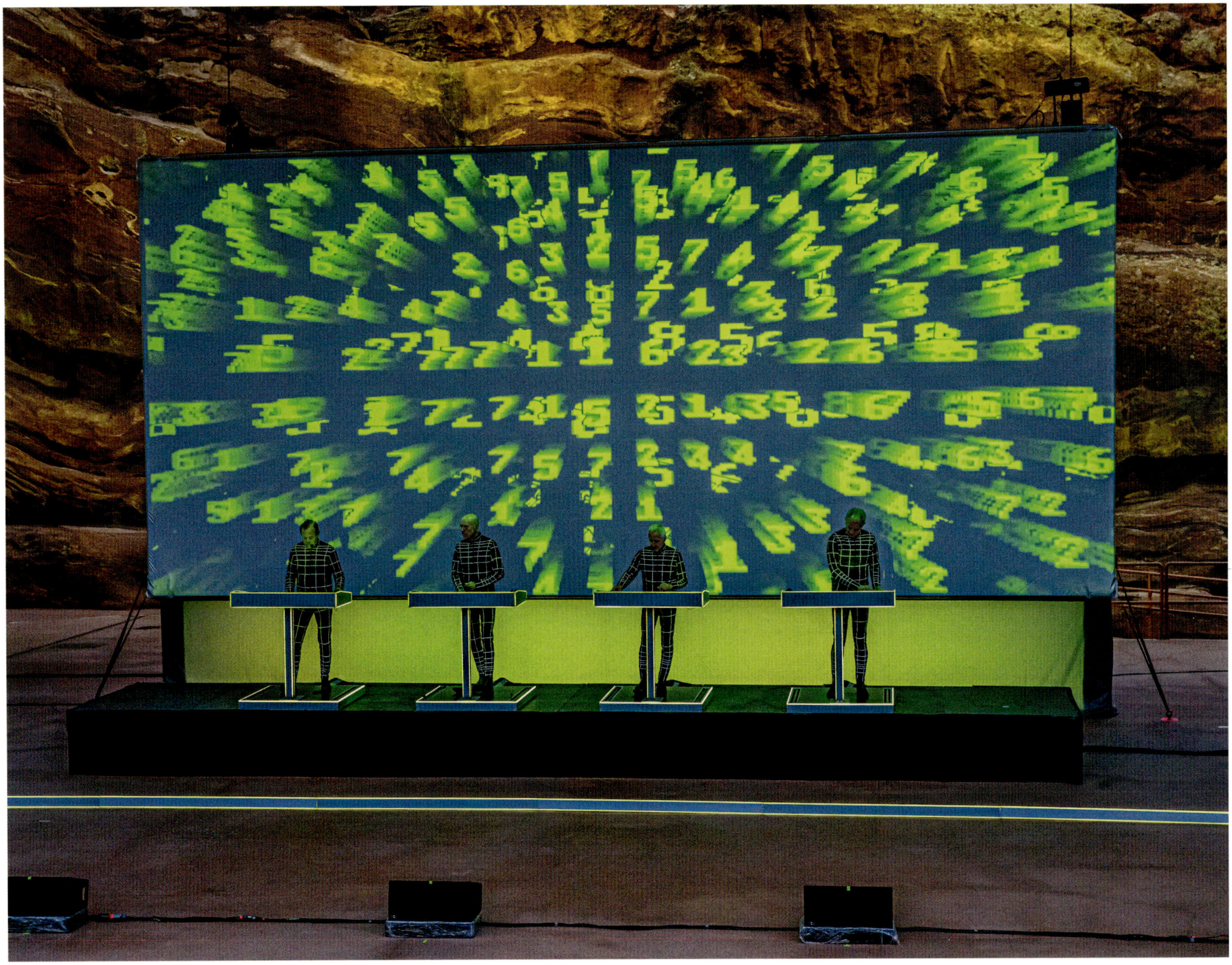

Kraftwerk, 2022; Radiohead, 2001 (right)

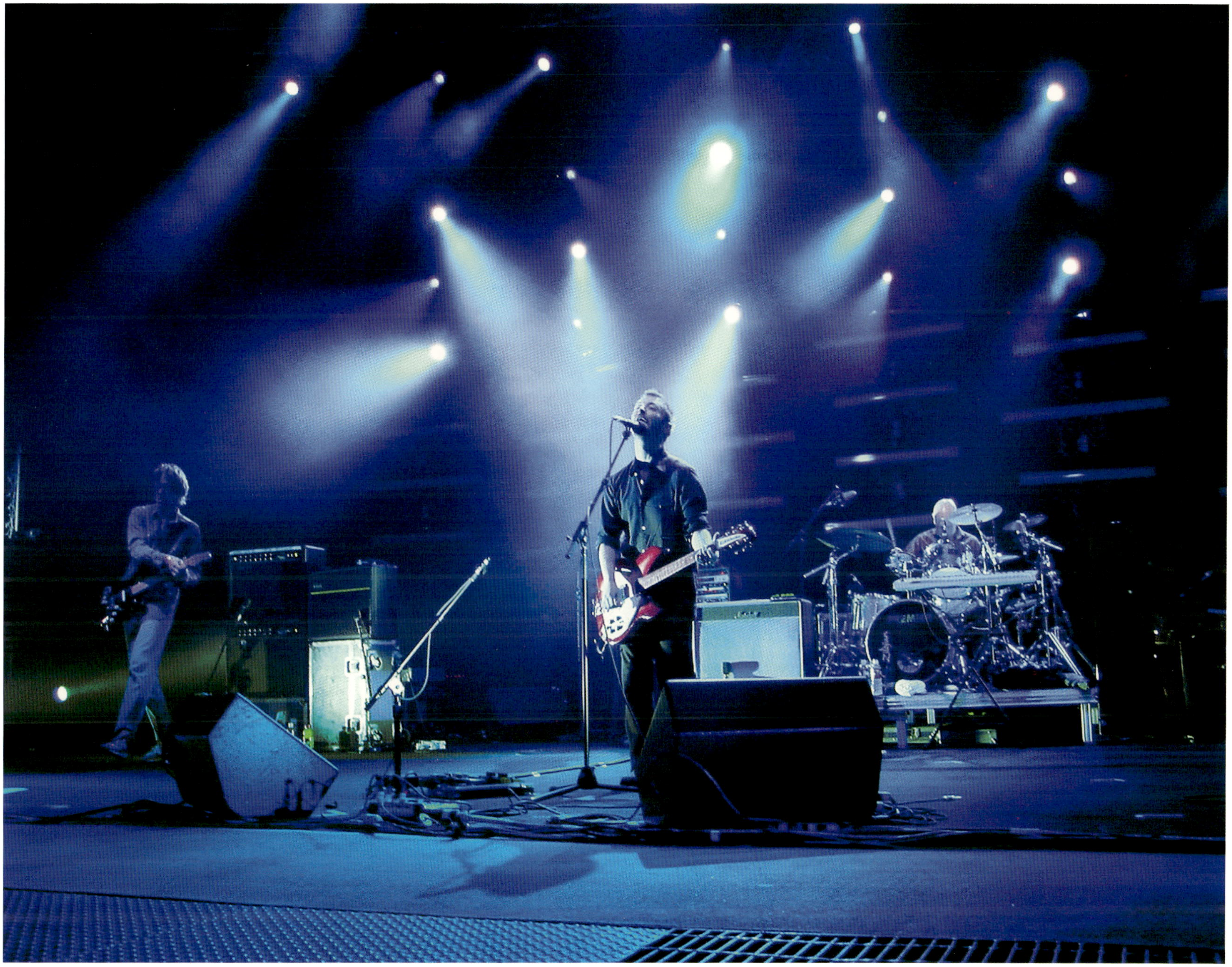

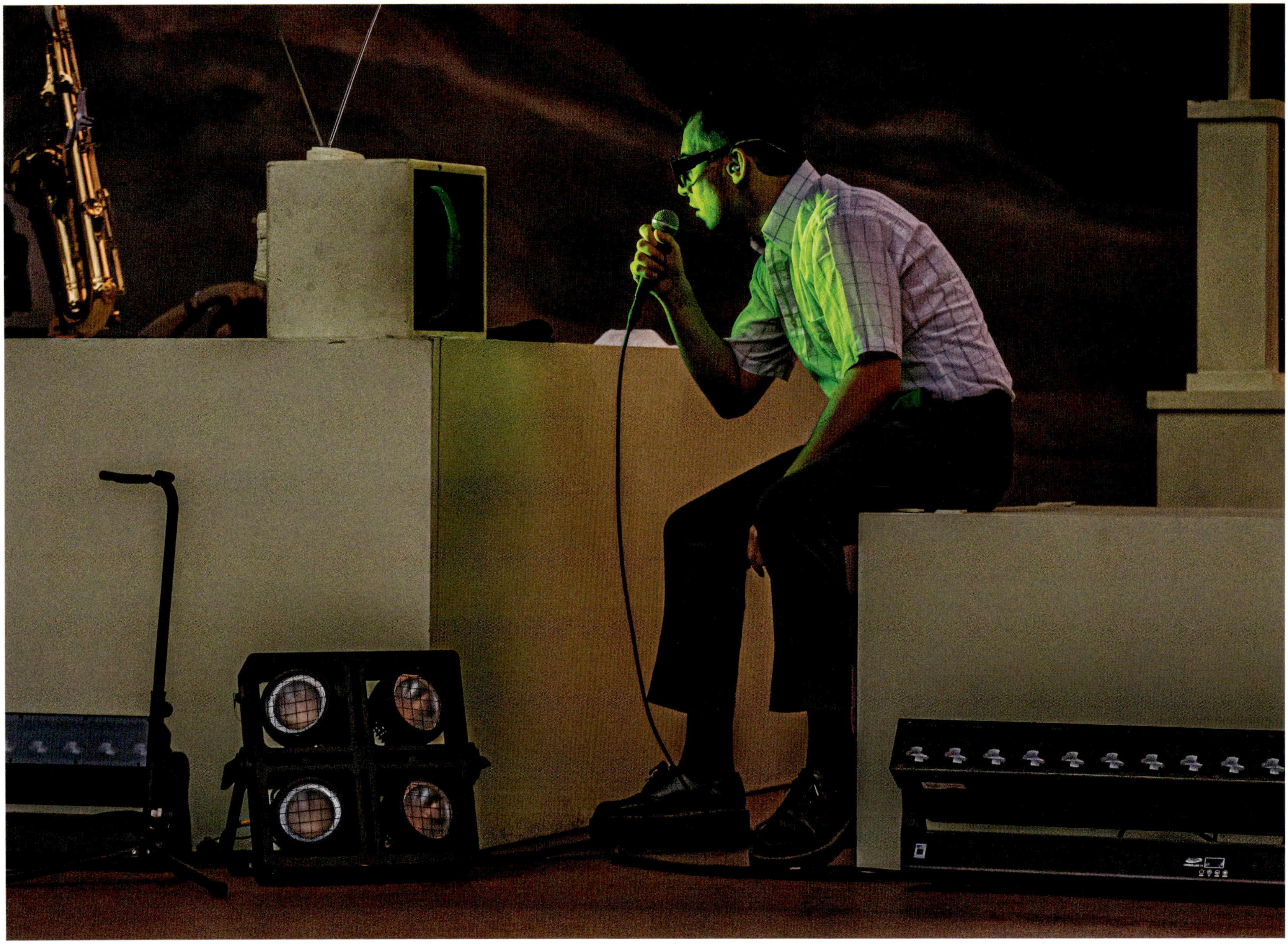

Bleachers, 2022; Billie Eilish, 2019 (right)

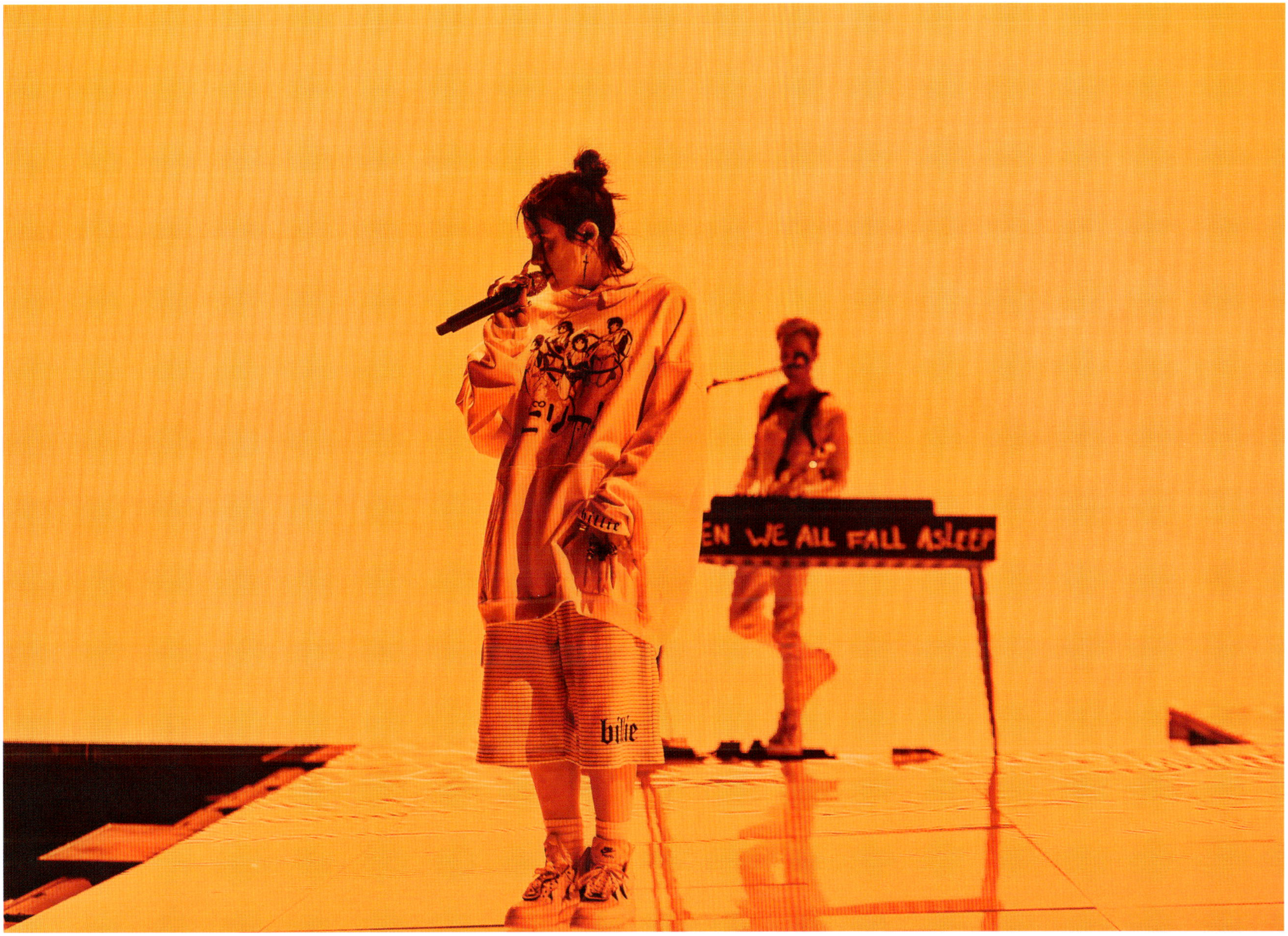
EN WE ALL FALL ASLEEP
billie

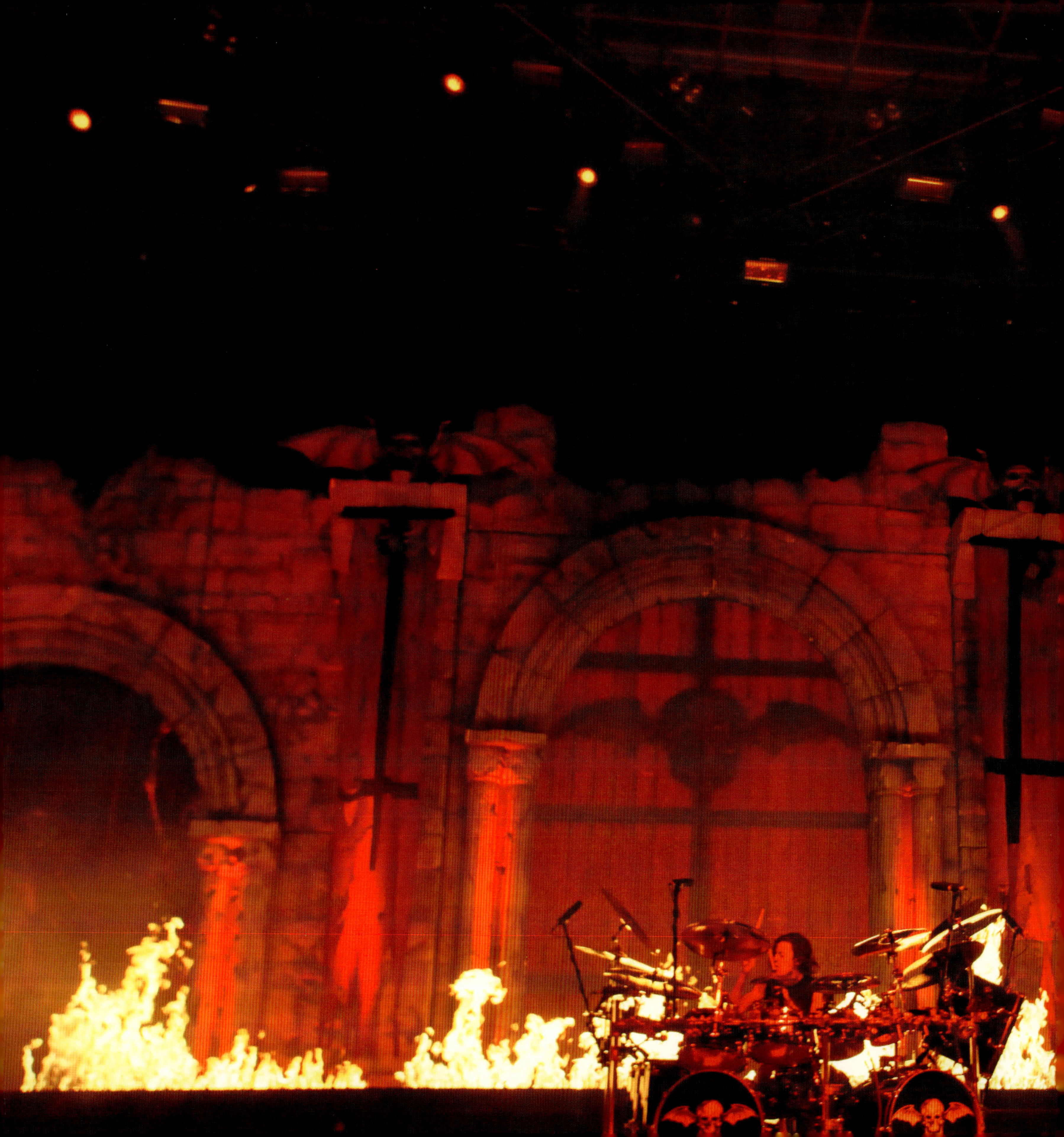

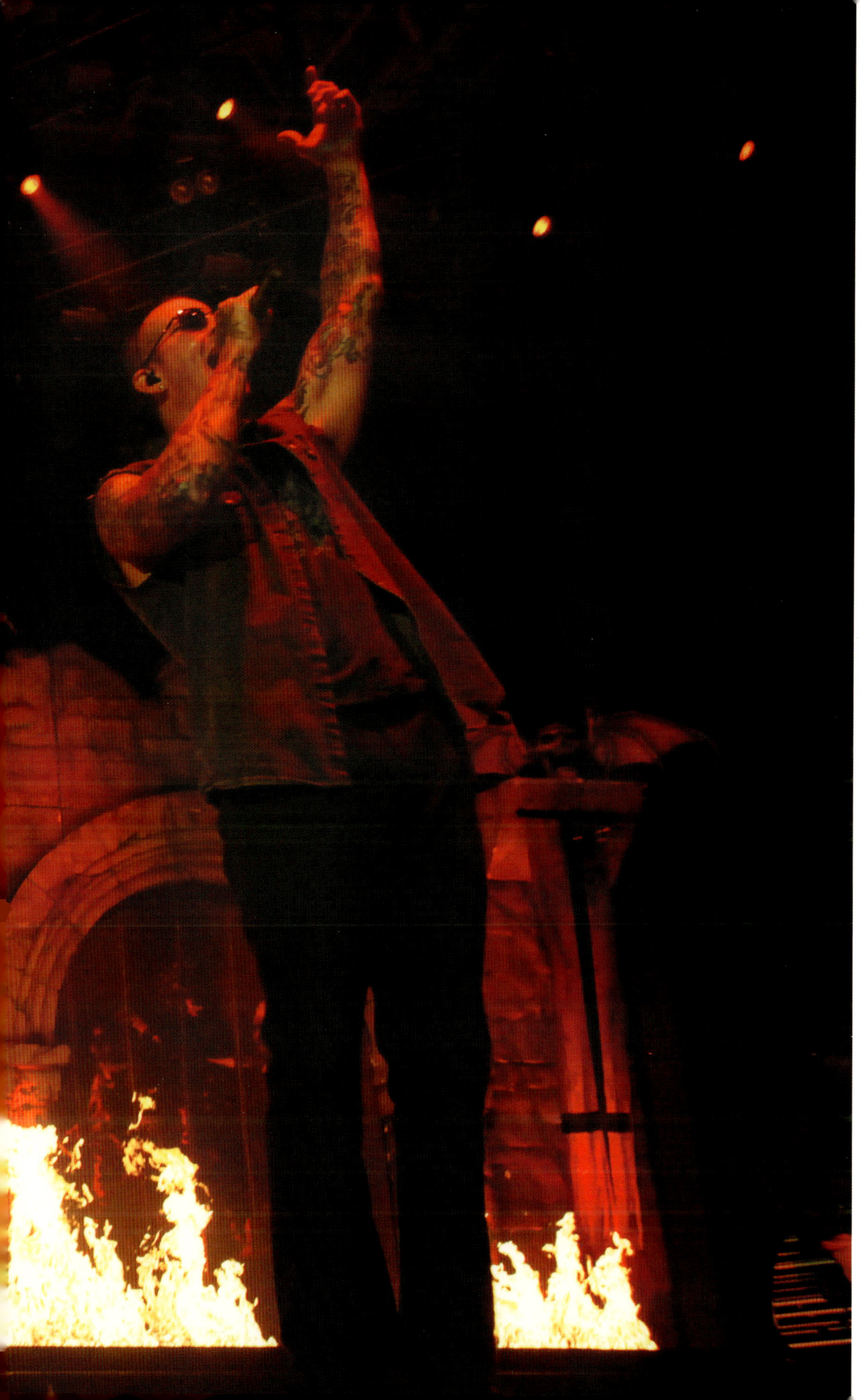

Avenged Sevenfold, 2014

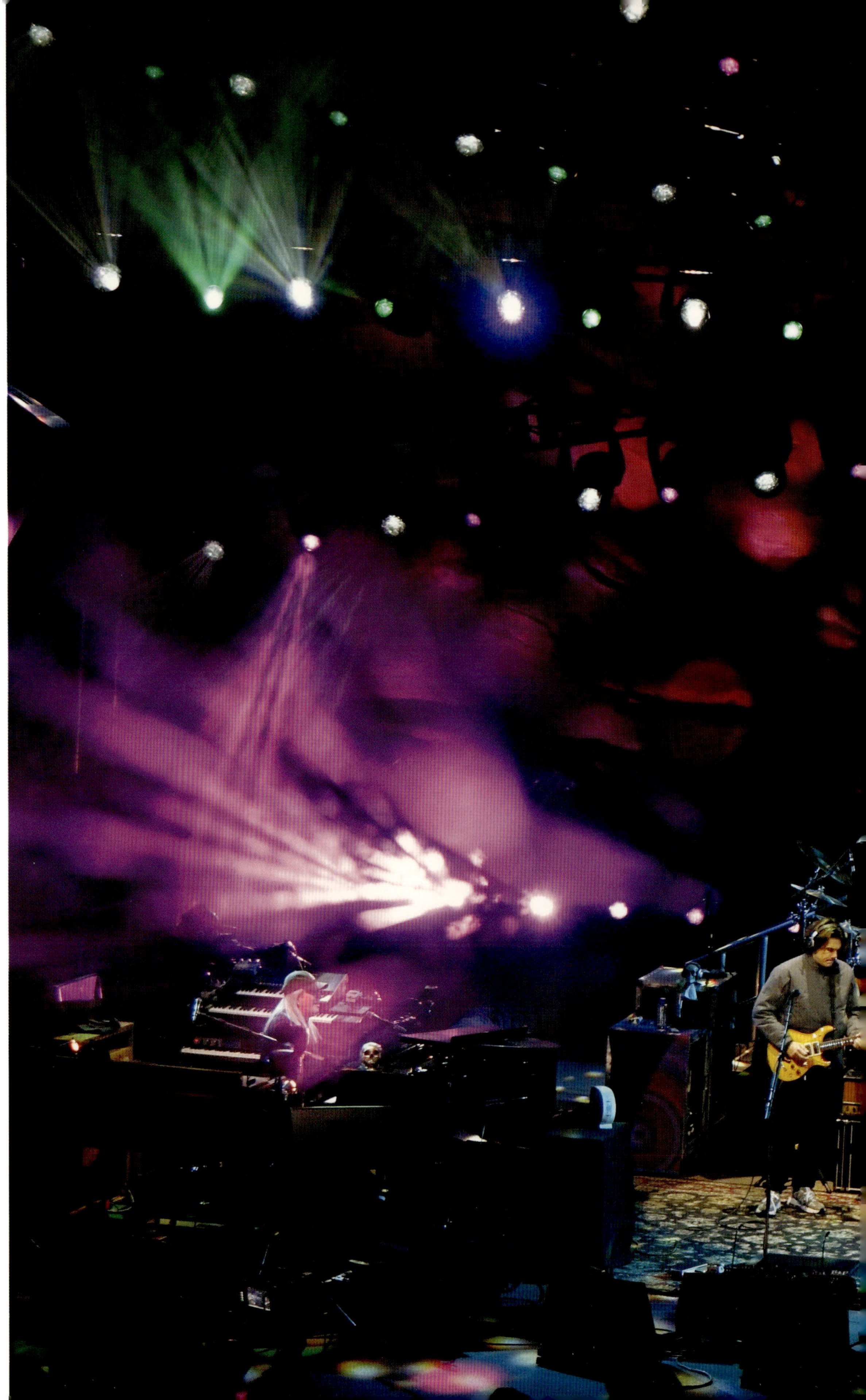

Dead & Company, 2021

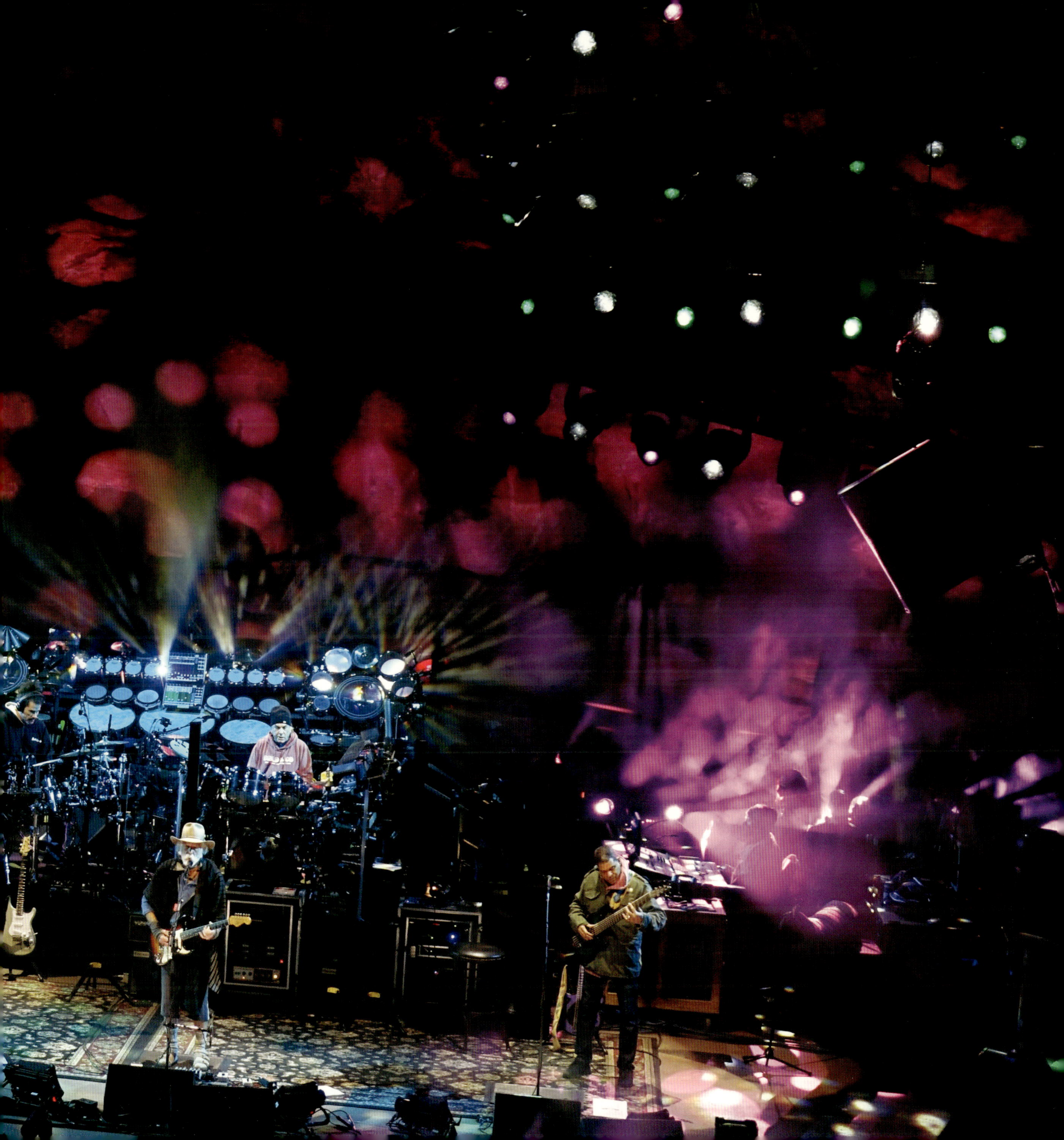

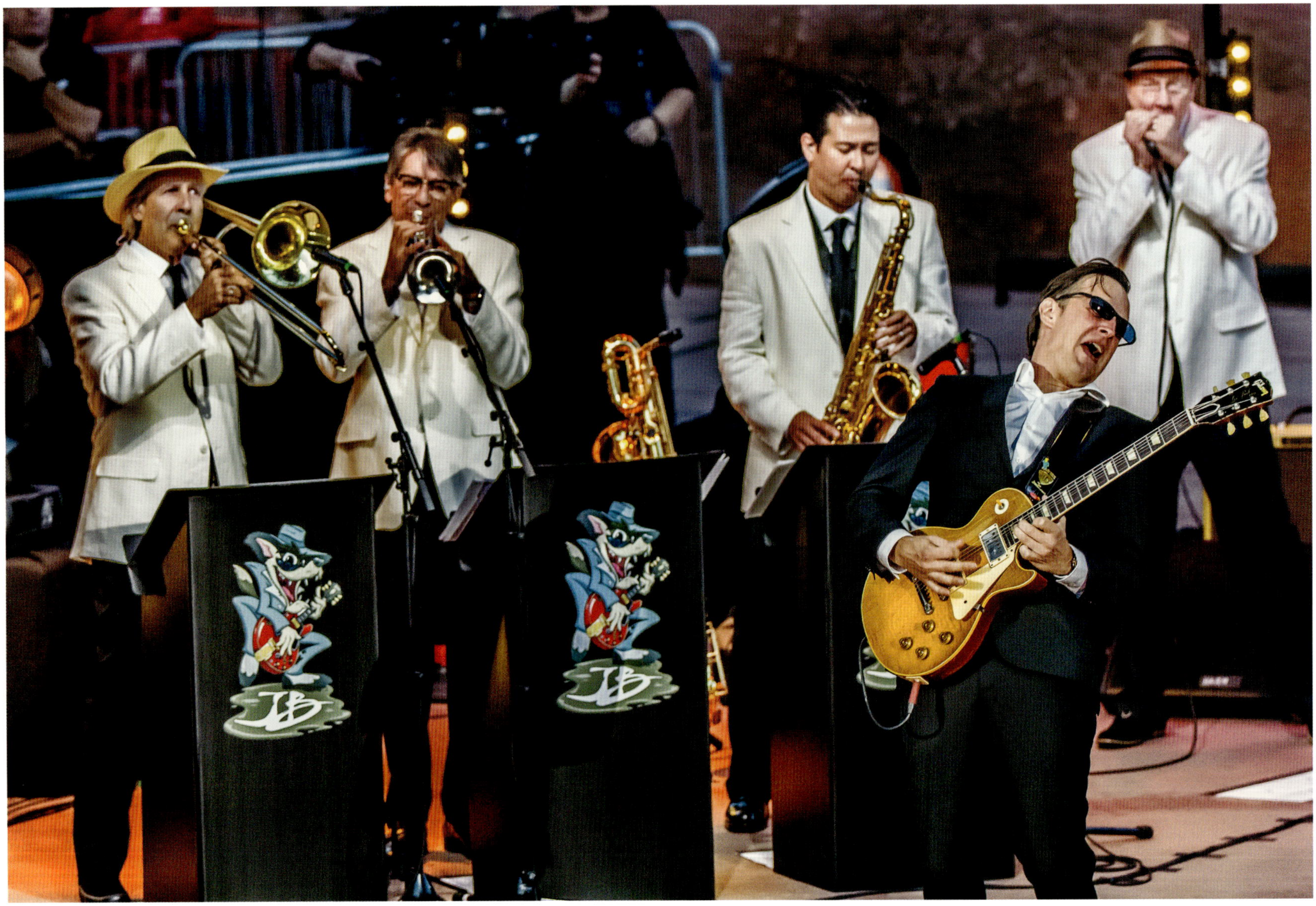

Joe Bonamassa, 2014; Warren Haynes with the Colorado Symphony Orchestra, 2013 (right)

Following spread: The Beach Boys, 2012

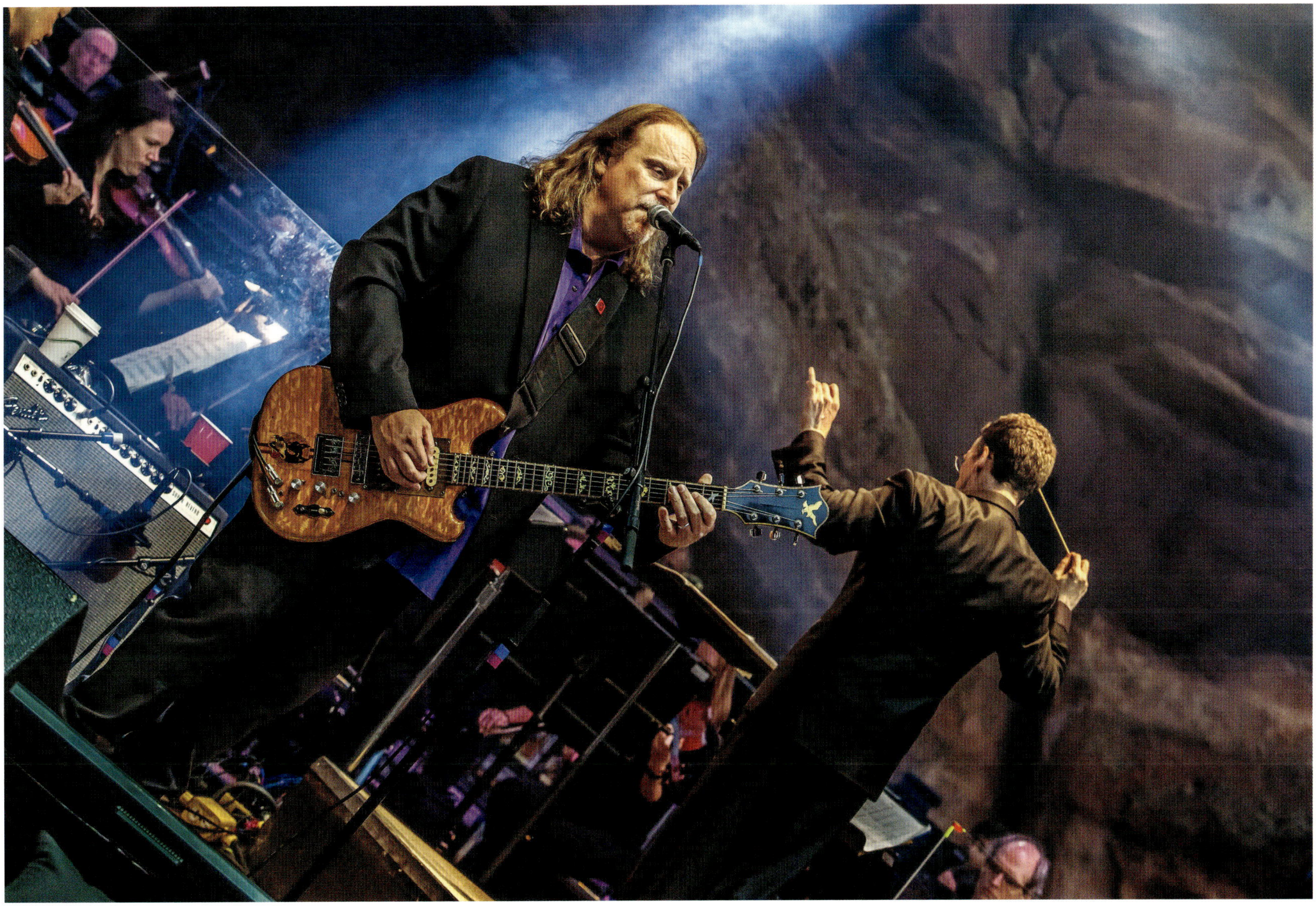

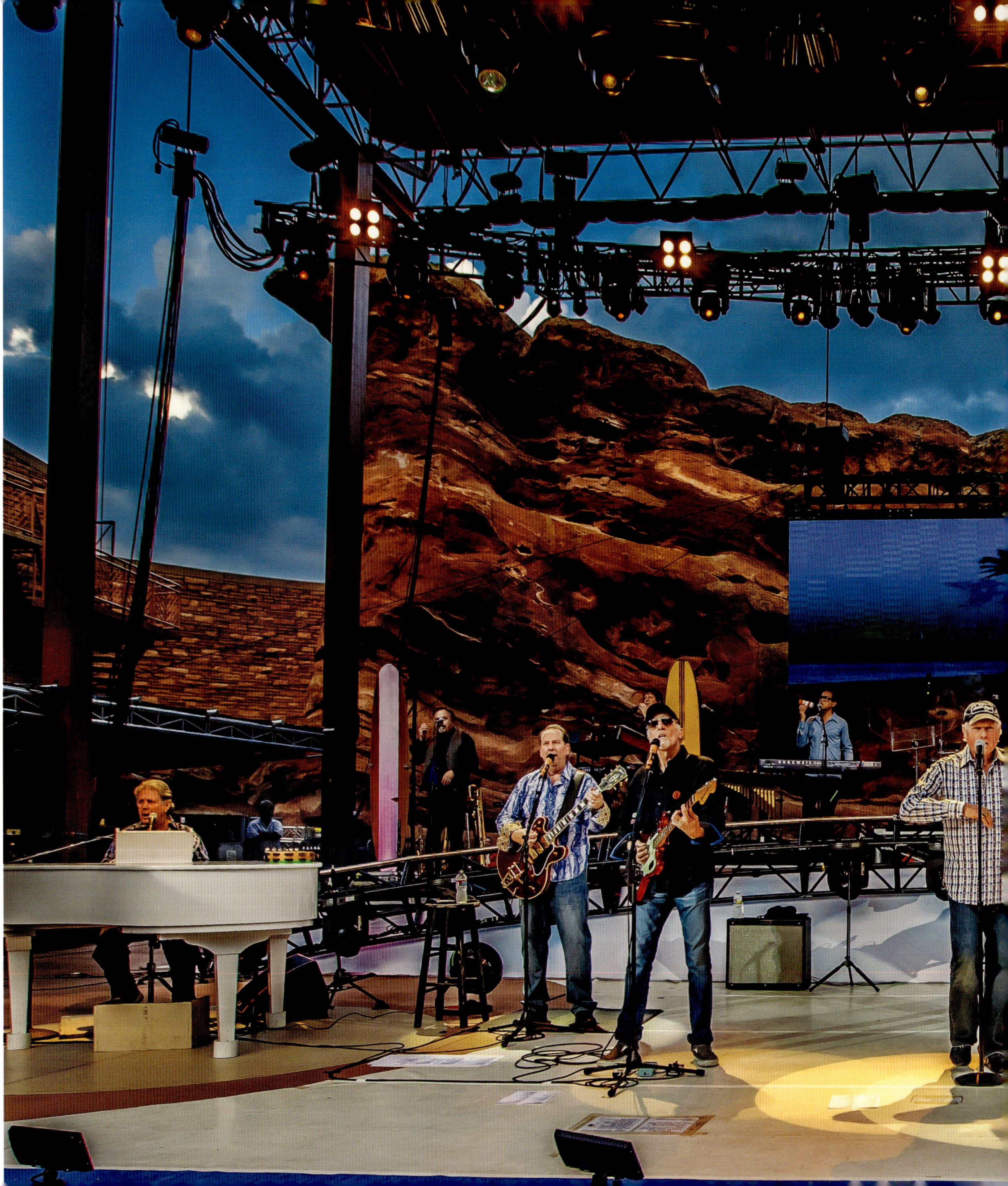

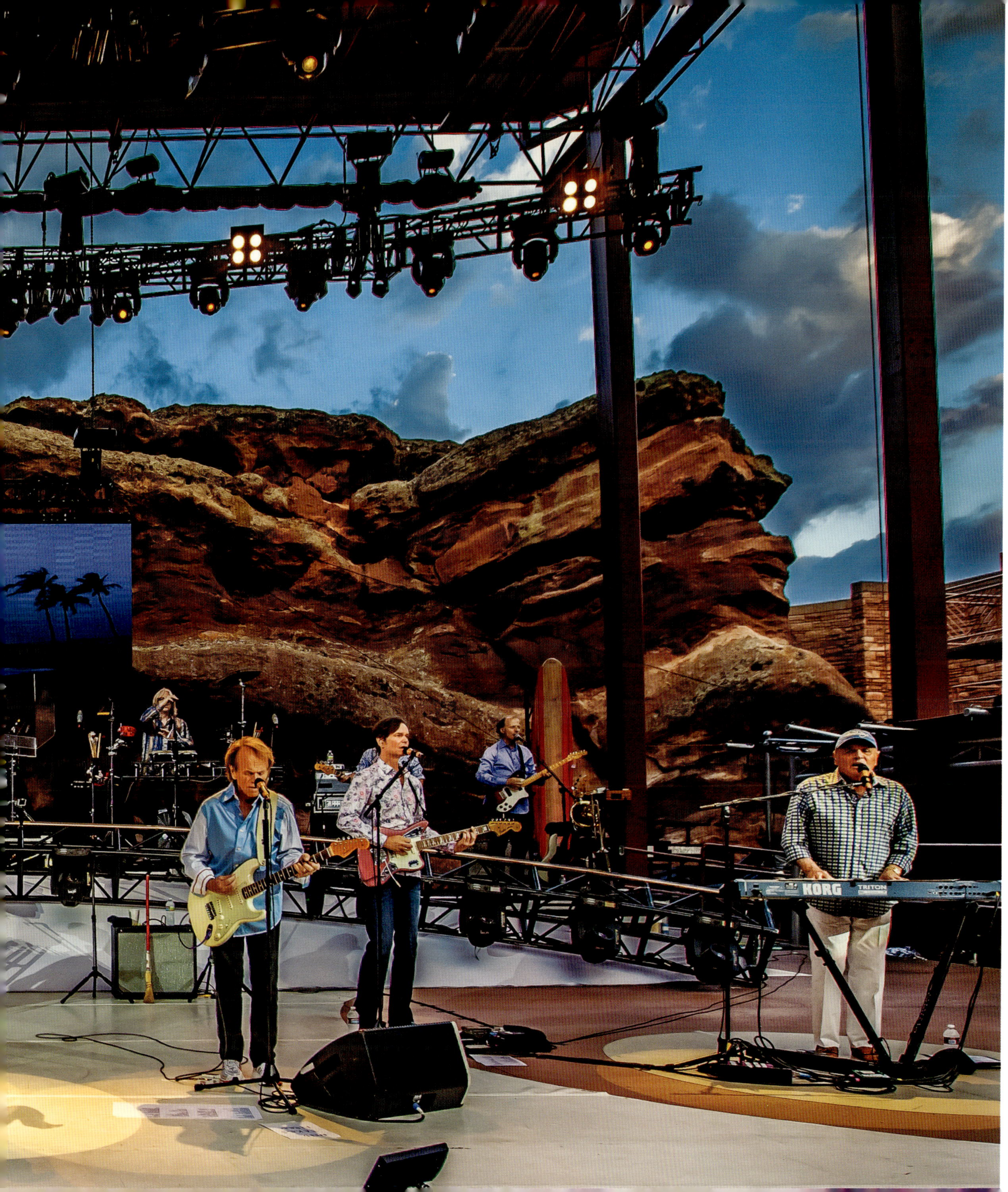
KORG
TRITON

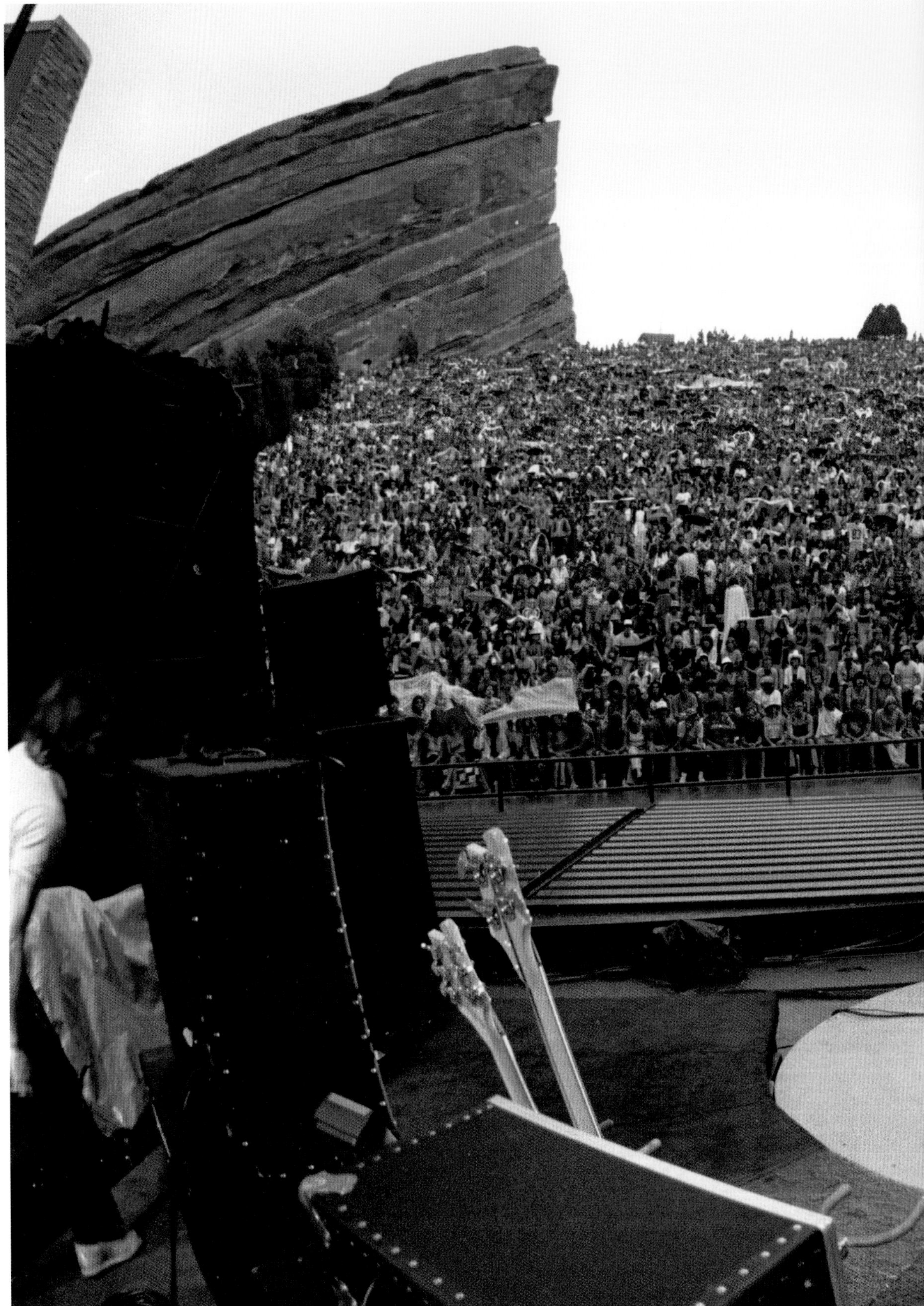

The Moody Blues, 1981

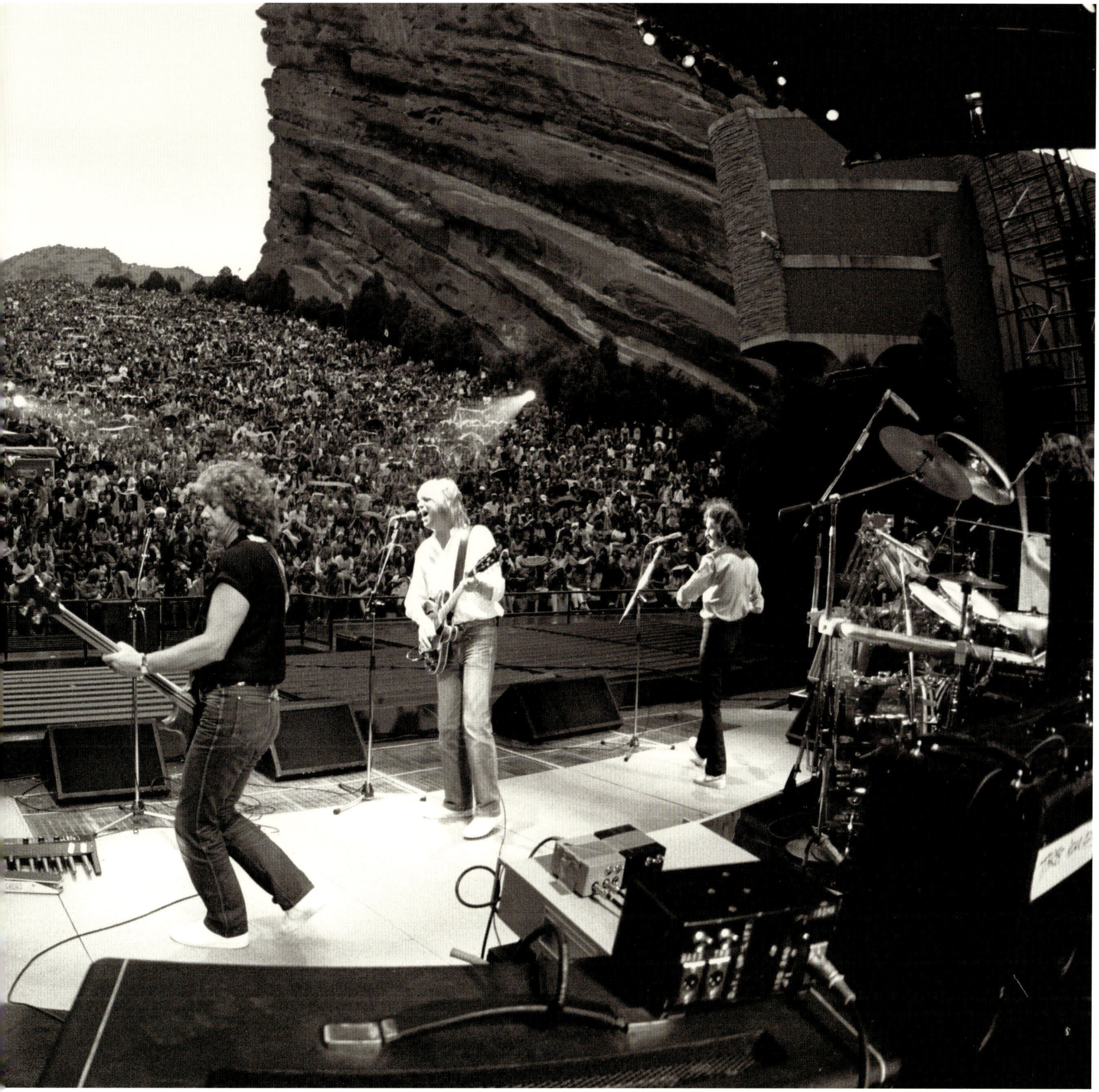

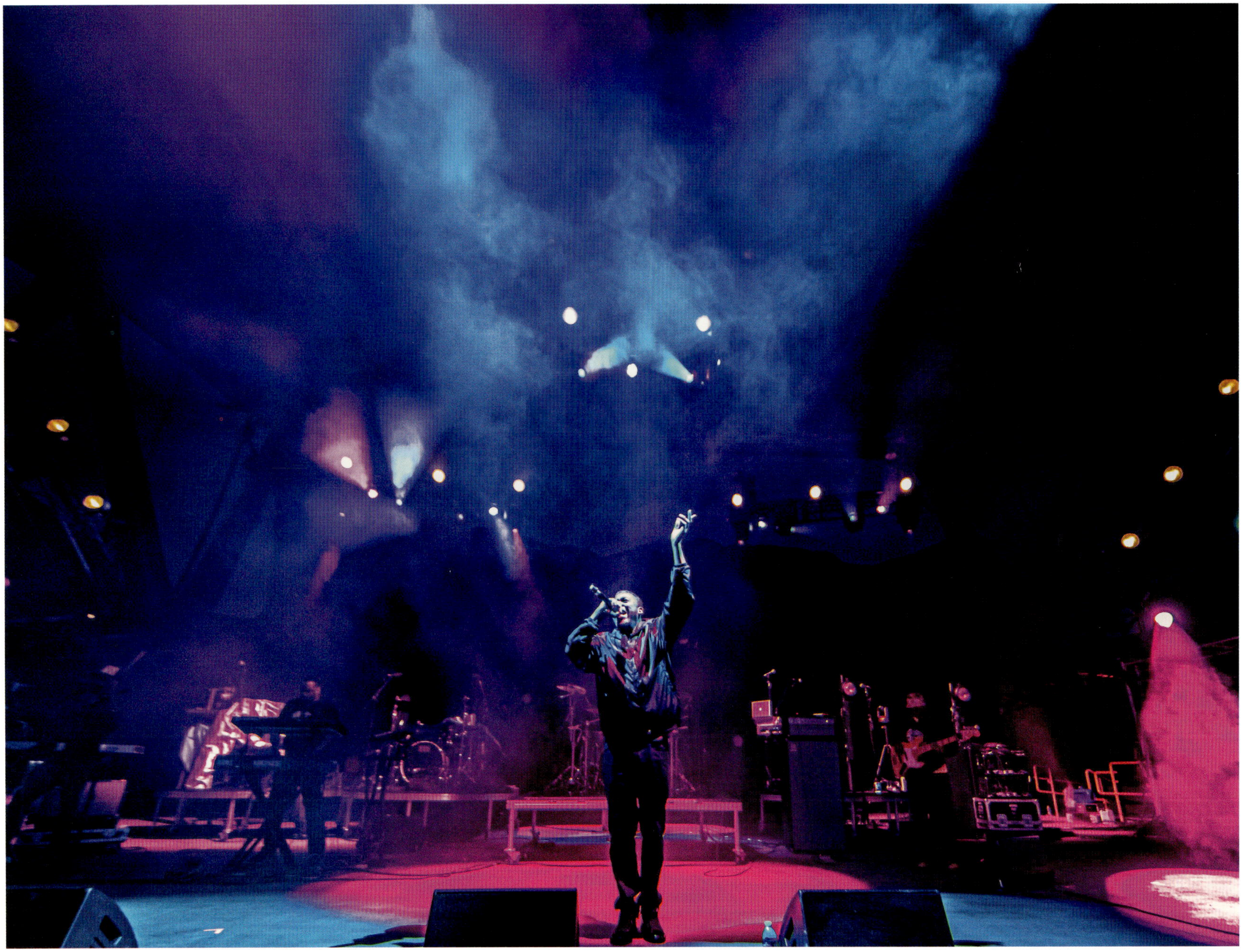

GZA, 2022; Trippie Redd, 2022 (right)

Following spread: String Cheese Incident, 2015

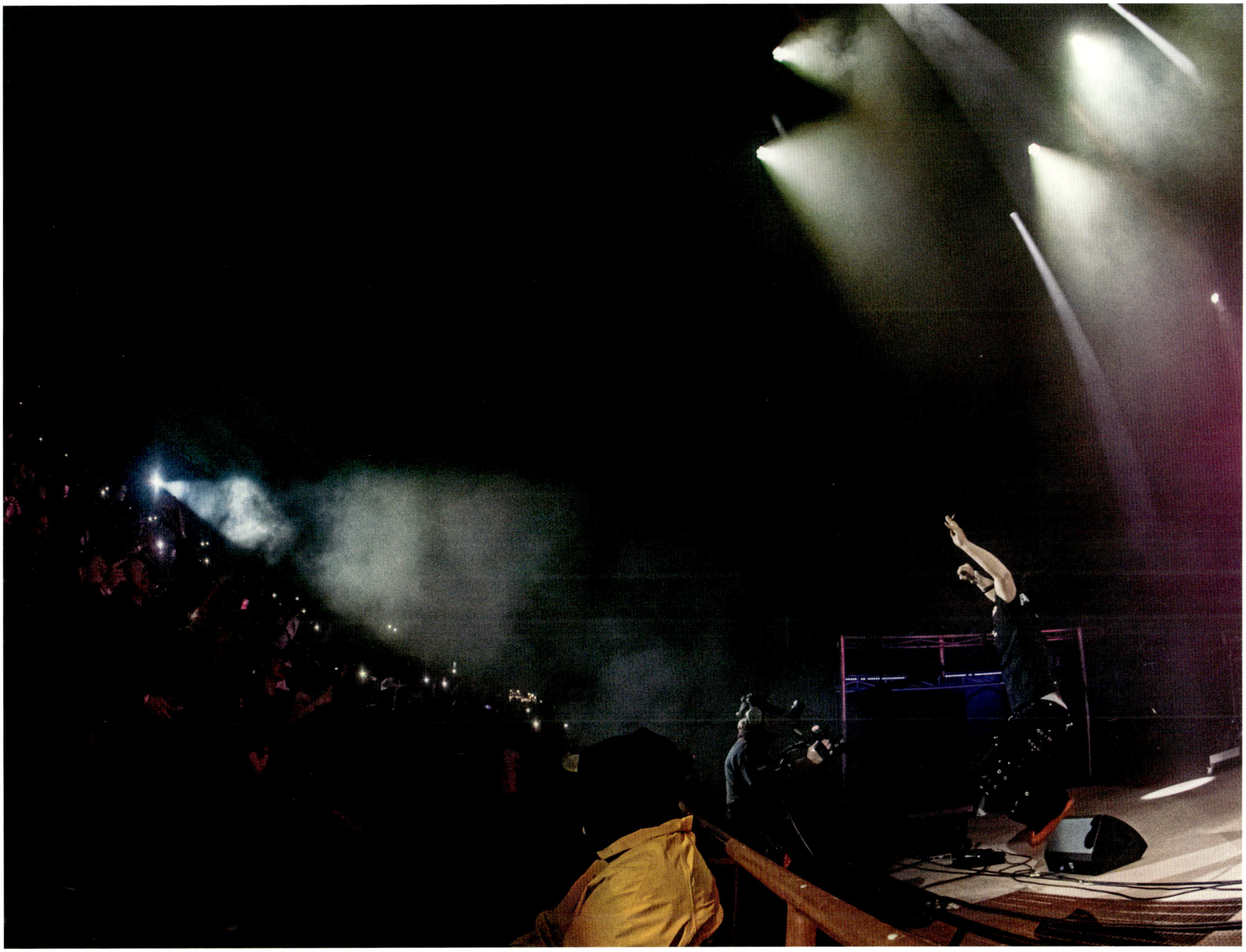

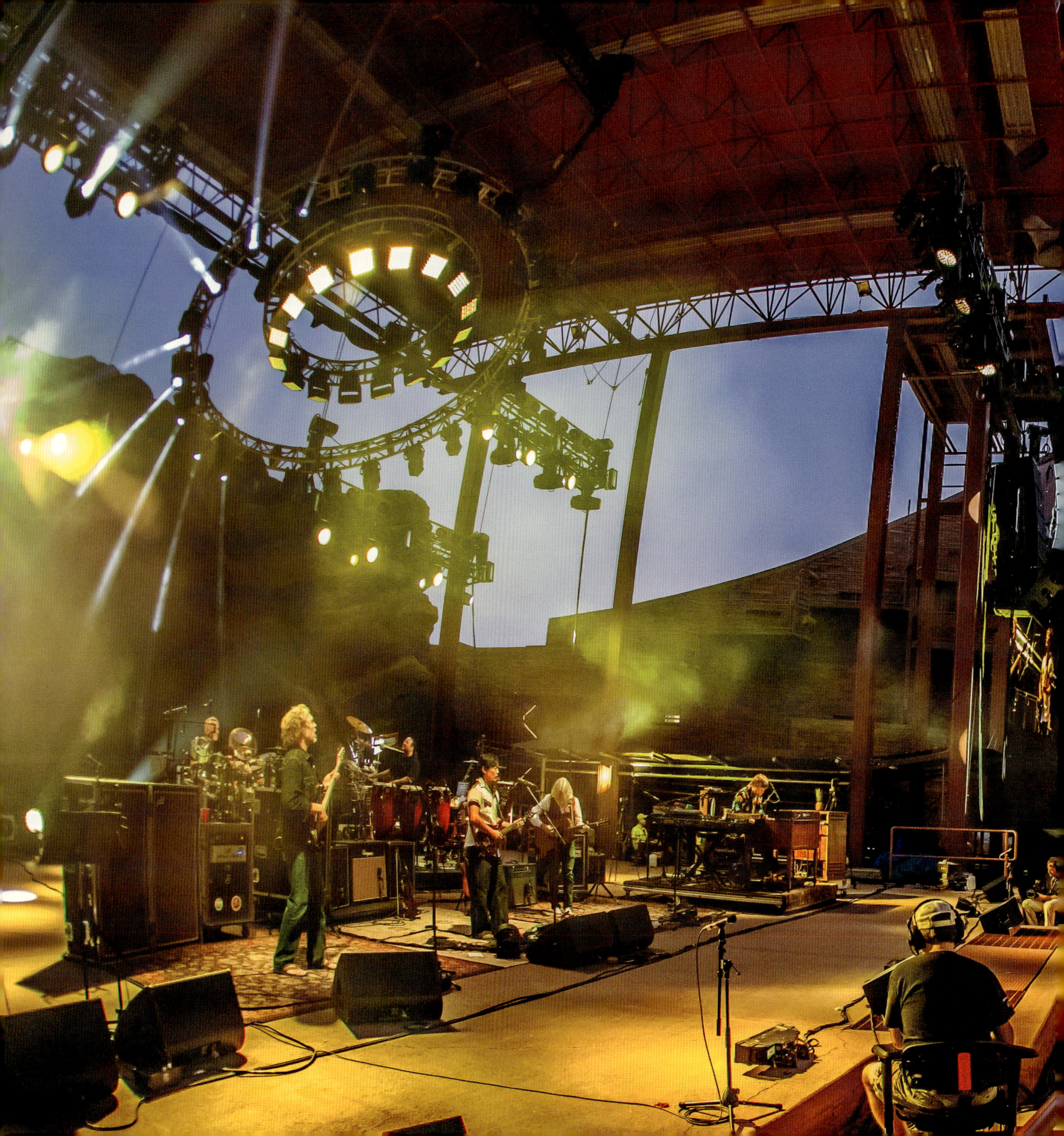

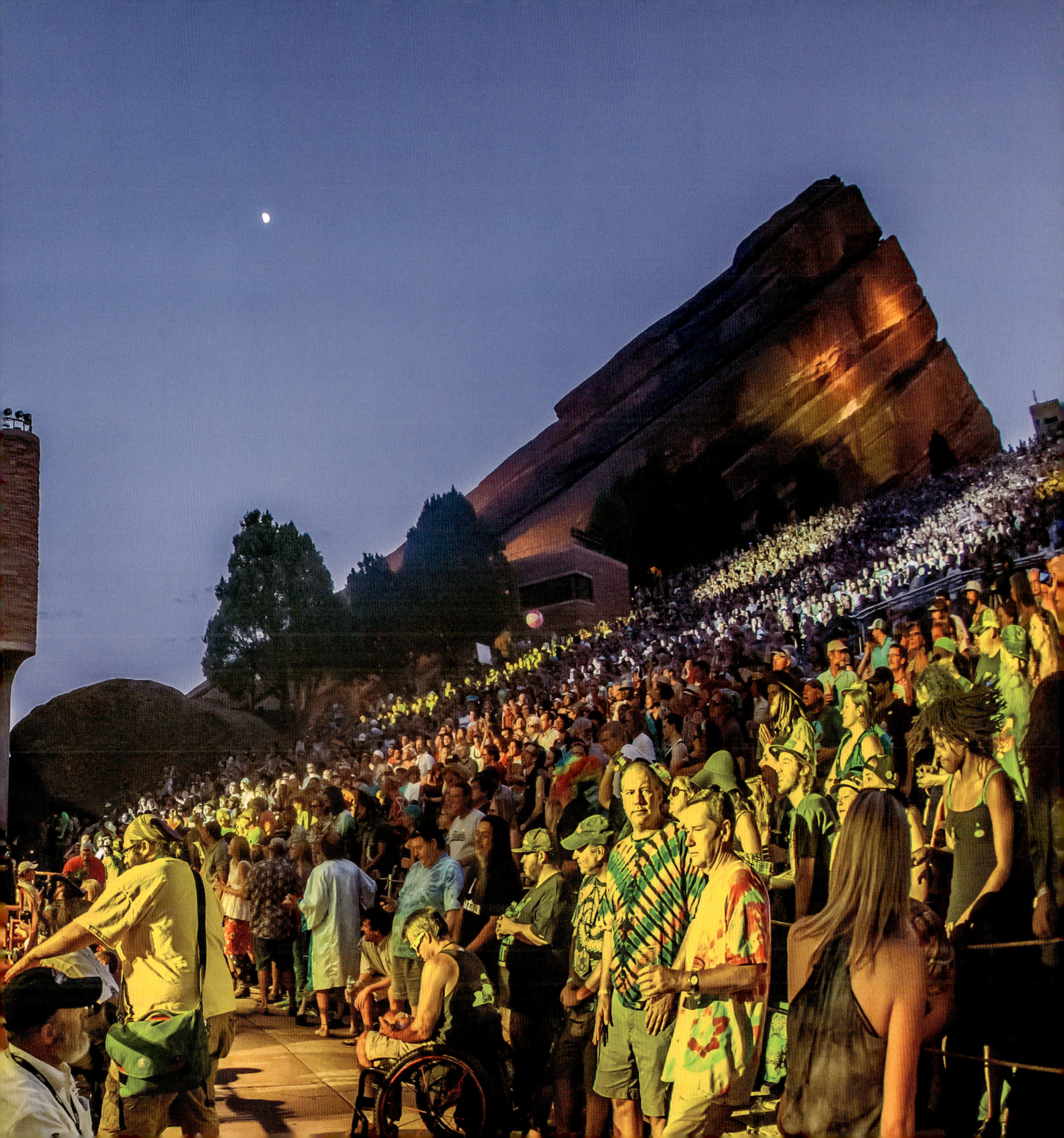

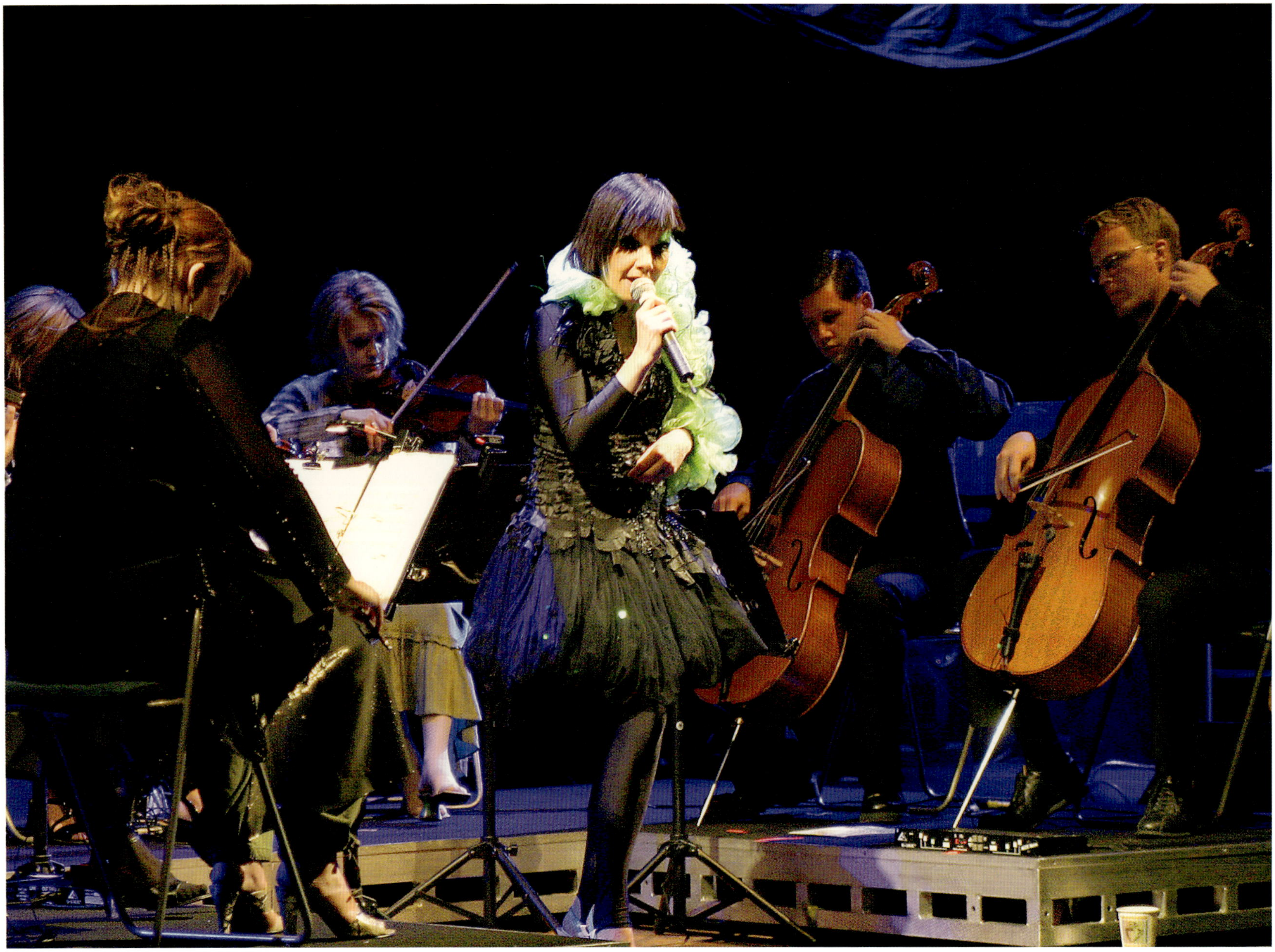

Björk, 2003; The Lumineers, 2013 (right)

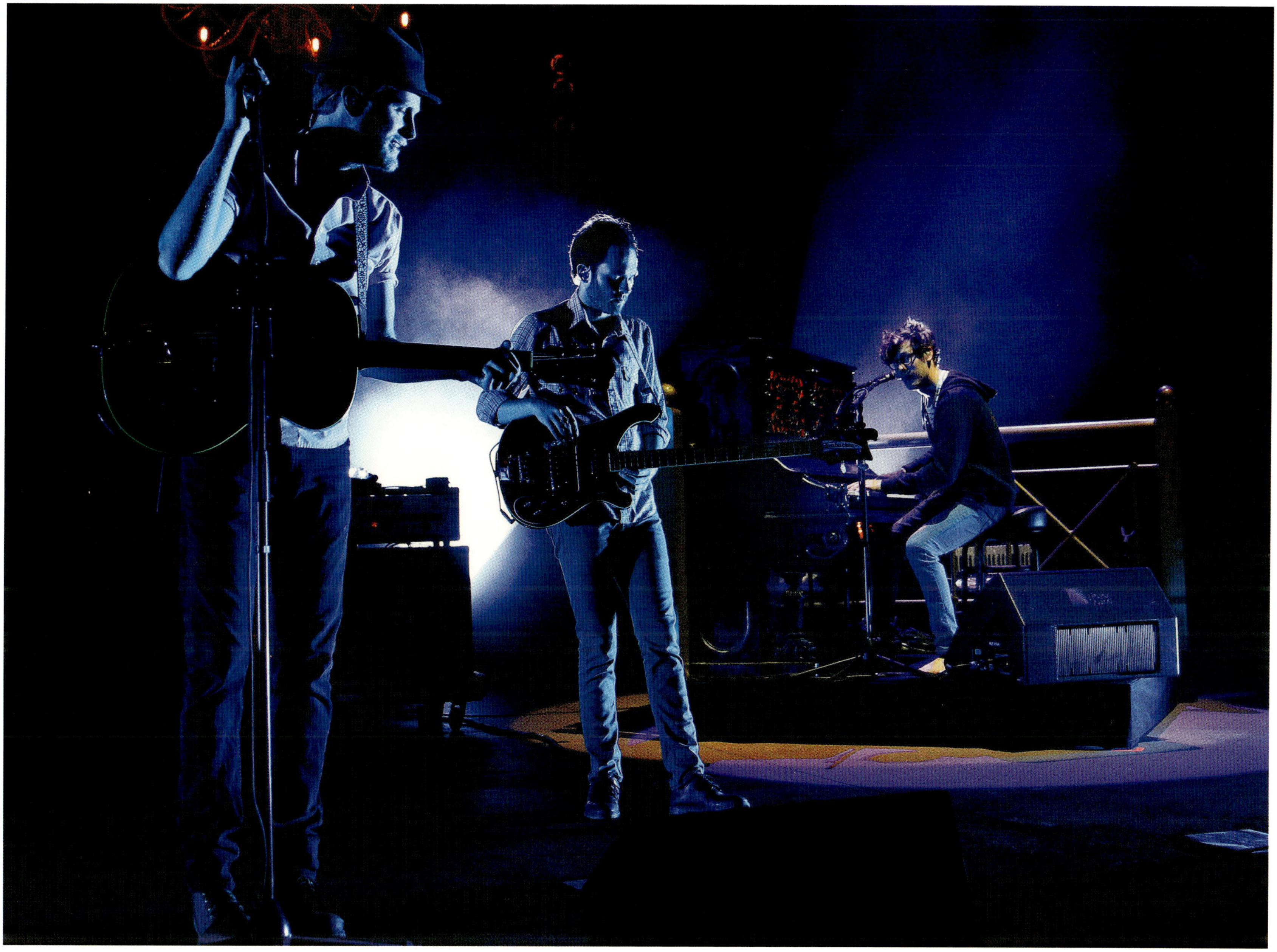

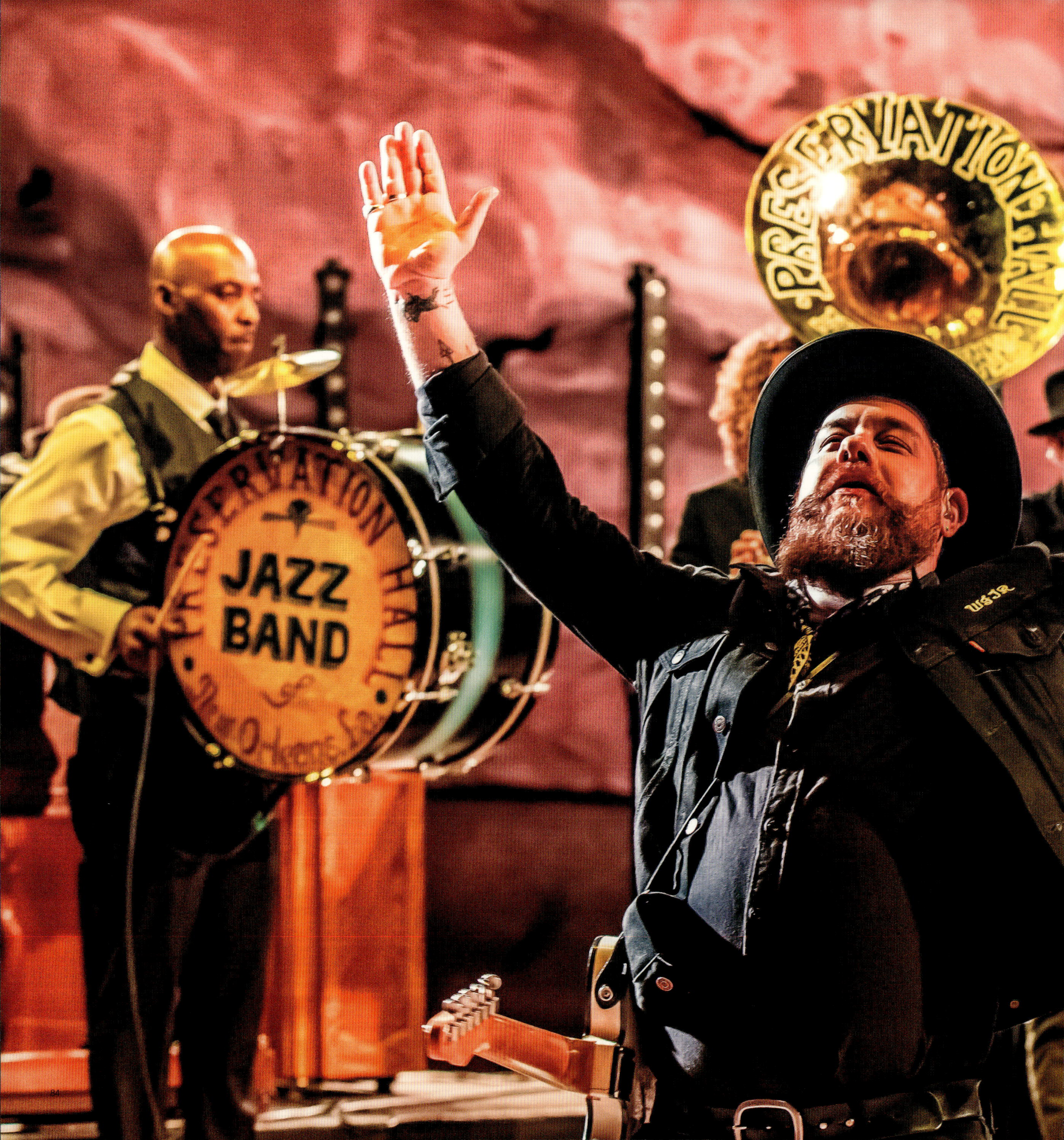
PRESERVATION HALL
JAZZ
BAND
New Orleans, La.
PRESERVATION HALL

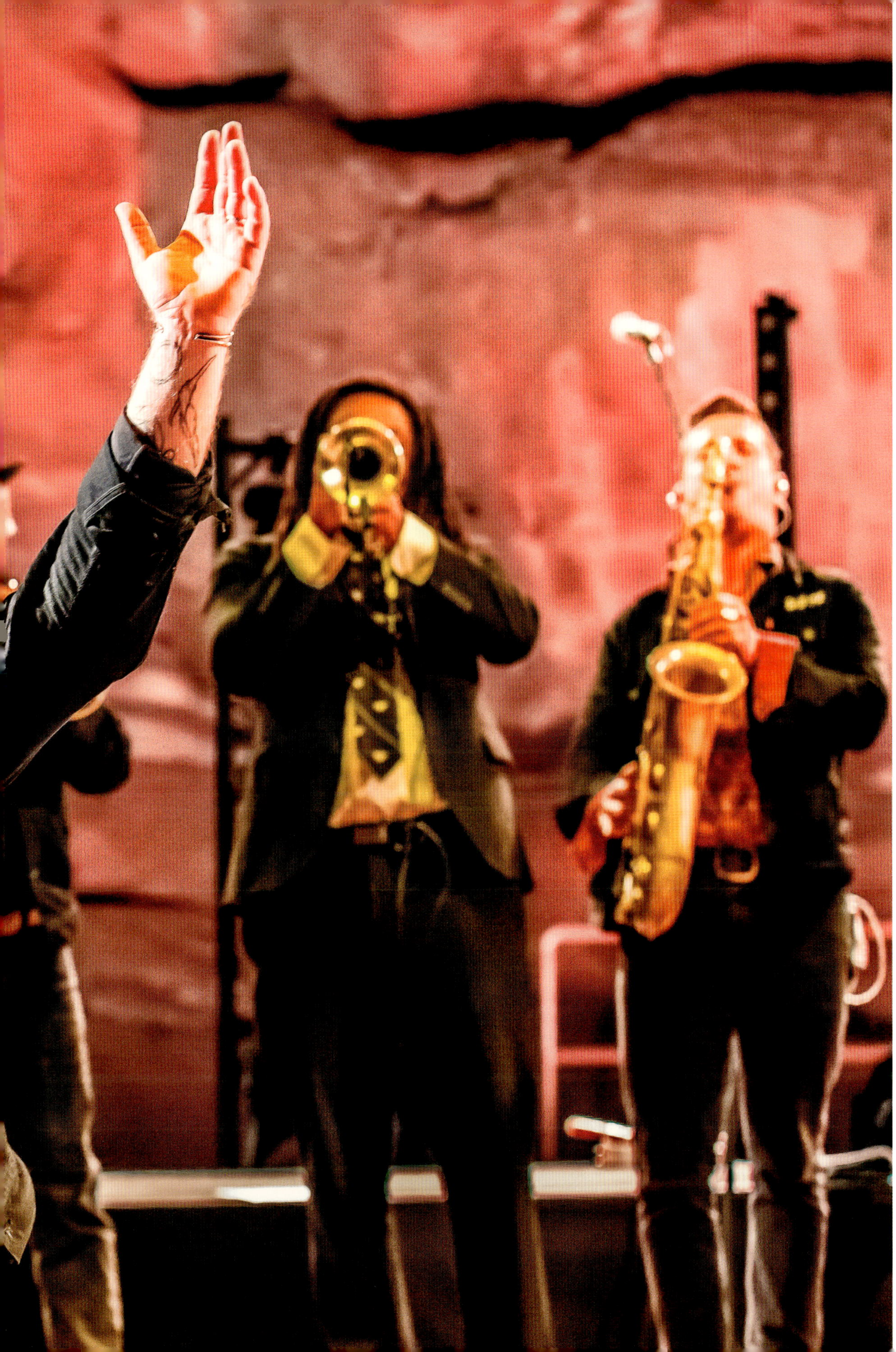

Nathaniel Rateliff & the Night Sweats, 2016

Following spread: Avett Brothers, 2014

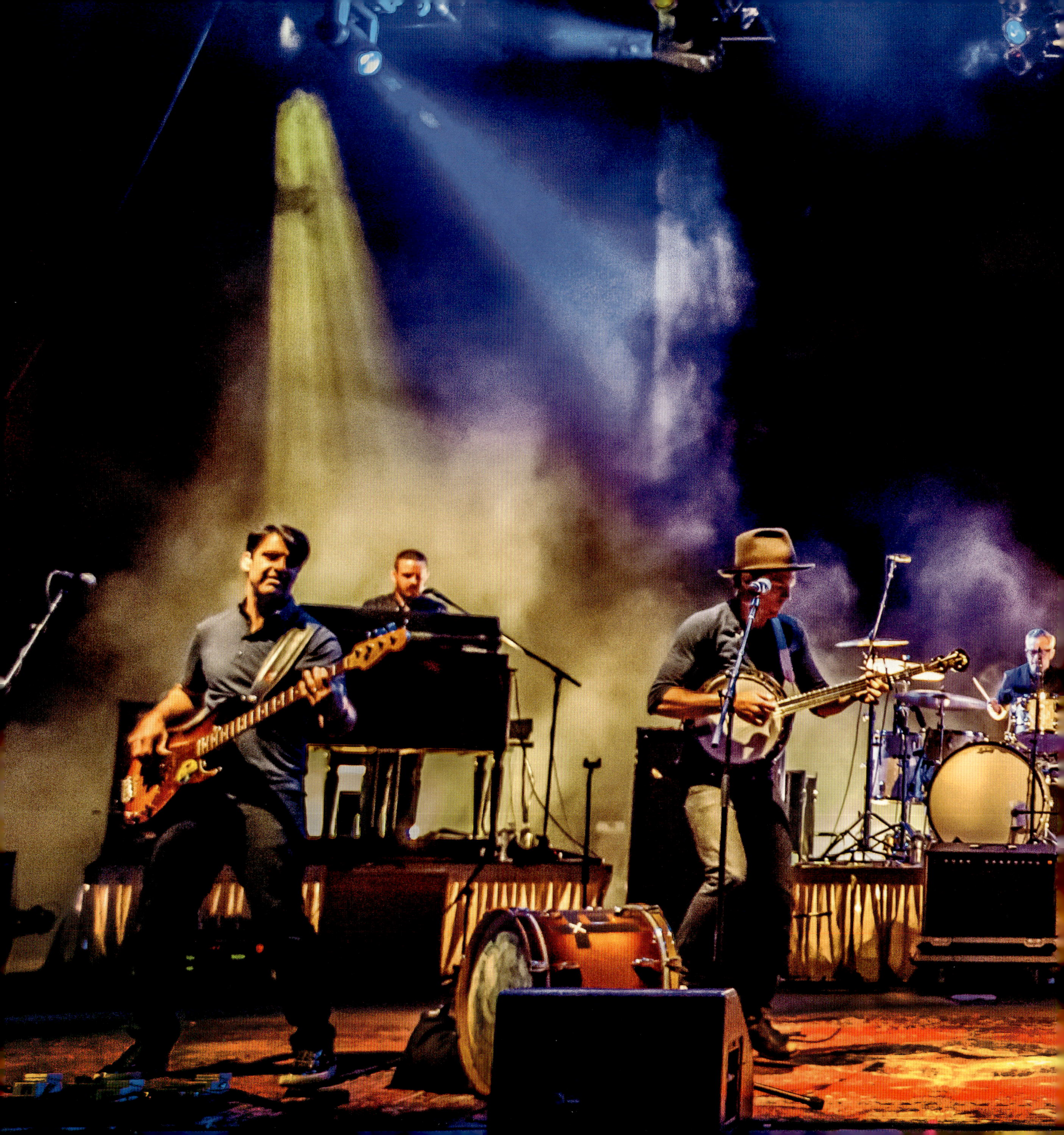

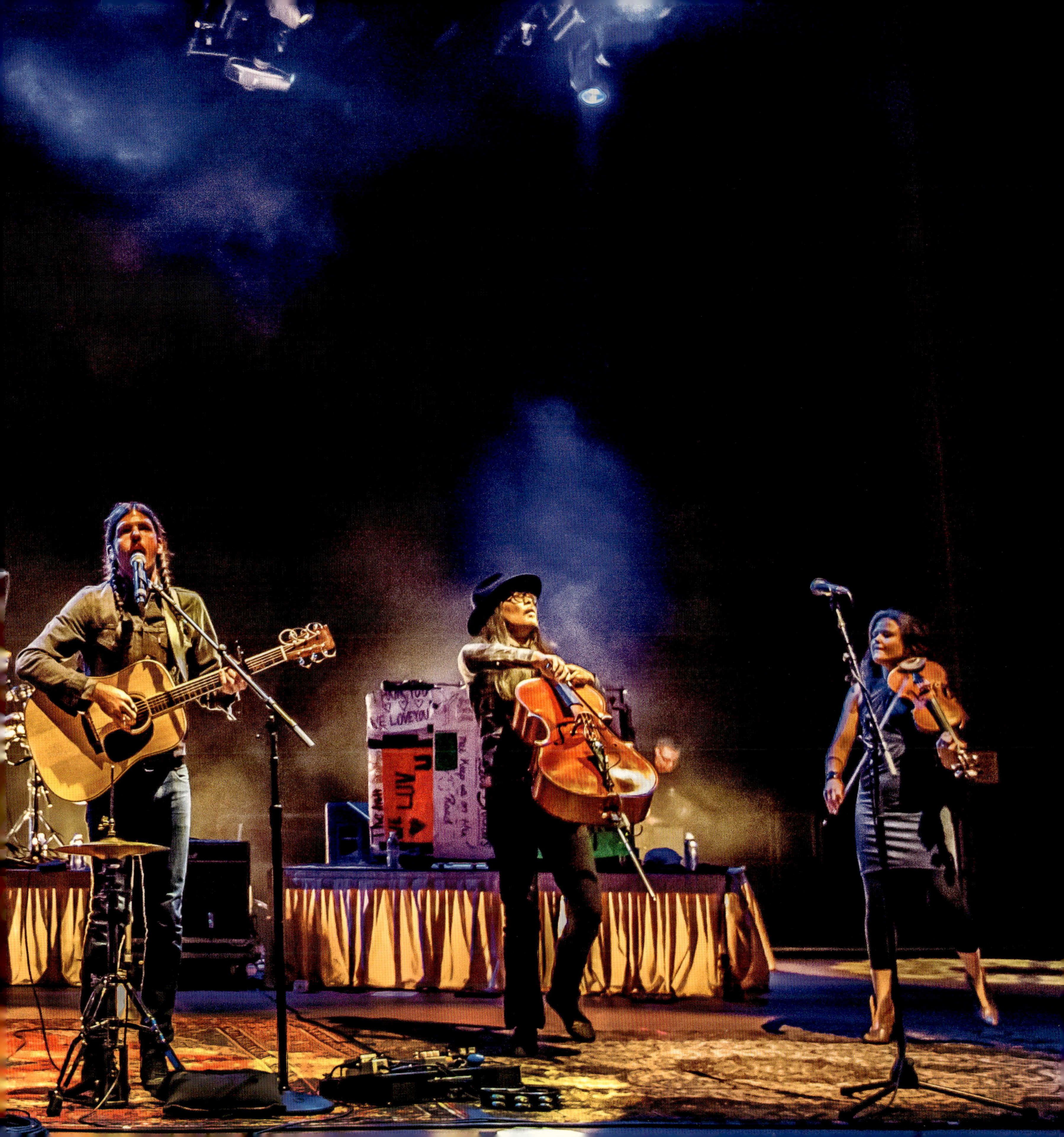

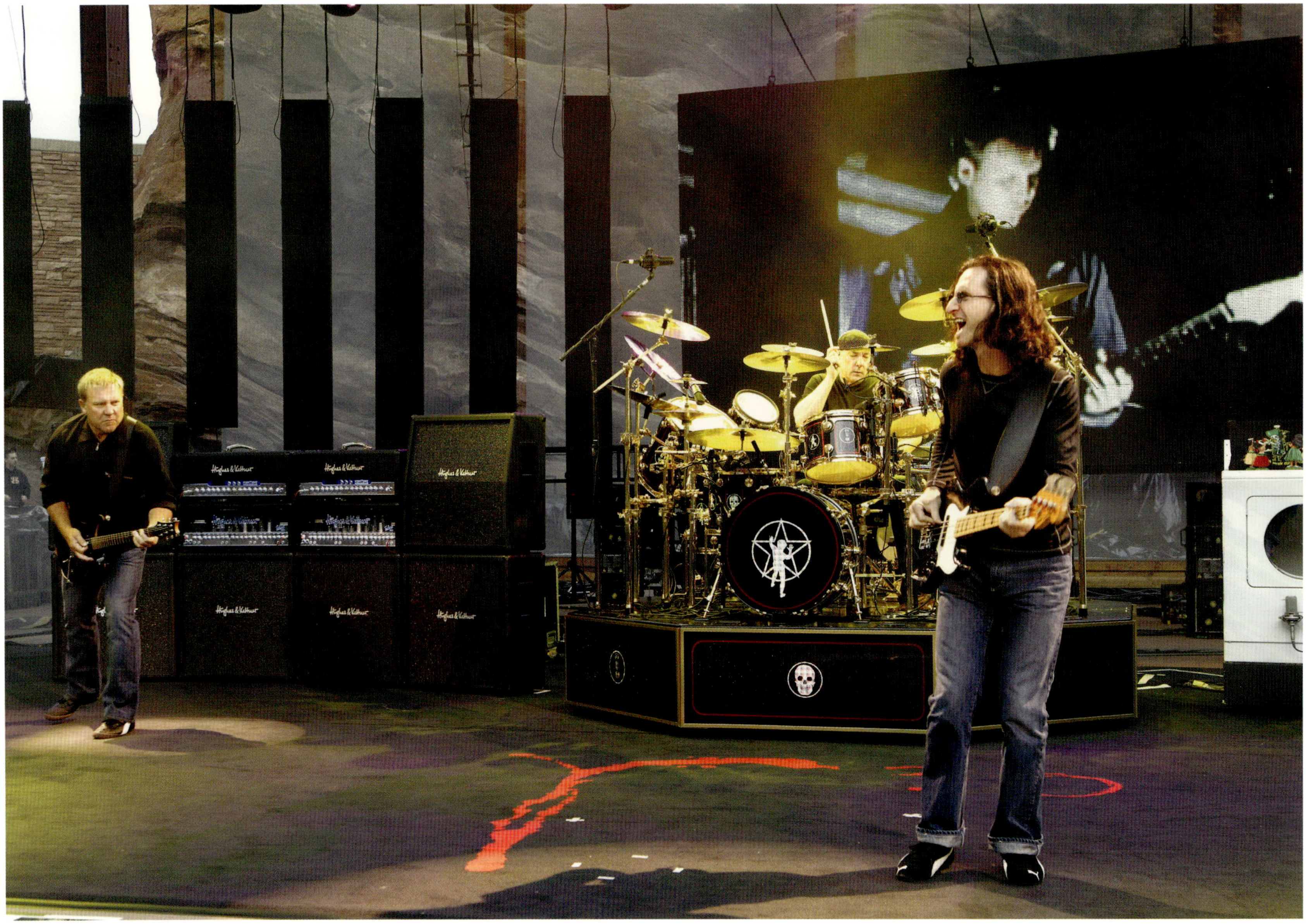

Rush, 2004; Mumford & Sons, 2012 (right)

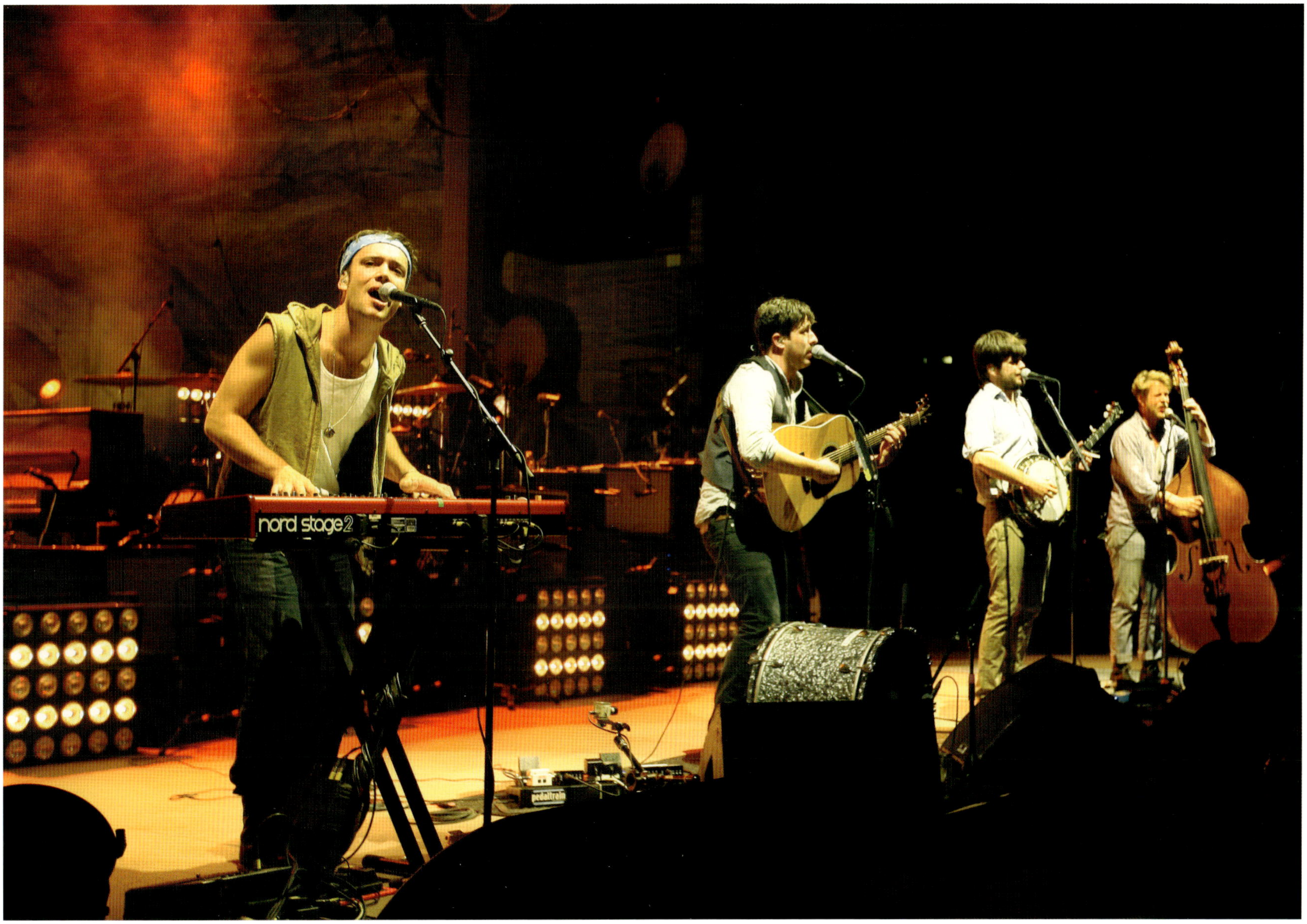
nord stage2

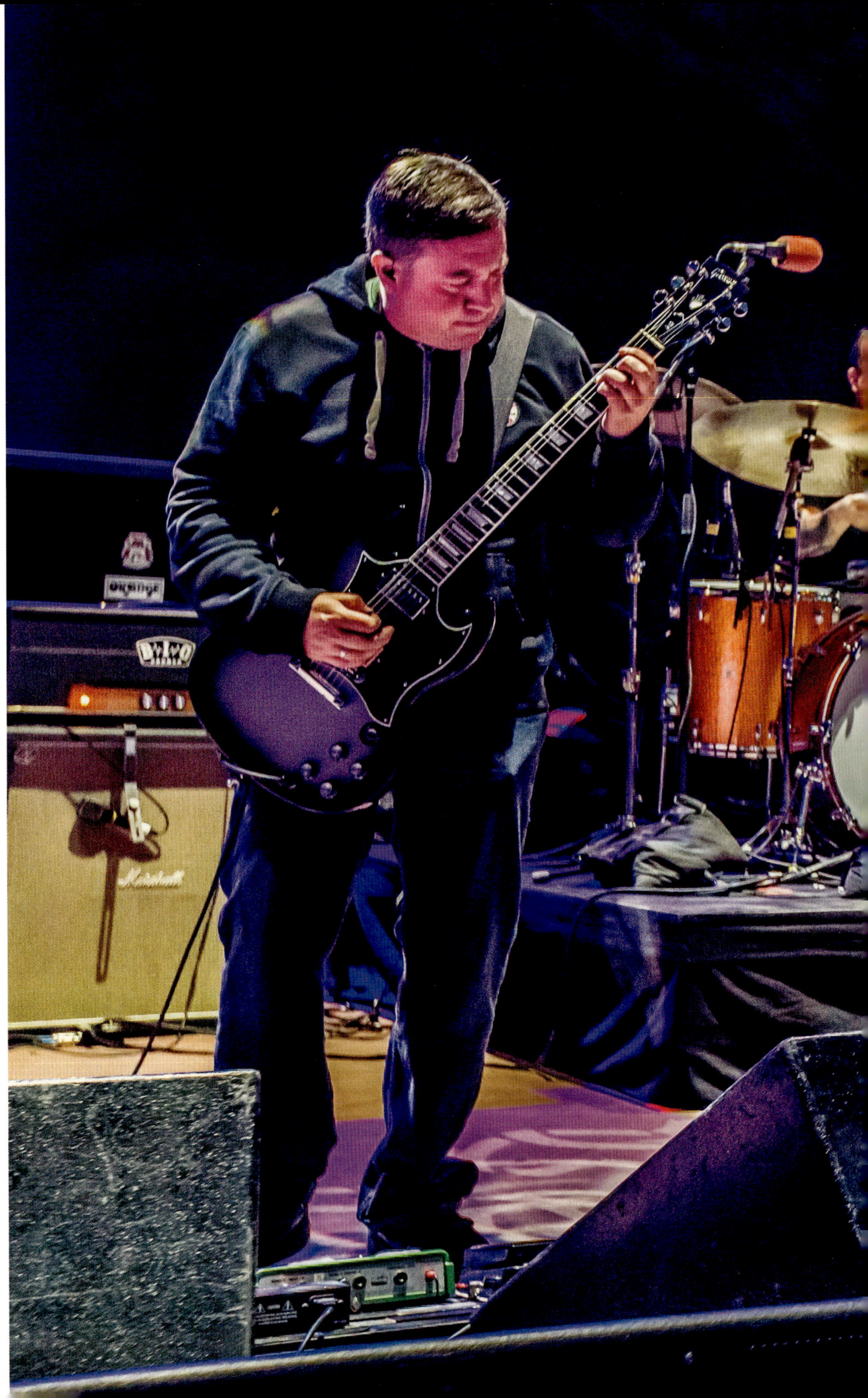

Clutch, 2015

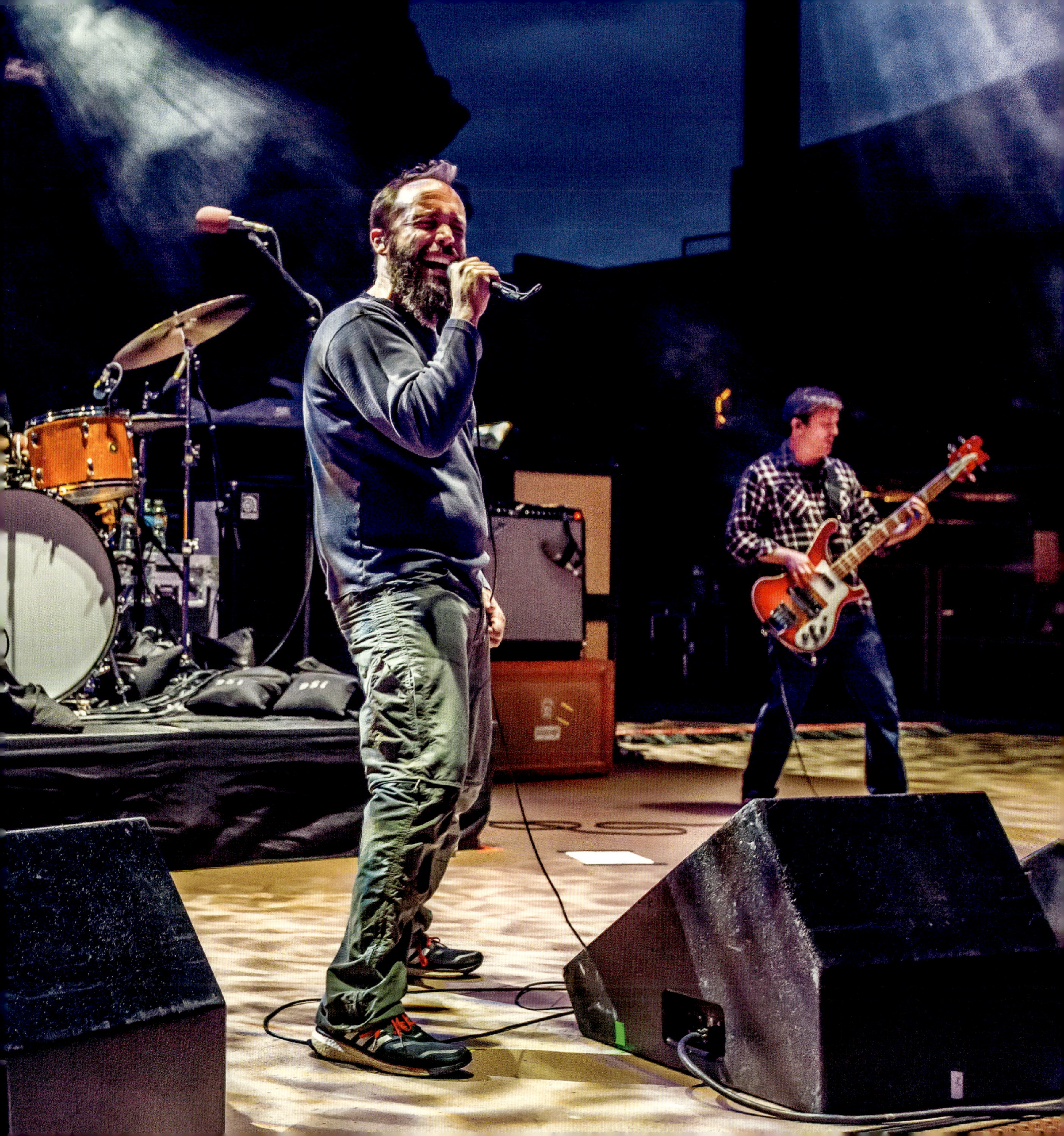

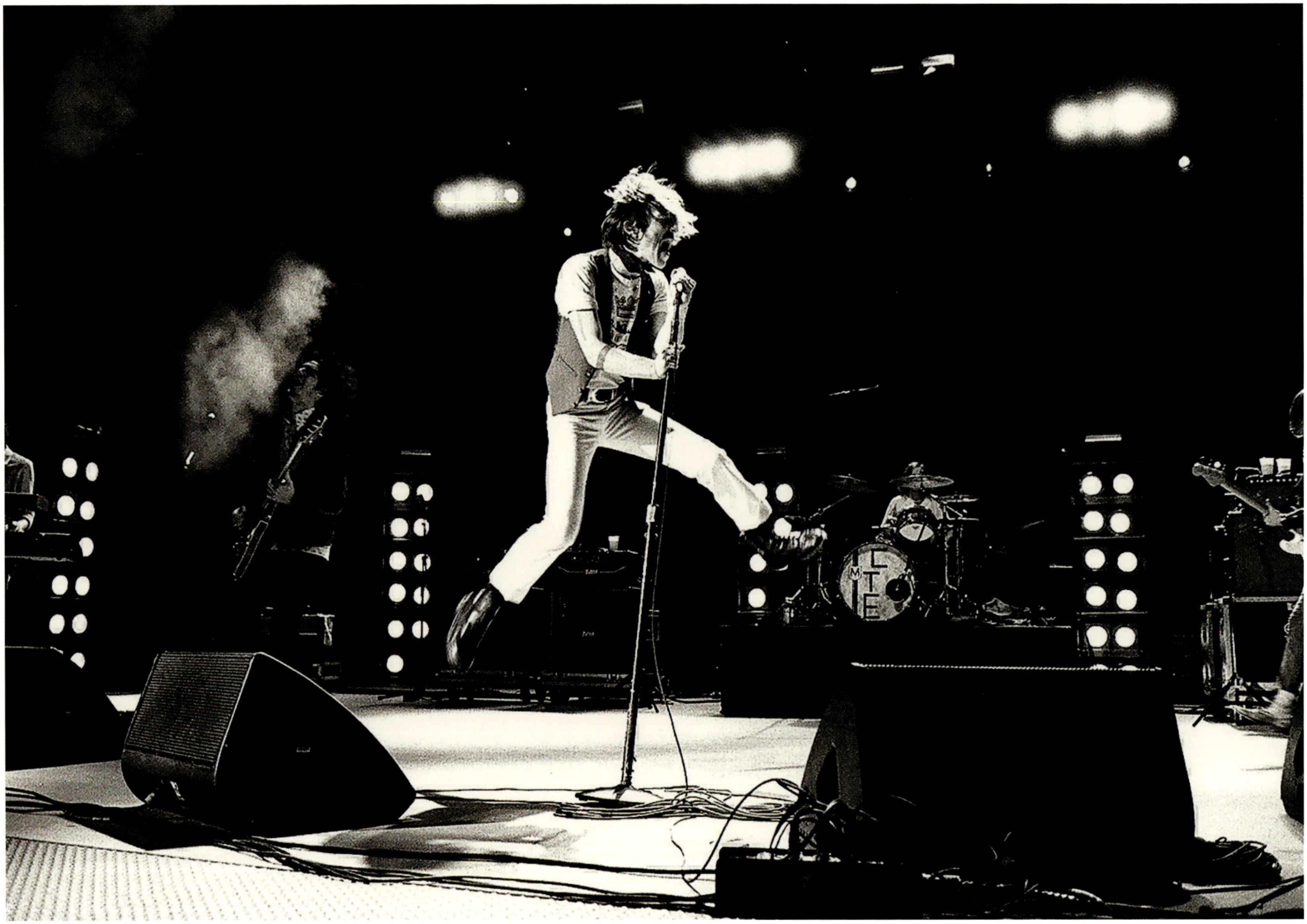

Cage the Elephant, 2015; Lynyrd Skynyrd, 1988 (right)

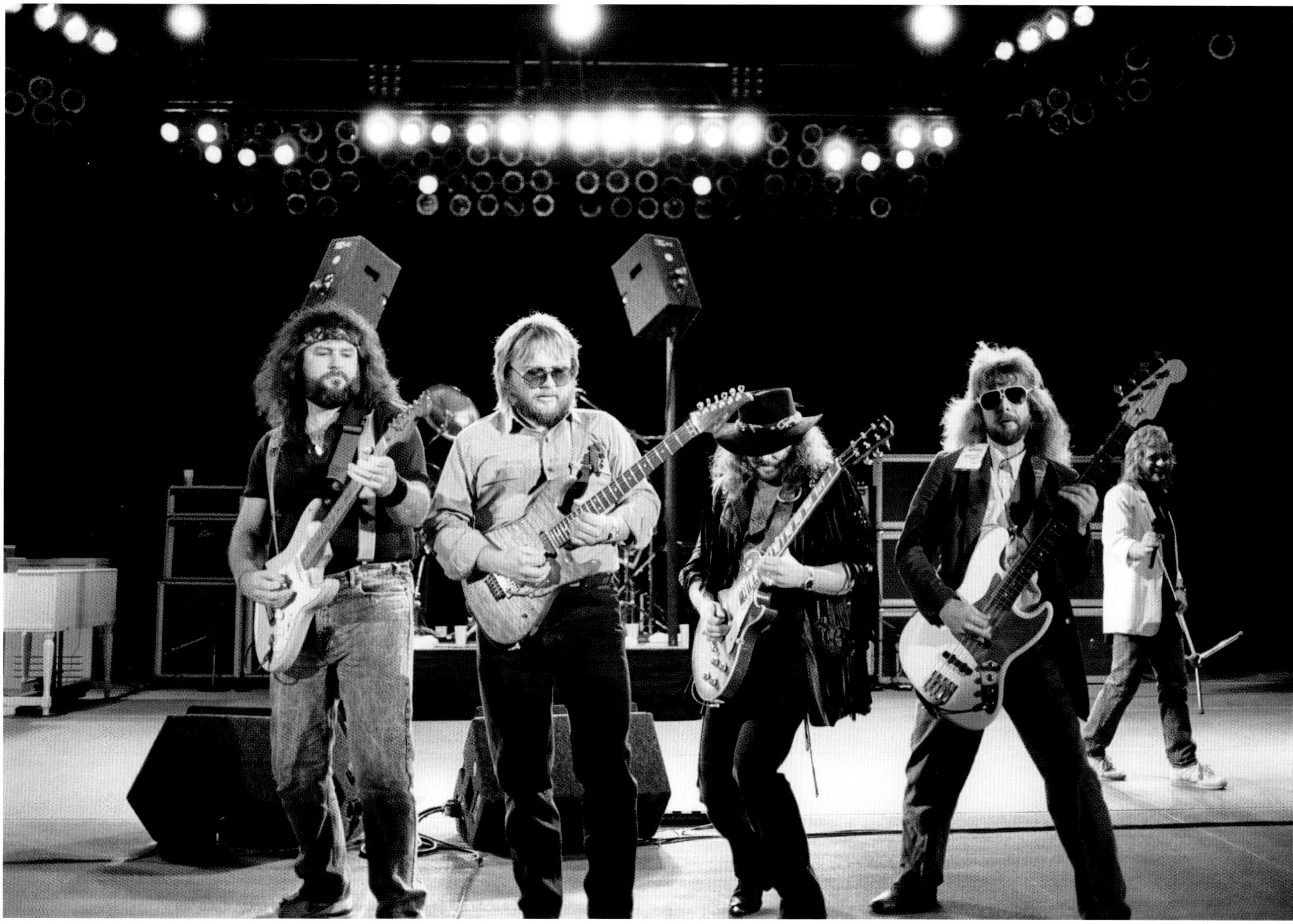

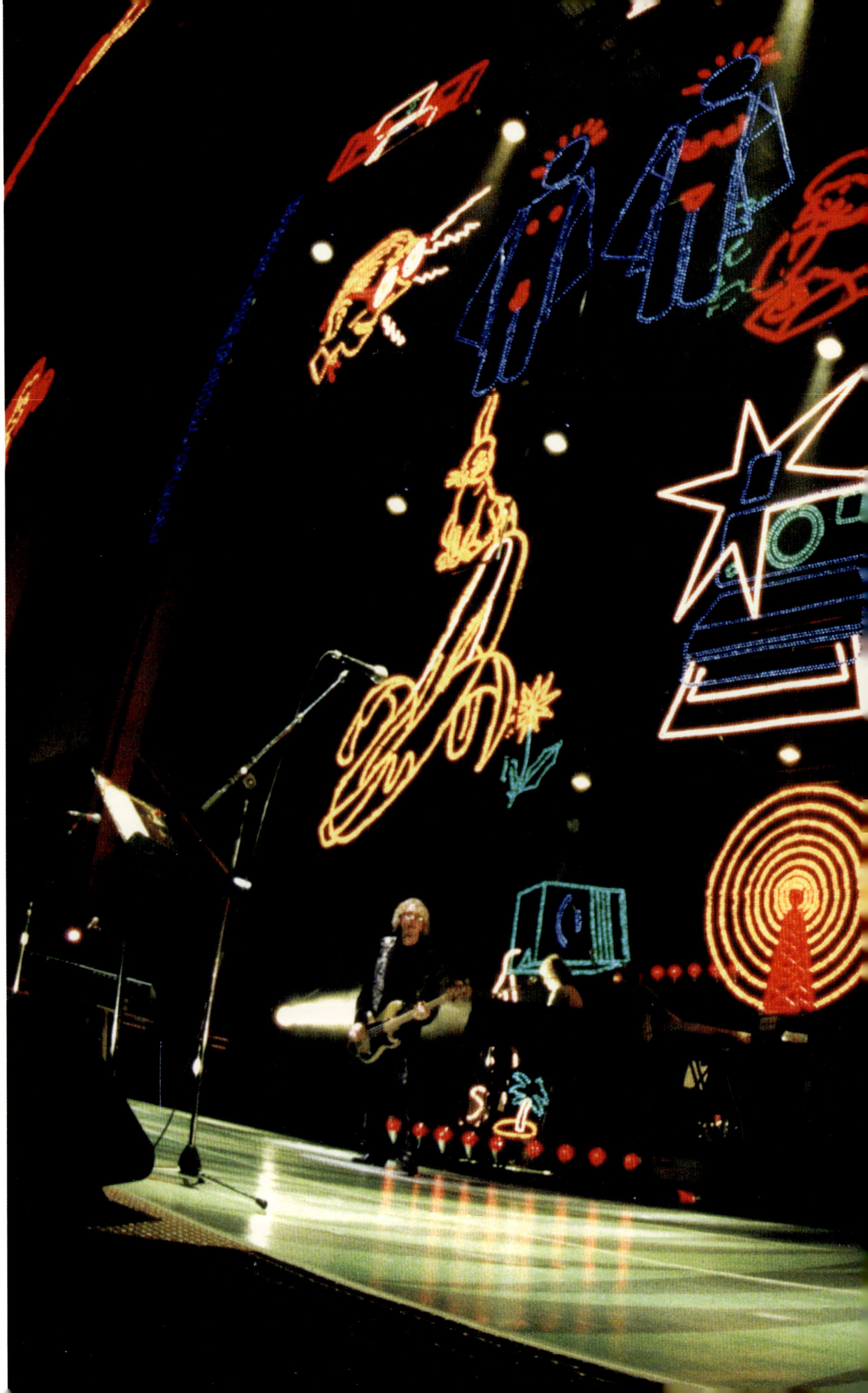

R.E.M., 1999

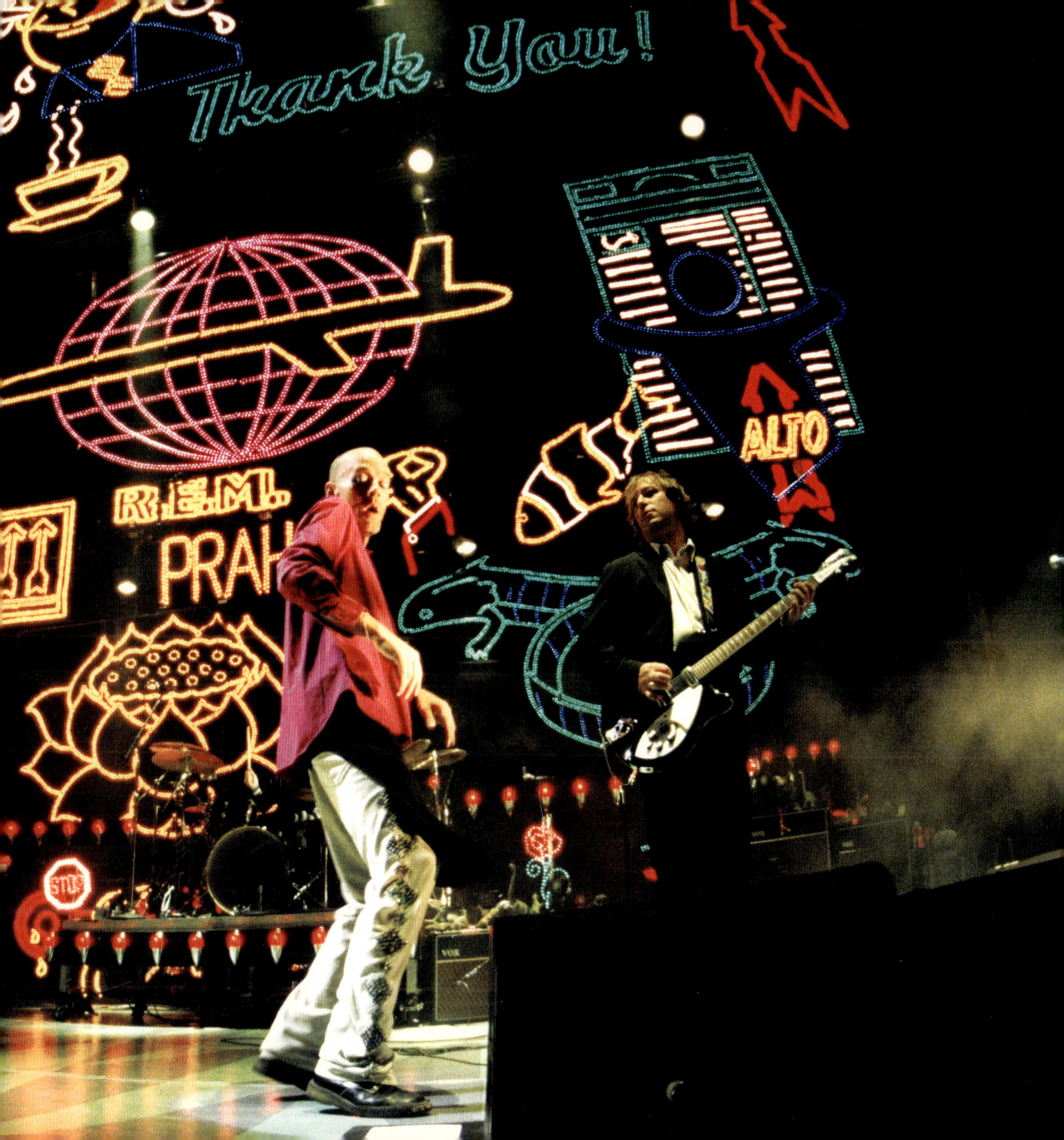
Thank You!
R.E.M.
PRAH
ALTO
STOP
VOX

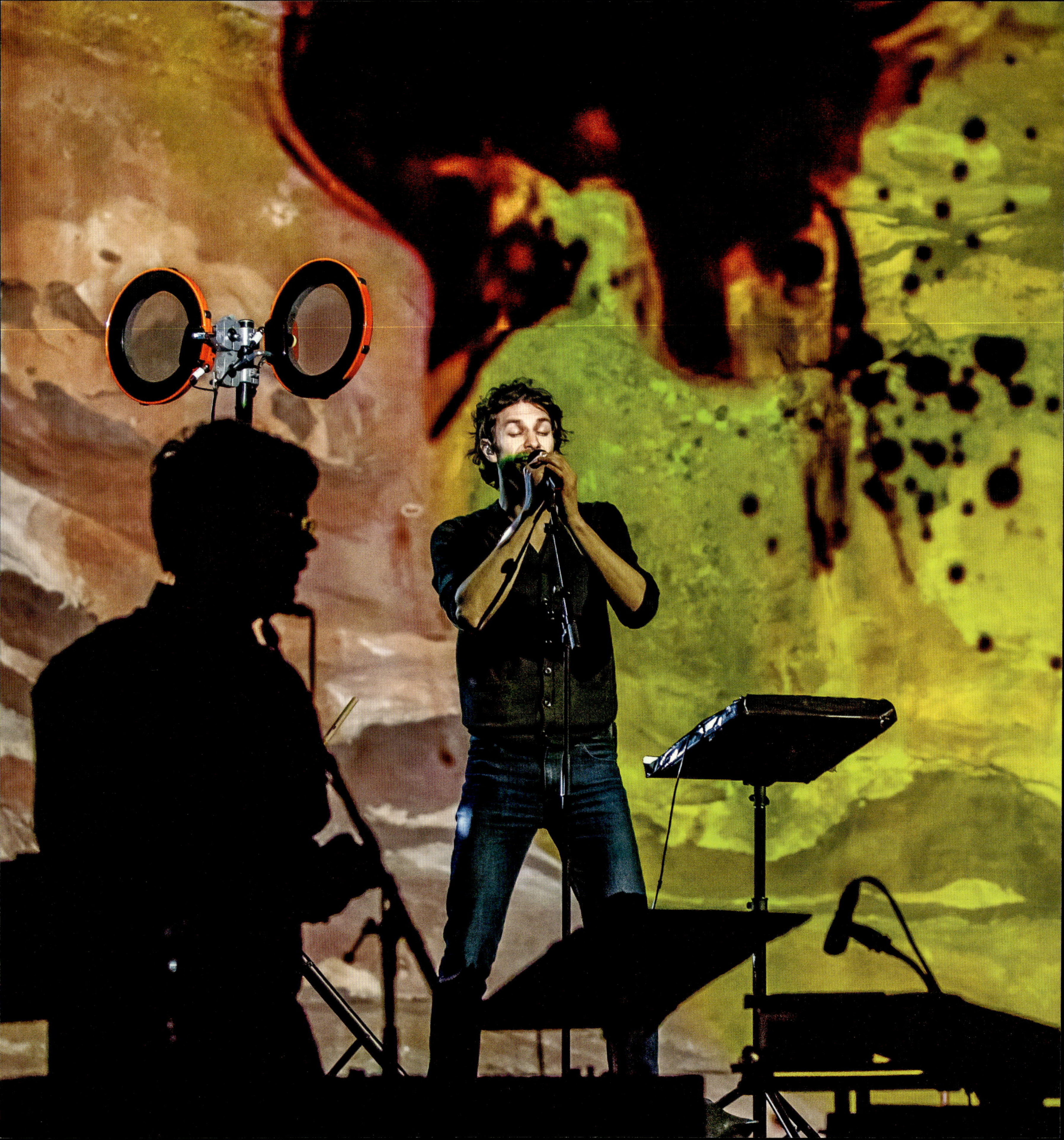

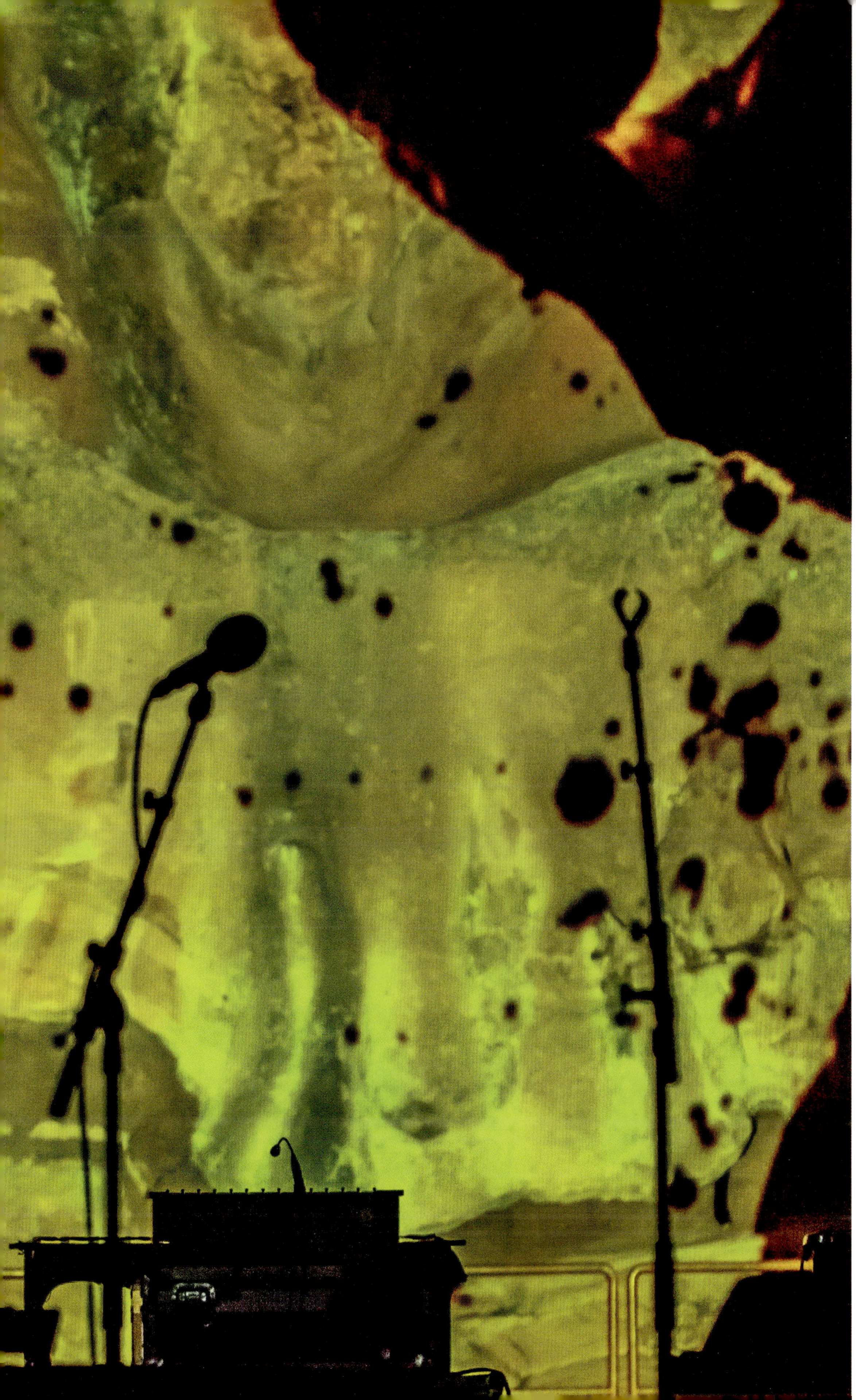

Gotye, 2012

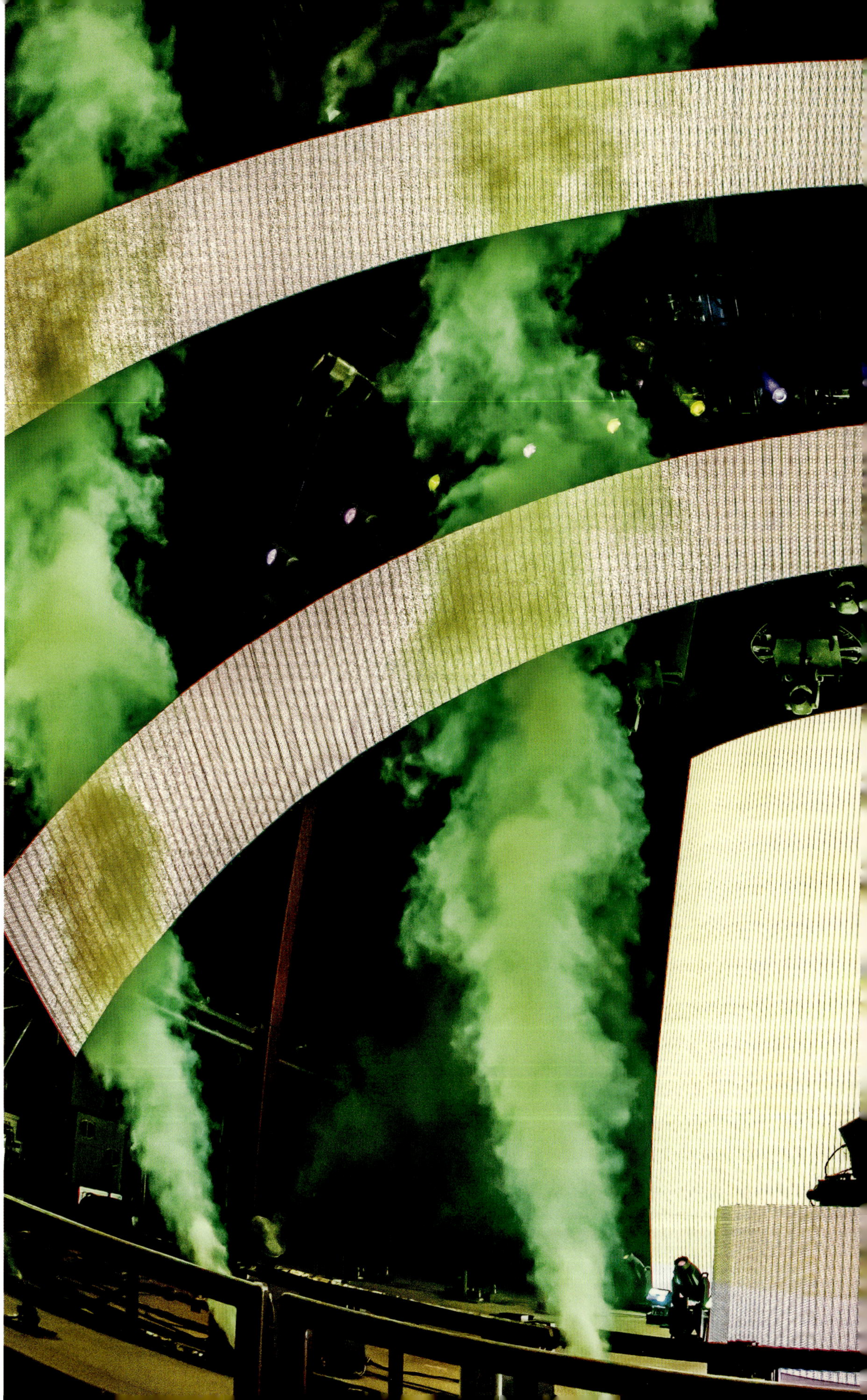

Marshmello, 2018

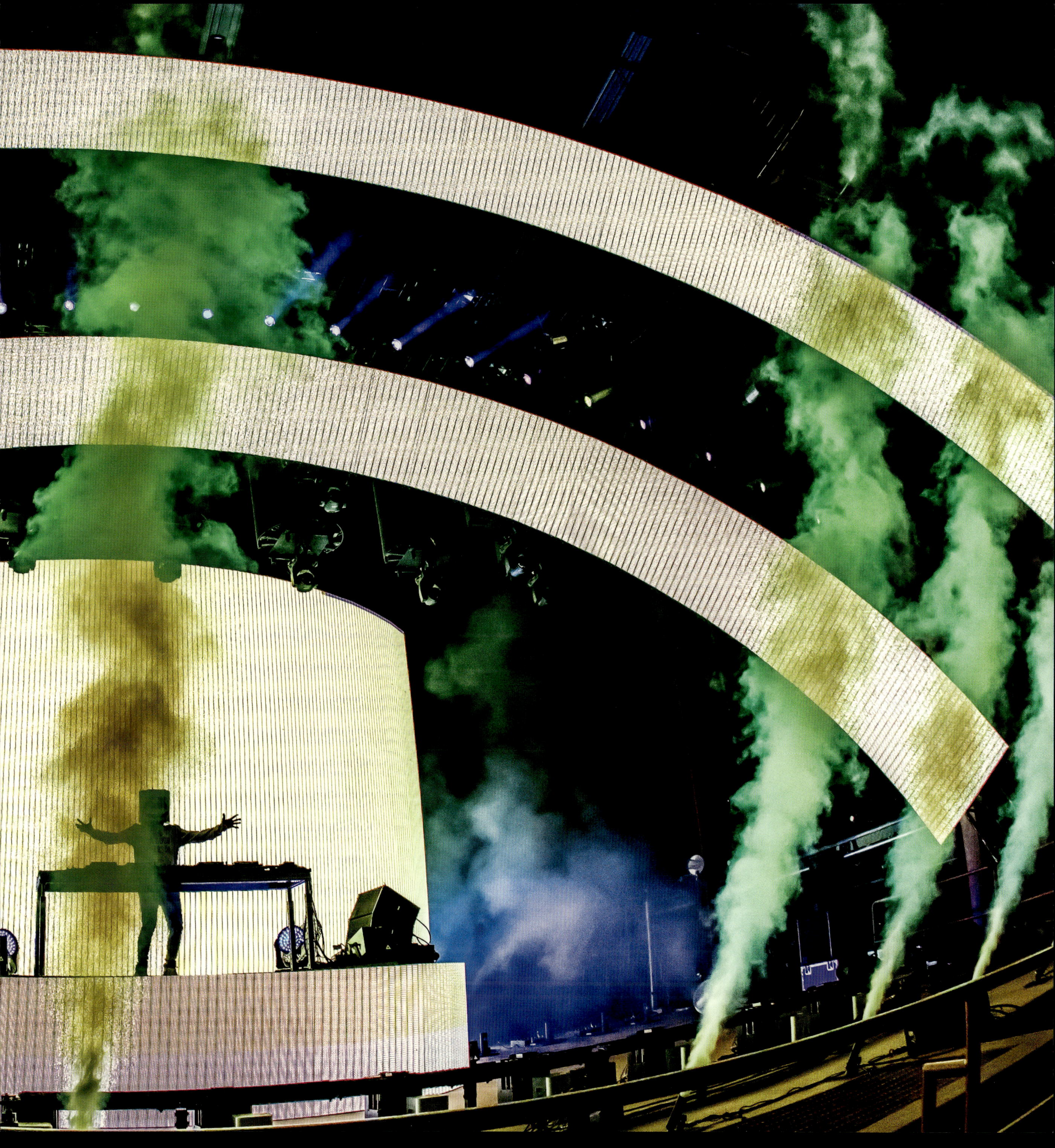

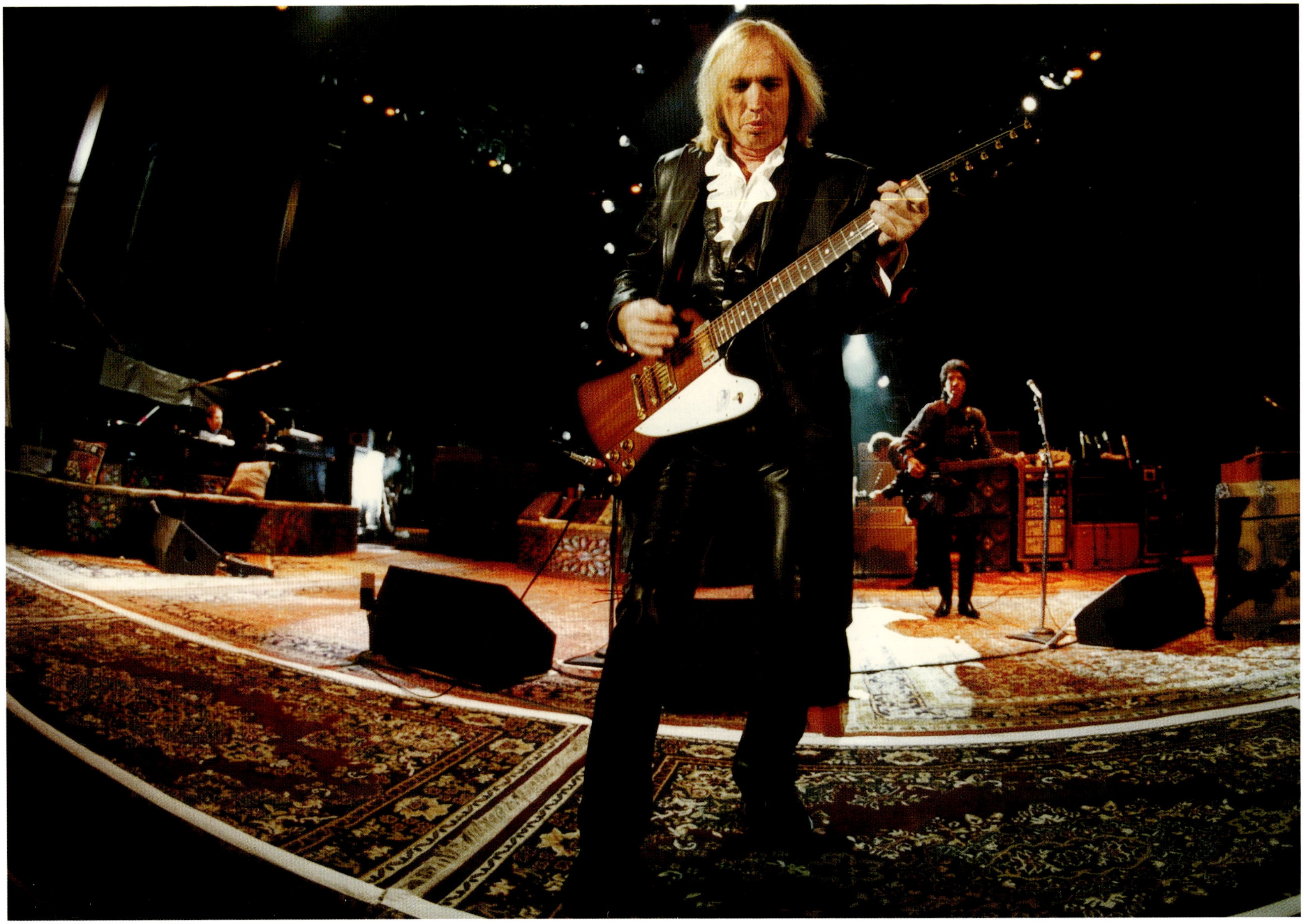

Tom Petty & the Heartbreakers, 1999; Poison, 1991 (right)

Following spread: Trey Anastasio, 2005

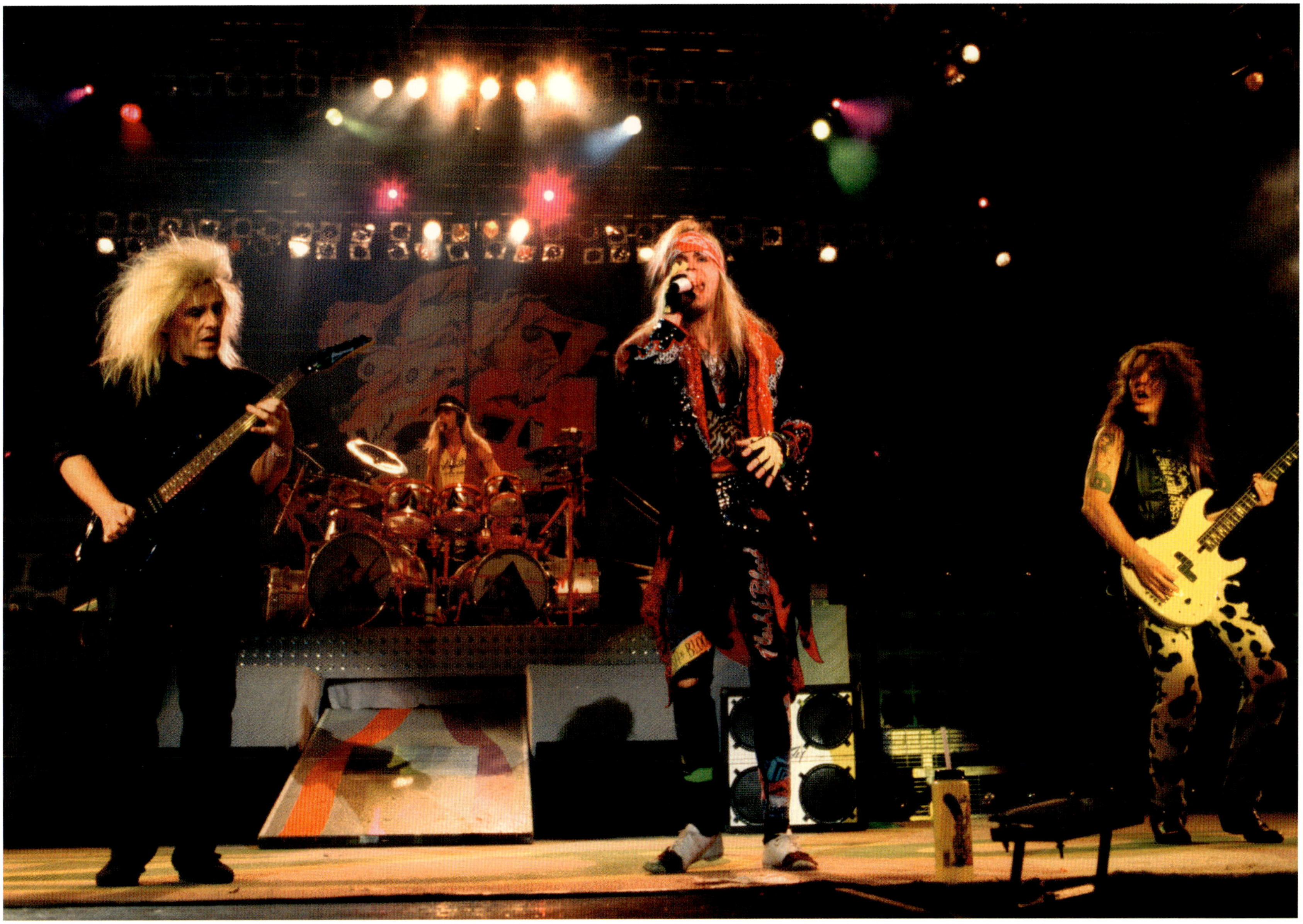

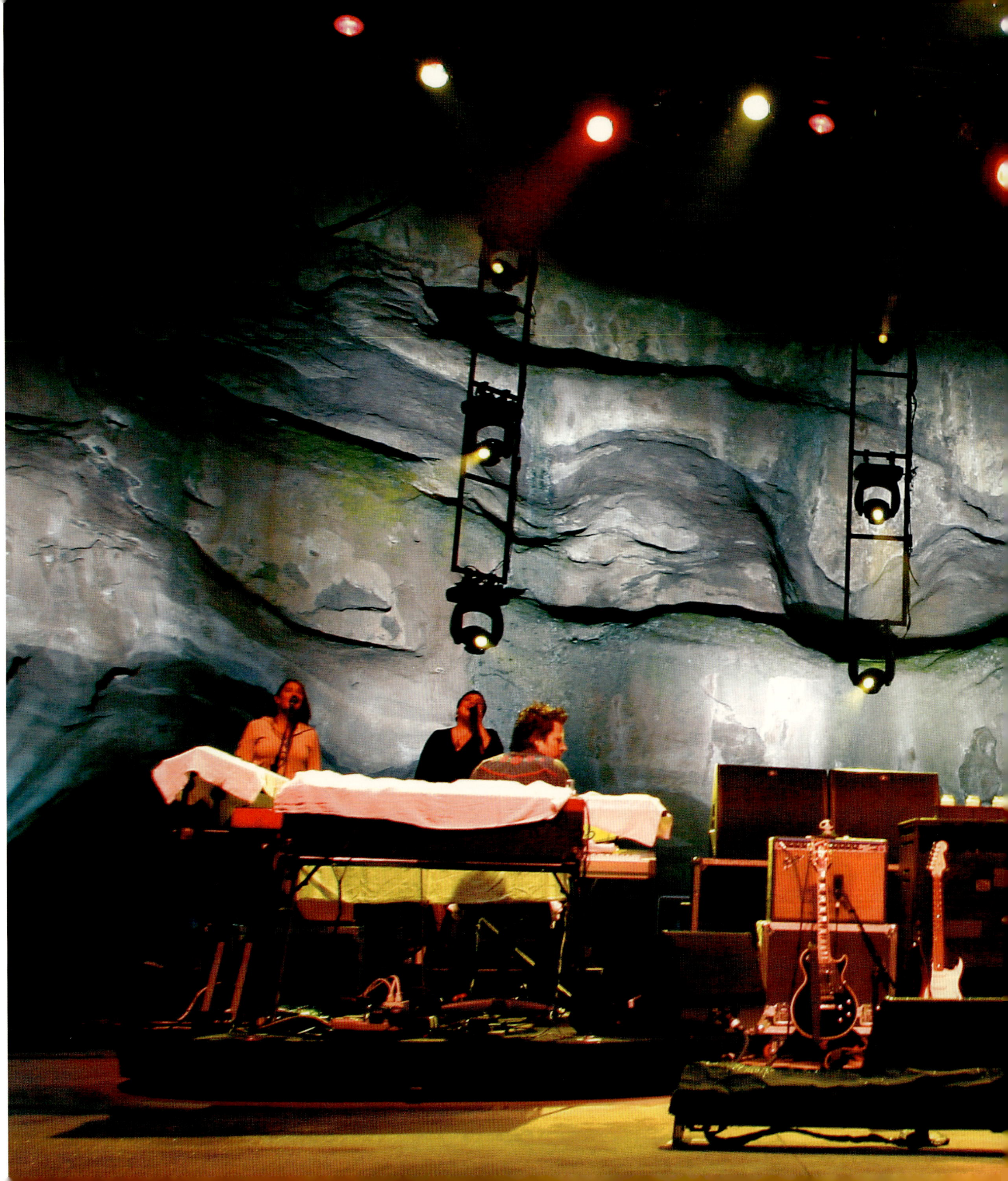

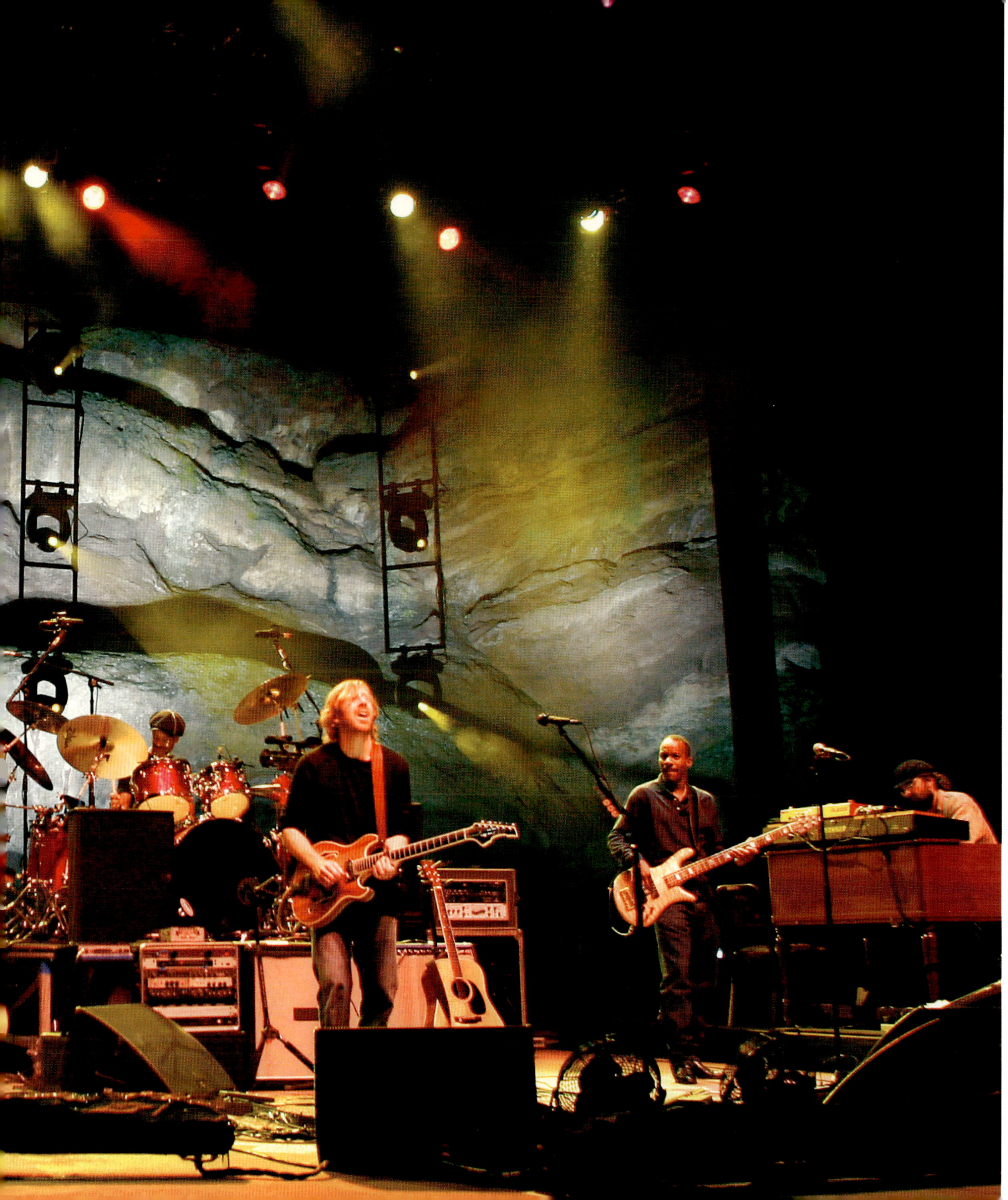

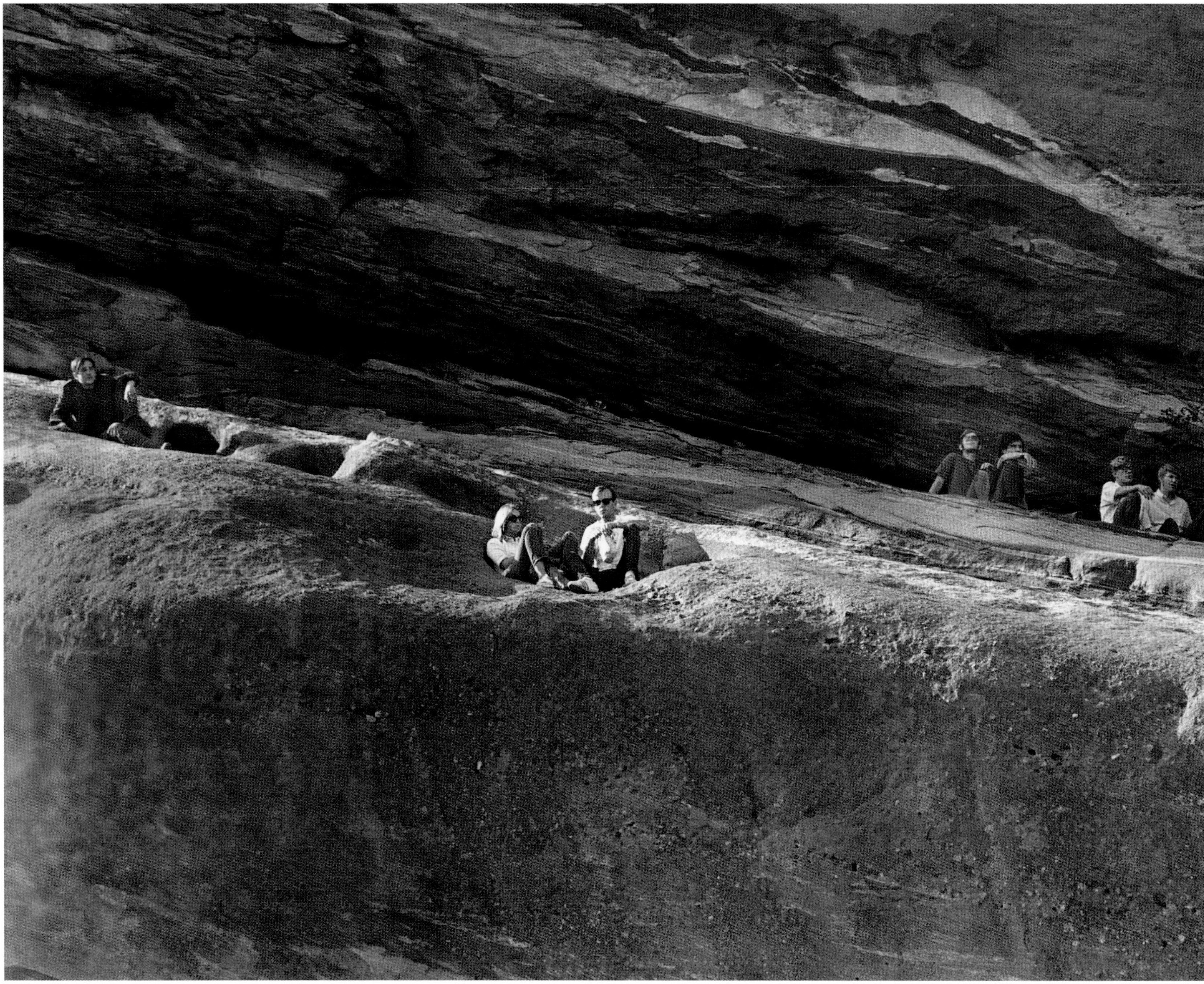

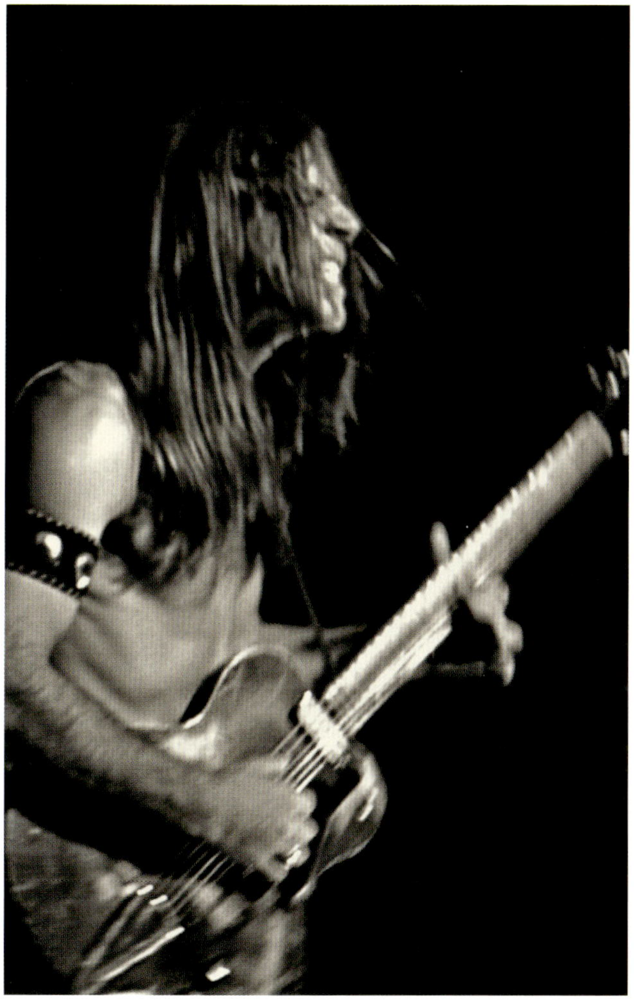

Unauthorized seating area, 1968 (left); Grand Funk Railroad, 1970

1970-1971
ROCKY TIMES

It was a time for drawing hard lines. Civil rights demonstrations, antiwar protests and student strikes flared up across the land. Music changed. Music mattered. For Denverites, the rock revolution was on, ready or not.

Fey kicked off the 1970 season with Ten Years After and Grand Funk Railroad for $4. By 3 p.m., the time at which those in attendance were required to show tickets in order to stay in the amphitheatre, the place was already one-third full, mostly with folks without tickets. With none available, discussion ensued about the possibility of moving the show to the larger Denver Coliseum.

But since Fey had fought the city long and hard to use Red Rocks for rock music, he averted disaster by appealing to the "brothers and sisters" to leave the stands and go back outside to return through the gates with their tickets. The ticketless complied, and they were invited to stay outside and listen to the music even if they couldn't see the performers.

On August 10, another capacity crowd greeted the power trio Mountain and the British progressive rock band Jethro Tull. Urban growth had pushed major roads into the west metro area, but concertgoers still had to negotiate winding roads to find a space in one of the parking lots, and then came a steep walk to get to the amphitheatre from the lower lots. But it was all part of the fun—the incredible beauty and excellent acoustics led Felix Pappalardi of Mountain to call Red Rocks "the most beautiful place we've ever played."

After that triumph, Jethro Tull would open the summer season at Red Rocks on June 10, 1971. In one of the most infamous events in Denver concert history, it resulted in a riot.

Rumors about potential unrest surfaced in the days leading up to the show. On that Thursday, an estimated 2,000 people who had not been able to get tickets went peacefully to Red Rocks to situate themselves on the surrounding rocks and hills to see and hear what they could, but there also was a militant faction determined to start trouble. Extra police were called in at 3 p.m. to control gatecrashers. At 5:30, the police, under orders from Lt. Jerry Kennedy, told the fans they would be allowed to sit on the hill behind the theater where they could hear the music, but not see the show.

The tumult started an hour before the concert was scheduled to begin, when a number of the "hill people" started to climb over the outdoor venue's back area in an attempt to get closer to the show; they swarmed the perimeter, walking over the bluffs and into the top parking lot.

The cops had warned the crowd that they would use tear gas if it

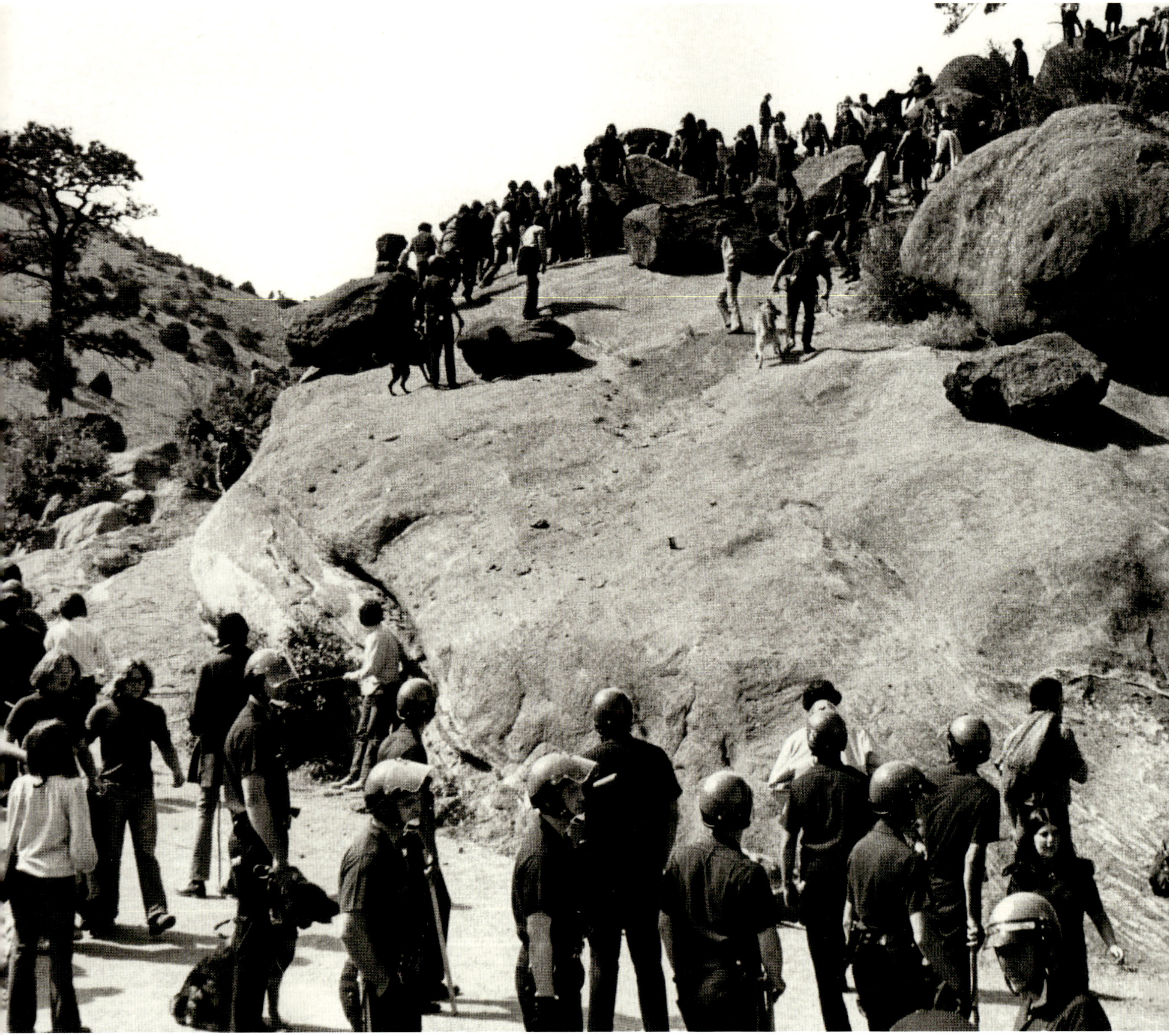

Jethro Tull concert riot, 1971

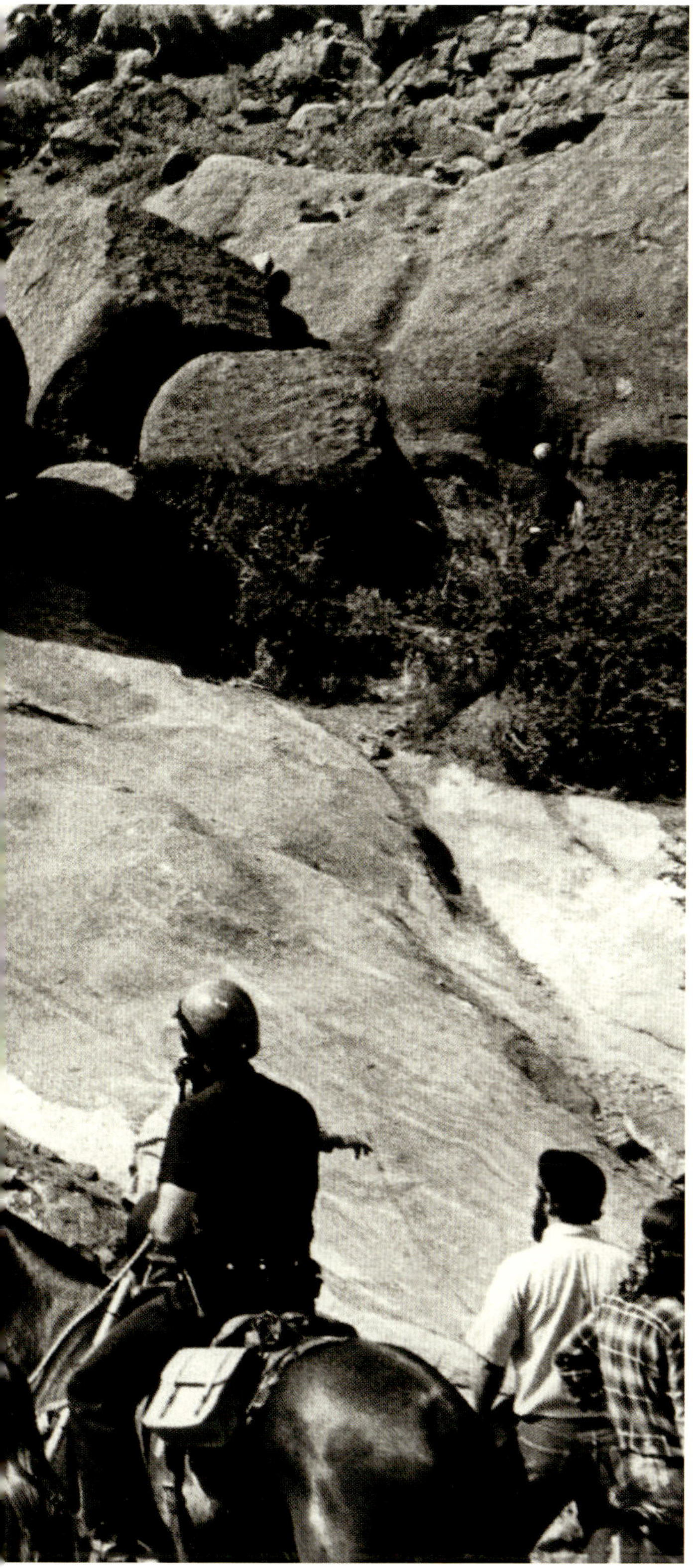

didn't disperse, feeling that the rough terrain would render any other way to maintain security impossible. A helicopter dropped the first volley in the upper area, but rather than deterring the disorderly throng, the tear gas incited further acts of violence. The crashers picked up bottles and rocks to use as ammunition against the police.

Adding to the problem, some of the gas began to fill the canyon-like shape of the amphitheatre, wafting over the paying crowd and collecting on the stage at an alarming rate—a situation that forced Livingston Taylor, the opening act, to make a hasty exit before finishing his set. "This is supposed to be music!," he cried. "What's going on here?"

While the police tended to injuries outside the theater, the medical staff attached to the amphitheatre had more problems than they could handle. Two doctors who went into the audience to treat severe injuries had their medical bags stolen, rendering them virtually helpless, while a small staff inside the aid station bandaged cracked skulls and revived those who had been overcome by the gas.

That the concert went on at all was a tribute to the perseverance of the members of Jethro Tull.

"We were leaving our hotel to go up to the show when we received word that there was a problem," flute-playing frontman Ian Anderson said. "We set off in our rented station wagons and were met by a police roadblock that tried to turn us back. We said, 'We're the band,' and we were told, 'There's not going to be a show, go away.'

"We thought that was ridiculous, so we managed to find a back route on a dirt road. We still had to make a fairly aggressive effort to get to the site—we wound up running a roadblock—and when we got there, we realized there was trouble going on outside. The police were trying to stop us from going to play—they felt that would make it worse. I said, 'Look, if you don't let us go onstage, not only are there going to be 2,000 people outside rioting, but 9,000 people inside are going to go crazy as well.'"

Reluctantly, the authorities allowed Tull to proceed. Anderson wandered on stage with tears in his eyes. The other members were also weeping and gasping for breath—keyboardist John Evan couldn't see his piano through the tear gas.

Undaunted, Tull played anyway. Anderson surveyed the Denver police chopper hovering in the distance dispensing periodic charges of tear gas at the rear of the assembly. "Welcome to World War III," he croaked, and the music, much of it from Tull's album *Aqualung*, went on for the next 80 minutes. Anderson was magnificent, stalking the stage and playing his flute like a man possessed, despite the circumstances.

"The gas made life very difficult in the amphitheatre itself," he said.

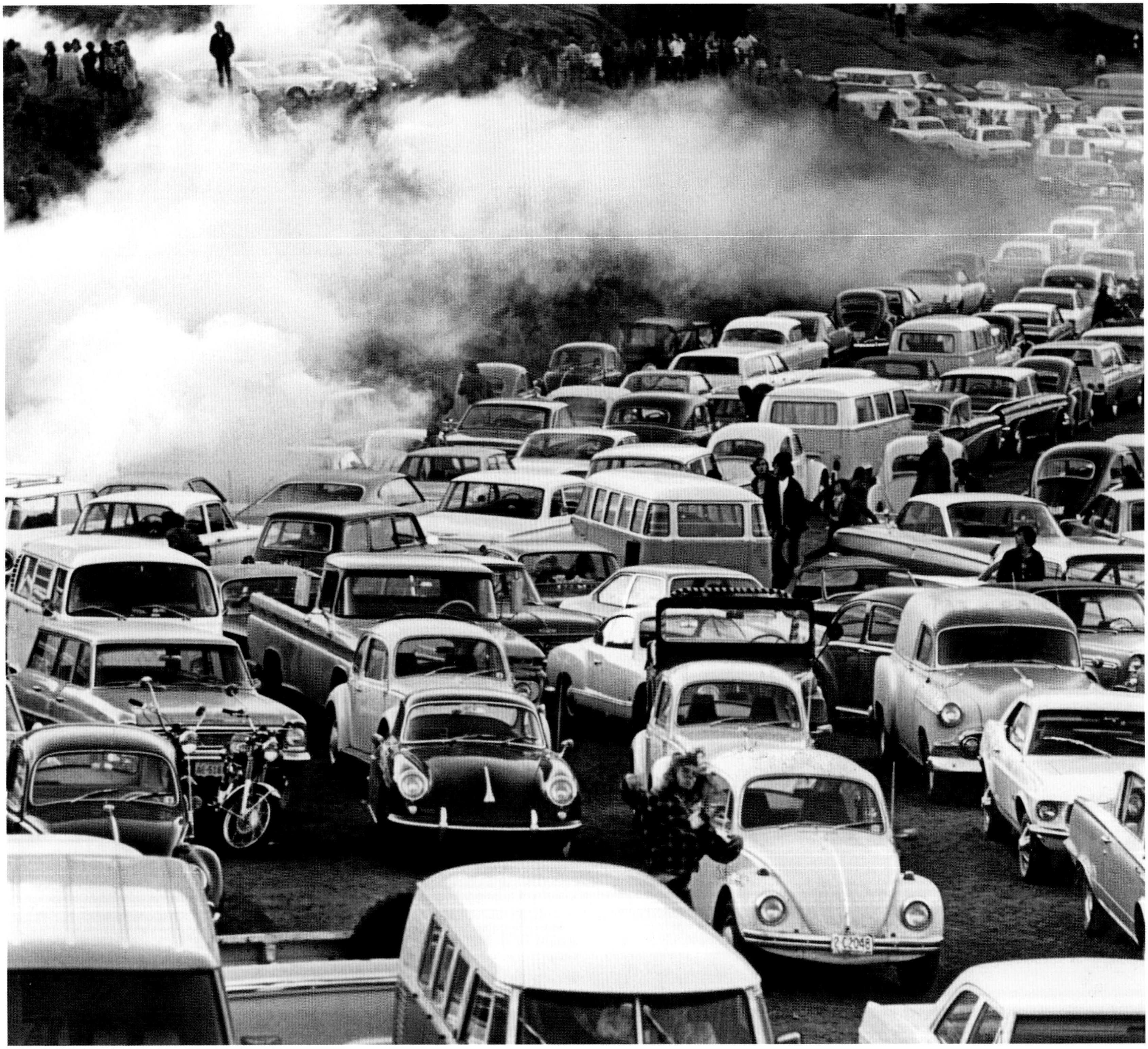

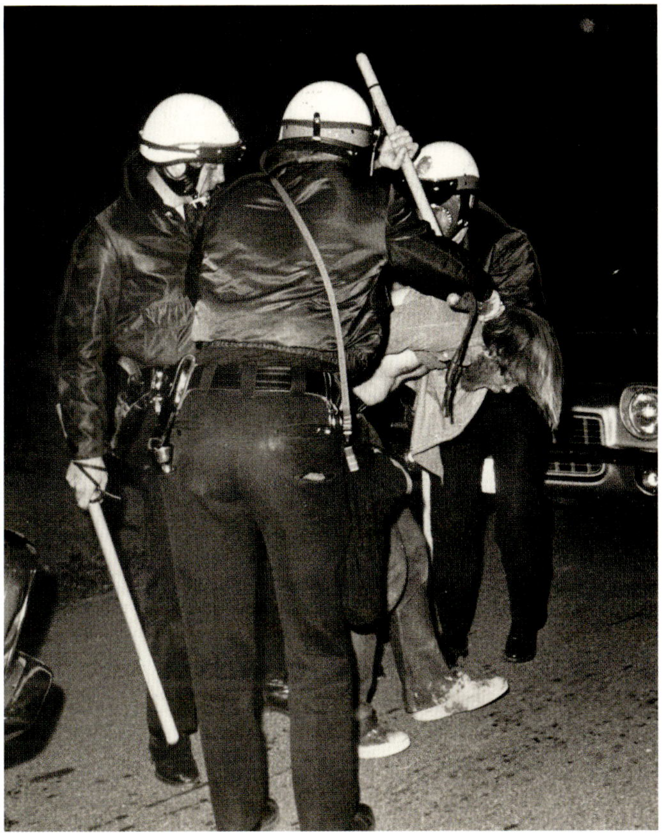

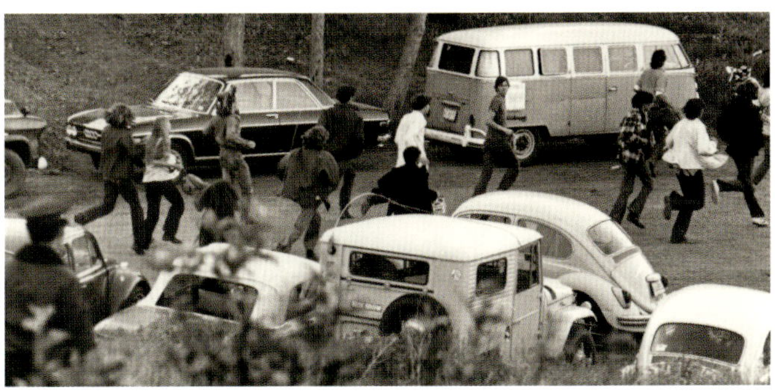

Jethro Tull concert riot (left, top, above), 1971

"The wind blew a cloud of gas over the audience to the stage. We had to stop several times. I remember seeing babies being passed down through the crowd so they wouldn't be affected by the gas. It was a horrifying sight. Happily, we were able to keep some sense of peaceful resolution with the audience. By playing the show, we kept the lid on what could have become a very dangerous situation."

The show at Red Rocks was one of drummer Barriemore Barlow's first dates with the band.

"Having slightly upset the police on the circuitous way up there, we had to be careful going down again—they saw us as the reason all this had happened," Anderson said. "We were hiding under blankets in the back of a rental station wagon, licking our wounds, lest the rather overly anxious local police decided to encourage a fray. They shined their torches in the station wagon looking for the longhaired British rock band. It was all a bit scary. Our eyes were streaming and we were coughing. Barrie turned to me and asked, 'Is it going to be like this every night?'"

In the wake of the riot, 28 persons, including four Denver policemen and three infants, were treated at area hospitals for injuries suffered in the disturbances, ranging from broken bones to gas inhalation. Dozens more—policemen, concertgoers and would-be gatecrashers—received treatment at the scene by a volunteer medical team. Twenty people, including three juveniles, were arrested on charges ranging from weapons violations to drunkenness to possession of narcotics. One parked car was overturned and burned, and several other vehicles were damaged.

The mayhem resulted in the cancellation of the remainder of the 1971 season—Judy Collins, Burt Bacharach, Rod McKuen and the Vienna State Opera Ballet. Sam Feiner, director of Denver's theaters and arenas division, said he wouldn't allow any more rock events at Red Rocks as a result of the disturbances—a ruling that held for years.

1972-1977
RETURN OF THE ROCKERS

The City of Denver banned any music more vigorous than soft rock from Red Rocks, but notable shows were still booked, including a Pete Seeger & Arlo Guthrie collaboration in July 1972. Later that month, an artist who would always be associated with Colorado and the city from which he took his name debuted at Red Rocks. John Denver was still ingratiating himself into the public's consciousness, and he used the occasion to debut a song that was four months from hitting the charts—"Rocky Mountain High."

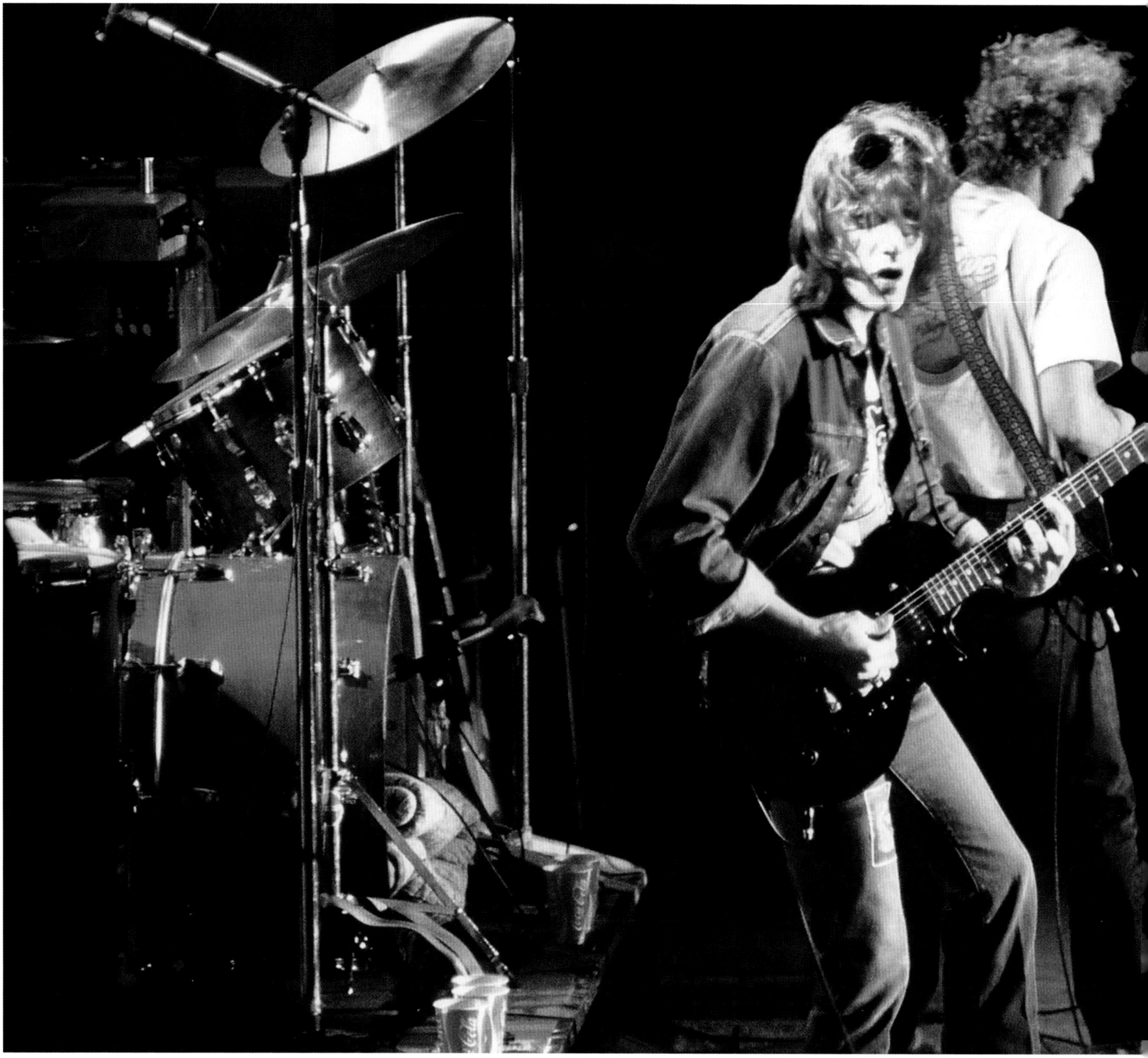

Eagles, 1975

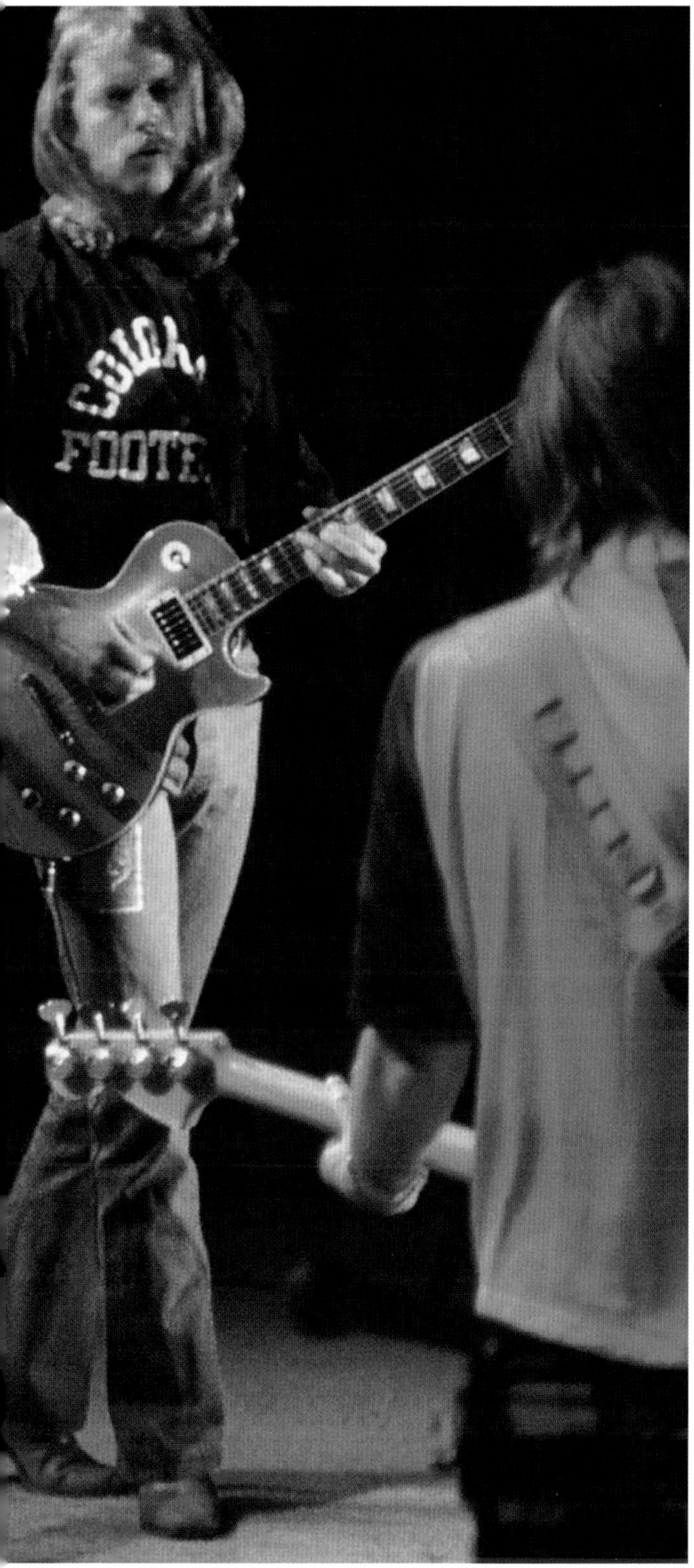

The following summer, Denver introduced "City of New Orleans" with mock indignation, noting to the audience that Arlo Guthrie's version, released six months later than his, had become "a giant hit record…really ticked me off." In singing "City," however, Denver forgot a line in the first verse and faked his way through it. RCA Records released the flawed performance as part of an expanded version of *An Evening with John Denver* on CD in 2001, four years after Denver's death.

In 1974, Denver was the first artist to play four consecutive nights at Red Rocks. Other mellow acts hit the outdoor stage—Joan Baez, Neil Diamond, Carole King, Roberta Flack and Helen Reddy. Joni Mitchell was scheduled to perform in September 1974 on the "Miles of Aisles" tour with Tom Scott and the L.A. Express, but a thick fog rolled in and transitioned to light snow, so she played the next night at the Denver Coliseum instead.

The summer of 1975 featured a Wayne Newton and Bob Hope show and an appearance by Doc Severinsen with the Denver Symphony Orchestra. The only disturbance occurred during a July performance by Gordon Lightfoot when someone threw an orange at him.

However, when city officials deemed the acoustic folk-rock group America an inappropriate act for the park, promoter Fey turned to the courts. While the case was ostensibly an attempt to quash the America concert, by extension the decision would determine whether the city could continue to dictate which acts would appear at Red Rocks. Over Sam Feiner's objections, Judge Robert T. Kingsley of the Denver District Court okayed the America show, calling the ban "quasi-judicial" and saying that the city had acted "arbitrarily and capriciously."

After the America concert took place without incident, Red Rocks opened up to rock music. Stephen Stills performed July 17, as did Linda Ronstadt August 6.

Also, the Eagles—just beginning a run of four consecutive No. 1 albums with *One of These Nights*—were booked for two shows, August 18 and 19. The band's original opening act, Dan Fogelberg, became too ill to perform, so Tom Waits, already in town to play the Denver nightclub Ebbets Field, was recruited to replace him. Although the idiosyncratic singer-songwriter had written "Ol' 55," which the Eagles had covered on one of their albums, Waits was a disaster; the crowd didn't warm up to his mongrel musical style.

What crowds were finding enjoyable, however, was getting high at Red Rocks, though some folks weren't equipped to handle it, judging by the lines at the aid stations. The hot sun and alcohol made for a lot of oblivious concertgoers. Bouncers served as a rudimentary form of security personnel; some were renowned for their "hit first, ask questions

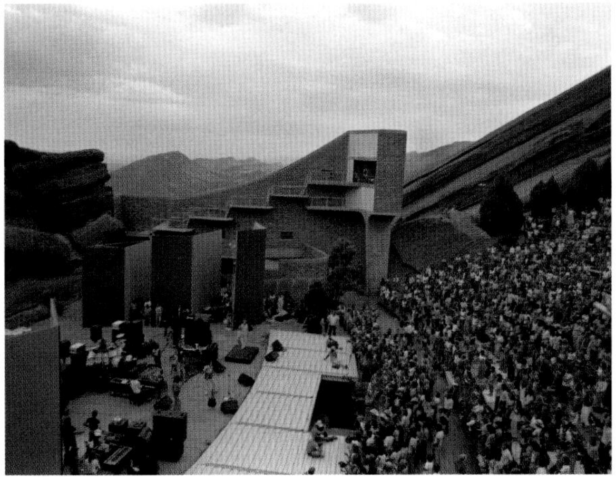

Jackson Browne (above, right), 1977

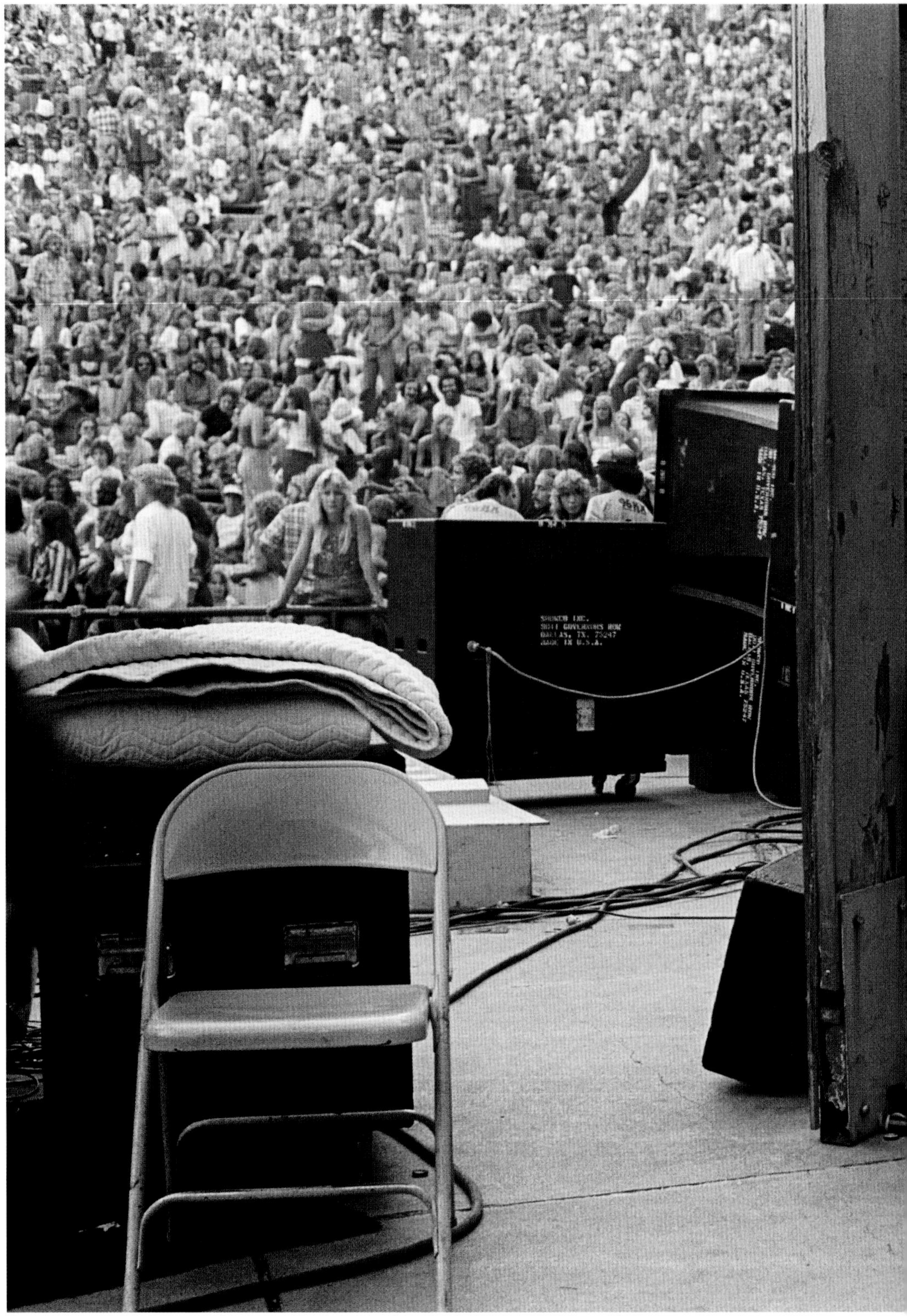

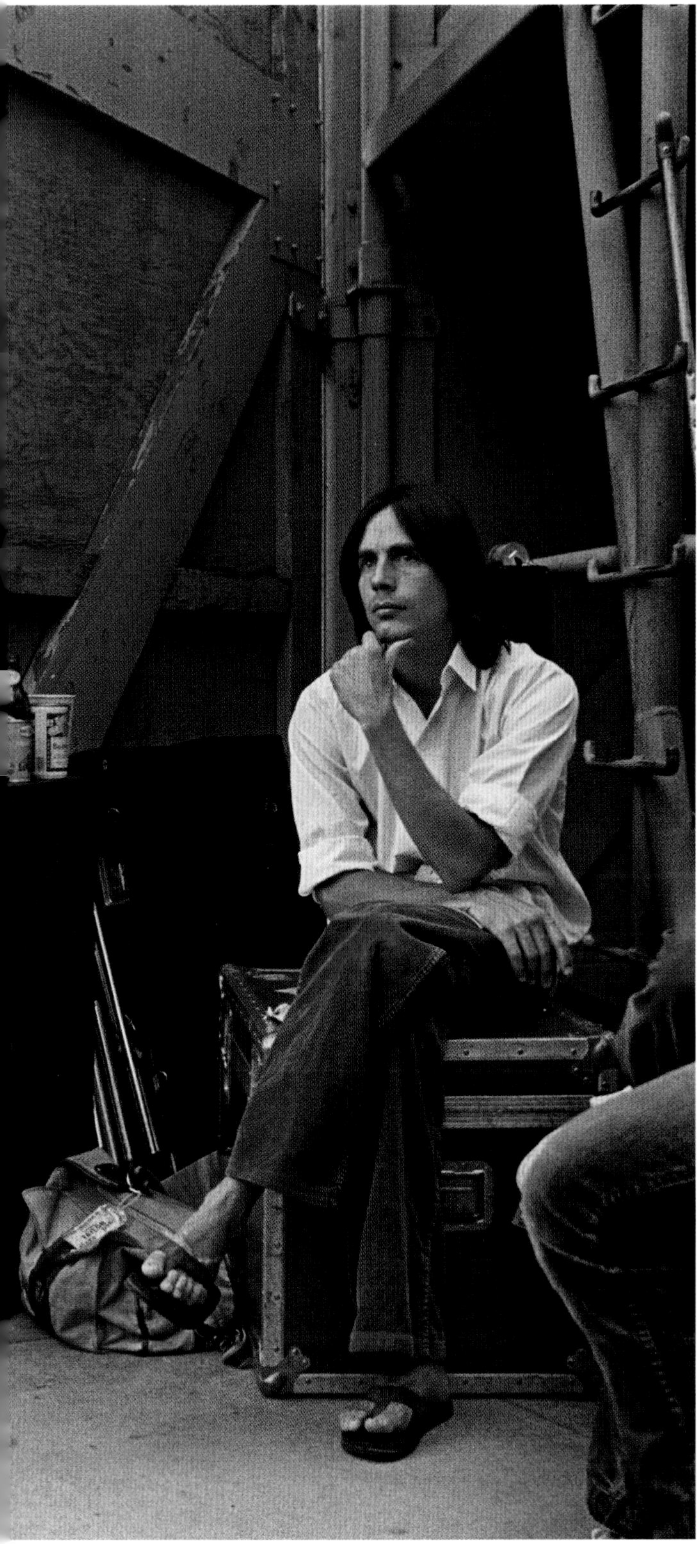

later" policy. The Open Clinic, a 24-hour crisis intervention hotline operated by Denver University students, was a foray into providing first-aid care. Eight to ten staffers would mingle with the audience in jerseys that read "No hassle, no heat" and assist kids if they were having bad drug experiences and tend to people who had fallen on or off the rocks.

The city couldn't overlook the revenue source derived from concerts. Fey's company created the "Summer of Stars" series, which became the heart of the Denver area's summer entertainment calendar, and Red Rocks turned into one of the busiest venues in the western United States. Fey, Feyline chief talent buyer Chuck Morris and Fey's chief assistant Pam Moore managed booking the acts, securing the available dates with the city, arranging alternate "rain-out" locations, getting the word out and the tickets on sale.

Poco performed at Red Rocks for the first time in 1977; the seminal country-rock band had finally cracked the top of the charts with its fourteenth album, *Legend*.

"I grew up in Denver, and only famous people played Red Rocks," co-founder Rusty Young said. "There are a few milestones in your life that you don't think you'll ever achieve but you wish you could. When I was playing in little bands in bars around town, I never dreamed that I'd be onstage at Red Rocks playing. Made mom proud!"

Jackson Browne recorded *Running on Empty*, his innovative concept album about life on the road, on a cross-country tour in 1978—onstage, backstage, in hotel rooms, even on the tour bus. The picture sleeve of his "Stay" single, which became a Top 40 hit, featured a photo taken at Red Rocks; it also appeared in the gatefold album cover. Opening for Waylon Jennings in May, Hank Williams, Jr. sang "You Love the Thunder" as rain poured down.

Comedian Steve Martin's tour stopped at Red Rocks in June 1978. Singer-songwriter Steve Goodman, in the opening slot, sat at the side of the stage, gazing at the people filling the amphitheatre and shaking nervously. His composure was quickly tested during his performance when a guitar string broke. Goodman audaciously kept on singing. But instead of continuing the song, he improvised rhyming lyrics for a new one on the spot, in the same key and rhythm as the interrupted tune. Meanwhile, he selected a replacement string, threaded it through its proper peg on the guitar and wound it up—never missing a beat of his improvised tune. Once he got the string in place and tuned, Goodman seamlessly segued to the original song—resuming at the same point he had interrupted it—and finished to thunderous applause.

Martin had exploded onto the comedy scene and become the most successful concert draw in the history of stand-up, earning the level of

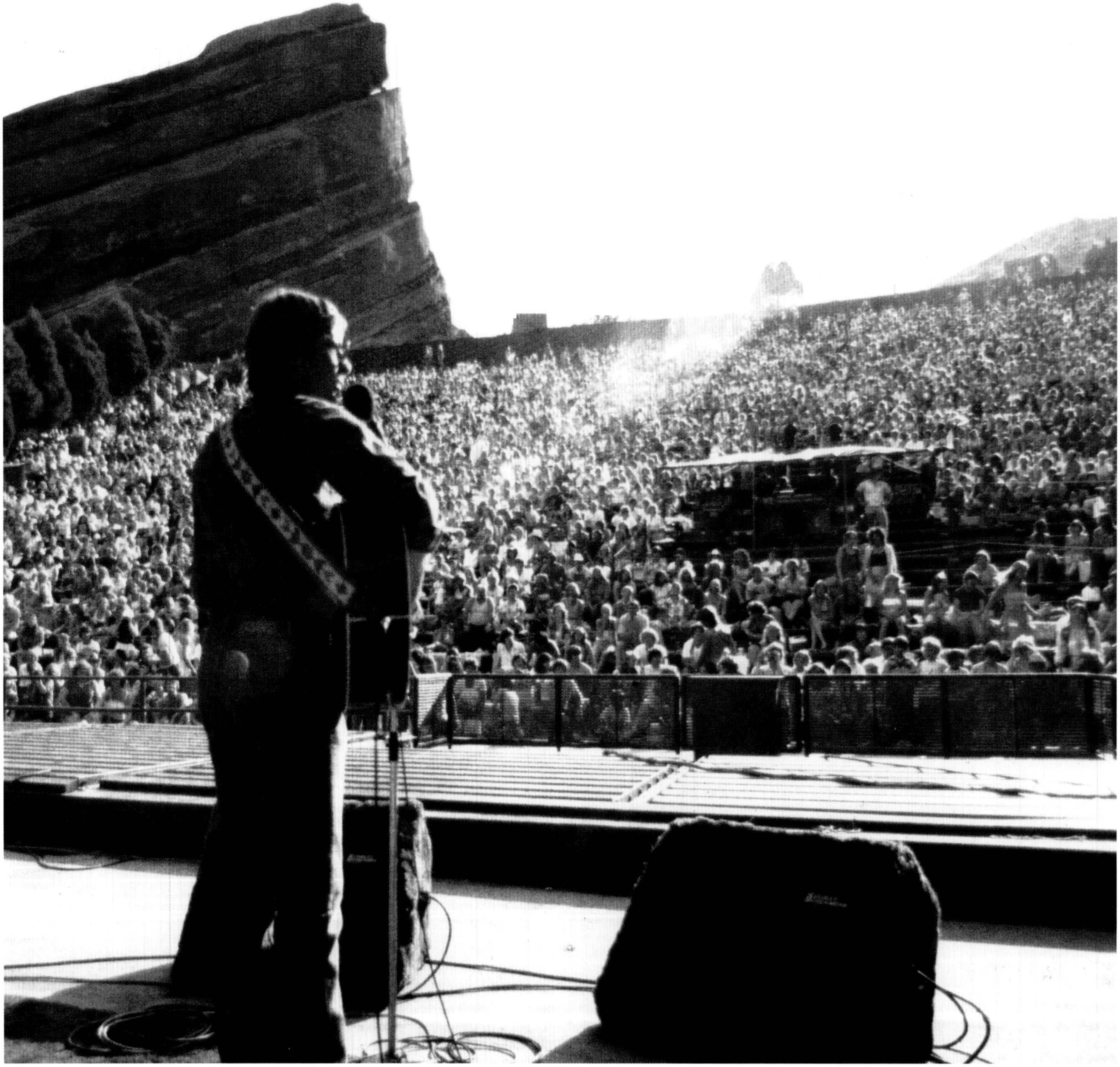

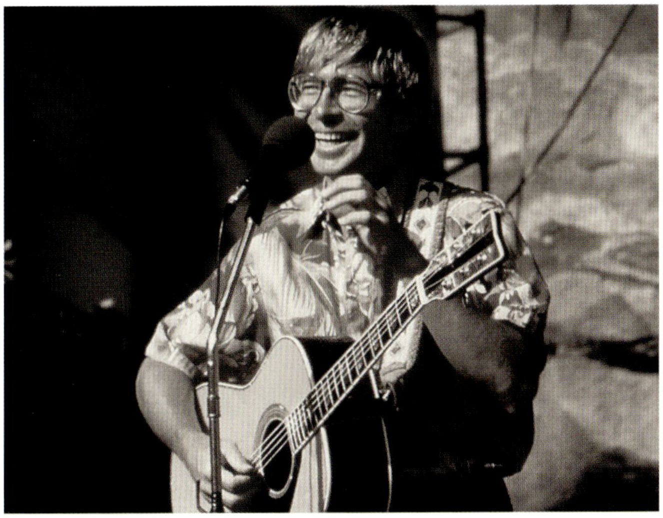

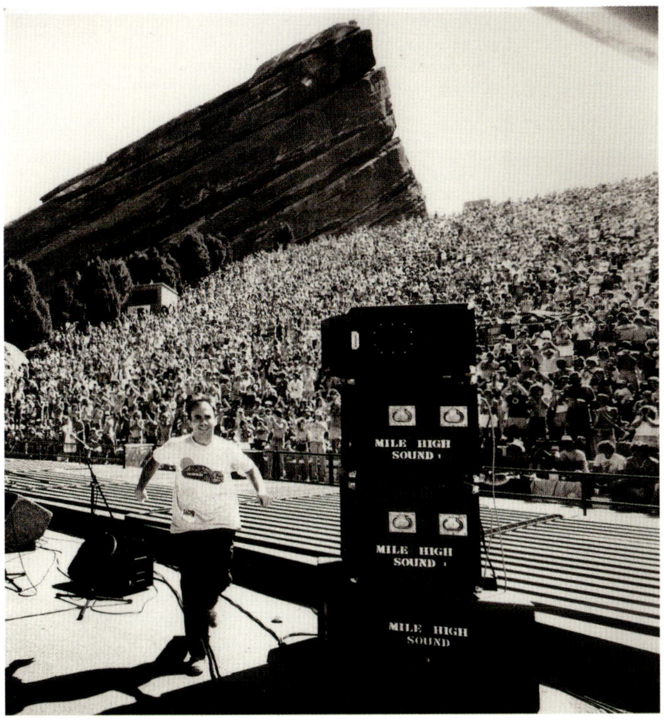

John Denver sound check, 1981 (left), 1982 (top);
Steve Goodman, 1982 (above)

commercial success usually reserved for rock stars. He recorded the second side of his comedy album *A Wild and Crazy Guy* during the Red Rocks concert, lovably catering to a roaring crowd in a frenzy of his *Saturday Night Live* bits and unique-to-him jokes. The record reached #2 on *Billboard*'s Pop Albums Chart; it was eventually certified double platinum and won the Grammy Award in 1979 for Best Comedy Album.

"Though my general recall of the period is precise, my memory of specific shows is faint. I stood onstage, blinded by lights, looking into blackness, which made every place the same," Martin recalled. "I don't really remember much about Red Rocks except watching Doug Kershaw and the Nitty Gritty Dirt Band as a fan. Beautiful place, though."

1978-1982
RIDIN' THAT RAIN

On June 20, 1978, Bruce Springsteen and the E Street Band made their Colorado debut at Red Rocks Amphitheatre in support of *Darkness on the Edge of Town*, his first release in almost three years. He had spent the interim battling his ex-manager, letting the *Born to Run* hype settle down and recording several albums' worth of songs. Only after weeks of cajoling by his manager and booking agents did Springsteen agree to his first-ever outdoor show. A gig in the wide open spaces? He was apprehensive about a lack of intimacy, dubious about the havoc that it might wreak among his sound crew and cautious of problems with audience communication.

Only 6,200 persons had the foresight to catch it, but on that Tuesday night, Springsteen put on a legendary performance, one that he later claimed was the best of the entire tour. The new songs—the opening "Badlands," "Prove It All Night" and "Racing in the Streets"—came to life as the kid from Asbury Park spat out the words, darted around the stage and exhorted the crowd, playing for three hours and three sizzling encores. Springsteen had the charisma of a kid who had just hopped out of his folks' station wagon and seen the mountains for the first time. He and his band managed to keep their Jersey sensibilities intact—"Nice place you got here…bunch of big rocks," Springsteen said with a laugh. The adoring audience rushed the stage, and Springsteen's loyalty to his new friends out West was incredible. "The idea is to deliver what money can't buy," he said.

With the Beatles, the Rolling Stones and the Who, the Kinks were one of the most influential bands of the British Invasion. By the mid 1970s, the band had refashioned themselves as hard rockers, playing arenas in

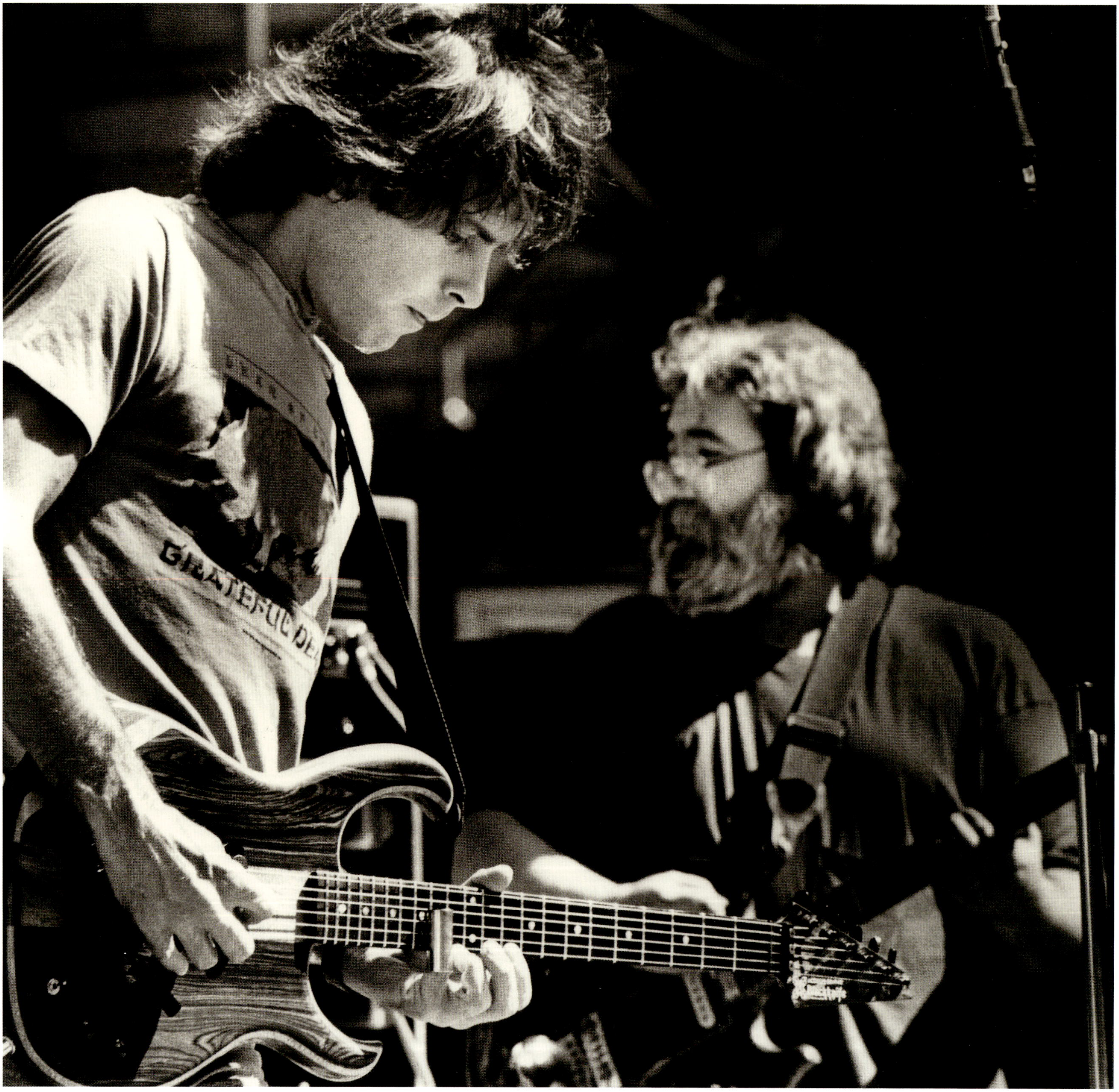
GRATEFUL DEA

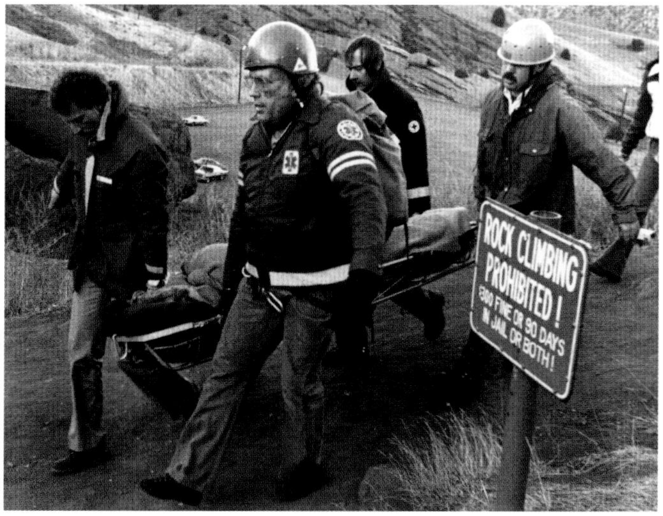

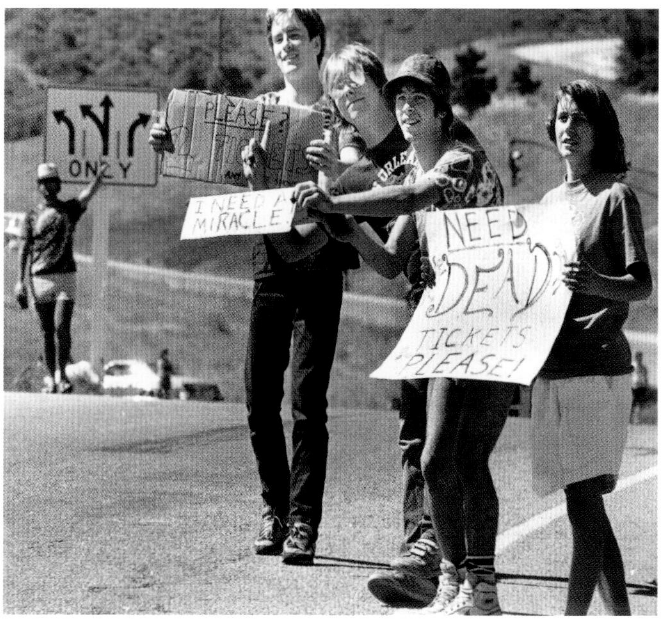

Grateful Dead, 1982 (left); rock-climbing fatality, 1979 (top); Deadheads, 1982 (above)

the United States. In support of *Low Budget*, the group's biggest American success, the Kinks performed at Red Rocks in July 1978.

"I remember having the oxygen at the side of the stage, because it's quite high up there. Geographically, it was just a spectacular place to play," Ray Davies, the band's leader and songwriter, said. "I was terrified of what the sound would be like, but I was really pleased and surprised with the good quality we got there, how acoustically pure it is. I've played Carnegie Hall, and that is not a happy place for rock music. But Red Rocks certainly worked for our band."

The Grateful Dead and Red Rocks started becoming synonymous, as the band considered the venue "a sacred place," likening it to Stonehenge and the pyramids of Egypt. The Dead were scheduled to play four days in 1978, but in two shifts (July 7 & 8 plus Aug. 30 & 31; the last show was moved because of rain). The band used Red Rocks as an instrument of sorts to take Deadheads to places they'd never been. One of them, basketball star Bill Walton, who a month earlier had just won his first NBA championship, hung backstage on crutches.

"We play better with more nights in the same place," venerable guitarist Jerry Garcia explained. "It's a cumulative thing as we adapt to the environment. The realities of touring keep you playing in a different venue every night. At Red Rocks, we played three nights in one place. It gave us fine-tuning possibilities that we couldn't do before, and the live show is what we really do."

"I was awestruck by the place when I walked in," rhythm guitarist Bob Weir added. "You can use all the 'power' you can get up there, because you're basically gasping for air if you're singing, or playing a horn—you just don't get a lot of air to work with."

For the Grateful Dead's 1979 show, the band's inimitable fans arrived in full force in and around Morrison. As soon as a Kris Kristofferson concert let out on a Saturday night, Deadheads began trying to camp at the park for Sunday night's performance, the first in the Grateful Dead's three-night stand. Police and park personnel spent Saturday night chasing as many as 2,000 illegal campers from the grounds; folks partied and did the windowpane dance around the bonfire at Chief Hosa campground. On Sunday, at least 200 people without tickets also tried to sneak in, which resulted in one man falling 35 feet to his death while trying to climb the rock behind the stage. All the while, thunderheads lit up in the distance.

"It will stand out until the day I die," drummer Mickey Hart said. "You couldn't see more than 20 feet into the audience. The front row was up to its waist in water because the drains had backed up. The rain and wind was coming at us perpendicular, whipping off of the cymbals. I saw

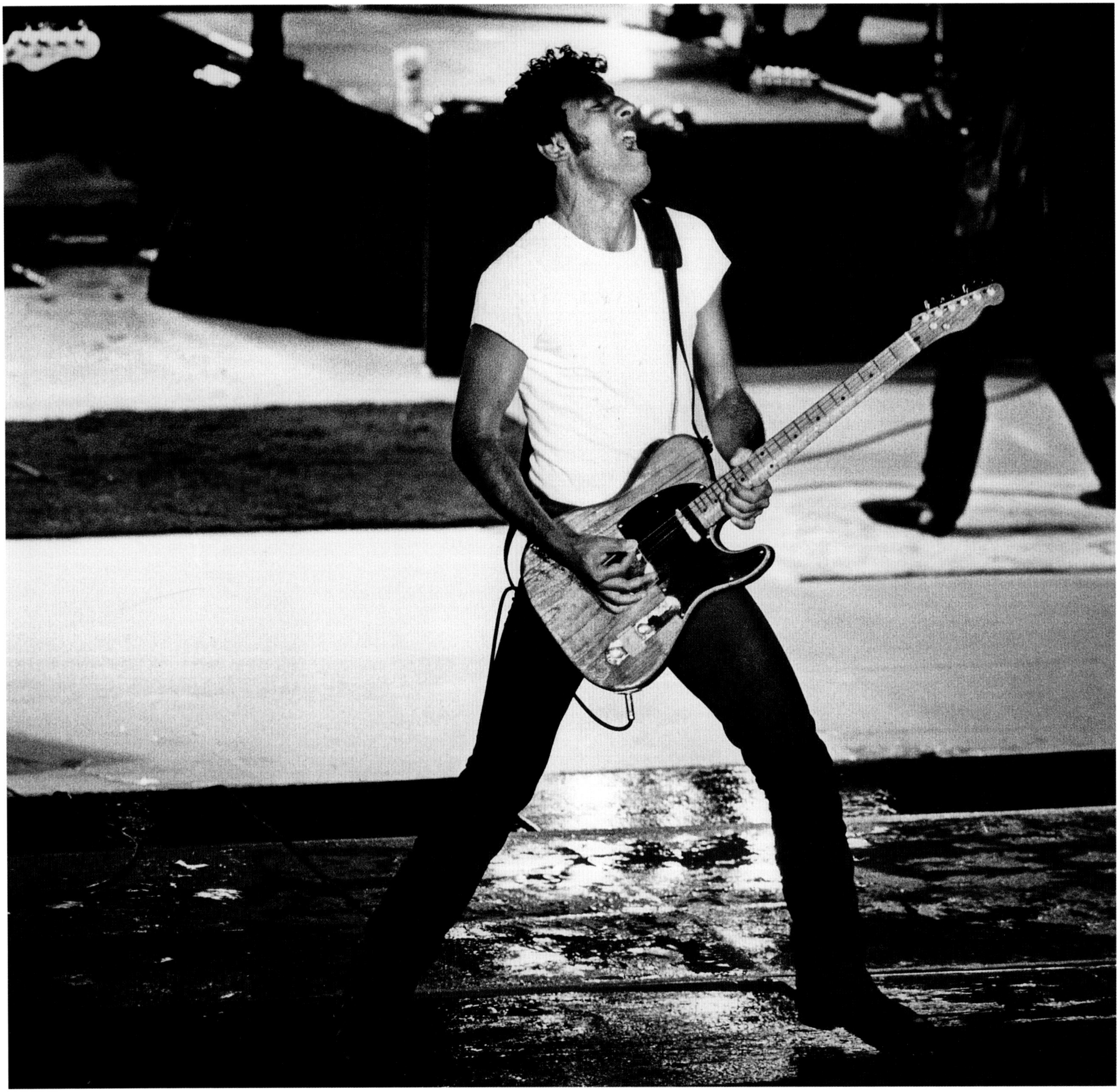

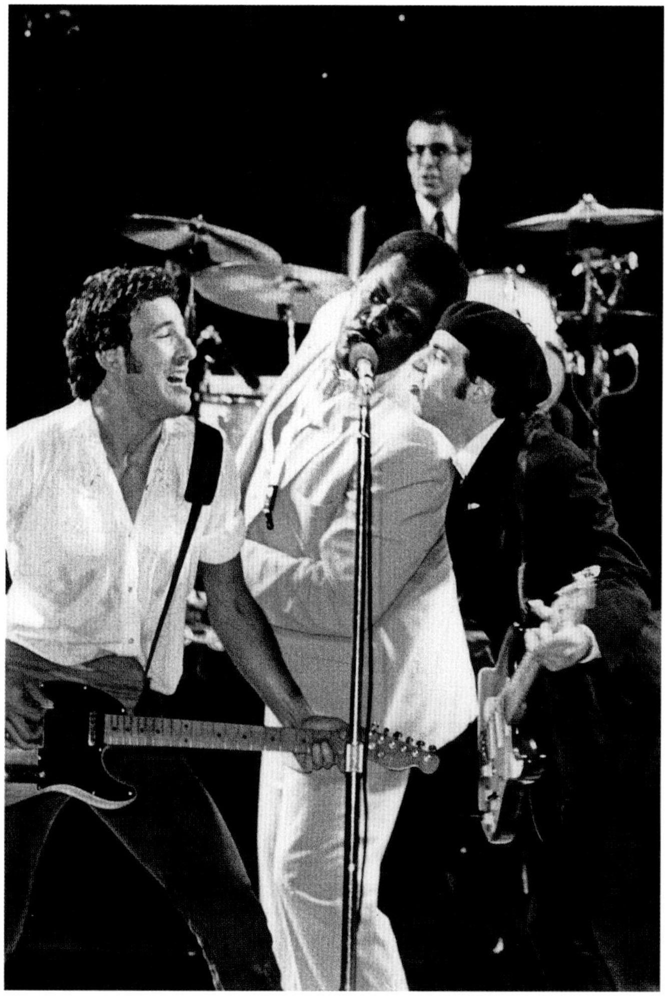

Bruce Springsteen & the E Street Band (left, above), 1981

Bill Walton and he took off his giant raincoat to dance. If you stopped playing, you died! It was so awesome to play against that awesome force of nature. You had to give it up to the moment. It was so much larger than the music." It rained the following day and the second show was moved to McNichols Arena in Denver.

TTS—the Commerce City-based firm contracted to produce all of Feyline's events—completed installation of a $100,000 stage cover at Red Rocks for the summer of 1981. The roof, a custom-designed aluminum grid with vinyl-coated nylon "skin," could be raised, lowered and angled for shade and water runoff. While protecting performers from the elements, it still permitted an unobstructed view for the audience.

But at the Joe Walsh/Cold Chisel show, winds whipped rain every which way, rendering the structure ineffectual and dousing everyone at one point or another. The rain fell hardest during Cold Chisel's set, and the Australian band made quite a favorable impression by refusing to cut its allotted time. Singer Jim Barnes screamed, "Fuck this rain!" while the band knocked out some frantic versions of songs.

Chuck Mangione played Red Rocks at sunrise and sunset that year. Doobie Brothers guitarist Patrick Simmons changed geographical references in "Black Water," the band's first No. 1 hit, singing about the "Denver moon" and "Colorado sky"; the crowd went understandably nuts.

During Bruce Springsteen's return visit to Red Rocks on July 16 and 17, 1981—his first outdoor shows since he played there in 1978—he learned rock 'n' roll is an indoor sport. On the first night, a torrential summer rainstorm drenched the audience. Springsteen opened with the Creedence Clearwater Revival classic, "Who'll Stop the Rain." The front of the Red Rocks stage had been ripped up to install plywood ramps, which Springsteen liked to use as springboards for his songs. During the opening chords of "Prove It All Night," Springsteen eyed the wet plywood warily. He finally jumped up with a splash, carrying his electric guitar, and...no sparks flew, no circuits shorted. The slick stage infused his signature flying knee drop with some spectacular extra yardage. It was the kind of physical performance one expected from an athlete or an actor, but it was just a skinny kid from the East Coast who had been all shook up by the magic of rock 'n' roll.

Midway through the 28-song set, Springsteen walked up to the edge of the dripping platform and tried to talk the crowd out of continuing—he thought a make-up concert on another night would be better. But much to his dismay, the people sitting in the puddles at Red Rocks shouted down the proposal in a spirited voice vote, and the show went on in an intermittent downpour. Springsteen opened the second

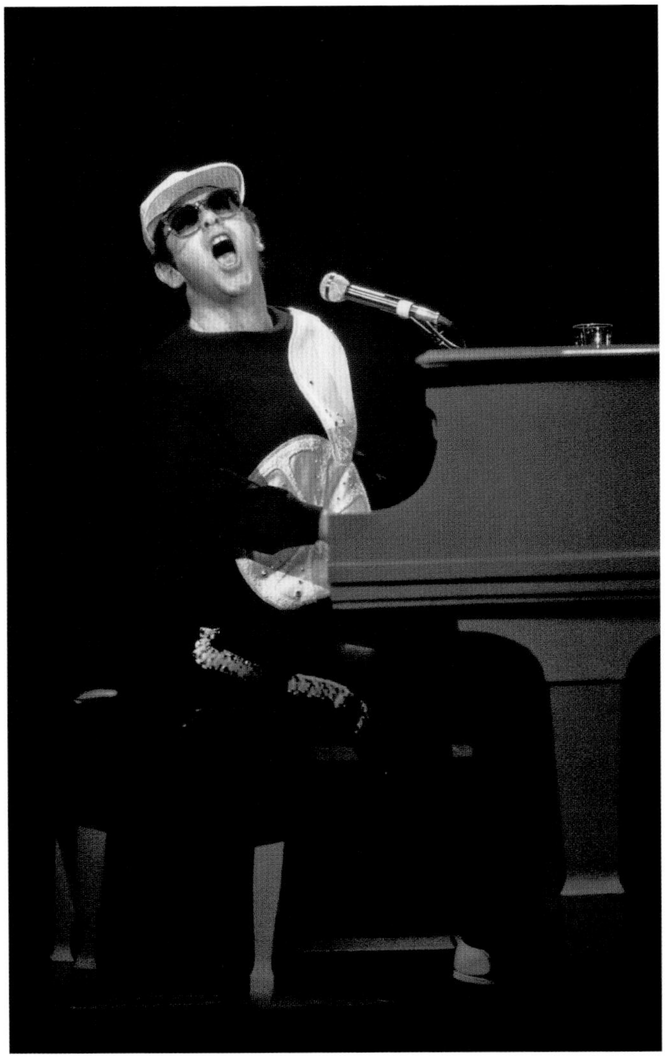

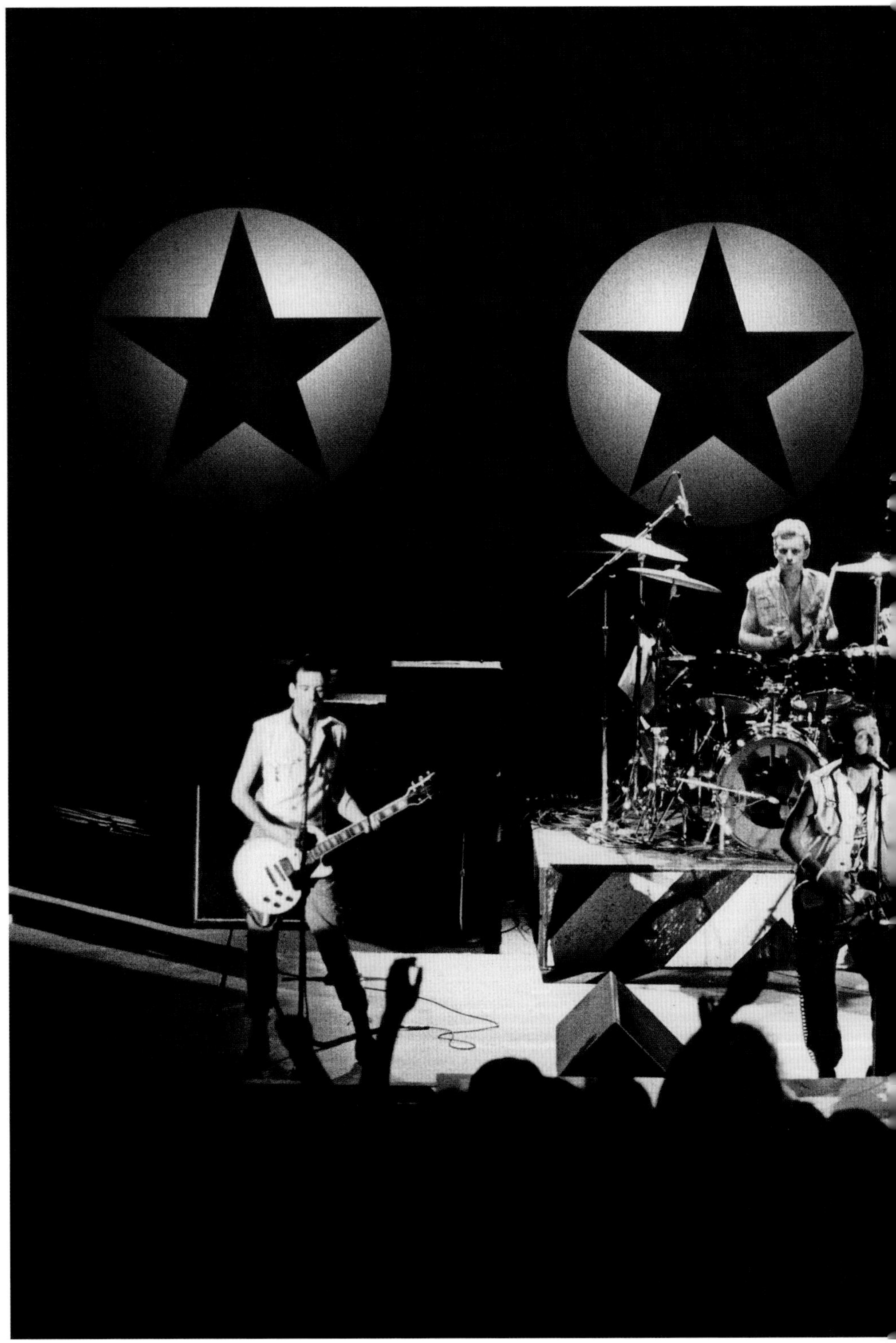

Elton John, 1982; the Clash, 1982 (right)

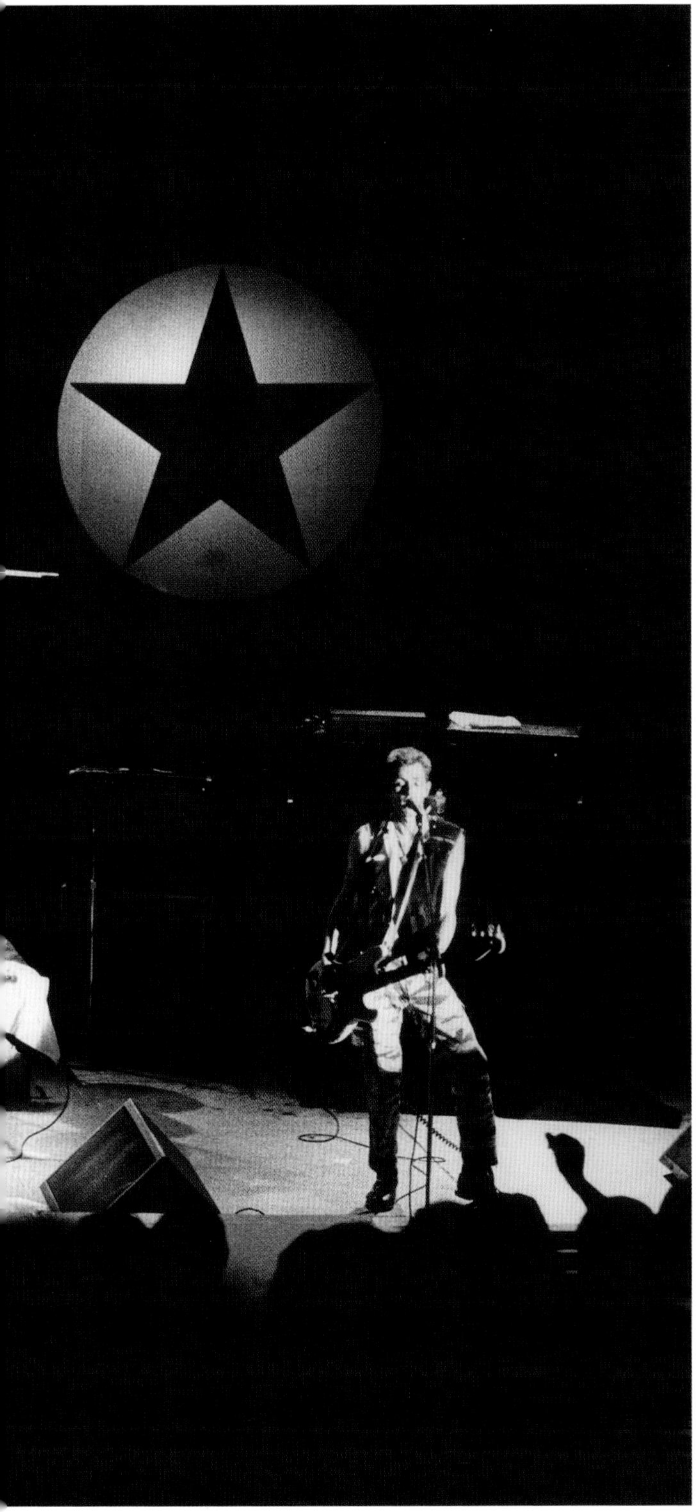

half by donning a sailor's cap for a one-and-only performance of the Frankie Ford classic, "Sea Cruise."

The end of 1981 brought a proposal to double the parking fee for patrons at Red Rocks—from $1 to $2. The following year, the city installed lights and posted attendants to patrol while adding another 500 spaces, bringing the capacity to 3,500 cars. Mayor Bill McNichols decided to bar Denver Police from acting as brokers for off-duty security; while off-duty cops could still moonlight, he wanted to make the promoters pay a salary to someone to handle this function.

One of rock's elite, Elton John, opened his American tour in 1982 with two shows at Red Rocks. John had recorded several of his 1970s albums at Caribou Ranch, the legendary recording complex outside of Nederland, so it was a homecoming of sorts.

Willie Nelson lived nearby in Evergreen; he drove to Red Rocks for his show barefoot and wearing a Hawaiian shirt, figuring he'd change backstage. Security initially wouldn't let him in, refusing to believe that the star of the show could look so unassuming.

Nothing short of a major event was expected when the Clash, one of punk rock's biggest acts, opened the second leg of their American tour by invading Red Rocks on August 9, 1982. The band had never appeared in Colorado.

But singer and guitarist Joe Strummer admitted he had no fun at Red Rocks. He explained the abysmal acoustics (some bass cabinets blew up during the first number) by noting the lack of a sound check: "When people have waited five years to see us, we're not gonna ruin the suspense in front of a mid-afternoon crowd by going 'Testing-one-two-three' into a microphone." Strummer never really cut loose onstage. He blamed his own poor performance on the weather ("Too cool and dry—I need it humid around my throat to get my voice worked up") and the stage itself ("There was too much space—I couldn't see the crowd").

Feyline's annual "Summer of Stars" release appeared as a pull-out newspaper section that fans used to map out their concertgoing plans for Red Rocks. All seating had been general admission until 1983, when it switched to reserved seating. After the initial concert in that plan, the Australian band Men At Work, got rained out, the first reserved seating concert at Red Rocks became Bow Wow Wow/English Beat/R.E.M. on June 1. People still streamed out of their seats to move near the stage, and promoter Fey quickly admitted that the new policy was a mistake, as most people liked the social aspects of meeting friends in the park. A long-standing configuration—two-thirds general and one-third reserved seating (a section of 20 rows in the middle of the venue)—resulted.

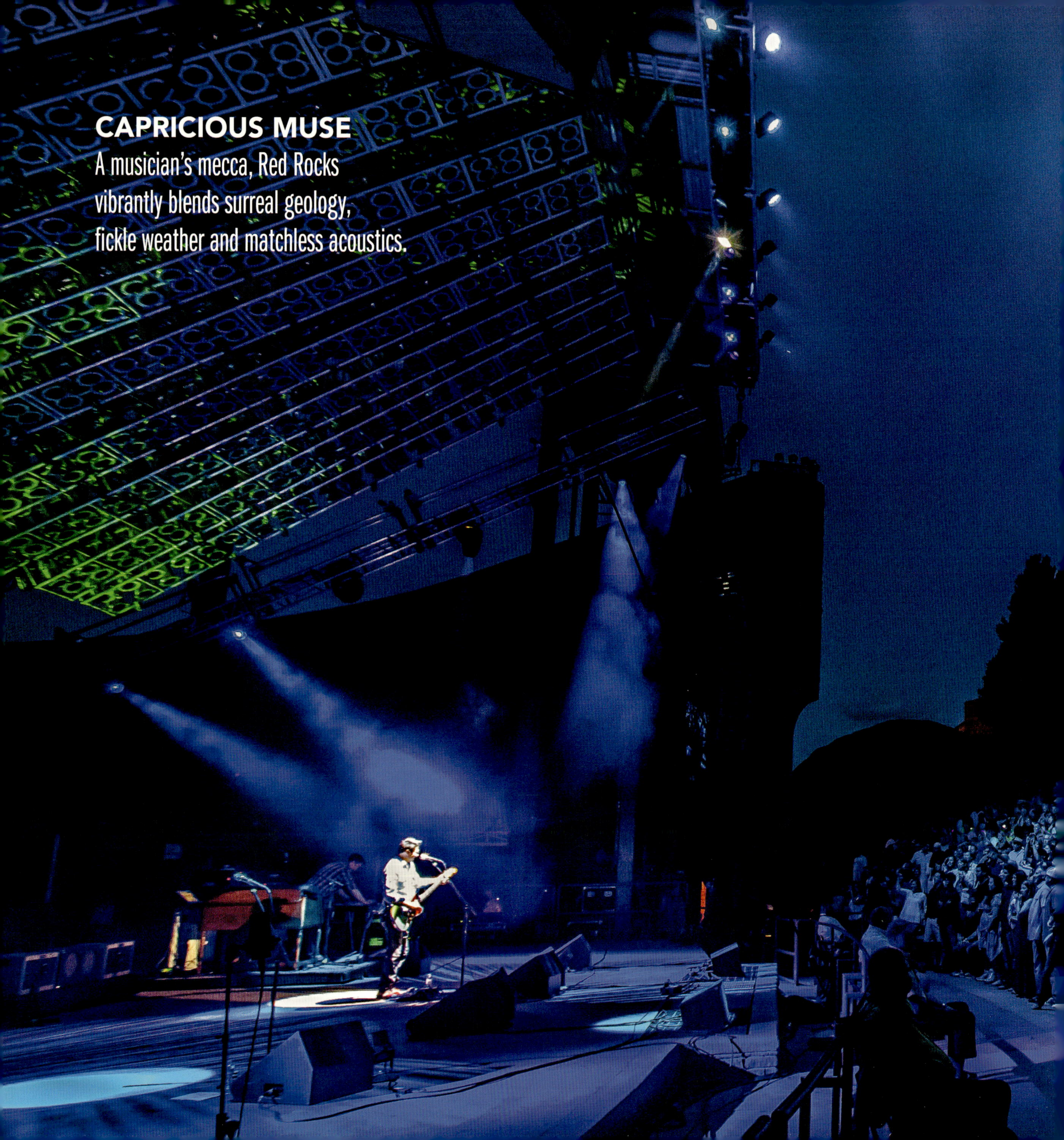

CAPRICIOUS MUSE
A musician's mecca, Red Rocks vibrantly blends surreal geology, fickle weather and matchless acoustics.

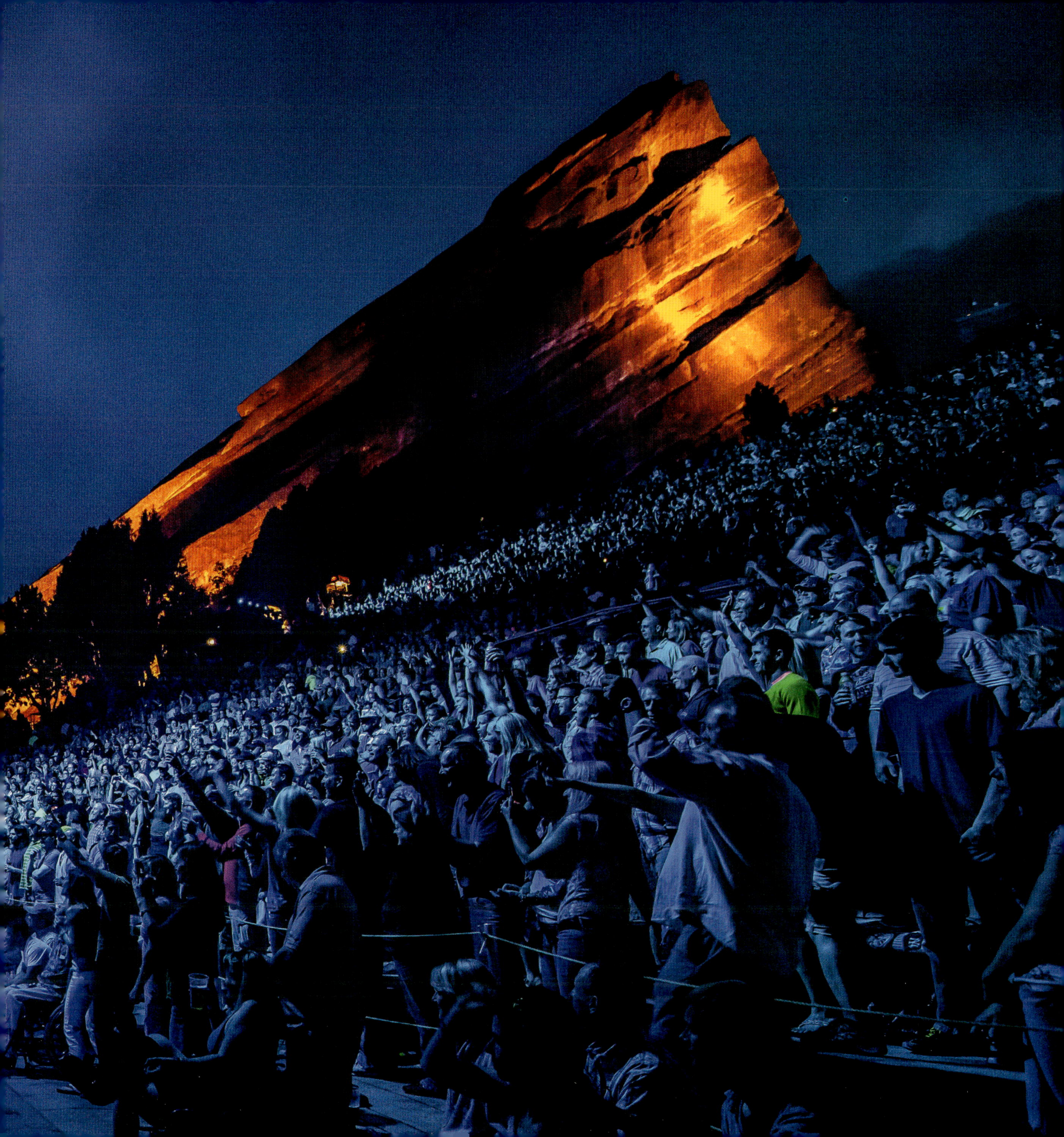

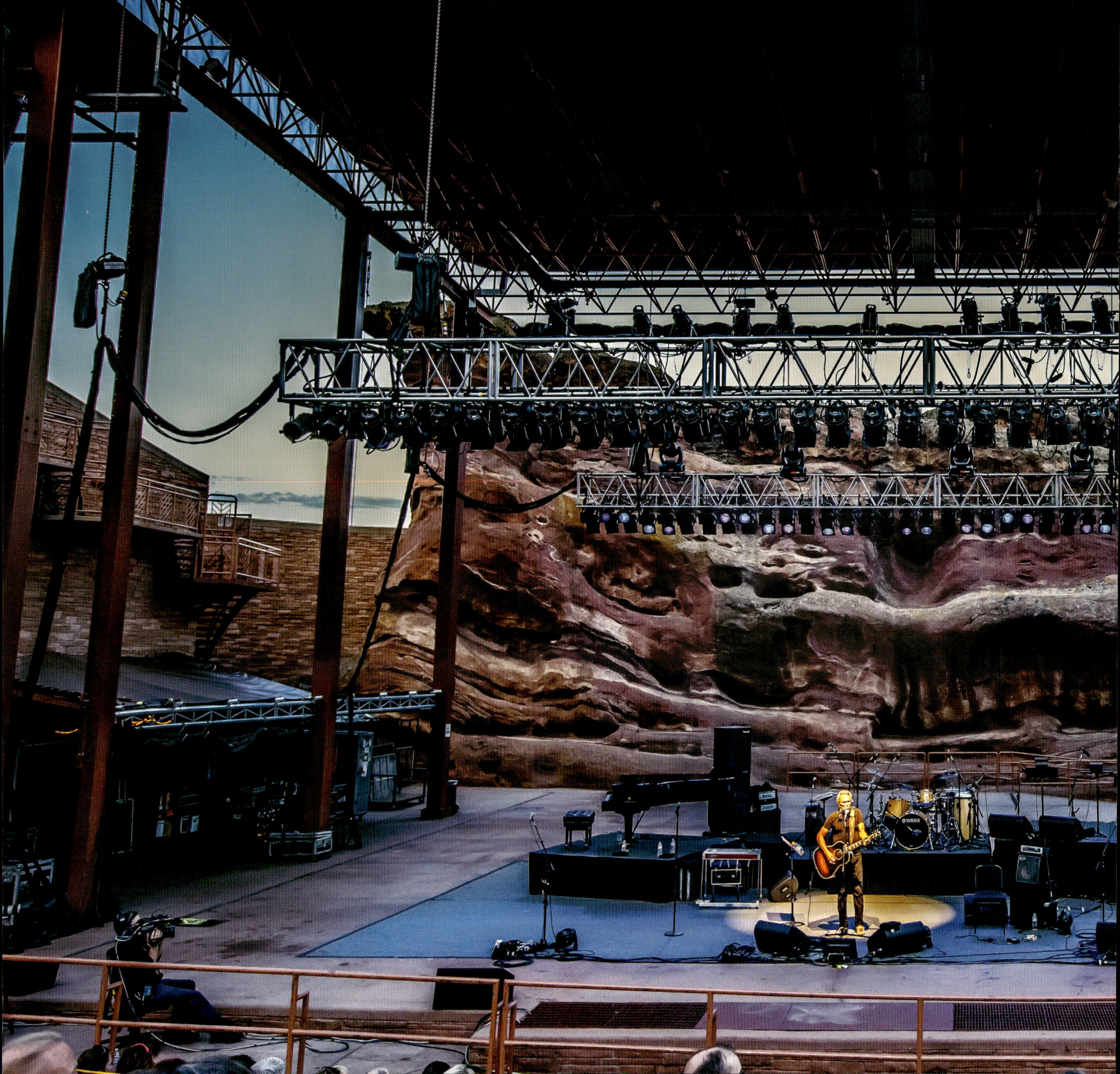

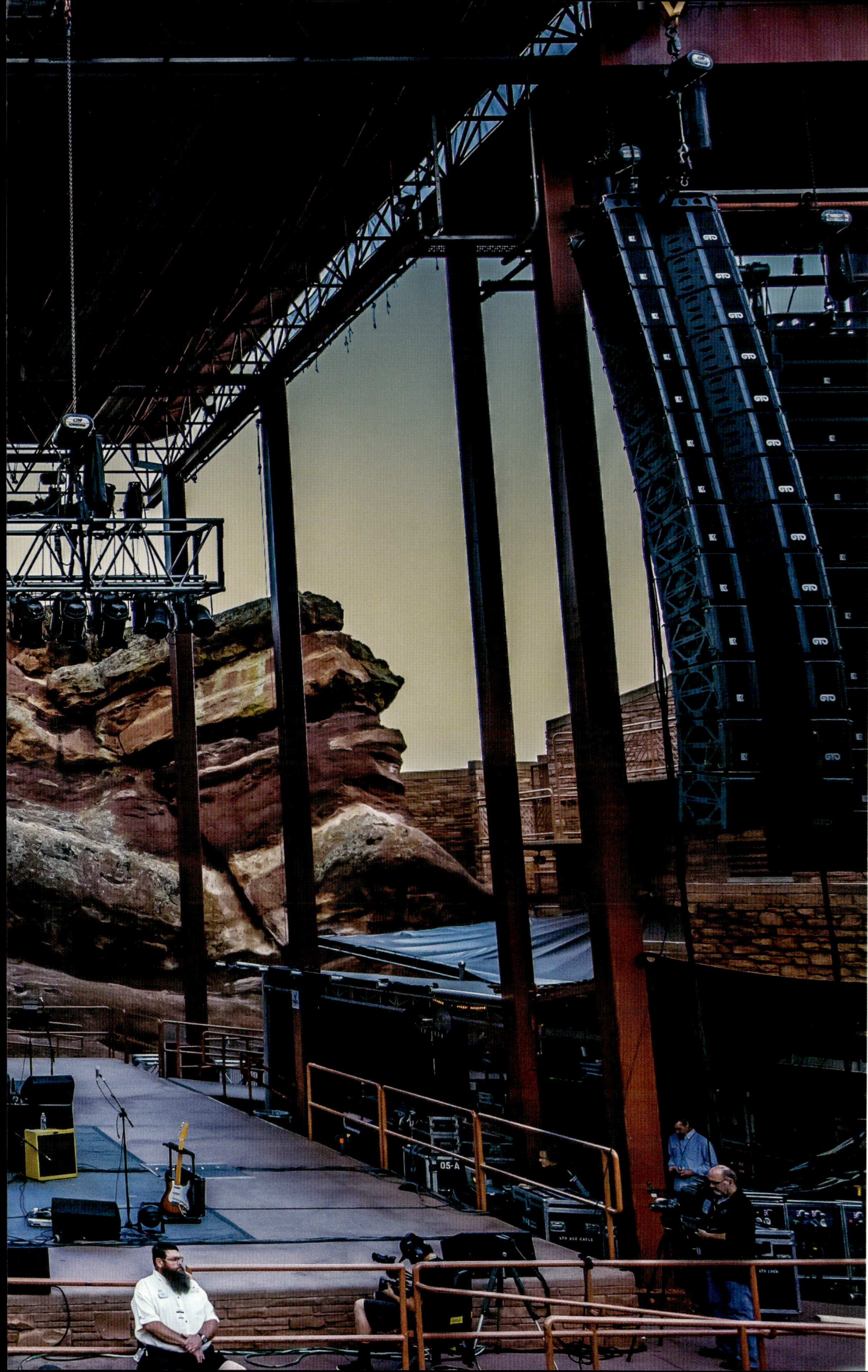

Kris Kristofferson, 2013

Previous spread: Big Head Todd & the Monsters, 2013

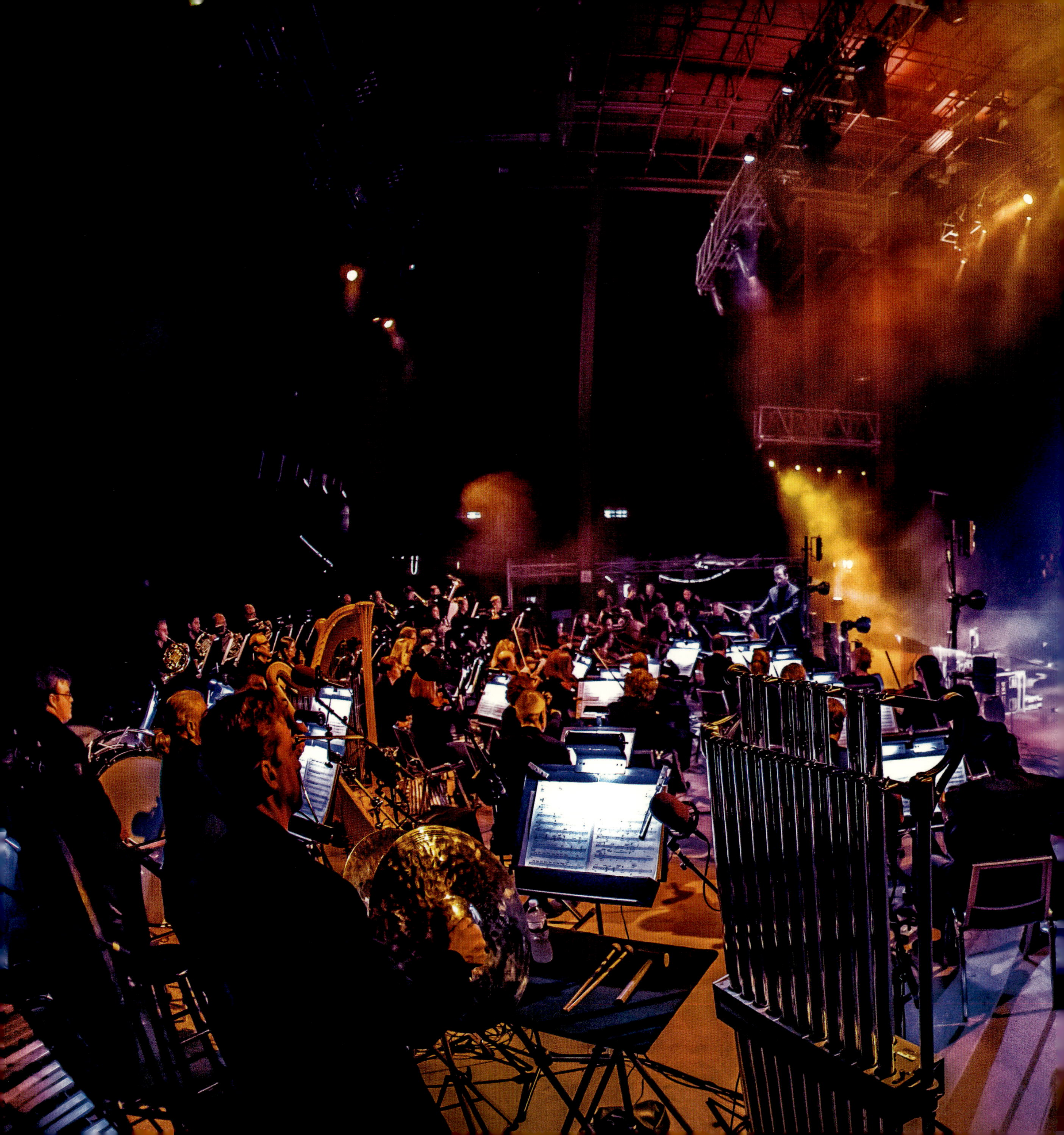

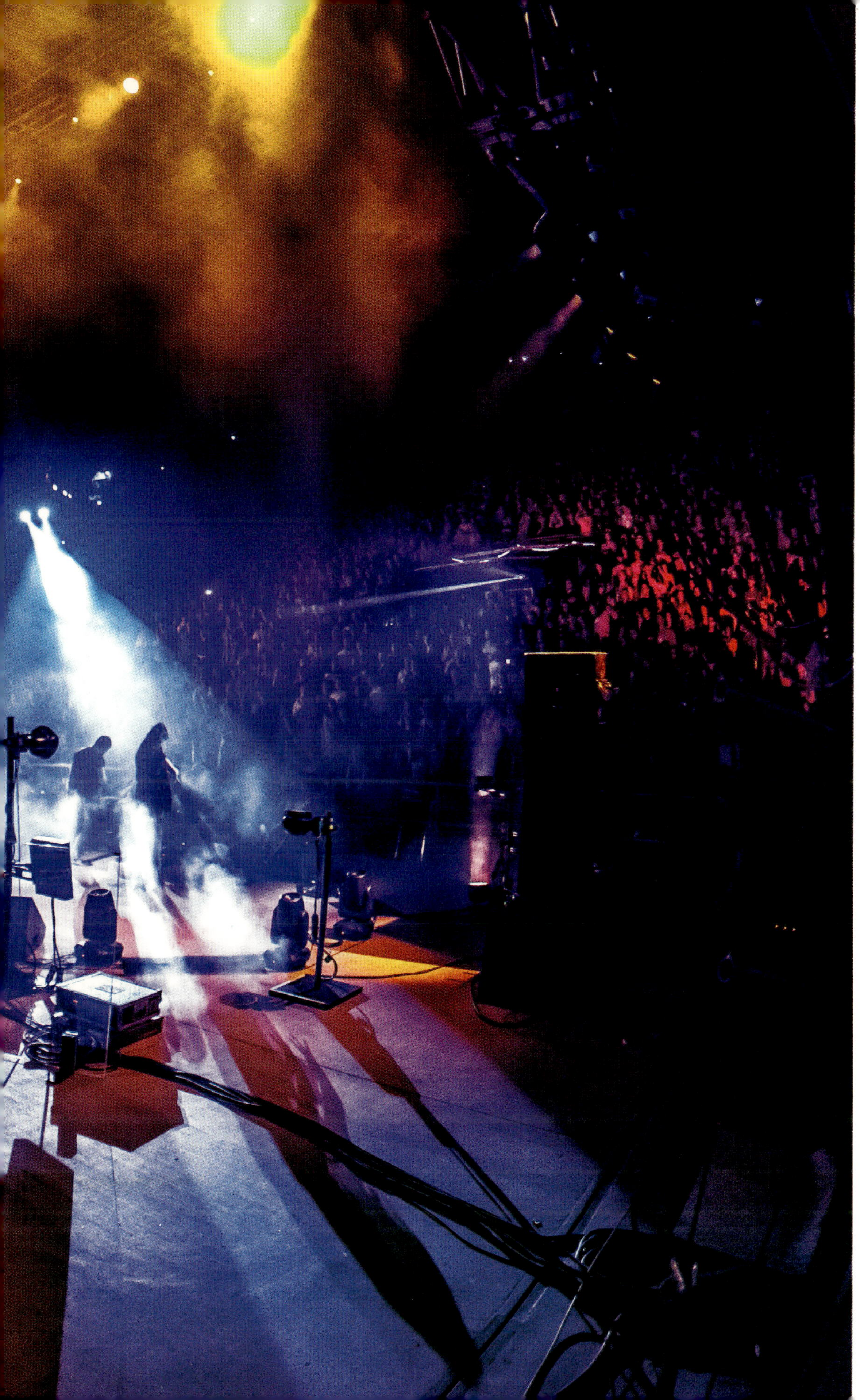

Rodrigo y Gabriela with the Colorado Symphony Orchestra, 2013

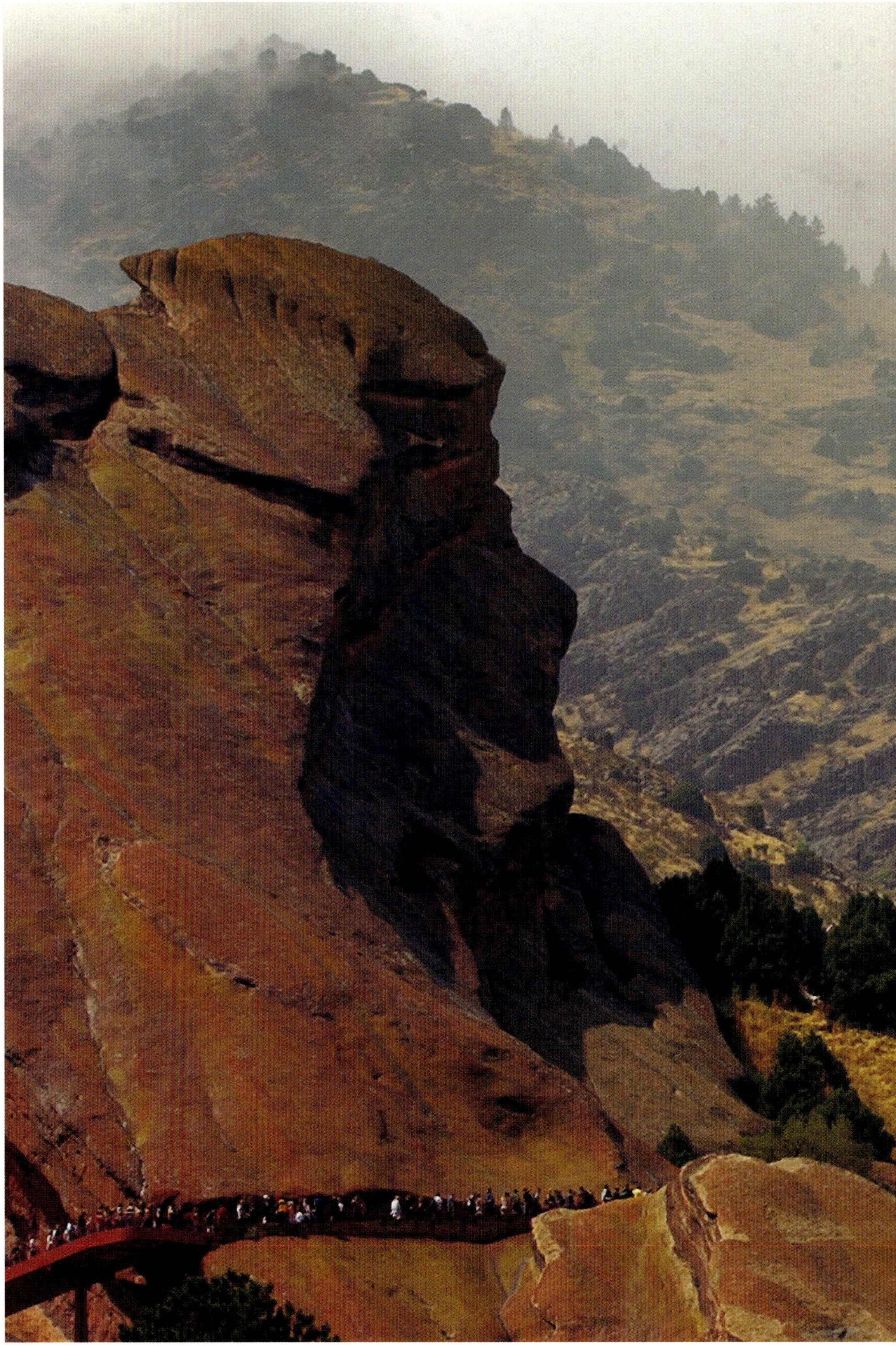

c. 2003

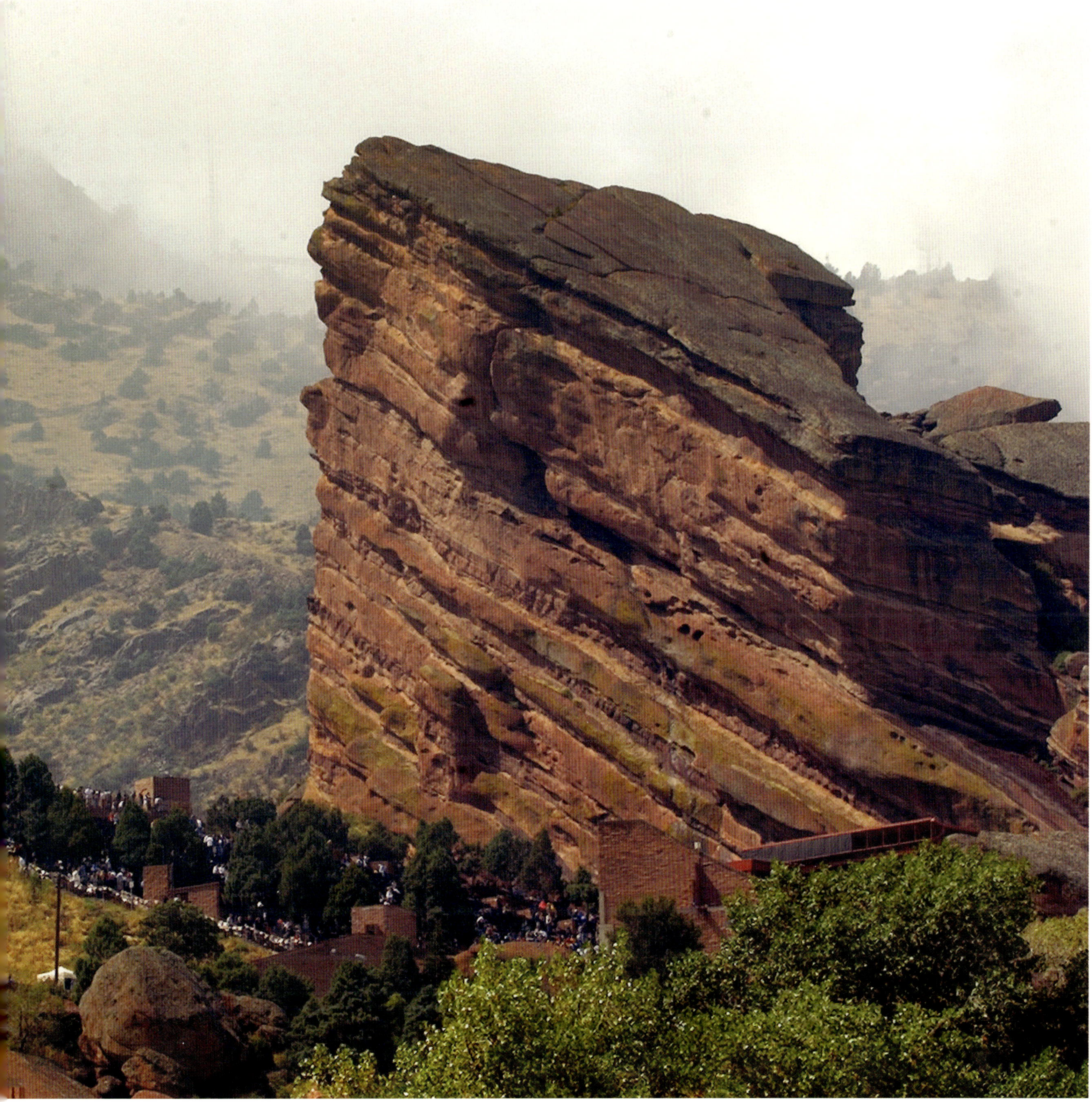

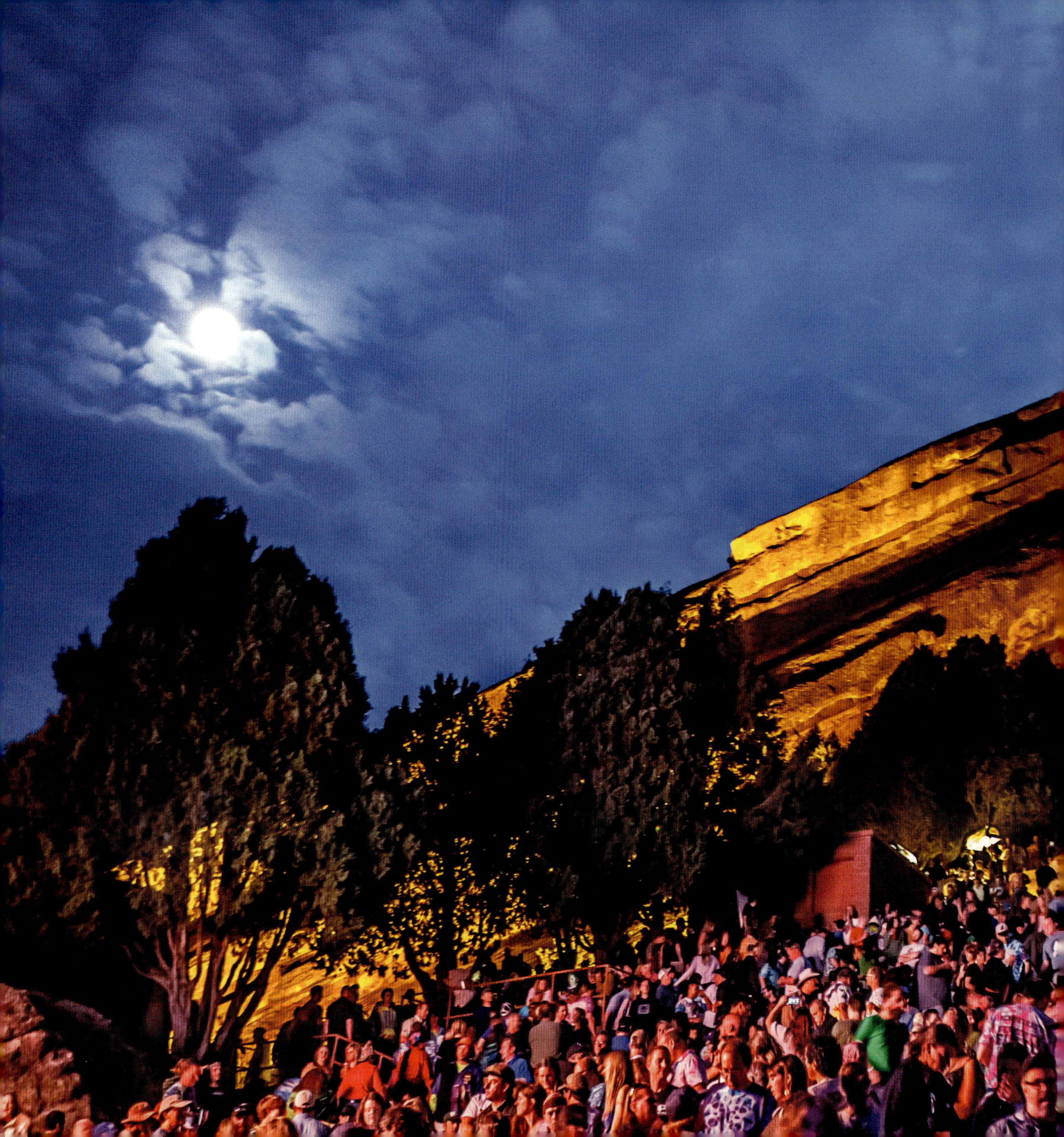

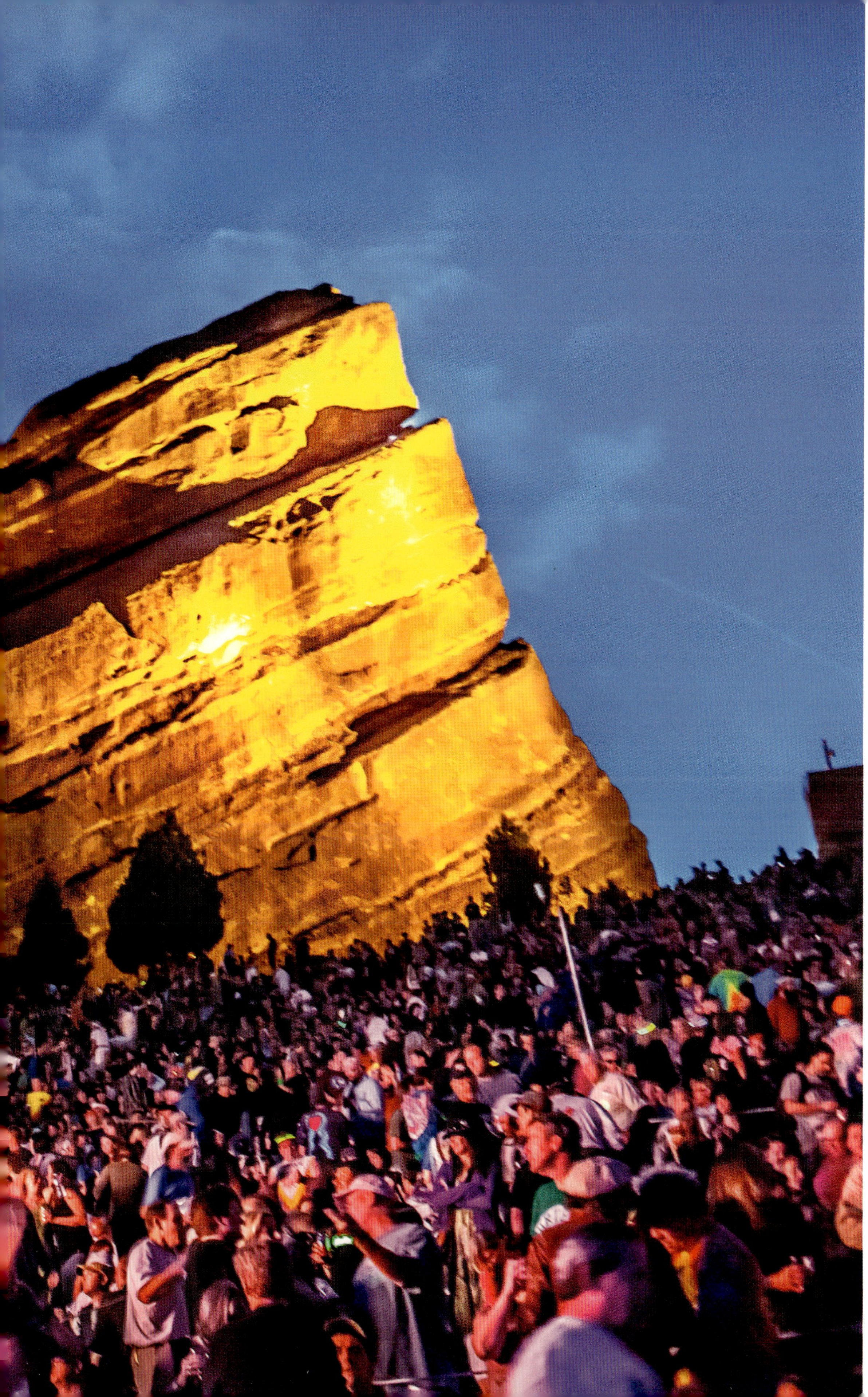

c. 2012

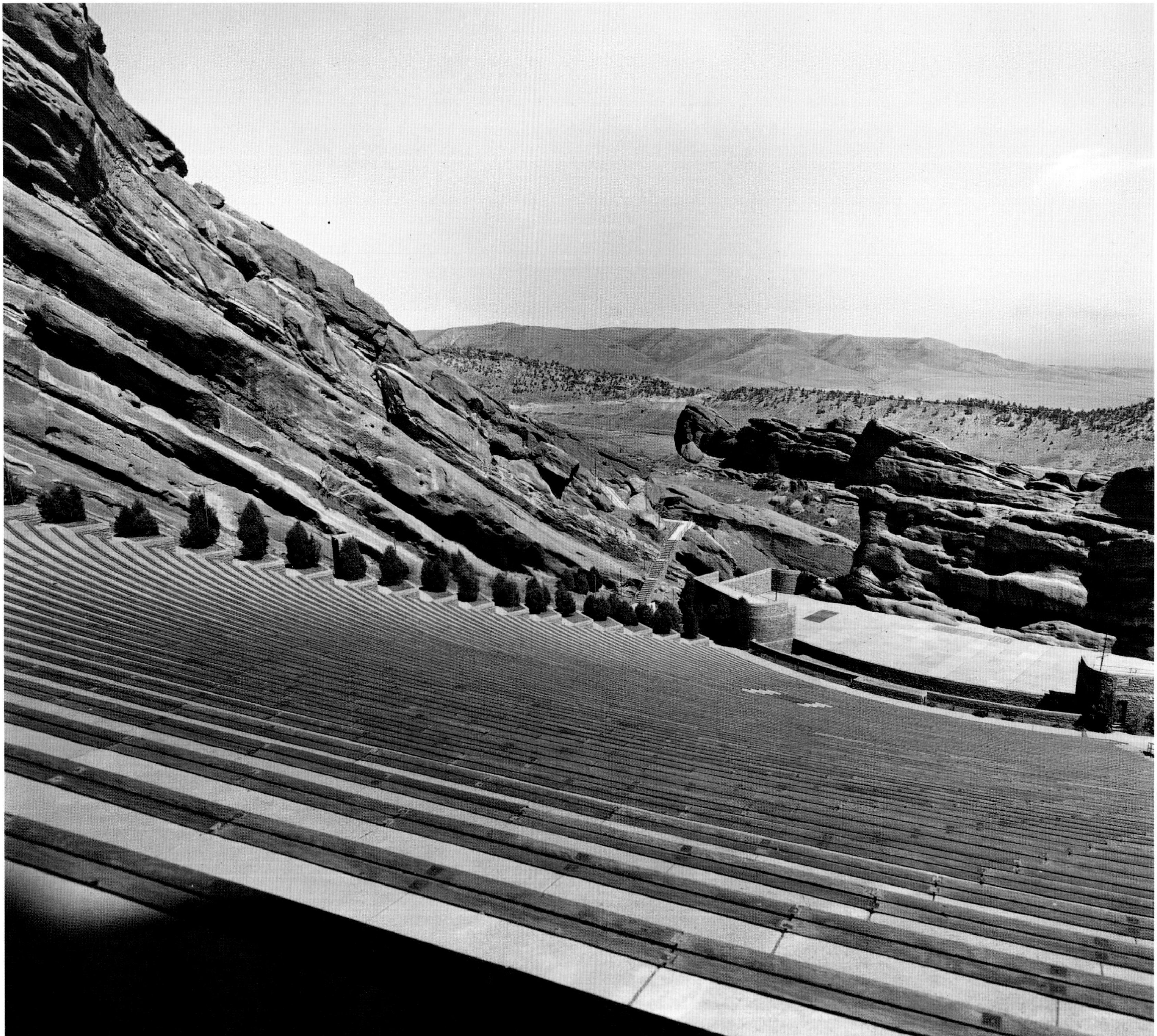

c. 1955

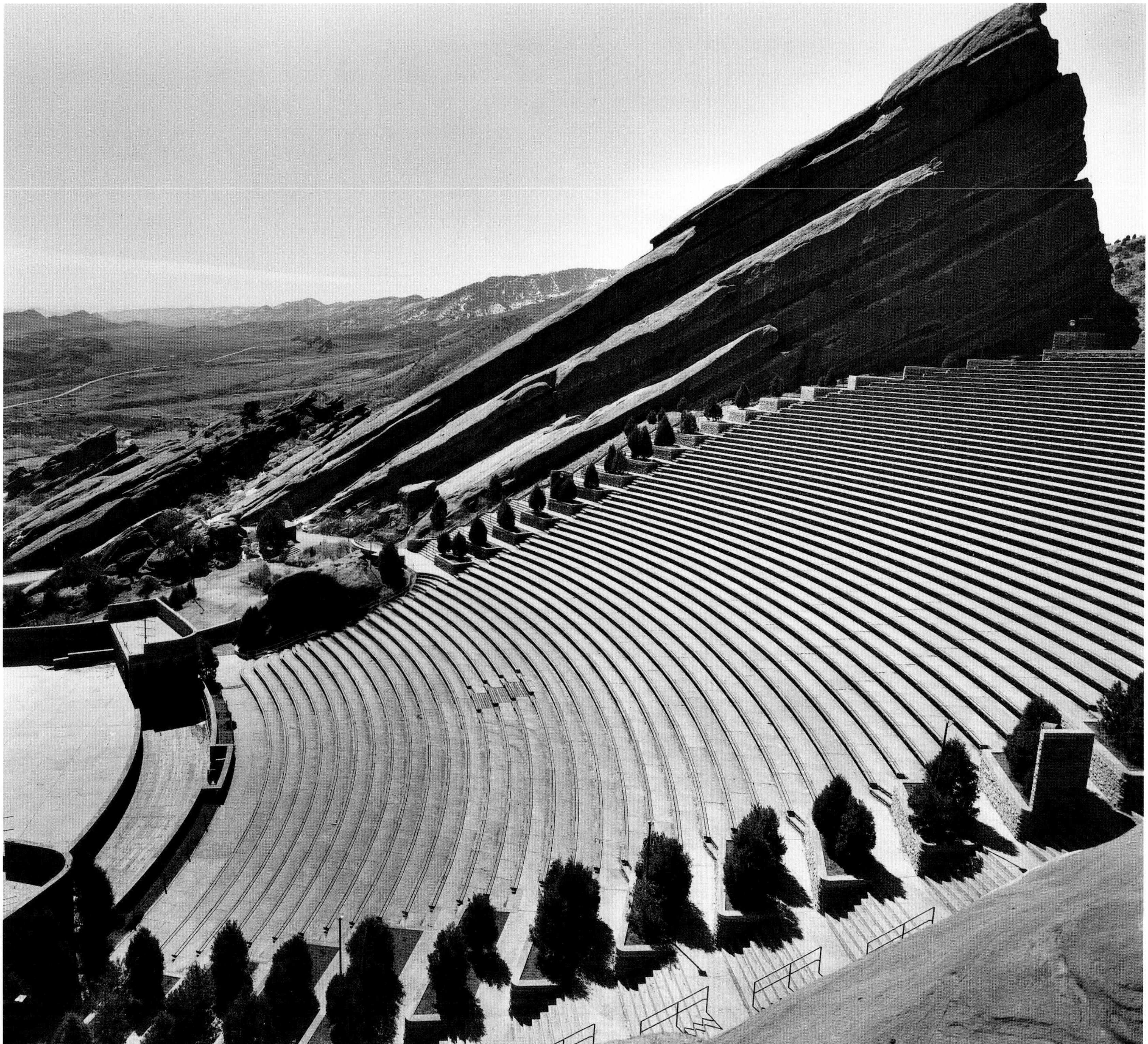

c. 1955

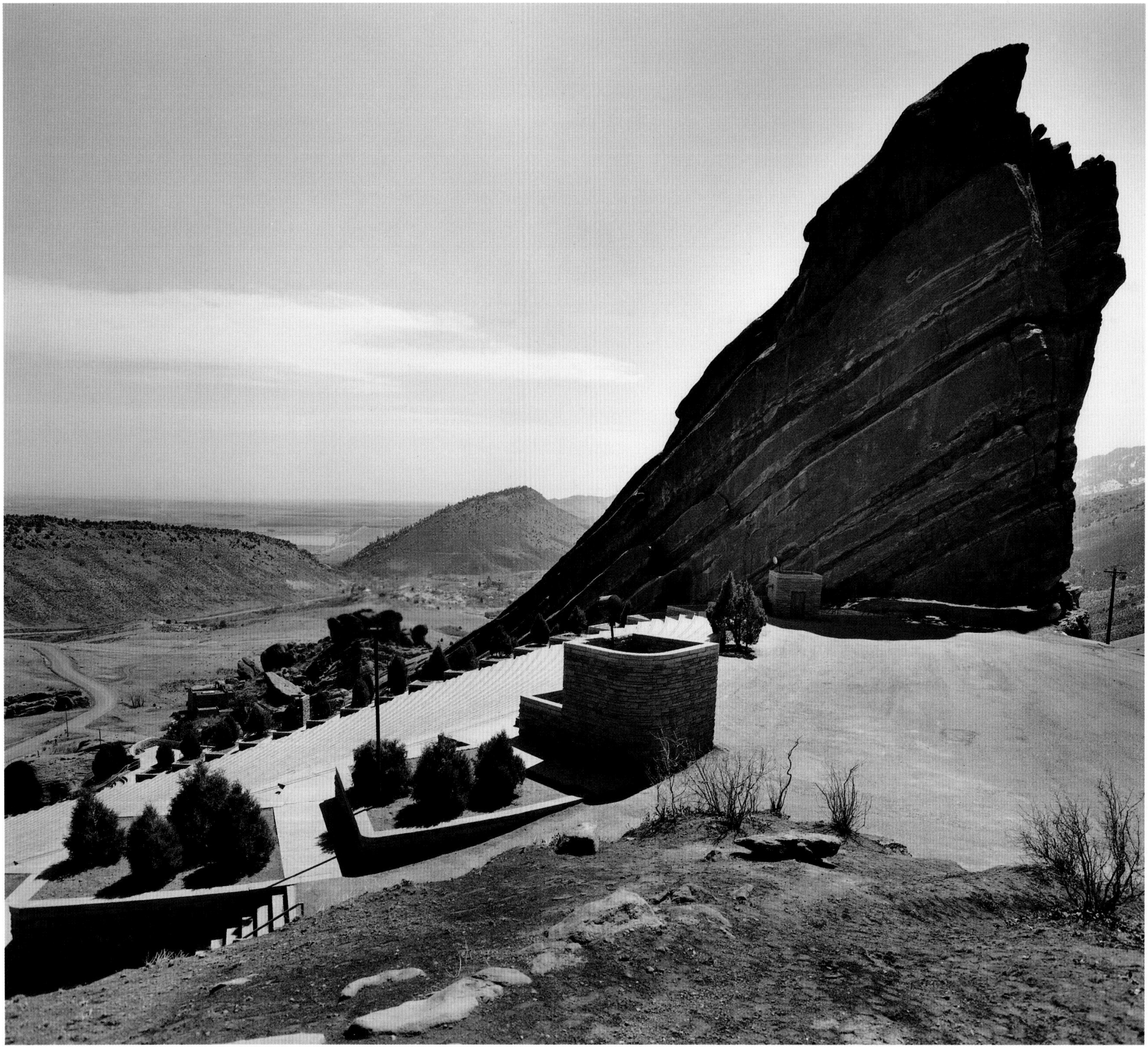

c. 1955

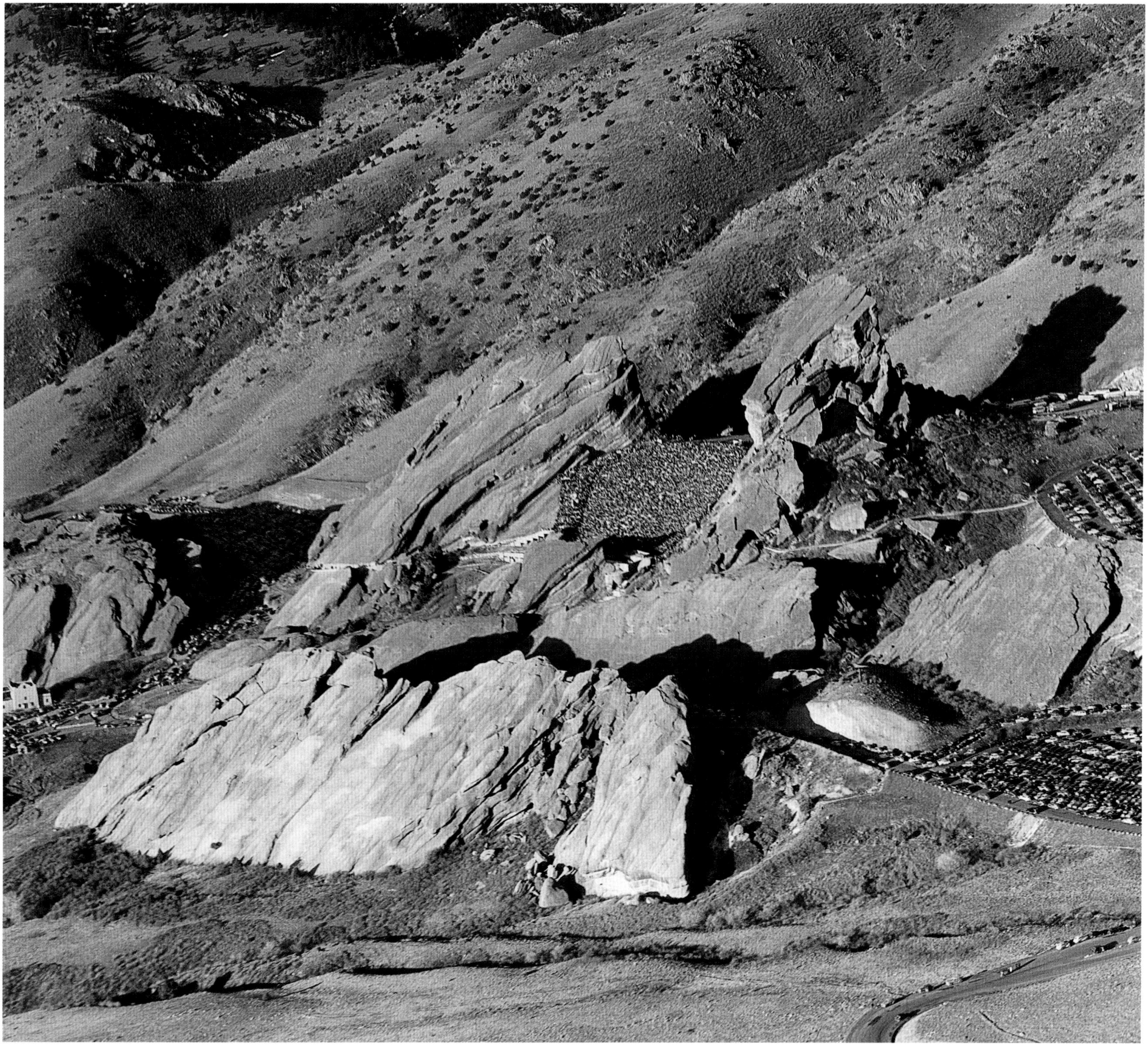

c. 1953

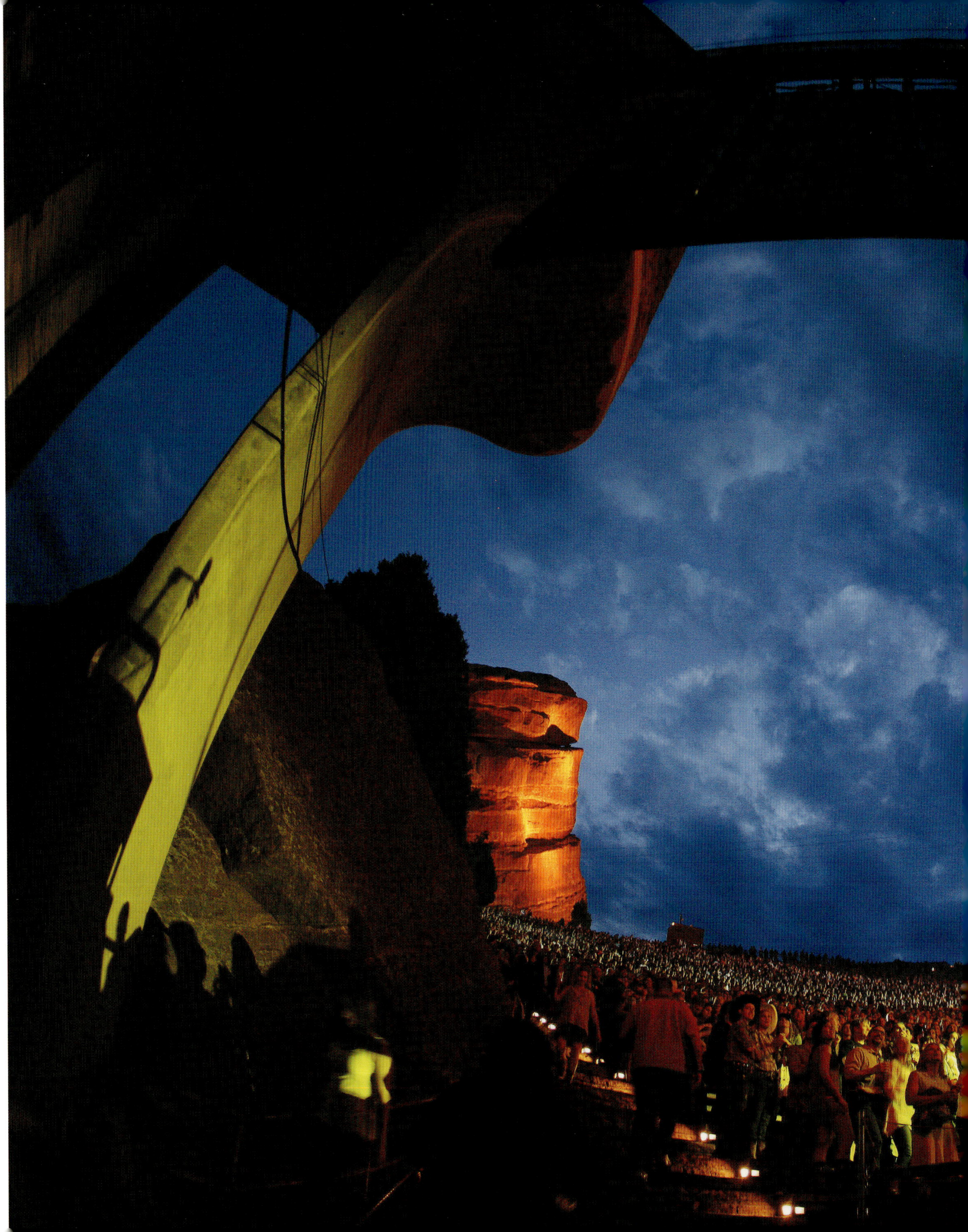

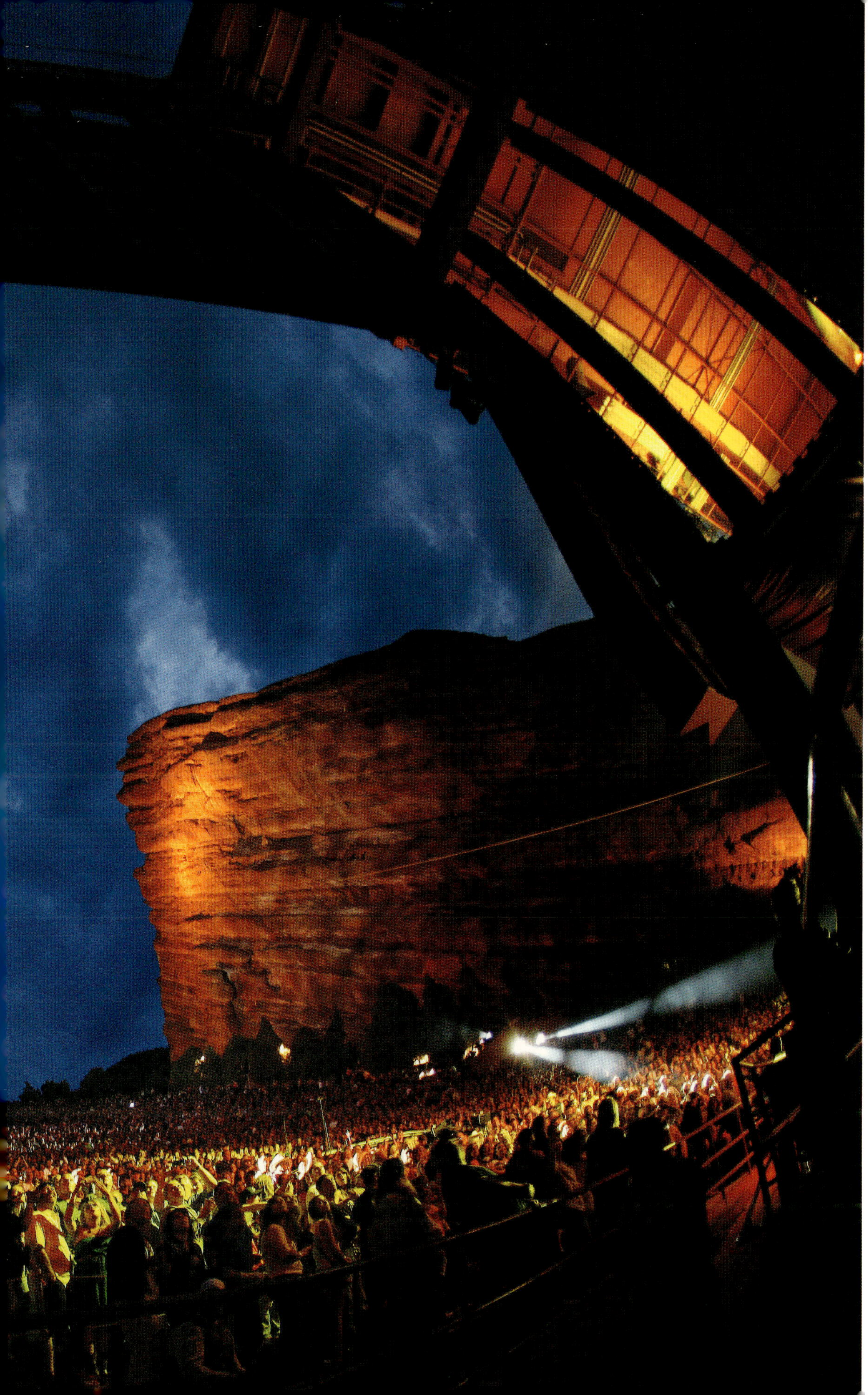

c. 2013

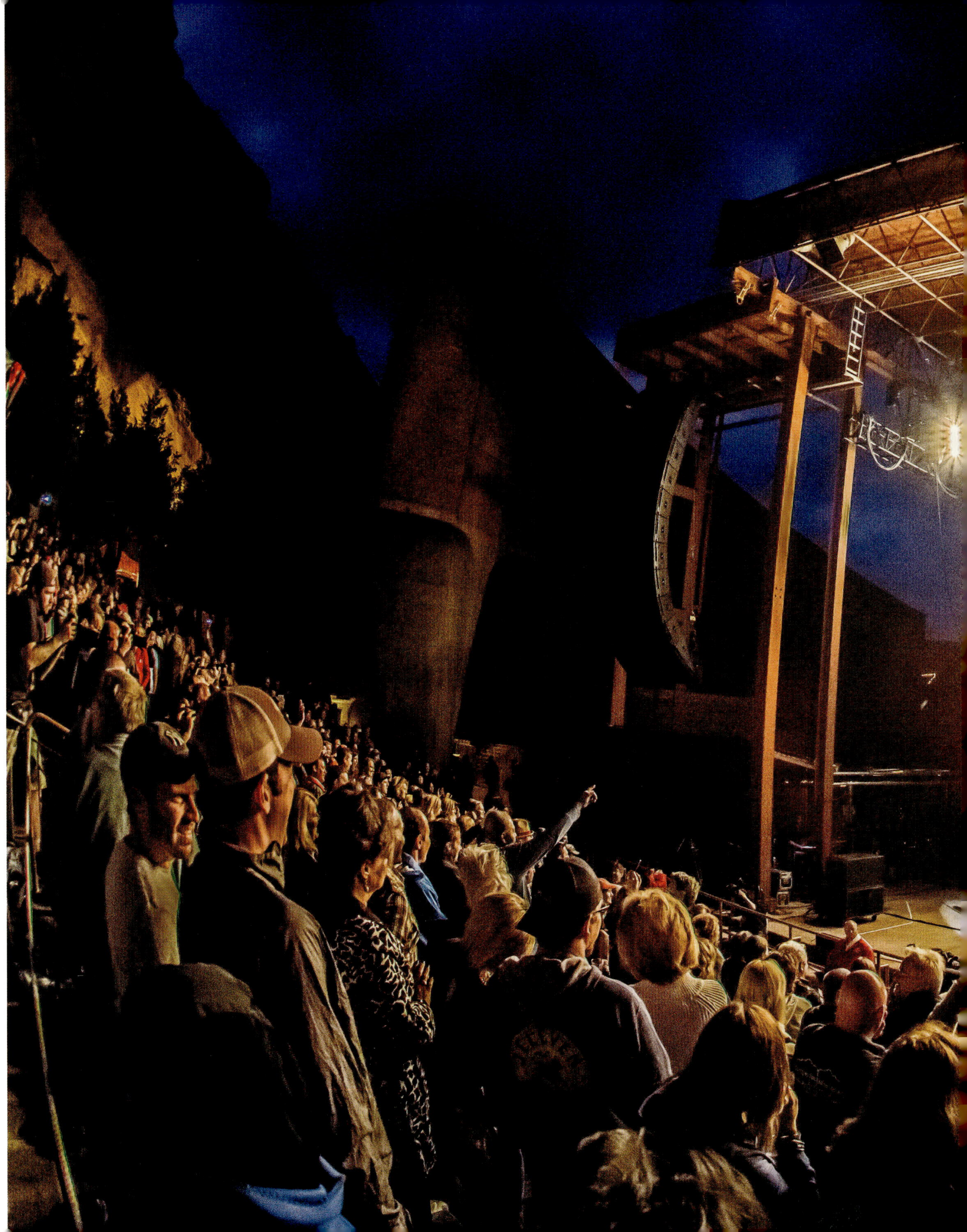

Lionel Richie, 2014

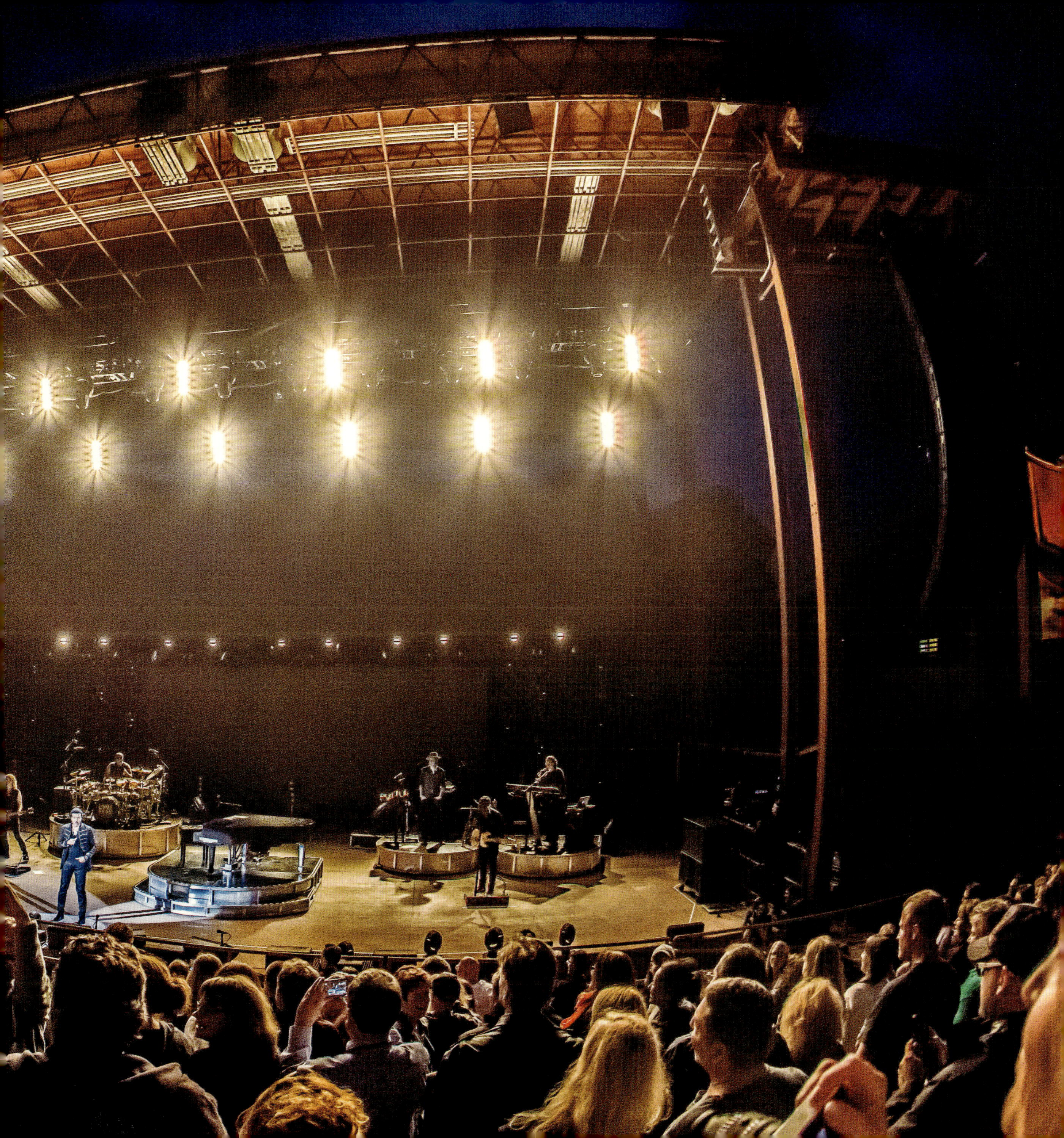

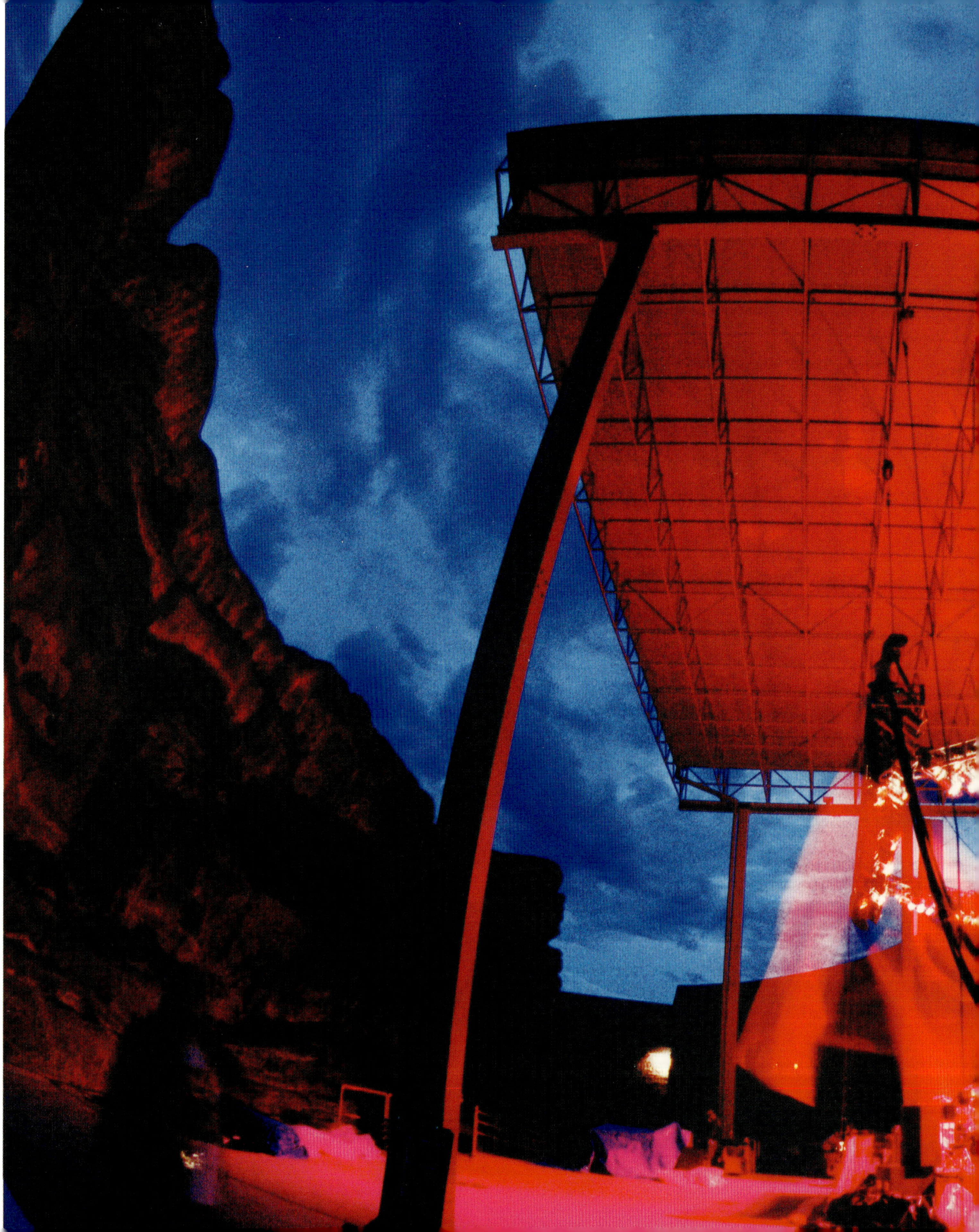

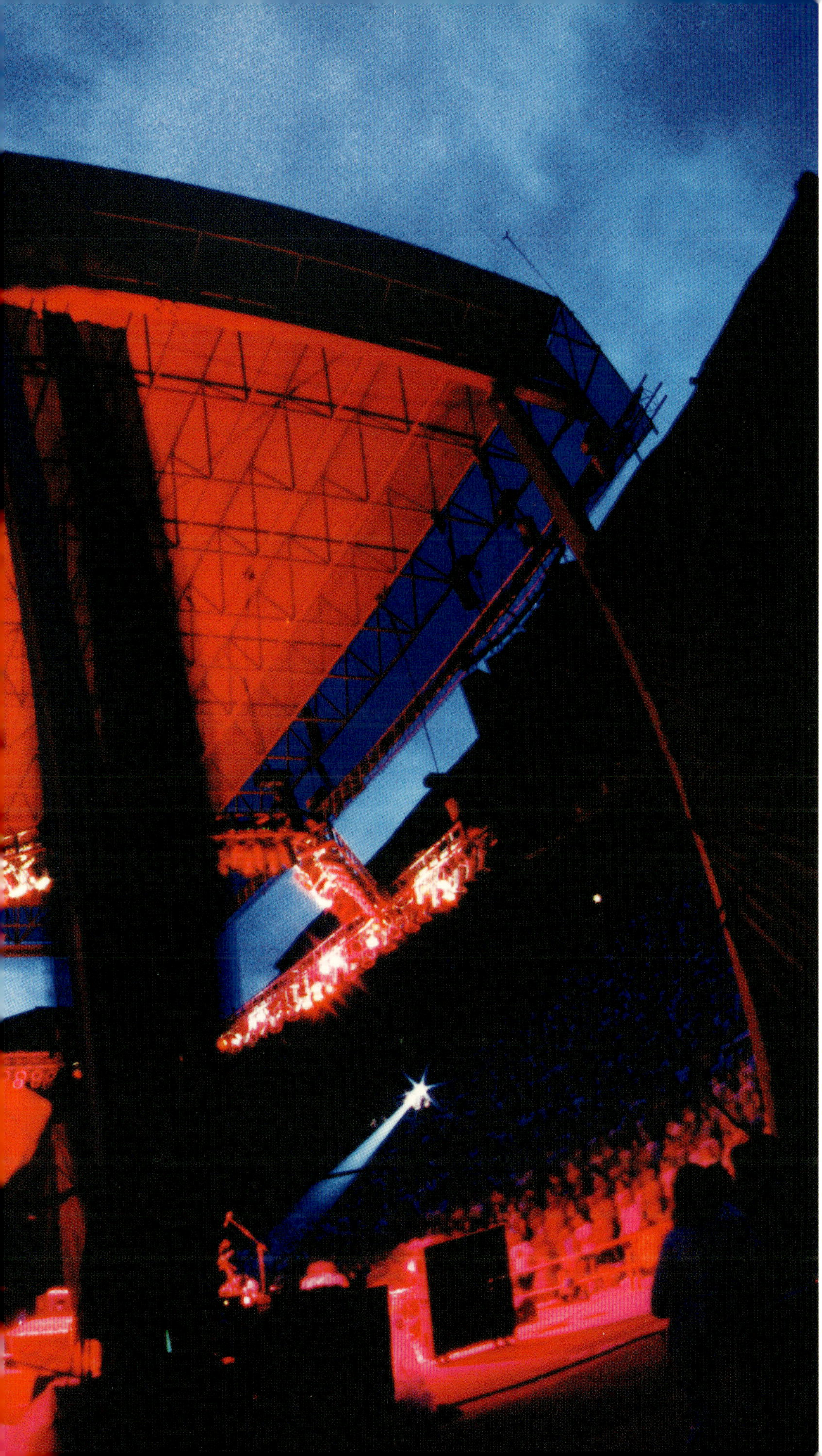

c. 2004

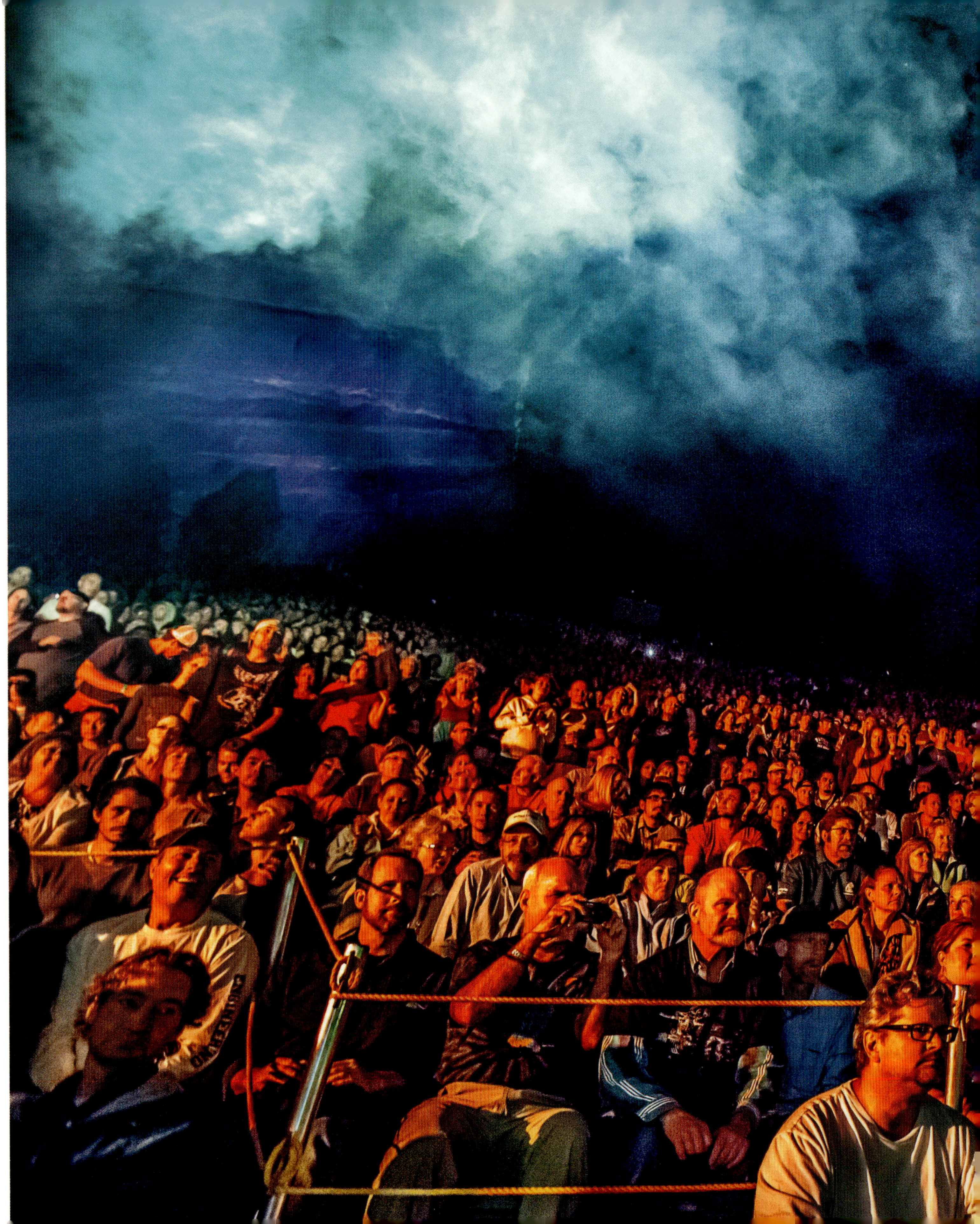

c. 2013

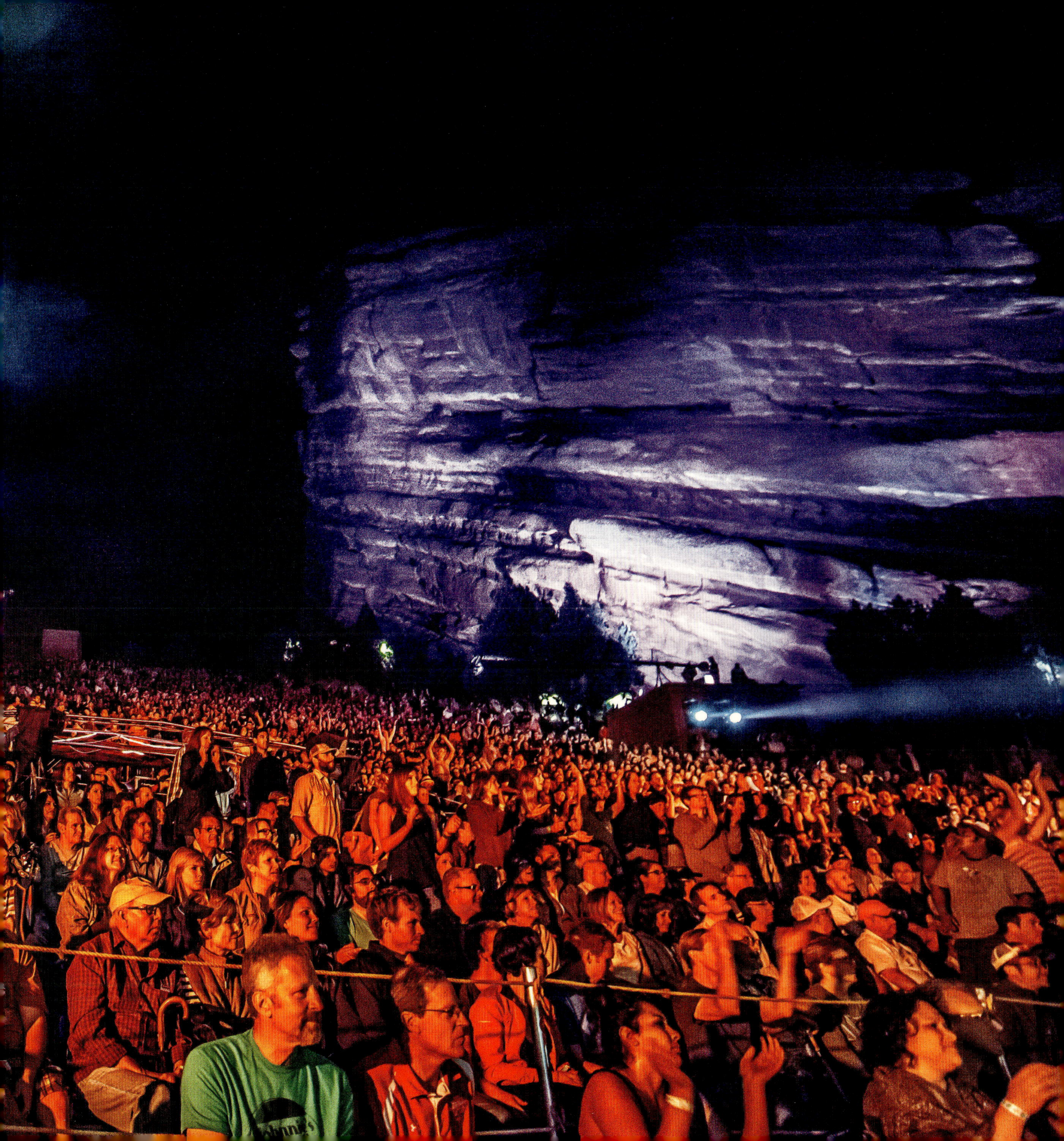

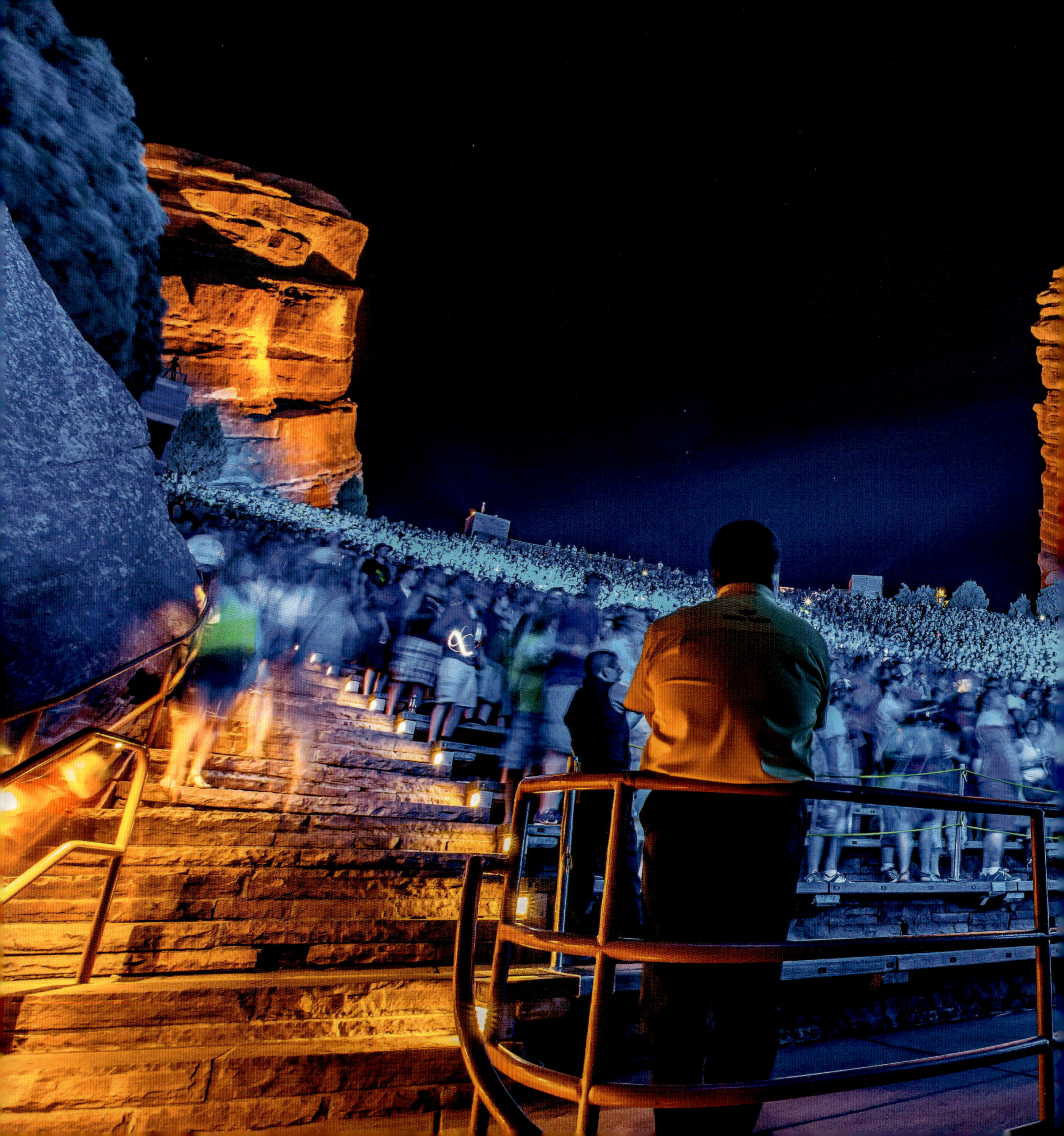

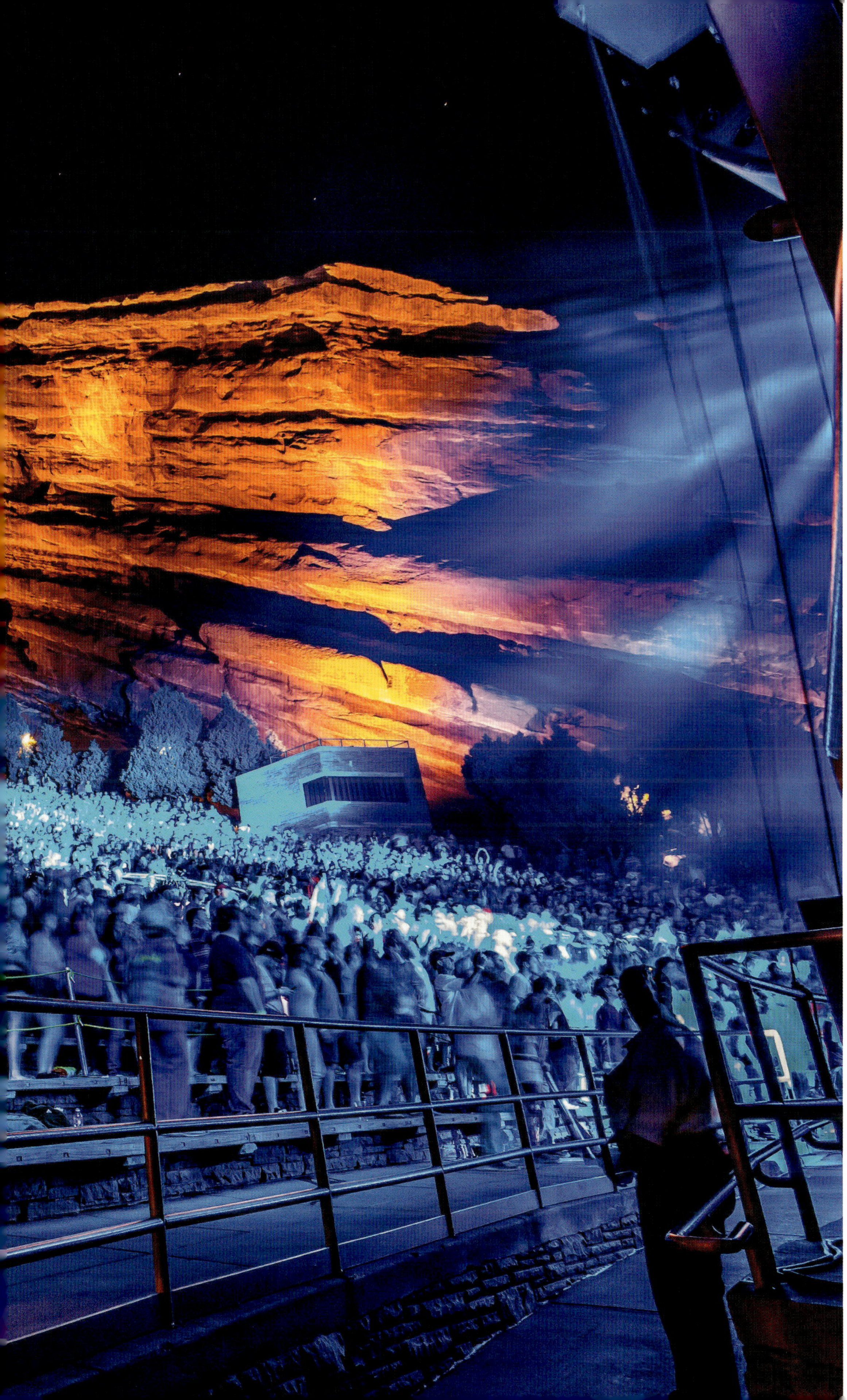

c. 2014

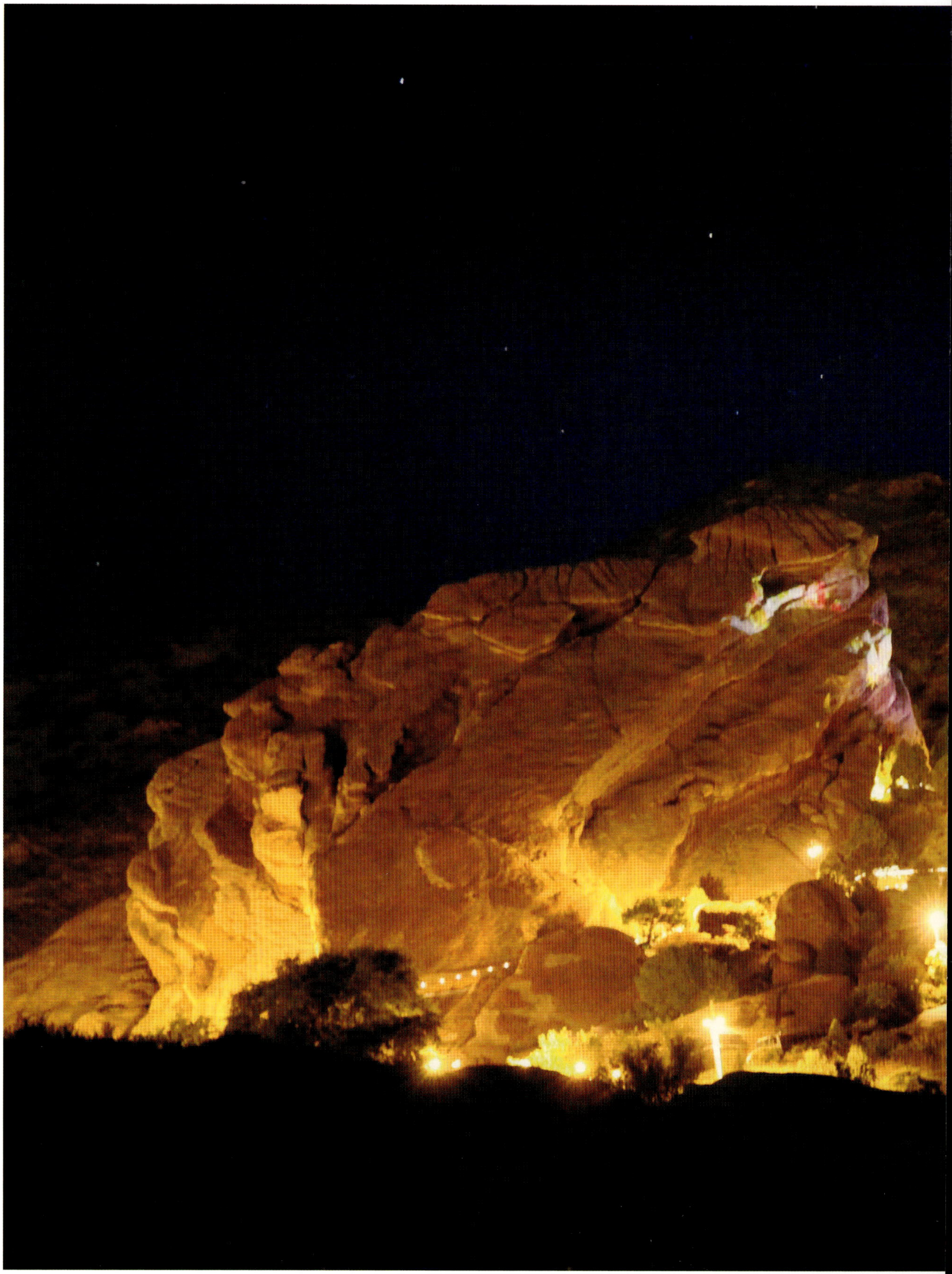

c. 2010

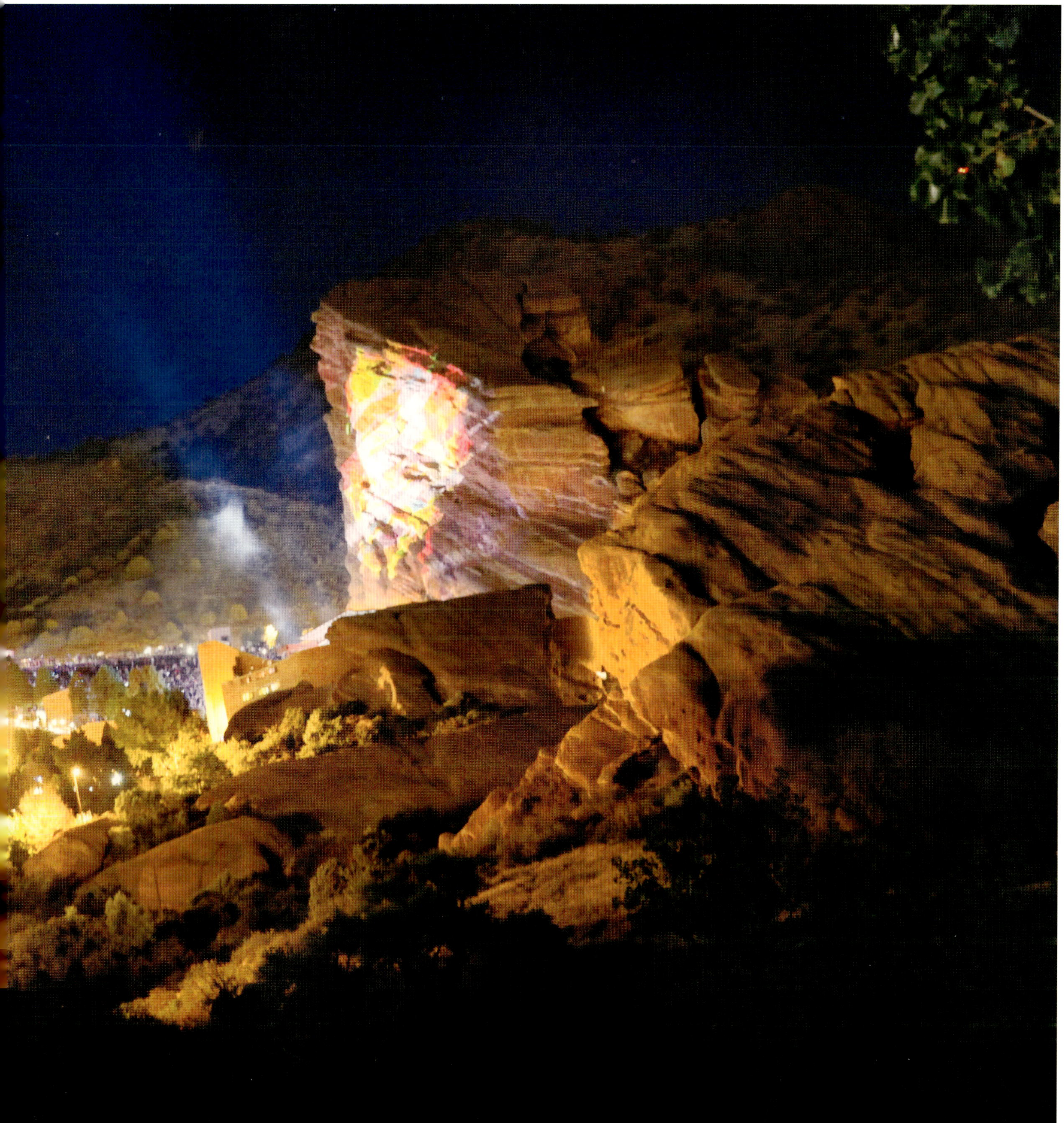

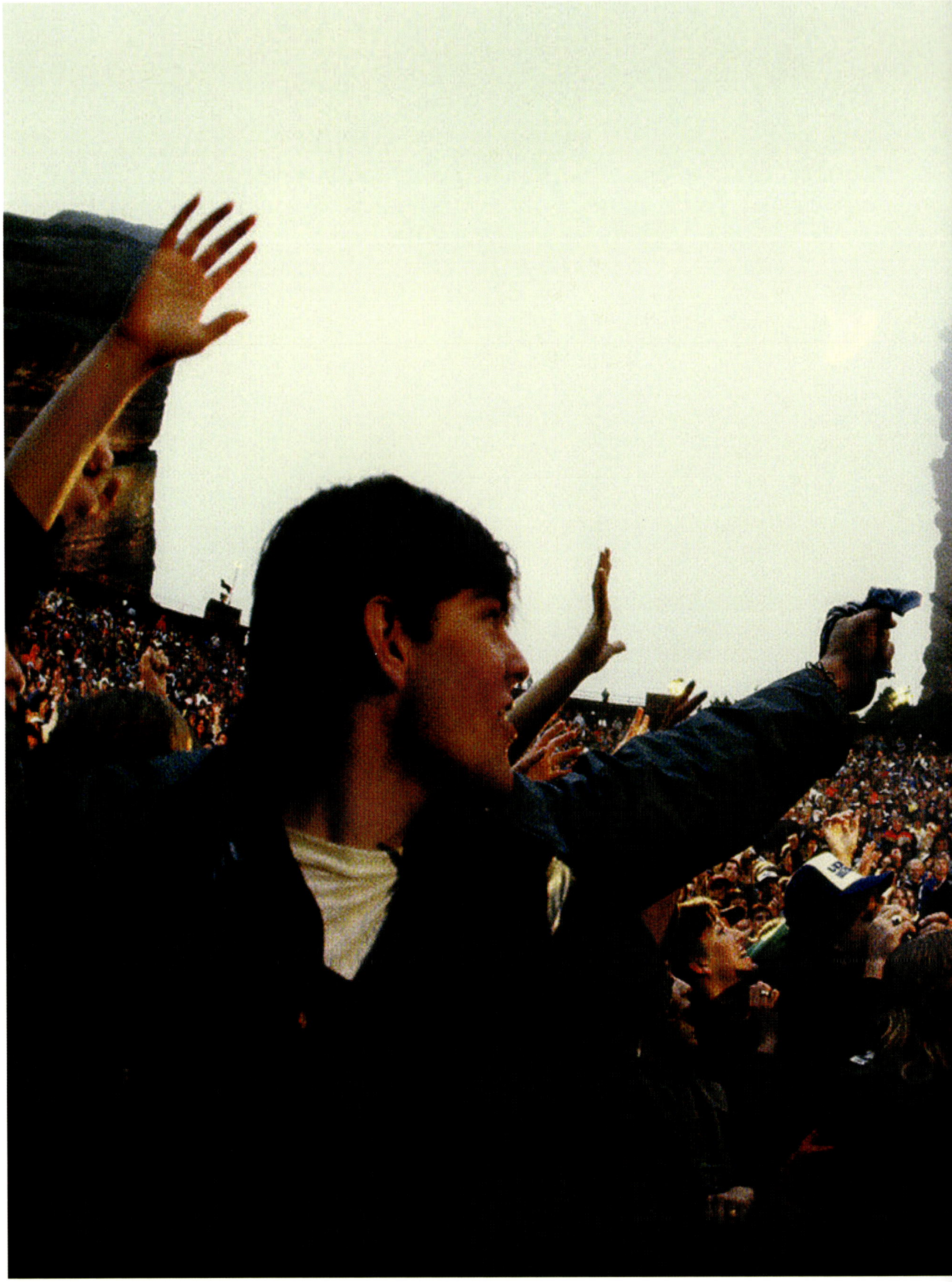

U2, 1983

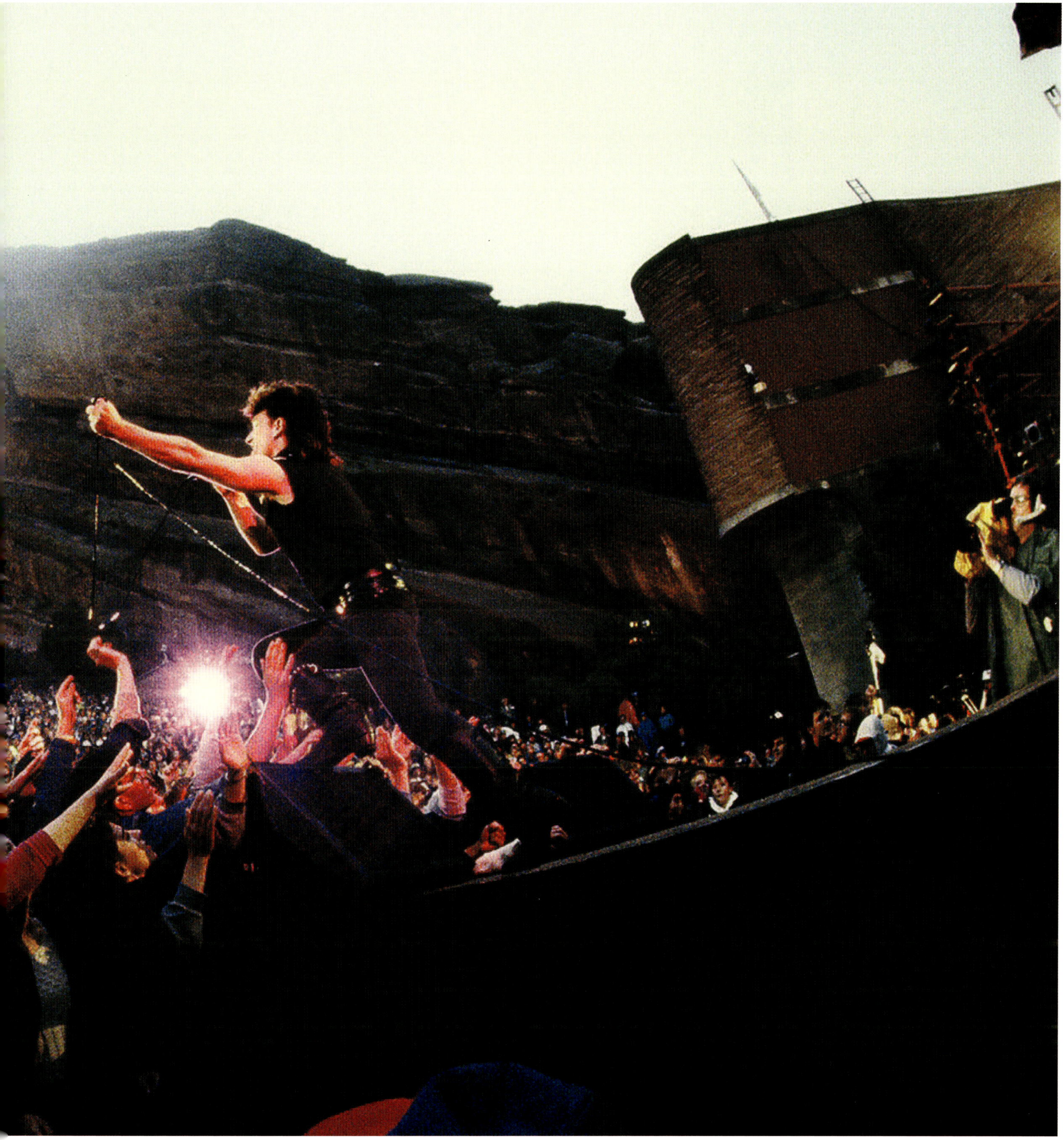

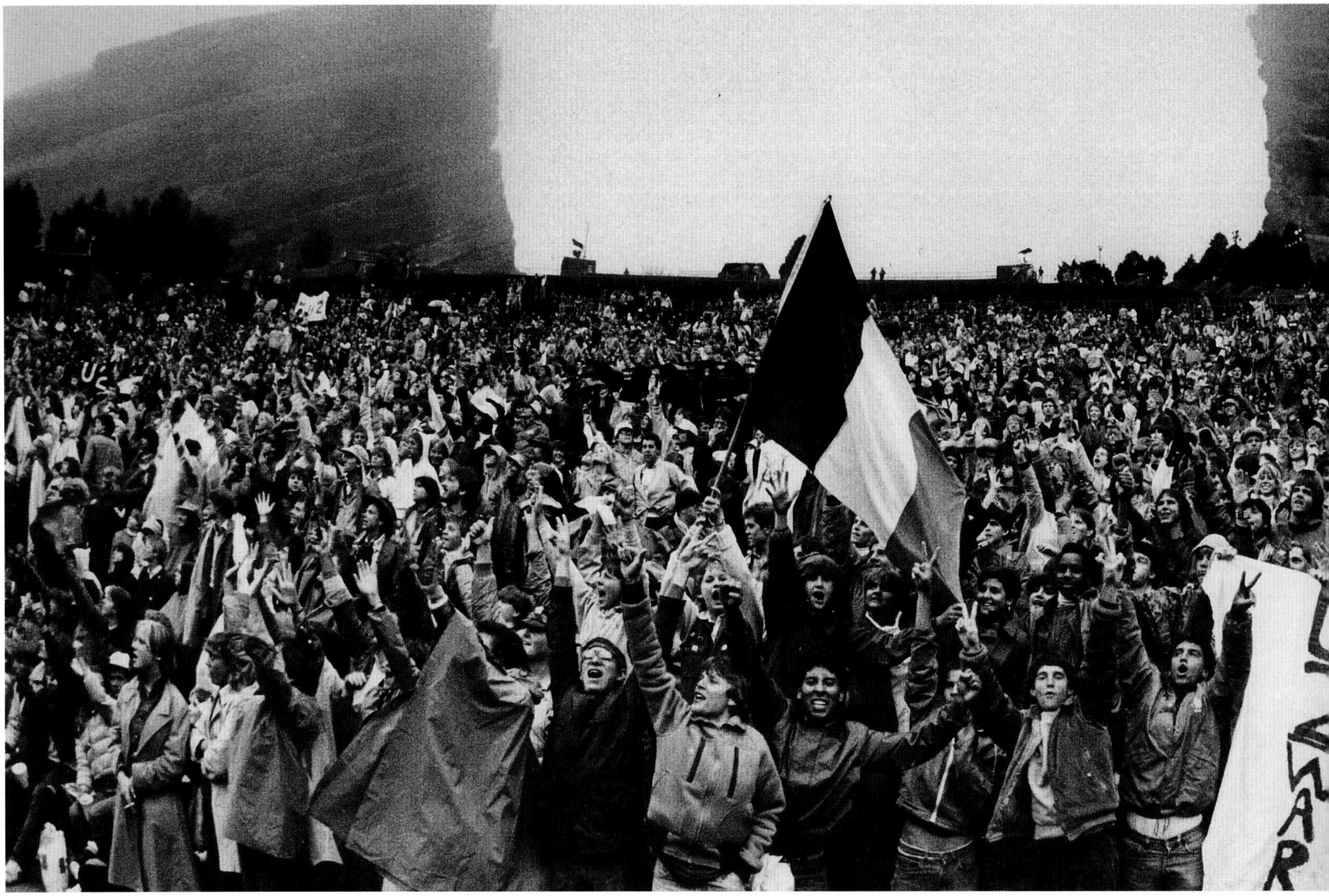

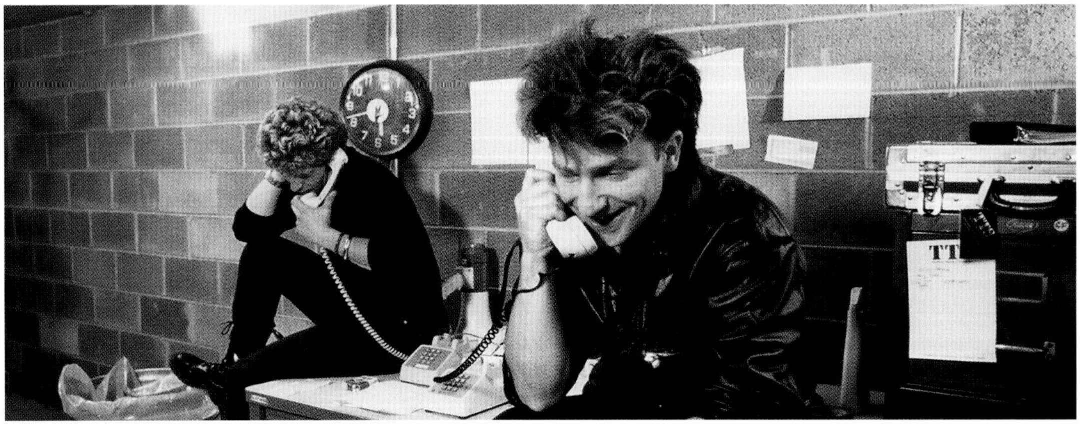

U2 fans (above);
U2 backstage
(left, right), 1983

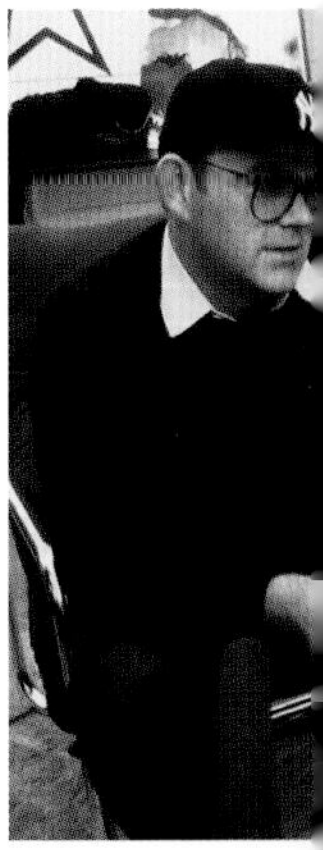

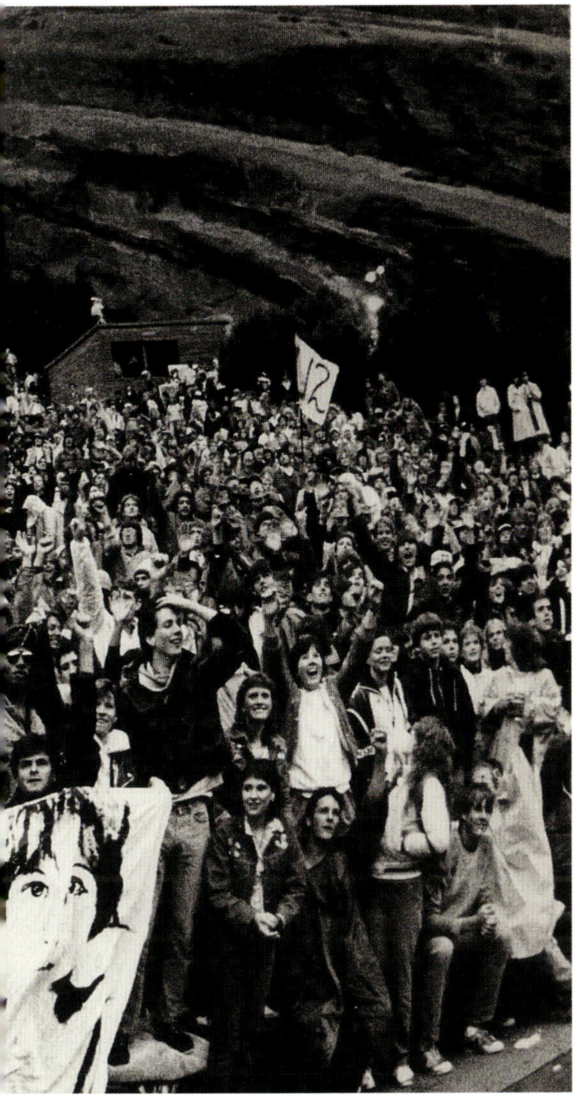

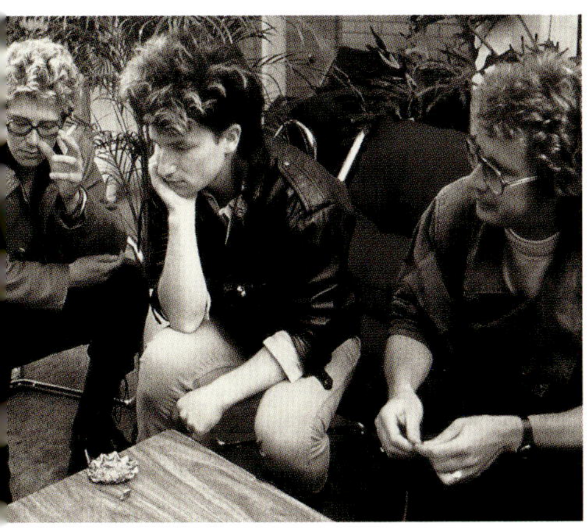

1983-1986
RED ROCKS GETS ITS CLOSE-UP

It took MTV's revolutionary all-video format of the early 1980s to cement the wonder of the Red Rocks setting in the popular imagination. The event took place on June 5, 1983 when U2 staged a famous concert video, *Under a Blood Red Sky*. But a lot of things had to go wrong in order for the show to come off so right.

In 1980, U2 had come through Denver on its first American tour, playing in Denver at the now-defunct Rainbow Music Hall. Promoter Chuck Morris knew the young Irish band was destined for greater things and wanted to show off Colorado's incomparable outdoor venue to the members. Three years later, U2 was booked into Red Rocks.

"It was the first tour where a record was doing quite well, a (writer and a) few people in radio got behind us—we might have made some money," lead singer Bono said. "We were going to invest it into in a film to record our victorious U.S. tour."

From day one, the planning and coordination of the operation proved to be formidable—no one had attempted such a project before. The natural beauty of the foothills meant no shortage of logistical obstacles. However, the band proceeded with the lofty plans. Gavin Taylor, the director of an avant-garde English video program, *The Tube*, flew over to oversee the filming. Steve Lillywhite, the famed producer of the band's albums, also arrived from Europe to record the live audio on location. The band commissioned numerous special effects, including bonfires on the rocks and backdrop.

But on the day of the show, miserable weather threatened to ruin the entire scenario. Temperatures dropped to 40 degrees at showtime, and a day's worth of drizzle evolved into a deluge. It was no place to be holding a concert, and it made for some tremendously difficult decisions.

"We heard that Barry Fey was coming into town...very, very cross, saying that this concert couldn't take place at Red Rocks," Bono said. "We had to explain to him there was no way we could afford for it not to take place. We had all our savings invested in it. We had to do it.'"

So U2 resolved to play without a warm-up act for whoever braved the weather. They then planned to do a proper performance in Boulder the following night with the Divinyls and the Alarm. Bono went on the radio—he called KBPI, KPPL, KPKE, KTCL and KAZY.

"I said, 'We're going to do the show tonight at Red Rocks. If you want to come, then come, and if you don't, then we'll do the show over again tomorrow indoors at the university in Boulder.'"

Out of the 6,000 advance sale, 4,400 ticketholders showed up to

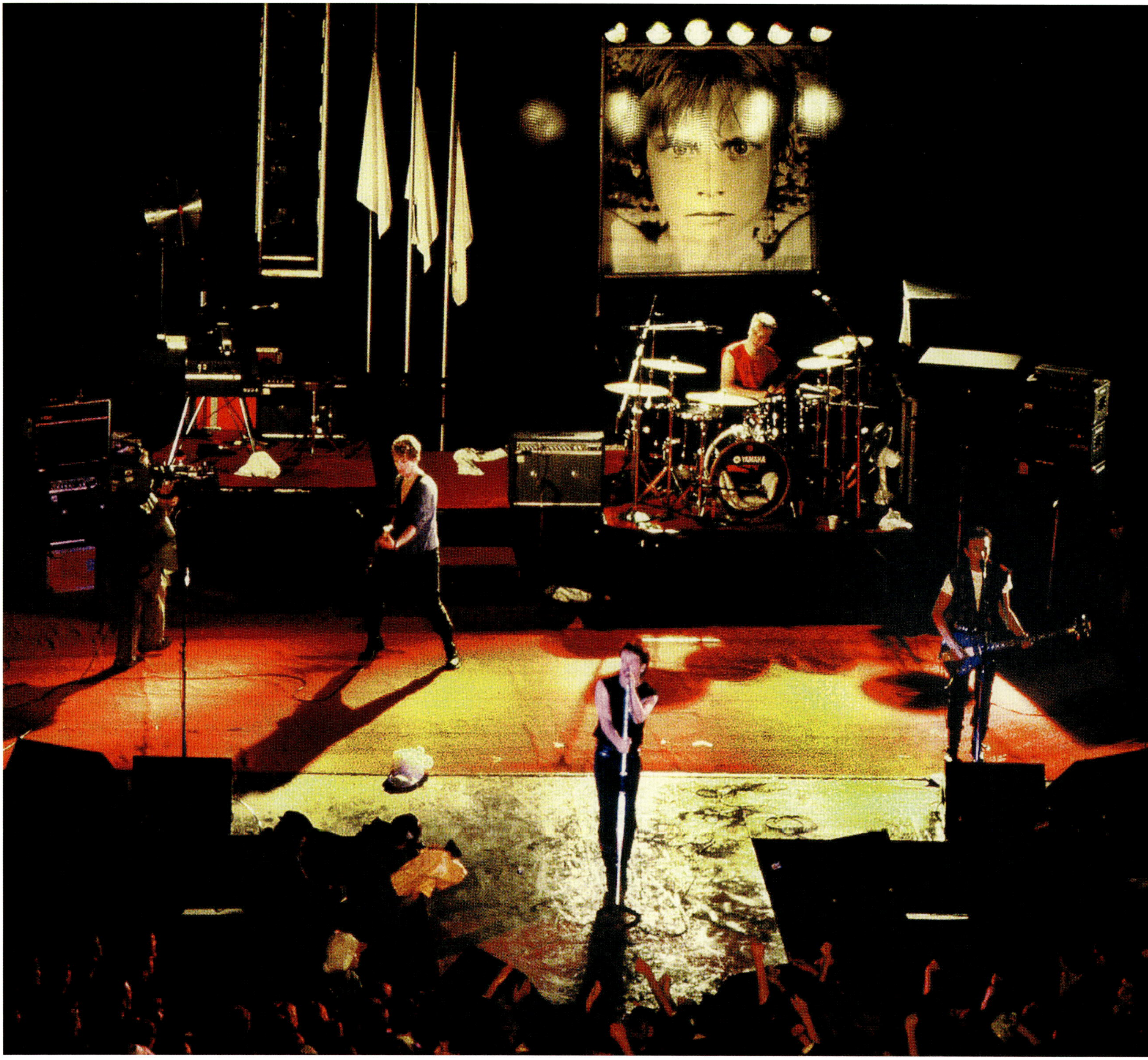

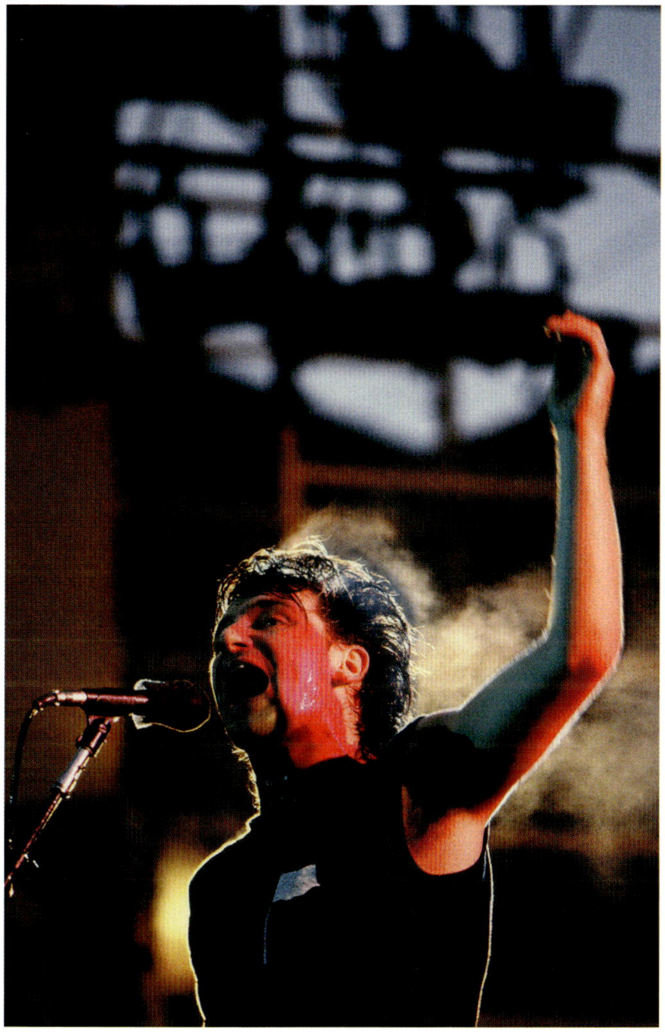

U2 (left, above), 1983

deal with the elements. U2 took the stage despite all of the logistical nightmares. "If only eight people turned up, we were still going to play like our lives depended on it," Bono said.

It's doubtful that any other band could have turned the adversity at Red Rocks so convincingly to its advantage. The event ceased being a concert after the second song. From that point on, it was more akin to a church service, a tangible exchange between a band fulfilling its promise and its soaked, shivering congregation of fans.

Later, the drama made its way to *U2 At Red Rocks* (a documentary that aired on Showtime) and *Under a Blood Red Sky* (the video and live album). The swirling fog that rolled in over the mountains gave the setting an eerie quality akin to a Scottish moor. The segments in which the band was delivered to the site via helicopter appeared to have come from the film *Apocalypse Now*.

And the concert pieces were exceptionally striking. During "Sunday Bloody Sunday," Bono immortalized his holy gladiator profile, unfurling and waving a huge white flag in the crowd against the hellish glow of the large flaming torches high on the cliffs surrounding the stage.

The mystic, against-all-odds performance was a spiritual and commercial breakthrough, and it turned U2 into A-list rock heroes.

"I'd like to thank the man who invented the wide-angle lens," Bono said. "He made the 4,000 people there look like millions."

"That was the turning point for us," guitarist the Edge reflected. "In Europe, nobody knew who we were. They saw this visually spectacular video and said, 'Who are these guys?'"

U2 wasn't the first act to recognize the problems with a notoriously wide range of atmospheric conditions. Ever since the first season in 1947, when radio station KOA was contracted to broadcast 5:45 p.m. weather reports the day of concerts, every generation of Red Rocks crowds knew to deck out in jackets, hats, scarves and blankets.

In 1984, the rainy Go-Go's concert suggested that the band's swimsuit garb on the cover of their second album *Vacation* would have been more suitable stage attire. As a storm nearly washed away a Eurythmics' concert in 1984, a soaked Annie Lennox stood in the drizzle singing "Here Comes the Rain Again," tossed aside her prop umbrella and knocked out the "Let it rain, rain, rain" fadeout, shouting the final chorus defiantly at the skies. Dave Stewart then drove away the clouds with an incendiary guitar solo. At the band's next Red Rocks concert two years later, Lennox captured an ironic moment by singing the first line of "The Last Time": "Well the first time that I saw you/You were standing in the rain." "Here Comes the Rain Again" was offered with clear skies, but Eurythmics chose not to employ a special opening effect

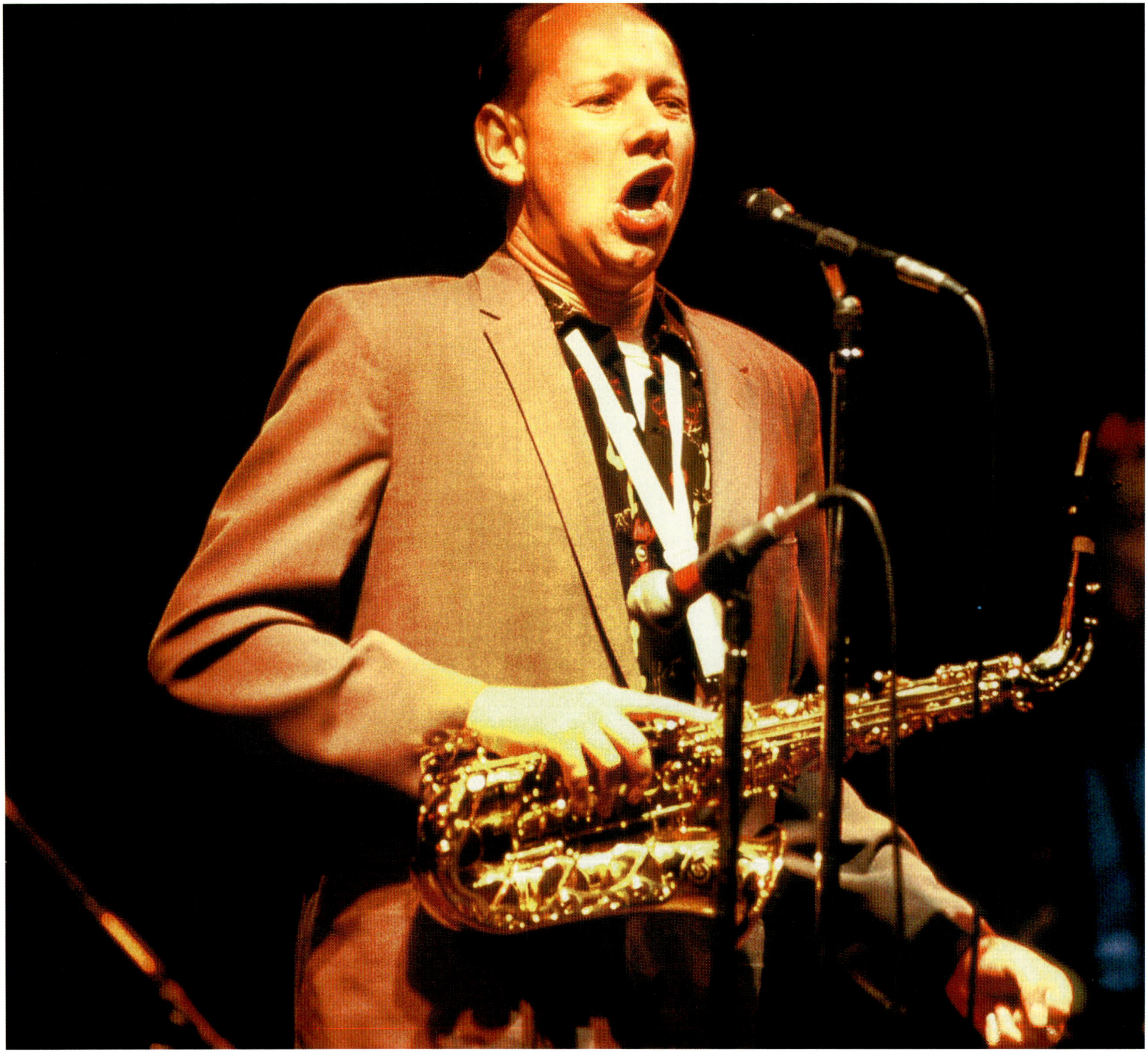

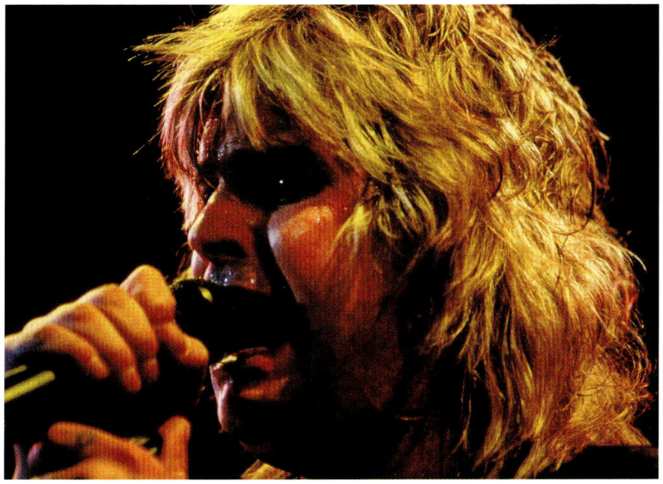

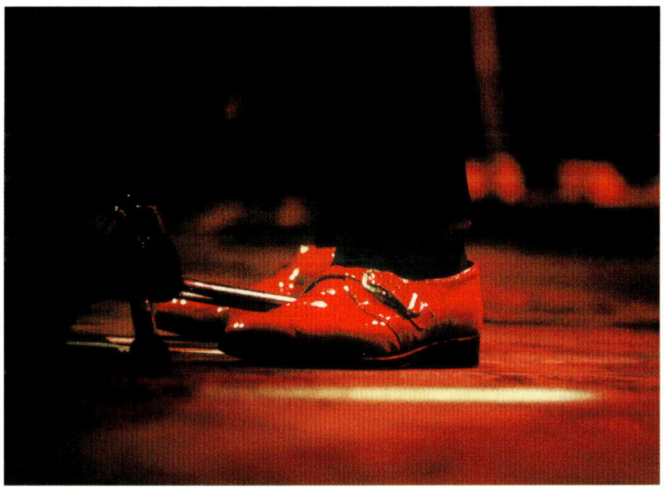

Joe Jackson, 1984 (left); Ozzy Osbourne, 1984 (top); Elvis Costello, 1984 (above)

utilizing a zippered curtain for fear of wind damage.

38 Special managed to attract its share of human battering rams to its 1984 show. "We had a lot of special effects that time, like lightning and lasers," guitarist Don Barnes said. "We sent 'em out in space and hoped they'd travel forever." Dio's ambitious medieval-themed stage shows took on Red Rocks in 1983 and 1984, and the band became one of the few acts that absolutely hated performing at the famous outdoor venue.

"Red Rocks is a beautiful place to go watch a sunset, and sometimes it's a wonderful place to go watch it rain," Ronnie James Dio, the diminutive singer, said with just a trace of sarcasm. "And have you ever tried getting an 18-foot dragon up the side of that mountain?"

Rain, cancellations and good music were all components of a Red Rocks "Summer of Stars" schedule, but the opening show for the summer of 1985 featured all three in good measure. The cancellation of opening act Andreas Vollenwider was an unfortunate last-minute circumstance. Actually, the Swiss harpist did make an appearance—all of 30 seconds to explain to the crowd that the rain made for "technical difficulties," leaving the music in the hands of headliner Joan Armatrading. His decision moved 500 baby boomers to request ticket refunds.

"It was my saddest moment as a performer," Vollenwider recalled. "I've played music all of my life, and it was the first show I've had to cancel for any reason. The crew worked the whole day, but the equipment was too delicate." Vollenwider got the whole place to himself in 1986; the gates opened late "due to the unique technical requirements for setup and sound check."

Golf served as a unique requirement for Huey Lewis, the lead singer of Huey Lewis & the News, one of the most iconic music acts of the 1980s. Lewis played golf in the mornings before concerts, and the title *Fore!* was ideal for the band's fourth overall album, released in 1986. His interest in golf was piqued the previous summer, when Huey Lewis & the News set a record with four consecutive sold-out shows at Red Rocks Amphitheatre.

"That was the year the PGA was at Cherry Hills," Lewis said. "I didn't know anything about golf at that point—I'd only played a handful of rounds. Here's Peter Jacobsen and a few pros at our show. 'Jake' was compelling—he knew all of our songs. He invited me to Sunday's final at the PGA. We went down for the hell of it, stood right there at the 18th green—it caused quite a fuss, actually. And then I got to play Cherry Hills on Monday, and I didn't realize then what a big deal that was. But I struck up a friendship with Peter Jacobsen that has lasted to this day." Teaming with Jacobsen, Lewis made his debut at the AT&T

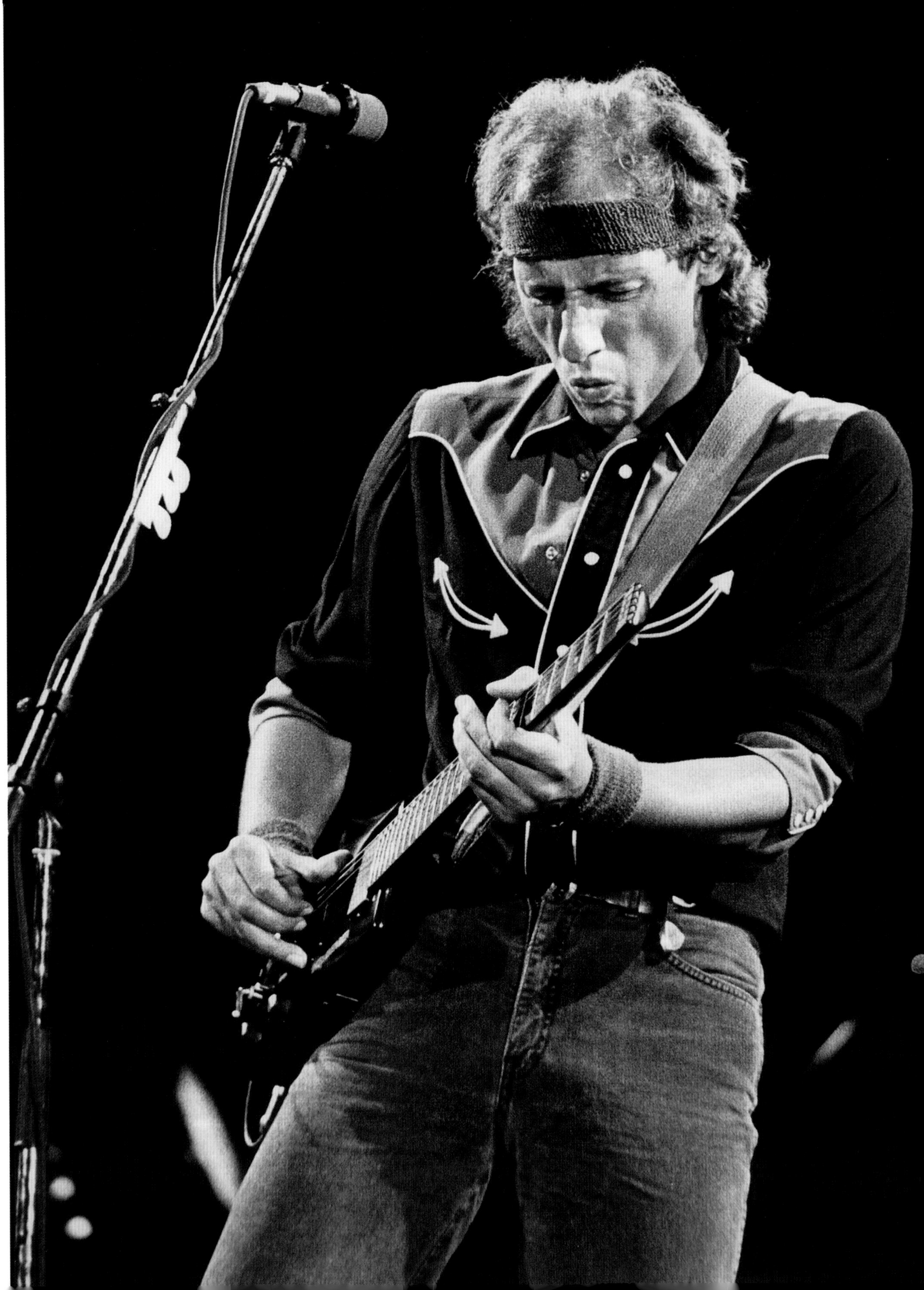

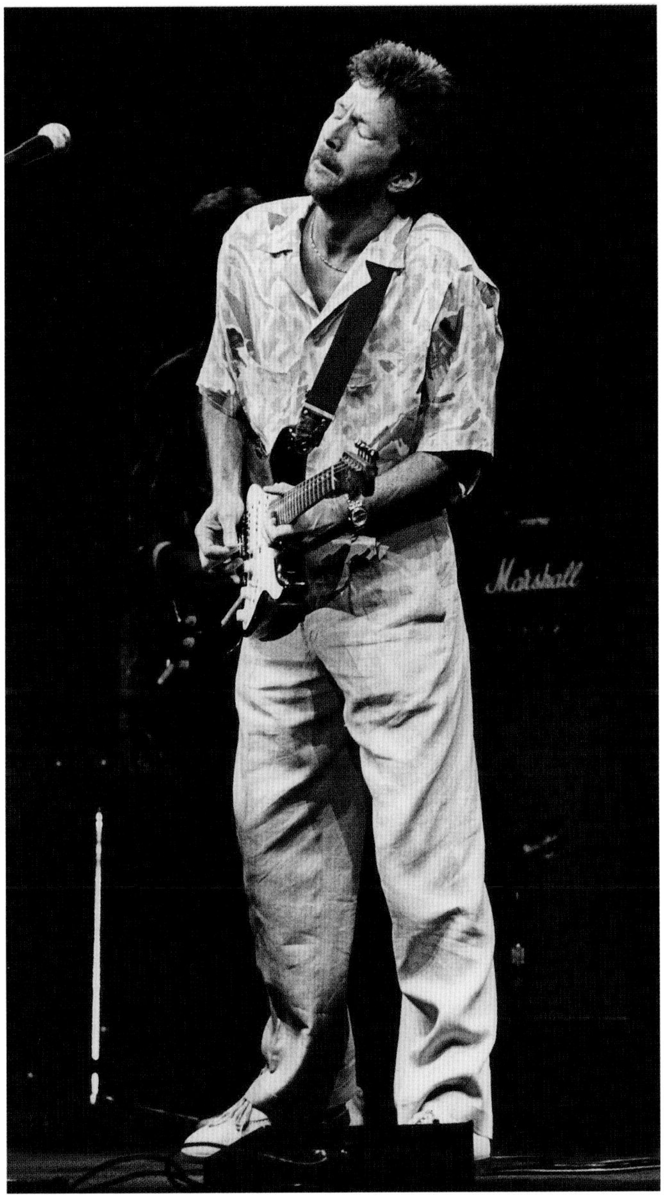

Dire Straits, 1985 (left); Eric Clapton, 1983

Pebble Beach National Pro-Am the following year and has attended the tournaments since.

Eric Clapton performed a sold-out show at Red Rocks on July 11, 1985—and scheduled an additional concert for July 14. The three-day break in his tour allowed him to appear in Philadelphia at Live Aid, the international famine relief fund-raising event consisting mainly of two concerts staged simultaneously in London and Philadelphia on July 13 and broadcast live on TV across the world.

"For most of 1985, I was out on the road promoting my *Behind the Sun* album," Clapton said. "We were booked to play Las Vegas the night before Live Aid, with shows in Denver on either side, so there were some pretty big leaps involved. I told my manager to cancel the Las Vegas show, and called Pete Townshend to say we'd do it." Clapton flew from Denver to Philadelphia and back again to fulfill his Red Rocks obligation, the hit single "Forever Man," spicing the proceedings.

Joe Walsh had been going through a musical menopause, wondering how his music stood up against the Duran Durans of the world, but that was no excuse for him to show up on the Red Rocks stage in August after apparently having had a few too many. A hot new technology had stirred public interest when Dire Straits performed at Red Rocks September 3 and 4, 1985. *Brothers in Arms* was the first album to sell a million copies on compact disc. "Red Rocks is a lovely venue," leader Mark Knopfler mused. "God, the audience there, such music lovers. That's the kind of show you get an awful lot of good memories from."

For several years after U2 eternalized Red Rocks Amphitheatre with *Under a Blood Red Sky*, other acts were apparently too intimidated to use the outdoor setting for filming. When INXS played at Red Rocks in August 1986, the members called for the production director and asked where the bonfires and fog were. They thought it came with the place after seeing the U2 video.

But Stevie Nicks broke the ice in 1986, when she filmed the final performance of her American tour at Red Rocks—where she had played two sold-out shows just eight weeks before. "They told me, 'You can't go back so soon and film there, nobody's gonna come,'" Nicks said. "I said, 'I can—you don't understand, this is a sacred thing to me and everybody will be there.'

"And it sold out. I knew in my heart where I should do my movie, where my feet are planted," she continued. "Every year of two I need to go to Red Rocks and spend some time, whether I'm performing or not. If I ever have children or grandchildren, if I want to explain my legacy to anybody, I'll put on my *Live at Red Rocks*."

Director Marty Callner, who had conceived of most of Nicks' rock

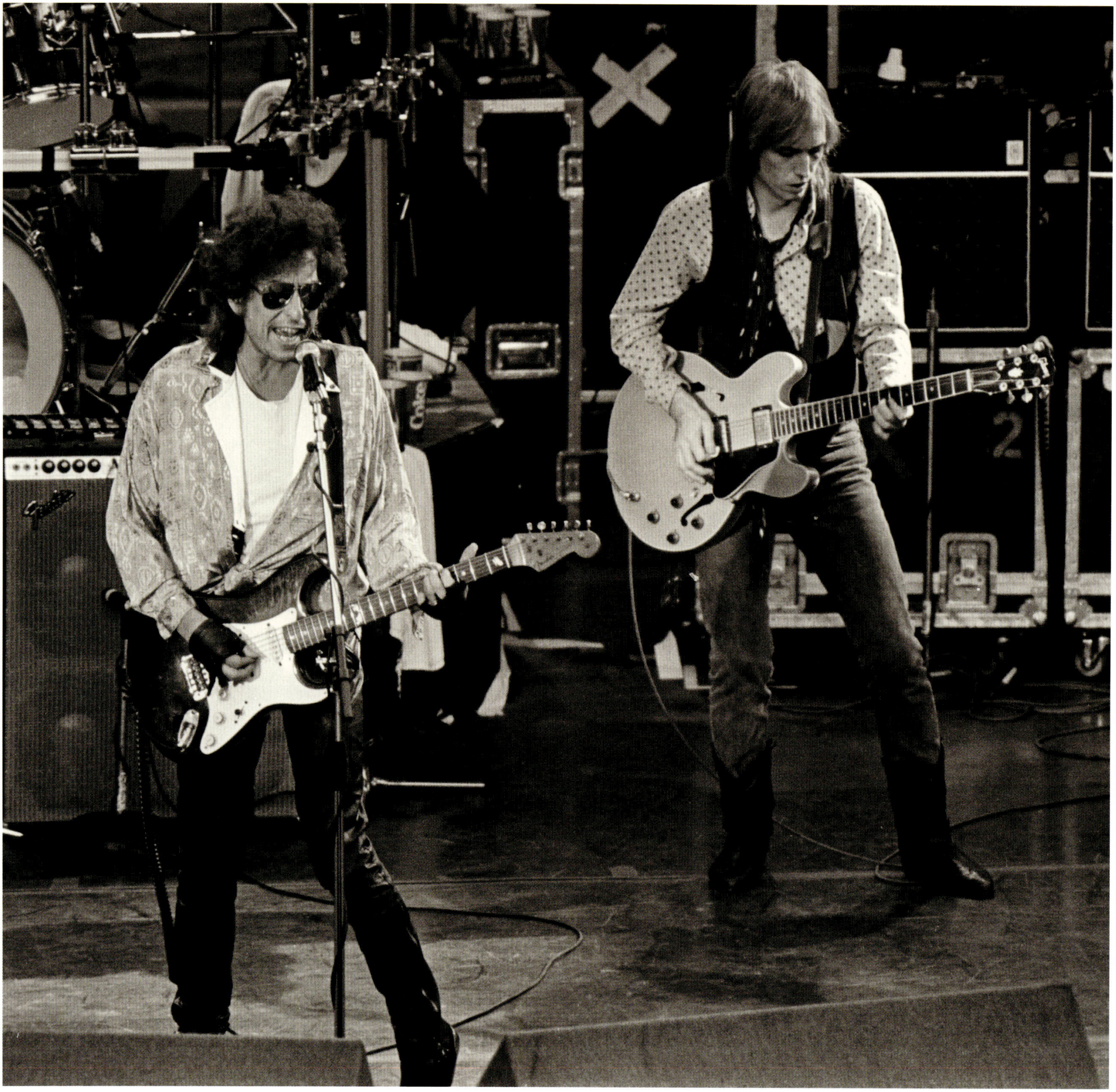

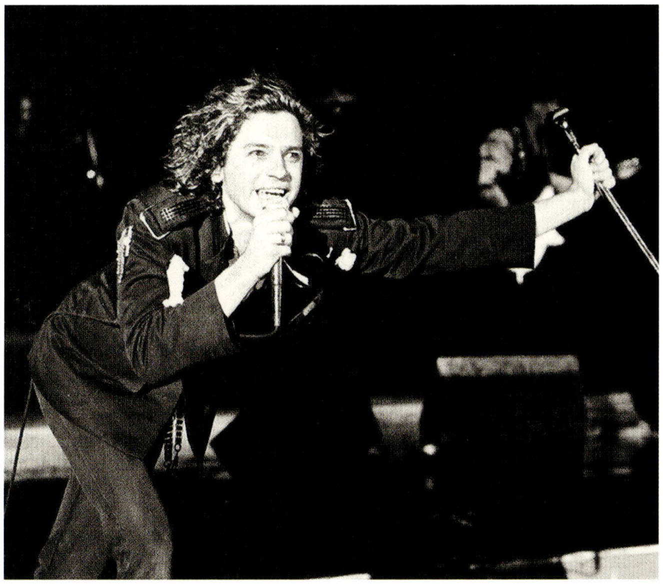

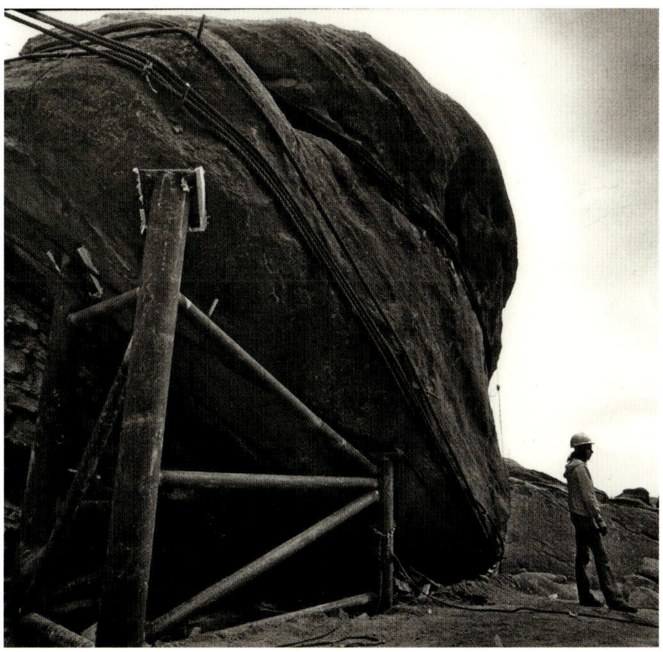

Bob Dylan and Tom Petty & the Heartbreakers, 1986 (left); INXS, 1986 (top); "Sundown" boulder, 1986

videos, turned Red Rocks into a giant natural sound stage. Backstage, production gear was jammed into every available space: extra audio equipment (a 24-track mobile recording facility was brought in from Los Angeles), pyrotechnic effects and the usual maze of cables and wiring that were part of any filming operation. It took Callner and his helpers three days to set up Red Rocks to their specifications.

Nine cameramen filmed around the stage and one zoomed above the park in a helicopter. And the sellout crowd wasn't even privy to the majority of the footage. Following the filming of the two-hour concert, the crews ate and then Nicks and her band embarked on another three-hour stint of shooting close-ups sans audience. The equipment wasn't completely loaded until 9:30 the following morning; another crew was just showing up to oversee an Oak Ridge Boys performance that night.

The resulting video aired on the Showtime cable network under the title *Give a Little*, then released commercially on video as *Stevie: Live at Red Rocks*.

Some controversy swirled around the use of special effects. The video included numerous sprawling shots of the mountains and surrounding area, but the directors took the liberty of embellishing the outdoor footage. During "Dreams," when Nicks got to the line "Thunder only happens when it's raining," flashes of lightning were superimposed over the Denver skyline.

The Red Rocks show had ended when 25 doves were released into the crowd. One of the birds refused to leave Nicks' hand—and fifteen minutes later she was still clutching the dove backstage and demanding that a separate cage be found for him.

"I want to find a good home for him," she said. "I want to visit him when I come back next time."

But Nicks kept him—only it was a her, named Rhiannon, of course.

"She wouldn't leave. I couldn't get her away, so I said, 'I guess this is my dove.' She lives with me, and I've since gotten two more," Nicks explained.

In 1986, Joe Jackson had to play the first part of his set in daylight, and the typically fun-loving crowd of 9,000-plus wasn't totally focused on his performance. And it bothered him no end. He disdainfully requested that no one speak while the band tuned up, and he chastised those who dared to chat during his song introductions. He finally adopted a self-deprecating tone and noted that he received a lot of reviews that found his surly attitude perturbing.

That June, a 315-ton, 20-by-30-foot sandstone boulder had cracked off of the north rock wall inside the amphitheatre. Luckily, nobody was using the park at the time and the boulder didn't damage any of the seats. It crashed some fifty feet towards the stage before lodging under a stone railing along the north stairs. Had it not stopped there, it would

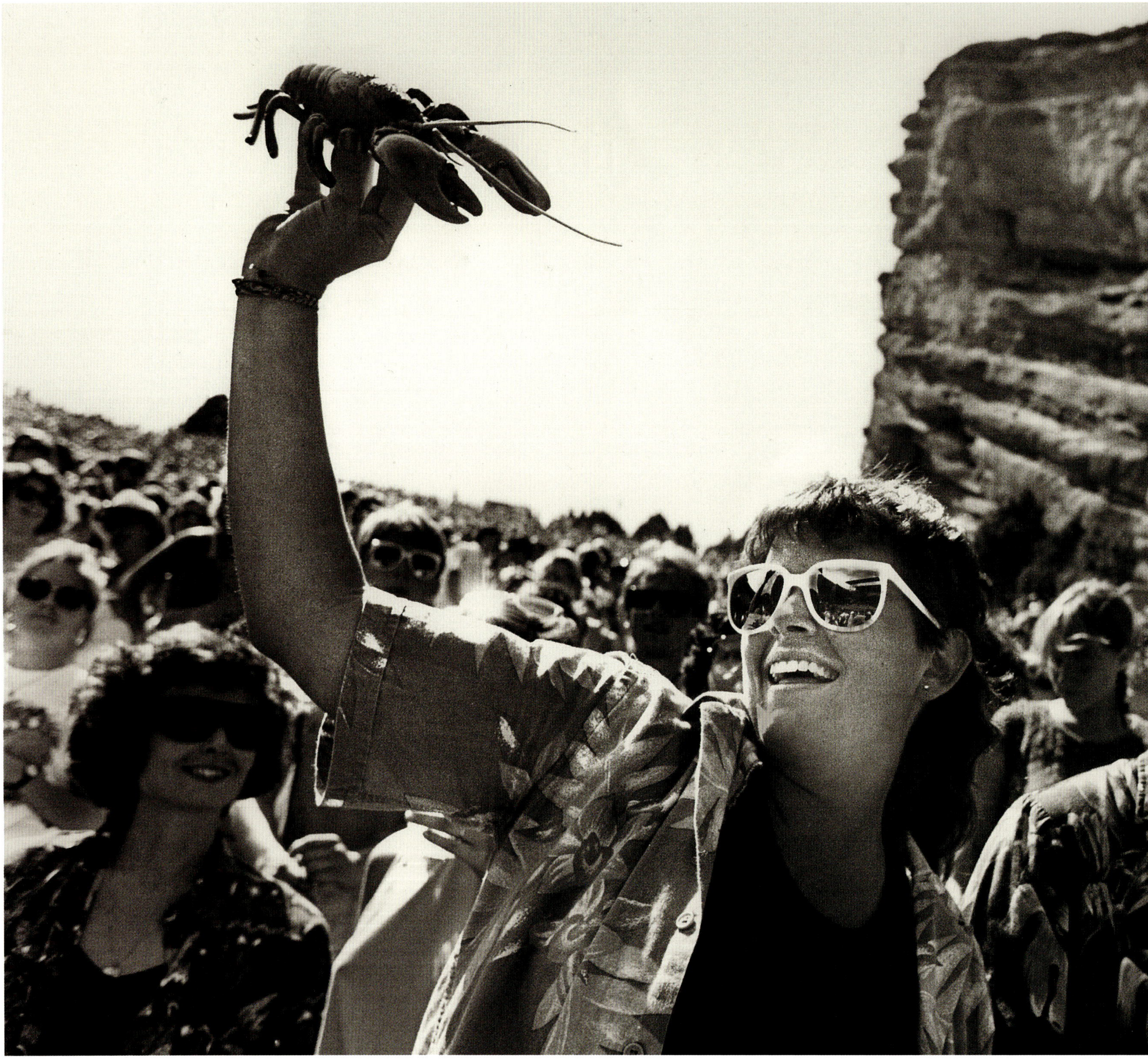

Parrotheads, 1986

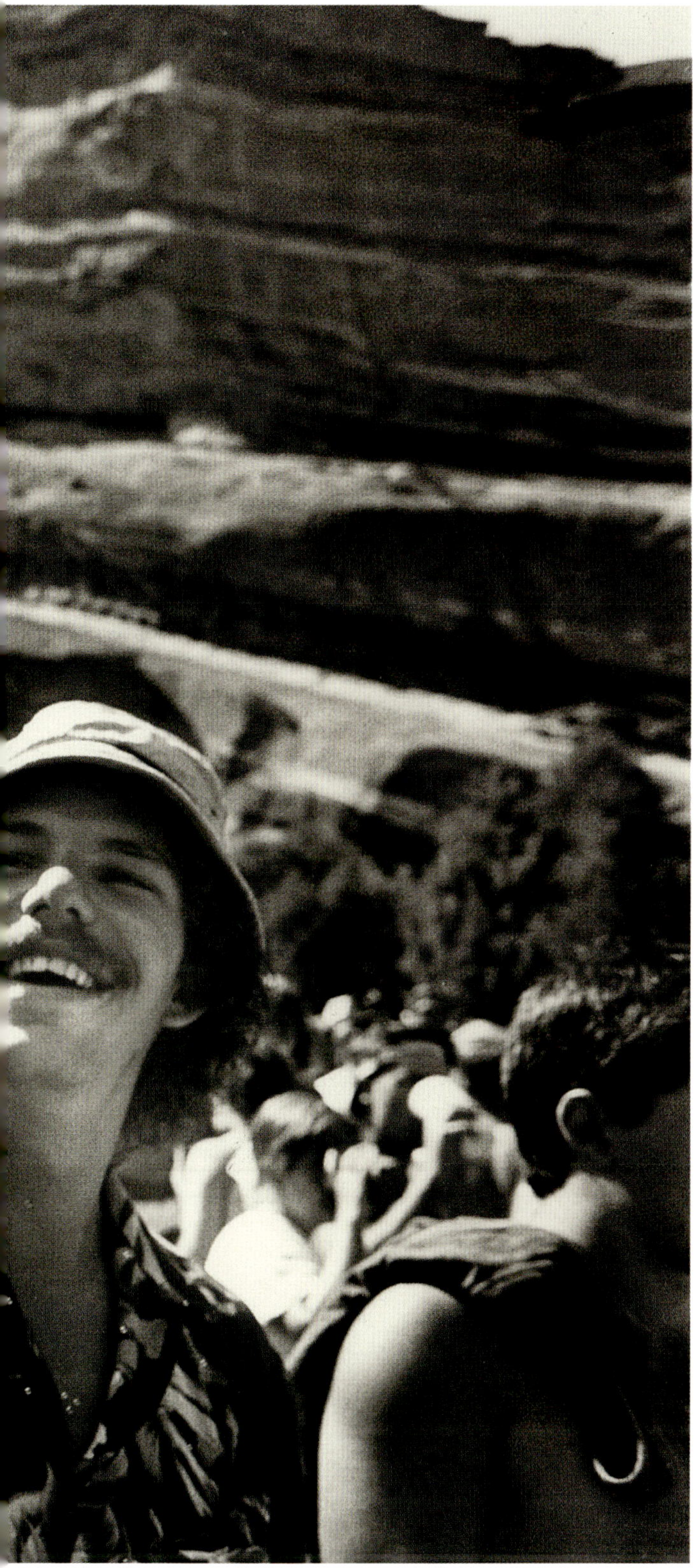

have likely wrecked the building that housed the restrooms and dressing rooms near the stage. The boulder (nicknamed "Sundown") couldn't be destroyed all at once without also destroying part of the stage. The following May, small amounts of dynamite and a lot of manpower were used to crush it bit by bit. The 60-day job cost an estimated $225,000.

1987-1991
NO FIDDLING ABOUT

Denver's entire flock of Parrotheads—as Jimmy Buffett's famed fans had anointed themselves—had alighted at Red Rocks in 1986 for their annual activity charitably described as cocktail aerobics. The Sunday afternoon show (the only daytime concert on the "Floridays" tour) provided the perfect setting for Buffett's fun-loving, chug-a-lug ideology. The event resembled an oversized backyard barbeque—shirts off, heavy imbibing and aromatic smoke filling the air. "I haven't seen this much white meat since Thanksgiving," Buffett surmised.

Red Rocks made artists aware that they had to schedule sound checks once paying customers had already been allowed into their seats. Doors opened early—2 p.m. for weekday concerts and at noon on weekends. But since most performers felt doing a sound check in front of an audience gave away part of their show or cut down on the excitement, they would often forego that formality. Besides, many of them were unable to get to Red Rocks from the airport in time to sound check.

But acts like Buffett, Dan Fogelberg, Jackson Browne and John Denver were exceptions—they'd do a couple of songs and joke with the audience to make sound checks an impromptu rehearsal/concert in the afternoon. In 1987, doors opened two hours later in order to make Red Rocks more easily secured for concerts. The gates opened the same time as the parking lots, so people holding general admission seats gained no advantage in arriving early.

That year, Buffett maintained his usual upbeat atmosphere for his cult of "cultural outpatients" dressed in "Caribbean soul" outfits. Band members muttered in amazement in the dressing room after two sold-out shows: "Did you see those guys 'mooning' us in the third row? These people are crazy." With the best show going on up in the seats, Buffett really had to compete to entertain.

The first rap concert at Red Rocks, with Run-D.M.C. and the Beastie Boys, took place in 1987. Backstage, the Beasties were imbibing Dusted Llamas, cocktails that blended everything in their contract rider (151 proof rum, pre-mixed Brass Monkey drinks, apple/grape/cranberry

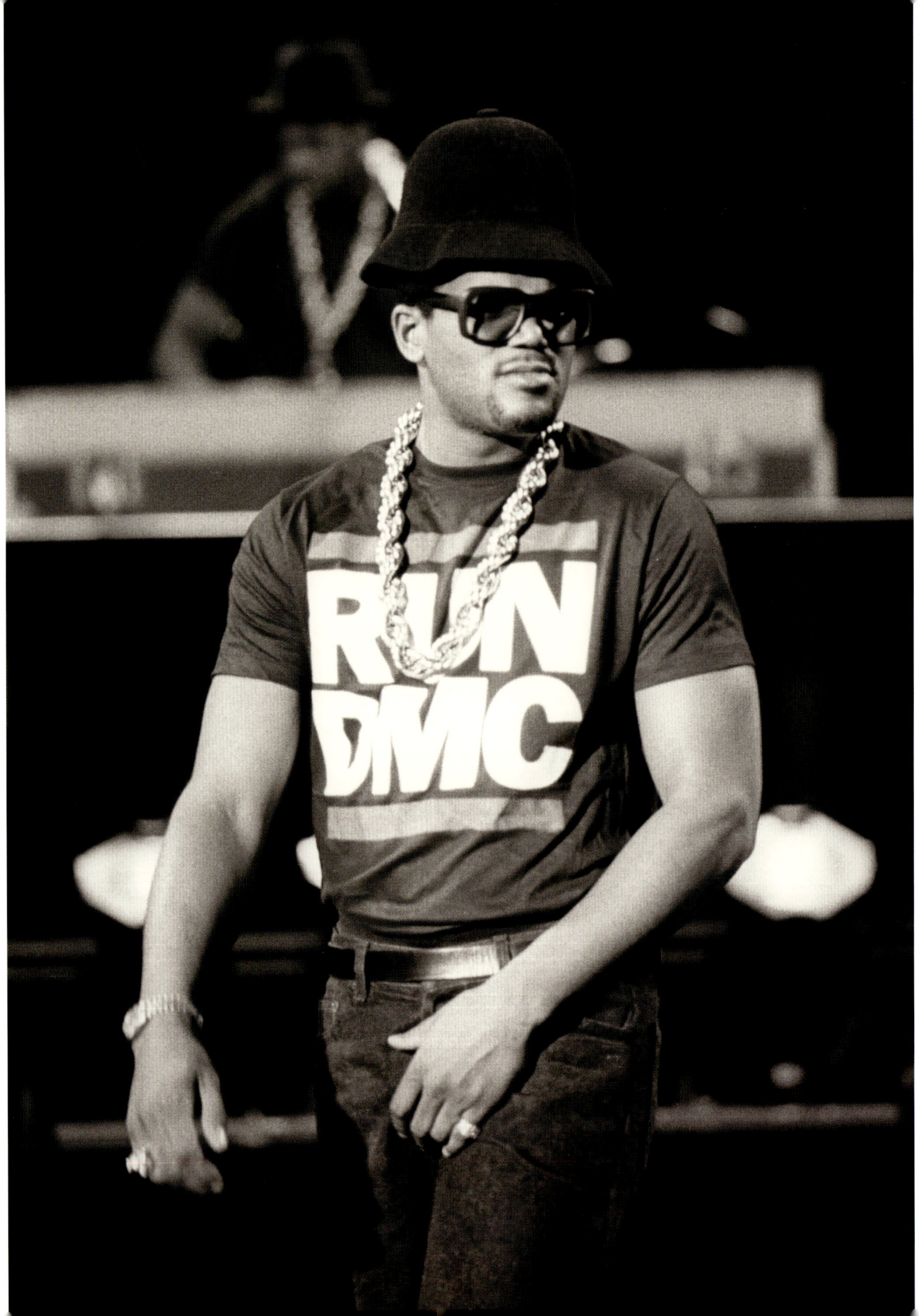
RUN
DMC

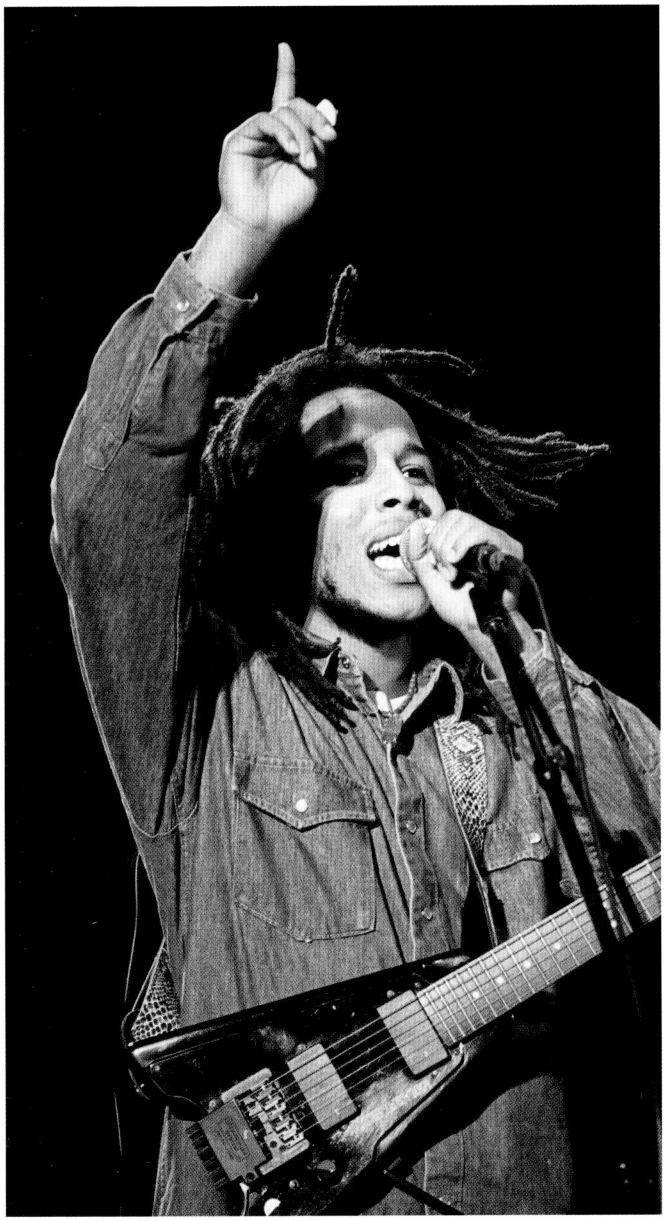

Run-D.M.C., 1987 (left); Ziggy Marley & the Melody Makers, 1989

juices, cream of coconut), and they were willing to share.

To shelter performers from the wind and the rain, a permanent roof was completed in time for the 1988 summer concert season, designed to minimize interference with existing sightlines of the rocks. In August 1989, fans watched a total lunar eclipse during Ziggy Marley & the Melody Makers' set.

But the era of 50-plus shows every summer at Red Rocks had come to an halt because of competition from Denver's newest outdoor venue, MCA's Fiddler's Green Amphitheatre in the Denver Tech Center. It began an unprecedented bidding war for major acts in Denver. Crosby, Stills & Nash played Fiddler's, and David Crosby weighed in: "What the fuck are we doing playing here when the greatest place in the world to play is fifteen miles away?"

In 1989, scenes for the movie *The Adventures of Ford Fairlaine*, a box office bomb starring Andrew Dice Clay, were shot at Red Rocks with Vince Neil of Mötley Crüe. That same year, Kip Winger, a Denver native, brought his self-named pop-metal band (along with Bullet Boys and headliner Cinderella) to Red Rocks.

"I can't believe it—it's two miles from where I grew up," Winger said. "I used to ride my bike up to Red Rocks and sit on the seats at the top, visualizing I'd play there one day—it was a major inspiration. It was amazing because the weather went through several changes during our set. I felt like, 'Wow, this is really the place to do a show.'"

The Nitty Gritty Dirt Band organized a 1989 show that featured the big cast of the *Will the Circle Be Unbroken: Volume Two* album.

"We did a short set and began to bring up the likes of New Grass Revival and Roseanne Cash," NGDB's Jimmy Ibbotson said. "Then John Hiatt joined us and the music began to rock, relentlessly. The crowd was into it like nothing I had ever seen before. In the back of my mind, I was a little worried that our old friend and neighbor, John Denver, was going to have to follow this. I didn't think that anyone could. His songs were smooth and soft by comparison and I worried that he must not have any fans in a crowd that liked the harder music so much.

"When the crowd quieted down after Hiatt's departure, I took the center microphone and announced Denver. He joined us to a standing ovation of unearthly volume. It was as though Christ had walked on to play at Elvis's birthday barbeque. Here was the ultimate home field advantage. Everyone was looking down at the lights of Denver below. We were looking up at faces that reflected that dazzling pride."

In 1990, Fleetwood Mac, Jimmy Buffett, Depeche Mode, the B-52's, Robert Plant and Bonnie Raitt all turned down big offers

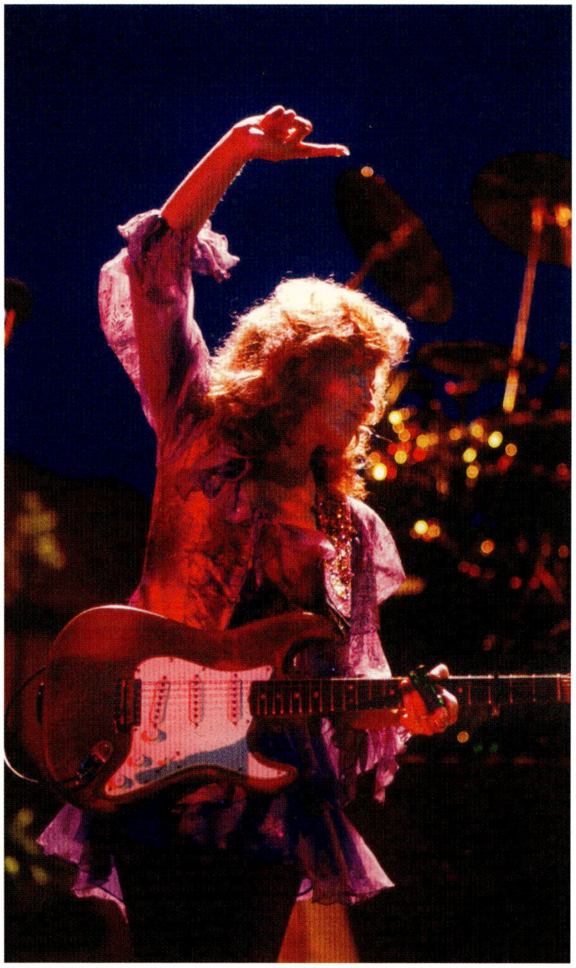

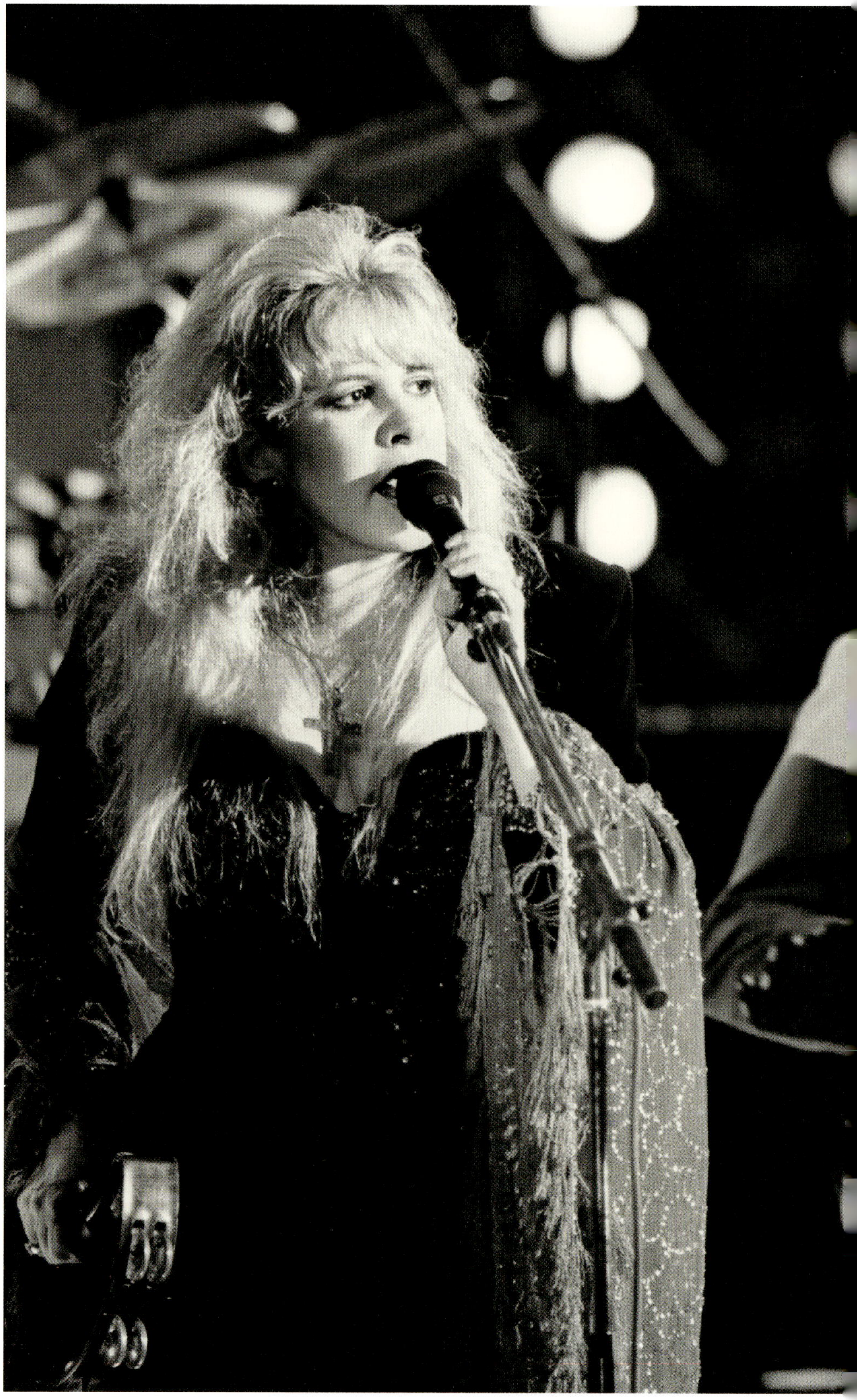

Bonnie Raitt, 1990; Fleetwood Mac, 1990 (right)

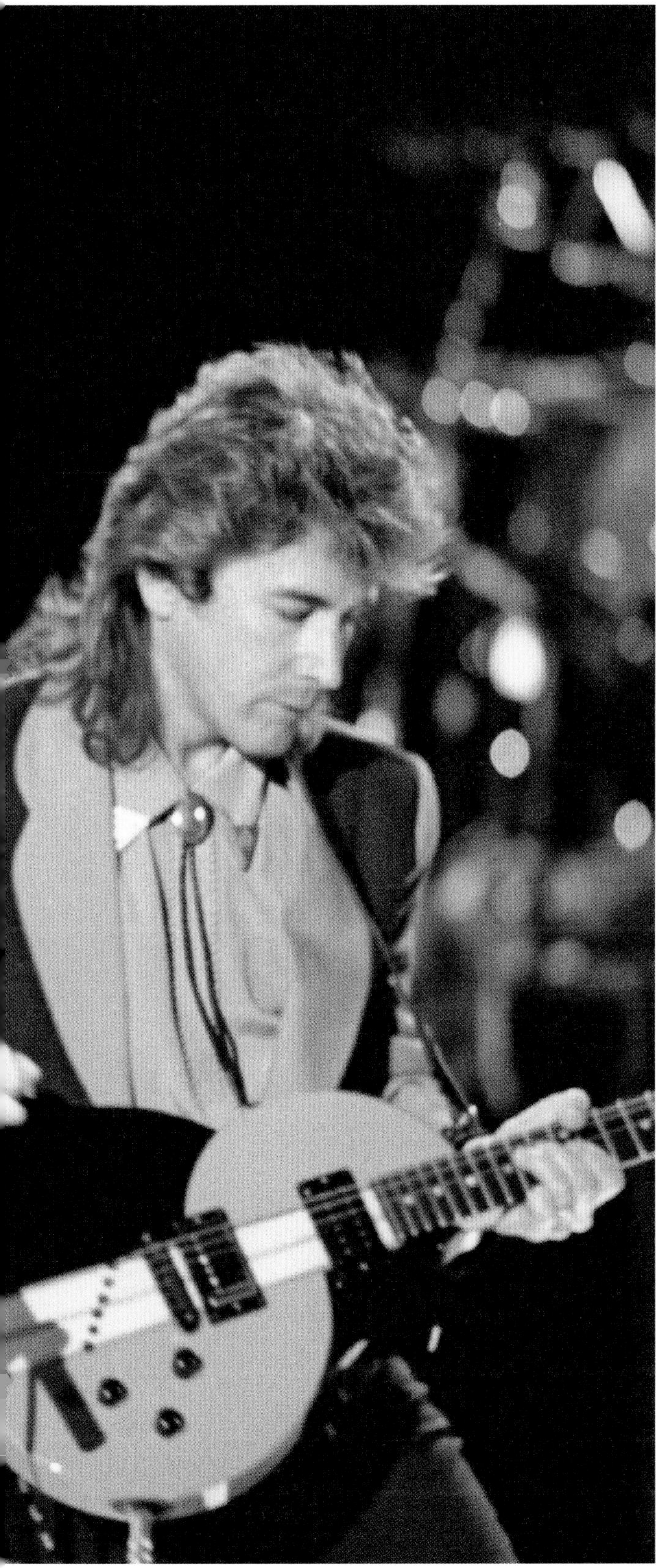

from Fiddler's Green and played two nights at Red Rocks. Buffett was overpowered by his fans' opinions. "Everybody expressed where I should play in Denver, which is why I played Red Rocks," he said. Raitt dedicated part of her set to blues guitarist and vocalist Stevie Ray Vaughan, a veteran of Red Rocks who had died in a helicopter crash two days before.

Buffett, however, returned at Fiddler's Green Amphitheatre the following year. "I can't put a show together when I see the number of casualties I saw backstage last year. People falling off the rocks, people on stretchers—it looked like a medical ward back there. If the front rows would sit down and behave themselves, if I didn't have to worry about that nasty combat zone, I'd play Red Rocks. It's still a wonderful place to play. But I'm not sure it's a solvable problem."

Dan Fogelberg performed solo at Red Rocks in 1990. "There are better sounding places, to be honest, but the audiences are respectful. There are some outdoor places I play that are as big for me as Red Rocks, but there's noisy stuff going on—they feature dinners, and people are popping champagne, smoking cigars—so they're not the ideal setting to do a folk show. Because Red Rocks is so steep, you can see people at the very top and make out their features. It's like looking at this huge animated poster."

In her Red Rocks performance that summer, singer-songwriter Rickie Lee Jones drew from her 1979 debut and her 1989 underground classic, *Flying Cowboys*, and sang "Love Is Gonna Bring Us Back Alive" with opening act Lyle Lovett. The set was issued as an archival release in 2001, *Live at Red Rocks*.

Performing at Red Rocks in September 1990, soul crooner Luther Vandross obviously preferred the warmth of indoor arenas to the outdoor venue—members of his entourage even wondered aloud if any bears or mountain lions might take the Red Rocks stage. When a chipmunk appeared in the dressing room, Vandross let out a yelp and ran away.

The vocalist felt an early evening downpour compromised his show, and he didn't wish to ruin the several thousand dollars' worth of costumes worn by his backing band. So he cut his two-hour set in half, leaving the stage after nine songs because of rain and drizzle. He offered no encore, or acknowledgment to dismayed fans, who jeered for a full five minutes after the house lights went up.

In 1991, "Reggae on the Rocks" featured three legendary reggae acts—Burning Spear, Steel Pulse and Jimmy Cliff—who stood for tolerance, justice and equality. But that apparently meant nothing for opening act Dread Zeppelin, led by lead singer Tortelvis, an Elvis

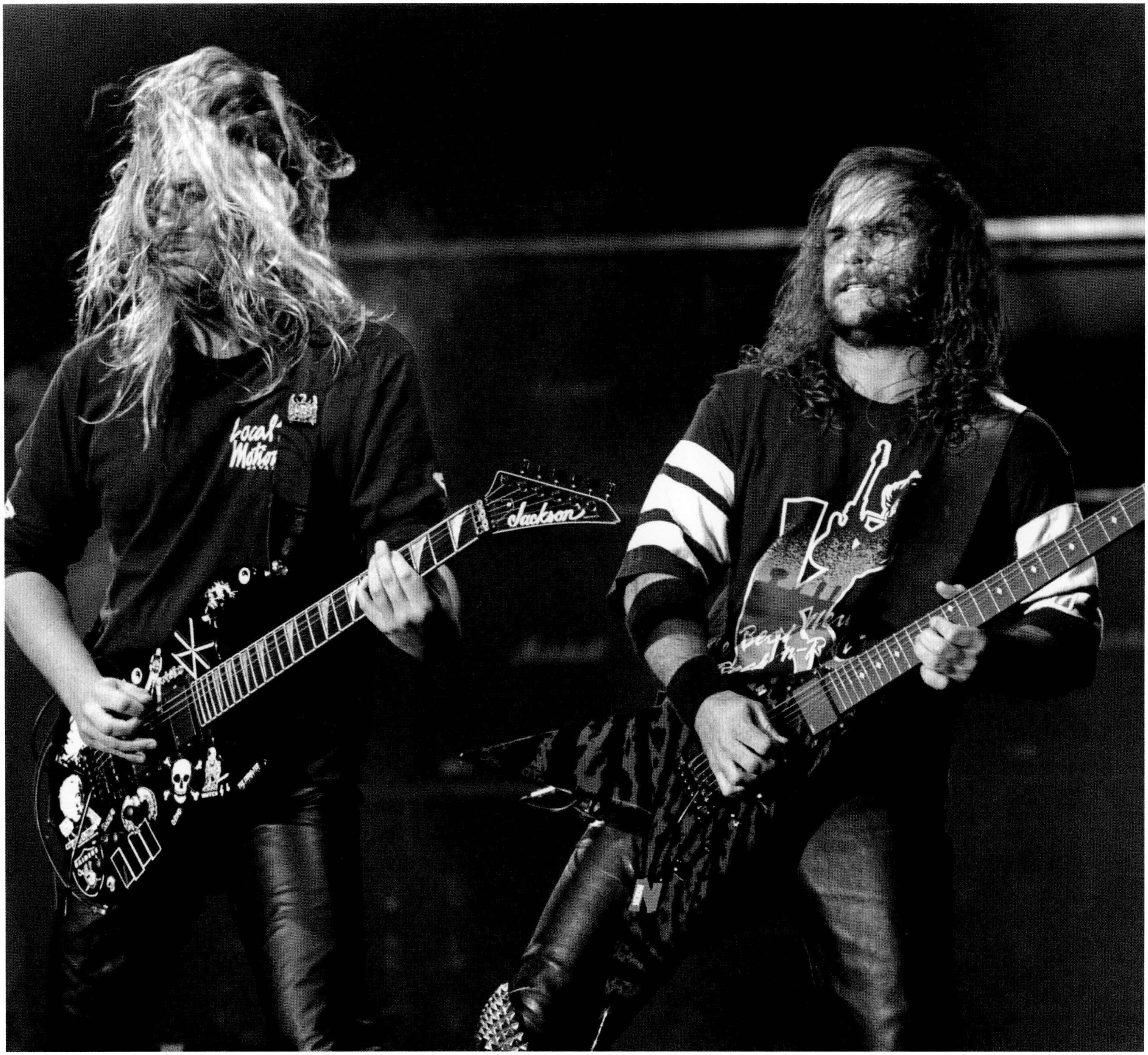
Jackson

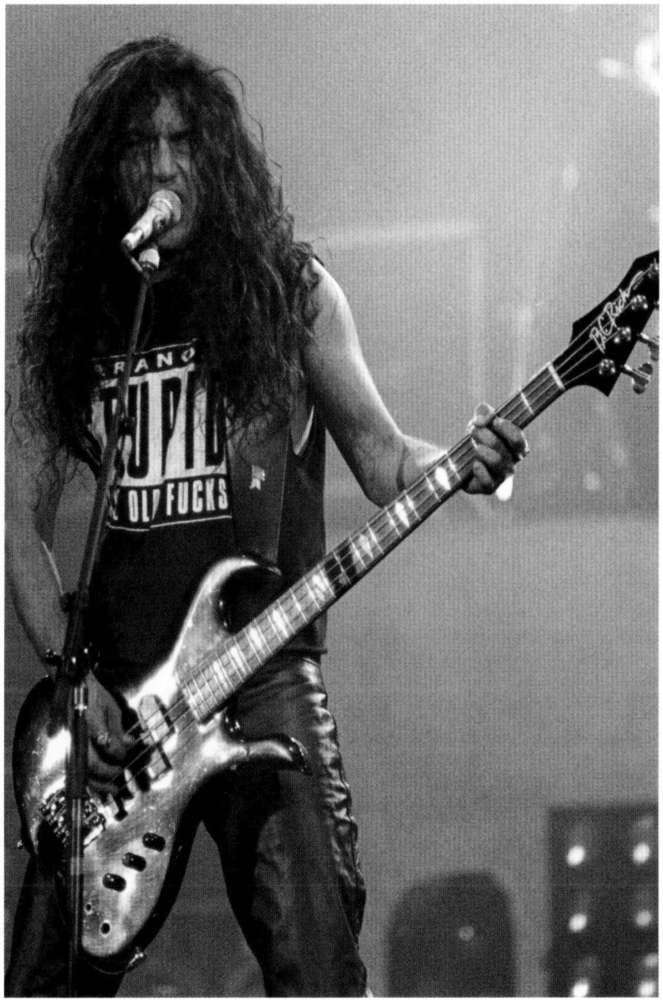

Slayer (above, left), 1991

impersonator singing Led Zeppelin songs to a reggae beat. The act got pelted with food and booed off the stage.

When 1991's "Clash Of The Titans" tour—co-headlined by Slayer, Megadeth and Anthrax—came to Red Rocks, the event's security risk potentially tripled. Speed-metal's fiercely aggressive music and hyper-rebellious attitude routinely drew wild crowds of kids slamming and ricoheting into each other, people toppling and scattering helter-skelter, heads and bodies getting bruised.

The bands were conscious of the physical danger the audience faced upon the unforgiving rocks. "There are always a few bad kids who show up to maim and punch," Slayer guitarist Kerry King admitted prior to the concert. "And there are a few bad bouncers, too, who come in just to whale on kids."

Two-thirds of the way through the performance, nine arrests had been made, but the police and the bands insisted that the Denver crowd was relatively well-behaved outside of a few drunks. With the help of first-aid staffers and Red Rocks security, the ungovernable incidents were toned down. A metro SWAT team was called in at 10 p.m. but remained outside the venue. The stage barricades were too high for kids to vault, and there was no "mosh pit" in front. But Slayer still had its share of crowd-control problems.

"Some of these people just don't know how to restrain themselves," King demurred. "The thing I hate most is when they start throwing things or spitting. Why do that to people you've paid money to see? It's degrading, the most ungrateful thing."

Serving up his 1970s hit songs to rowdy kids in 1991 and 1992, Steve Miller cited the Red Rocks audience as his drunkest.

"The majority of the audience is so young, we have a little bit of a hard sell on a few things," Miller explained. "They love trotting along with the songs on my *Greatest Hits* record, and if the set doesn't go in the order of the album, they're not sure why. The whole joint's too noisy—it's not the right atmosphere to play something new. It's 'Fuck you!' and they go get a hot dog—and the show goes *phfttt*."

Red Rocks had become a mecca for artists wanting something different for recording and filming; in 1991, the Stray Cats' Brian Setzer did a Budweiser commercial on stage with the "guitar granny." The city developed a master plan to carry Red Rocks into the next century, emphasizing the growing demand for more restrooms, merchandising points of sale, food and beverage locations and standard amenities. Improvements included re-covering the stage surface, widening the backstage roads, revamping the catering and crew areas and renovating the artists' dressing rooms by assimilating some of the ancient rocks.

ARTISTIC INSPIRATION

The sandstone temple's otherworldly magic routinely elicits exceptional performances and singular portraiture.

Go-Go's, 1982

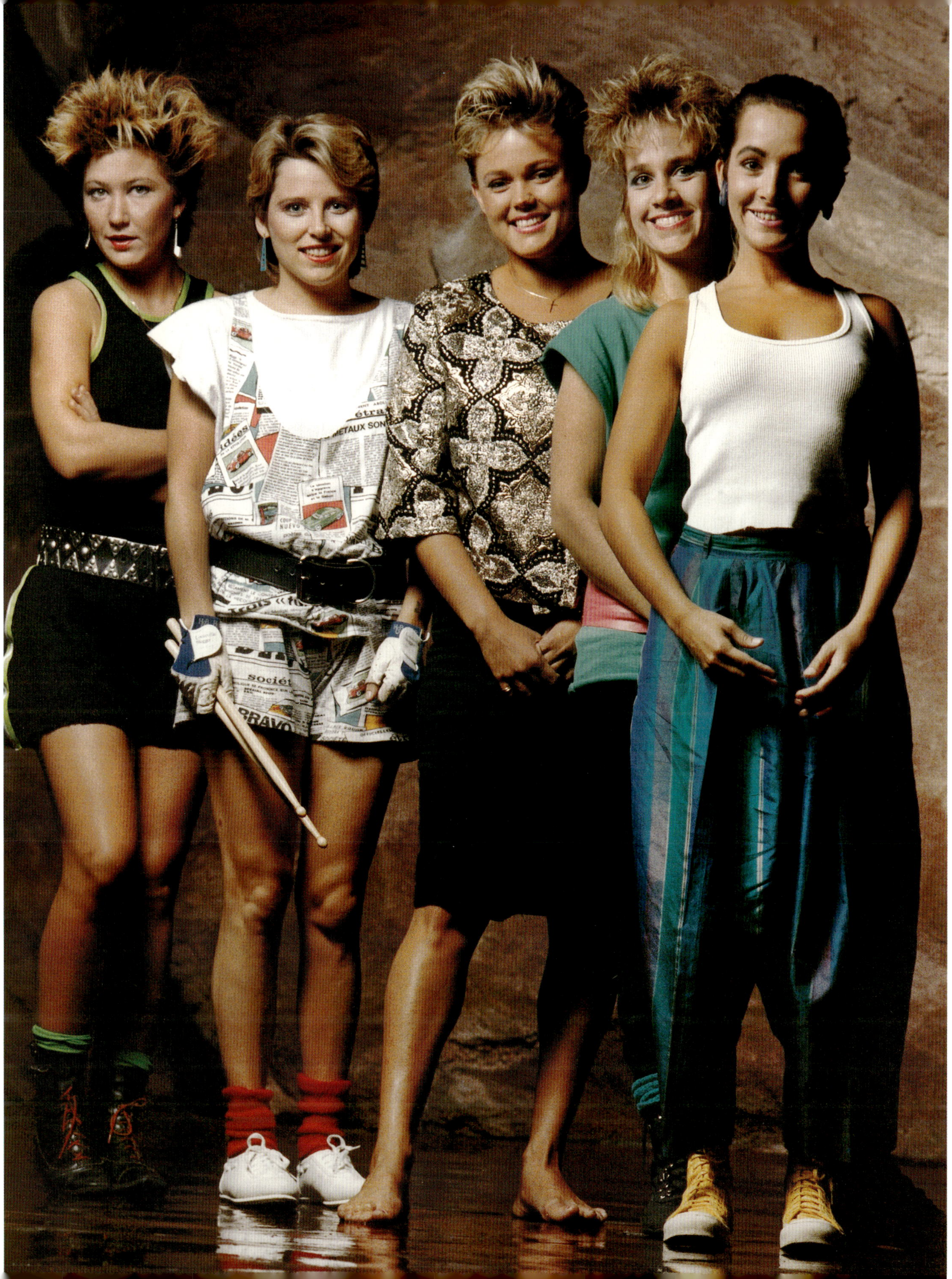
BRAVO

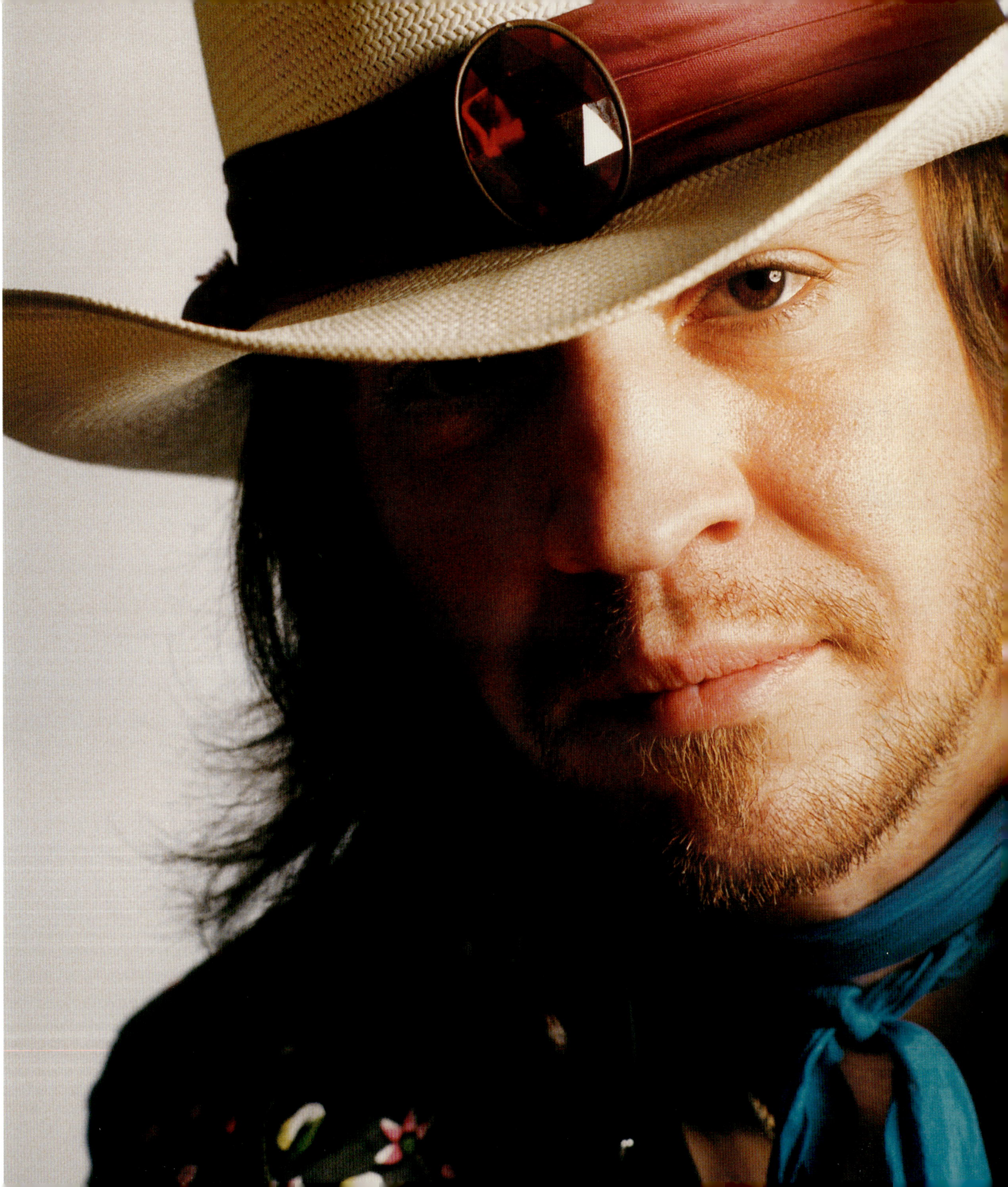

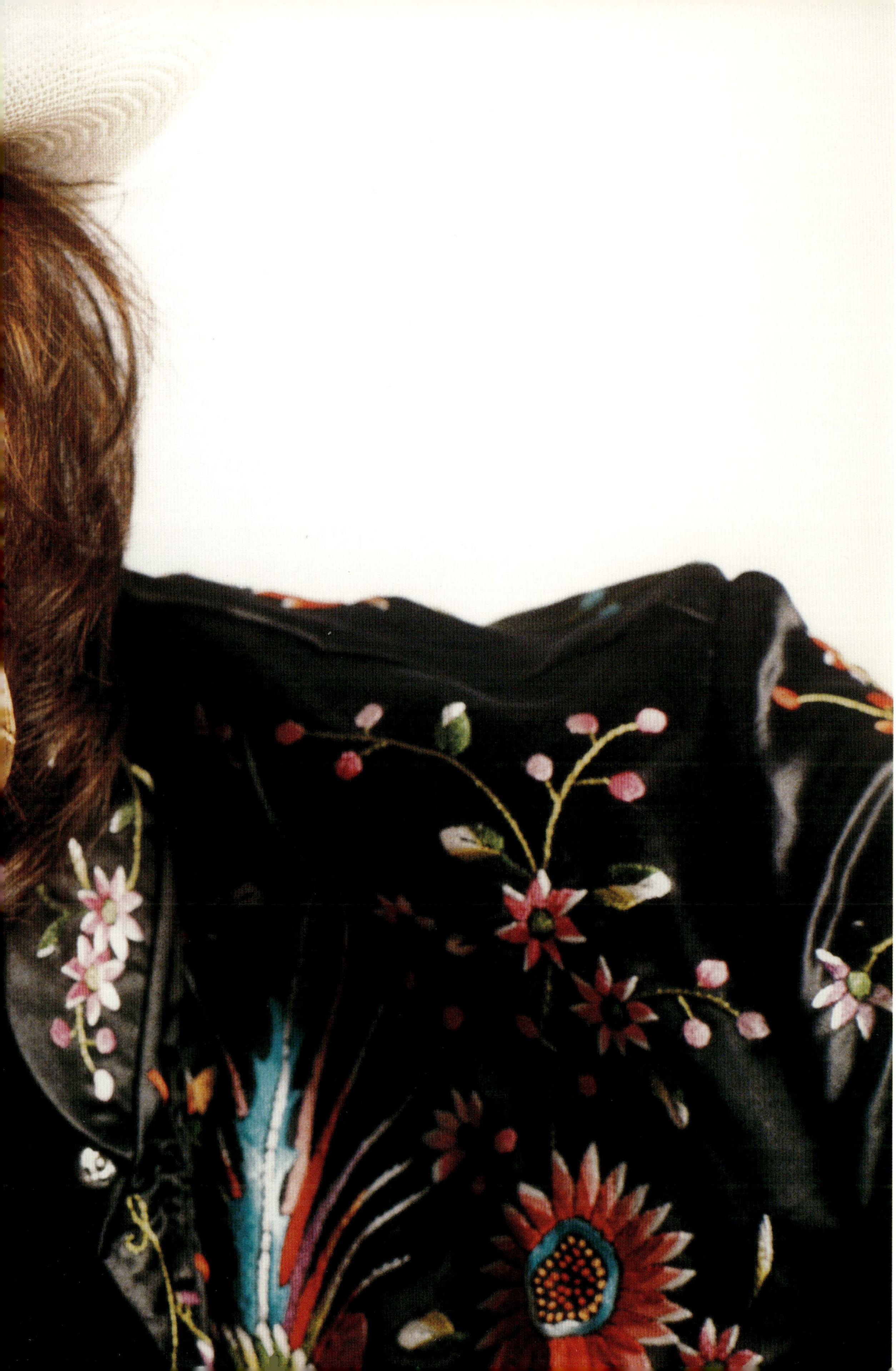

Stevie Ray Vaughan, 1985

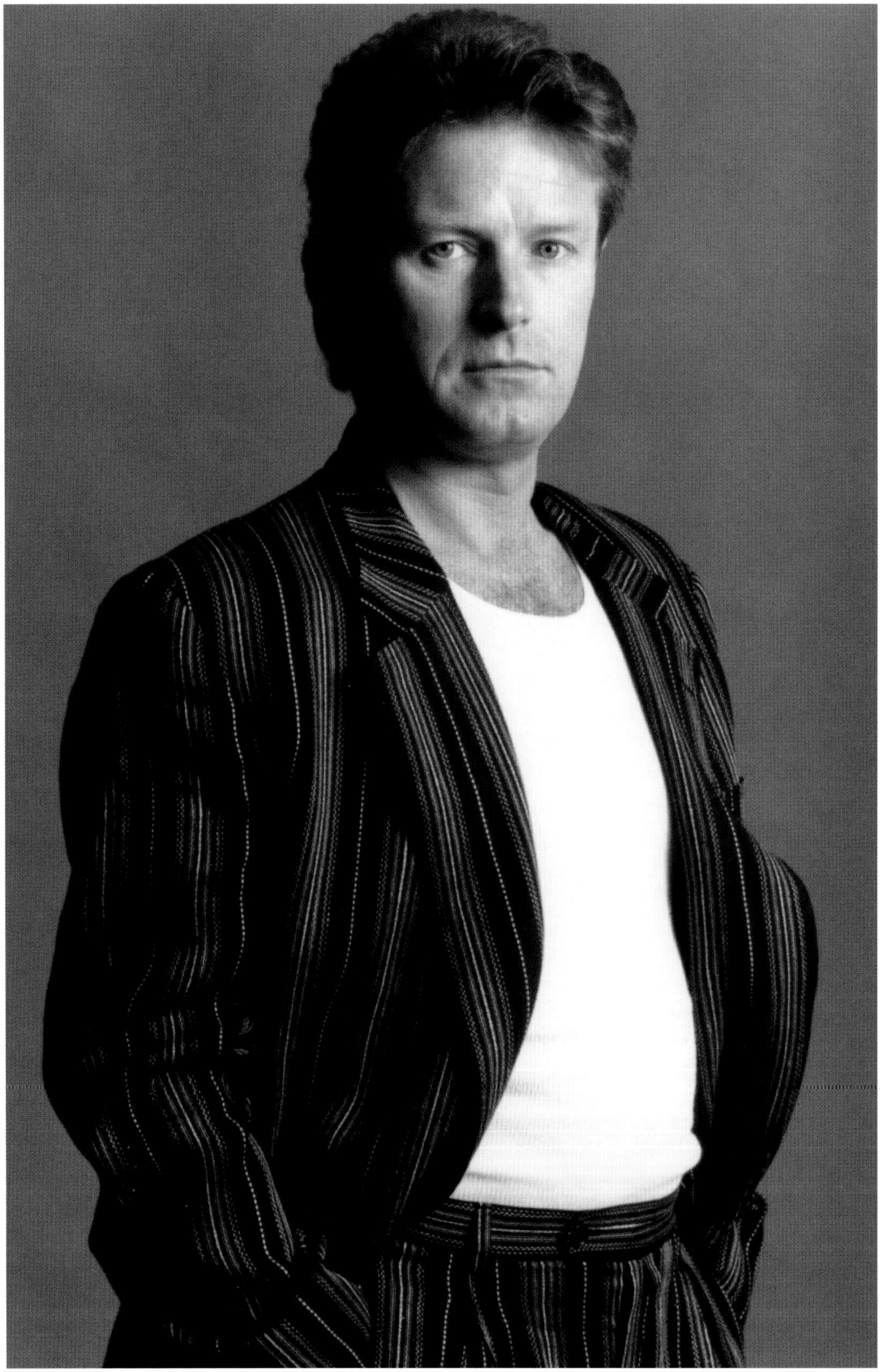

Don Henley, 1985; Billy Idol, 1984 (right)

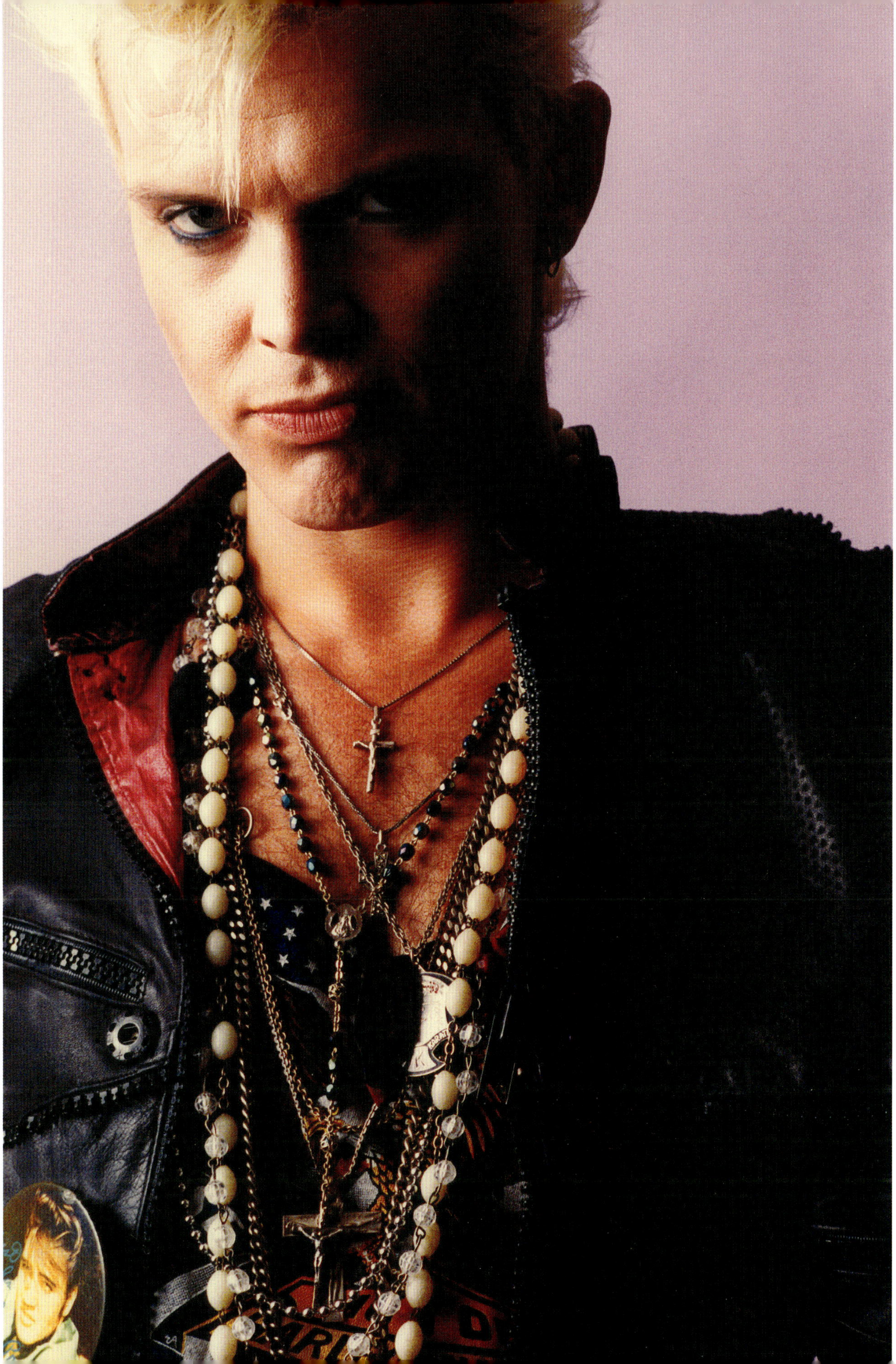

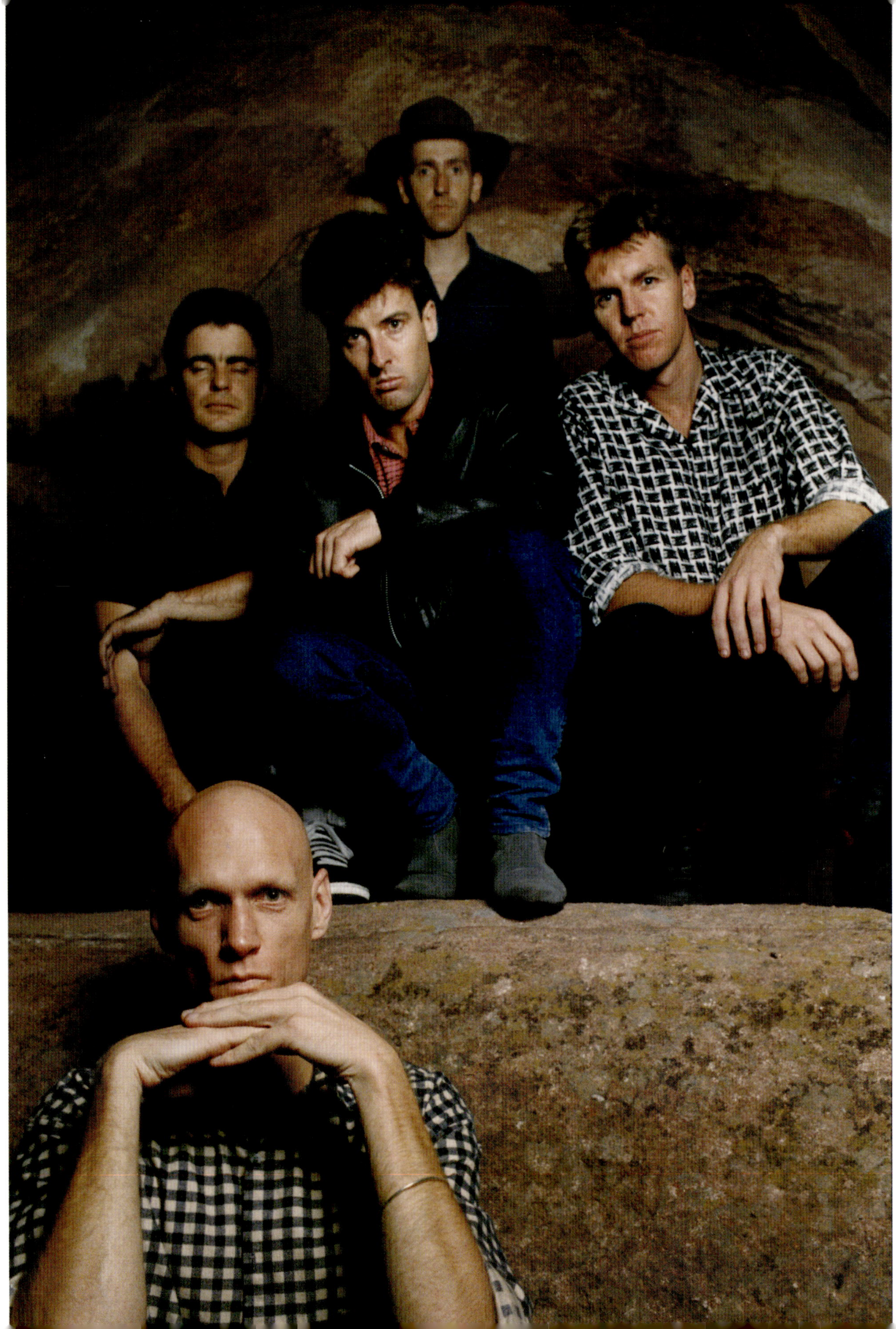

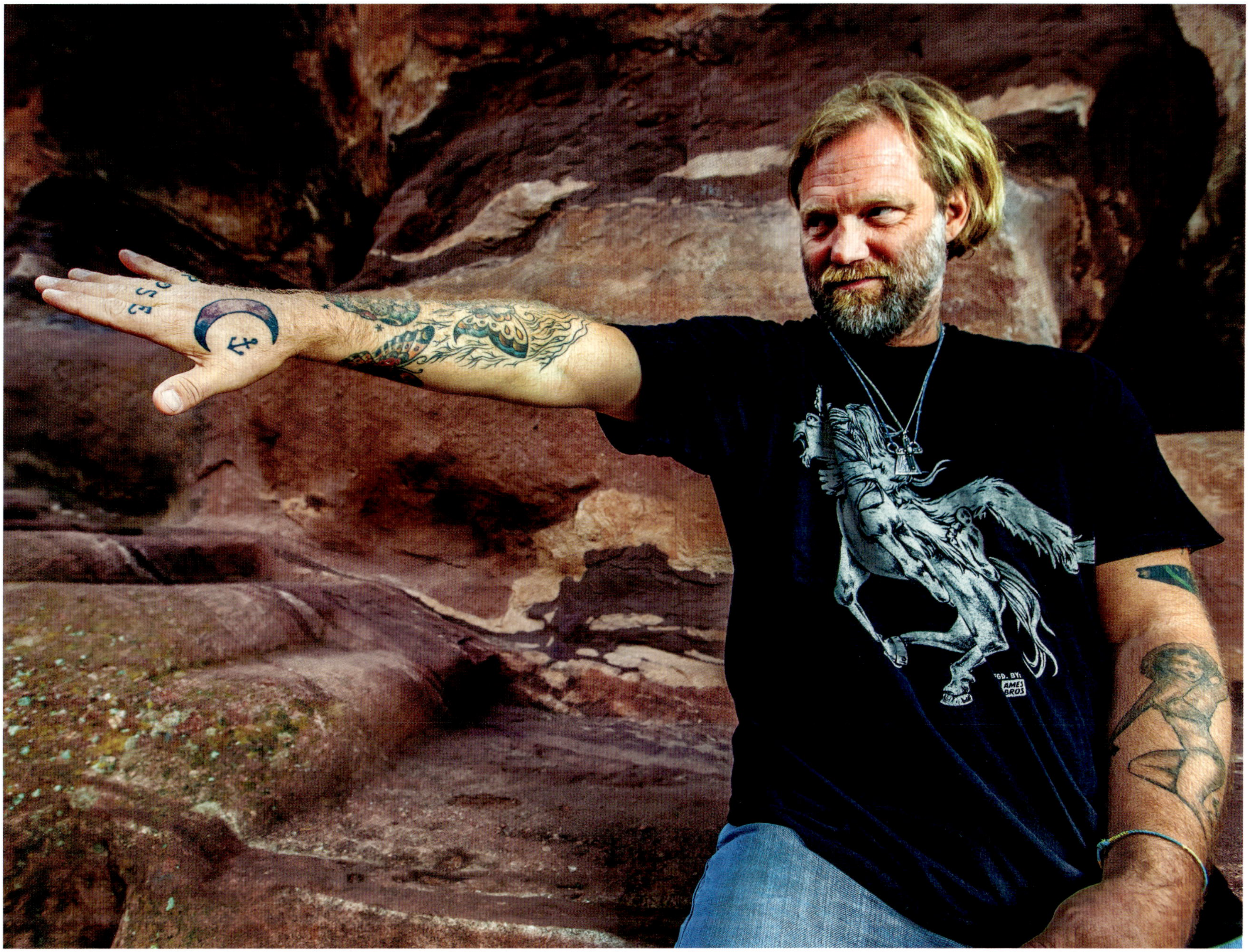

Midnight Oil, 1985 (left); Anders Osborne, 2013

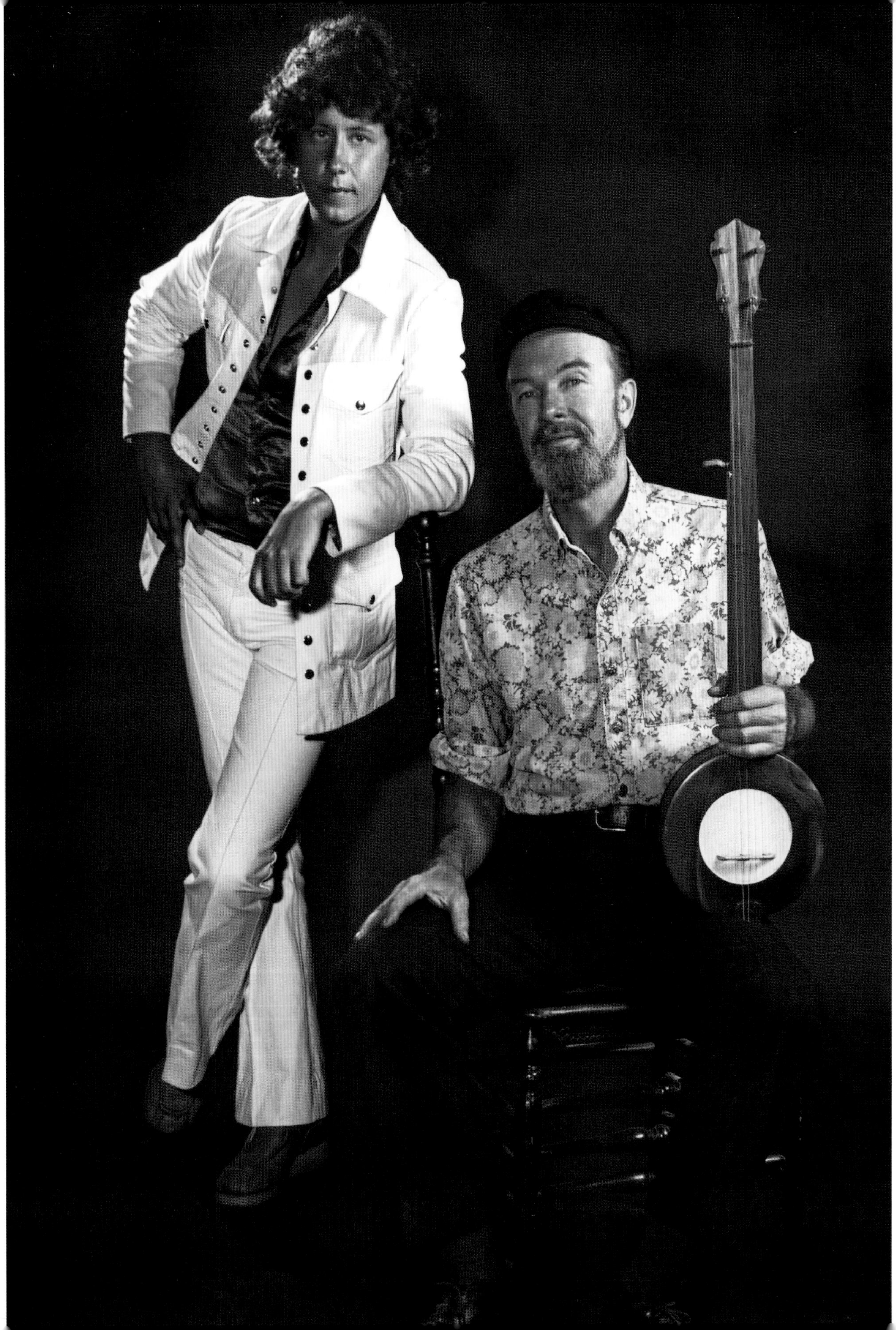

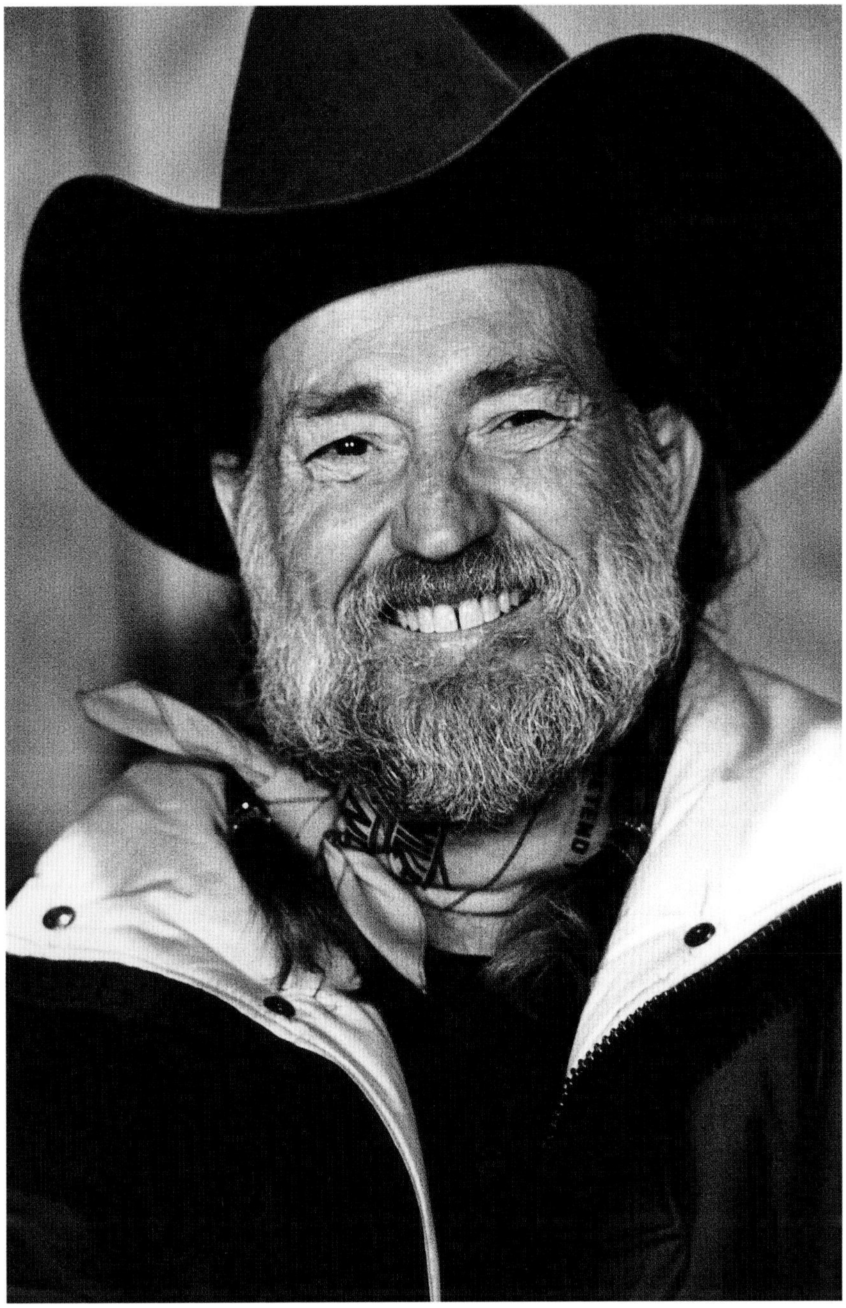

Arlo Guthrie and Pete Seeger, 1969 (left); Willie Nelson, 1982

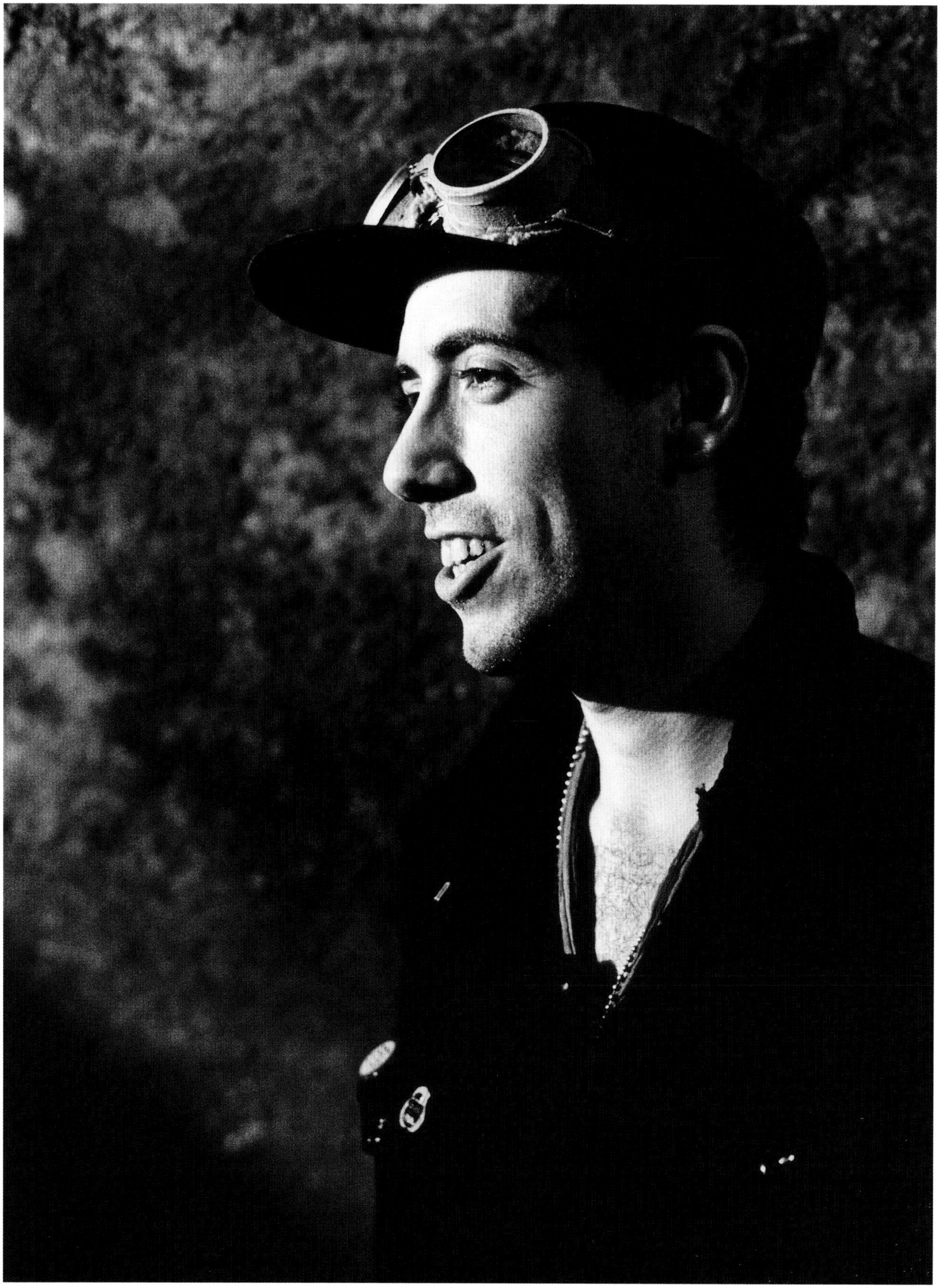

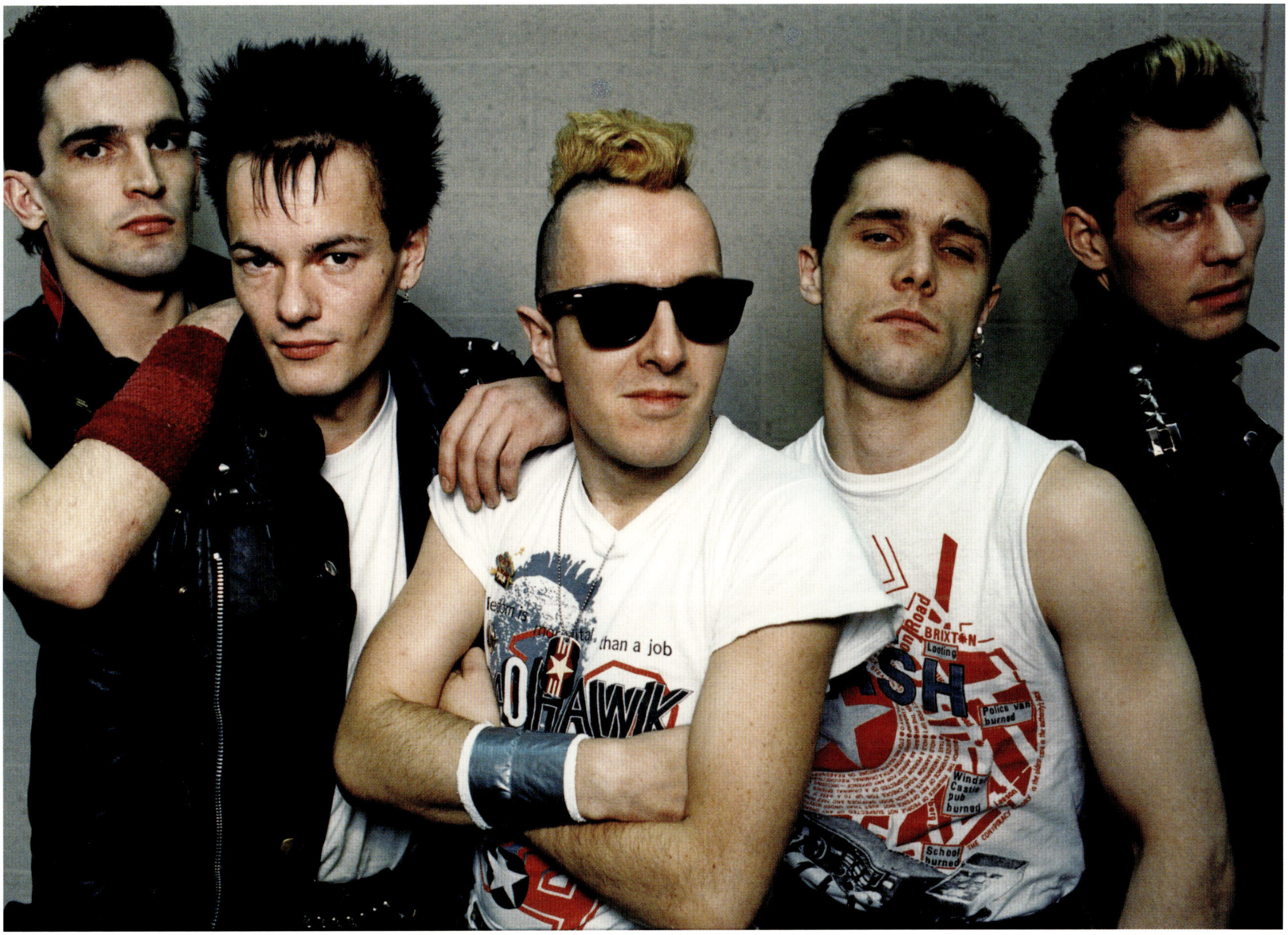

Mick Jones of the Clash, 1982 (left); the Clash, 1984

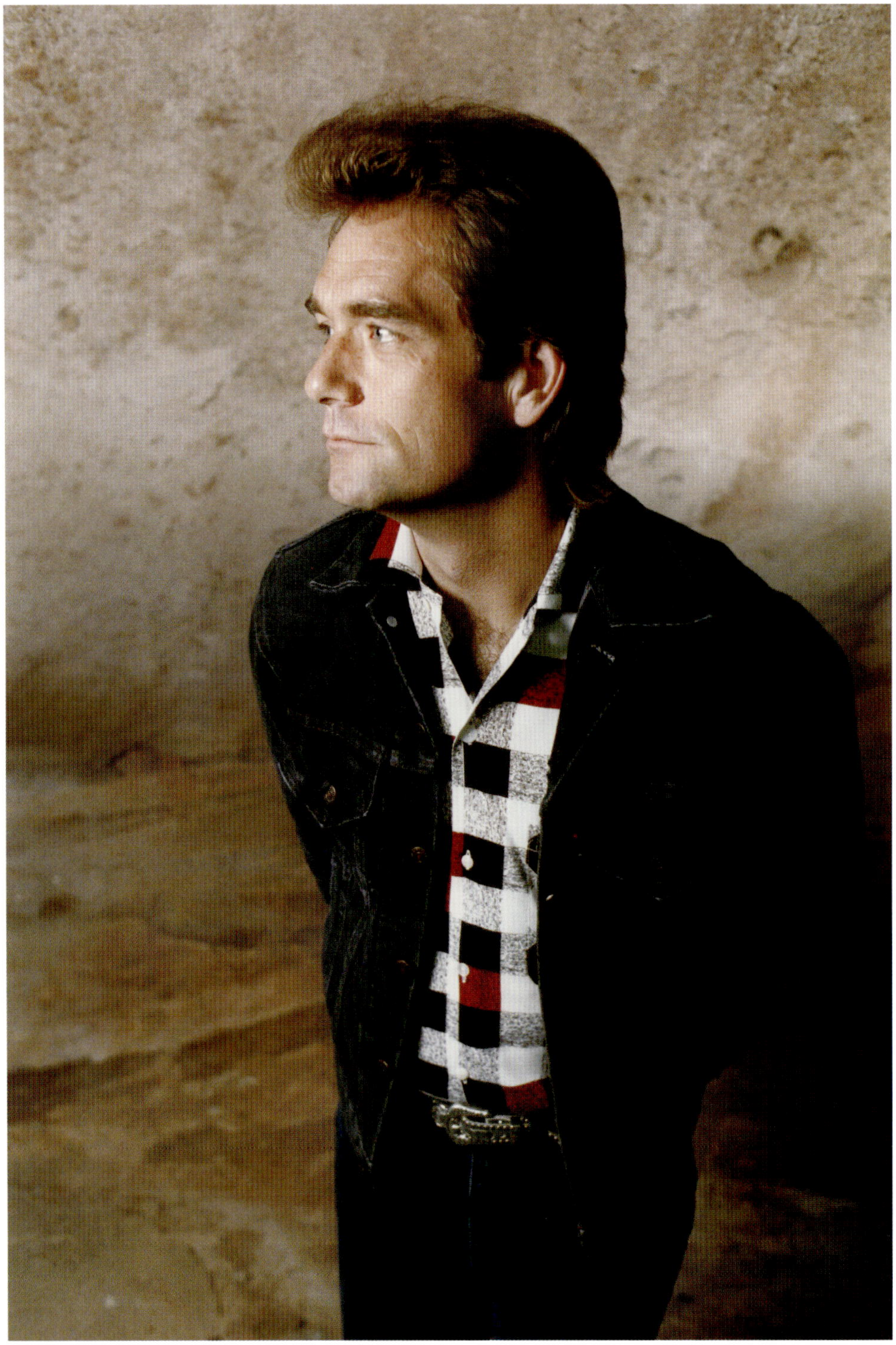

Huey Lewis, 1985; Sting, 1985 (right)

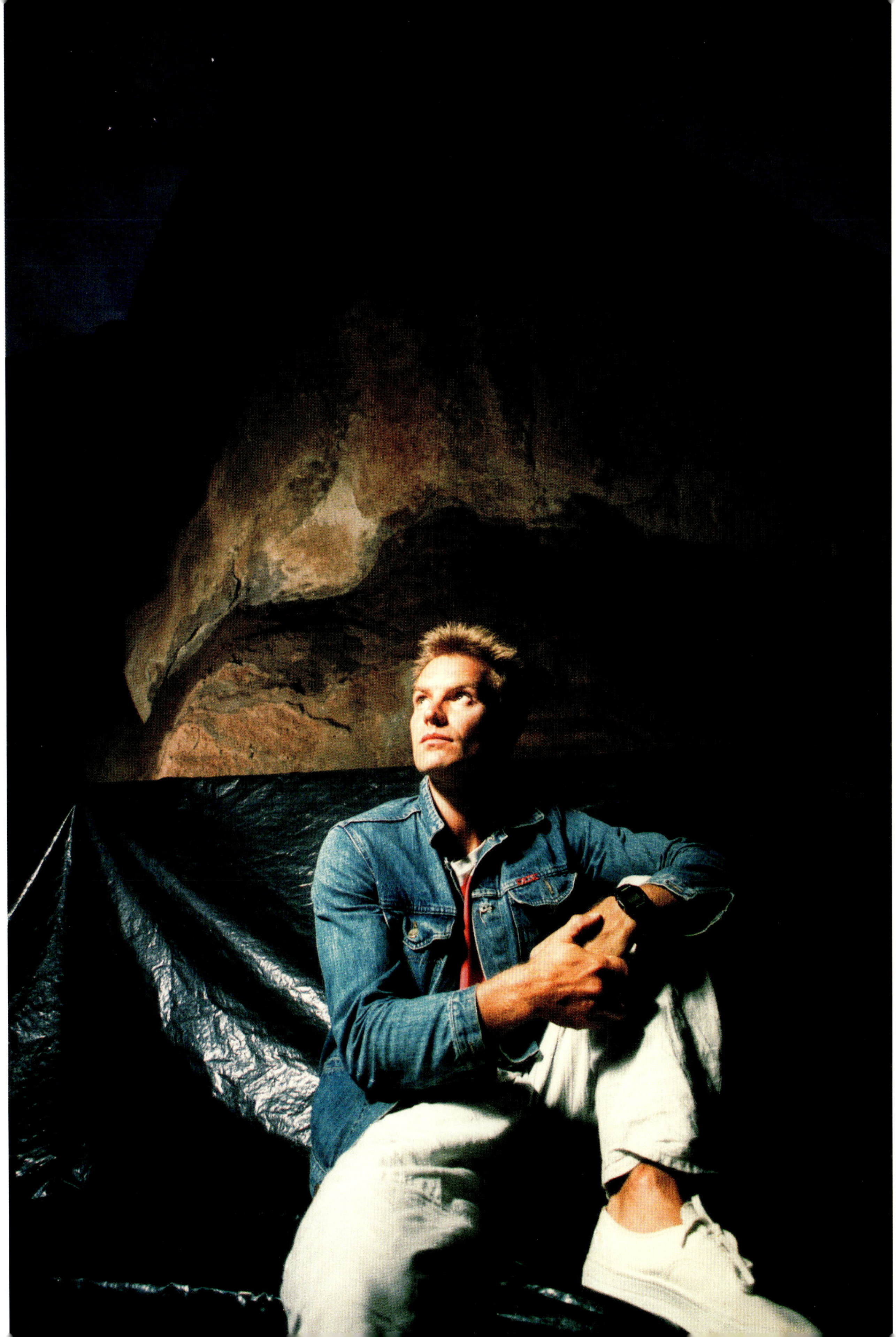

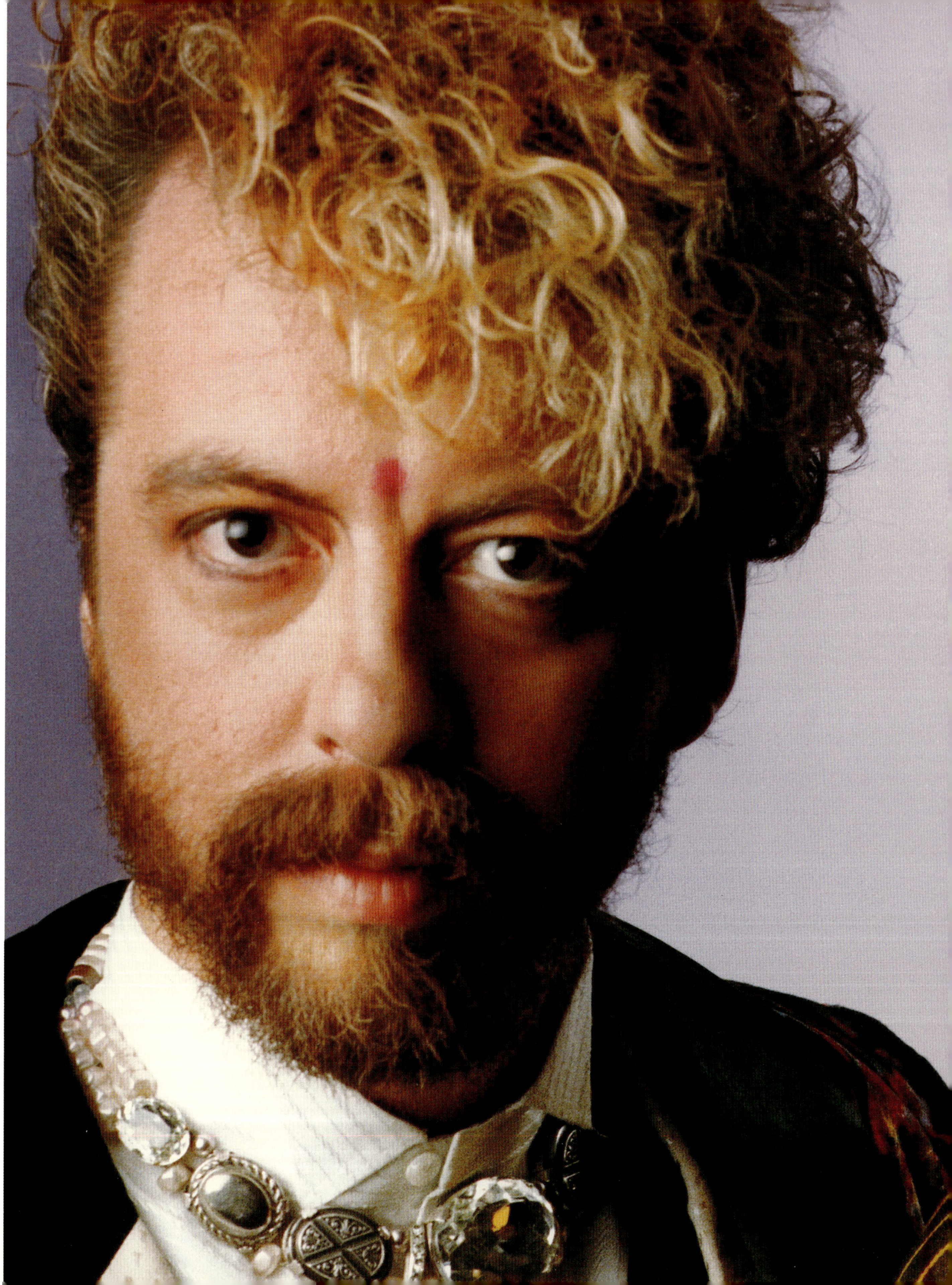

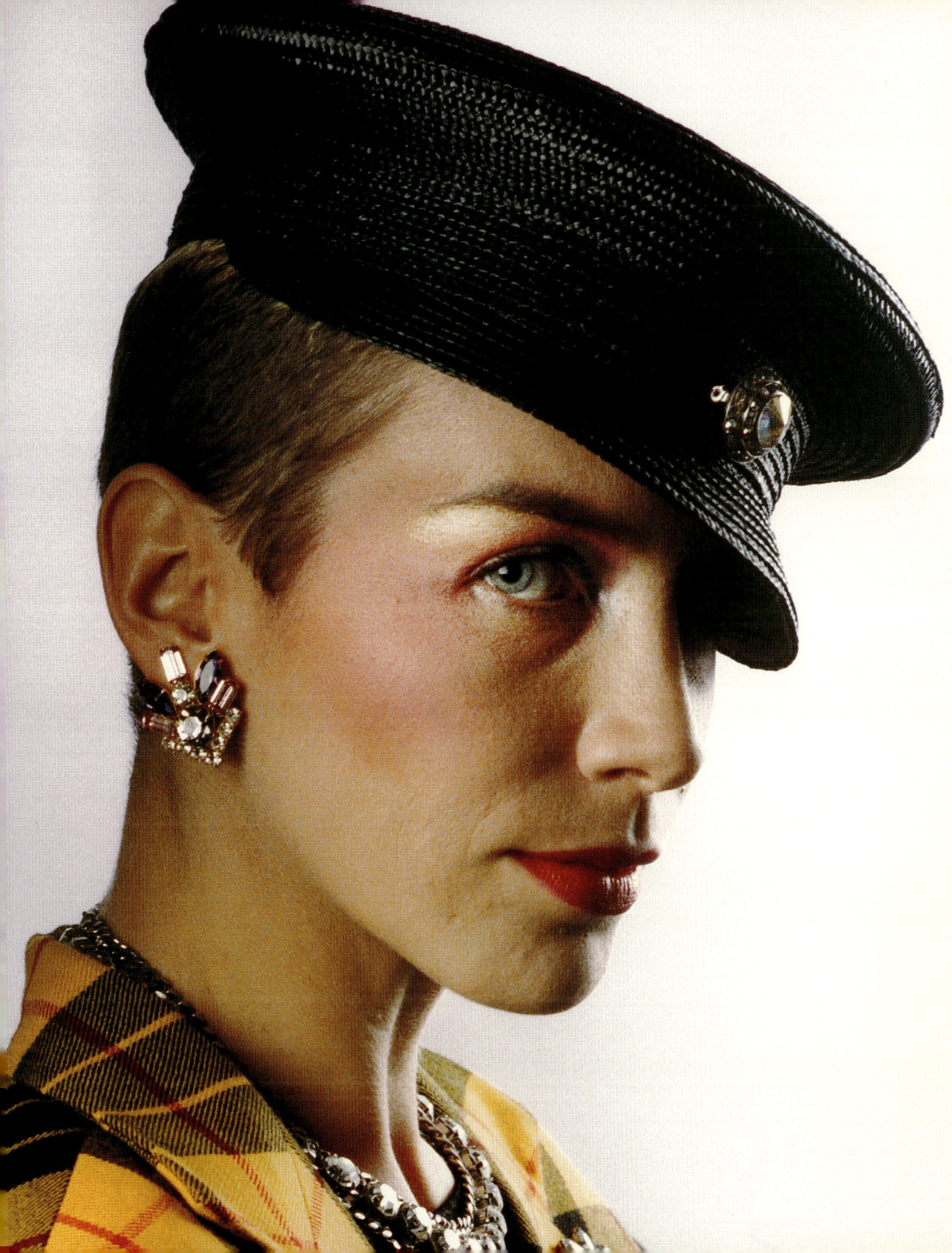

Eurythmics, 1984

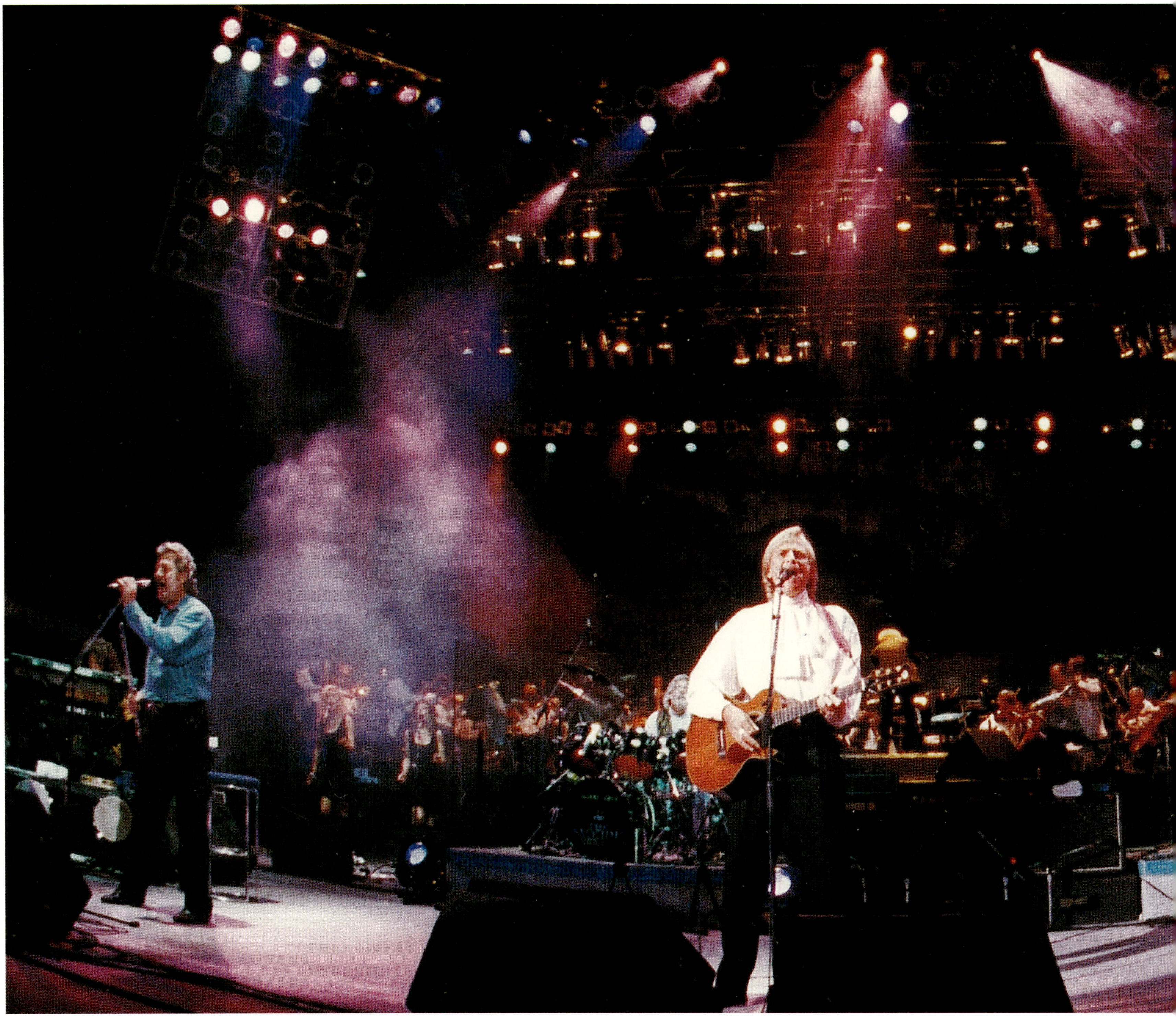

The Moody Blues with the Colorado Symphony Orchestra, 1992

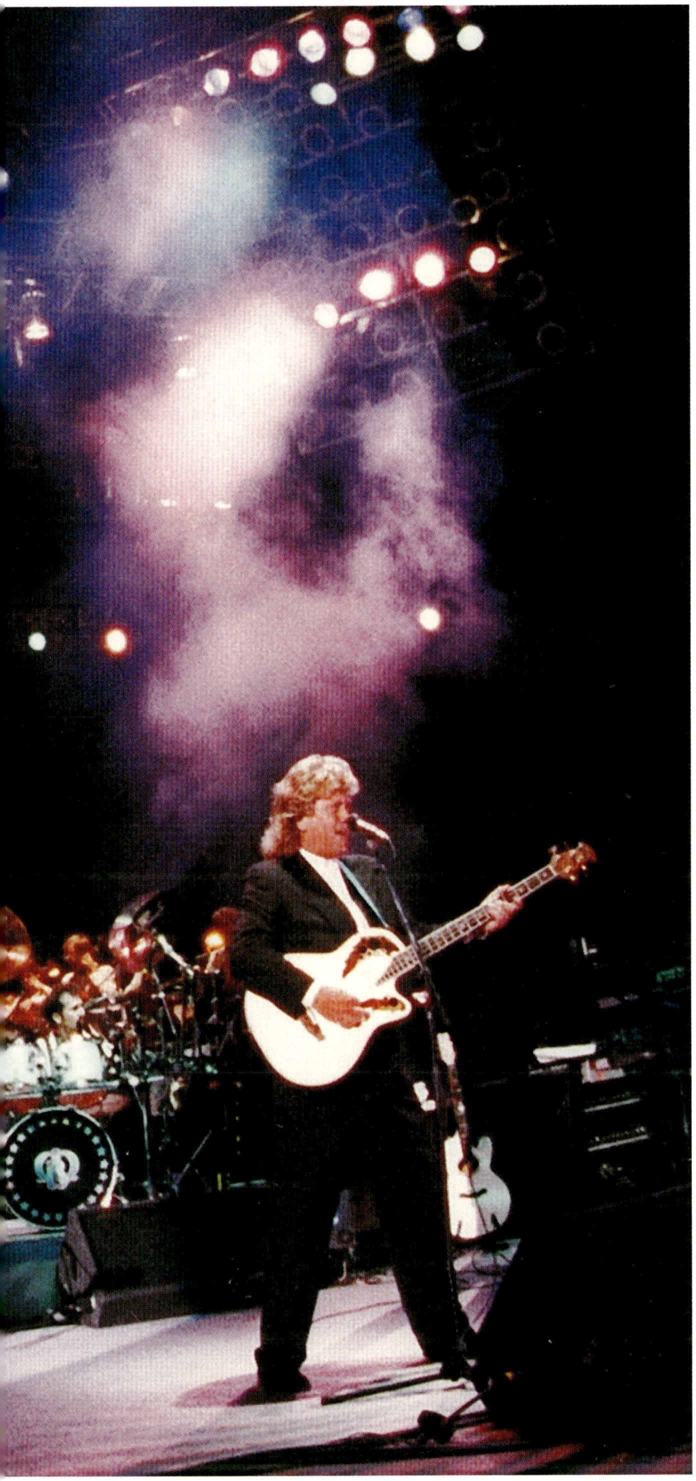

1992-1995

SYMPHONIES AND STARS

At Red Rocks Amphitheatre on September 9 and 10, 1992, the Moody Blues debuted a concept to celebrate the 25th anniversary of *Days of Future Passed*. Recorded in 1967, that landmark album featured the classics "Nights in White Satin" and "Tuesday Afternoon," as well as the talents of the London Symphony Orchestra in what came to be regarded as the first blending of rock music with orchestral accompaniment. A quarter-century later at Red Rocks, the band paired with the Colorado Symphony Orchestra for a live video and album.

"In the absence of a record company revitalizing the achievement of *Days of Future Passed*, we figured we'd do it ourselves," singer-guitarist Justin Hayward explained. "We thought we'd work with an orchestra before a live audience—we'd never done it. And Red Rocks had been a favorite venue of ours—it's a stunning, beautiful setting."

The first night, the Moody Blues recreated their majestic studio sound as originally envisioned. The CSO began by performing an overture of passages from the band's songs. They built to the climax of "Nights in White Satin," then softened. Drummer Graeme Edge entered from the side of the stage and walked to a microphone. As the orchestra played "Late Lament" and he recited the words, "Cold hearted orb that rules the night," the moon shone over Red Rocks like a perfectly placed prop.

The grandeur of the event was matched by rare moments of nerves. Hayward came in too early on part of "Tuesday Afternoon," and Edge later admitted, "I was in such a blue funk that night. Red Rocks was the first time I'd been the drummer for 80-odd people. If all they had was 'tadpoles on washing lines' (sheet music), they were going to stick with that.

"So I was concentrating on staying with the orchestra, really concerned of speeding up or slowing down a little. Most of that concert, the only thing I heard was myself going 'one-two-three-four, one-two-three-four'!"

The evenings resulted in a career moment captured in *A Night at Red Rocks with the Colorado Symphony Orchestra*, a successful album and subsequent PBS television special. In its wake, the Moodies enjoyed another period of great success—the band ranked as one of the decade's top concert draws, playing with orchestras throughout the United States and Europe.

After an August 1992 rainstorm, rocker Melissa Etheridge put on a supercharged show at Red Rocks. "This is one of my favorite

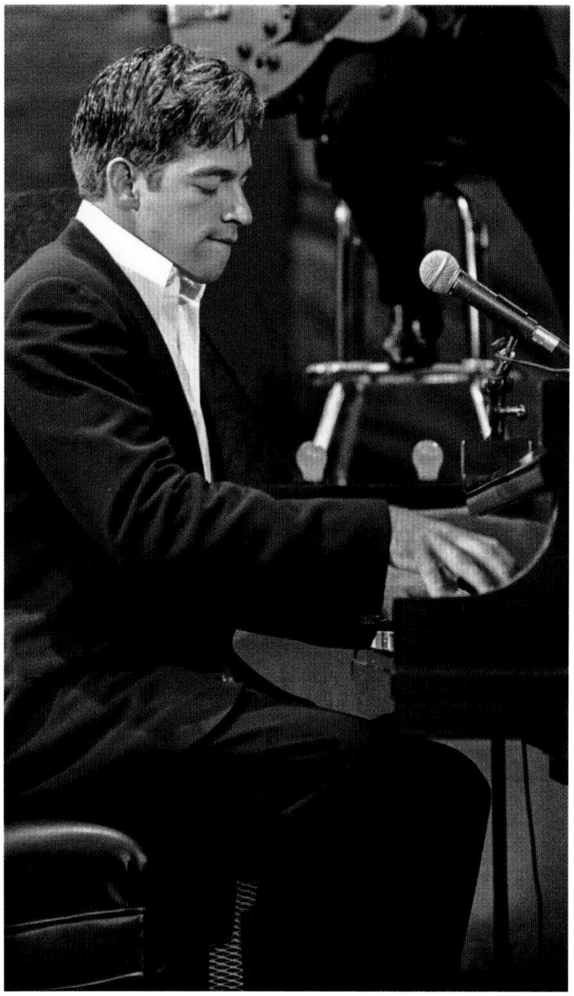

Harry Connick, Jr., 1992;Lyle Lovett, 1993 (right)

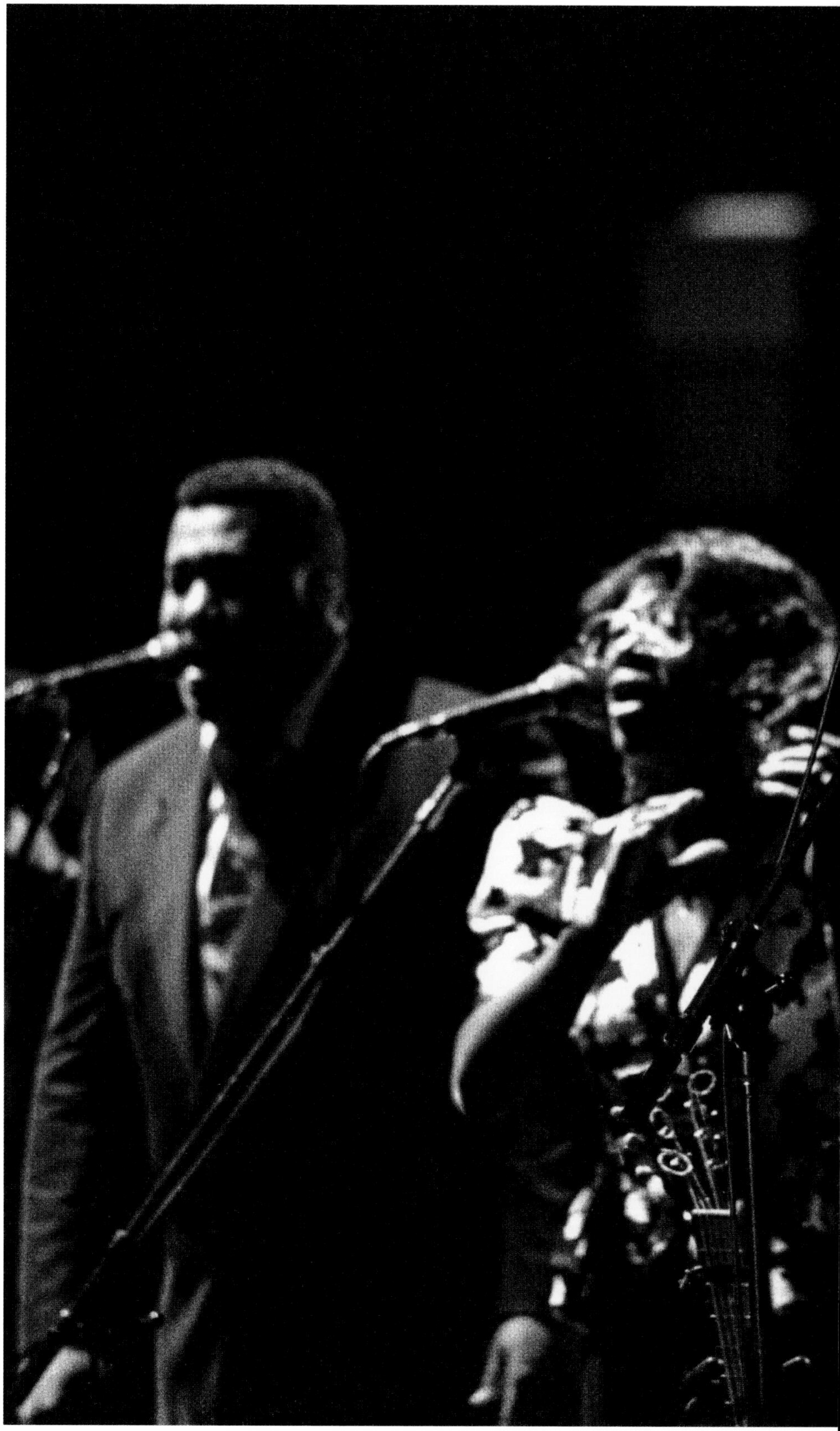

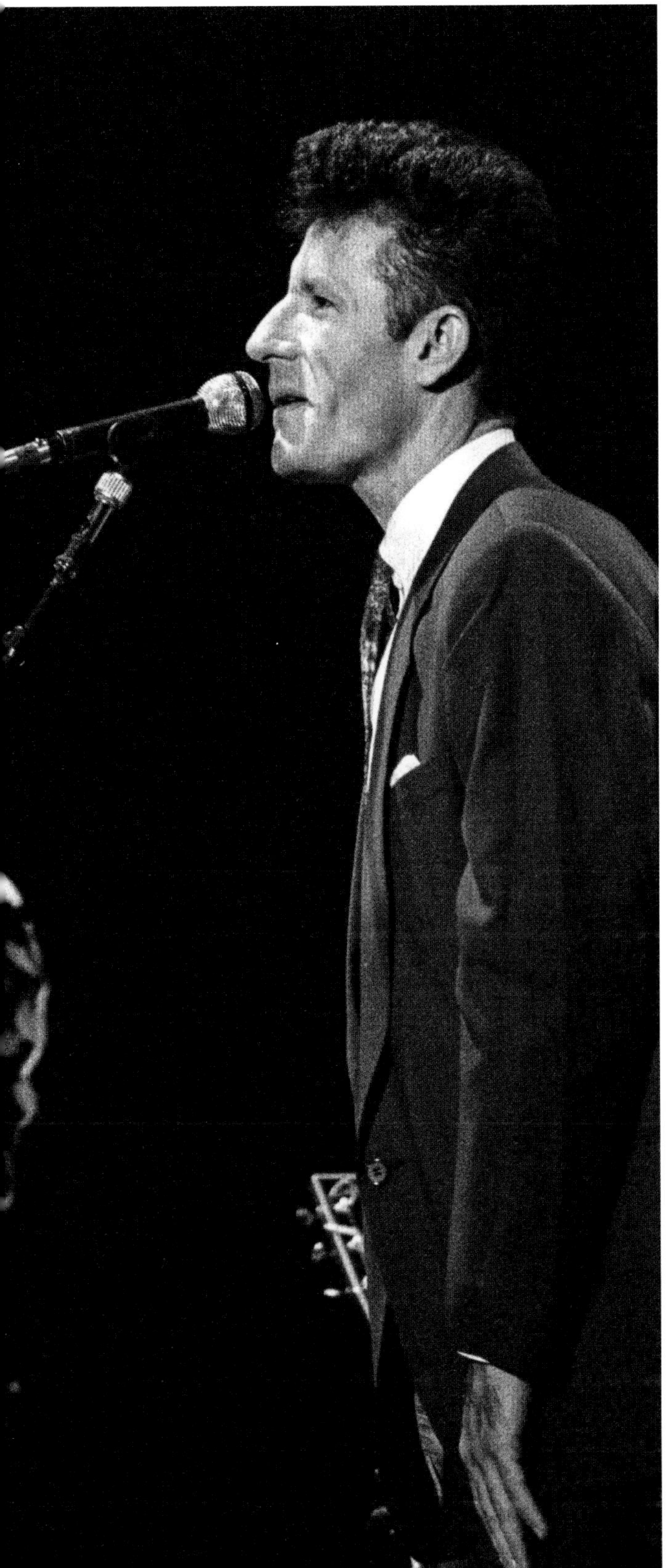

places to play, bugs and everything," she said as she struggled to get an insect out of her eye. "This place is so pretty it makes you want to sing." Etheridge had a sizable lesbian following, and women threw their bikini tops and jogging bras on stage. "They don't do that for me," lamented opening act Jeffrey Gaines.

On his "No More Tours" trek in 1992, Ozzy Osbourne took the Red Rocks stage during a torrential rainstorm and immediately dumped a cooler of water over his head to get right in there with the drenched crowd. "Now we're even," he crowed. Osbourne performed "Changes" backed by Zakk Wylde on piano, and a live performance clip of the ballad hit MTV the following year.

Harry Connick Jr.'s wit and showman's instincts made his debut performance at Red Rocks look effortless; he likened the venue to Adventureland at Disney World.

Jill Sobule, a Denver native, returned to Colorado to open for Crosby, Stills & Nash. "My record company wouldn't put out money to tour this summer," she said. "My manager also manages Crosby, Stills & Nash, so I begged him—'Can I play the Red Rocks date? It's my dream!'"

The headline act on the H.O.R.D.E. (Horizons of Rock Developing Everywhere) festival appearance in 1993 was Blues Traveler, a group that emerged from the vanguard of jam bands to become a Fourth of July fixture at Red Rocks, interrupted only in 1999 when frontman John Popper was hospitalized.

"It began on the 3rd and Fourth of July with the Allman Brothers Band in 1992," guitarist Chan Kinchla recalled. "Of course, we'd heard of Red Rocks—my first experience was watching U2's famous 'Sunday Bloody Sunday' video on MTV when I was a kid. But from the very beginning of the band, we had great support in Colorado, way before we had any following at all in the rest of the country. Even before we played with the Allman Brothers, we went there and just putzed around on the stage and pretended we could be playing a show there. To us, the people are just as incredible as the venue. It's such a great high-energy, open, rocking crowd of really mixed, diverse people. The opportunity to play there so many years in a row is just insane to me, something I'm thankful for.

"After we opened for the Allman Brothers, someone said, 'When the fireworks come, we've got to go up to the top.' So a bunch of us climbed all the way up and watched the Allman Brothers with the fireworks crackling in the background. And since then, every year I've been down on the stage playing. When the fireworks start going off, the crowd goes nuts, and it always makes me a little jealous. But I have

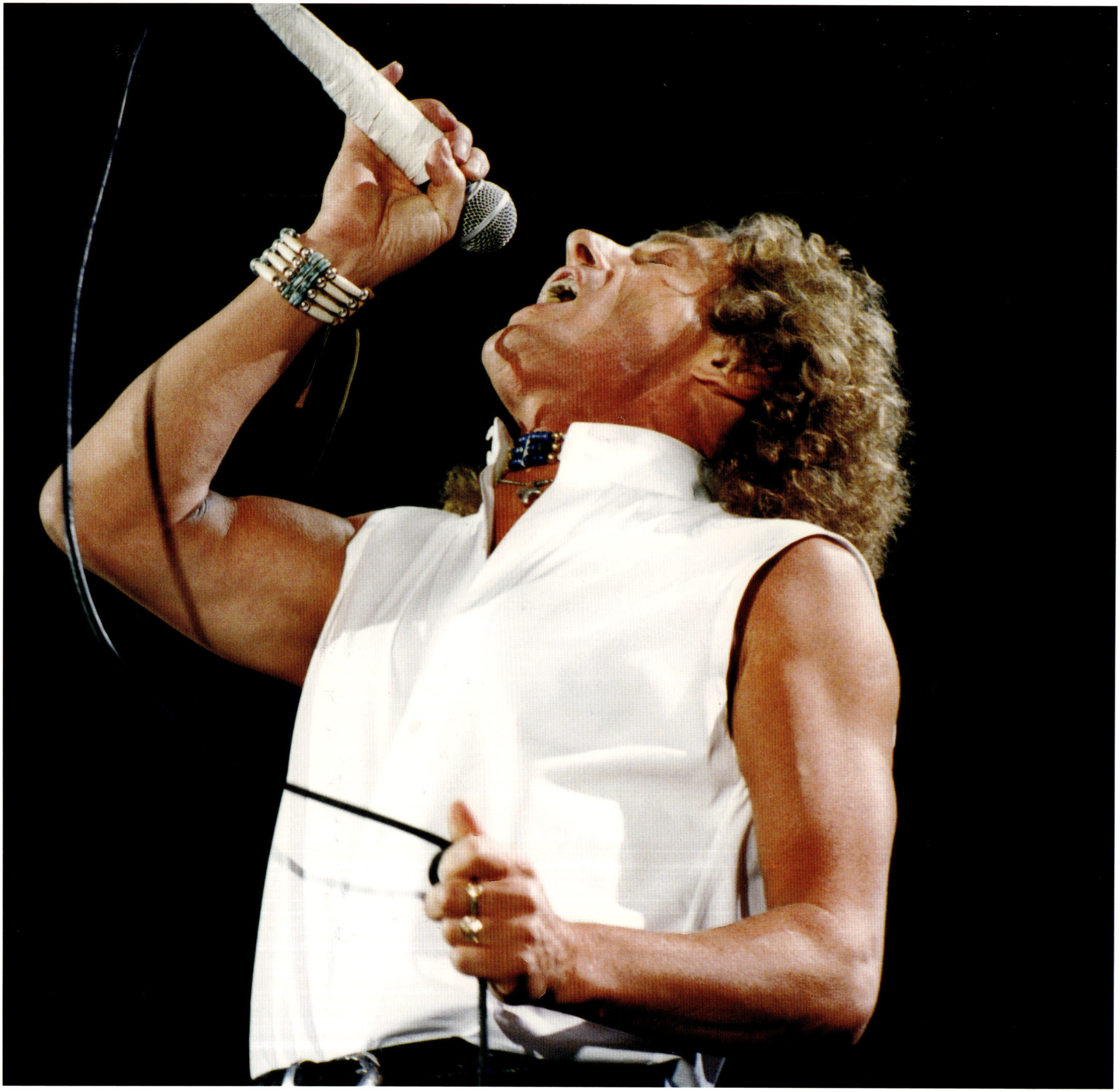

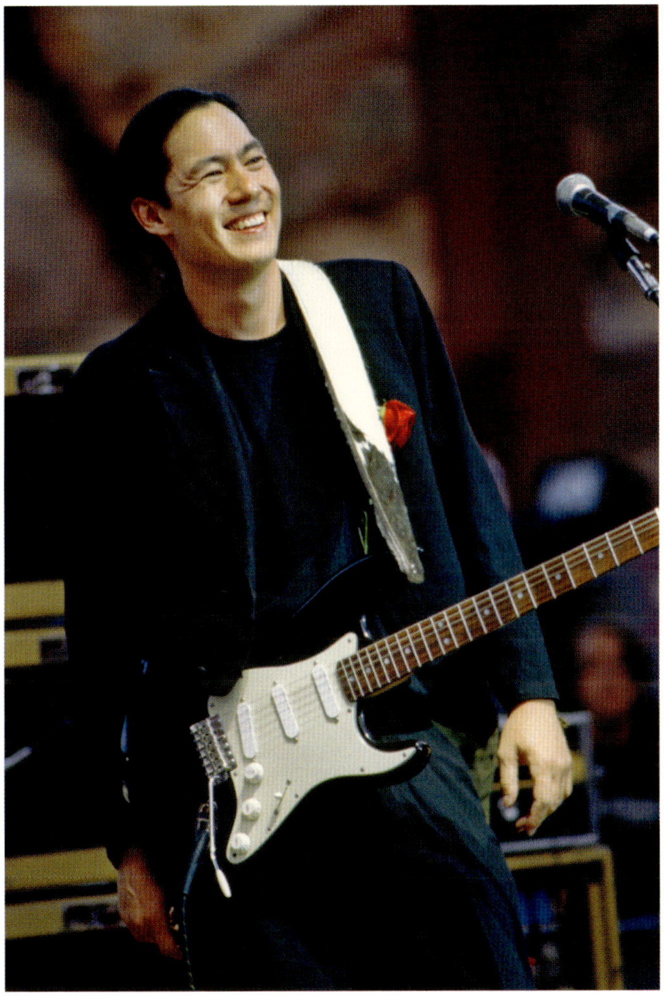

Roger Daltrey, 1994 (left); Big Head Todd & the Monsters, 1993

that memory—I know what they're screaming about!"

Lyle Lovett had been married to actress Julia Roberts in the summer of 1993, and celebrity junkies went bonkers when a willowy blonde in a dress introduced Lovett's Red Rocks show. It was his personal assistant in drag, and the singer-songwriter and his band took the stage to a tape of "The Crying Game."

"There is something about the majesty of the place that inspires everybody who works there—they are so proud to be associated with Red Rocks," Lovett mused. "That kind of spirit is a nice thing to see. It's obvious that it's beautiful, but when you talk to the people who take care of it, you really see that it means something to them. How great would it be if the whole world felt that way about their jobs?"

That year, Crosby & Nash performed with the Colorado Symphony Orchestra at Red Rocks. "The beautiful journey to Red Rocks is insane," Graham Nash said. "And then you stand on that stage and you're faced with those gigantic rocks on each side—to play those songs in that setting with that orchestra is totally unique. I'll never forget it."

The opening of the 1994 Summer of Stars was special because Colorado had never had local heroes on the scale of Big Head Todd & the Monsters. The band played two sold-out shows at Red Rocks—the first was cold and wet, but the sweet "thanks for coming" at the finish made it all worthwhile. Frontman Todd Mohr said performing at Red Rocks was overwhelming—he was in the audience when U2 had graced the same stage eleven years earlier, during its iconic *Under a Blood Red Sky* performance.

"It's great to see a show at Red Rocks, but to play a show here is a different story," Mohr said. "It's not big relative to some other places, 9,000 people or so. But the way it's laid out is menacing—everybody's stacked right on top of you. It's an intimidating, overwhelming, awesome experience."

Ticket sales were slow for Roger Daltrey's performance at Red Rocks, but the Who singer's project had the merit of a live 60-piece local orchestra; the *Quadrophenia* material filled the venue with an awesome power.

"Concertsonics" was an experimental stereo broadcast of celebrated British band Yes' show at Red Rocks—a special mix was beamed direct from the stage to headphones and Walkman-type FM receivers. The regular sound system unfortunately overpowered the mix.

The speed and brutality of metal music surely irritated the hell out of moms and dads; to them, it was the sound of a chain being put down a disposal. But there was an audience that did "hear" the fist-in-the-face noise, and Pantera, Sepultura and Prong offered plenty

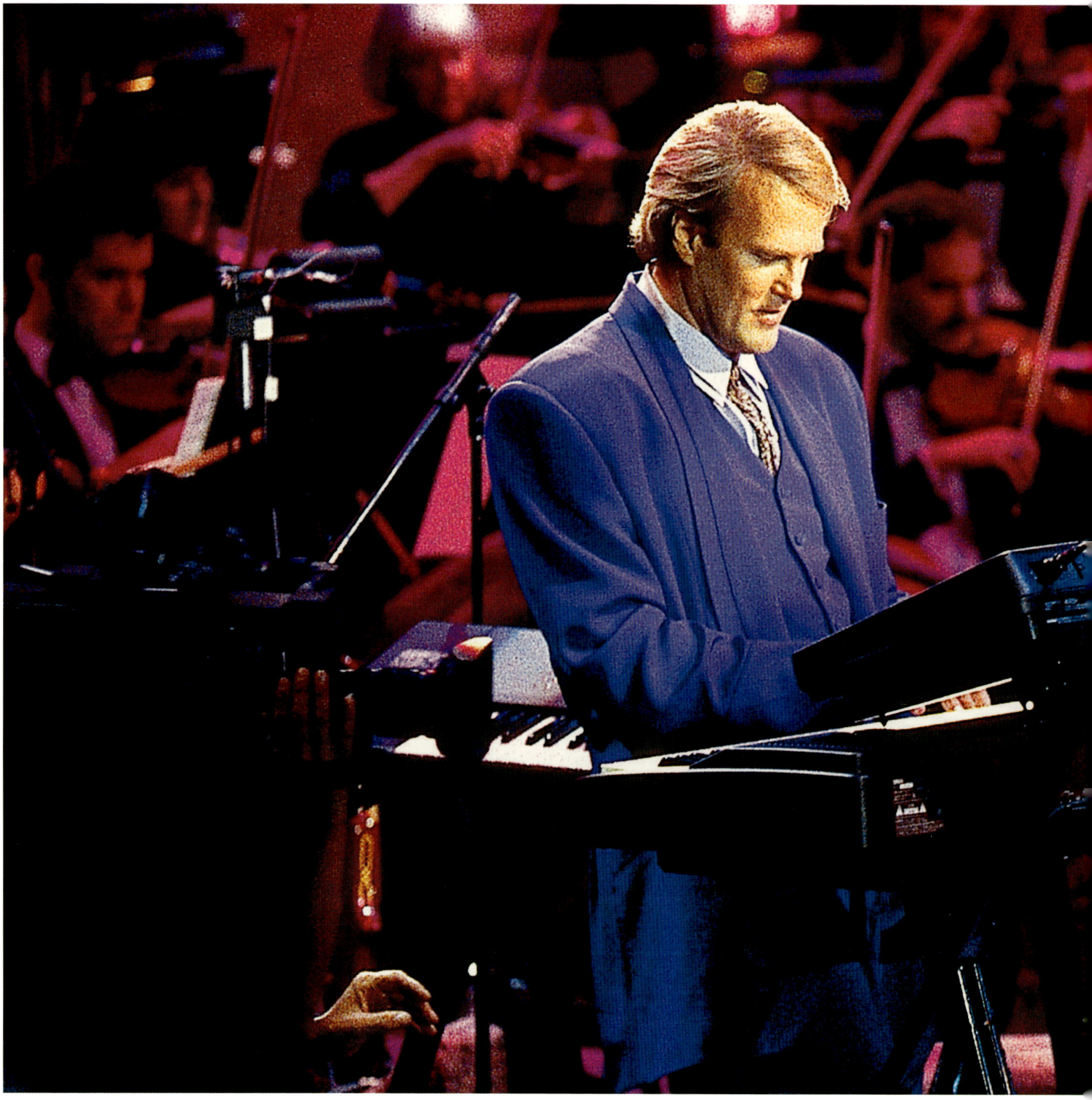

John Tesh with the Colorado Symphony Orchestra, 1994

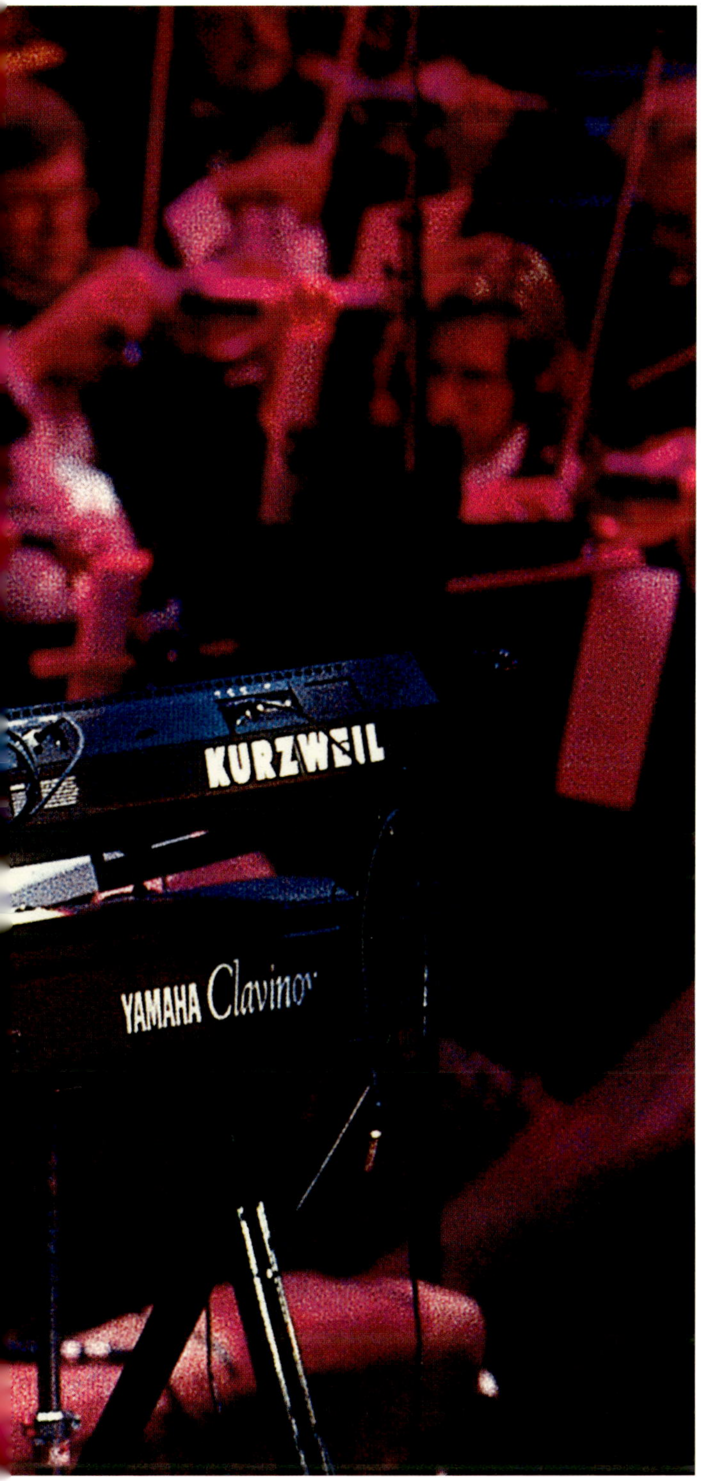

of cheap thrills to a crowd of 6,000 at Red Rocks in 1994.

For 90 minutes, Pantera frontman Phil Anselmo screamed profane lyrics about religion and sex over guitarist Dimebag Darrell's abrasive riffs. A throng of aggressive kids (some actually wearing mouth guards) surged relentlessly, restrained by security. To get pumped up and ready to rage onstage, a rabid Anselmo had worked out and boxed with a sparring partner.

In contrast, drummer Vinnie Paul seemed to be getting downright sentimental before the concert.

"A friend took me up here a while back when we played the Gothic Theatre," he recalled. "It was as the sun was going down, and it was just beautiful. I was like, 'Someday I'm going to play this place.' For our band to move to that level is really an achievement and a lot of dreams come true."

Television made John Tesh an household name when he was the square-jawed co-host on *Entertainment Tonight*. But Tesh daringly left the security of *E.T.* and its seven-figure salary to concentrate on writing and recording music. His breakthrough came when he appeared at Red Rocks in concert with the Colorado Symphony Orchestra on August 18 and 19, 1994.

Tesh gave a "personal tribute to sport and to the athletes who dedicated themselves to competition." Near the beginning, a whole slew of children surfed a massive flag above the heads of the crowd. Dancers and Olympic medalists Nadia Comeneci and Bart Connor performed gymnastic routines specially choreographed to Tesh's music, and volcanic explosions erupted on the sides of the stage. Tesh financed the stage production himself and released the album and video through his own company.

"I didn't want to do the show at Red Rocks," Tesh divulged. "When we got to the business management stage, they had a meeting with me and said, 'You just can't do this. It's absolutely impossible. The orchestra's going to be too expensive and there's a chance of rain—and you can't get rain insurance.' I didn't think we could afford to light the place. The budget increased to $1.5 million.

"But I had seen U2's *Under a Blood Red Sky* video and I knew the Moody Blues had done something there, and I had visited and totally fallen in love with the place—I was sold. Fortunately, my wife (actress Connie Selleca) was really cool with it—it was really a family decision—so I took my TV money and borrowed more money from banks to do it."

Selleca came to town, got altitude sickness and ended up in the hospital. Pianist Tesh and his eight-piece ensemble battled the weather

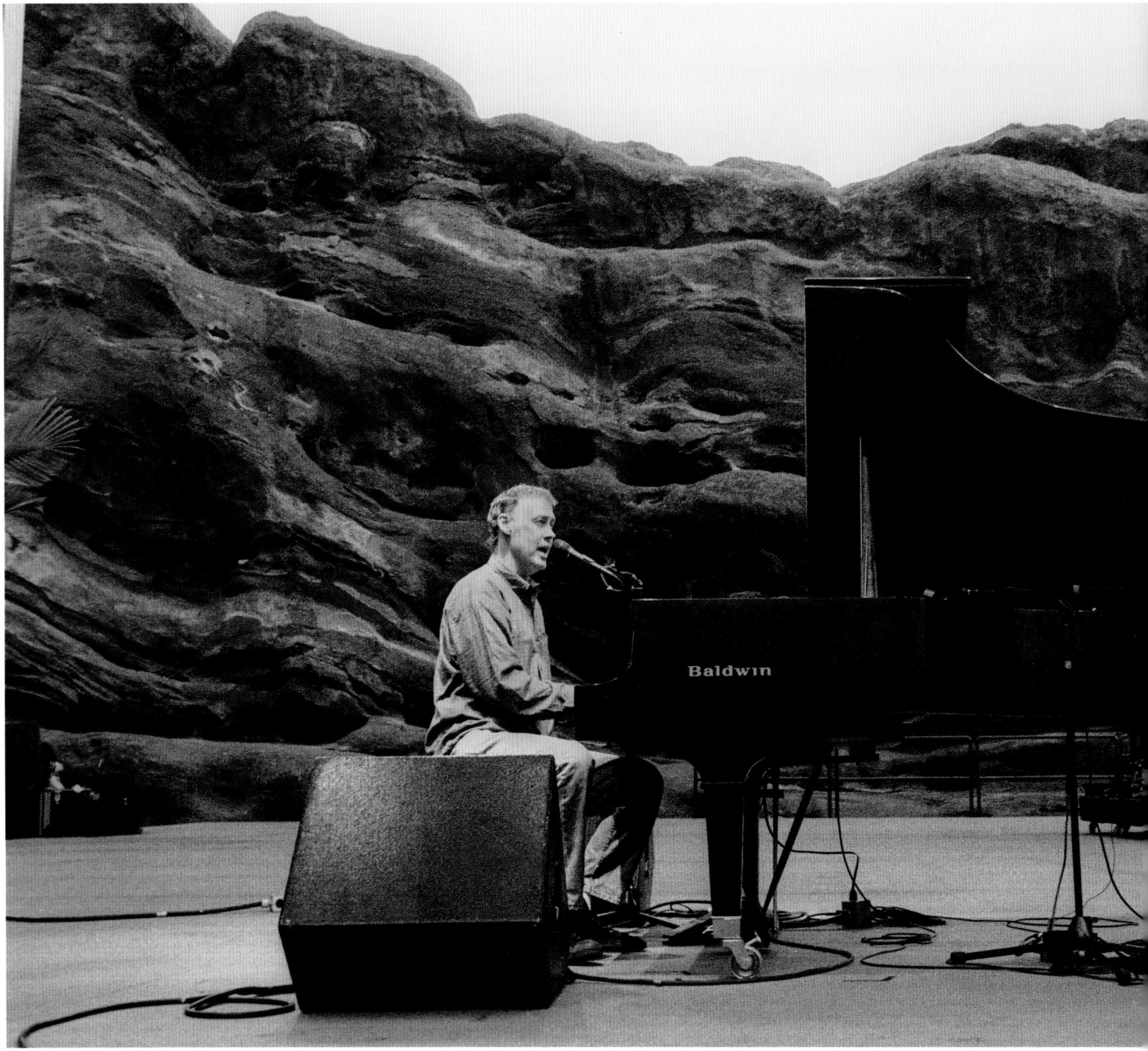

Bruce Hornsby, 1994

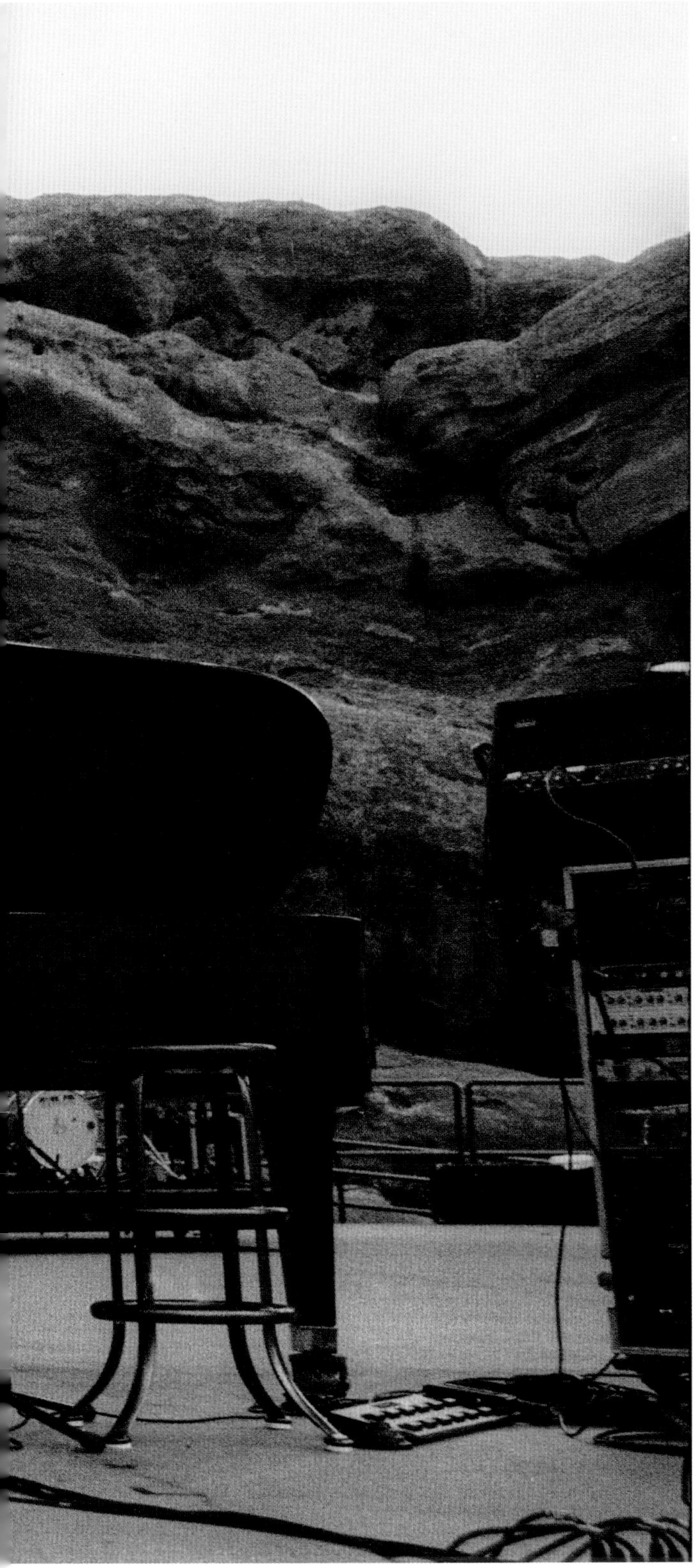

gods during the making of his opus. "Of course, in the middle of the concert, it started pouring. Then, on the second night, the temperature dropped twenty degrees and everything went out of tune. Trying to mix that thing afterward was ridiculous."

First broadcast on PBS stations nationwide in 1995 and repeated endlessly during pledge drives, *John Tesh Live at Red Rocks with the Colorado Symphony Orchestra* was a hugely successful release. The video reached double platinum sales and the attendant album went gold.

Bonnie Raitt got her father, Broadway legend John Raitt, to join her at Red Rocks in 1994 for encores of "They Say It's Wonderful" (from *Annie Get Your Gun*) and "Oklahoma!" "I wanted to show you where I got it from," she told the sold-out crowd.

Backstage, she introduced him as "the high tide of the gene pool," and an admirer asked the 77-year-old about belting out show tunes at altitude. "Anywhere!" he exclaimed, recalling the time he performed *Shenandoah* at Elitch Theatre in northwest Denver with a hole drilled in his impacted sinuses.

His daughter's array of songs, a blend of folk, blues and rock, found her in a reflective mood. But she had to stop "Circle Dance" in mid-song, her crew busting butt to move her out of the wind and rain. She then briefly donned an "I was rained on at the Rocks" orange poncho—"I've never played a blues song in one of these, but I'm a road cone for you, baby!" With the protected stage area shrinking ("I thought I was in a playpen," she said later), she saved a sad, gorgeous encore of Richard Thompson's "Dimming of the Day" for the end of the rain.

The ebullient onstage personality and playing of Bruce Hornsby made him the perfect choice to open for Raitt, and the wet weather didn't bother him during his hour-long set. "I just turn it into show biz," he said backstage. Indeed, he improvised a Leon Russell-esque take on "Raindrops Keep Fallin' on My Head."

In 1994, ZZ Top's sound gear got flooded in the middle of a show at Red Rocks, a circumstance that even veteran crewmembers had never experienced. The guys in the band weren't contractually obligated to reschedule the date (it was an "act of God" in legalese), but they did.

There was a meaningful tribute in the days following Jerry Garcia's death in August 1995—Lyle Lovett broke from the set list, opening his show at Red Rocks with a solo acoustic version of the Grateful Dead's "Friend of the Devil."

The special package tour of the summer was the Chieftains, the Grammy-winning veteran Irish folk group, and Sarah McLachlan, Canada's bewitching 27-year-old alternative-rock diva. Onstage at

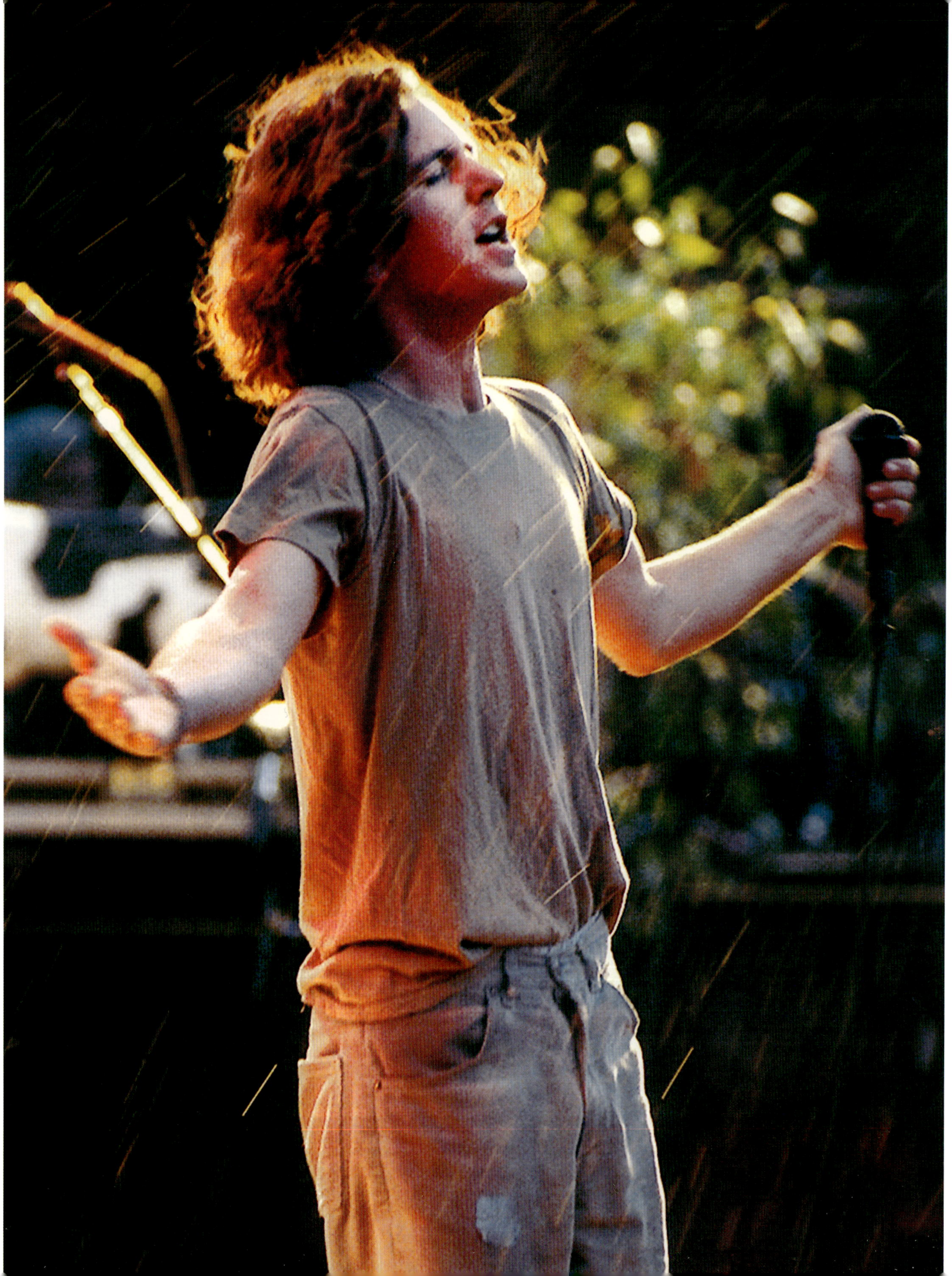

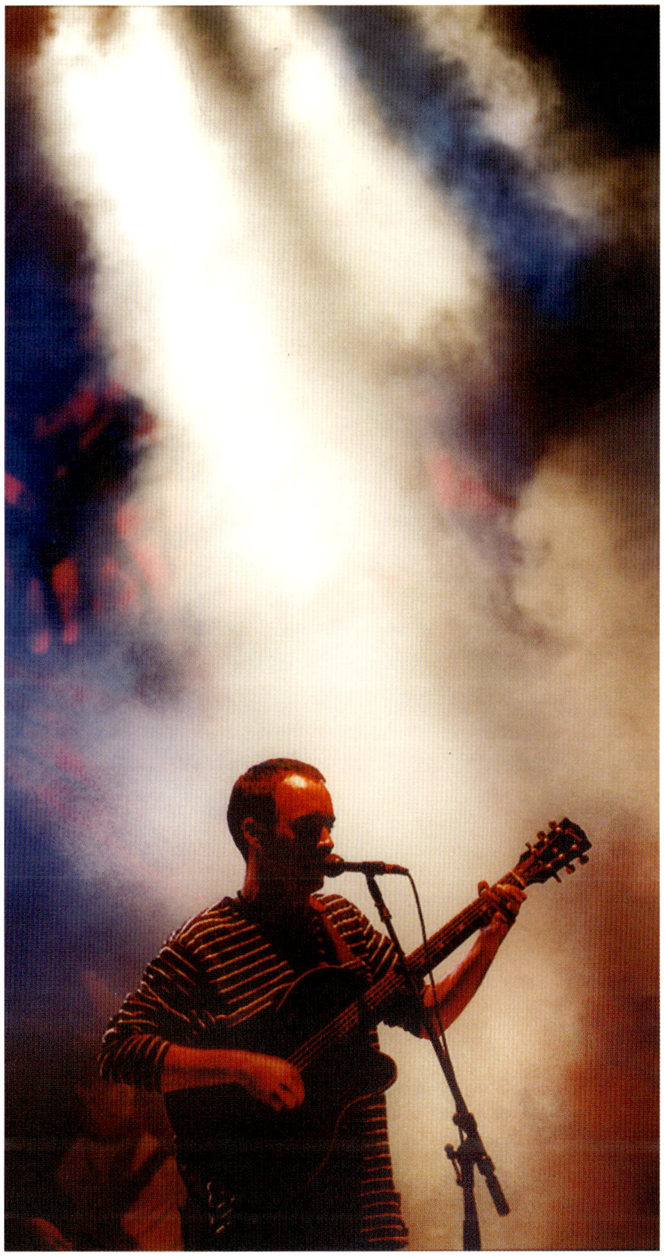

Pearl Jam, 1995 (left); Dave Matthews Band, 1995

Red Rocks, everyone was dancing in the rain during a kitchen-sink finale of "Did You Ever Go A-Courtin', Uncle Joe."

Dave Matthews Band's *Live at Red Rocks 8.15.95*, released in the fall of 1997, was the first in a series of live albums the band issued to give fans an alternative to the many bootlegs on the market. It landed in the Top 10 and sold a million copies with barely a flicker of marketing and promotion.

"We just felt it was a good way to give something back to the people who care about the live shows, including the improvisational elements," Matthews said. "It's not that we have a problem with bootlegs, because we have no intention of stopping people from bootlegging our shows. The trouble comes with the idea of some guy who doesn't really give a crap about the band or the music, just simply trying to cash in on an easy buck."

The double live album was an unedited soundboard recording. Perhaps as a nod to the fact that the band was performing in Colorado, snippets of John Denver's "Sunshine on My Shoulders" cropped up in both "Proudest Monkey" and "Recently."

In 1994, Pearl Jam had taken on Ticketmaster in congressional hearings, accusing it of running a monopoly. The following year, the popular Seattle quintet began shows on the national concert circuit without contracting with the ticketing agency. Before canceling its trouble-plagued tour, Pearl Jam performed at Red Rocks Amphitheatre for two nights in June.

The first night, singer Eddie Vedder entered the stage on an old bicycle and remarked, "This place sucks…obviously that is the furthest thing from the truth. Just like us going back to Ticketmaster is the furthest thing from the truth."

The second night, the members performed the first six songs seated, experiencing some of the effects of the altitude and taking a different approach from the previous night. They got frustrated while sitting down—guitarist Stone Gossard declared, "Alright, fuck the seats" and they dumped the chairs as they launched into "Last Exit." Vedder, the reluctant messiah, had a parting comment: "Thanks for coming up to the mountain with us."

1995 also saw the first live transmissions on the Internet at Red Rocks, for the Hootie & the Blowfish concert; a tour stop by the reformed Sex Pistols (the punk band didn't even try to pretend it was anything but a cash grab); and a performance by Alanis Morissette, the new darling of alternative-rock, who specifically requested the chance to do her thing in the country's most breathtaking live-music setting.

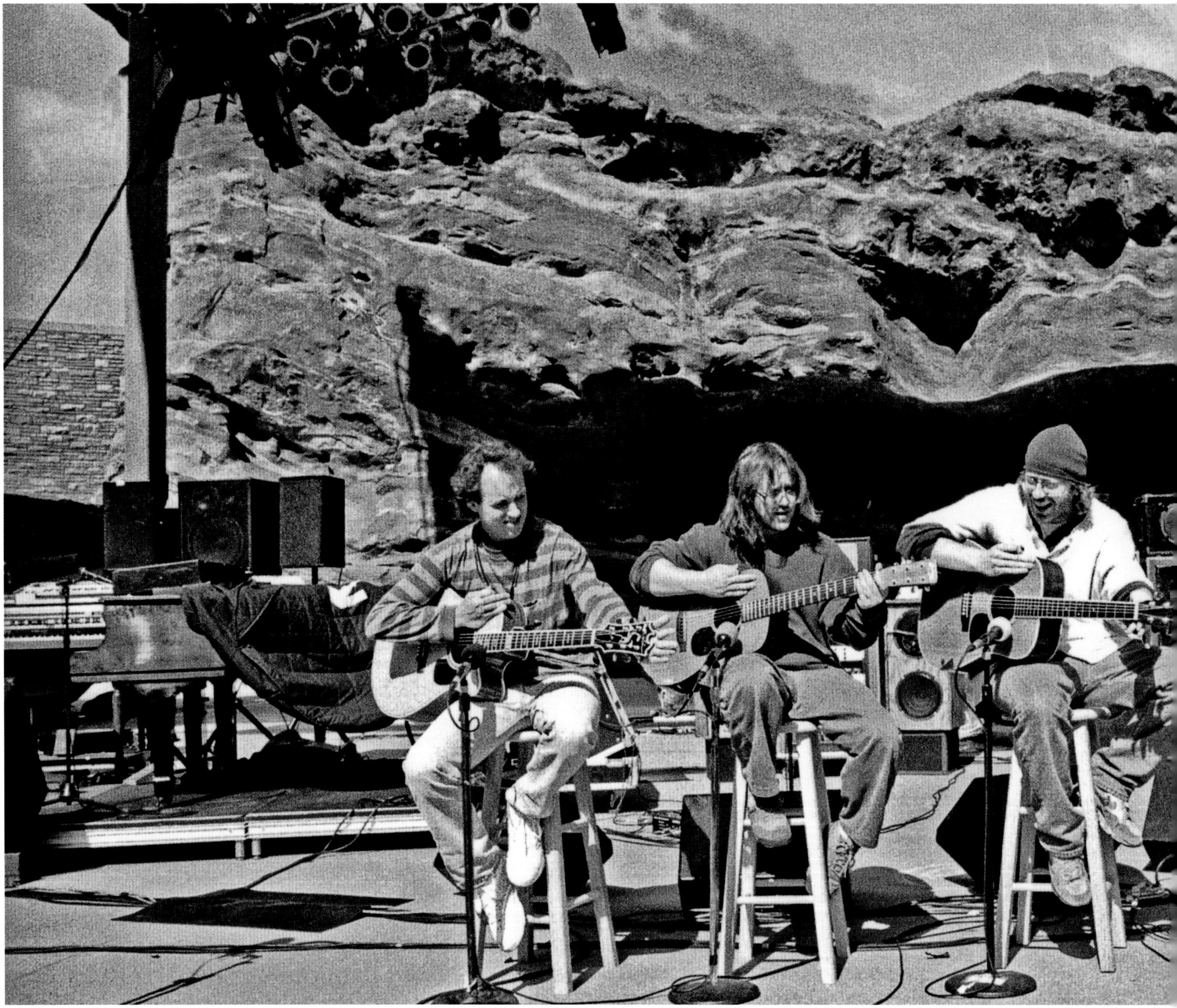

Phish rehearsal, 1995

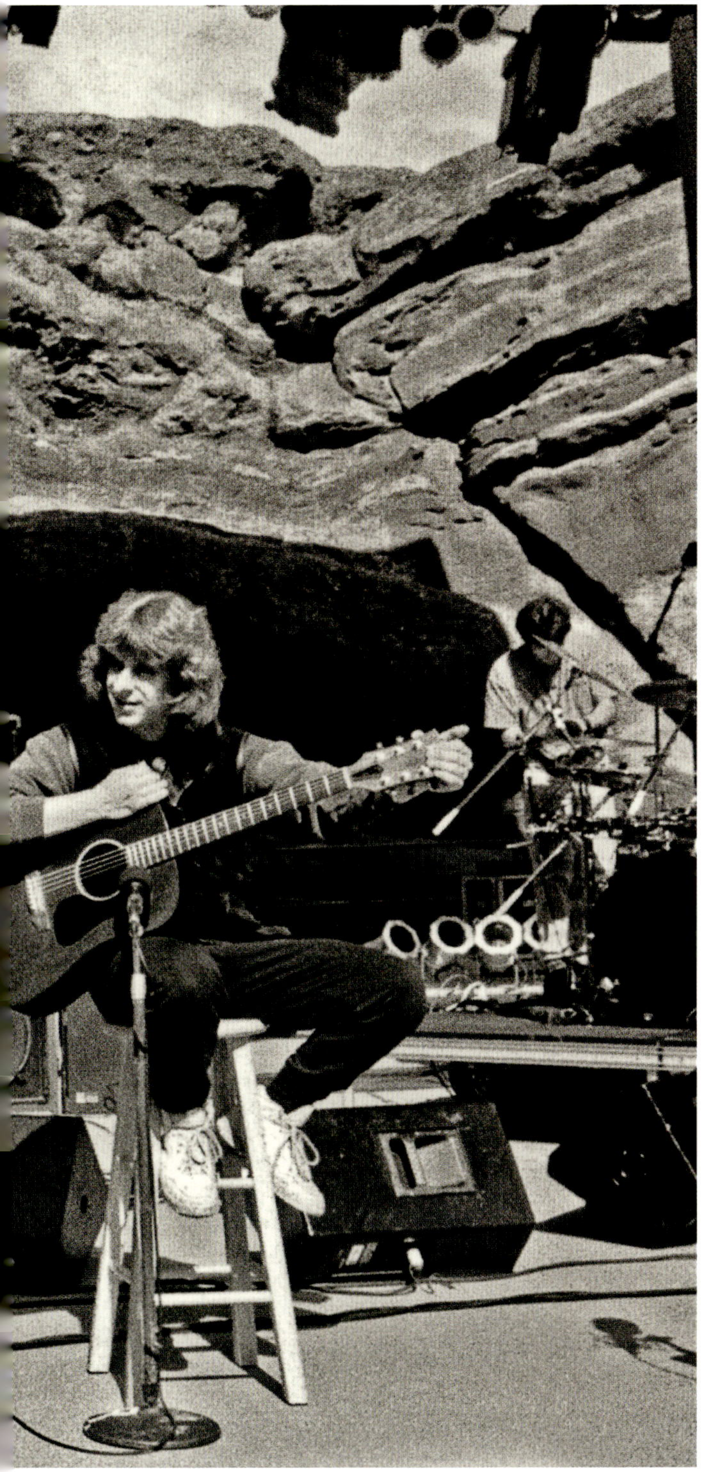

1996-2000
ROCKING INTO THE MILLENNIUM

The left-field success story of the 1990s, Phish was one of the most popular concert draws in America. The determinedly eccentric Vermont quartet was beloved by an army of noodle-dancing, sandal-wearing, tie-dyed nomads who basked in a kind of musical and social culture that hadn't manifested itself since the demise of the Grateful Dead. In that idiosyncratic spirit, during Phish's 1993 show at Red Rocks, drummer Jon Fishman and his mother, Mimi, both played the Electrolux vacuum cleaner, "Mama Phish" displaying her prowess on "Purple Rain."

But there were growing pains. When Phish played the first of four sold-out gigs at Red Rocks Amphitheatre in August 1996, a contingent of itinerant fans from across the nation couldn't get tickets to the shows but came to Morrison anyway, looking for a "miracle"—a free ticket to the show of their dreams. Few had more than a car or campground to stay in, and the overflow packed the streets.

Despite months of planning—Phish had its own security expert—things deteriorated when a truck accidentally hit and injured a 21-year-old Phishhead from Pennsylvania. A mob formed, dancing to the beat of bongo drums and chanting at armed police, who shut down the main road into town for a time as they tried to move the gathering, estimated at more than 400, out of downtown. Bottles were thrown and a melee broke out. Several people were injured, and officials reported ten arrests. Some of the kids felt the police had overreacted and punished the larger group of fans for the bad acts of a few; locals had a differing view.

Phish keyboardist Page McConnell looked back at the Red Rocks affair with displeasure, sorrow and acceptance. "In preparing for Red Rocks, we knew there was a potential situation there, and we met with all these people to make sure we were doing all we could to make everything as smooth as possible, where our fans would be low-impact on the community. We pledged money and support to make it go as well as we could. And nobody bothered to accept it, I guess.

"We can't prevent everything all the time. And when a situation does happen, it's a shame that it gets blown out of proportion—I saw it on CNN—because more often than not our fans are really peaceful, nice people and not troublemakers."

With singles like "All Mixed Up," "Don't Stay Home" and their biggest hit, "Down," the guys of 311 won 1996's alternative-rock sweepstakes. Thanks to radio station KBPI's support, 311 headlined

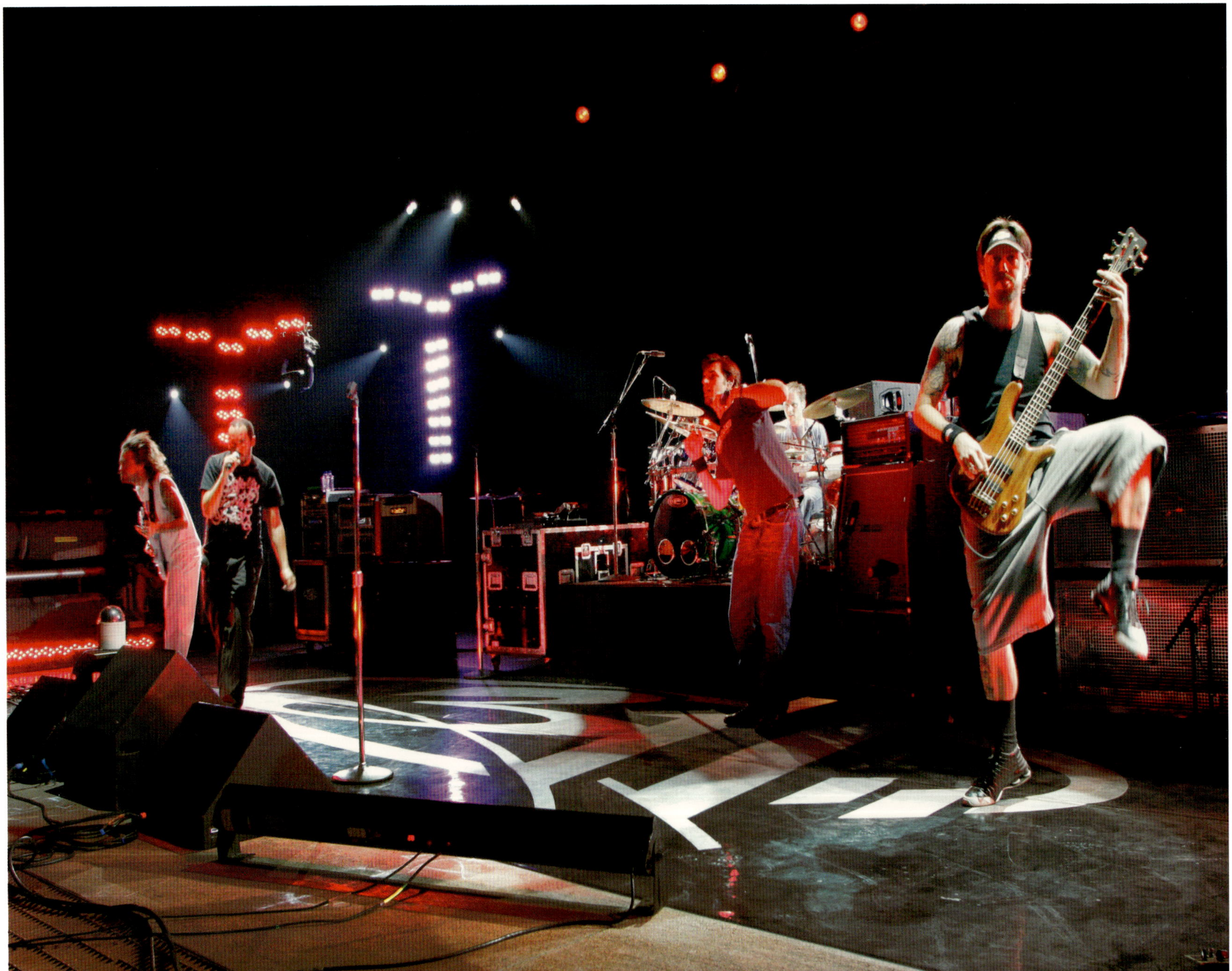

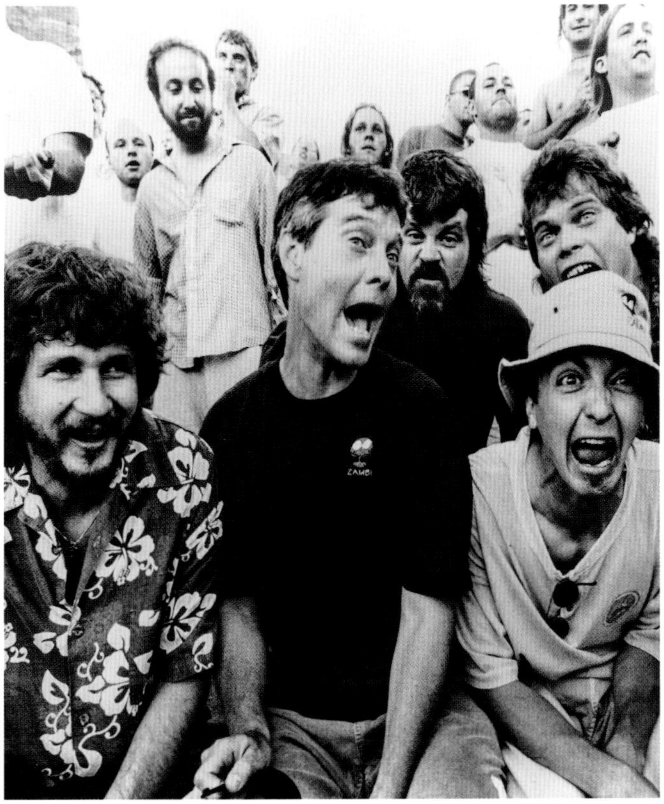

311, 1996 (left); Leftover Salmon, 1996

a sold-out show at Red Rocks. "We played in California during the day, and then we hopped on a private jet, flew to Denver and played our Red Rocks show," drummer Chad Sexton said. "We played two shows that day—that was kinda cool."

The band then released a long-form home video of live gigs, *Enlarged to Show Detail*, that was certified platinum. "We tell a story in the video," vocalist/guitarist Nick Hexum said. "When we were moving to L.A., we stopped to see some friends in Denver and hung out for a day. Then we drove by Red Rocks, actually made it up there, stood on the stage and said, 'Yep, someday we're going to play here.' That was before we were signed, in 1992. You get really ecstatic when your dreams are coming true."

Beer was sold at select concerts in 1997. The following year, the Smokin' Grooves tour stopped at Red Rocks; on the bill were the politically charged rappers Public Enemy plus Busta Rhymes and the Fugees' Wyclef Jean. Boukman Eksperyan's *Live at Red Rocks* archived the Haitian band's appearance at "Reggae on the Rocks" in 1998.

A multi-artist showcase landed at Red Rocks in September 1999—Bonnie Raitt, Jackson Browne, Shawn Colvin and Bruce Hornsby played two shows. "Every now and then the elements at Red Rocks plot against the musicians in an attempt to sabotage and gleefully impair the use of hands, throats, and even eyes during a performance, and those two shows were an archetypal case in point," Hornsby said. "The winds sprinted back and forth, across and through the stage area like a Carl Lewis-Alvin Ailey collaboration, and the temperature dropped like Ferrigno's barbells after the clean and jerk, creating the most difficult performing environment I've ever experienced.

"The worst part for me was the cold, making it very difficult for me to play the piano with any feeling, or actually have any feeling at all in my hands. Someone, probably one of the crew members with a creative mind, came up with a great solution and duct-taped a hair dryer to the left end of the piano so it blew hot air across the keyboard area, giving me a nice warm haven in the icy stage area to play in. I don't know how the other musicians played in these conditions—maybe it's time for the Red Rocks crew to create portable hair dryer 'stations' that can be strategically placed next to performers' hands."

While it wasn't recorded for conventional release, MTV Online broadcast the July 1999 KTCL "Rave on the Rocks" show via Real Audio and Real Video, one of only two gigs that Fat Boy Slim and the Chemical Brothers performed together that summer. "Rave on the Rocks" was an annual event that brought a slate of

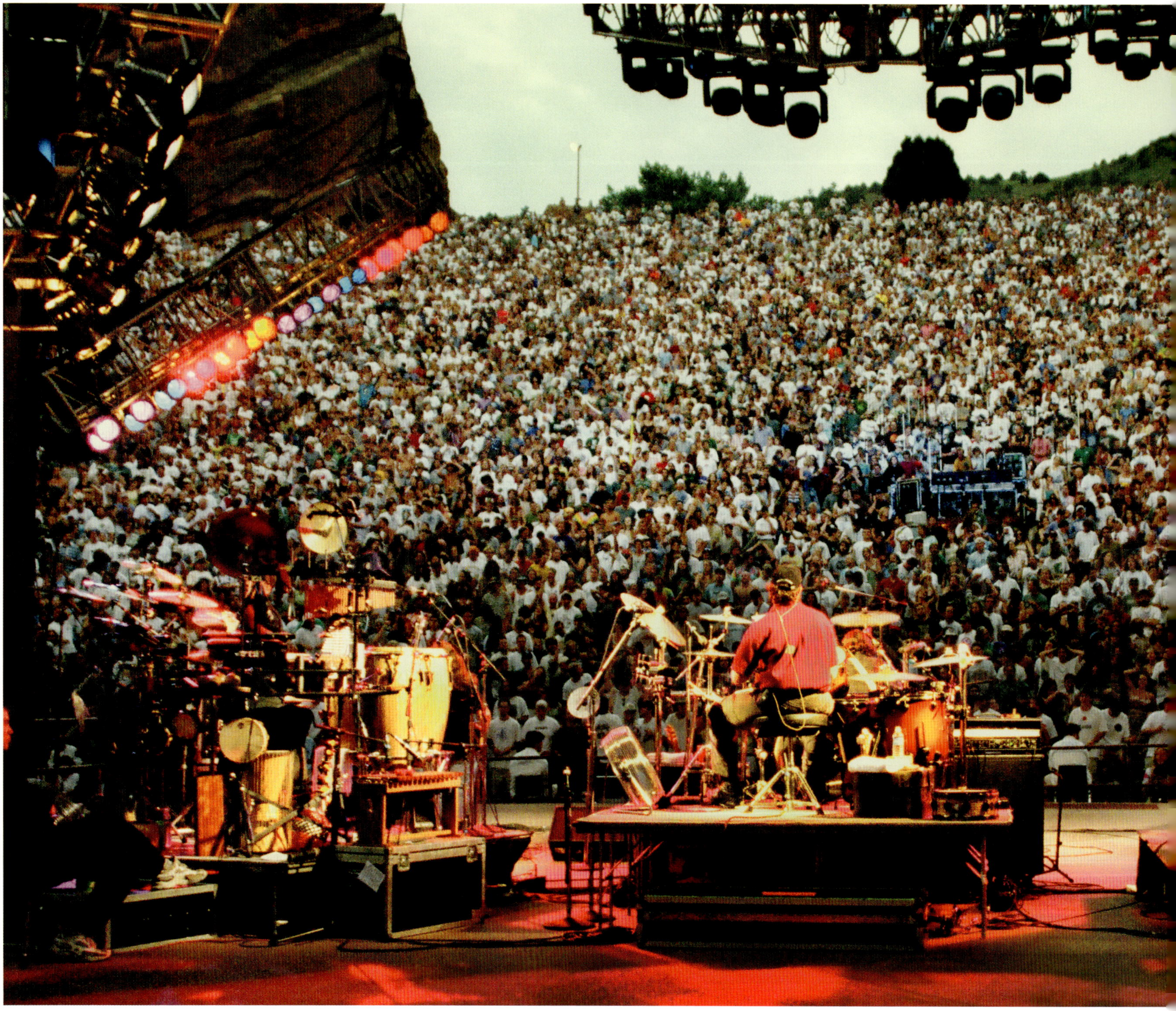

Widespread Panic, 1999

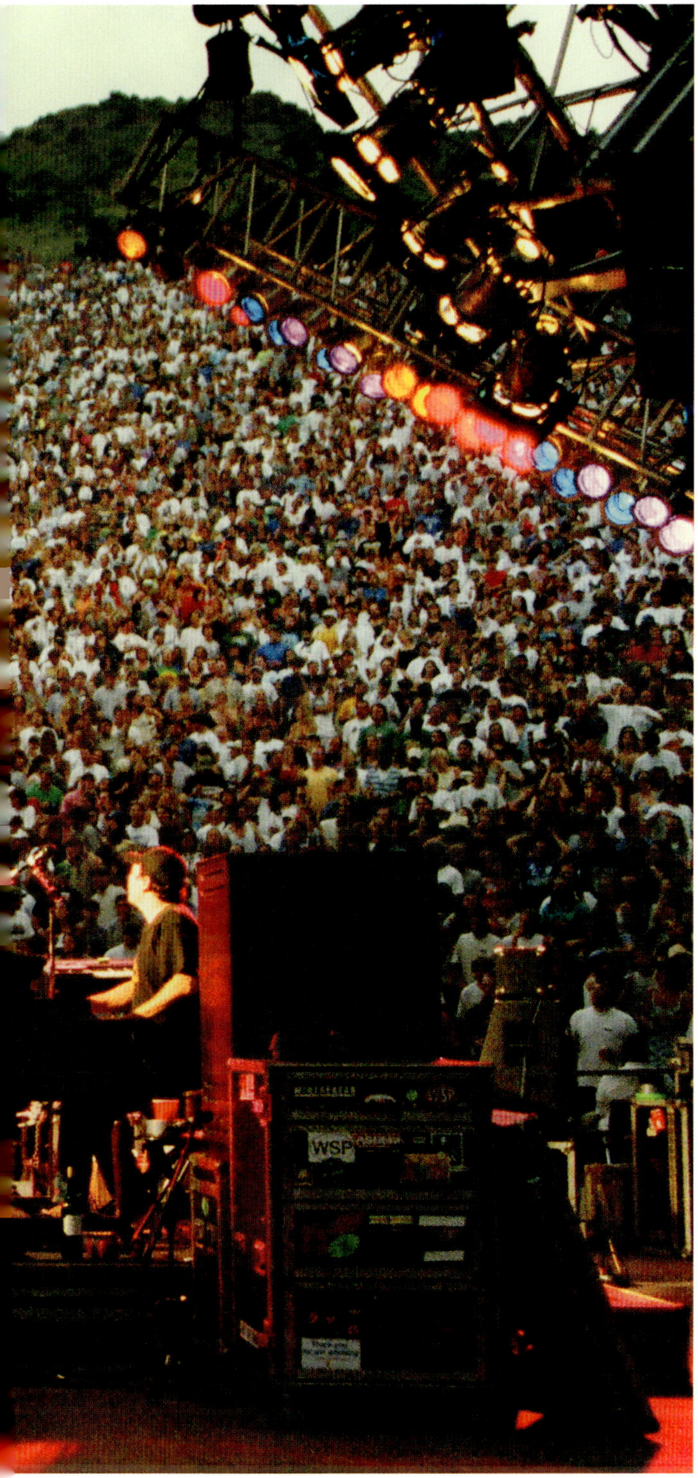

international DJs to Red Rocks, but Congress passed the "RAVE Act" (subsequently known as the "Illicit Drug Anti-Proliferation Act of 2003"), which held concert promoters liable for criminal activity at their shows—including drug use.

That frightened the keepers of Red Rocks, and they declared that no show with the word "rave" in the title could appear at the venue. That prompted sponsor KTCL to change the event's name to the cheeky "Weekend of E" (which the radio station steadfastly maintained stood for "electronica" though it clearly suggested Ecstasy, the raver's drug of choice), but the title proved equally objectionable. In 2003 the moniker finally settled on Global Dance Festival.

In 2000, an Earth, Wind & Fire concert at Red Rocks was cancelled mid-event because of record heat—the day's hot sun apparently melted the band's equipment.

Neil Young's acclaimed "Music in Head" tour included three nights at Red Rocks in September 2000. While short on hits, the set covered a wide range of phases from Young's career. His performances appeared on *Road Rocks Volume I*, a live album from the outing. The DVD audio and video editions, titled *Red Rocks Live, Friends & Relatives*, featured more than twenty tracks captured at the famed venue. As seen in the video, while the wind whips Young's hair in his face, the crowd seems unfazed by the lashing rain it endured.

Since its beginnings in the college town of Athens, Georgia in the early 1980s, Widespread Panic developed into a perfect example of a grassroots phenomenon. Without the support of radio or MTV, the neo-hippie jam band used touring and the Internet to expand a vast, dedicated following. During the late 1990s, the sextet took aim at the Colorado market, and fans quickly got on board. The band's 2000 summer tour kicked off at Red Rocks Amphitheatre, and the three shows (some 27,000 seats) sold out in 44 minutes. Photos of Red Rocks appeared prominently on 1998's two-CD live release, *Light Fuse Get Away*. The band established sellout records at the venue.

"We'll hang at Red Rocks for multiple nights, and we'll play all different songs, and that's what keeps us excited—and it's what keeps the fans going, too," Panic's John Bell said. "Music, getting together, skiing, drinking beer, mountain climbing—there are a lot of those types in Colorado. Our game plan is that we don't have a game plan. And folks at Red Rocks appreciate that more than anybody else."

John Mellencamp returned to the venue in 2001 and shared a similar sentiment. "I've played Red Rocks a thousand times, and the effect is always the same—looking up at all the people. I find myself watching them more than I should."

PROMISED LAND

Every musical artist aspires to play Red Rocks, and the fortunate ones know the joy and privilege of performing there.

ZZ Top, 2007

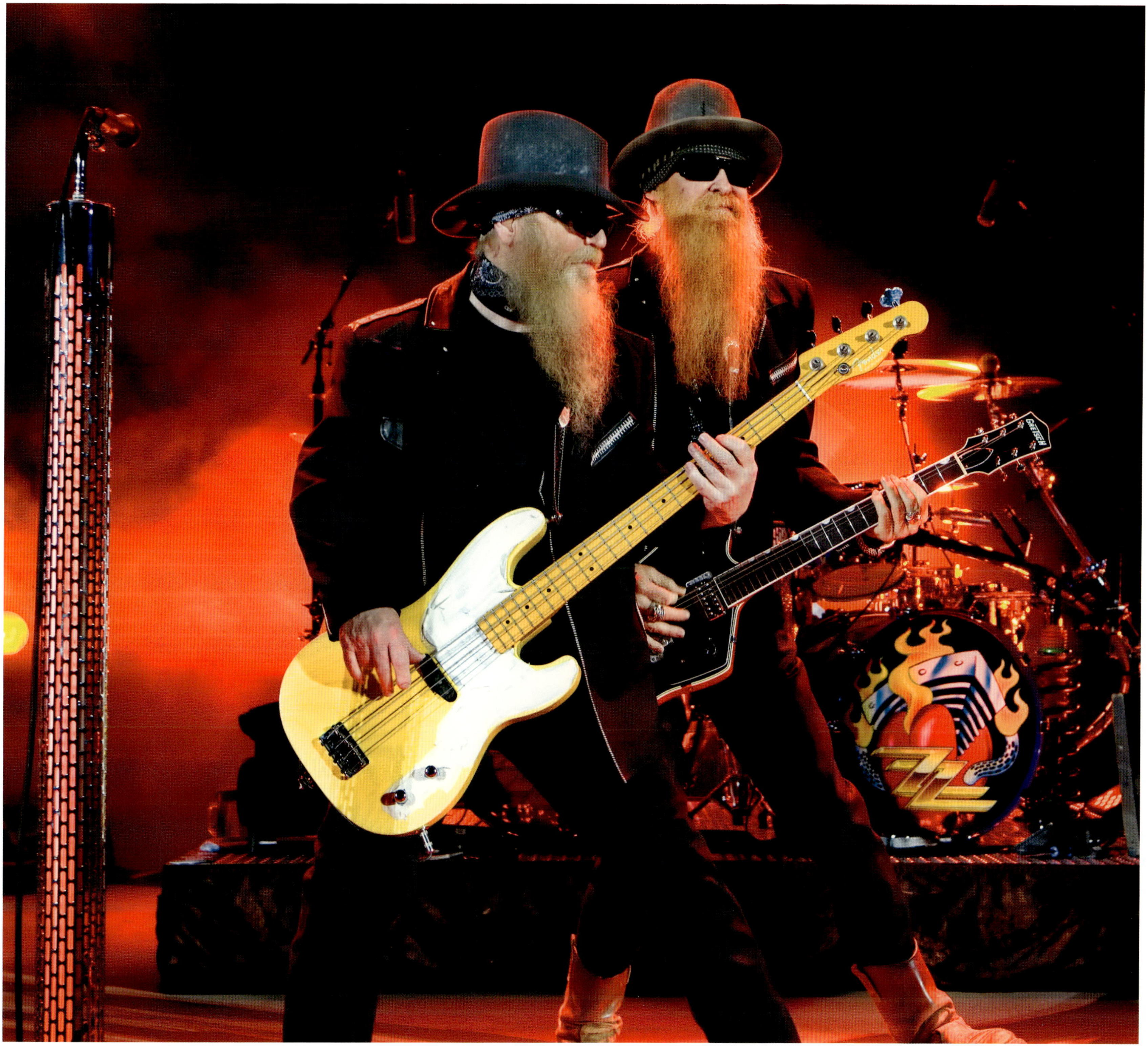
GRETSCH

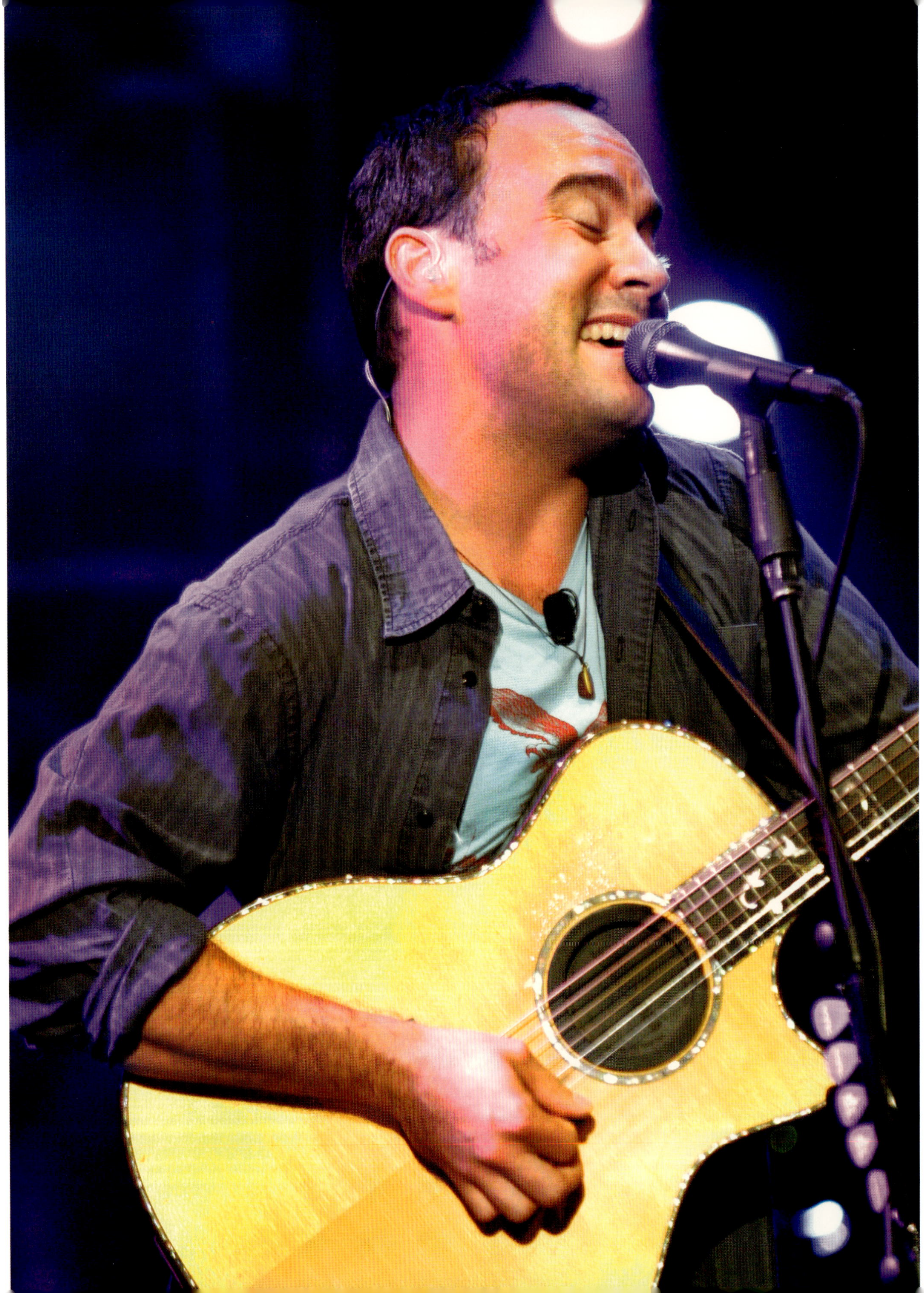

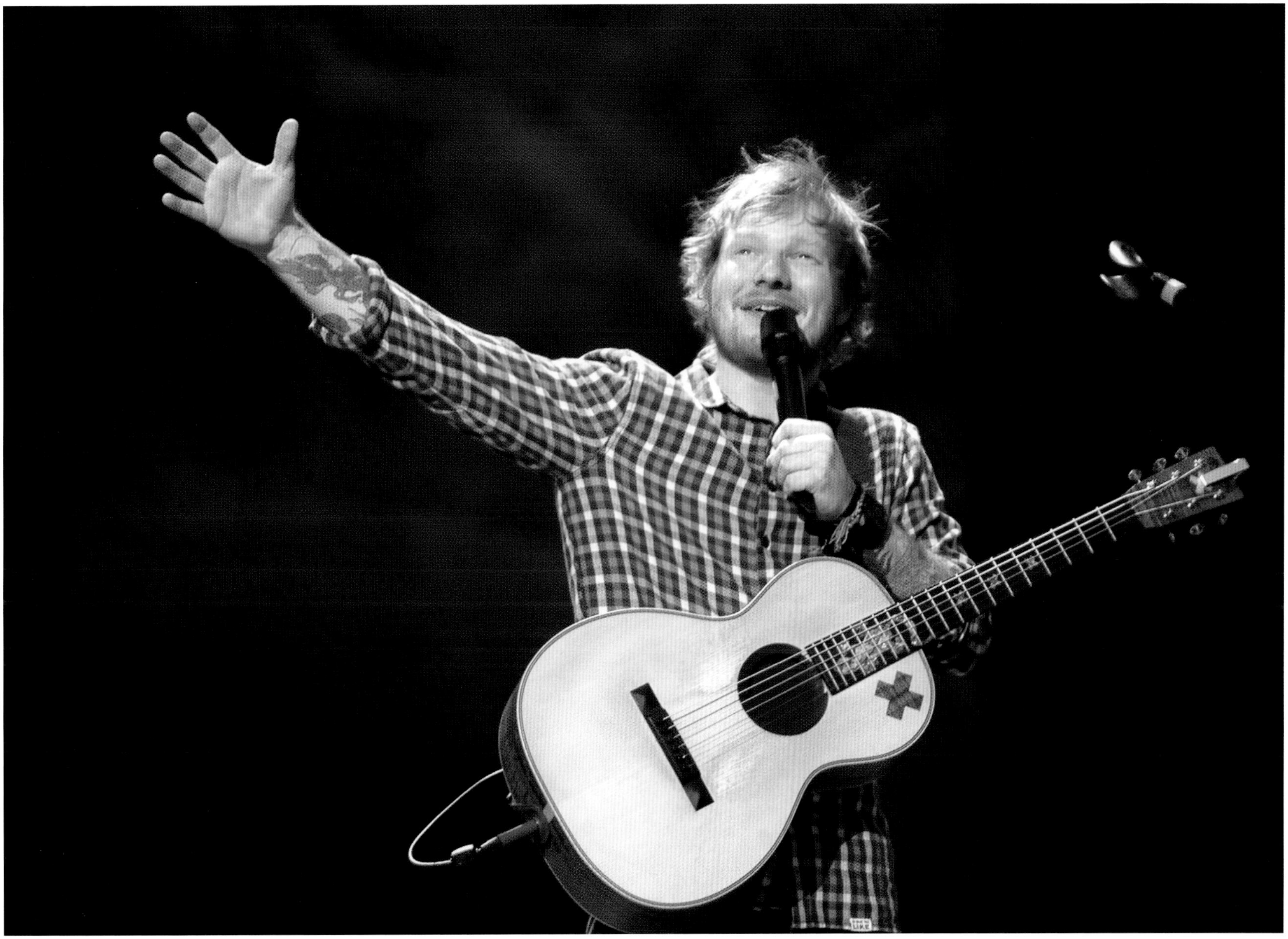

Dave Matthews Band, 2005 (left); Ed Sheeran, 2015

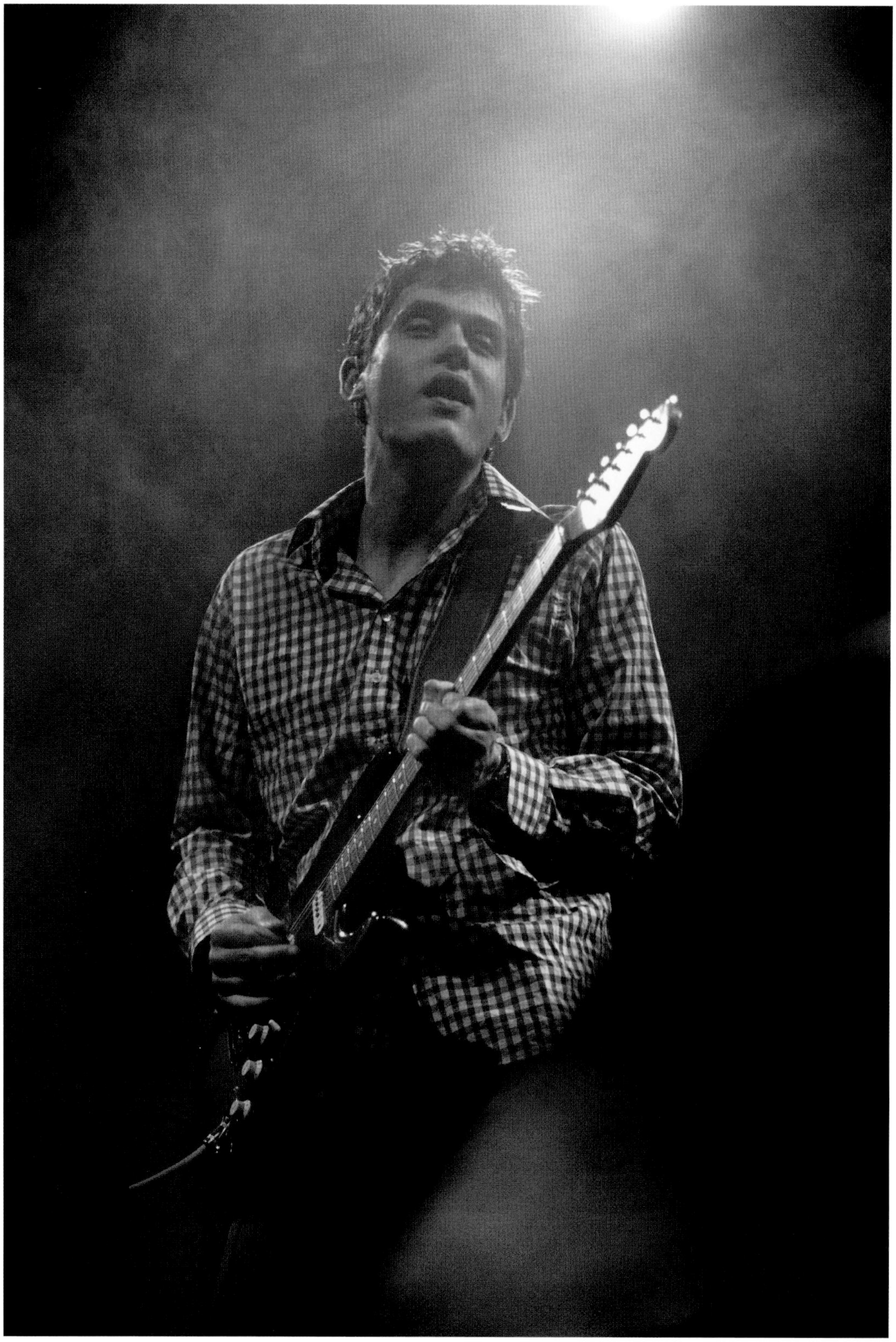

John Mayer, 2006; The B-52's, 1983 (right)

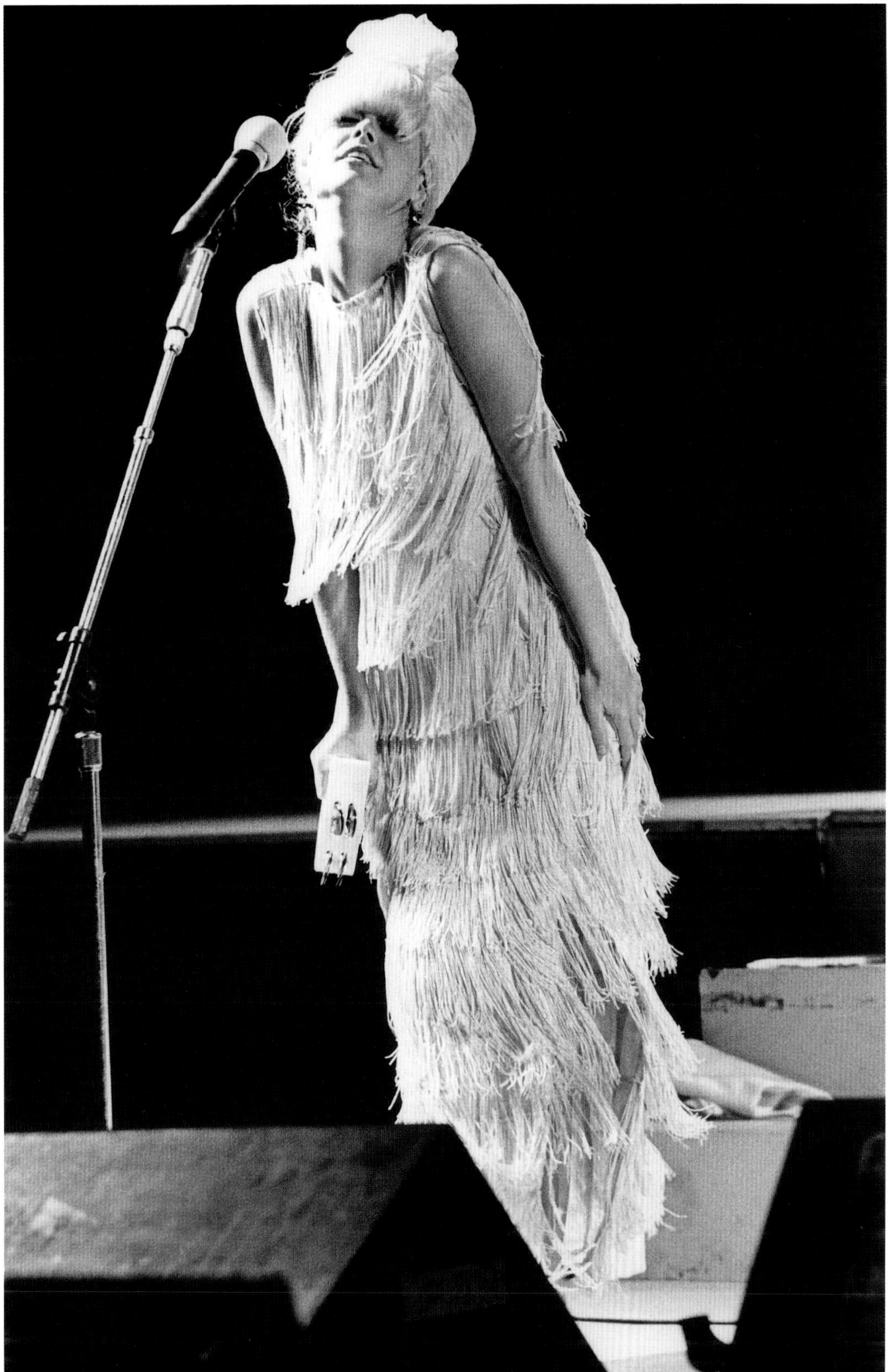

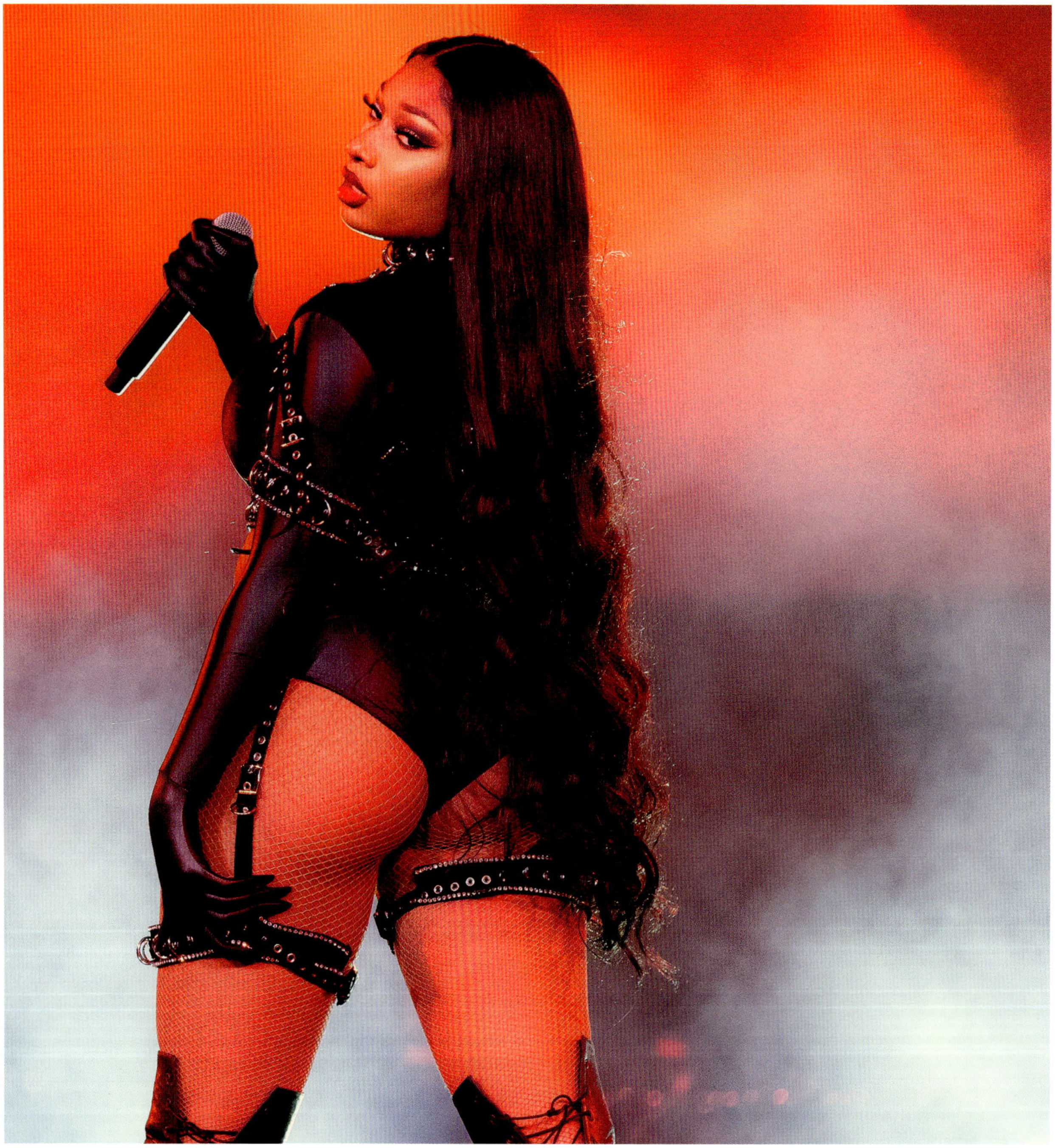

Megan Thee Stallion, 2020; Steve Winwood, 2014 (right)

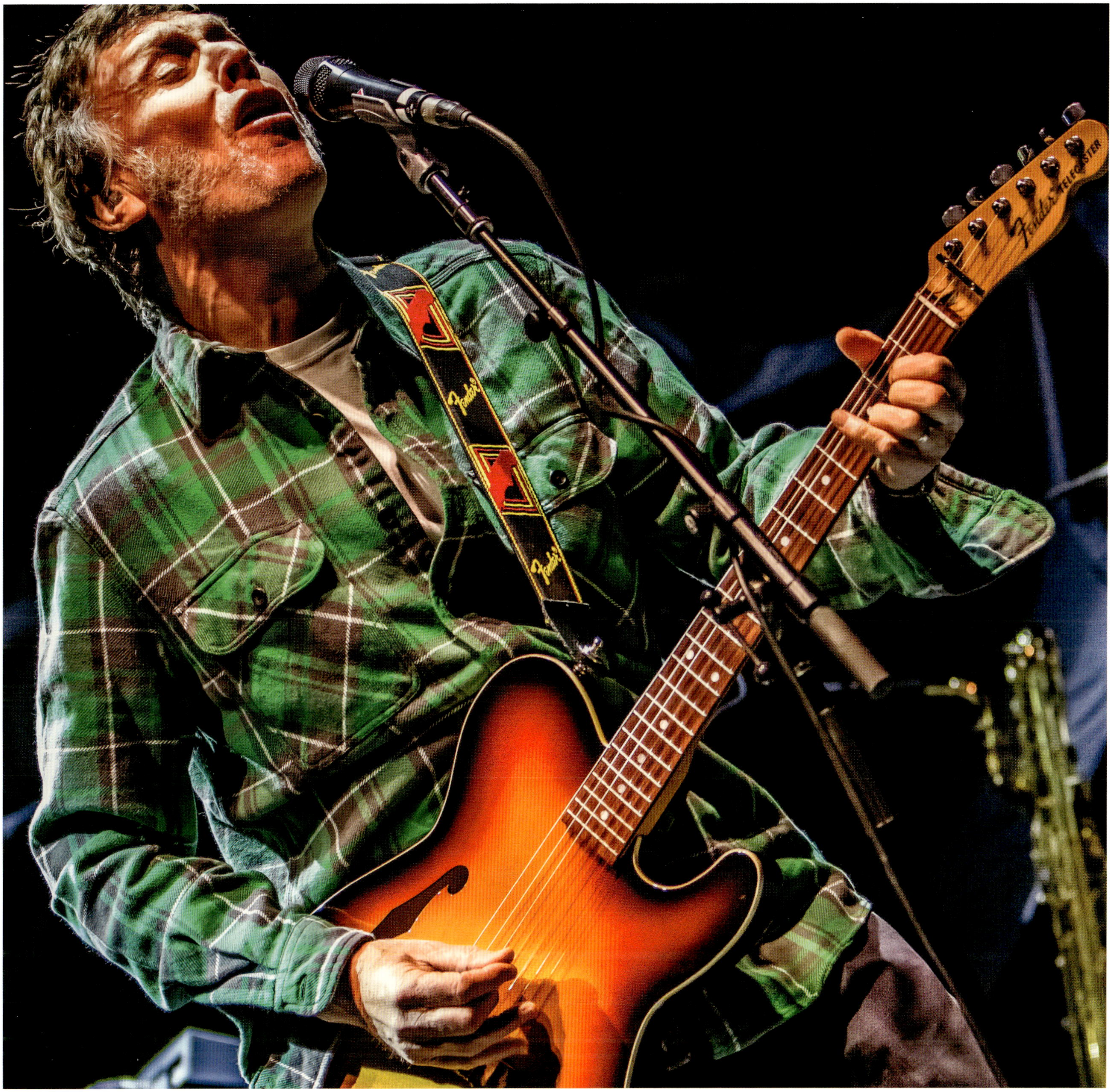
Fender TELECASTER
Fender
Fender

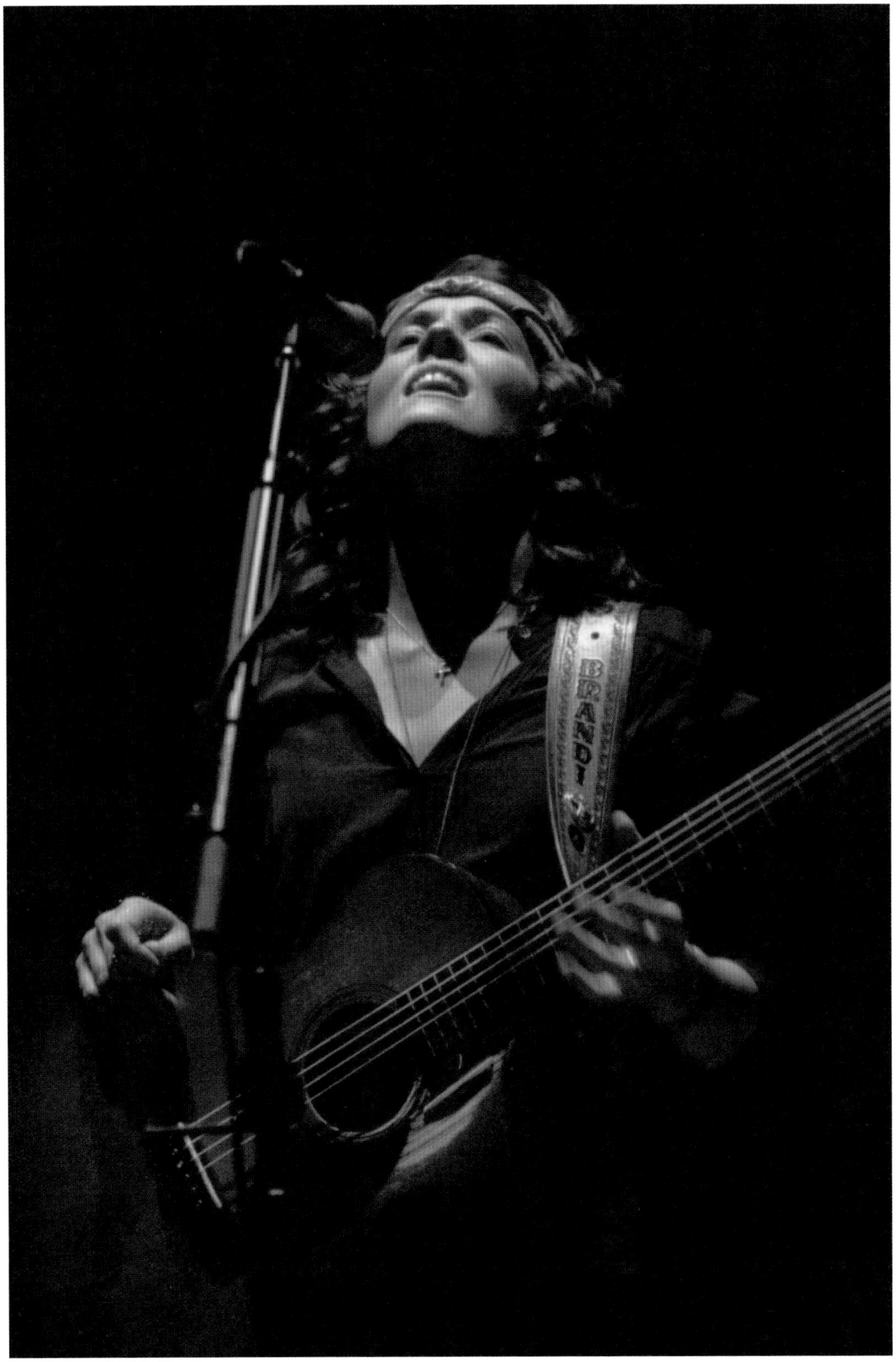

Brandi Carlile, 2013; Judas Priest, 1986 (right)

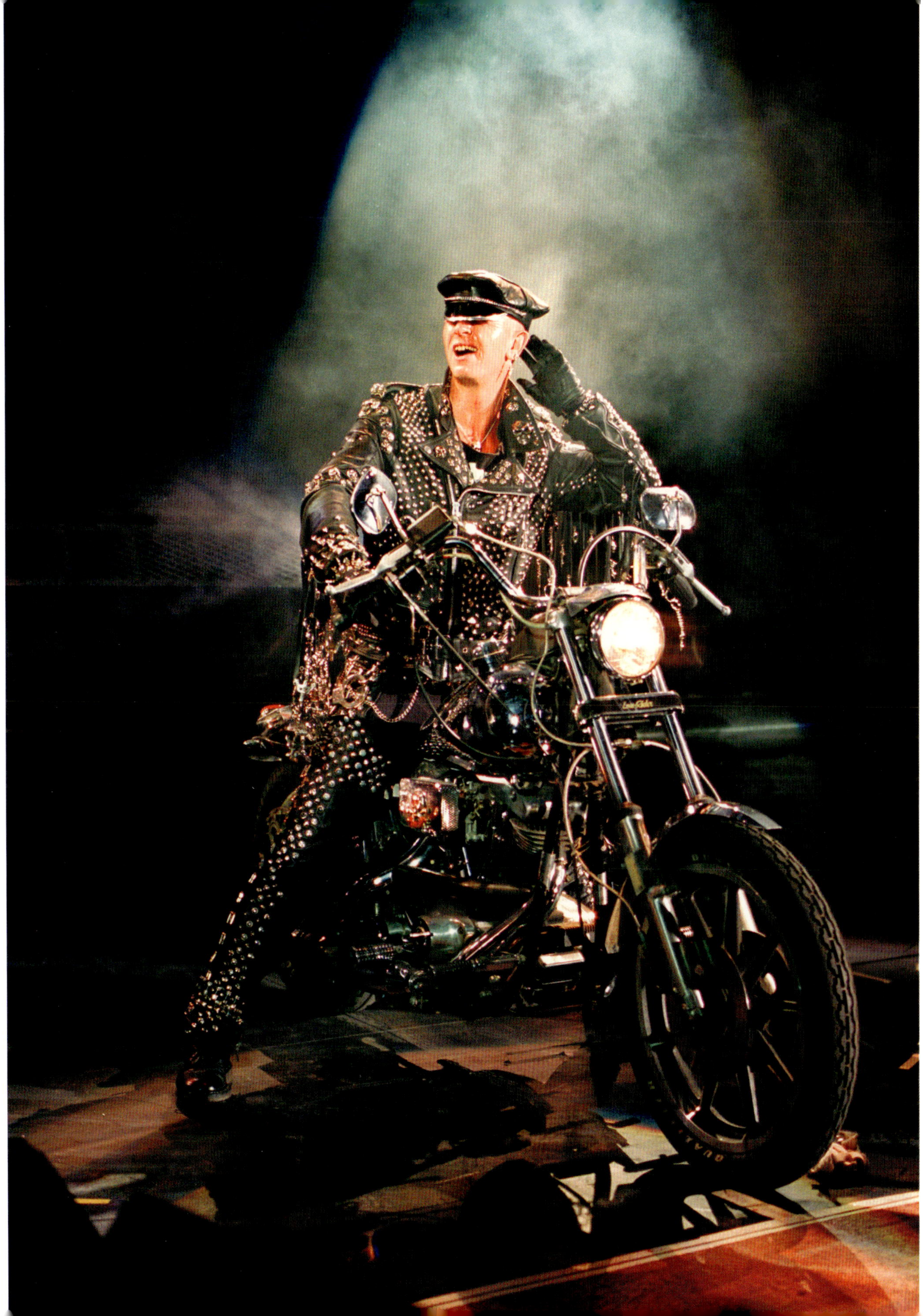

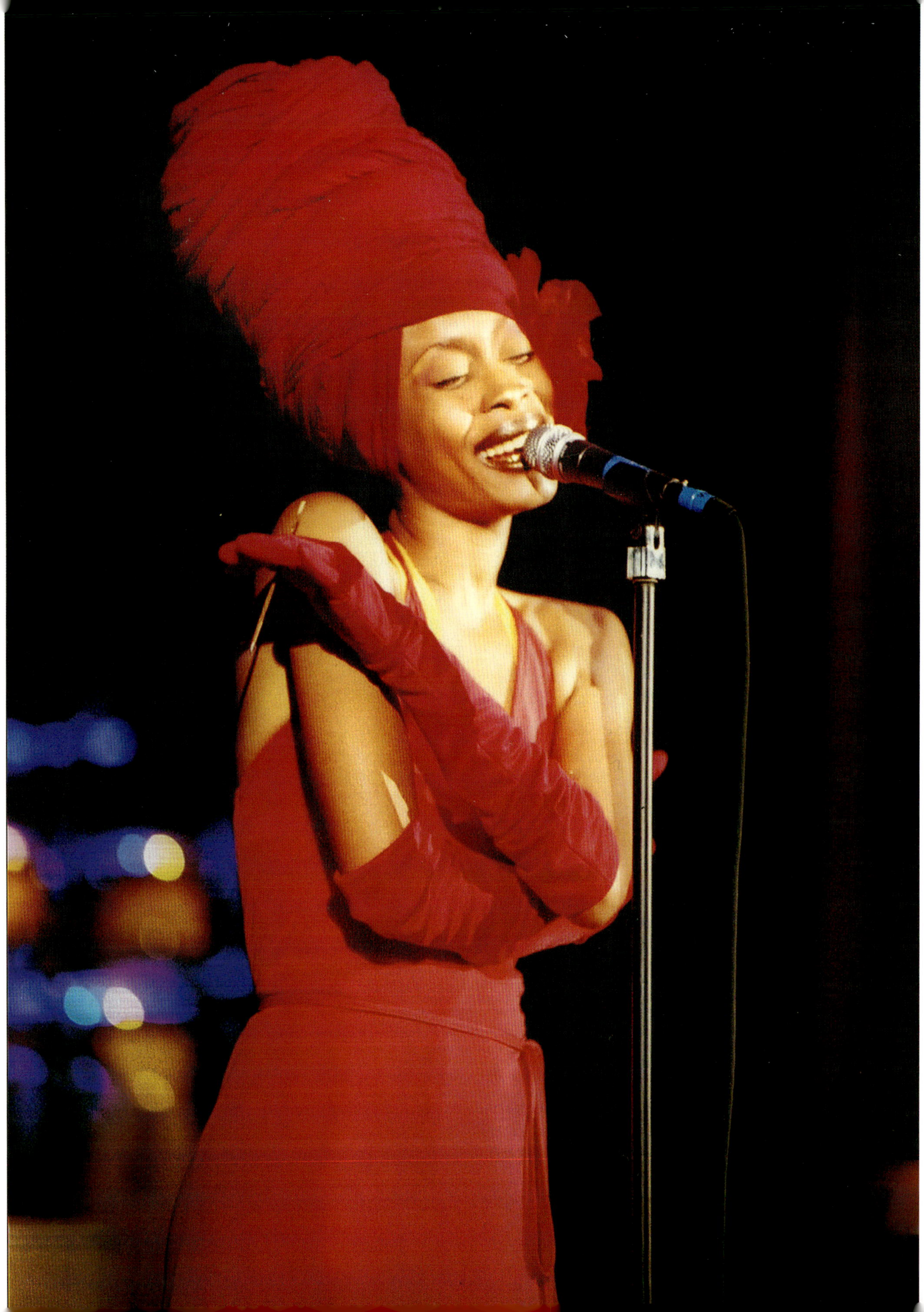

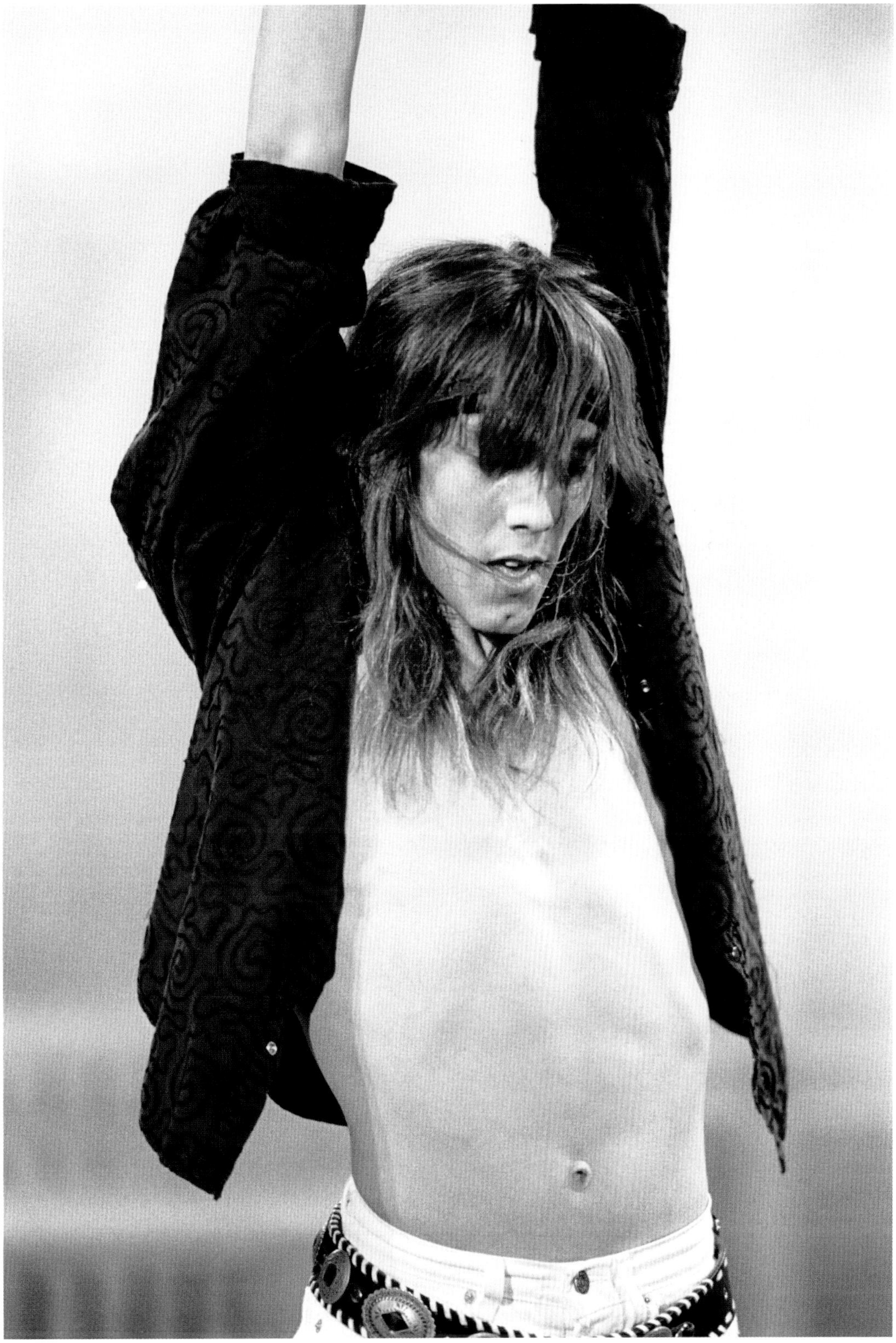

Erykah Badu, 2001(left); Tesla, 1989

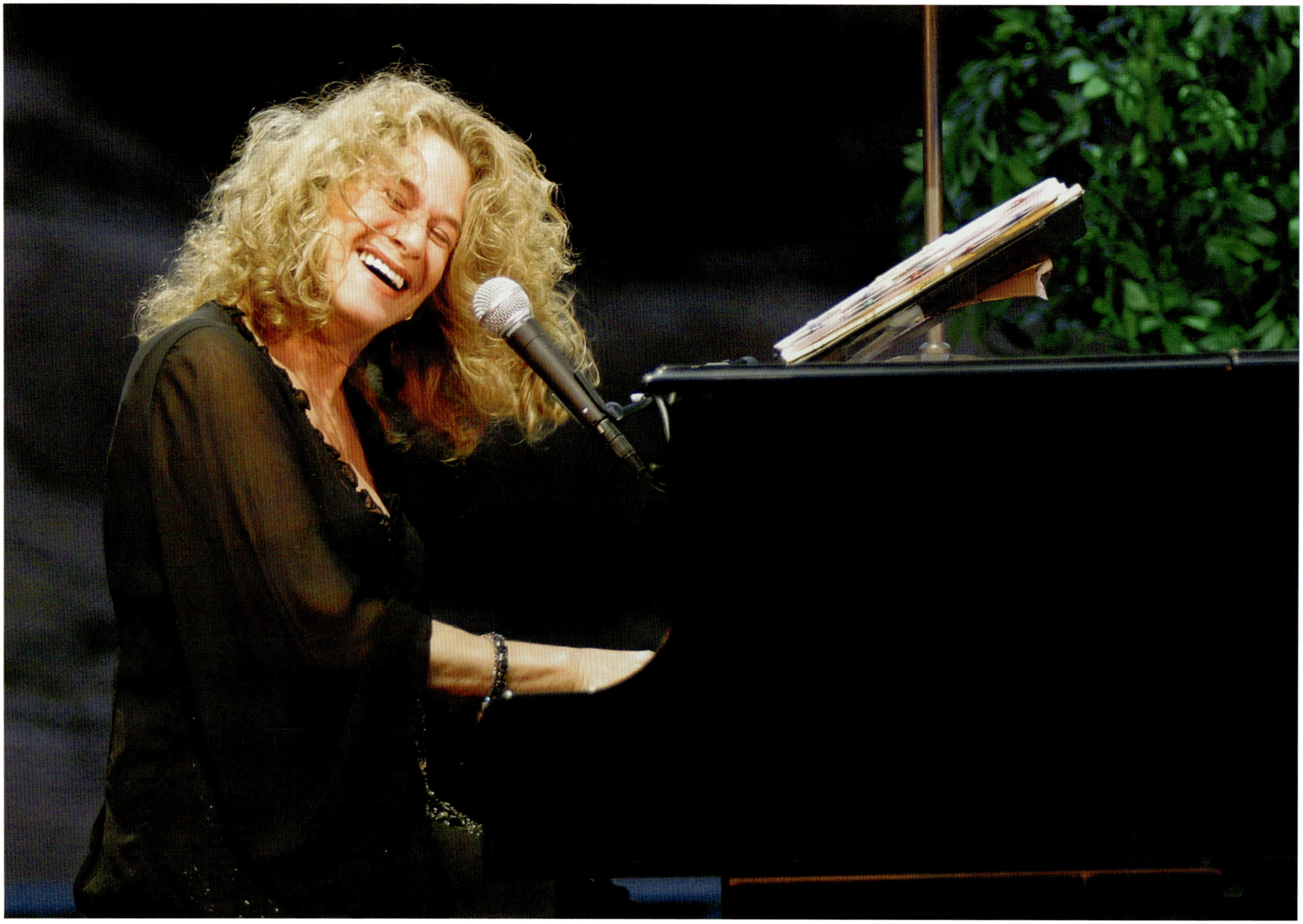

Carole King, 2005; James Taylor, 2001 (right)

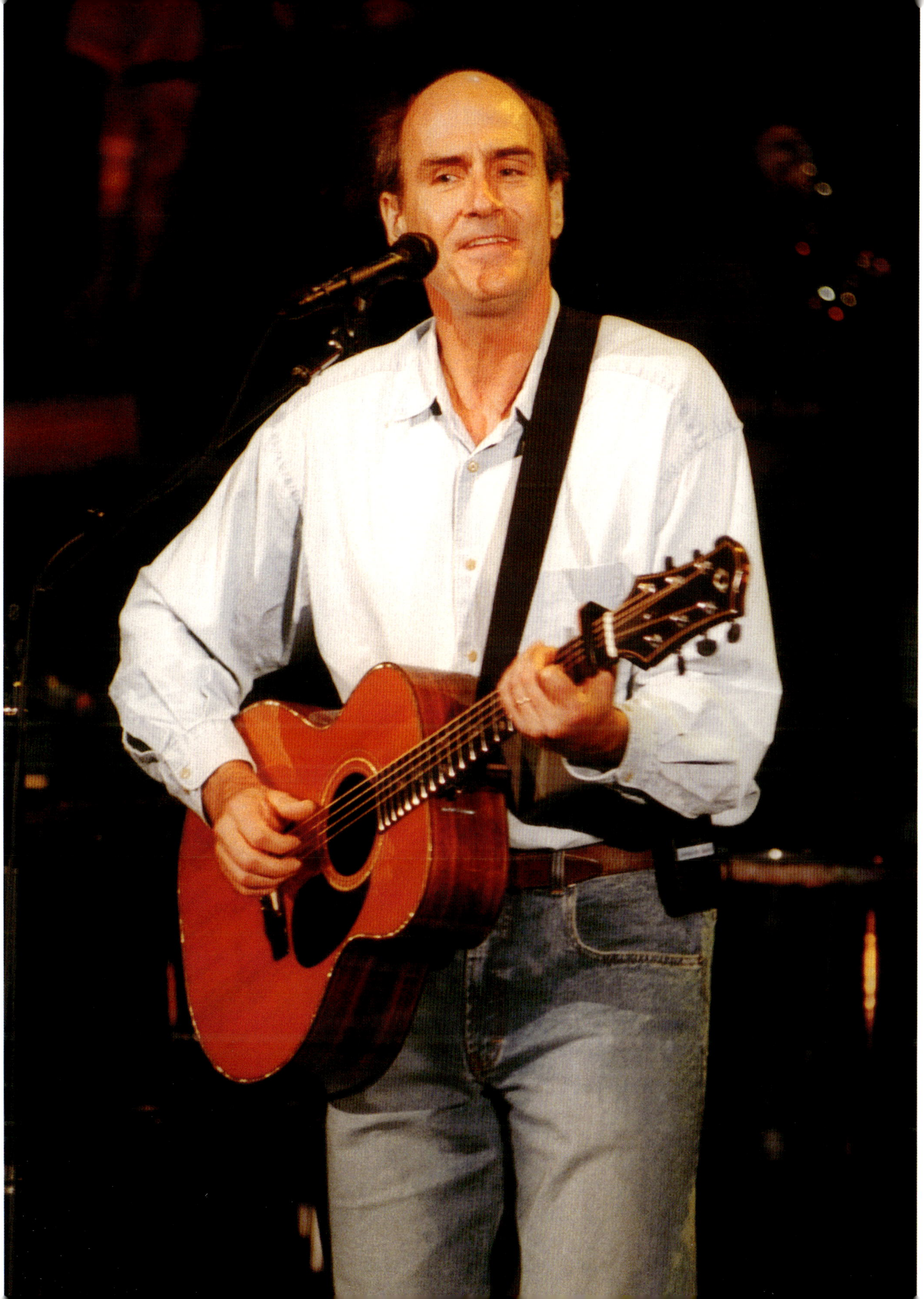

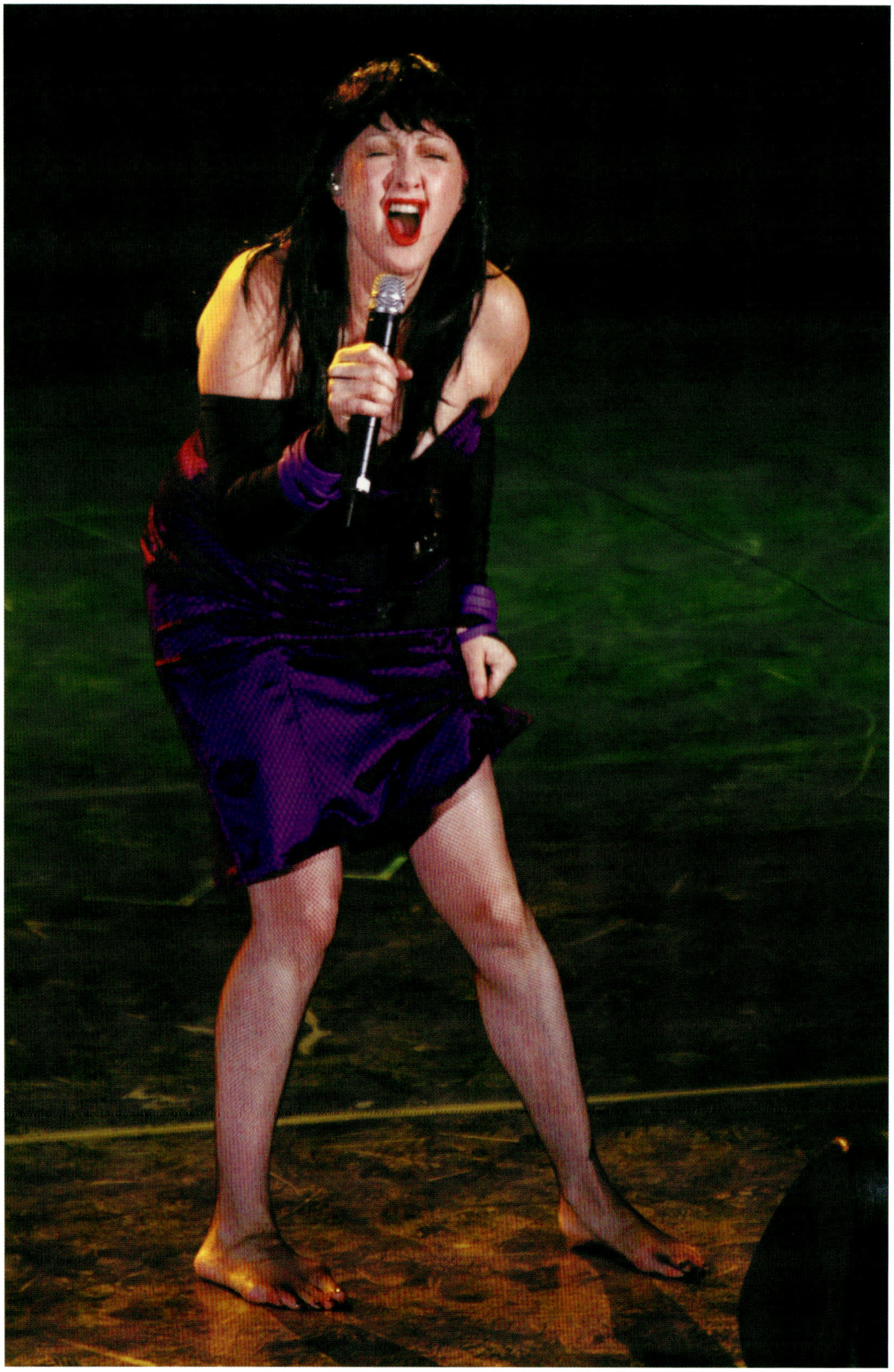

Cyndi Lauper, 2007; Debbie Harry, 2007 (right)

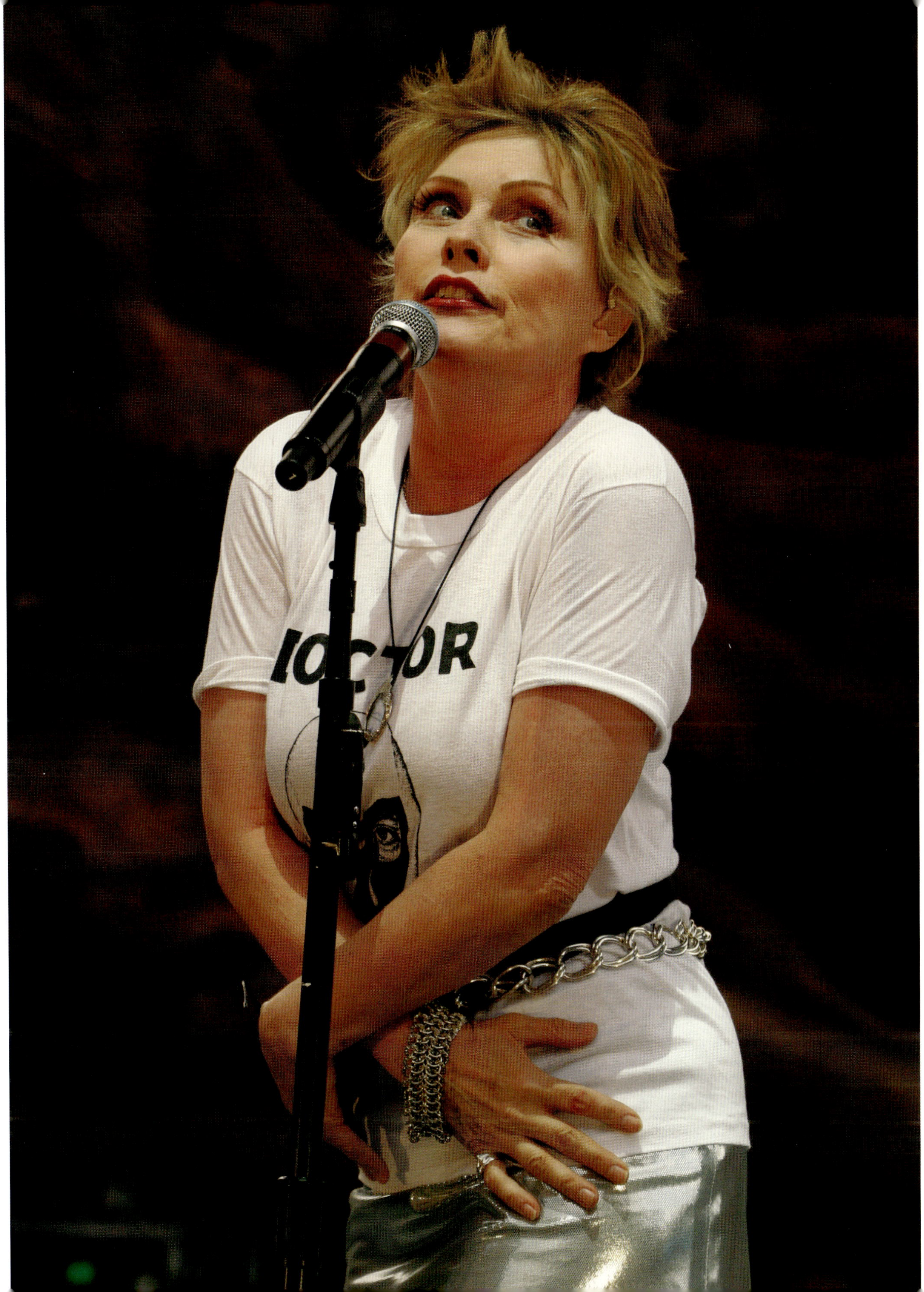

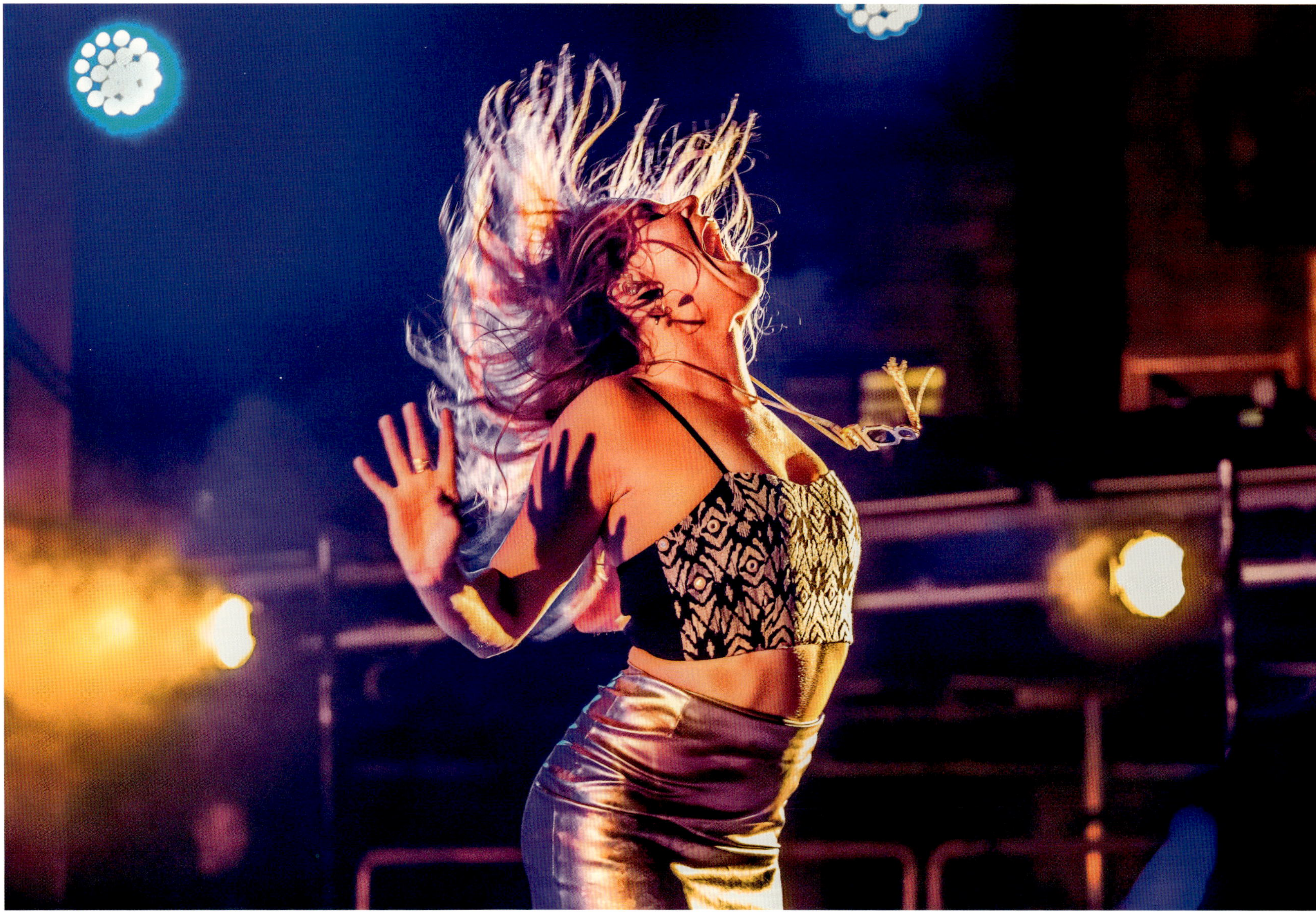

Grace Potter, 2015; Michael Franti & Spearhead, 2015 (right)

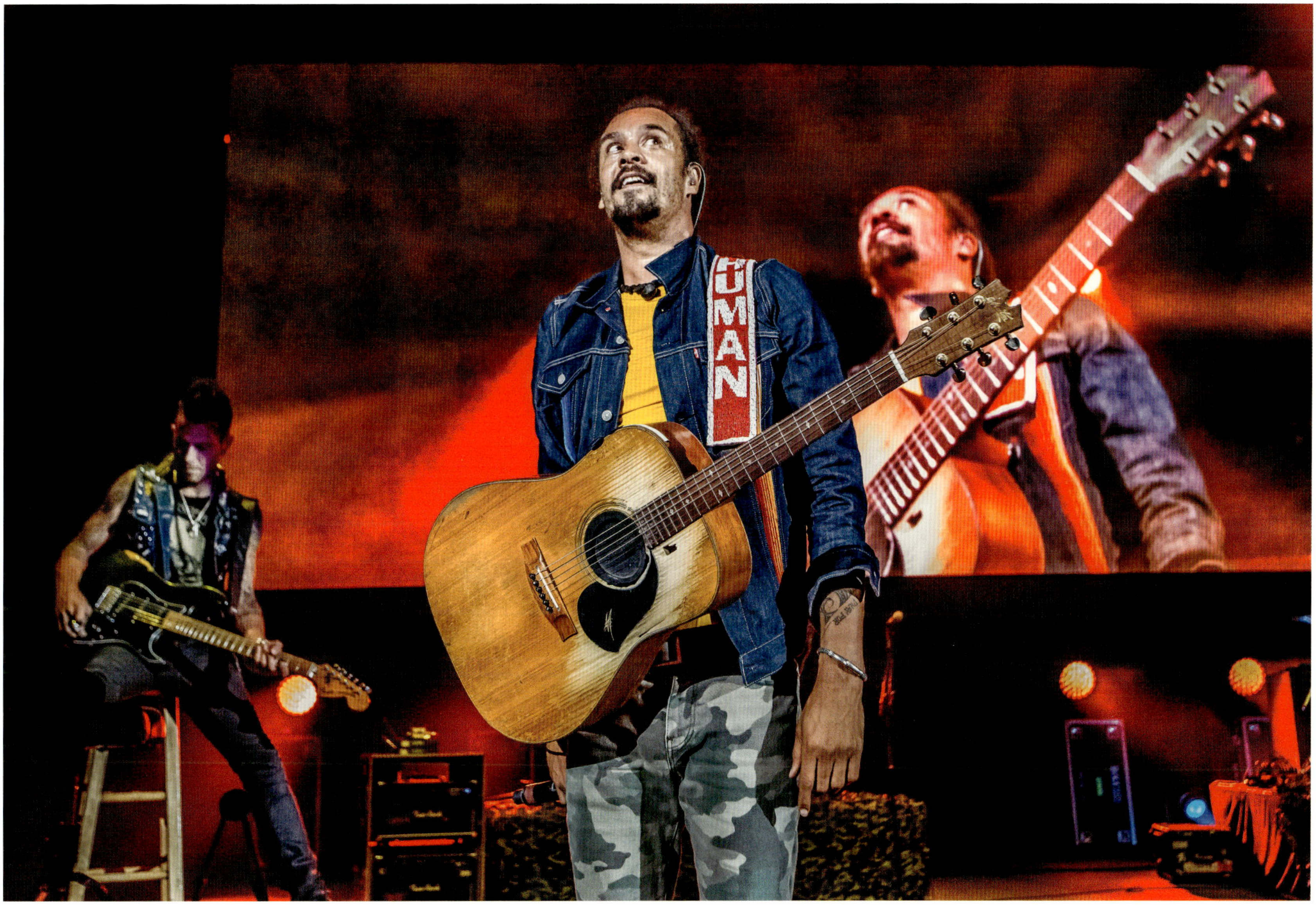

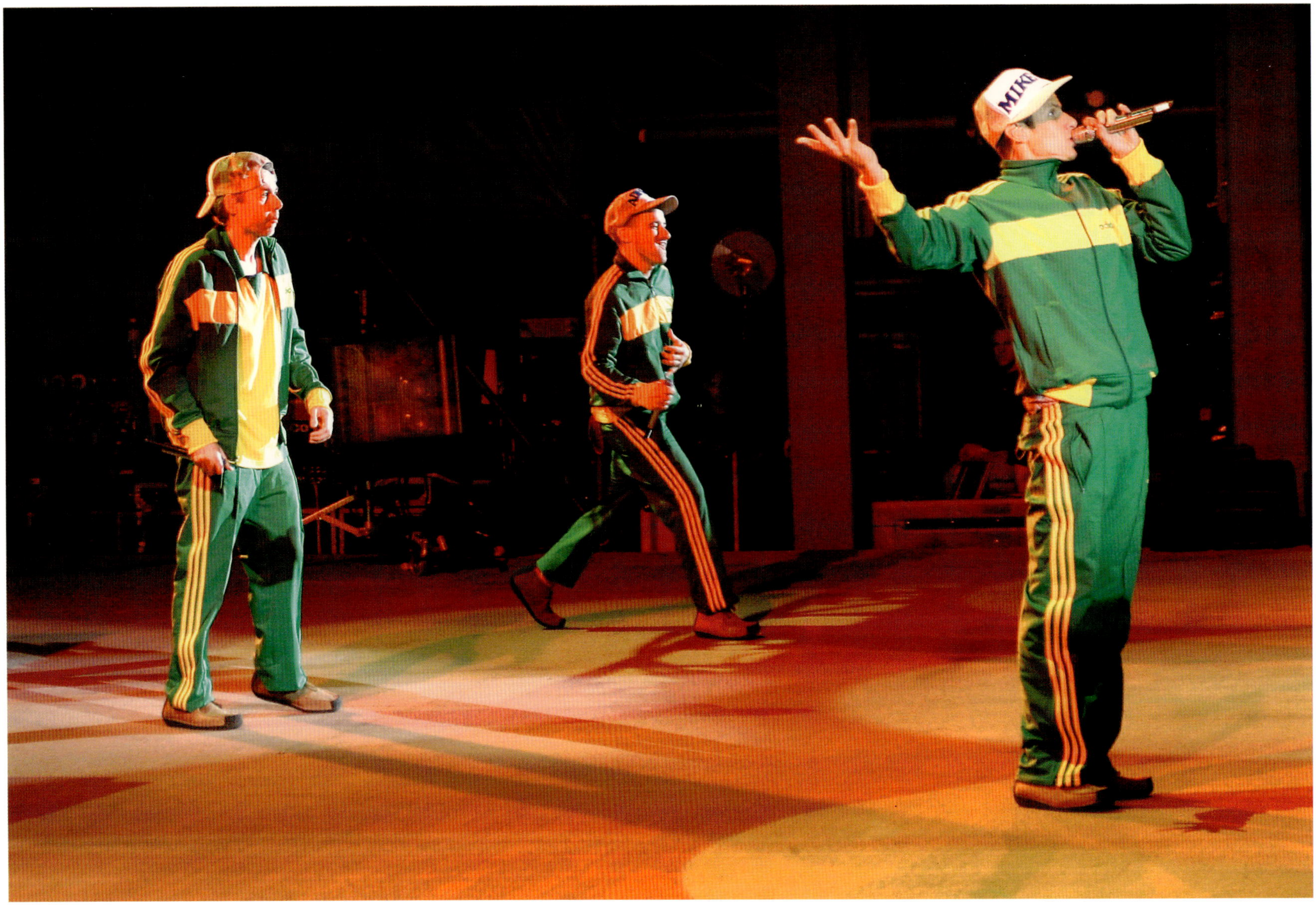

Beastie Boys, 2004; Dio, 2002 (right)

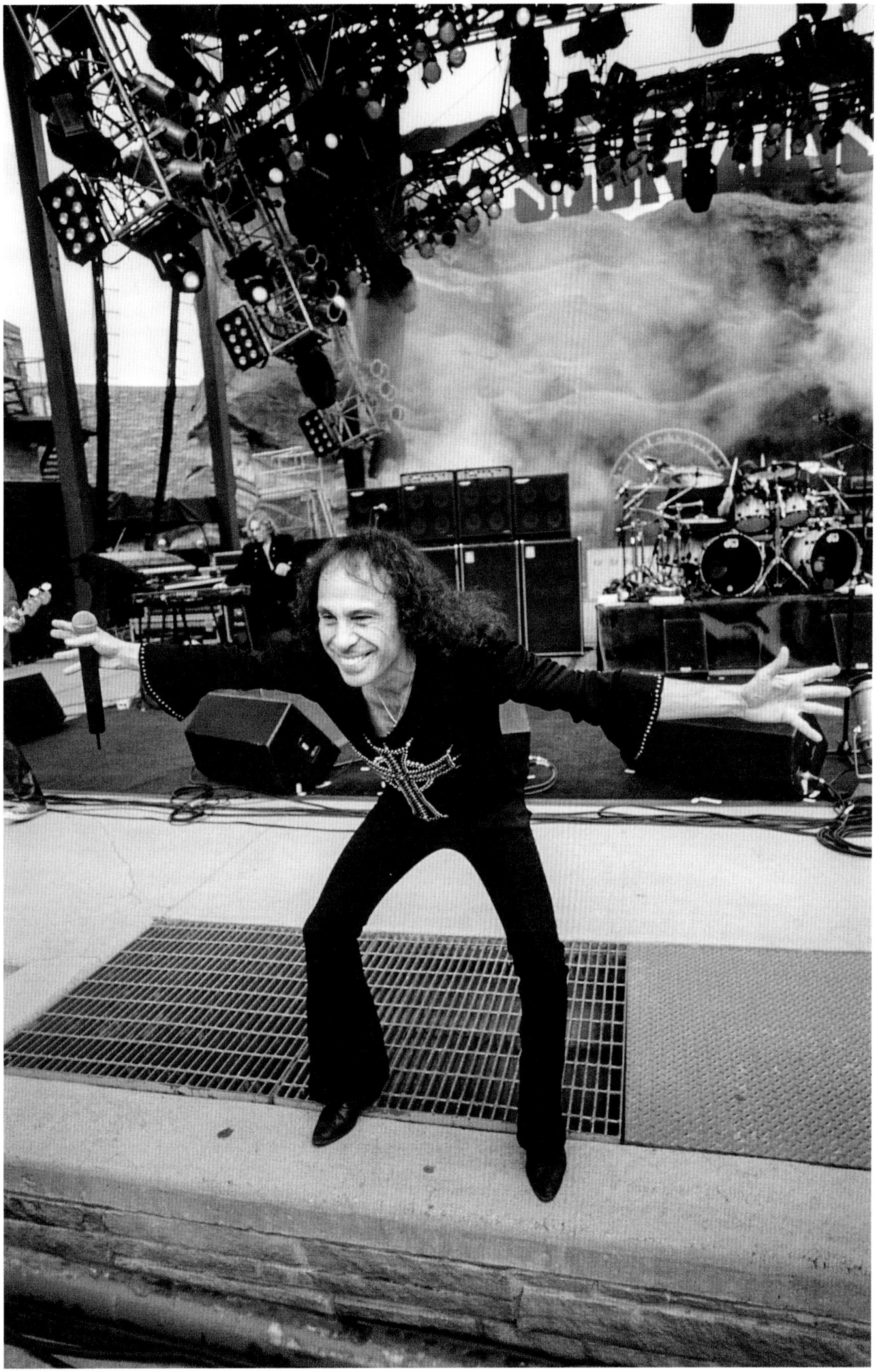

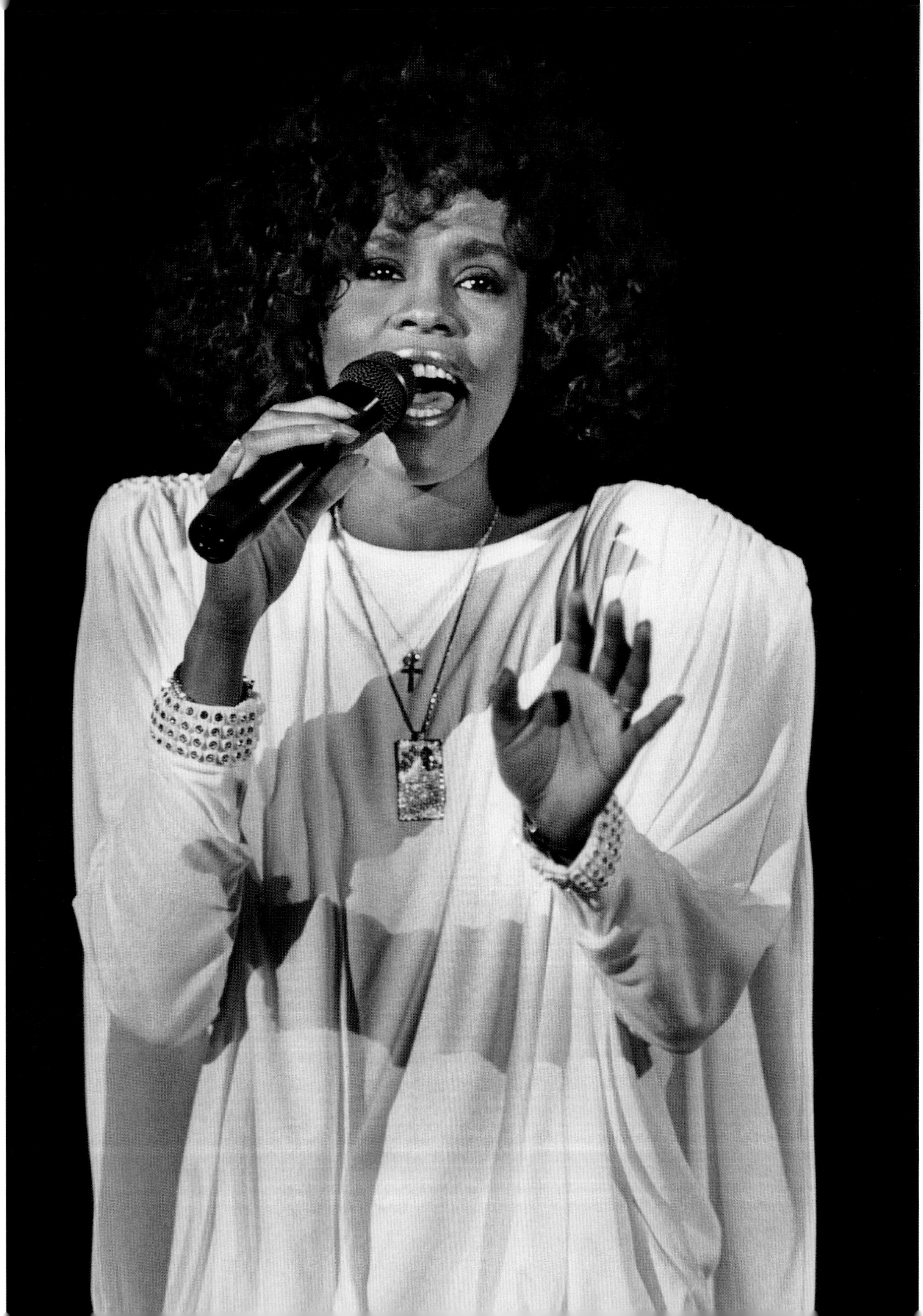

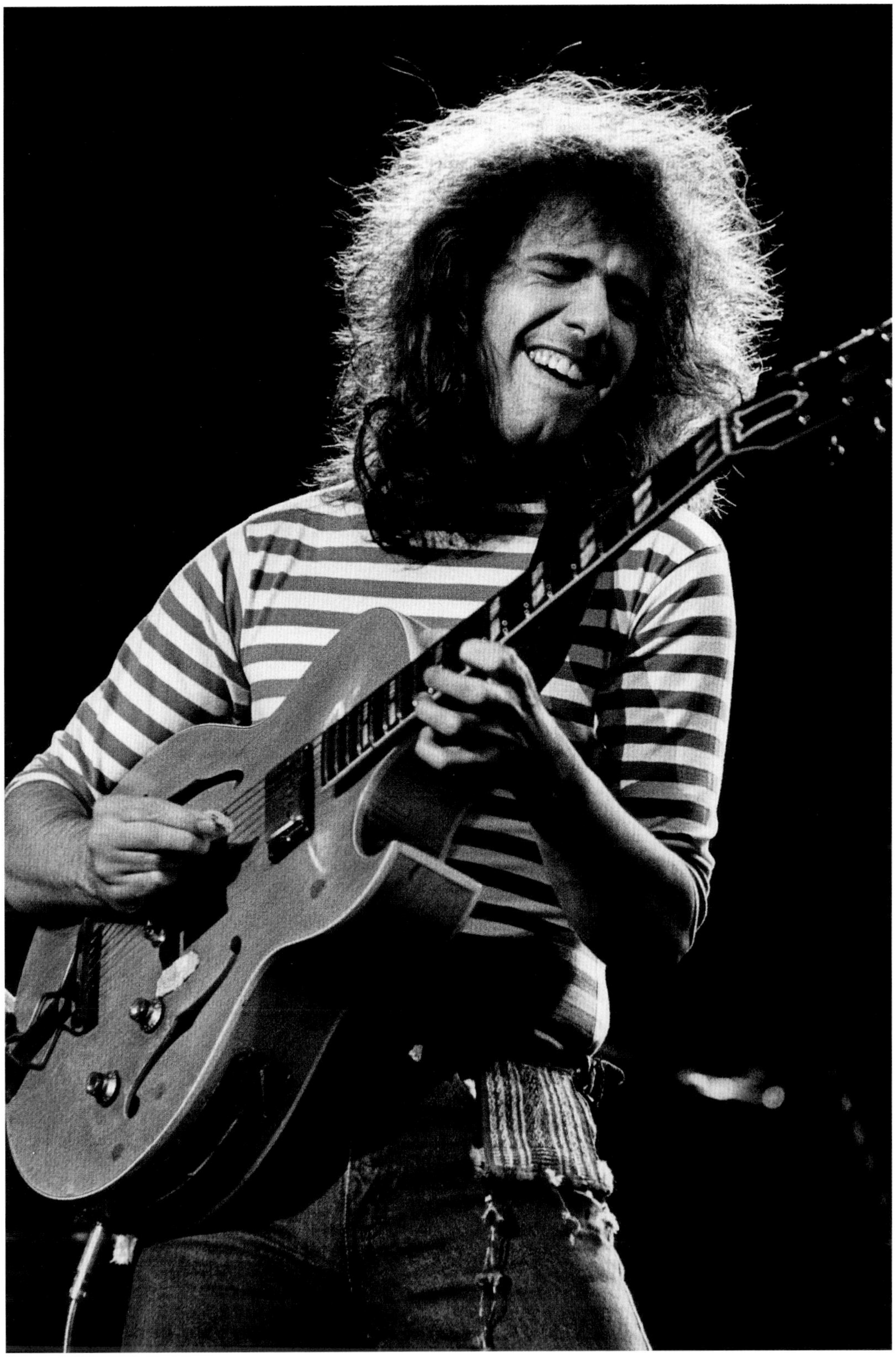

Whitney Houston, 1986 (left); Pat Metheny Group, 1982

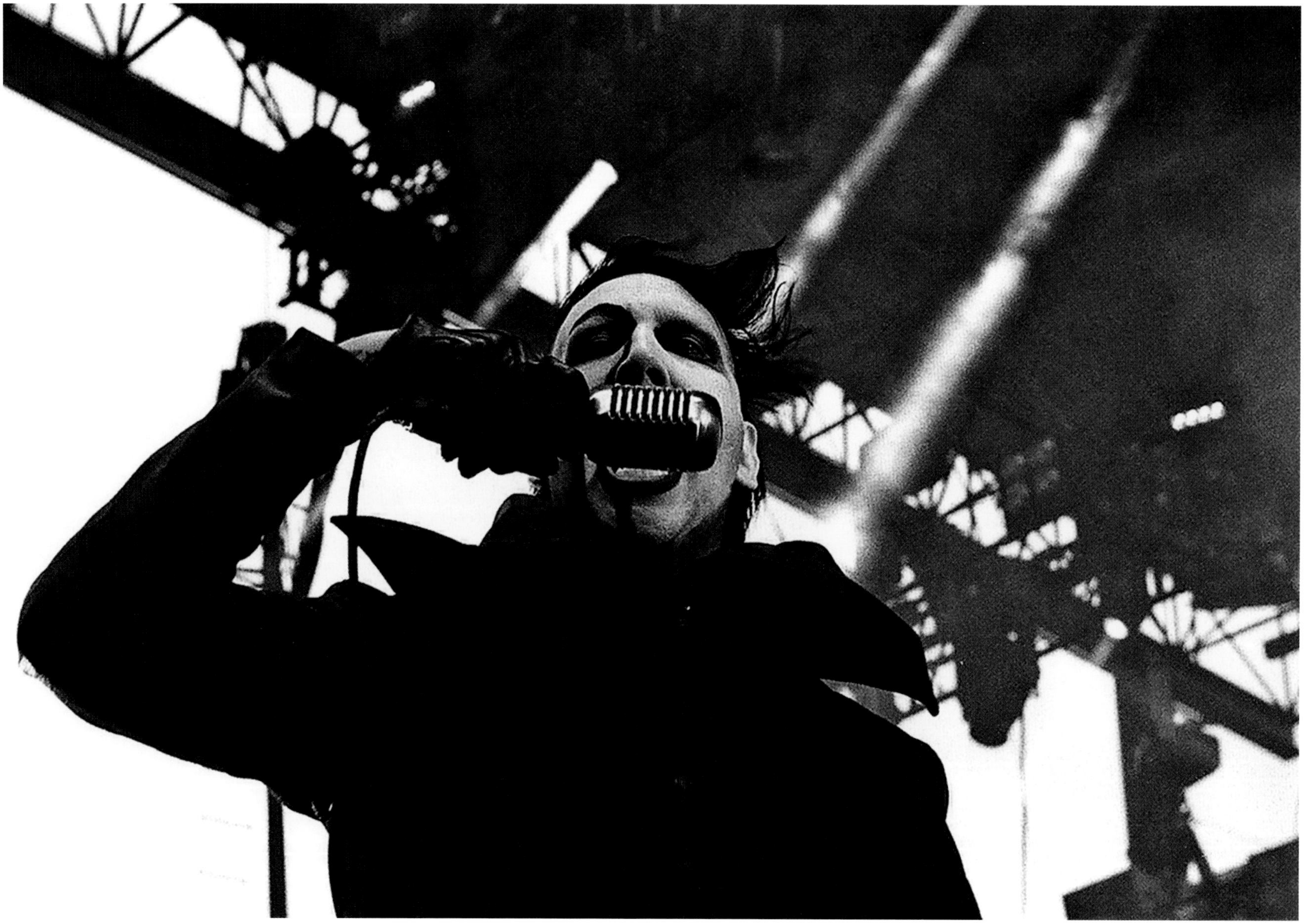

Marilyn Manson, 2015; Al Green, 2007 (right)

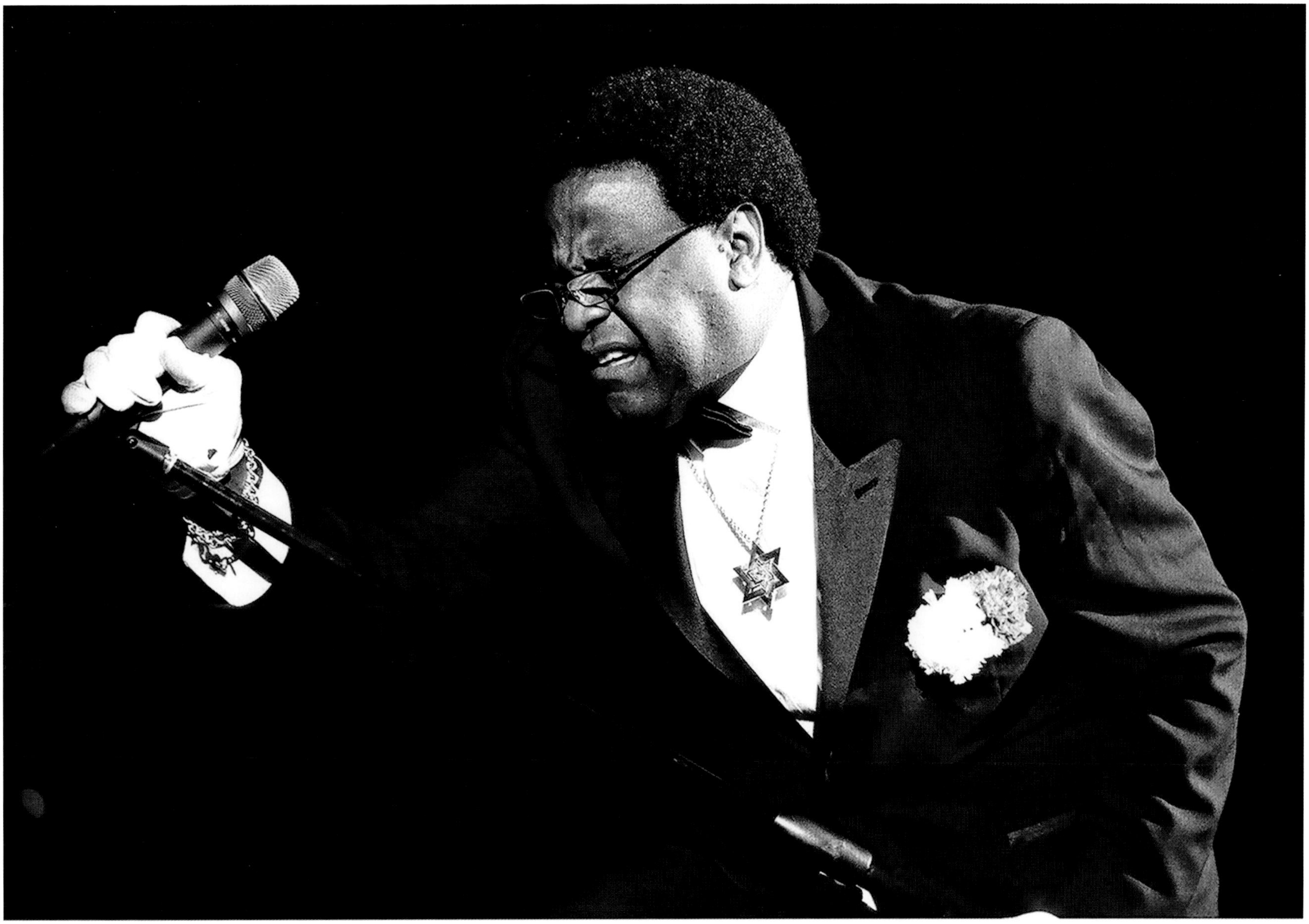

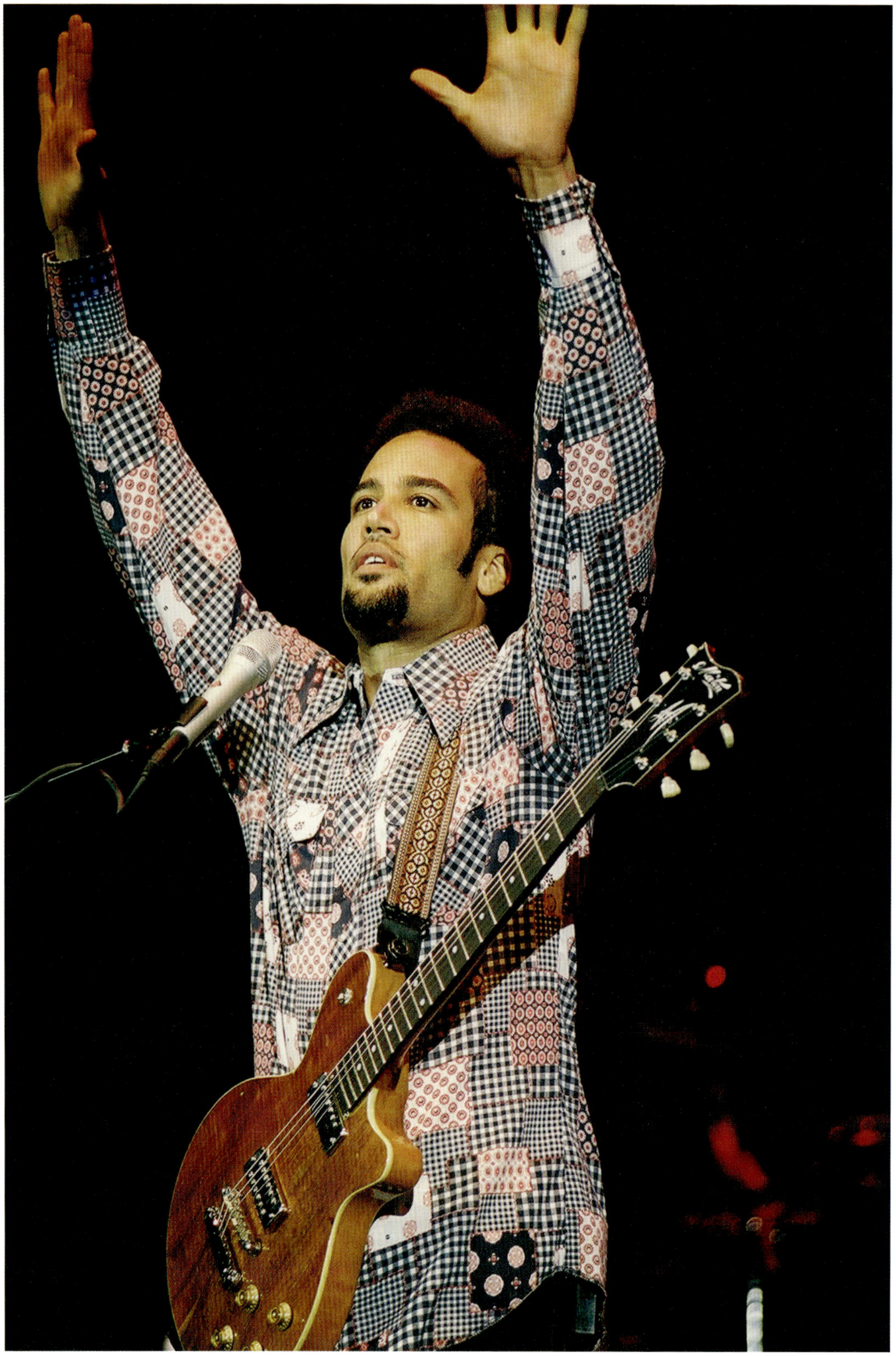

Ben Harper, 2003; Florence + the Machine, 2012 (right)

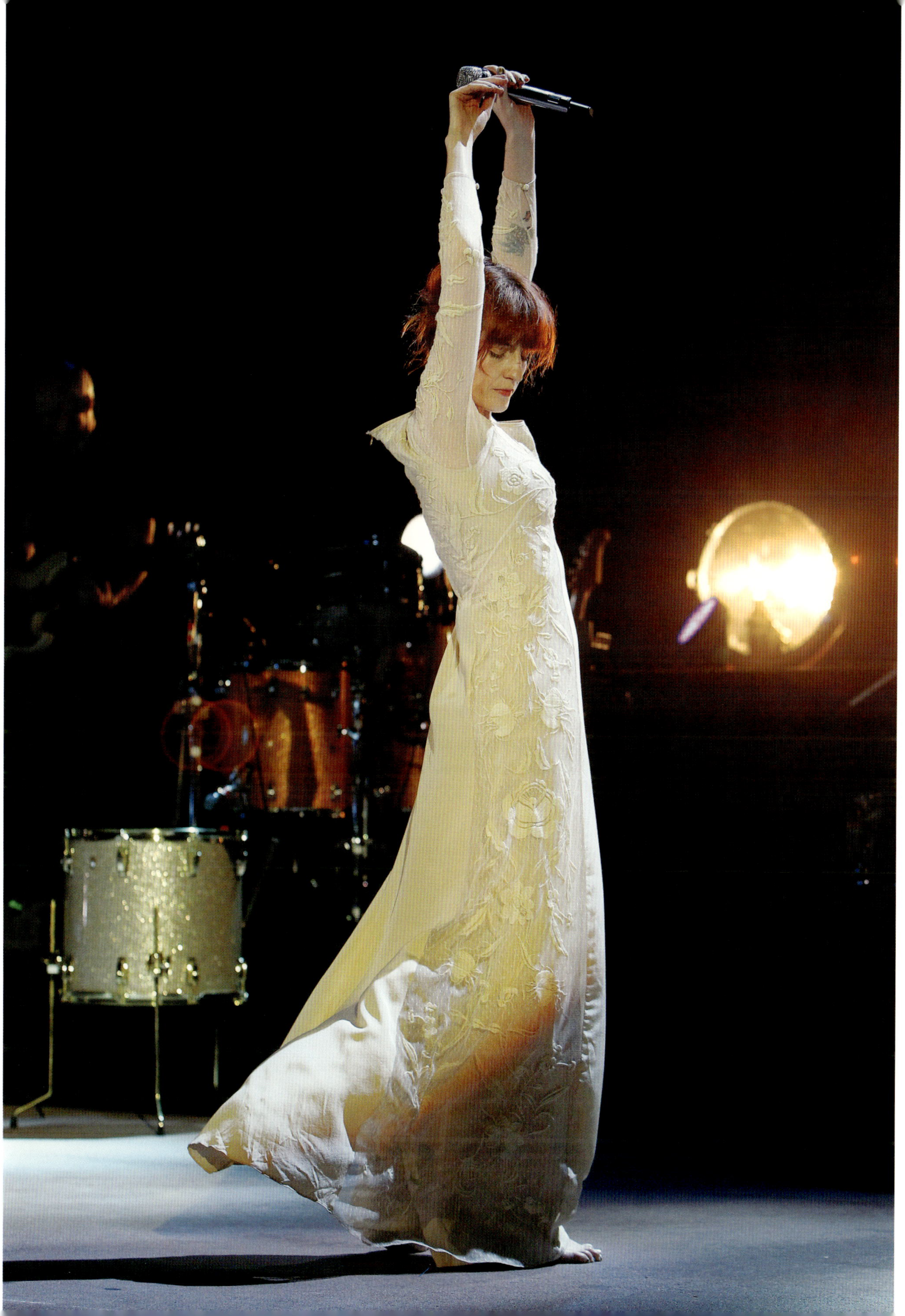

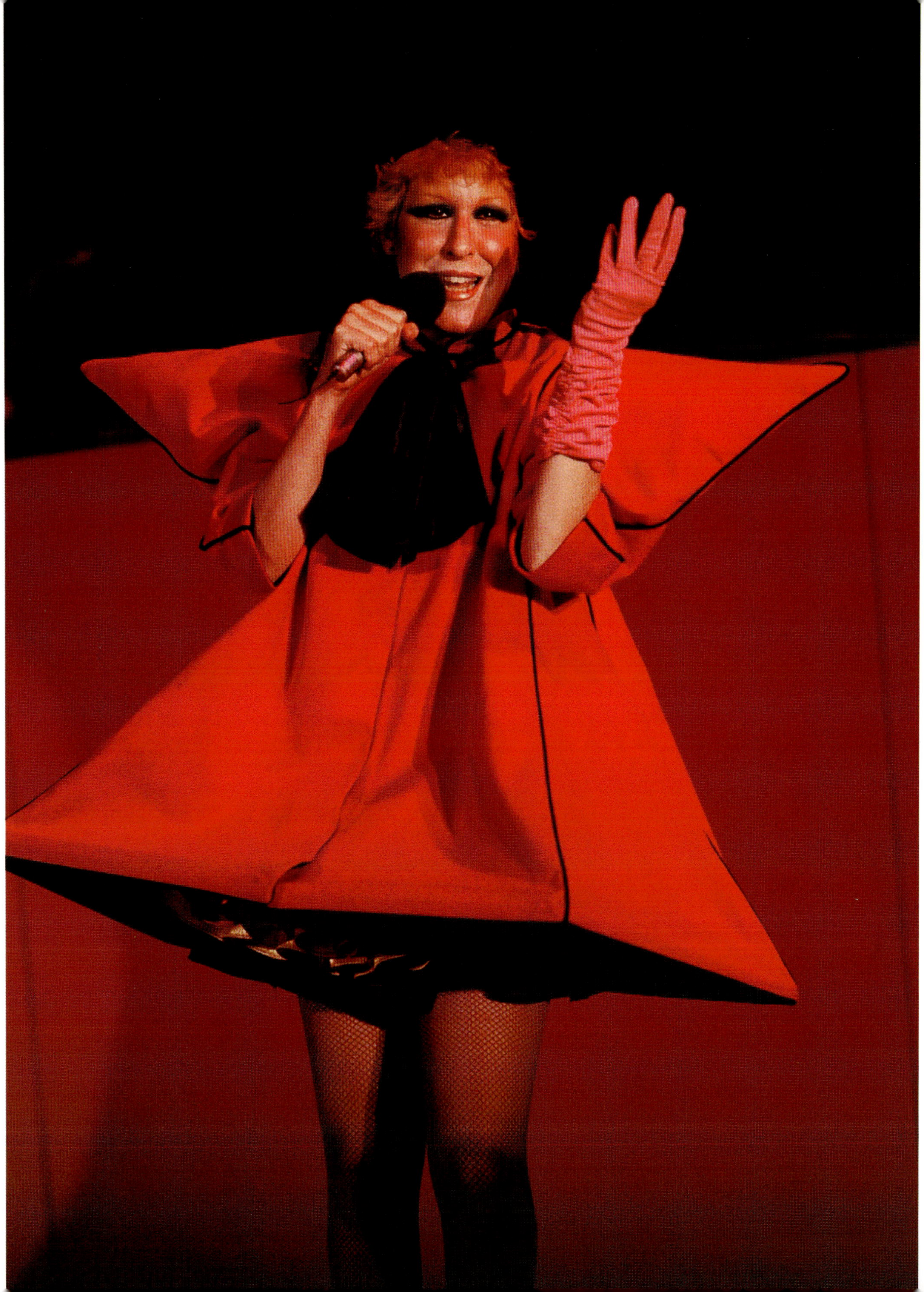

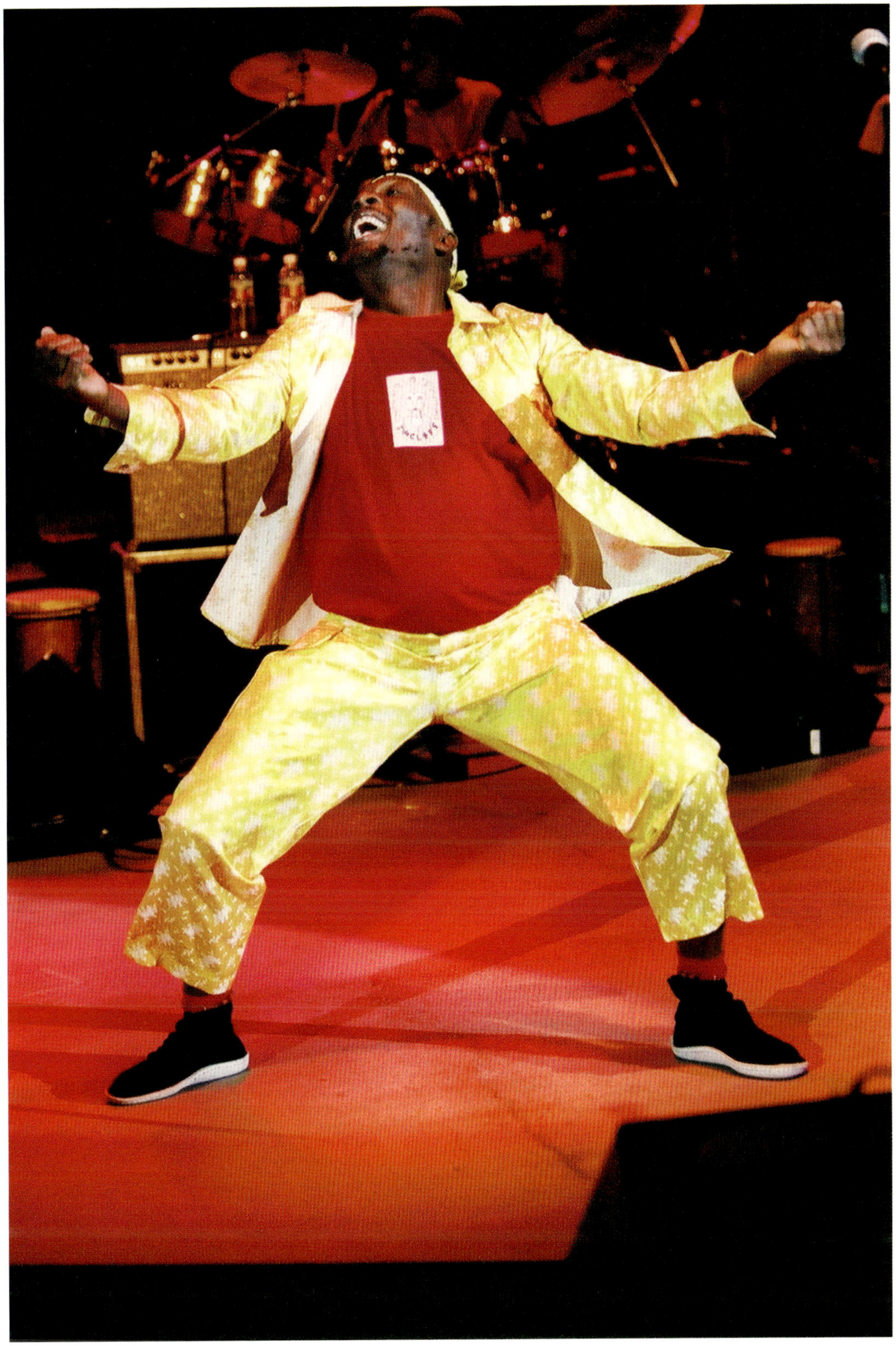

Bette Midler, 1983 (left); Jimmy Cliff, 2003

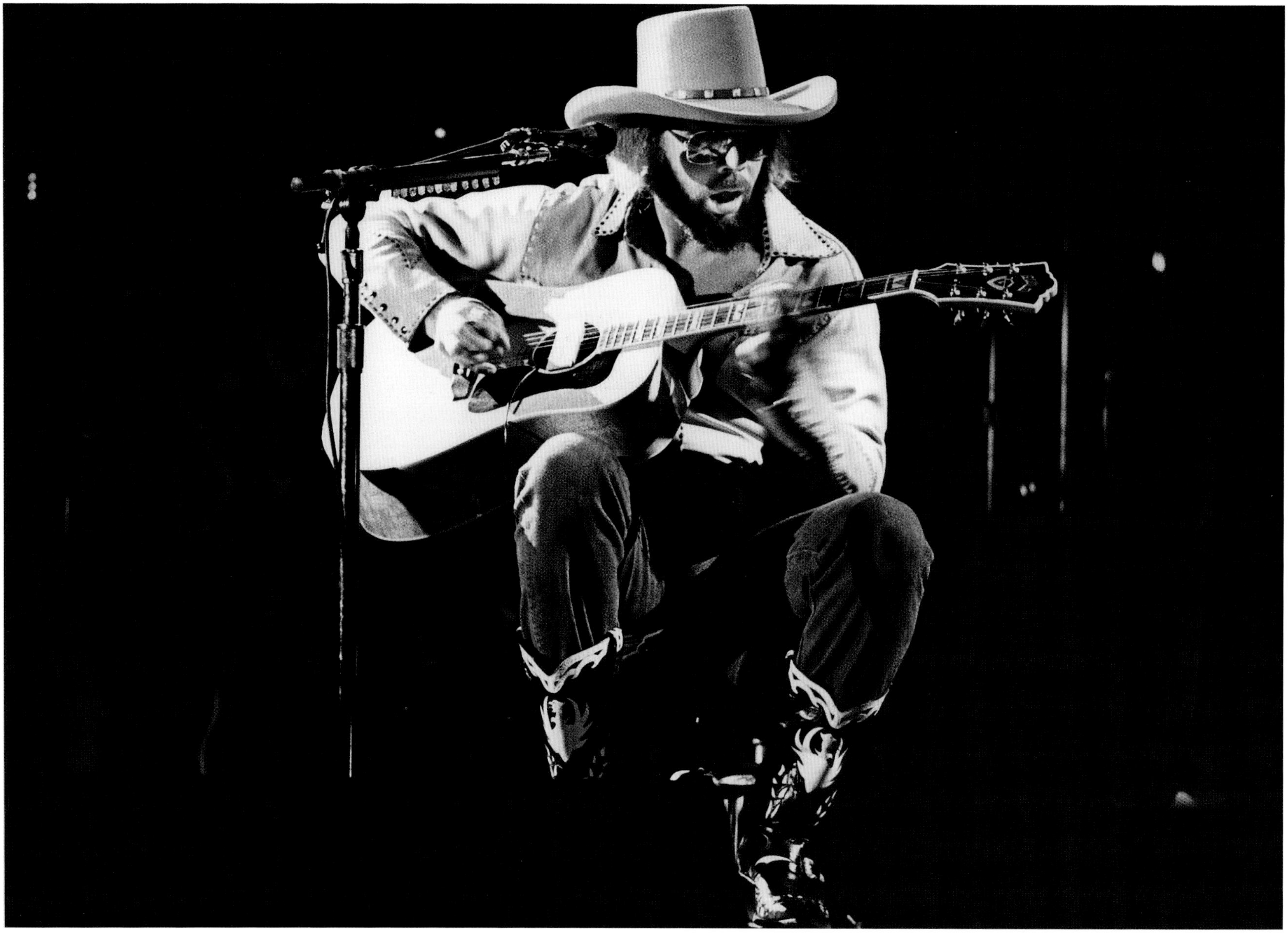

Hank Williams Jr., 1984; Miranda Lambert, 2005 (right)

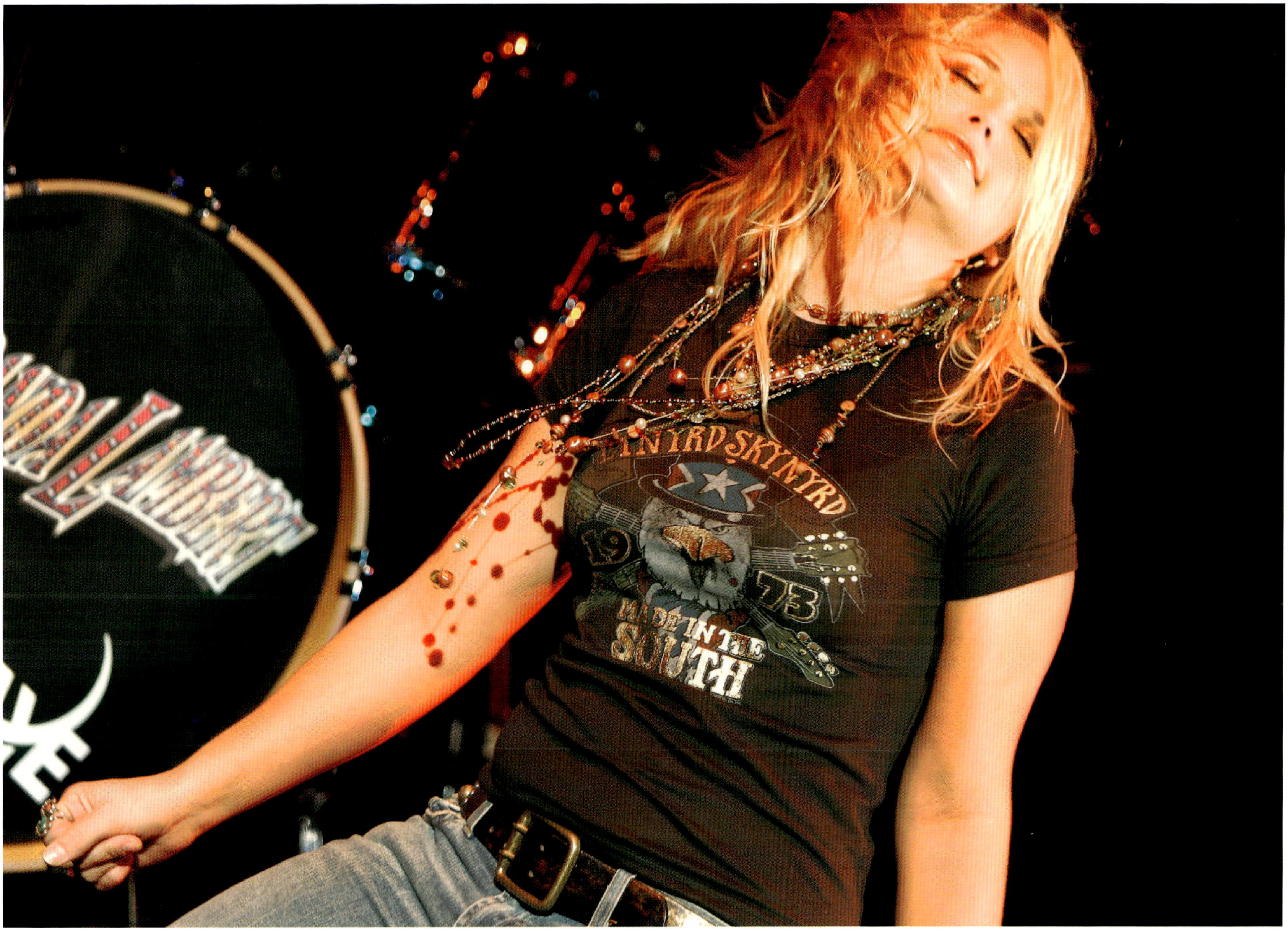
SKYNYRD
19
73
MADE IN THE
SOUTH

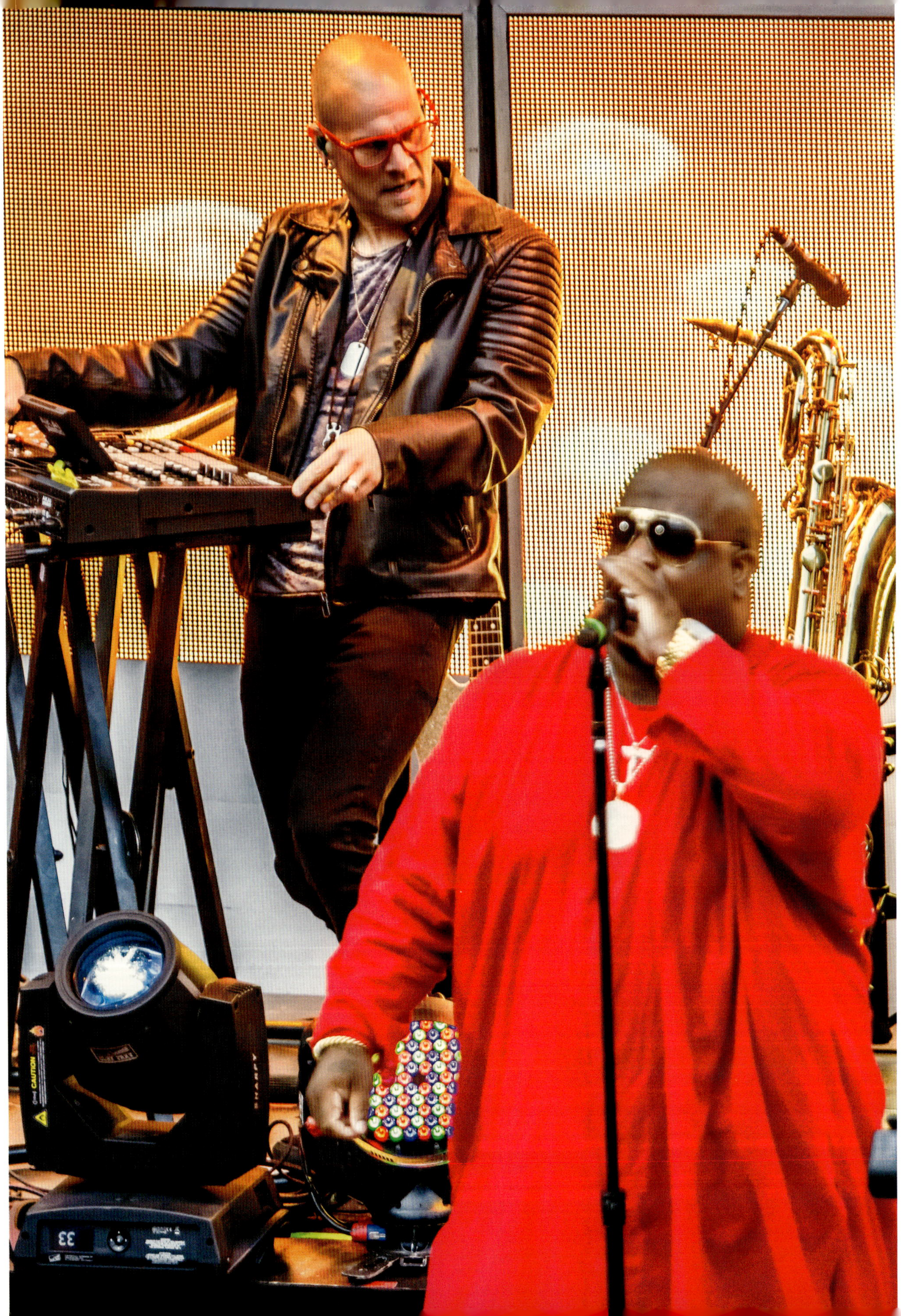

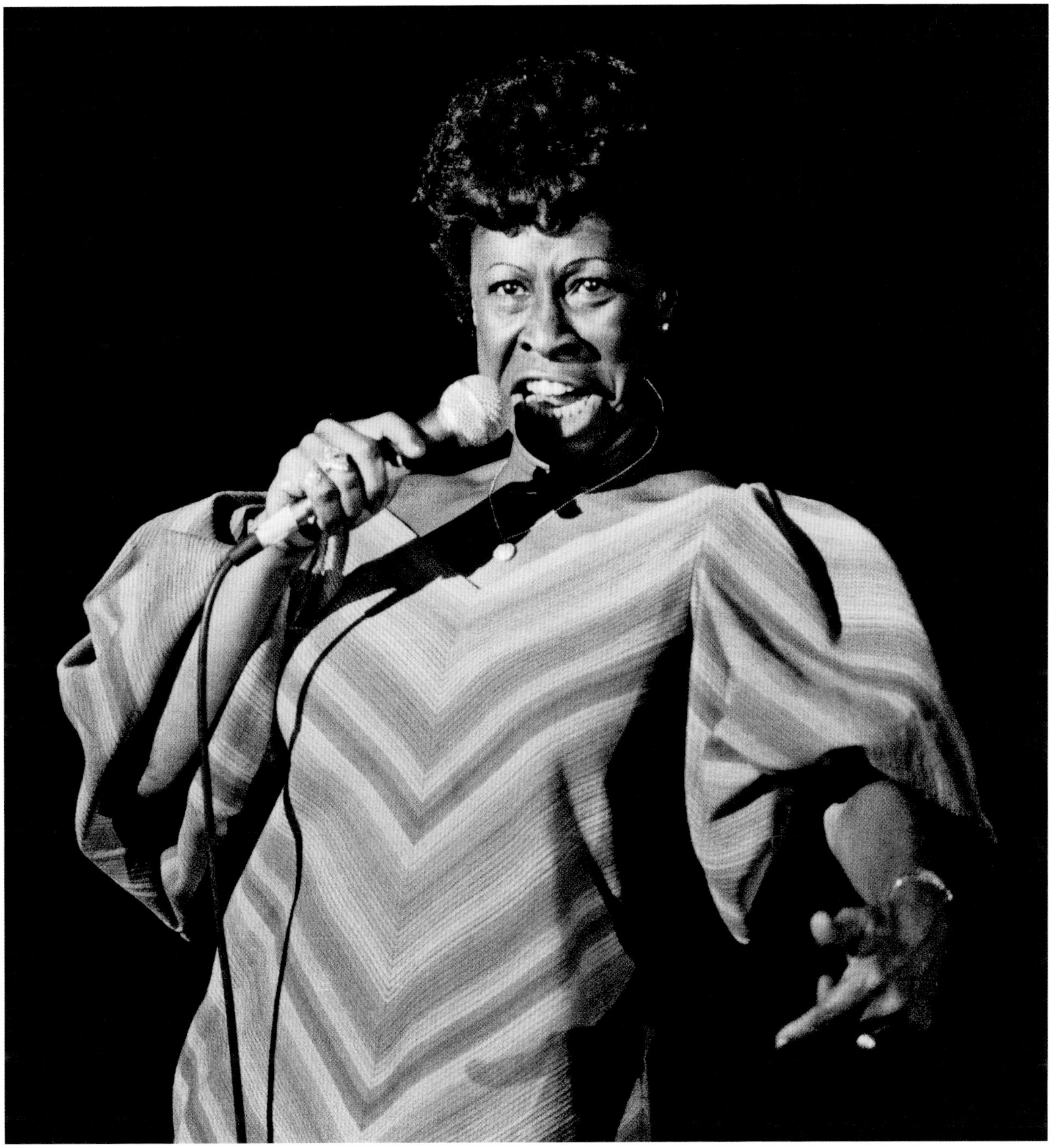

CeeLo Green, 2014 (left); Betty Carter, 1982

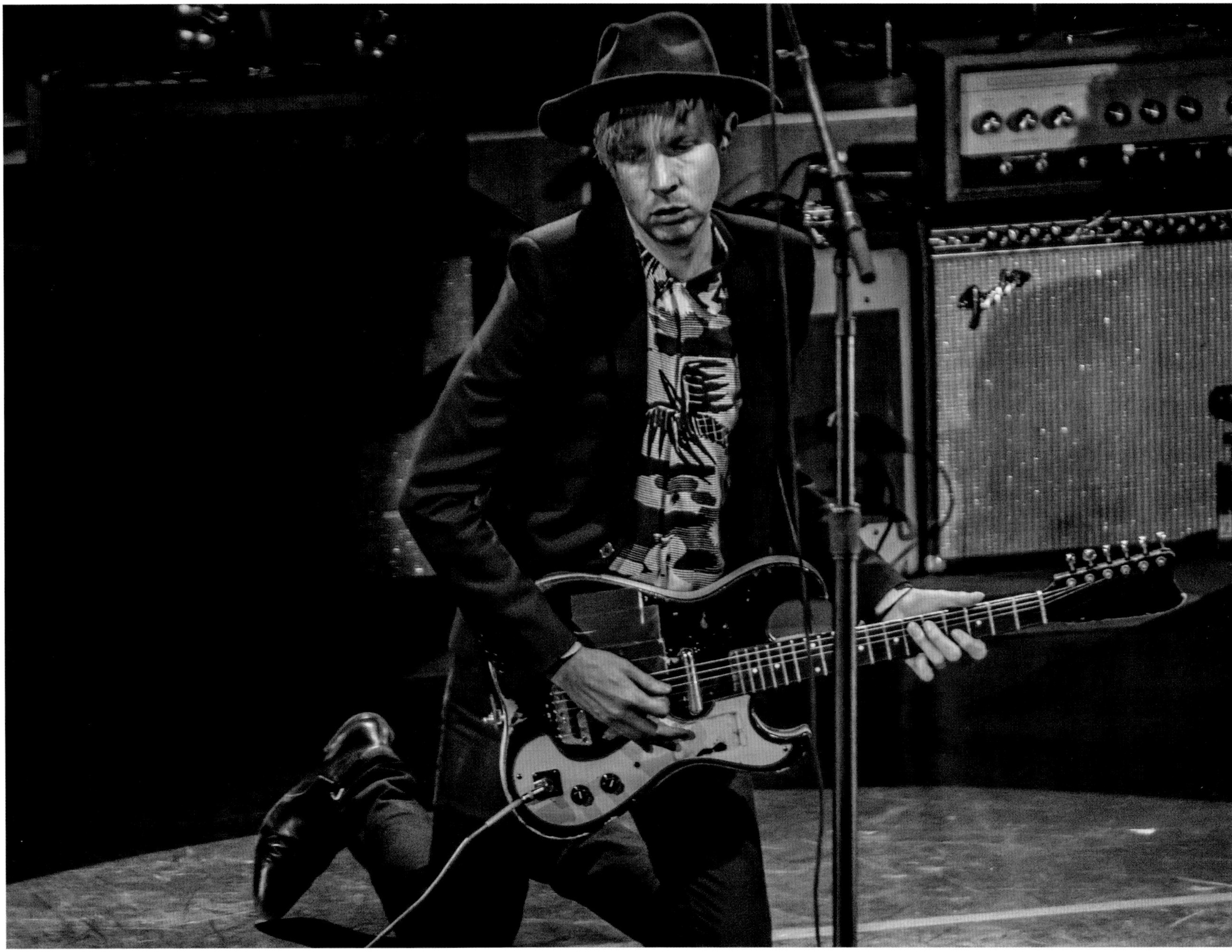

Beck, 2014 (above); k.d. lang, 1996

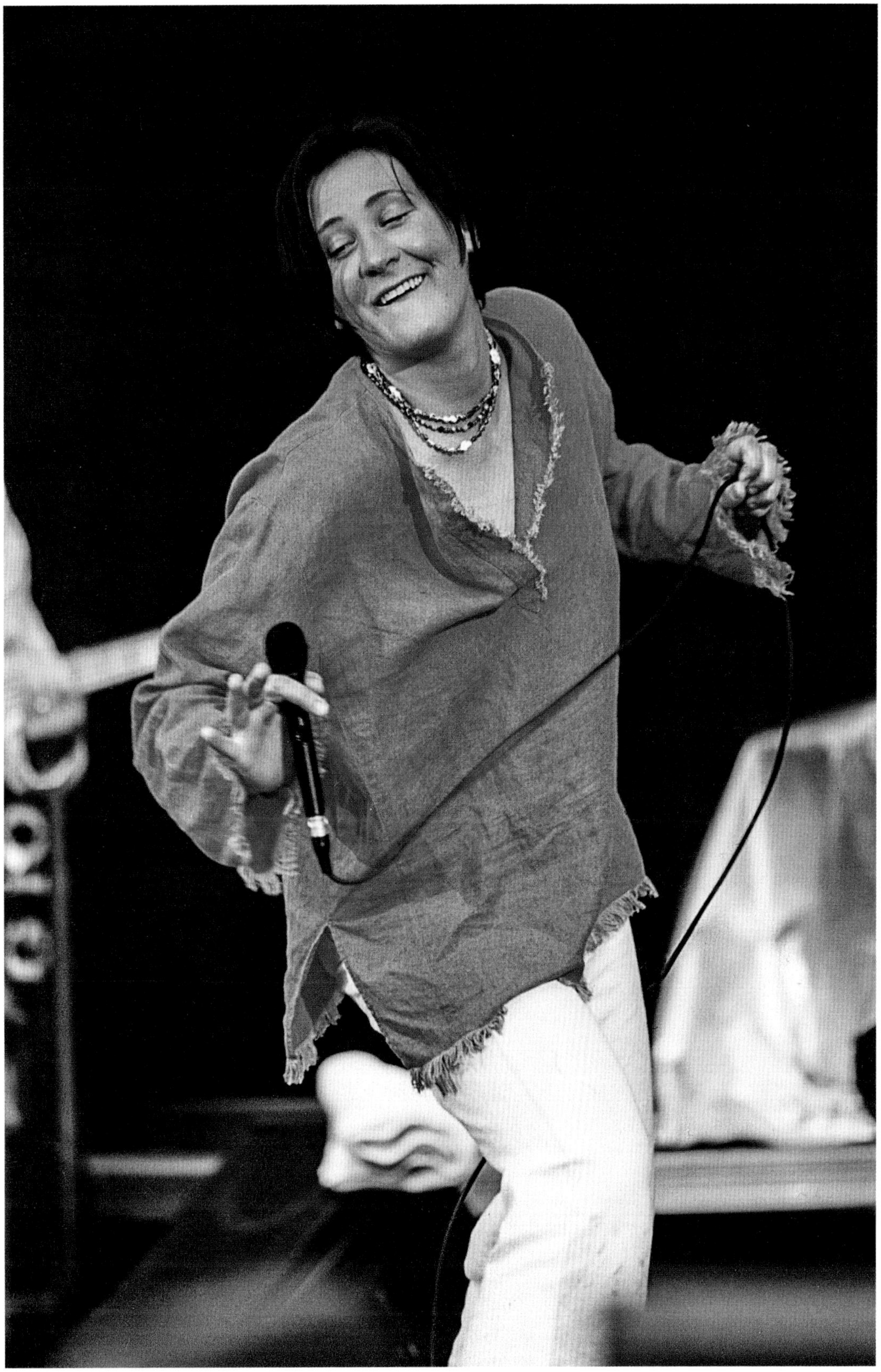

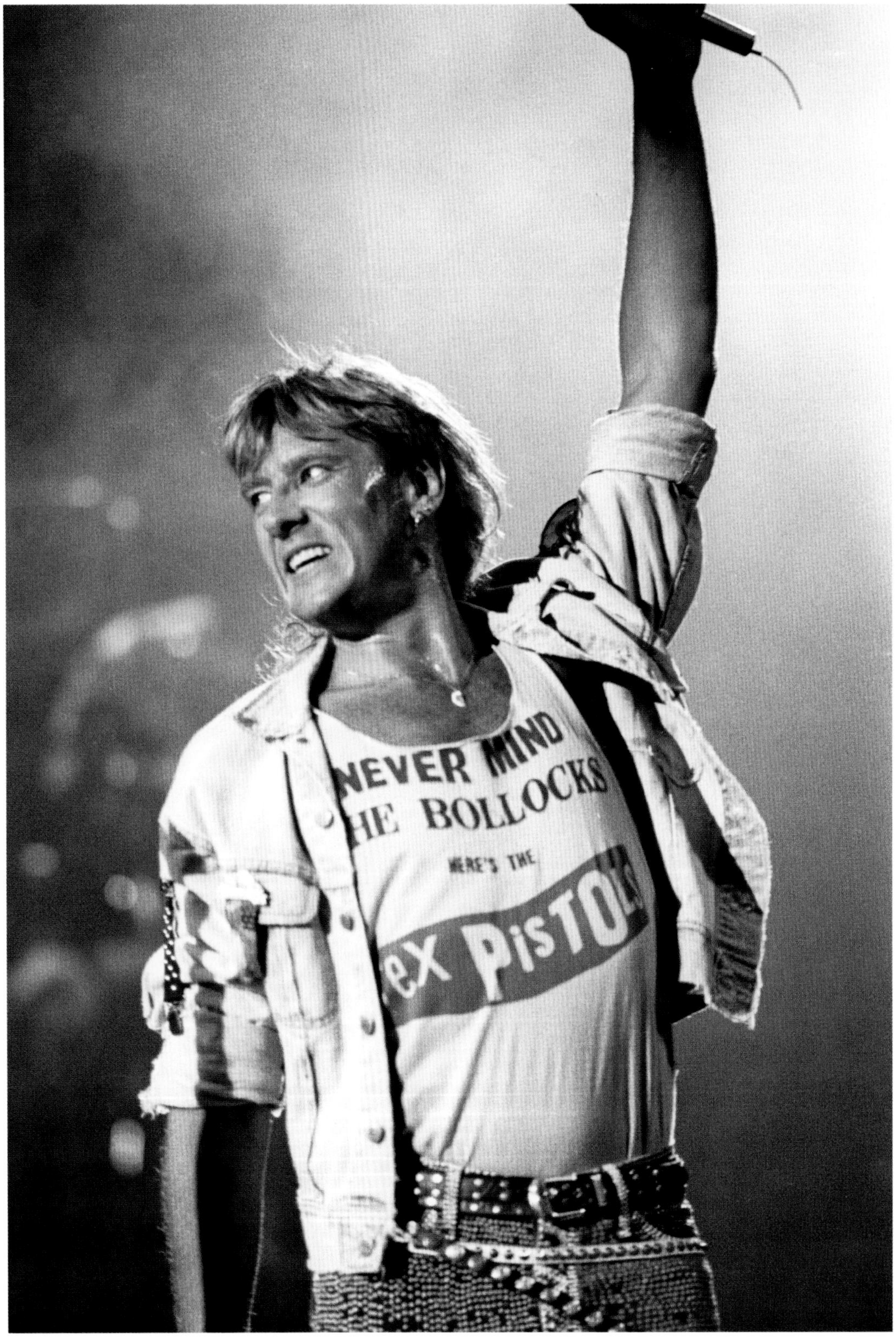

Def Leppard, 1988; Robert Palmer, 1986 (right)

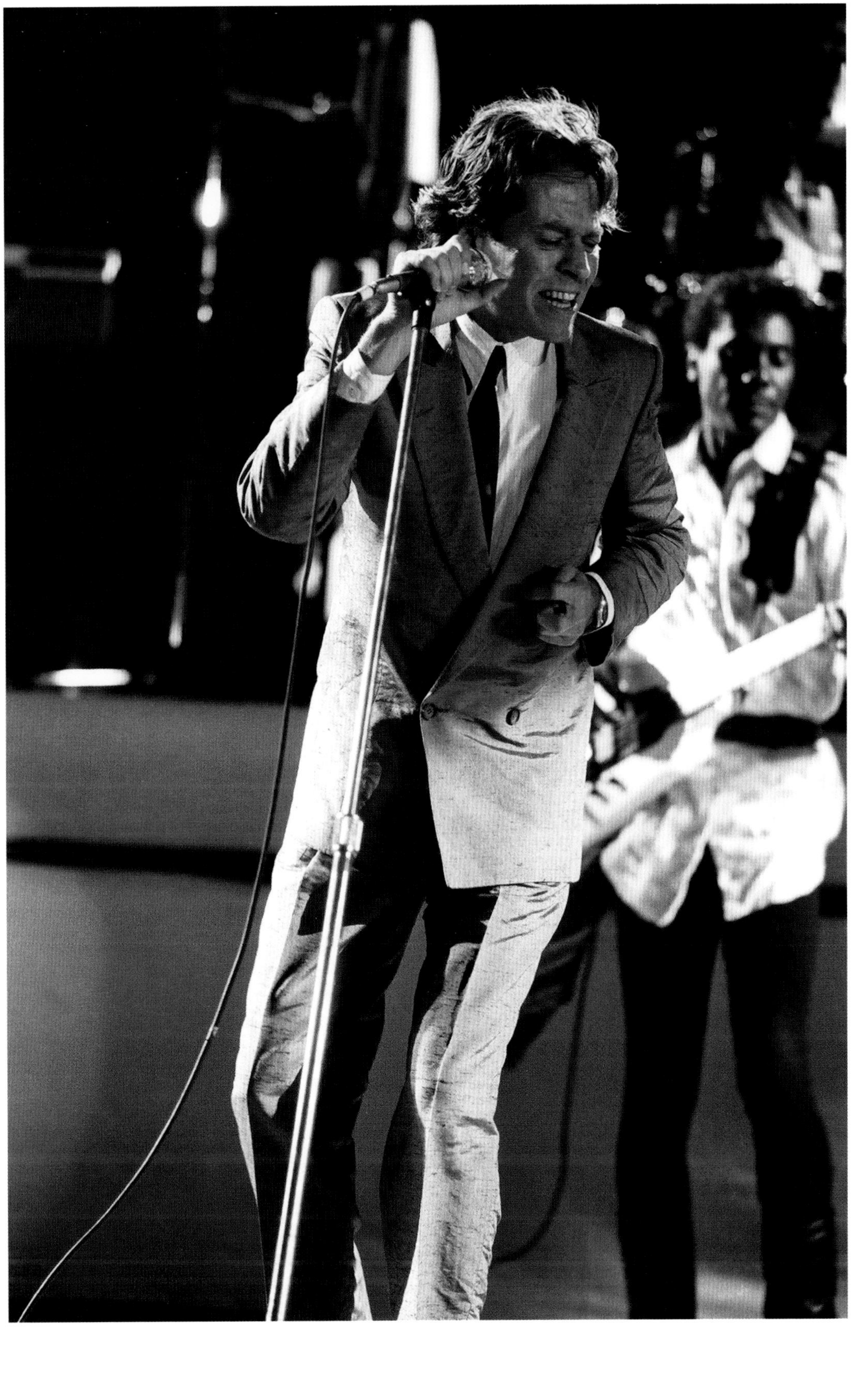

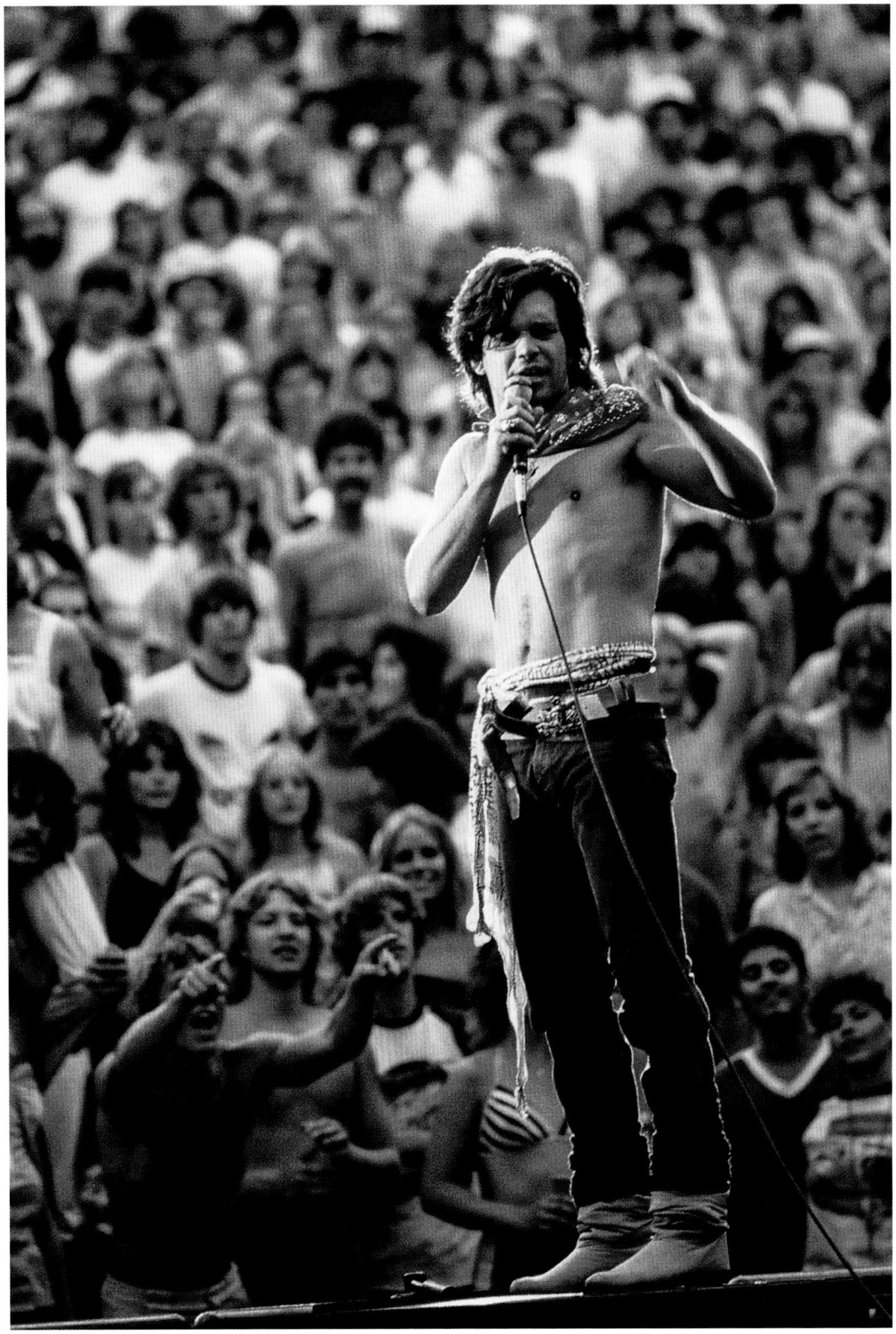

John Cougar, 1982; Jimmy Buffett, 1987 (right)

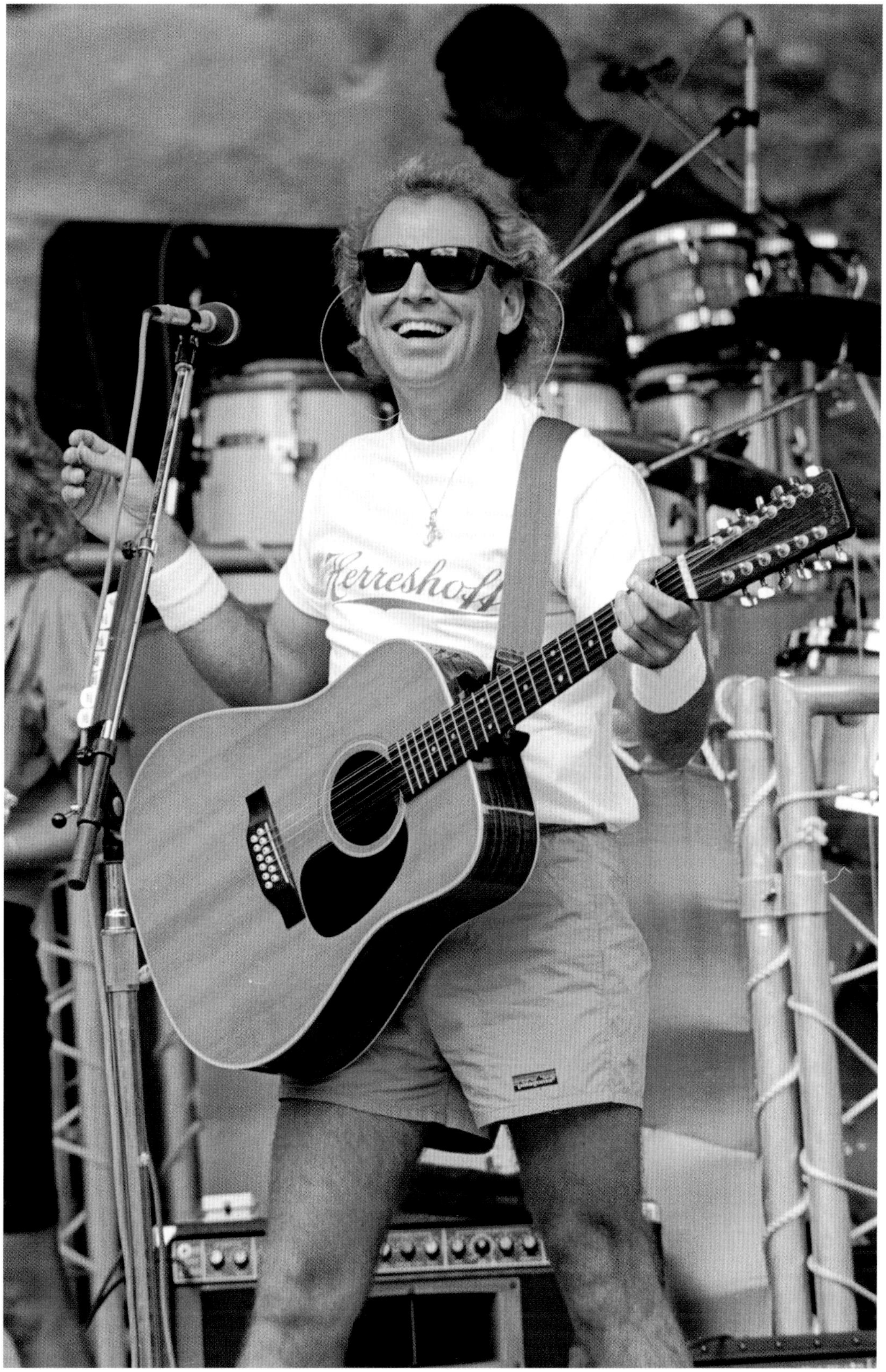
Herreshoff

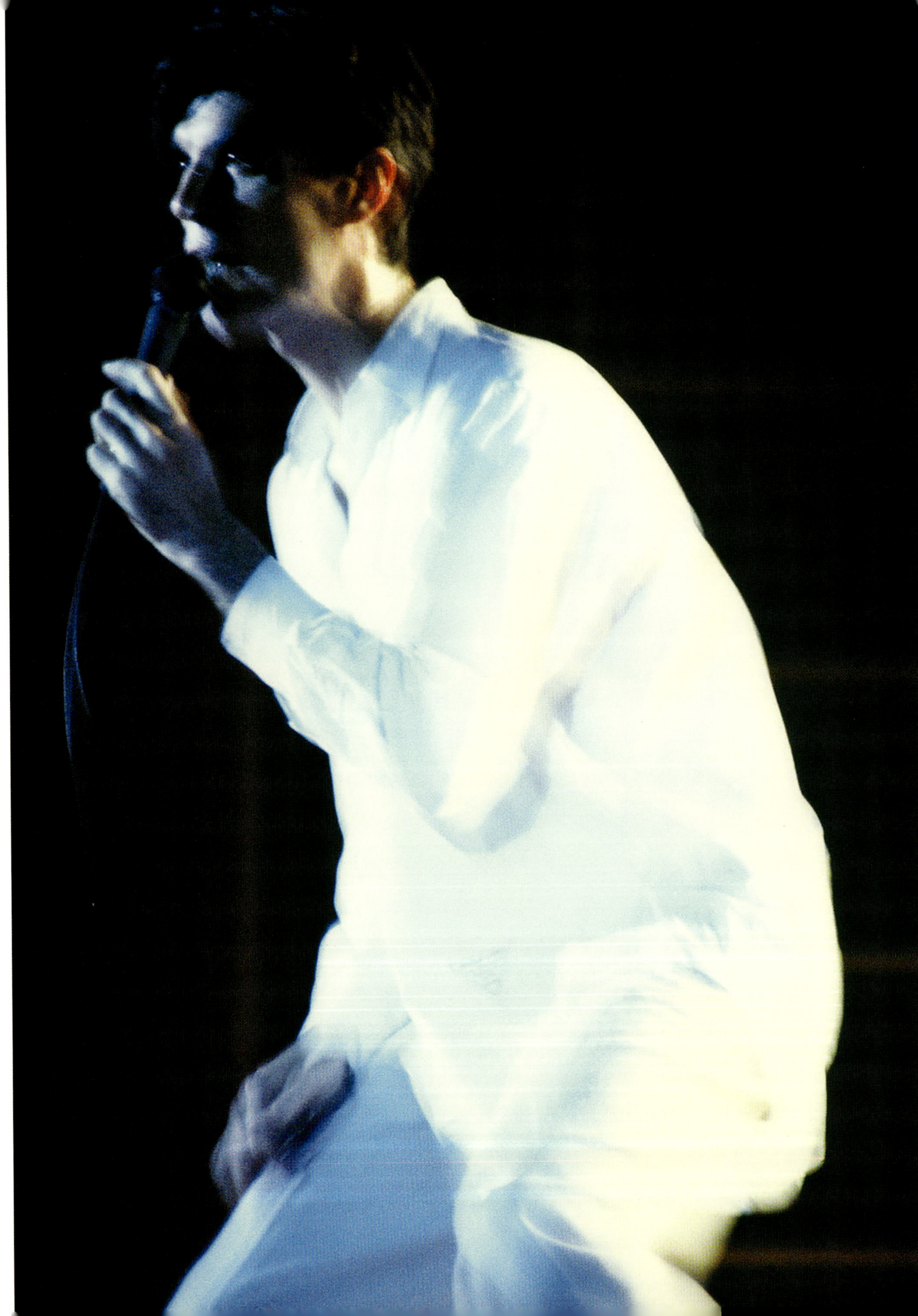

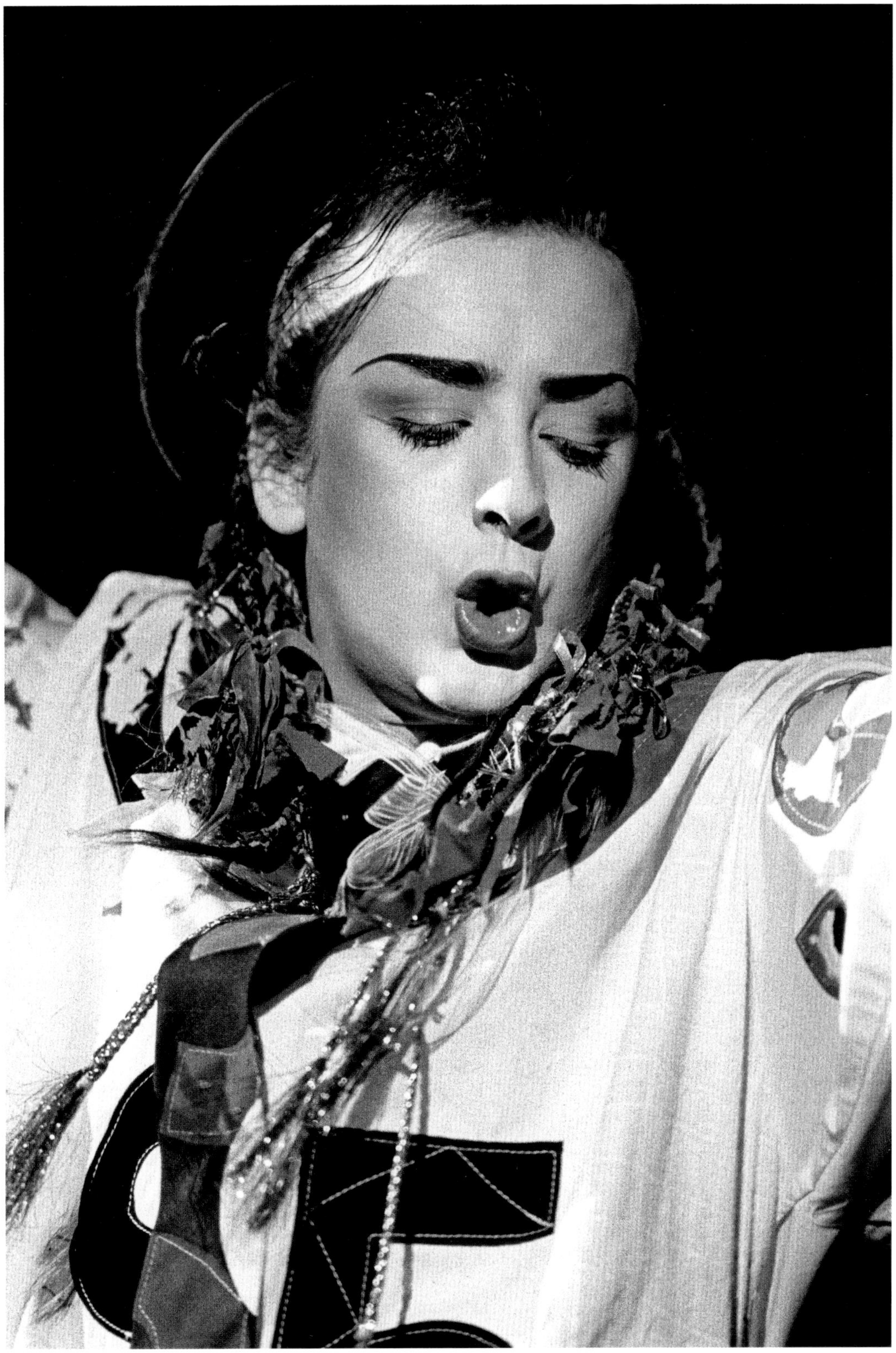

Talking Heads, 1983 (left); Culture Club, 1983

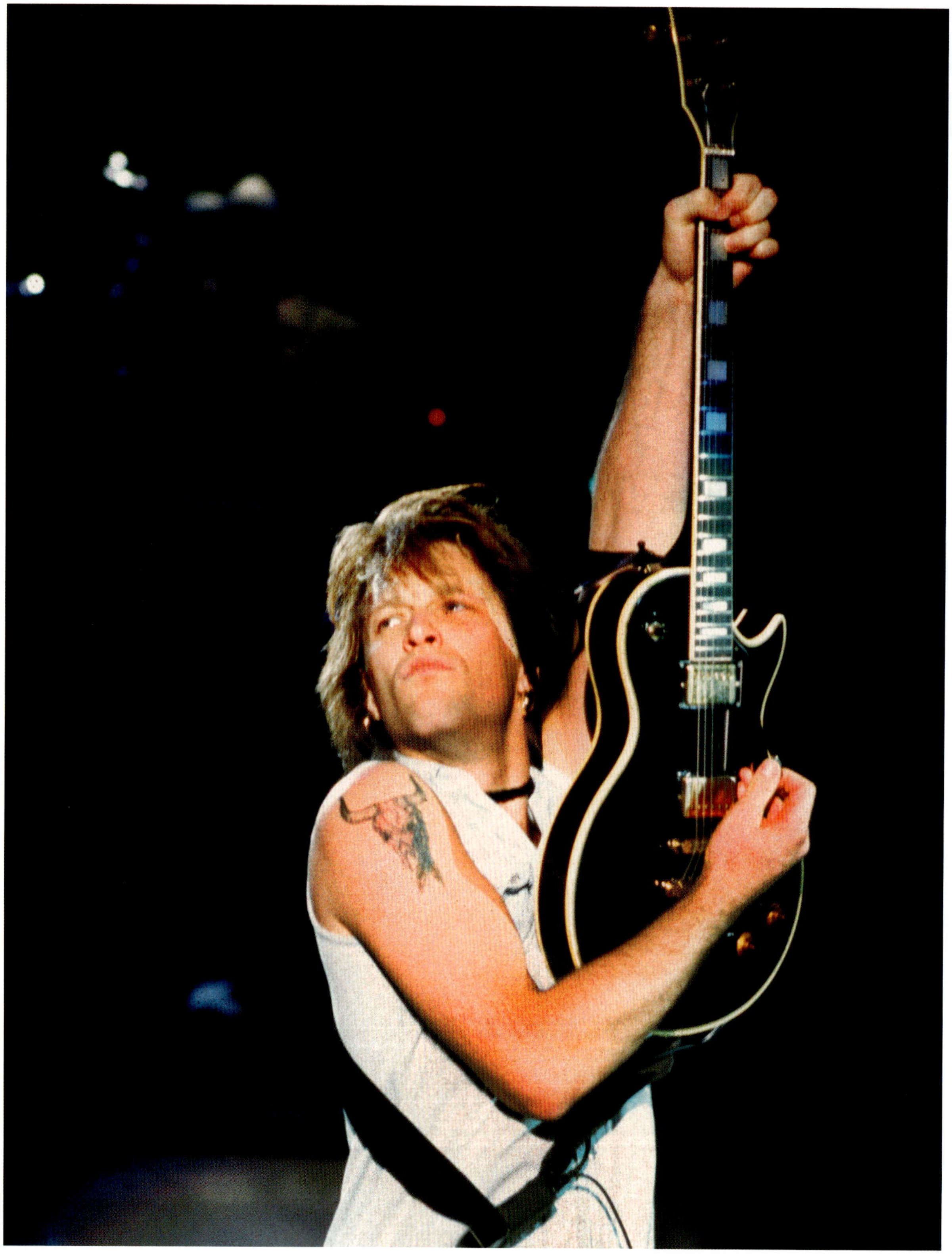

Bon Jovi, 1993; Kid Rock, 2004 (right)

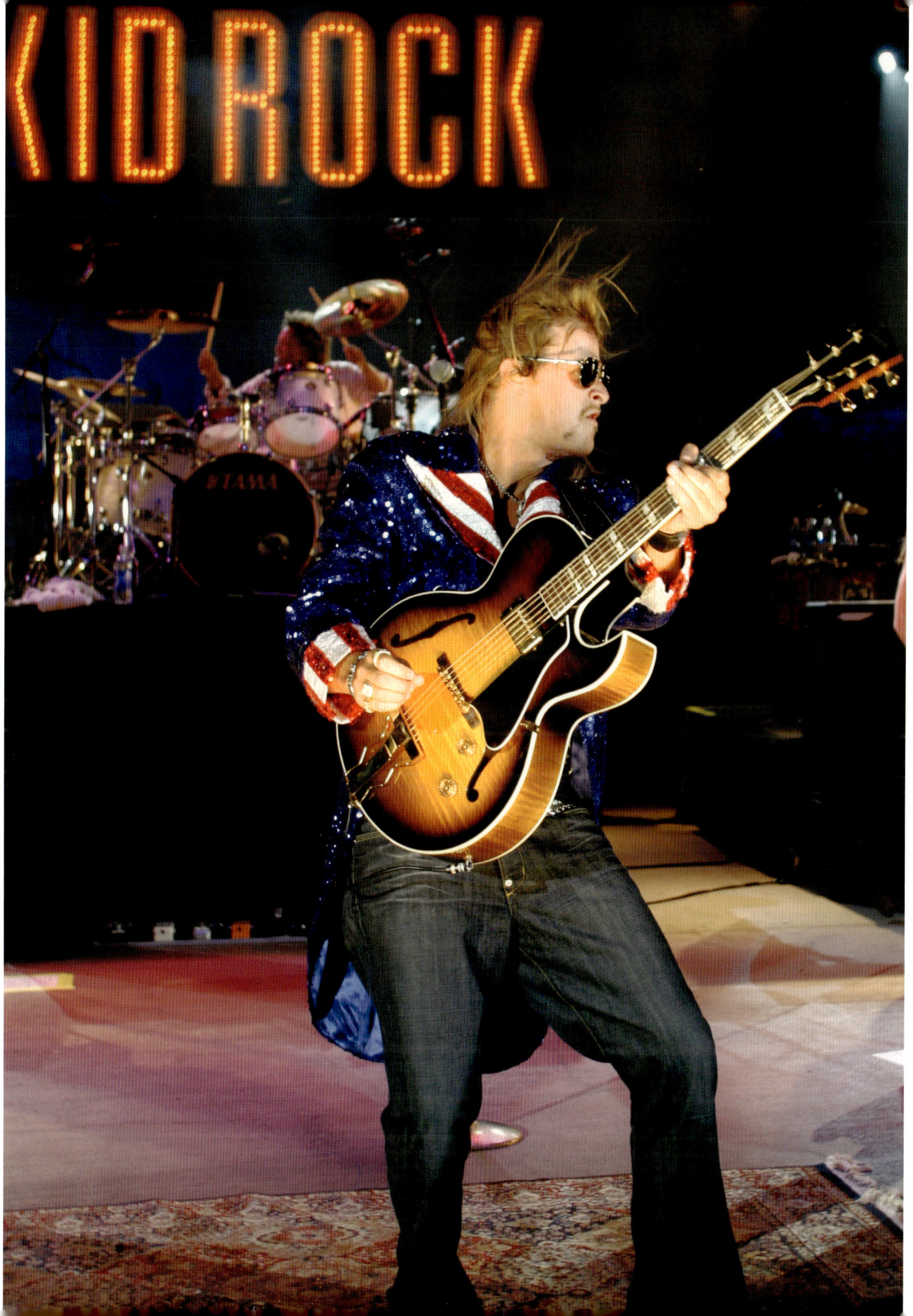
KID ROCK
TAMA

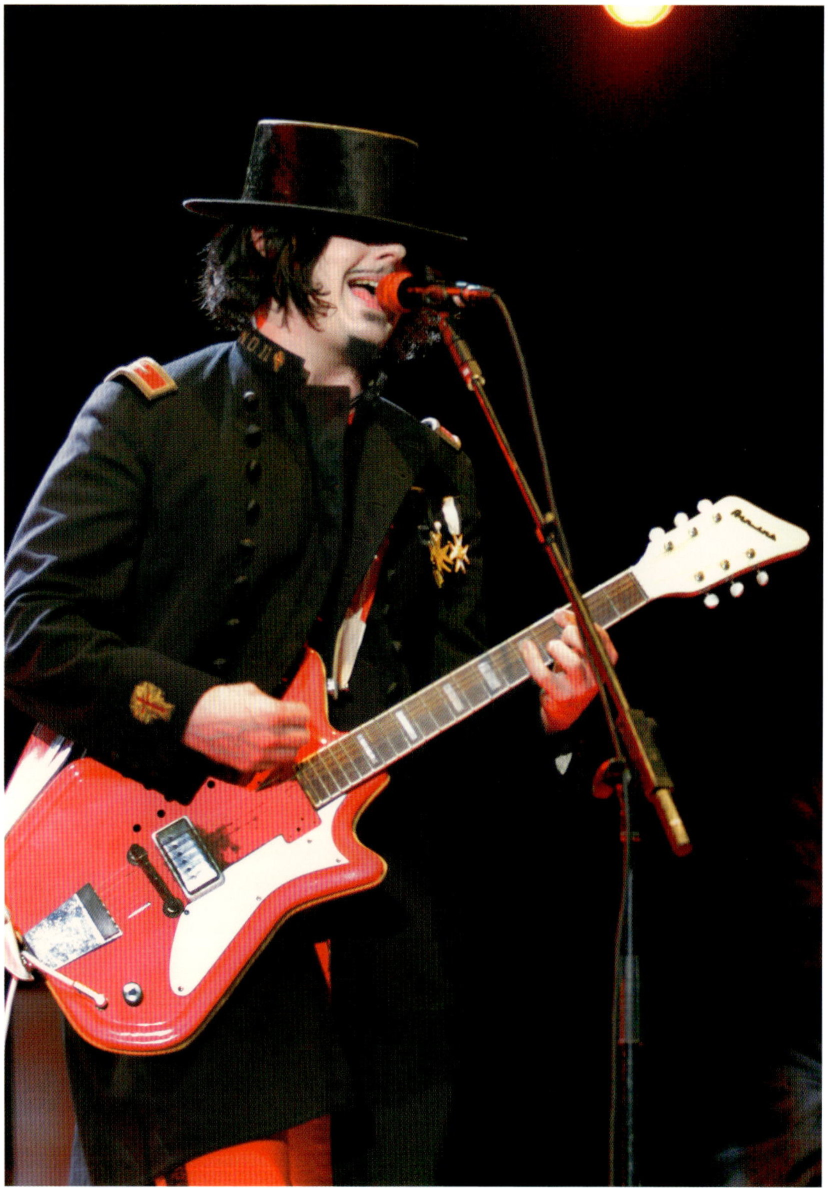 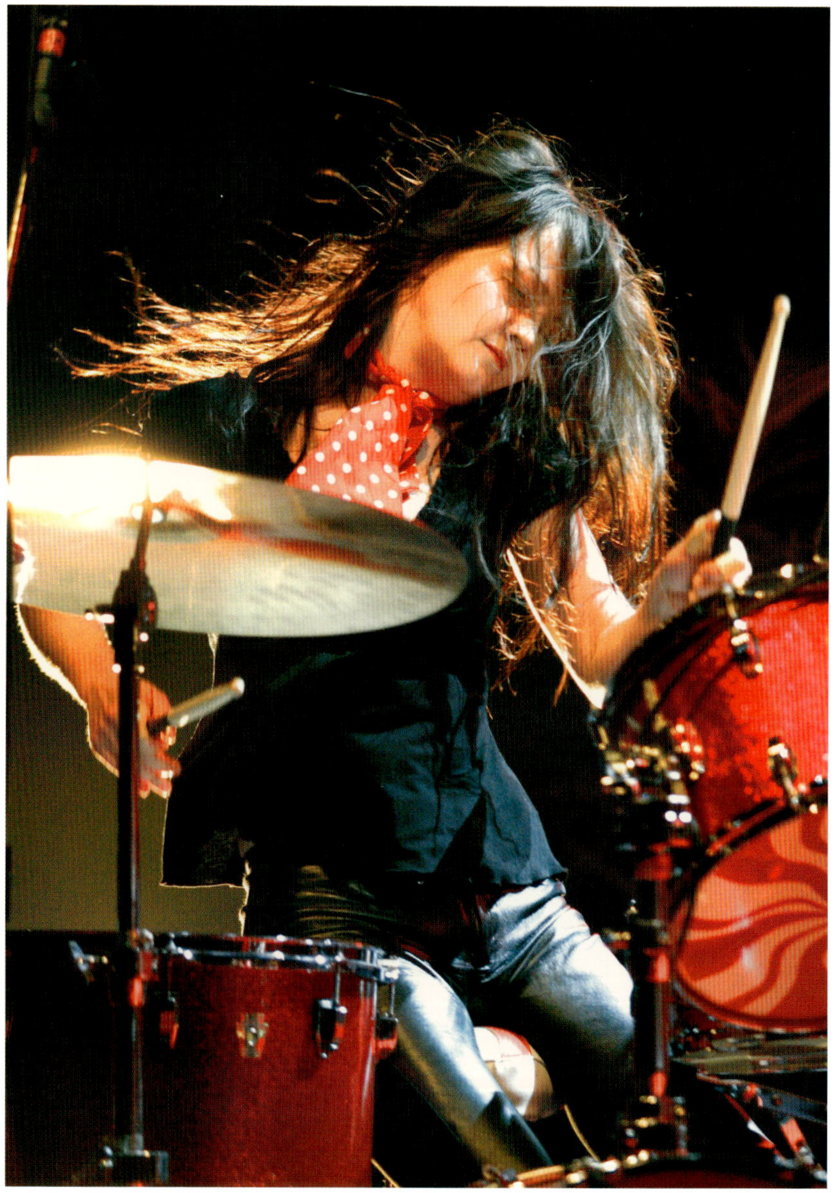

The White Stripes, 2005; Greta Van Fleet, 2019 (right)

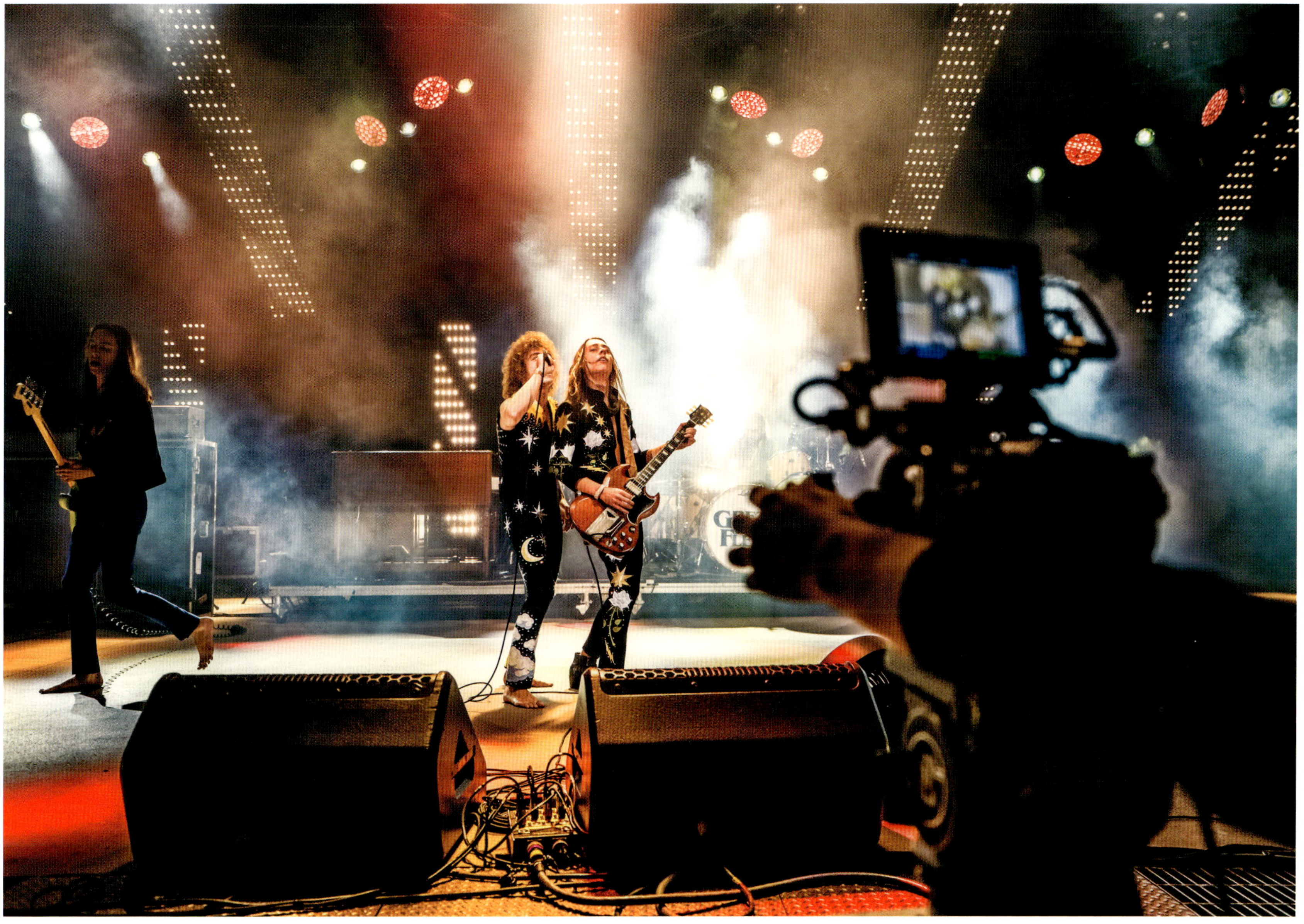

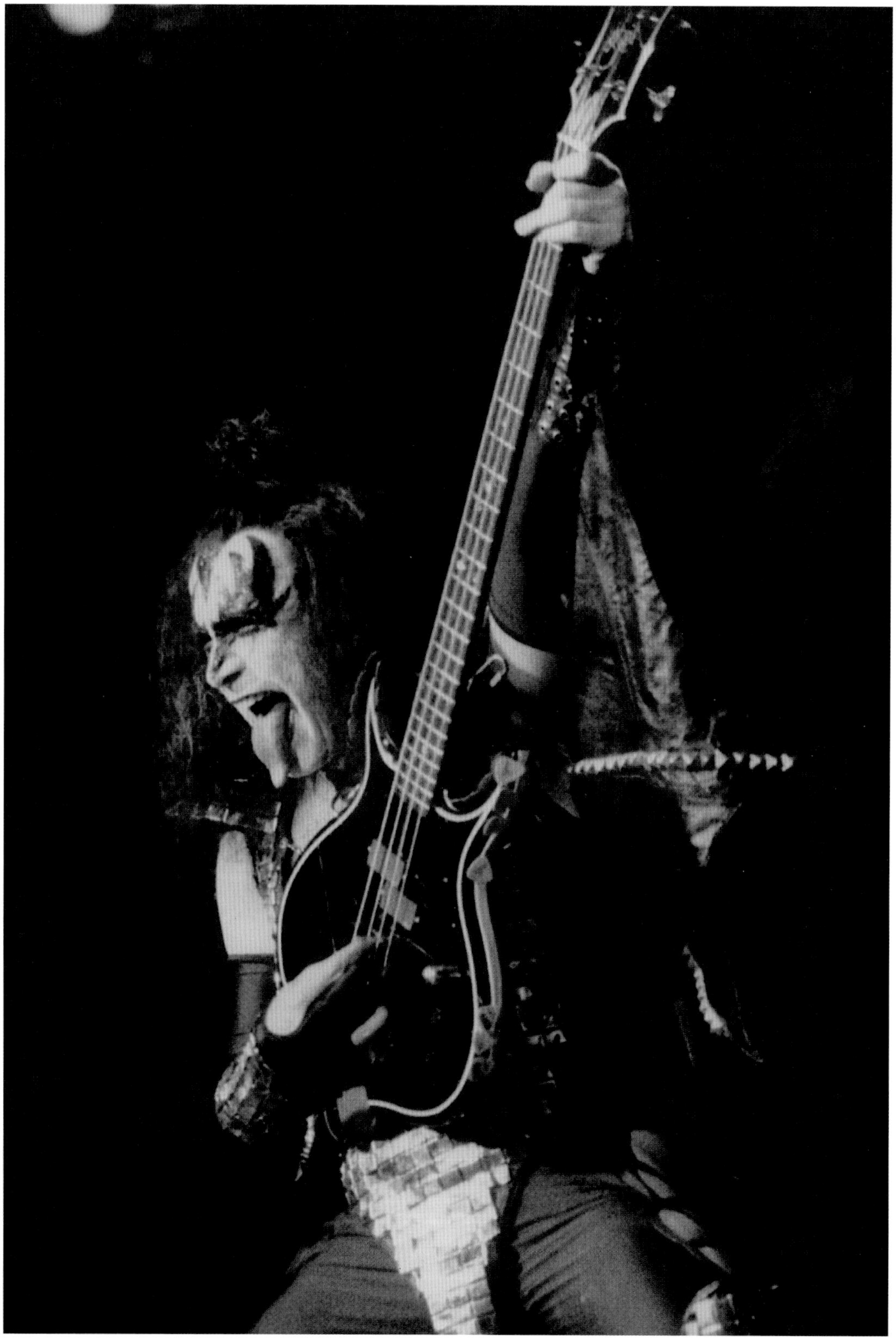

Kiss, 1990; King Sunny Ade, 1983 (right)

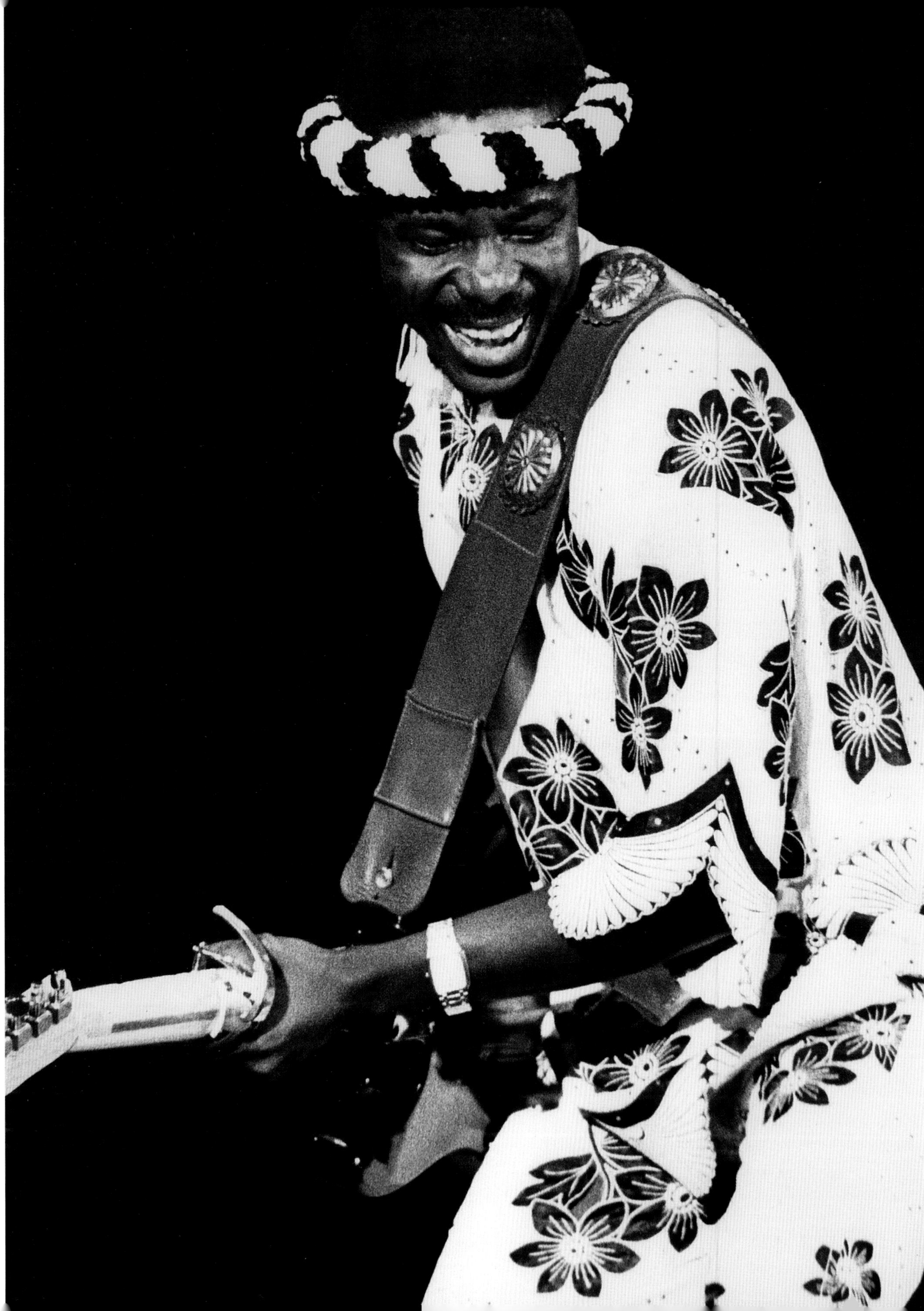

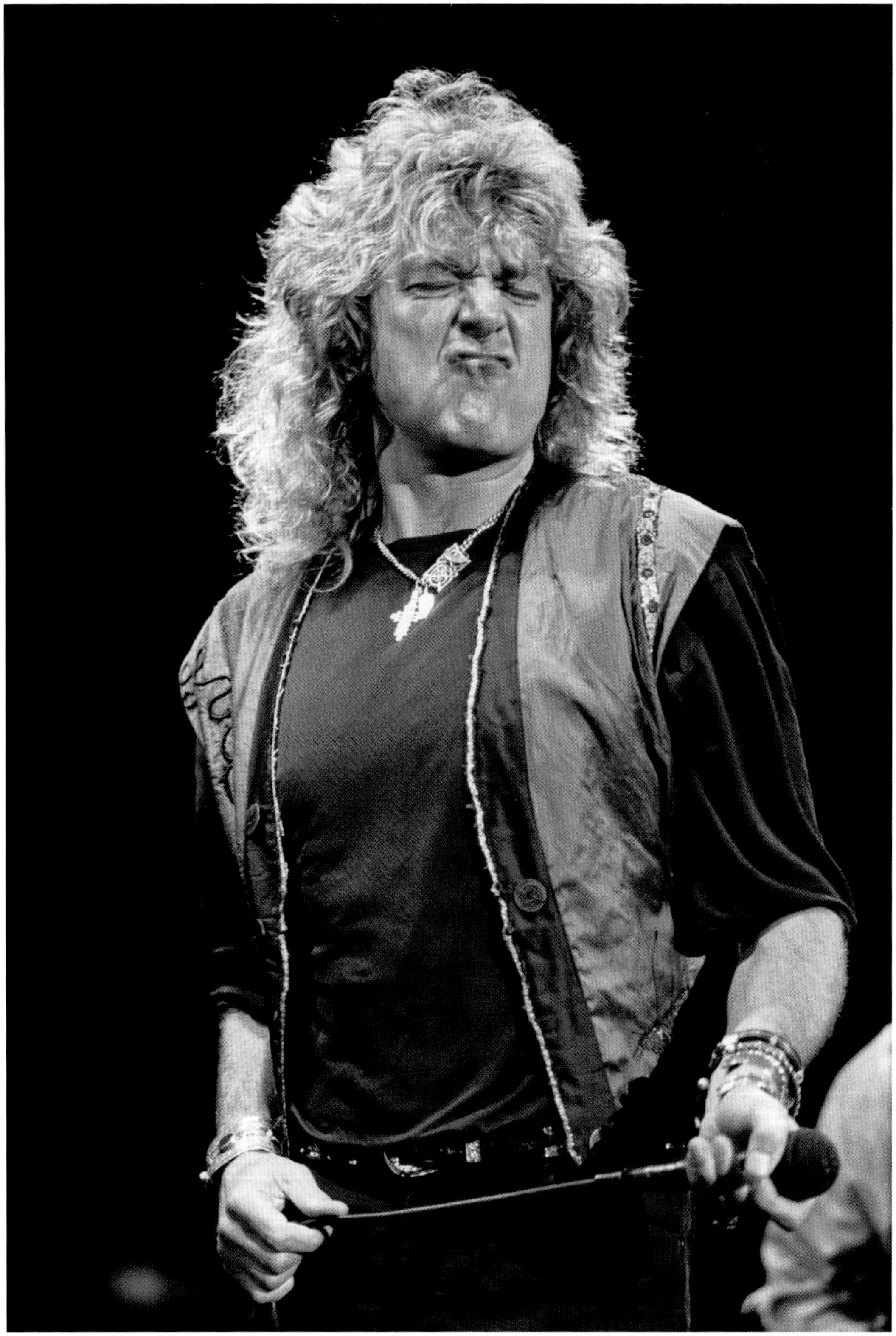

Robert Plant, 1988; Mariah Carey, 2003 (right)

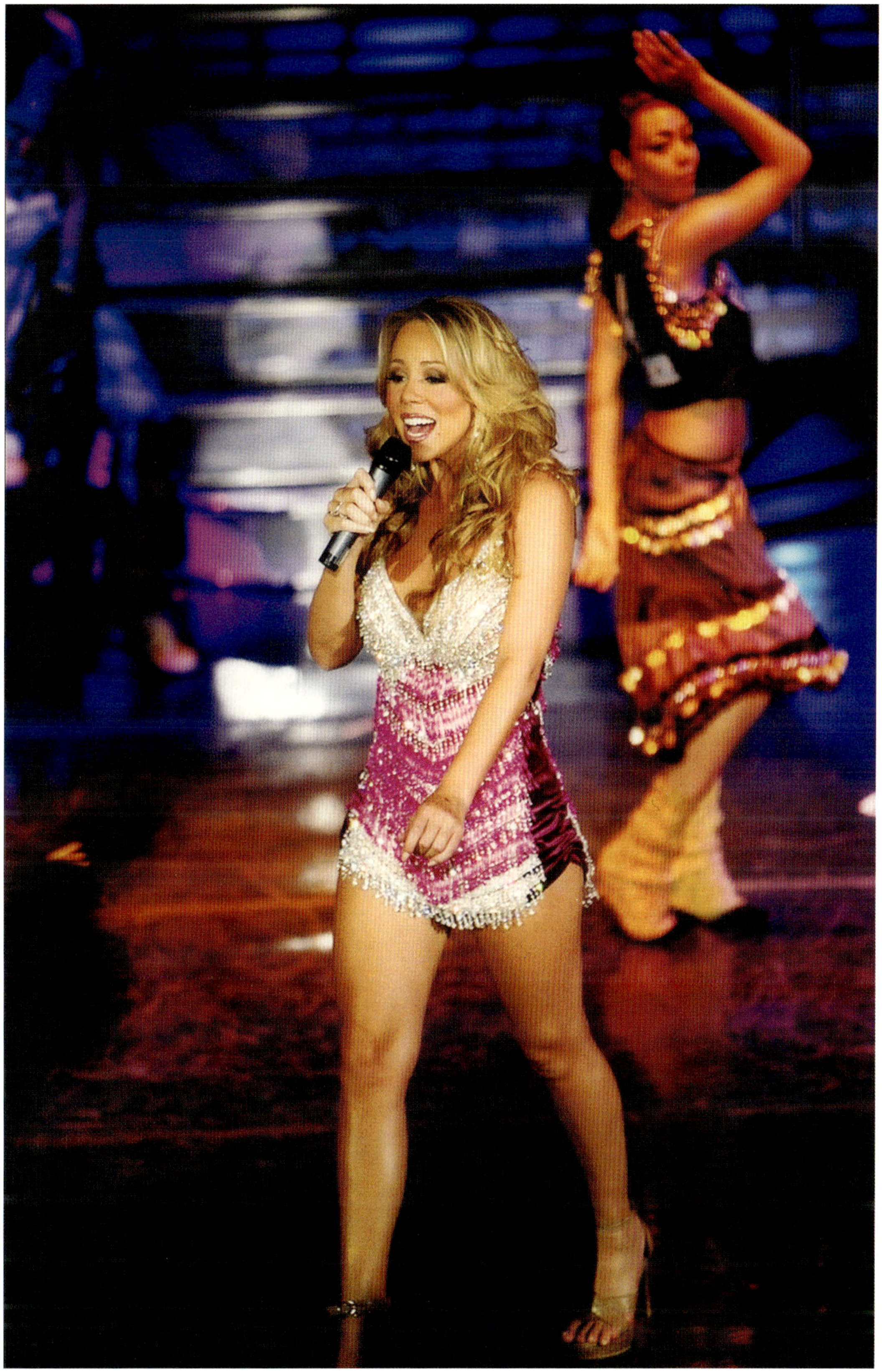

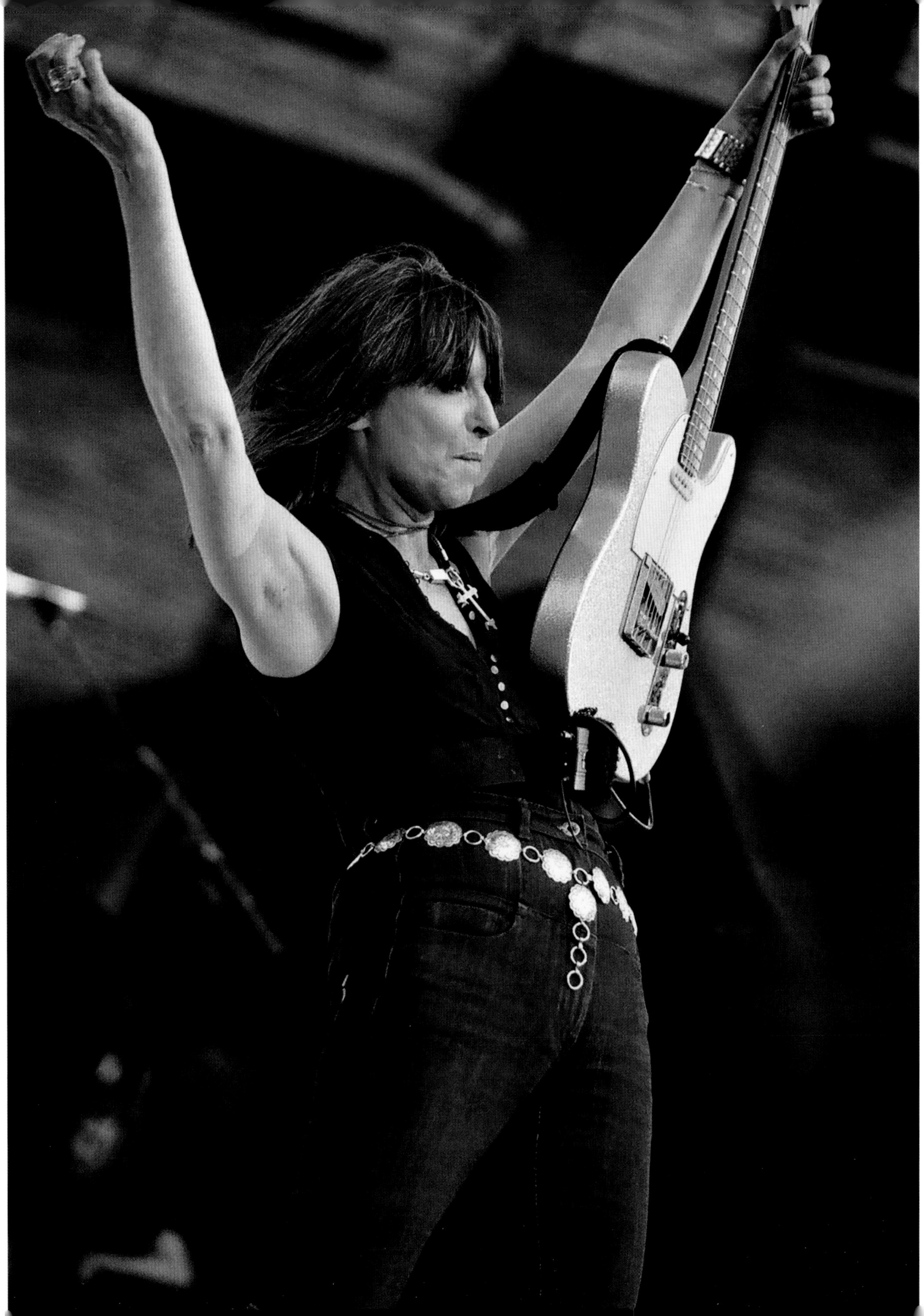

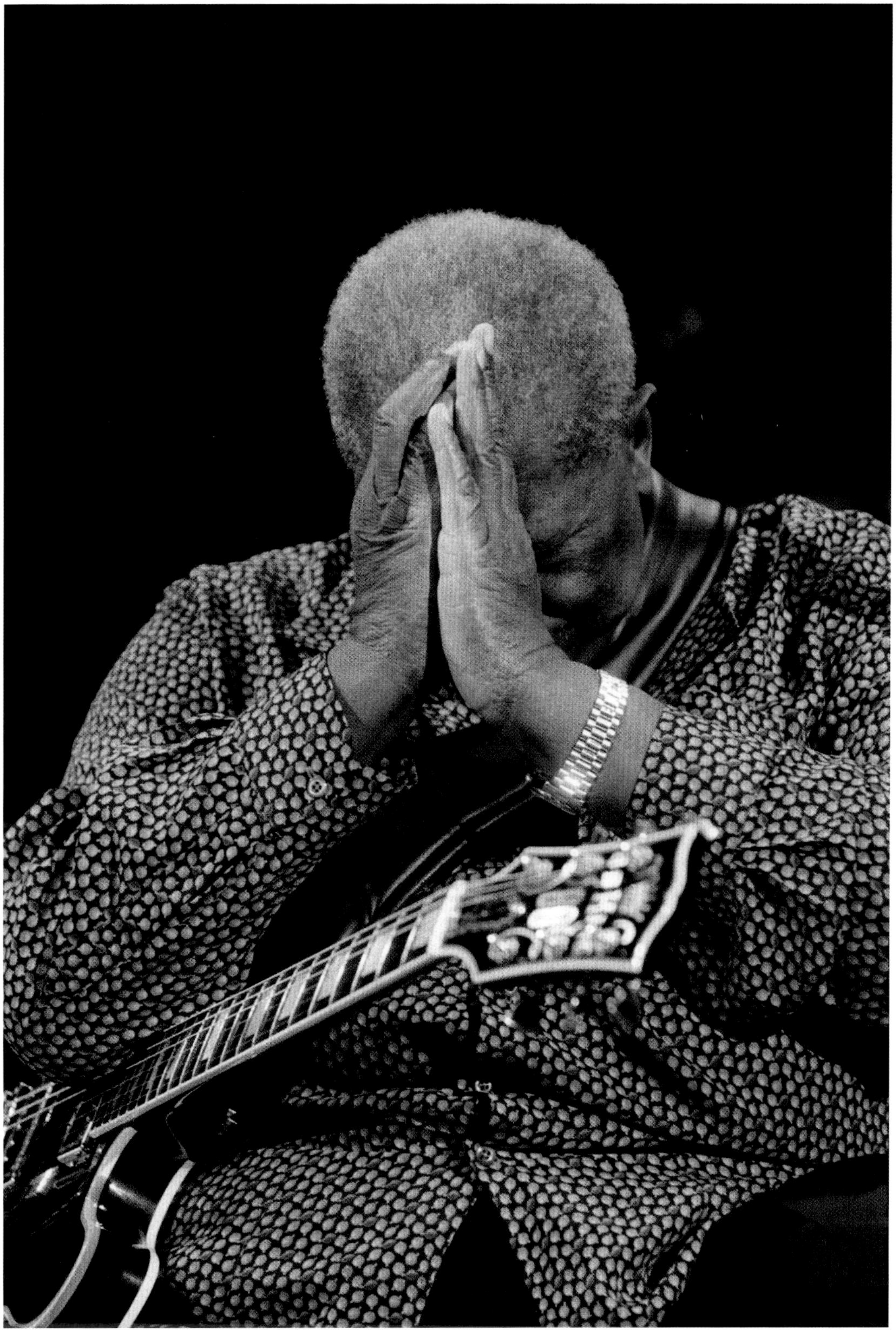

Pretenders, 2007 (left); B.B. King, 2007

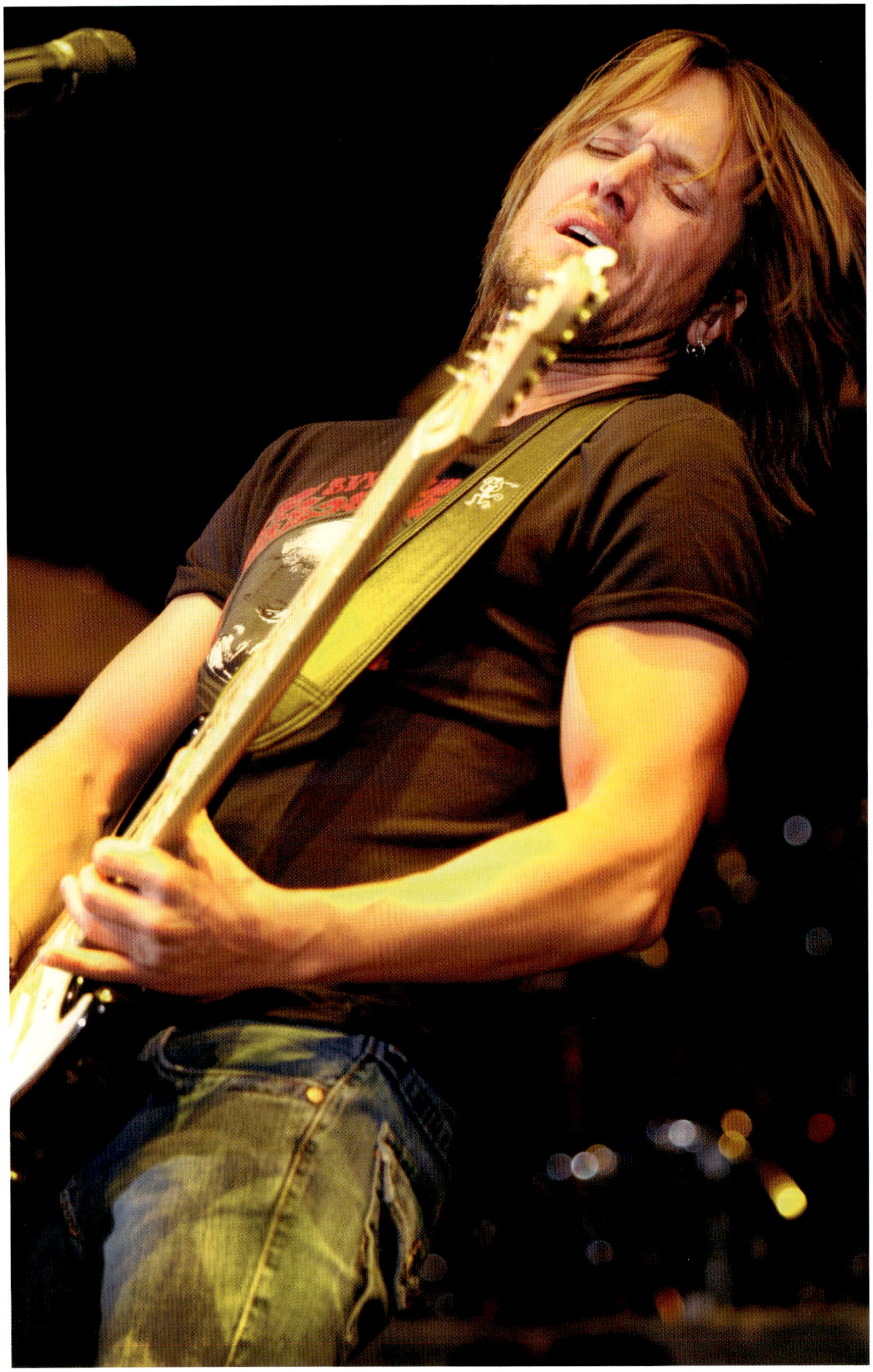

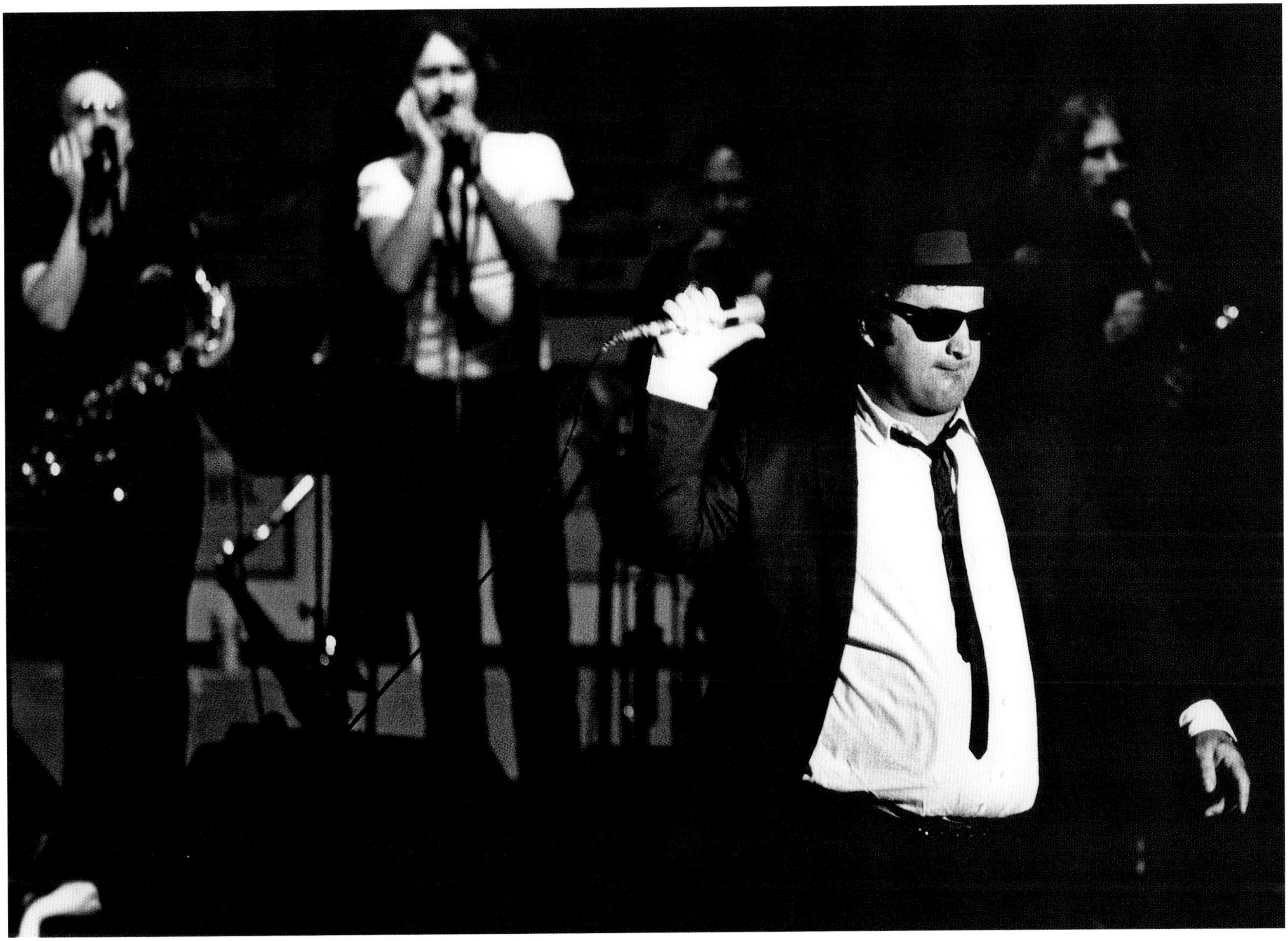

Keith Urban, 2005 (left); The Blues Brothers, 1980

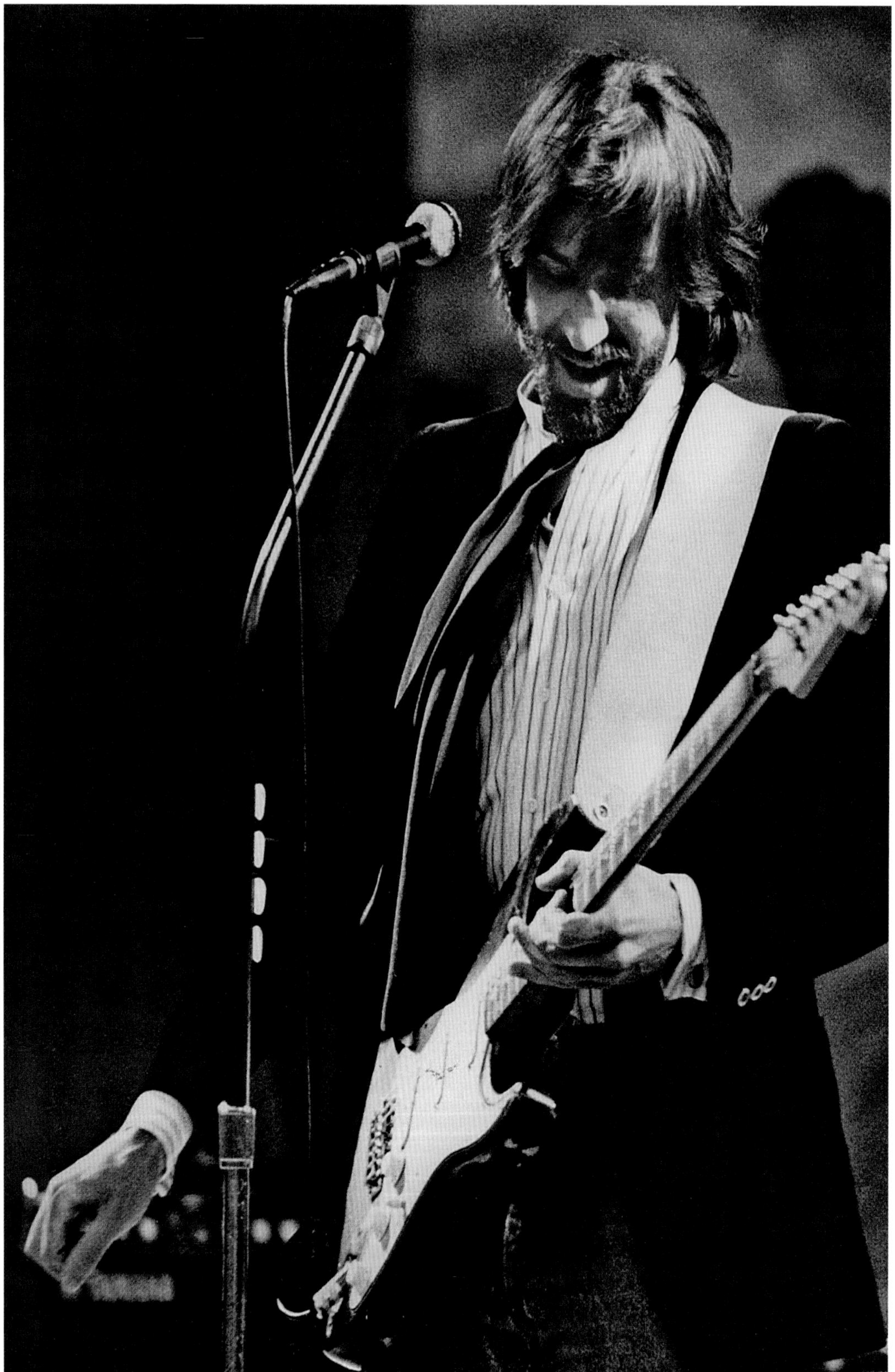

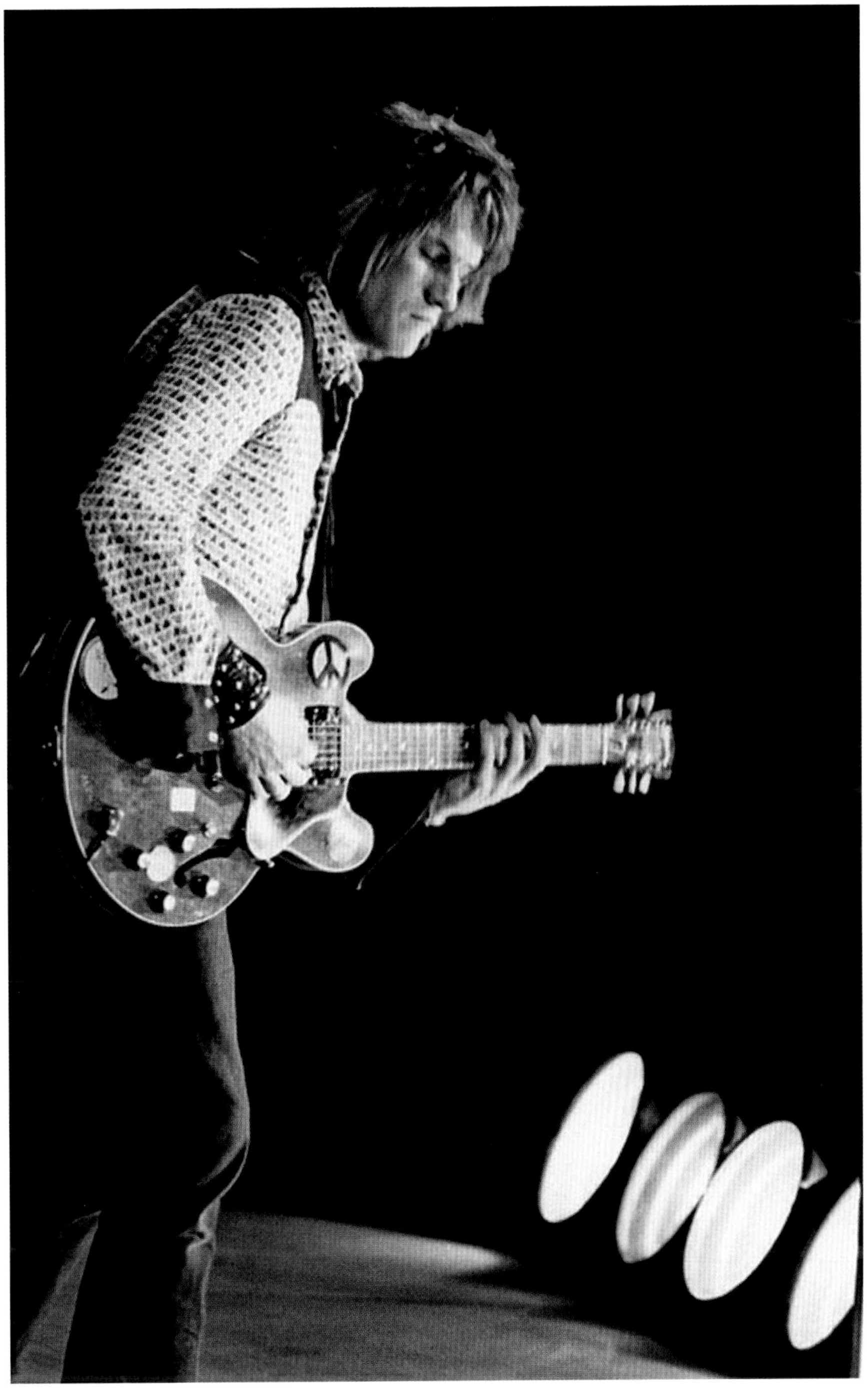

Dan Fogelberg, 1984 (left); Ten Years After, 1970

Neil Young, 1987

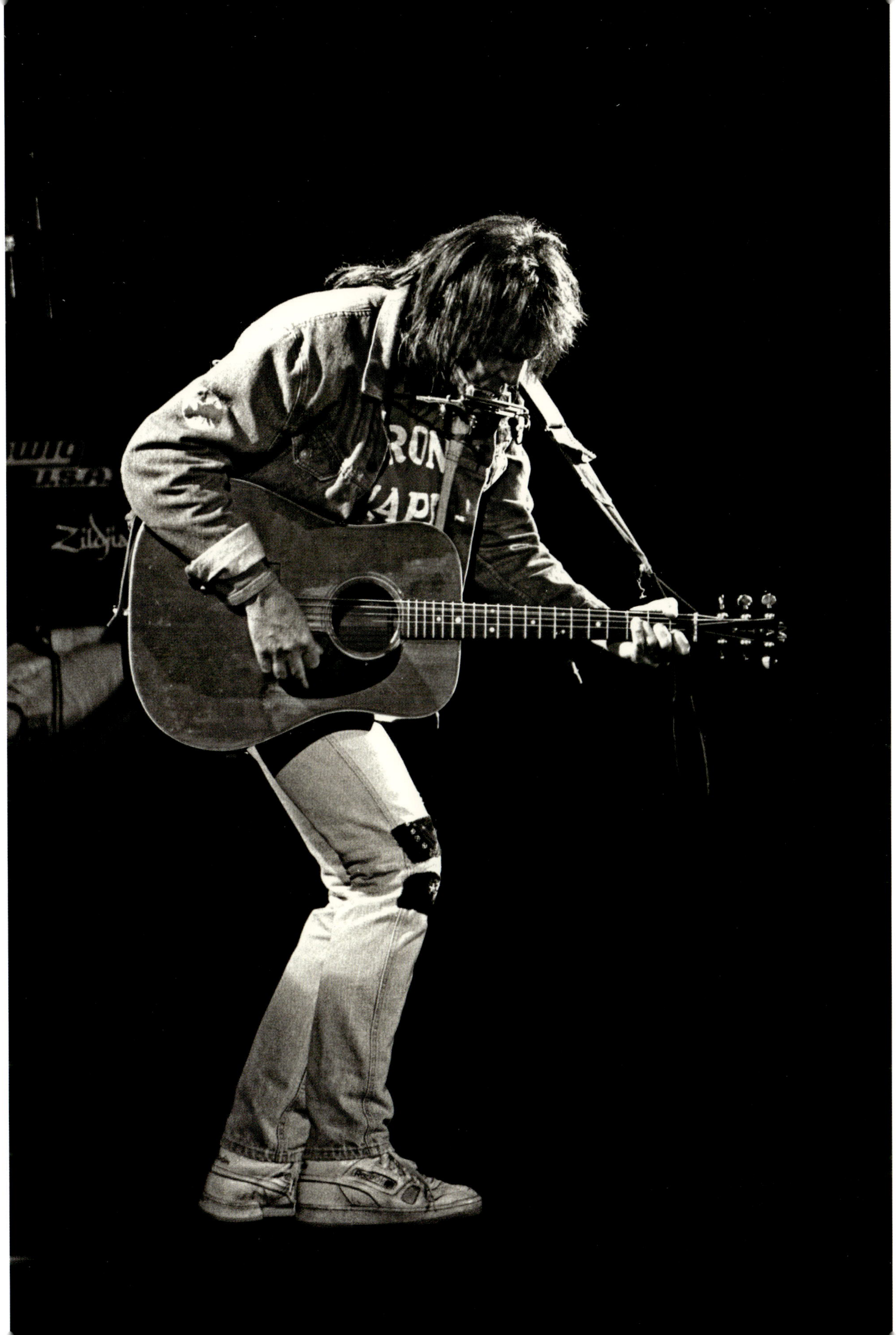

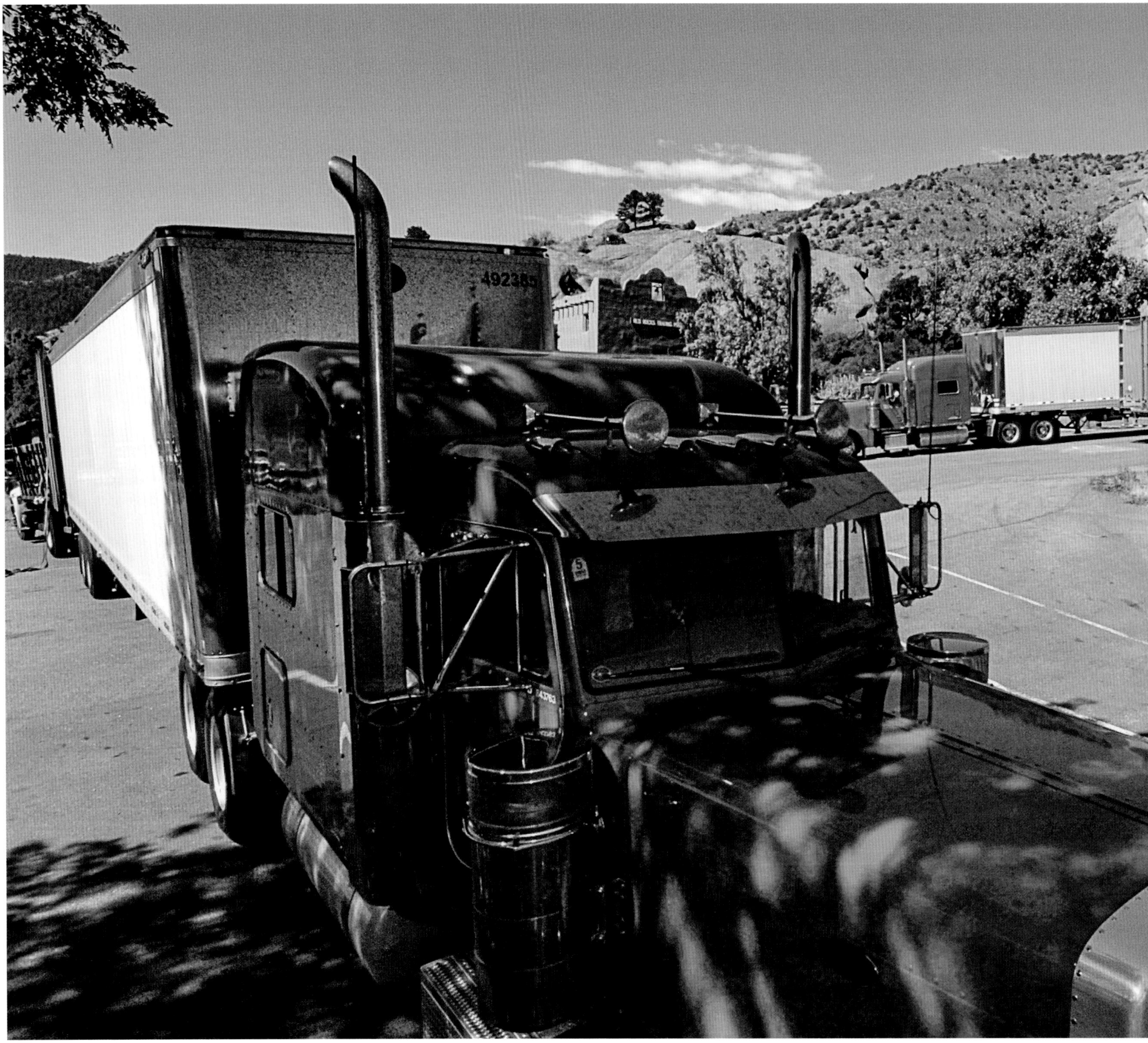

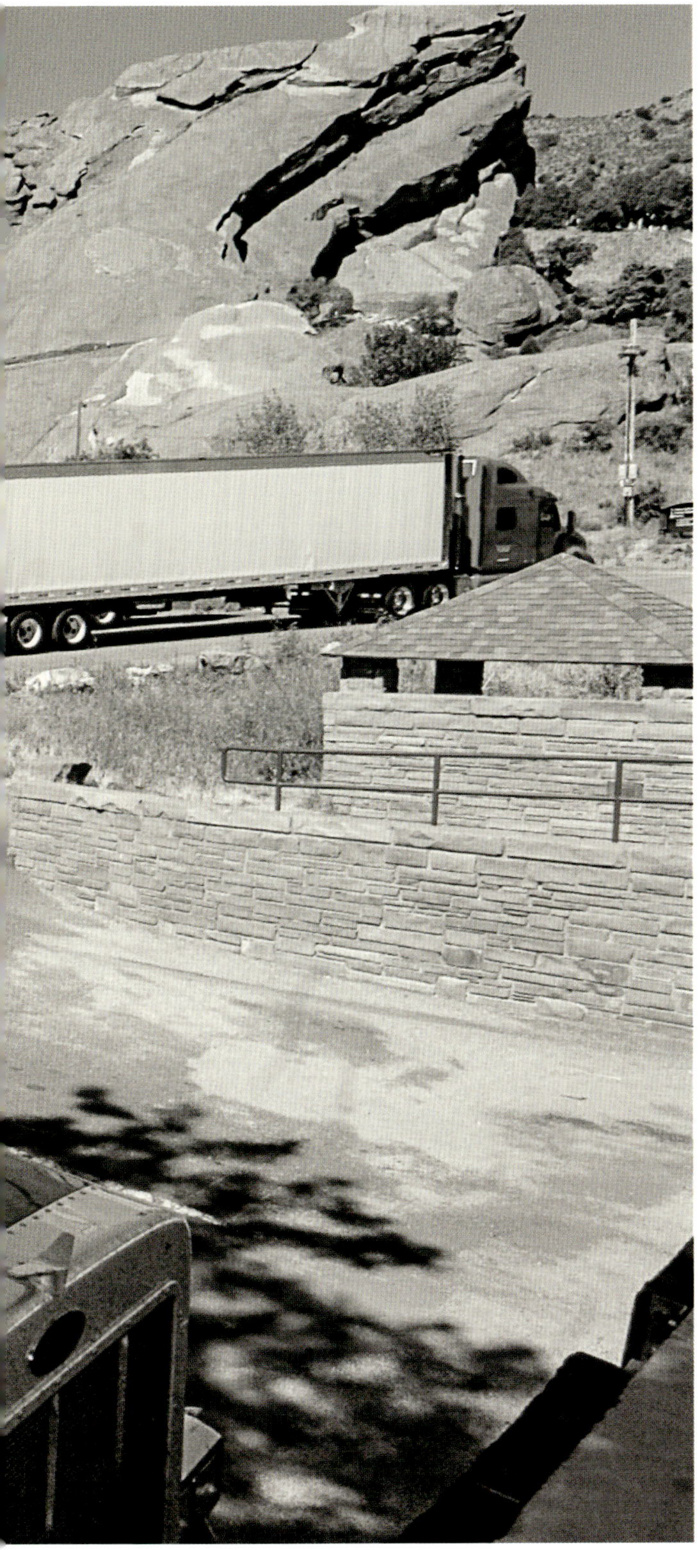

2001-2005

IT'S A LONG WAY TO THE TOP

Performers from all musical genres come to revel in Red Rocks' incredible beauty and natural acoustic quality. But to those hard-working roadies on a production crew in charge of getting equipment up to that stage, a Red Rocks date is the worst possible stop on an already grueling schedule.

On the road, acts play an average of four to six shows a week, anywhere from 100 to 200 shows in a tour run. Their production crews get accustomed to modern indoor and outdoor facilities in major markets, which are usually built like Denver's Pepsi Center and Fiddler's Green Amphitheatre. They can back their six or so 45-foot semi tractor-trailers simultaneously as close and as level to the loading dock or stage area as possible. Large numbers of men and machines move the masses of equipment—lighting fixtures, speakers, dimmer racks, smoke machines, sound-mixing consoles, stage set-pieces, even bicycles and cases of wine—out of the semis and onto the stage and dressing rooms very quickly. They usually complete the task in an enclosed, weather-protected environment.

Not at Red Rocks.

The bands' semis and the large sleeper buses carrying their road crews are too large to make it up the hill to the stage area, so they have to park down in a lot by the Trading Post. Roadies start the day by removing the semis' contents and reloading onto 18-foot stake bed trucks that can handle shuttling up the steep, narrow winding back road, which is approximately 200 yards long and rises at roughly a 30-degree incline. No one seems to have measured, because they don't want to know. Otherwise, it would be characteristic of the "5,280 feet above sea level" signs that Denver sports teams put in visitors' locker rooms, ostensibly to induce altitude sickness in opponents.

"The crew is facing that extra challenge of turning a Red Rocks day into an ordinary day. They're definitely not the same thing," guitarist Warren Haynes said. "We had a situation in the early '90s with the Allman Brothers. Our PA system was loaded onto a smaller flatbed to get it up the hill. The truck stalled, and half the PA tumbled down into the valley. We had to do the show with the other half of the equipment. It wound up being a great show anyway, but that was one of the hazards of the environment."

The back loading dock area is also unforgiving. The stake bed trucks have to turn around and back up to a ramp at the stage left entrance, with mere inches of clearance on each side. Look away from the curb

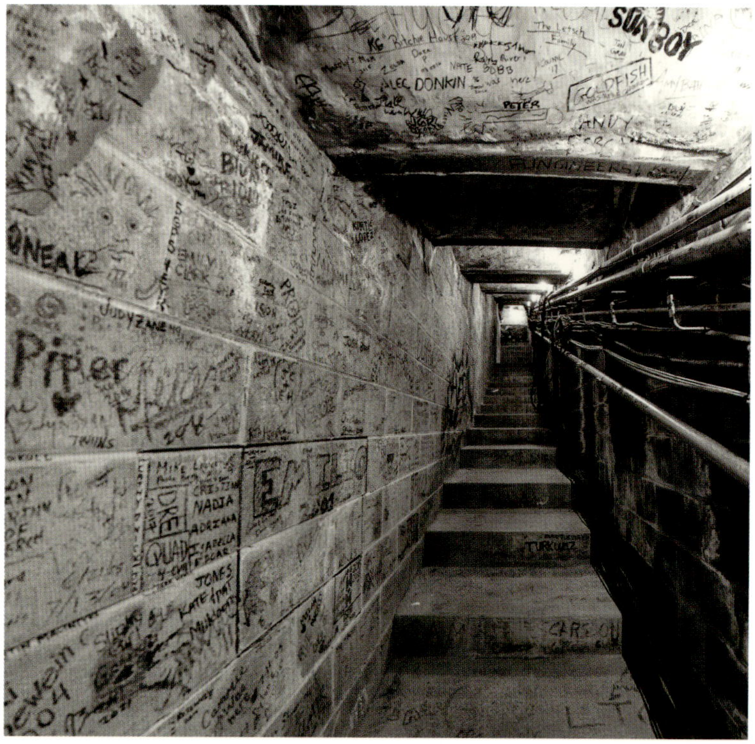

Underground tunnel; "the sled" (right)

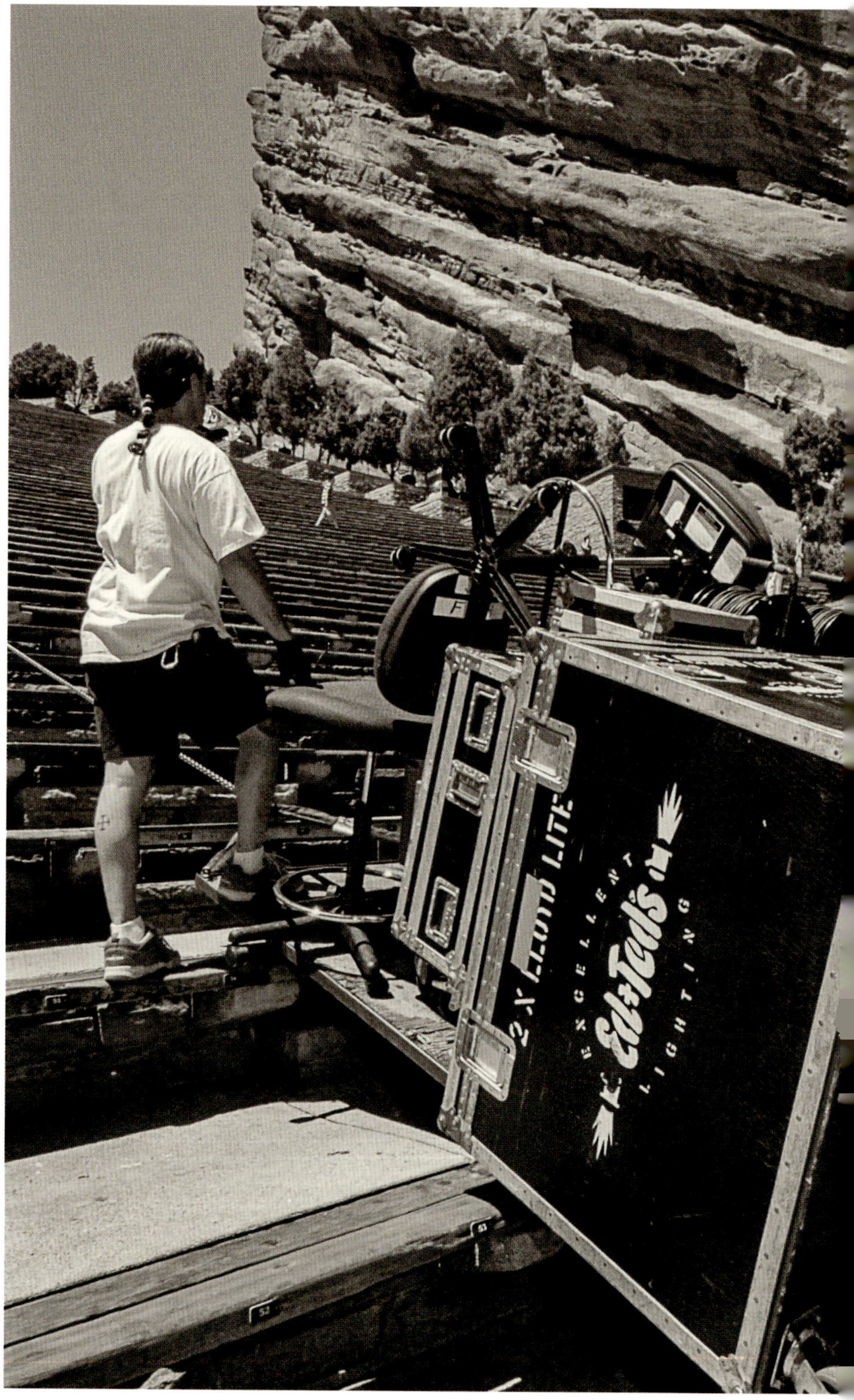

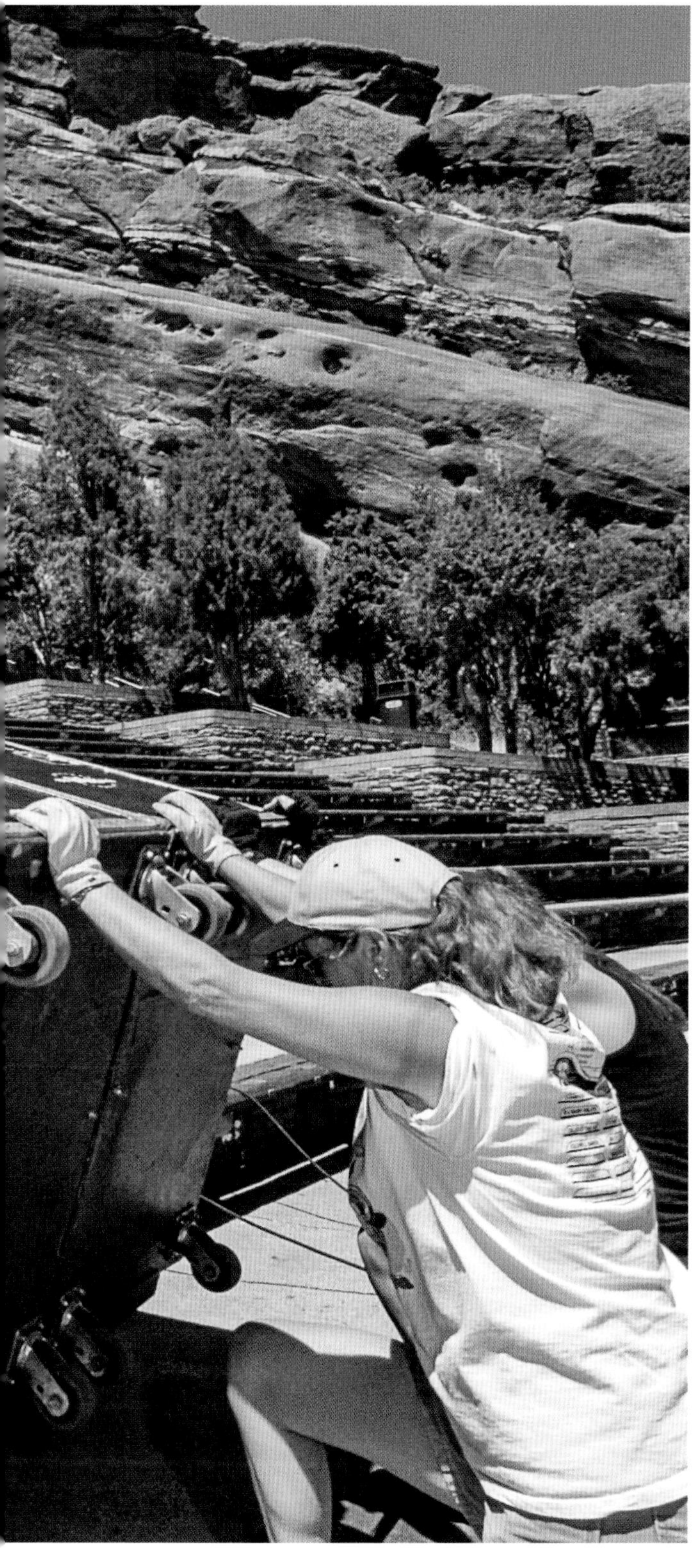

and you're on the rocks. A driver who once backed in a 26-foot flatbed without turning around is a legend. Workers roll the gear off the truck onto another ramp, and then push it up one more level to get on the main performance area.

The mandatory method of unloading from the trucks progresses approximately fifty percent slower than normal, but work on the stage is not hindered because the stage crew works at about the same pace as the intervals between the arrival of each new batch of equipment. Local 7, the Denver local theatrical, stage and film exhibition union, has contributed greatly to the organization of the setup and takedown of shows at Red Rocks, and provided a consistent house crew that can troubleshoot any challenge—from accommodating eight trucks for Mötley Crüe with two flying drum kits, to trying to get Carole King's grand piano onstage.

There are other unique problems at Red Rocks. The mix position—where the sound engineer sets up a few rows into the crowd—sits out in the open, vulnerable to inclement weather. Gear is pulled via "the sled," 19th century-style, for the front of the house; prior to that it was carried by hand. The underground tunnel to access the mix position from backstage, while cleaned up considerably from the days when a rattlesnake could be found lurking behind a rock, remains a challenging place to run cables.

And while it's usually clear by the time the show rolls around, there's more often than not a rain shower between 3 and 7 p.m.

Yet the grand setting of Red Rocks trumps everything. If a crew is unhappy, the artists are not.

"I love Red Rocks because there is some kind of strange, powerful electrical energy there," Sheryl Crow noted in 2003. "There are people who are sure it's the whole connection to the Native Americans, but we always have really wacky, odd little things happen with our gear. One time, during 'Strong Enough,' all of a sudden this man's voice started coming out of my amp—bizarre. I guess it was radio frequencies. We had a whole lighting rig go out once."

At a Jackson Browne show with special guests Keb' Mo' and Steve Earle & the Dukes in July 2003, a storm knocked out the power grid, not just at Red Rocks, but in the town of Morrison and surrounding areas. Torrents of water cascaded down the aisles. The stage manager didn't even have amplification to tell the crowd the concert was being called, but people figured it out in a hurry.

"It was the birthday of one of the road crew members, so we were going to sit around and play a little music in the catering area," Browne recalled. "The venue manager took me aside and said,

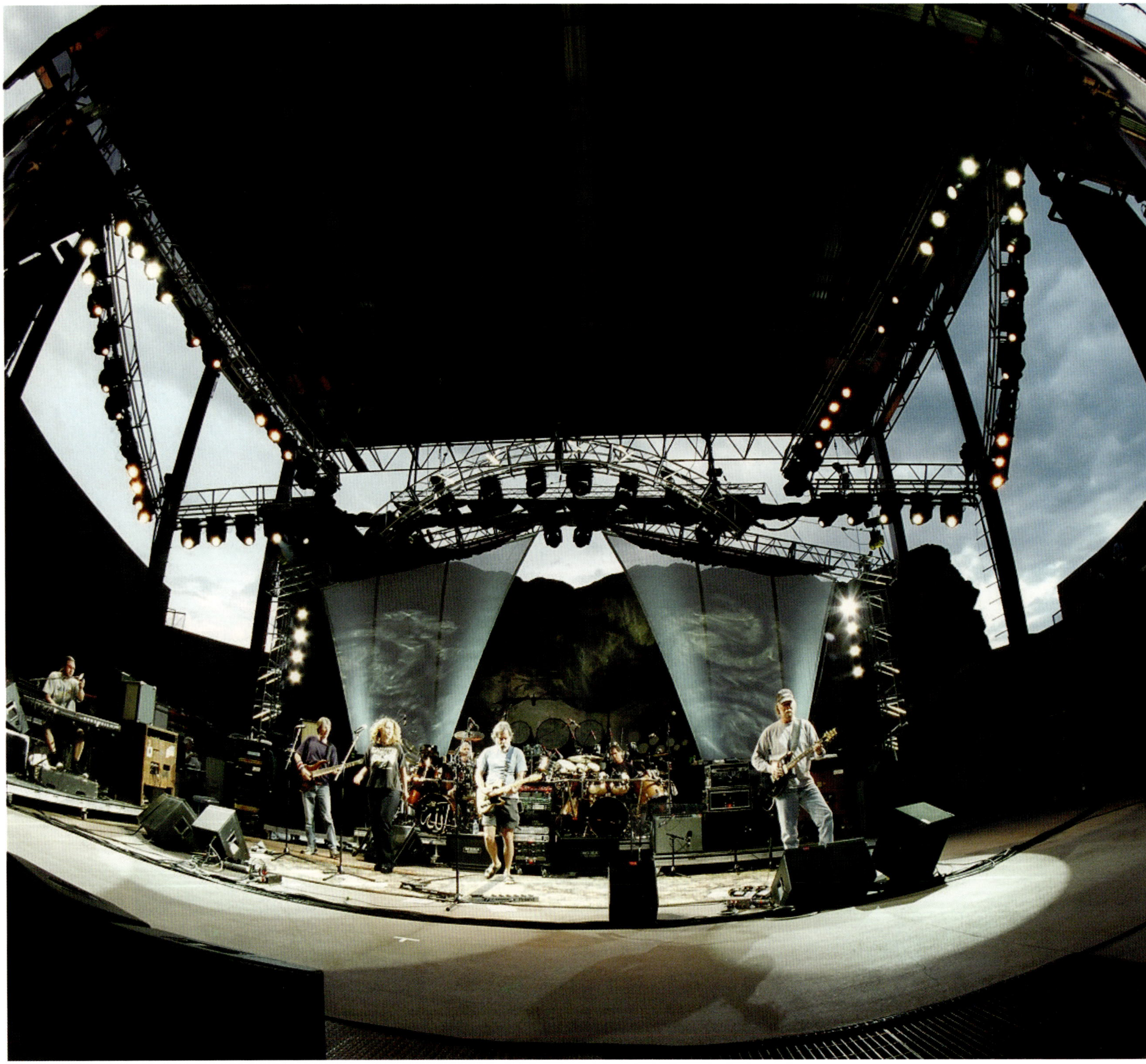

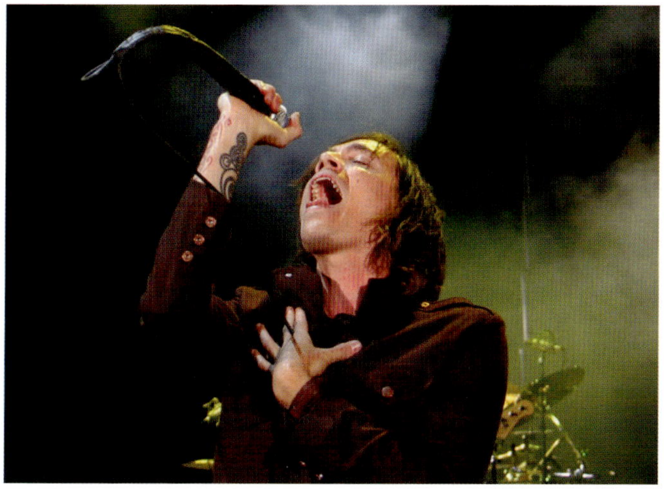

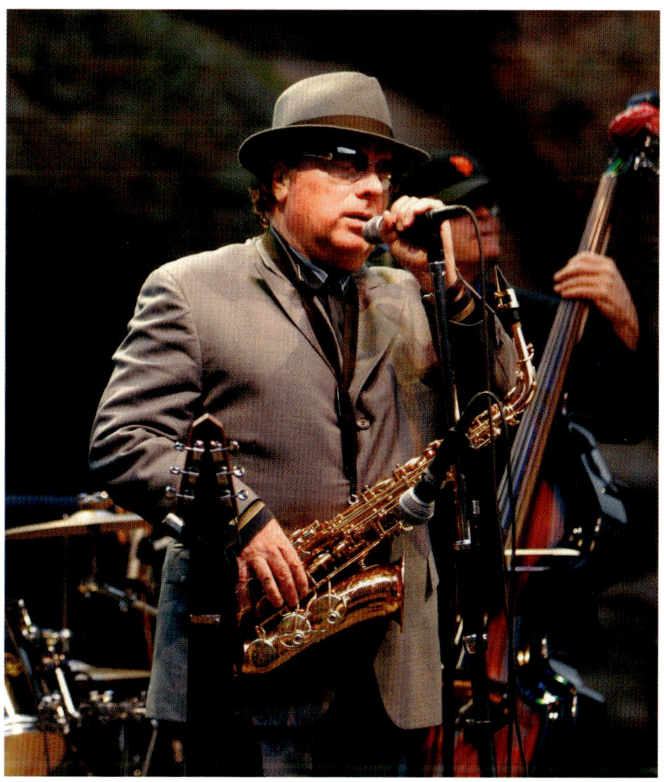

The Dead, 2004 (left); Incubus, 2004 (top); Van Morrison, 2005 (above)

'You don't get it. We're 30 (feet) underground. We're on backup emergency generator power that will last for no more than 40 minutes. You won't be able to see the hand in front of your face. Get out now!' We got the message!"

Boston's 2003 stage show was something to behold. It resembled a toxic urban wasteland, and the band brought out its big guns with a giant "phantom" pipe organ player and a lighting rig that lowered and turned into a guitar spaceship with smoke and afterburners. But singer Brad Delp didn't care if it all made it to the stage or not. "Why bring anything? The place itself is so stunning," he said with a shrug.

In addition to the ongoing tradition of "Reggae on the Rocks" (the annual celebration in 2002 featured Sly & Robbie), "Blues on the Rocks" and "Rave on the Rocks," there had been opera on the rocks, jazz on the rocks, even raza on the rocks. But "Film on the Rocks" didn't exist until the 2000 season. In a highly successful move, classic Hollywood films were paired with appropriate local music acts in a series, such as the Hot Tomatoes Orchestra and *Casablanca*.

The park's $14 million Visitor Center opened in April 2003. In addition to a gift shop, restaurant and private party space, the 30,000-square-foot center featured an interpretive hall on Red Rocks' musical history. As architect Burnham Hoyt had attempted to blend the walkways and dressing rooms into the rocks as unobtrusively as possible when he designed Red Rocks in 1936, the architecture firm Sink Combs Dethiefs carefully revisited the design plan when the Visitor Center was added.

Civic activists had prevailed upon the Landmark Preservation Commission to reject the city of Denver's proposal to sell advertisers the rights to project corporate logos onto Red Rocks' sandstone monoliths, Ship Rock and Creation Rock.

"I hope they never give Red Rocks a corporate name," Lyle Lovett noted. "But Red Bull would be my choice, just for the poetry of it."

Live on the Rocks, a DVD and live album by Blues Traveler, was recorded at the band's annual Independence Day show in 2003. In 2004, Incubus recorded *Alive at Red Rocks*, a long-form live concert DVD. The Dead, a band composed of former members of the Grateful Dead, played five shows at Red Rocks on its 2004 summer tour.

The legendary allurement of Red Rocks managed to escape some performers. Halfway through her set on a chilly night in late September 2004, jazz-pop siren Norah Jones commented in a small voice, "I can't feel my toes."

And after a quarter-century absence, Van Morrison returned to Colorado—and gave his first-ever performance at Red Rocks on June 10, 2005. To members of the sold-out crowd, the match of locale and

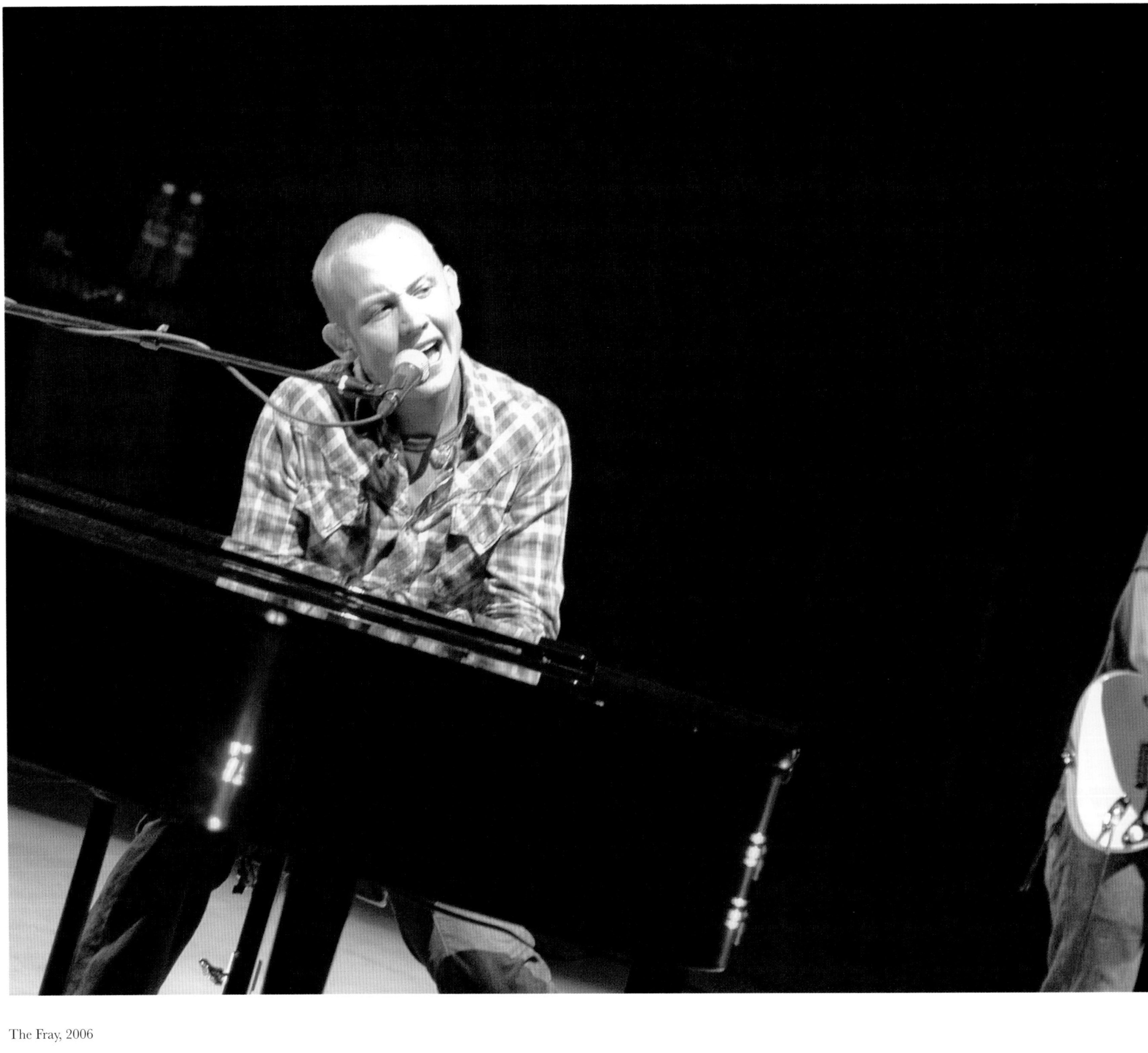

The Fray, 2006

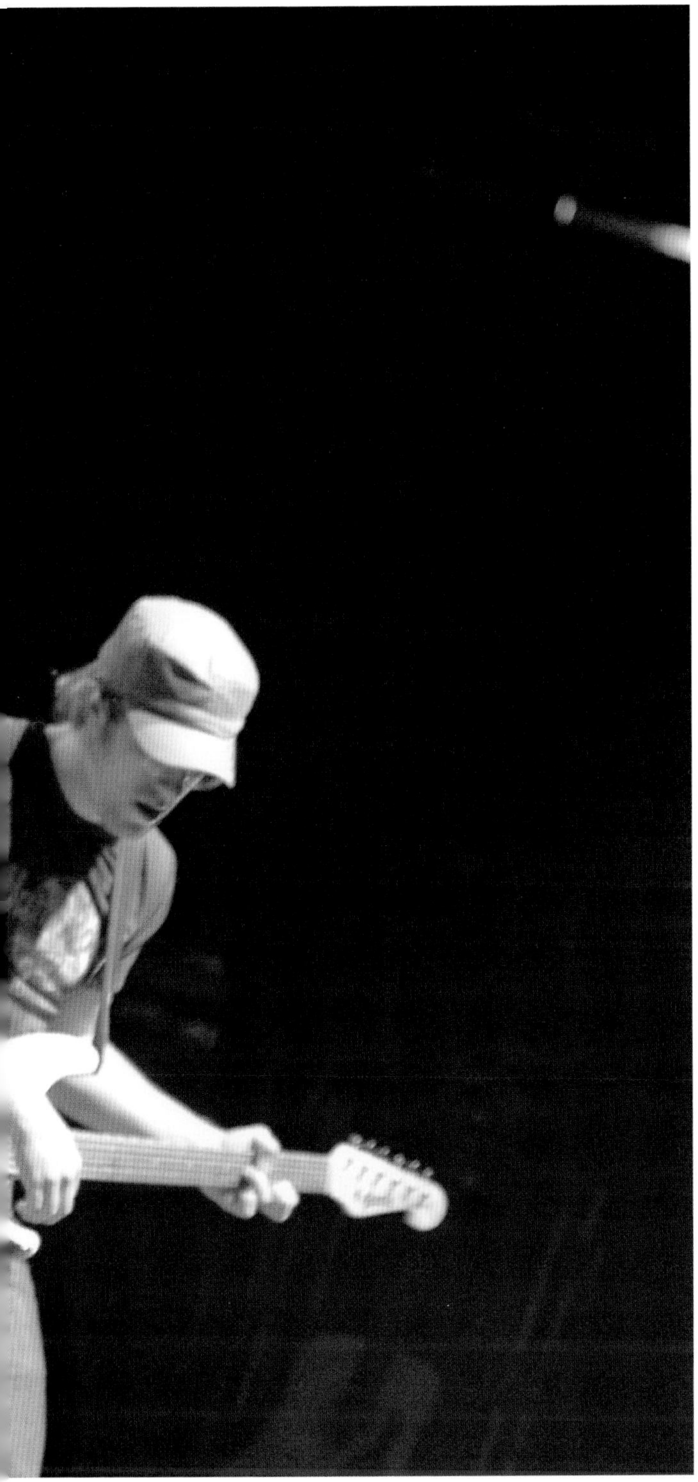

performer featured two legends, two inspirational sources of unequaled music, and an extraordinary ticket price—$158, the highest in venue history. Each ticket also came with a specific directive: "7:30 sharp."

The mood was lousy backstage, as rain had fallen all day, but the showers gave way to a night that was merely brisk when showtime rolled around. Outside of the dressing area, Morrison observed, "I'd rather play a 400-seat club than a place like this!"

The enormously gifted and notoriously petulant artist never spoke between songs. Instead of the expansive staging most acts go for, Morrison and his crack band crammed into the middle of the stage, all within arm's reach of each other, as if they were performing in a small nightspot. He stood rigid, eyes closed, arms at his sides, clenching and unclenching his left hand. Was he deep inside in the music, or counting down the minutes to the end? Morrison played exactly ninety minutes and strode offstage.

That September, the Dave Matthews Band performed three concert at Red Rocks, and offered to stay an extra night and headline a Hurricane Katrina benefit concert with New Orleans' own Neville Brothers. All of the money raised during the sold-out show—food, drink, t-shirts, tickets, parking—was contributed to the hurricane recovery effort. The city of Denver waived the Red Rocks rent and seat tax. Dozens of workers, from police, firefighters and paramedics to stagehands, concession stand workers and parking lot attendants, donated their time.

"This is just part of an effort by everyone all over the country to rebuild one of the cultural centers of the world to its former grandeur," Matthews said.

Starting in 1995, all the major artists who played a concert at Red Rocks Amphitheatre left with "A Piece of the Rock"—a special award unique to each year and given as a going-away gift in remembrance of the experience. John Haertling was the man behind the works. In 2005 alone, Haertling and his team created 130 awards in a warehouse district near Louisville. Each was one of a kind, handcrafted from some combination of rock, metal, wood and resin, and then engraved with each recipient's name. All shared the common regional flagstone.

Another kind of trophy was sought when reality TV infiltrated Red Rocks—the ninth installment of CBS' *The Amazing Race* made a stop in 2005, starting and finishing the competition-based show at the same location for the only time.

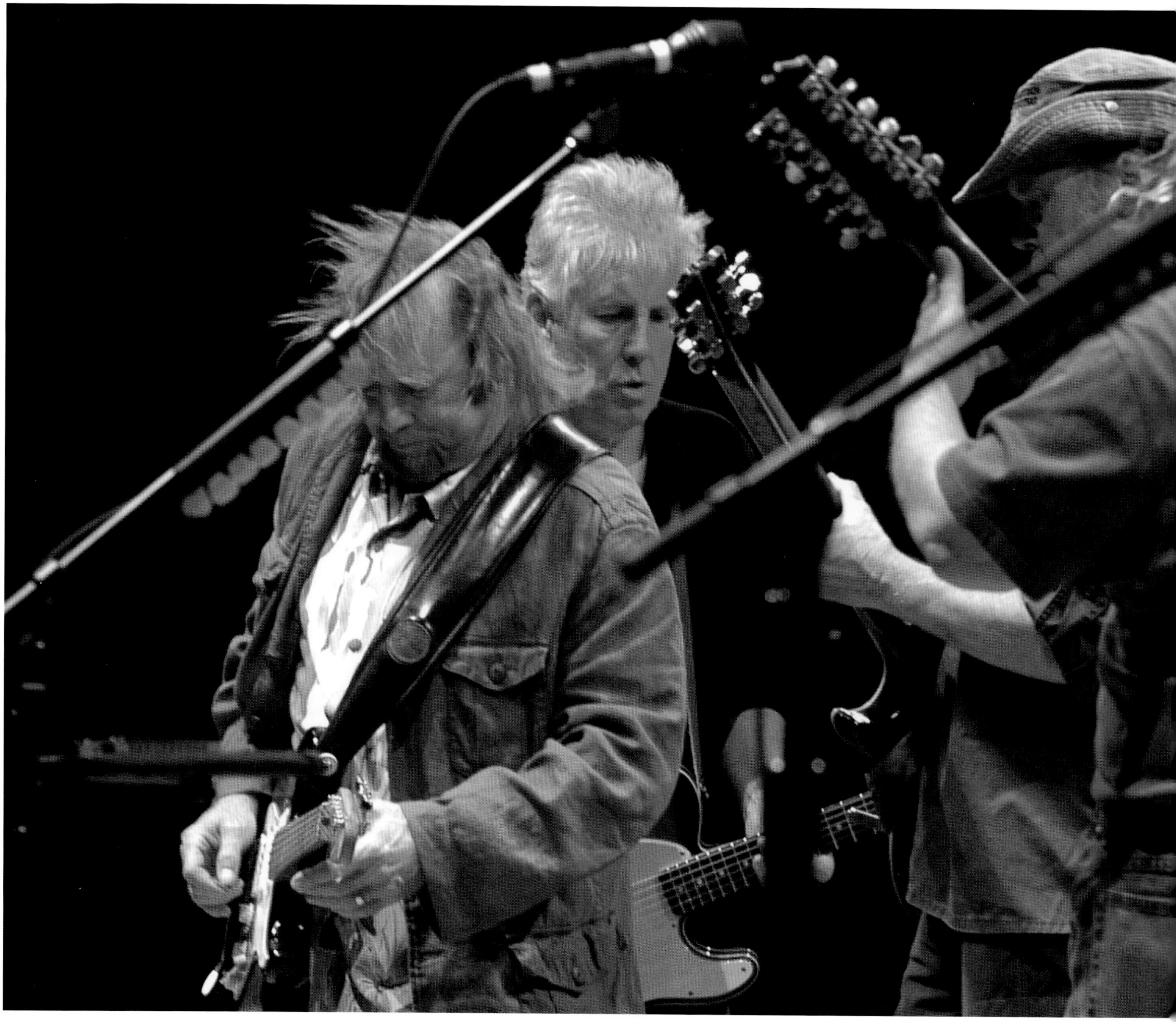

Crosby, Stills, Nash & Young, 2006

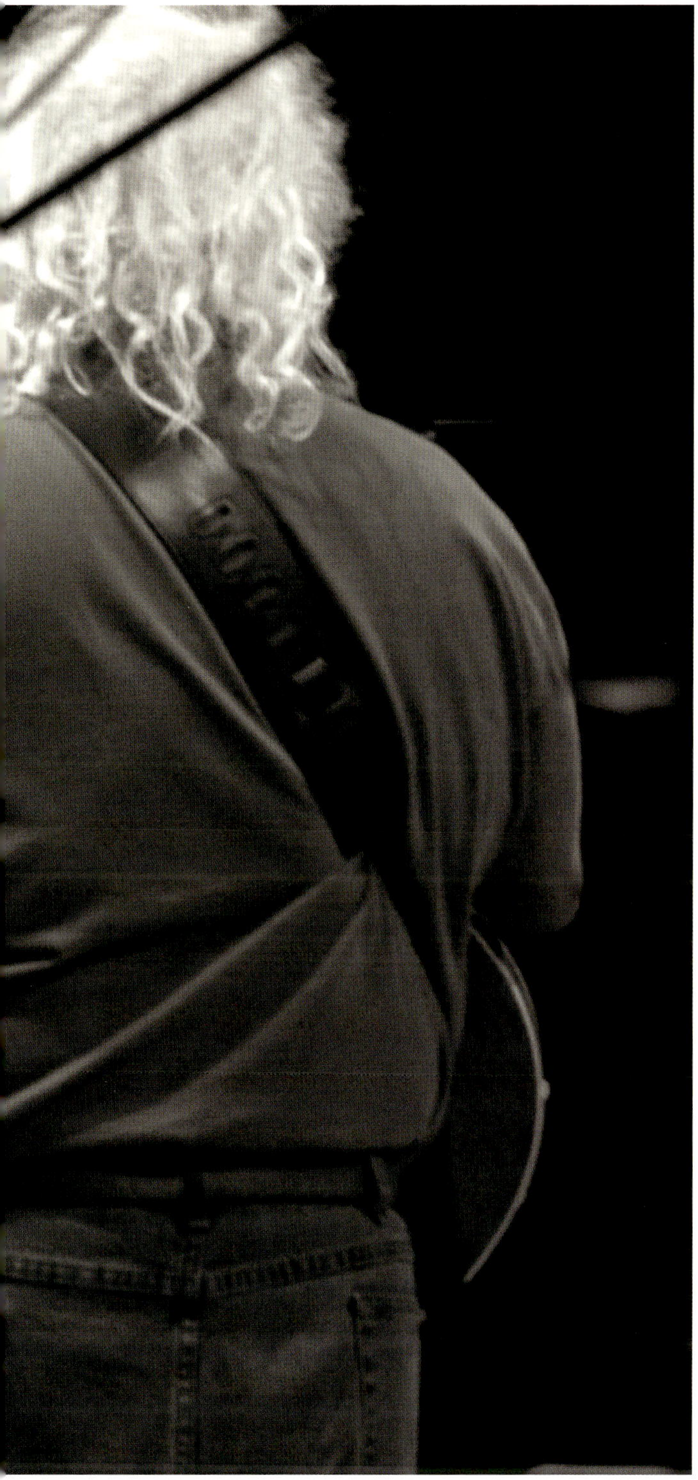

2006-2019
SOLID AS A ROCK

The Allman Brothers' 2006 pilgrimage to Red Rocks was a two-night package, the last shows of the band's summer tour. Mother Nature made her statement on the first night, September 1, encircling the venue with large rain clouds that unleashed a long soaking. Temperatures plummeted to the low 40s. Conditions started to affect the stage.

The road crew prepared a large steel box structure, then surrounded it with tarps on the sides and on the top, creating a "roof" for Gregg Allman and his keyboards. Large holes were cut on the sides so that the players and Allman could retain eye contact. The structure—Warren Haynes deemed it "the hut"—prevented some from seeing Allman at all.

Despite the challenges, after the show—which featured keyboardist Danny Louis of Gov't Mule perched next to Allman in a sassy rendition of "The Weight"—Haynes remained sanguine. "Red Rocks is possibly the most spiritual venue in the world," he said. "It's hard to have a bad show there. It doesn't matter if the elements are stacked against you, or you could be exhausted and ready to go home—as soon as you walk on stage, the magic starts happening. There's no denying it."

Also in 2006, Neil Young joined Crosby, Stills & Nash at Red Rocks for the first time. The following year, shows booked for the Red Rocks season featured old favorites such as Blues Traveler, Widespread Panic and Big Head Todd & the Monsters; icons such as Buddy Guy, Lyle Lovett and Bob Dylan; and new talent such as the Killers, Spearhead and local heroes the Fray. All were part of a lineup that only enhanced Red Rocks' nearly mythical status.

"It was a huge honor to play in the same place as the Beatles, U2 and Tom Petty," Isaac Slade, frontman of the Fray, said. "Plus we had six Denver bands open up for us. It's amazing to be able to help them."

At a Starbucks-sponsored "Carved in Stone" concert, the Old 97's were forced to play the first half of their set sans frontman Rhett Miller, who had just landed at the Denver airport after enduring some circuitous routing.

"I got some gray hairs that day," Miller said. "I was looking forward to playing Red Rocks more than any show in a long time. I learned a lesson—don't fly in day of show."

In 2008, Widespread Panic extended its record for the most consecutive sellouts at Red Rocks Amphitheatre, with 32. "I look out from my vantage point on the stage," keyboardist John "Jojo" Hermann said. "The rocks that jut up from the stage look like giant, great red sharks. The shark on stage left, he's even got a little eye and a little nose. I savor our yearly

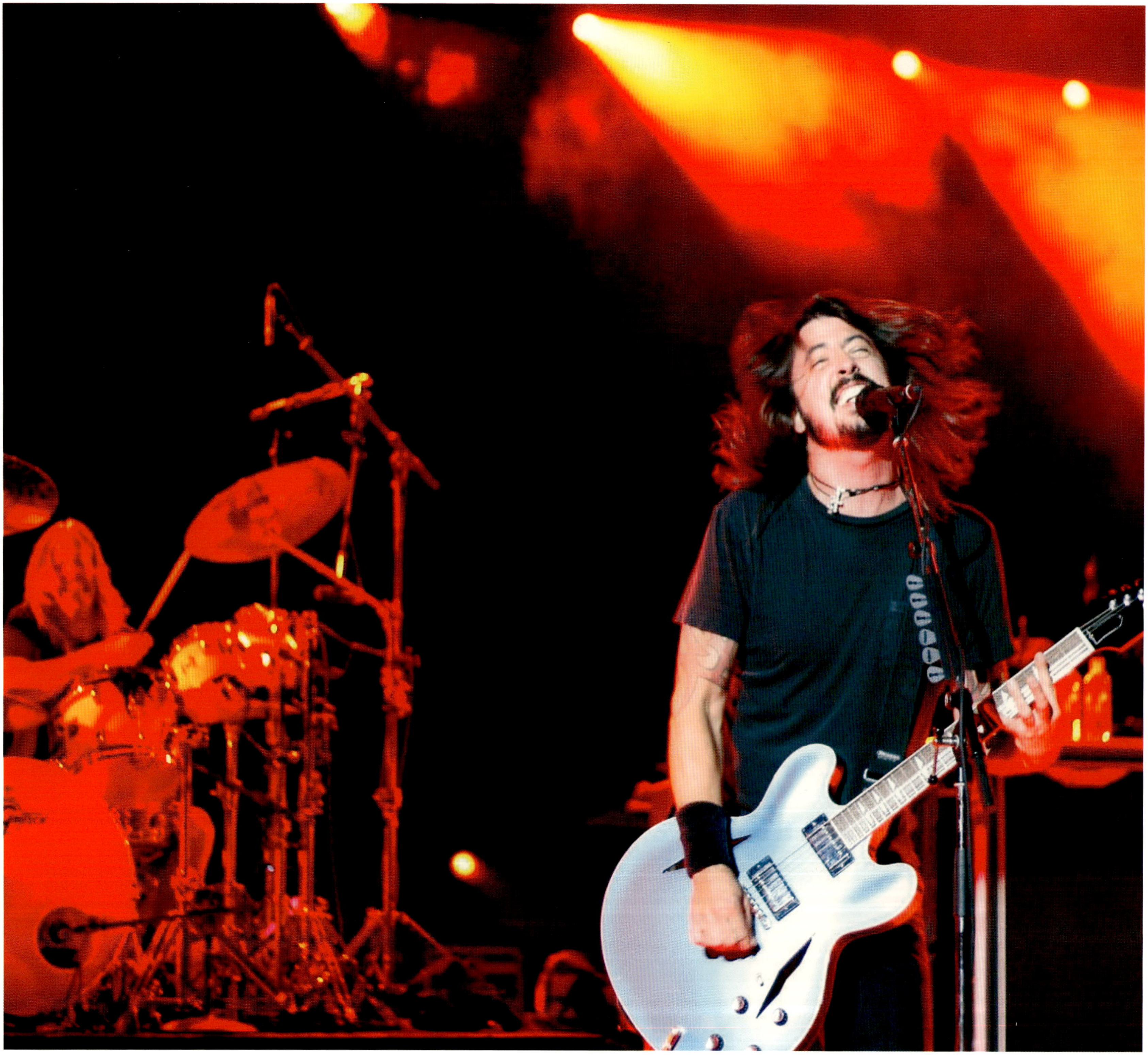

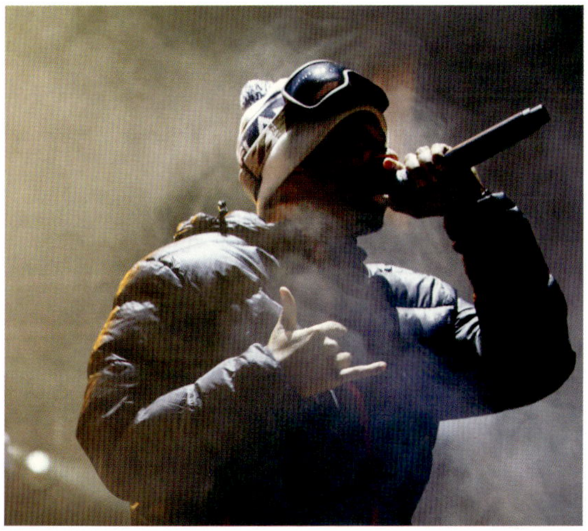

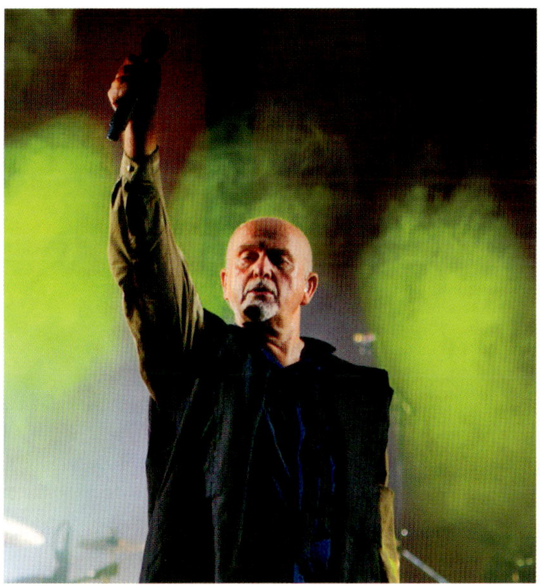

Foo Fighters, 2008 (left); "Winter on the Rocks," 2014 (top); Peter Gabriel, 2012 (above)

Red Rocks thing. The Colorado audience is so hyped up, and it makes you feel really good and connected. I can't imagine our lives without it."

A downpour hit Peter Gabriel's Red Rocks show in June 2011. He wryly noted, "When you are in the bosom of nature, you need to be careful of what you wish for." Three months later, a group of music fans was hit by falling rocks during "Baraka," the final song of Sound Tribe Sector 9's encore. The resulting whiff of litigation prompted yearly rock-stabilization work.

Red Rocks concerts had been scheduled as late as September 30—in 2000, the "Red Bull Rock 'N' Air" event featuring 311, Pennywise and an extreme-sports demonstration featuring a ramp covered with 40 tons of man-made snow. However, the ramp buckled under the weight, scrapping that portion of the show, leaving skateboard and BMX legends Tony Hawk and Matt Hoffman to go vertical on the half-pipe.

The risk of bone-chilling drops in temperature presented the biggest problem with holding concerts that late in the season. But in 2012, Red Rocks' first-ever "Winter on the Rocks" show was booked on January 27. Atmosphere and Common performed in freezing temps before a packed house.

"It seemed like a joke at first because, obviously, it's winter," Atmosphere's Sean "Slug" Daley said. "Then we quickly learned they weren't joking. The only thing I can grab onto is that we're from Minnesota, so we've played outdoors in the winter before."

Before Red Rocks kicked off its 2014 summer concert season, it had to address complaints of window-rattling sound levels during shows that churned out the pulsating tones, heavy drops and chest-crushing bass of electronic dance music (EDM). Neighboring residents and administrators in the town of Morrison and Jefferson County reported disturbances when EDM returned to Red Rocks—not only citing shows going late into the evening, but higher decibel levels and sub-bass frequencies that were disturbing those who lived as far as a half mile from the venue.

Over time, the Red Rocks team conducted studies and implemented changes to sound levels and event-ending times, drafting a good neighbor policy in time for the 2014 concert season. With dozens of EDM artists playing the venue, the ensuing years brought additional modifications. Most significantly, at the fixed front-of-house mix position, Red Rocks set up a monitoring system to measure sound pressure levels, providing a performer's sound engineer real-time data to manage the decibels.

In 2014, Easter Sunday landed on the pot-lover's highest holiday—April 20, or 4/20 in stoner lingo. The coincidence resulted in two completely different celebrations on the same day—the annual Easter Sunrise Service, the first performance of each season, transitioned into rapper

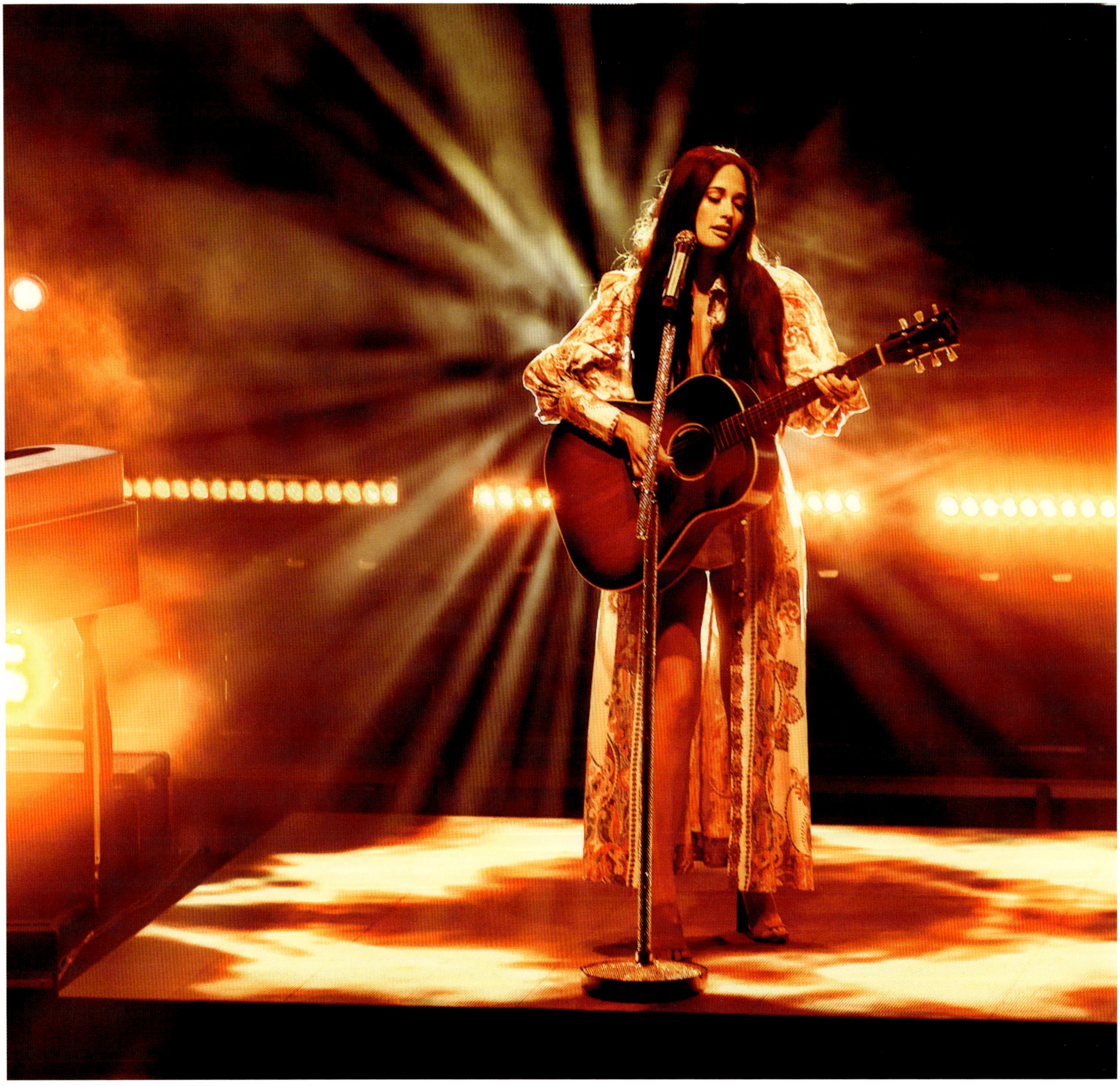

and marijuana activist Snoop Dogg's 4/20 concert. Later that summer, in a parking lot following a "Feed the Rocks" concert, a man fired multiple rifle shots into an SUV carrying hip-hop artist Schoolboy Q. Three people were injured.

Red Rocks headed into one of its best seasons in 2015, with more than 100 shows populating the schedule. Thanks to concert promotion companies AEG Live and Live Nation, a packed roster of talent—from indie shows (Ryan Adams, Iron and Wine, Morrissey) to metal (Mastodon, Slipknot, Lamb of God) to country (Lindsay Sterling, Grace Potter, Tim McGraw) to first timers (Sam Smith, Idina Menzel, Ed Sheeran) to Blues Traveler's twenty-first edition of its Fourth of July Tradition show—meant a performance nearly every day or night from April to October. In August, the National Park Service and Department of the Interior designated Red Rocks Amphitheatre a National Historic Landmark. Why it took so long was anyone's guess.

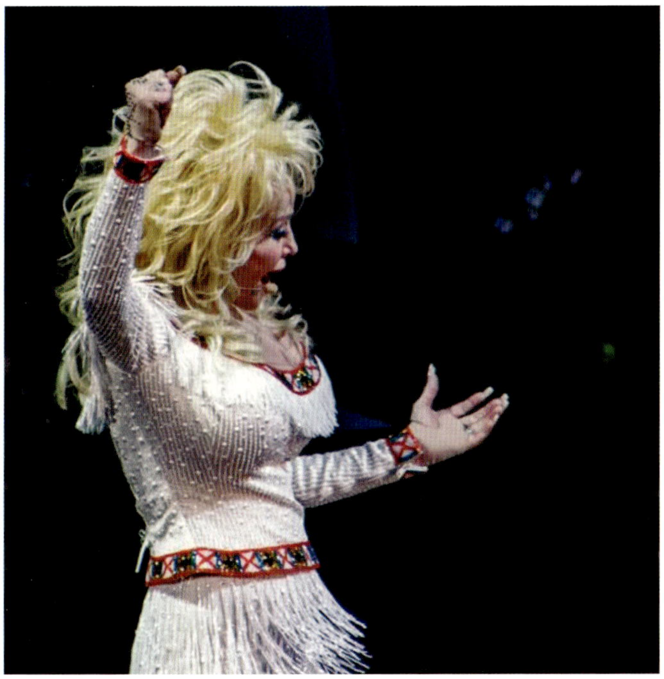

Kacey Musgraves, 2019 (left); Dolly Parton, 2016

Artists, concertgoers and staff looked to 2016 and the 75th anniversary of Red Rocks' dedication. For the fourth time in as many years, a new record was set for the number of shows booked. The legendary mountain venue looked nothing like it did at the first concerts. During the day, when Red Rocks wasn't hosting performances, there was an exhausting amount of athletic activity—folks running up and down the steeply inclined aisles and seats, practicing yoga, CrossFitting.

In 1941, musicians hung their clothes on nails; now they composed their set lists under pictures of Red Rocks greats. Artists now had use of a backstage kitchen and showers. Sound towers, light towers and box seats in the planter spaces on the sides of the seating areas had also been added. Attendance had grown every year, as had the number of vendors and service providers hawking apparel, blankets and souvenirs, as well as food and drink beyond the burger-and-soda standard.

The 2018 season saw major pop, EDM and hip-hop artists come to Red Rocks. The bands that garnered multinight stands tended to play roots, bluegrass and jam-band music—Avett Brothers, Umphrey's McGee, String Cheese Incident, Tedeschi Trucks Band and Greensky Bluegrass.

In 2019, 17-year-old Billie Eilish made her Red Rocks debut, managing her brooding bedroom pop during a dreary downpour. On the heels of her dominant performance at that year's Grammys, both musically and awards-wise, Kacey Musgraves had grown her discerning country-rock fan base, expanding the capacity for her Red Rocks show. At 75, Diana Ross came off a late-winter Las Vegas residency for a July performance at Red Rocks, where she revisited hits from a career that began as leader of the Supremes in the '60s.

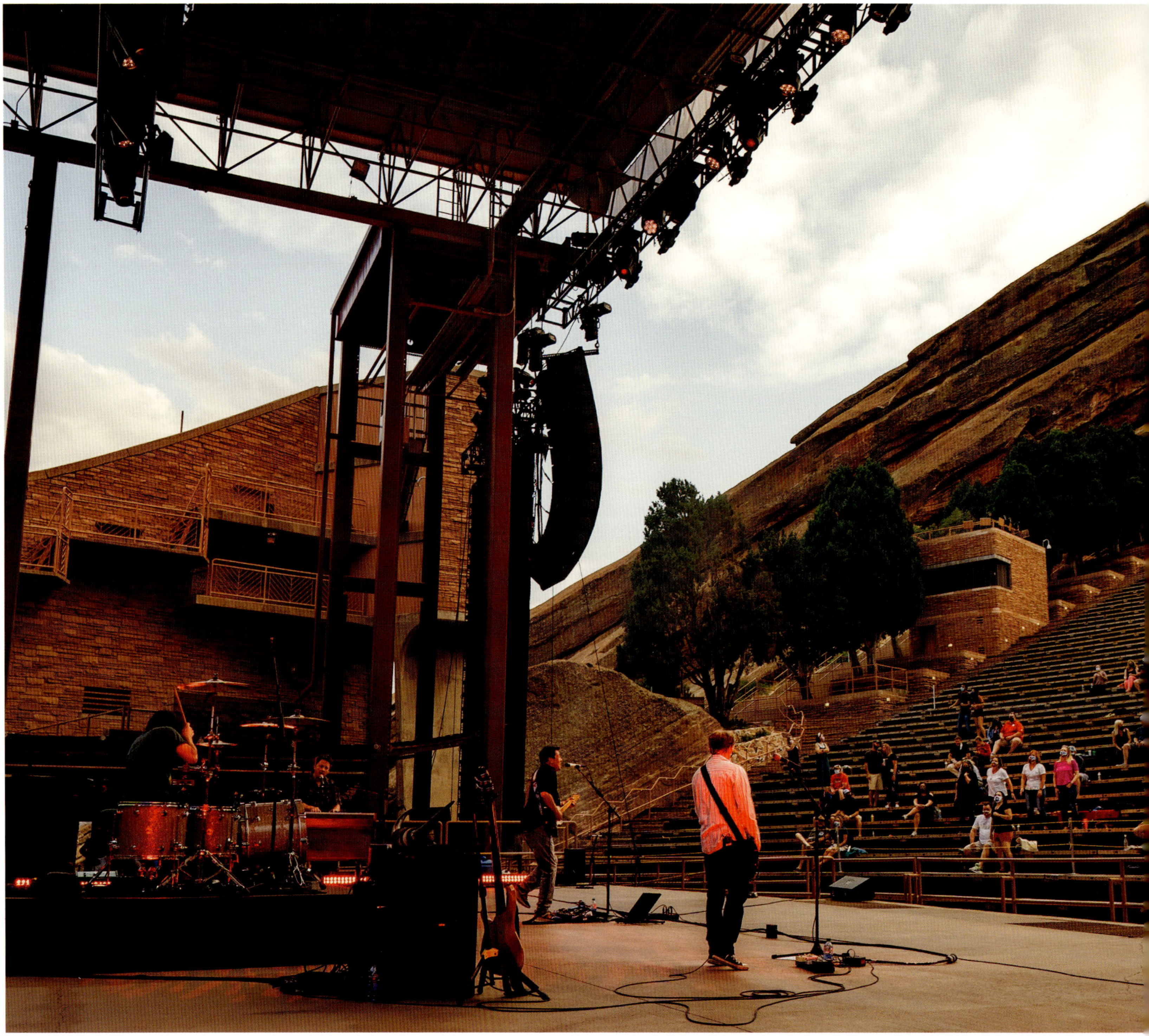

Big Head Todd & the Monsters, 2020

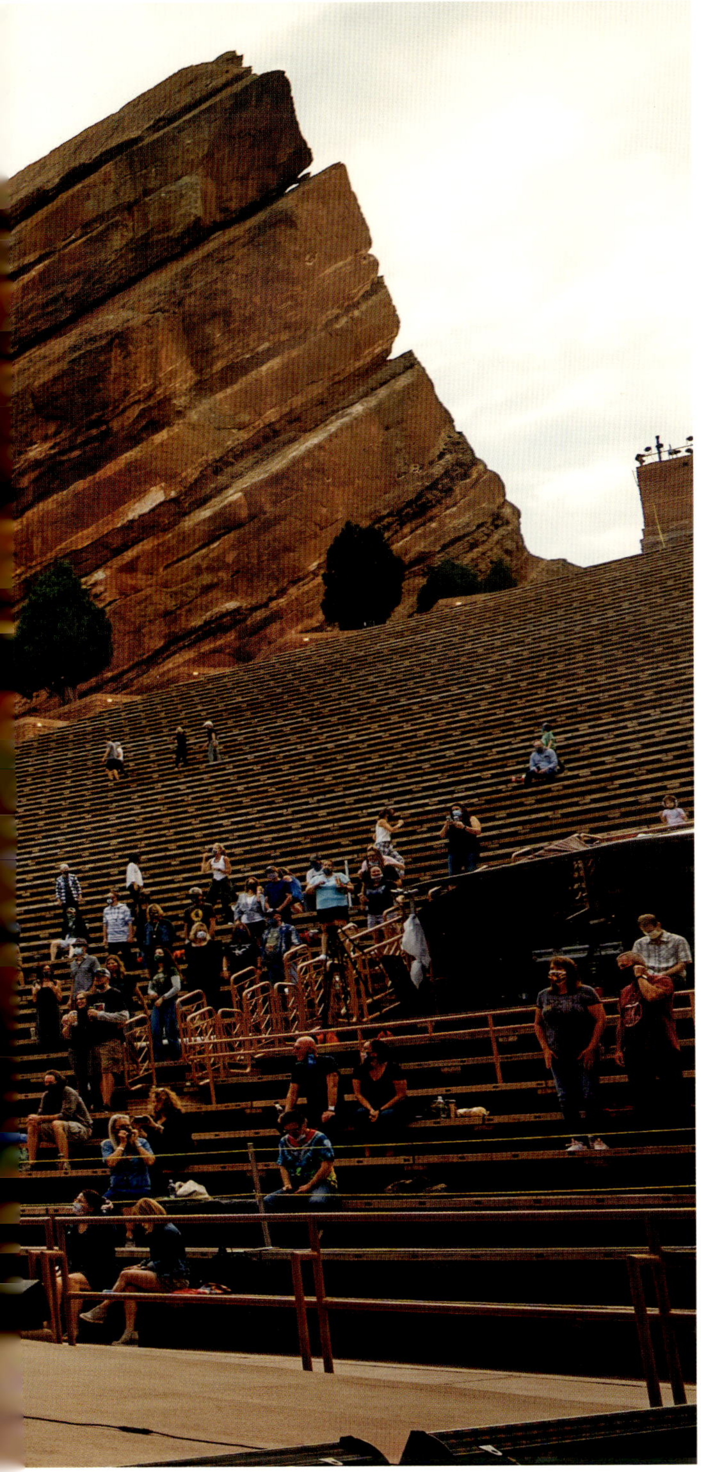

2020-2022

HEARD IMMUNITY

Red Rocks was open at full capacity for Winter on the Rocks on Jan. 31, 2020. And then the COVID-19 pandemic brought live music and entertainment to a screeching halt. Most of the concert season was postponed, but the state granted the venue a variance to COVID-19 restrictions, and a handful of shows took place for audiences of 175 people, including performances by the Colorado Symphony Strings, which played "Acoustic on the Rocks" shows in July and August following social distancing guidelines.

Virtual shows were streamed live. The Colorado Music Relief Fund launched with a "Banding Together" event—performances from iconic locations across Colorado and beyond, and Nathaniel Rateliff opened the show with a performance of "Time Stands" in an empty Red Rocks.

Megan Thee Stallion headlined a virtual three-day festival, "Visible's Red Rocks Unpaused." A photographer from *Vogue*, the fashion publication, captured her backstage wardrobe decisions before she took the stage with no audience in sight wearing a crop top and hot pants with studded garter belts and thigh-high boots.

"In a year with hardly any live music, it felt surreal to perform a show at a venue as iconic as Red Rocks," the rapper stated. "I had an idea for a look that would pay tribute to Lara Croft, but in my own Stalli style—it looks so bomb onstage under the lights."

"Red Rocks at Home" was a free virtual event live from Red Rocks, and Big Head Todd & the Monsters played a pair of concerts in September after Nathaniel Rateliff & the Night Sweats' run.

"Five nights with 175 people, and one night where we recorded the show with no audience—it was the maximum capacity in Denver city limits, and technically Red Rocks fell under those guidelines as a mountain park," Rateliff said. "There was a heaviness to those performances. The pitch of the seating that seems to turn 10,000 concertgoers into 100,000, the experience of looking up and seeing all those people and it just looks massive—that's why Red Rocks is my favorite outdoor venue to play. With no audience, it was pretty intense. In the stillness, you could feel the severity of what was going on in the world. How we were experiencing it onstage made us think about what was happening globally."

The 2021 season began under the shadow of the COVID-19 pandemic, with reduced capacities, seating charts promoting social distance, on-site vaccinations and uncertain fans and tours. The jamtronica band Lotus opened the summer with a four-night series in April, the first major shows at Red Rocks following the COVID shutdown.

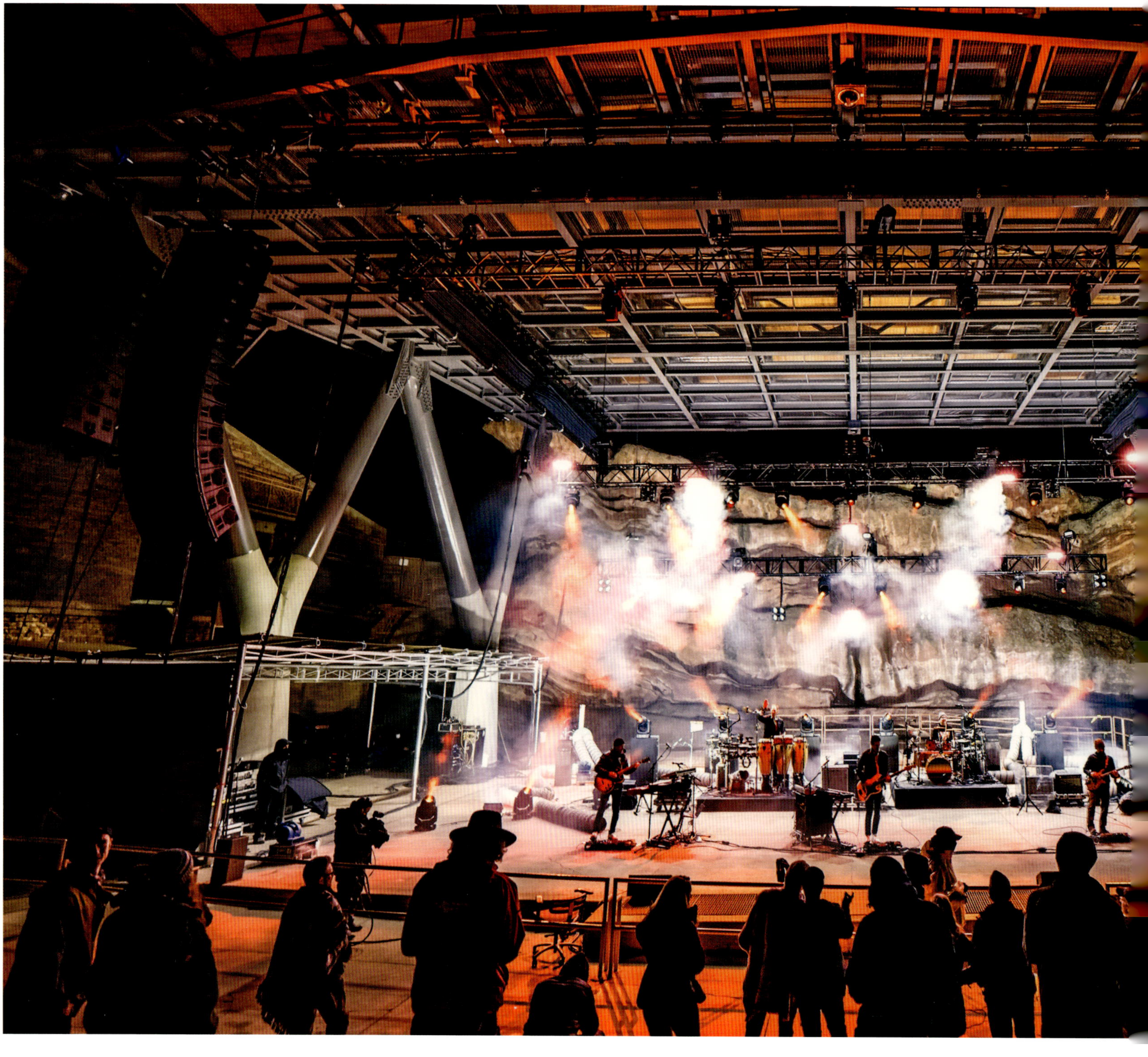

Lotus, 2021

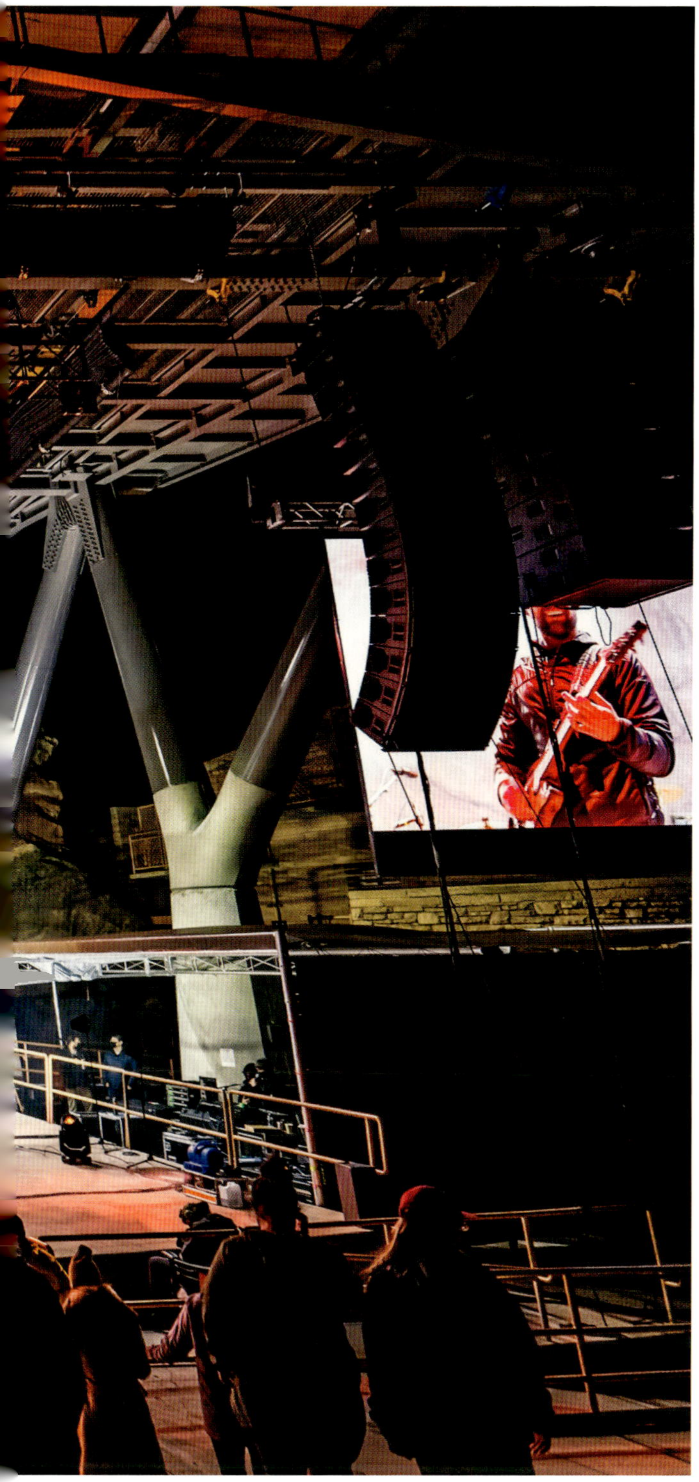

"Lotus had been lucky enough to headline Red Rocks over a dozen times in the backyard of where I grew up, from playing in full-on snowstorms to a special Talking Heads tribute," guitarist and keyboardist Luke Miller mused. "We were able to squeeze in a show during the pandemic, September 2000. Red Rocks had to reduce staff, they only let the miniature audience of 175 people come. As months went on and income was zero, no one knew how long it was going to last. I ended up helping a friend with his gourmet mushroom farm up in Conifer.

"When things lifted in April 2021, we came back. Usually when Lotus plays Red Rocks, we have multiple openers, one night. This was just us, four nights in a row at limited capacity, every other row. There hadn't been music at Red Rocks. You could just feel the energy in the air."

The only upside to the pandemic was the construction of a new stage roof. The renovation, schedule to begin in November 2020, got a head start in the last week of September. The original roof, built in 1988, had outlived its life expectancy, and the renovation was part of the Elevate Denver 10-year bond program to enhance city infrastructure. The new roof provided more protection from the weather for musicians and performers, a safer platform for stagehands and riggers, and more weight capacity for lighting and sound equipment via a cable-mesh system. It was built with more natural materials to blend into Red Rocks' scenery without sacrificing functionality.

Working around public health orders, performances with larger capacities—first 2,800 and then 6,300—continued through the spring of 2021. The live music industry had been booming prior to the coronavirus pandemic, and Red Rocks regained its pre-lockdown vibrancy, with a plethora of new artists and the return of some old favorites. A June concert by Americana artist Shakey Graves was the first near full-capacity event at the beloved venue since the onset of the pandemic, representing an important milestone on Red Rocks' return to normal operations. Those who helped the venue run, such as stagehands and concessionaires, could get back to work.

Highlights of the season included a six-night stand with electronic music artist and producer Zhu. Members of the Grateful Dead returned in the Dead & Company configuration, and singer-songwriter Dermot Kennedy, rapper Playboi Carti and comedian Bill Burr all headlined for the first time.

Digitization had stimulated a demand for events hosted at Red Rocks. Compared to traditional radio and purchasing recordings, streaming provided an easier connection to music, driving concert attendance for a wide variety of artists, not just the elite ones who made the charts. *Billboard* magazine named Red Rocks Amphitheatre as the top-grossing,

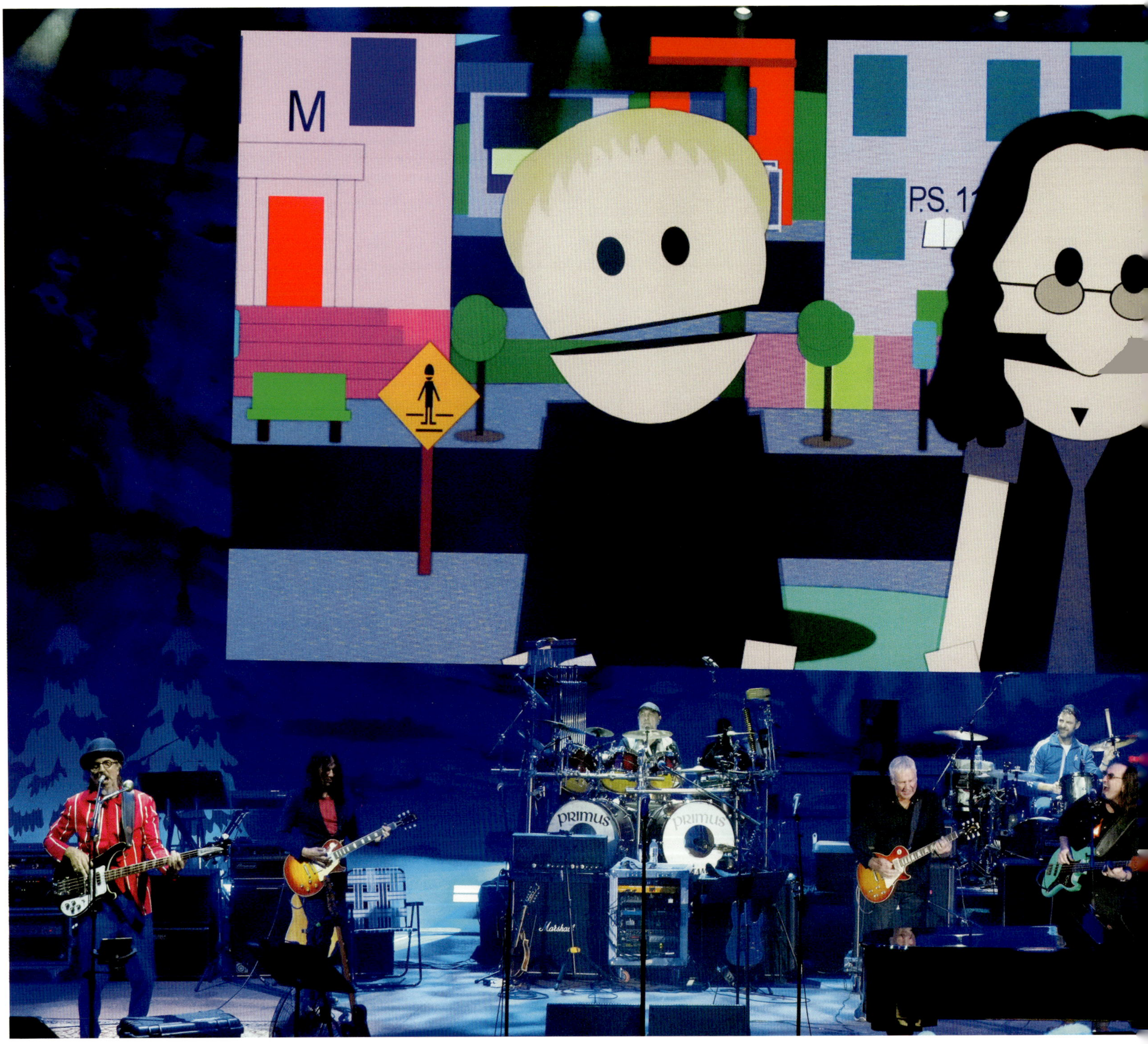

South Park 25th Anniversary Concert , 2022

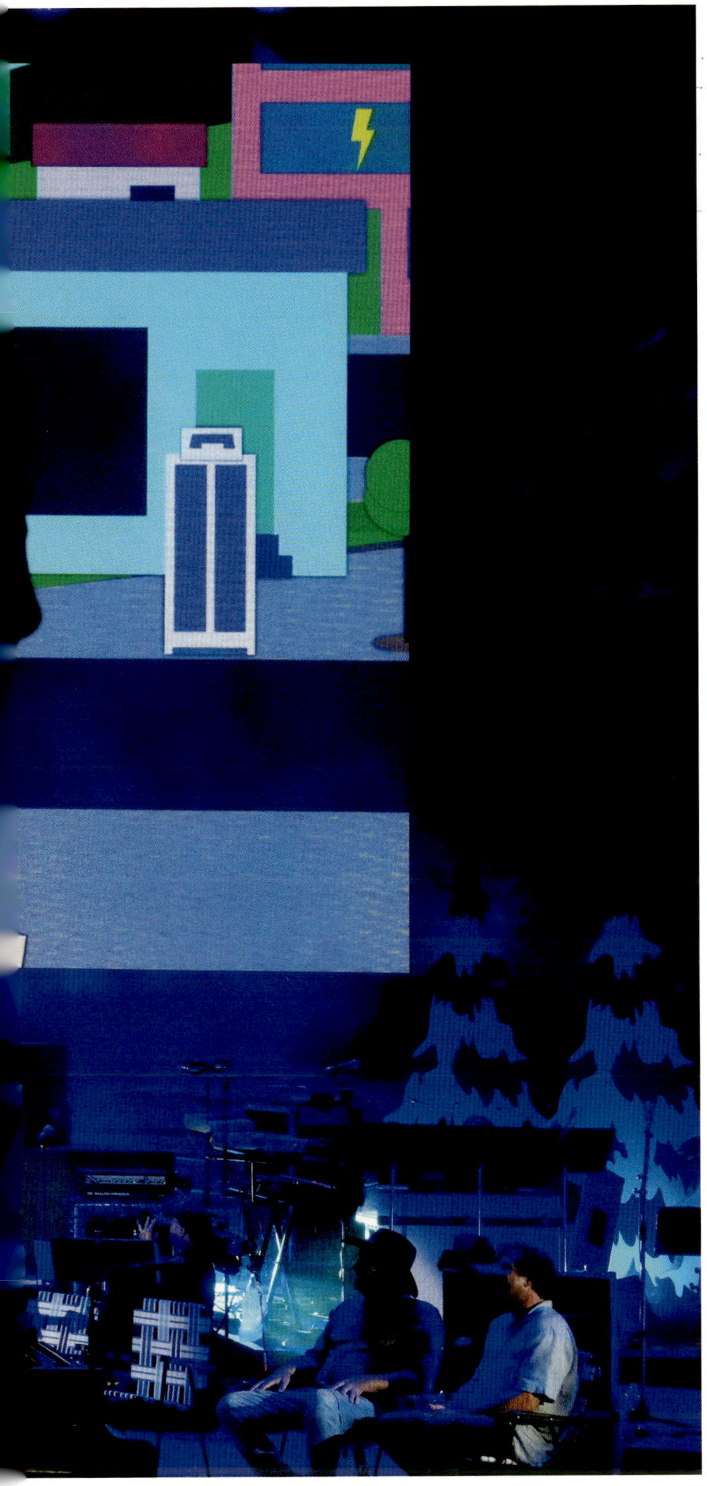

most attended concert venue of any size, anywhere in the world for 2021—the venue's 80th anniversary. Red Rocks broke its own season record (2019's 168 shows per season) by hosting 233 ticketed paid events, including 177 concerts, 20 yoga/fitness programs and 36 movies in the Film on the Rocks series.

As of 2022, Widespread Panic, in another three-night run in the heart of summer, extended the record for the most concerts in the venue's history, with 66 total appearances. The Chicks (née Dixie Chicks) stopped at Red Rocks, having risen back to prominence after releasing *Gaslighter*, the all-female country trio's first studio record since 2006.

To celebrate the 25th anniversary of *South Park*, the popular animated sitcom, creators Matt Stone and Trey Parker brought the party to Red Rocks. Two concerts were held, with Primus and Ween taking part in the celebration. The second night, Colorado Governor Jared Polis came onstage to proclaim "South Park Day." After Primus performed a take on "Blame Canada," Rush members Geddy Lee and Alex Lifeson made a surprise appearance, sitting in on "Closer to the Heart," with Stone living out a dream by performing on a second drum set.

"We're so excited to come home and play at Red Rocks, a place that's been known for hosting the most legendary artists and musicians—until now," Stone and Parker cracked.

As permanent as it seems, Red Rocks Amphitheatre never stops changing—a seamless blending of the ancient and the modern, of Mother Nature's endowment and human ingenuity. Red Rocks enters the future as a geological and acoustical marvel, a natural performance space where the sounds of Stratocasters and Stradivariuses, sopranos and Steinways, all resonate with a fidelity that's every bit as extraordinary as the spectacular setting. The world knows Red Rocks, a mecca in the mountains—not only for artists performing on its storied stage, but also for the hundreds of thousands of annual visitors who come to marvel at its unique, hard-finned beauty.

And while so much has evolved on the musical landscape since the opening performances of 1941, the prehistoric and surreal appeal of Red Rocks remains timeless, an attraction unto itself. The venue is as much the star as the procession of performers who have appeared there—sometimes more so.

It's a jam that will go on forever. ■

THE FAITHFUL

For nigh on a century, the fans who flock to Red Rocks have remained as essential to the experience as the artists they come to see.

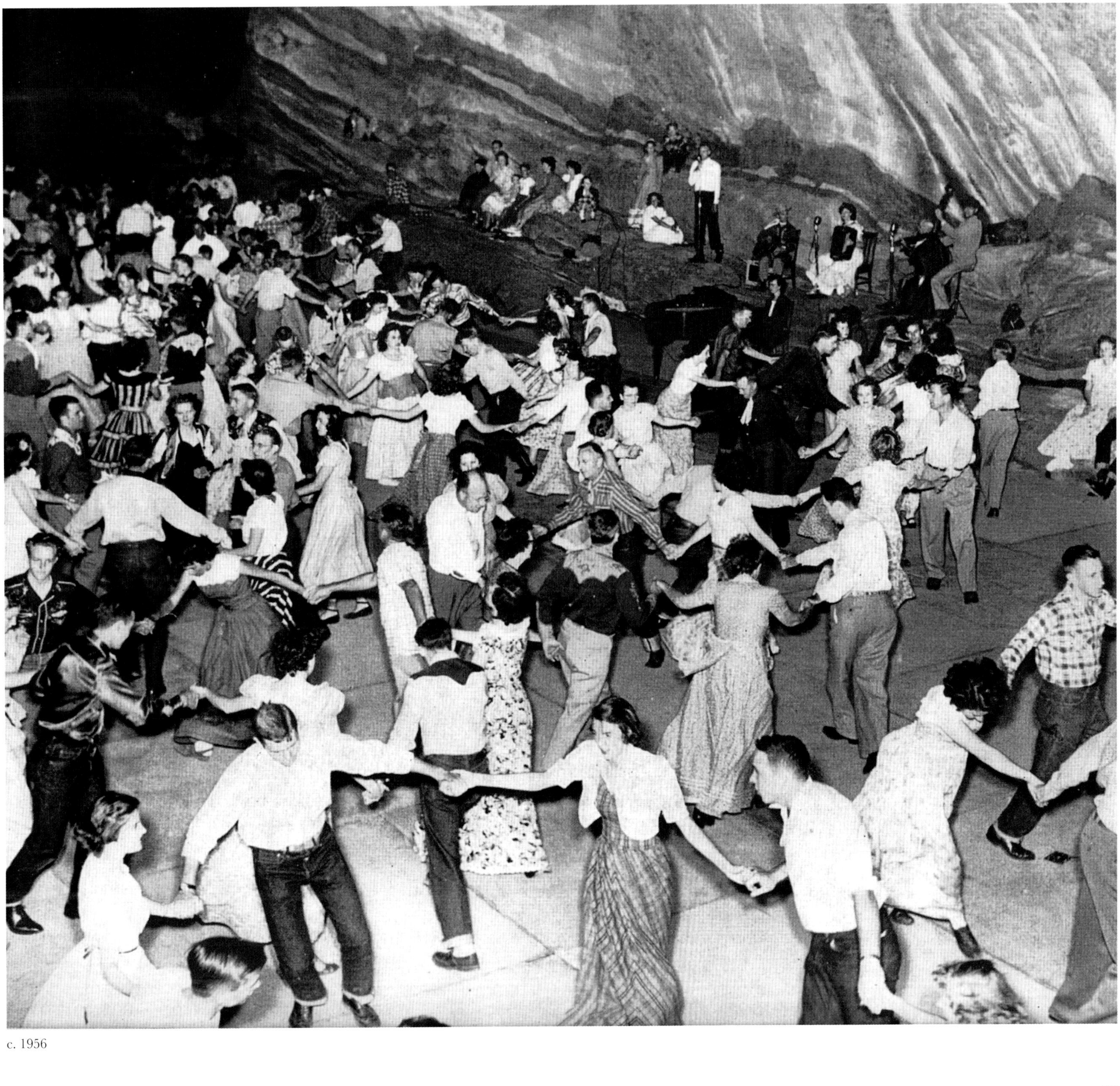

c. 1956

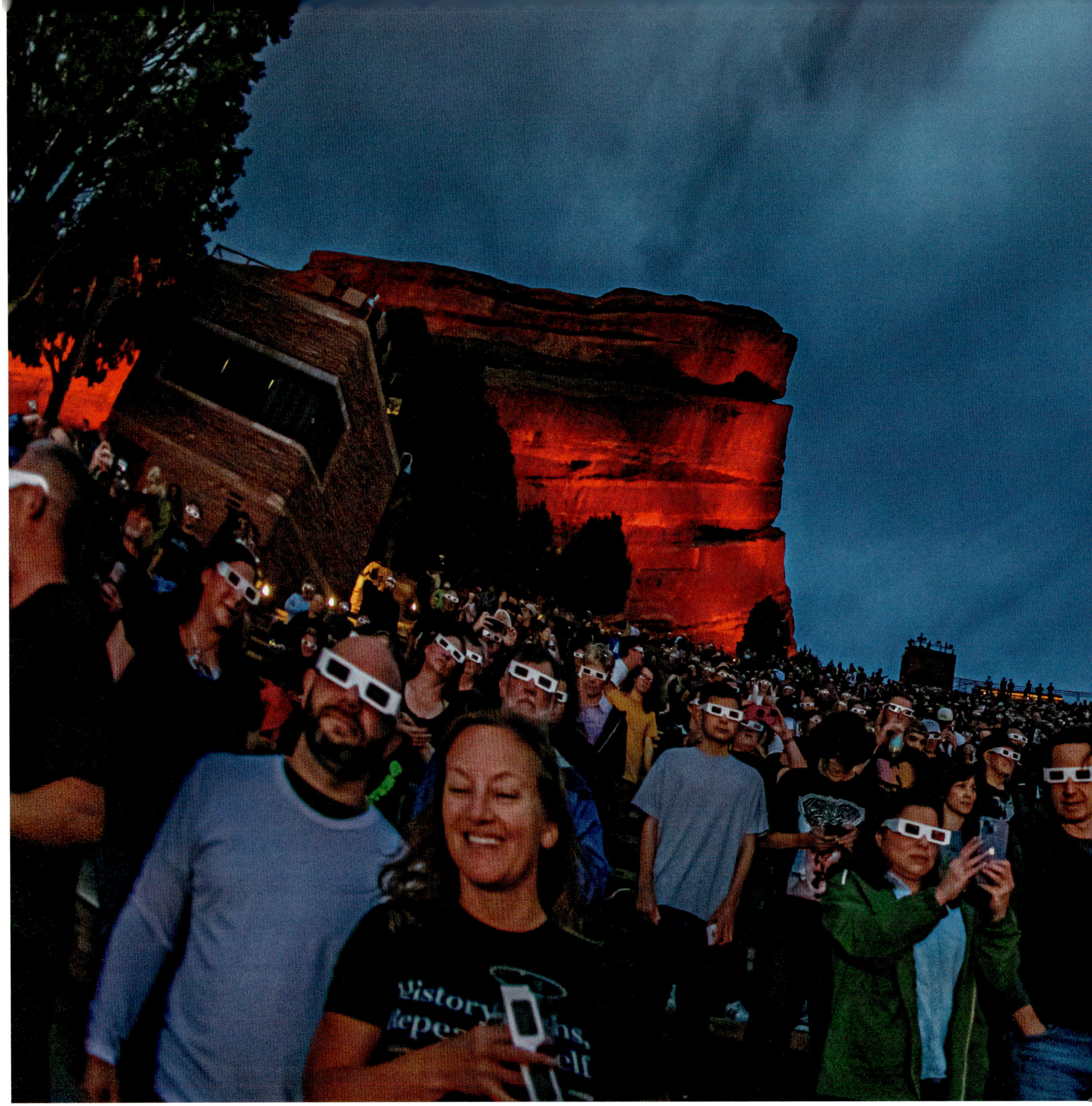

c. 2022

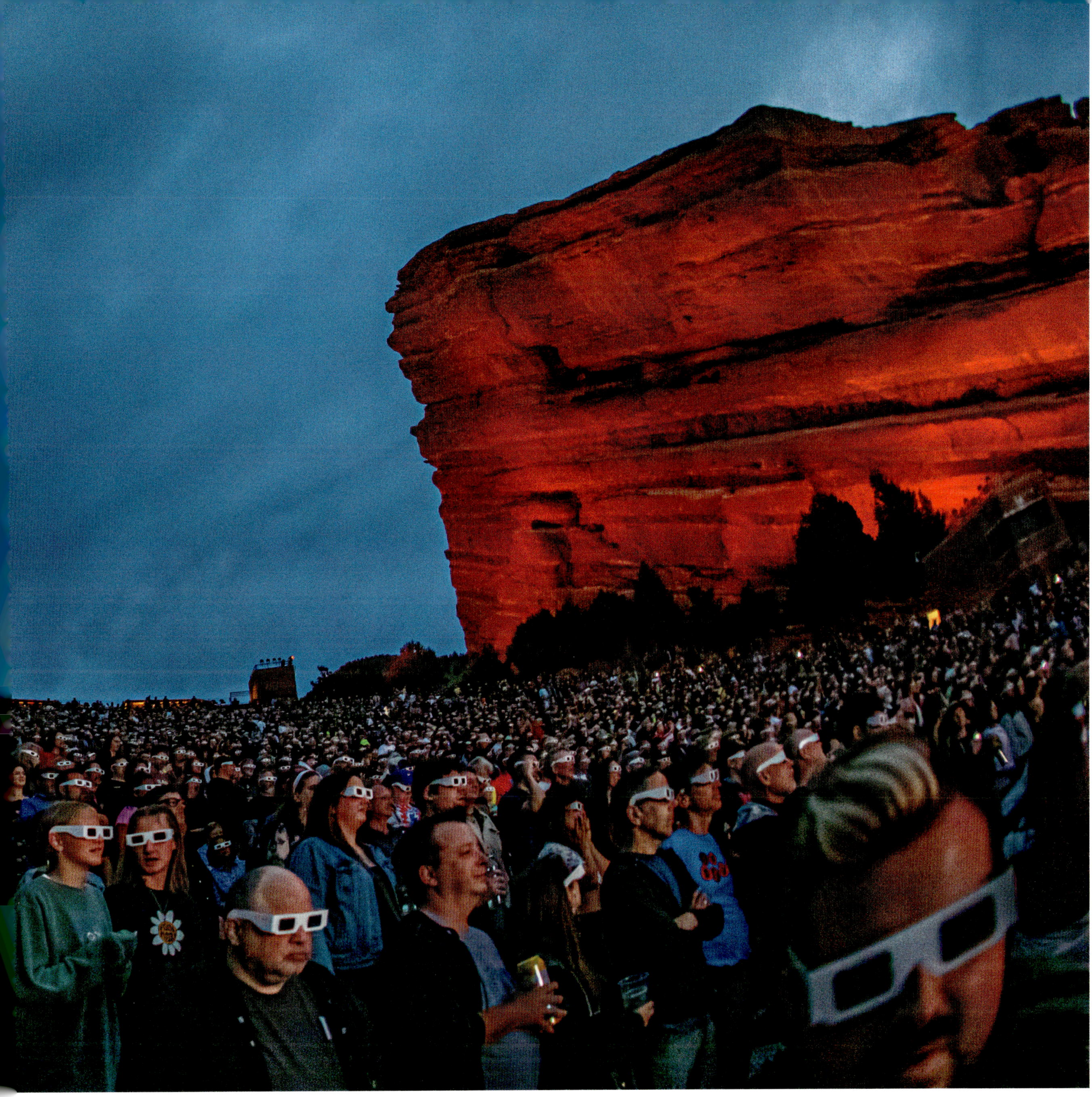

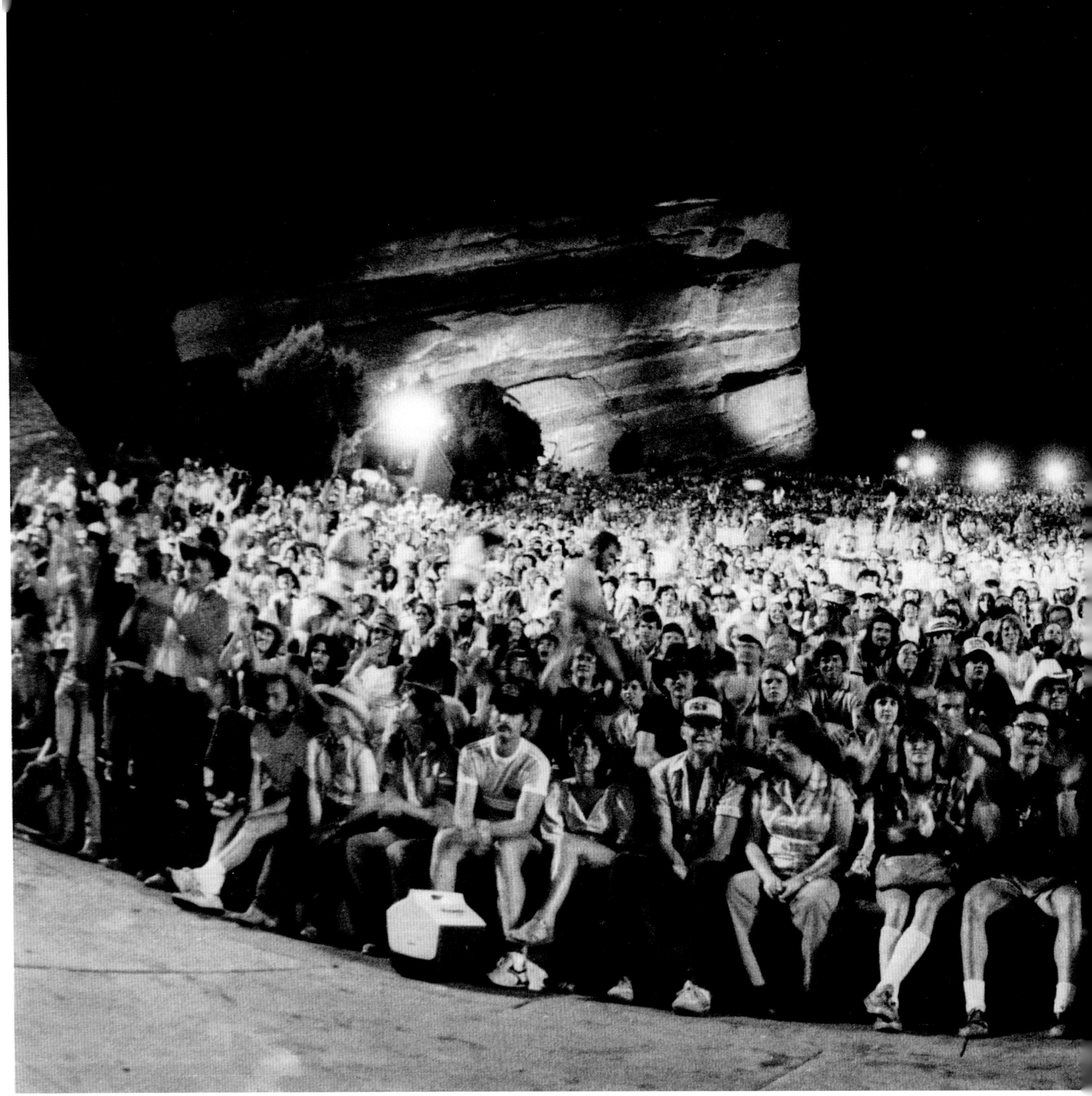

c. 1995

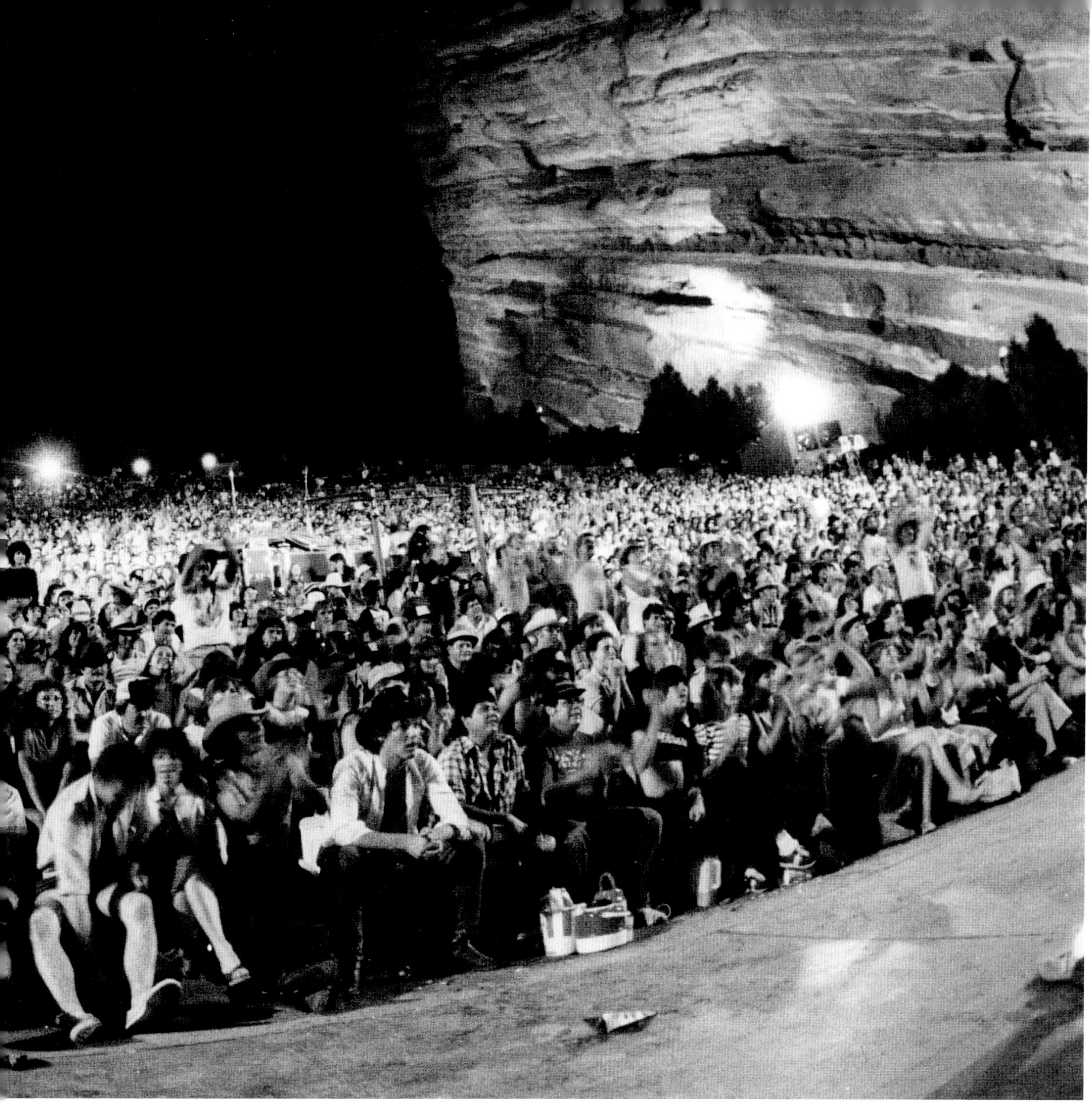

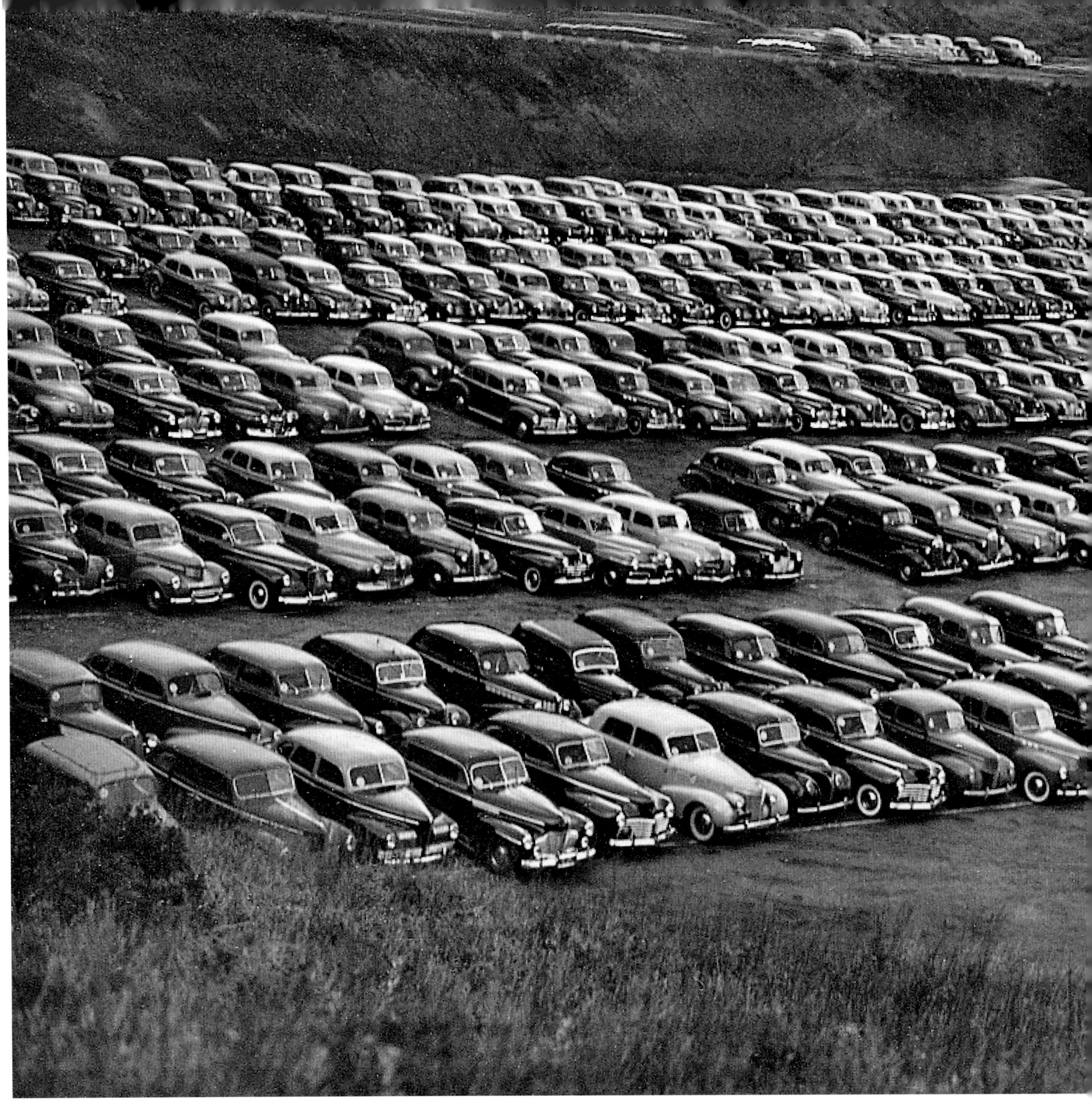

c. 1947

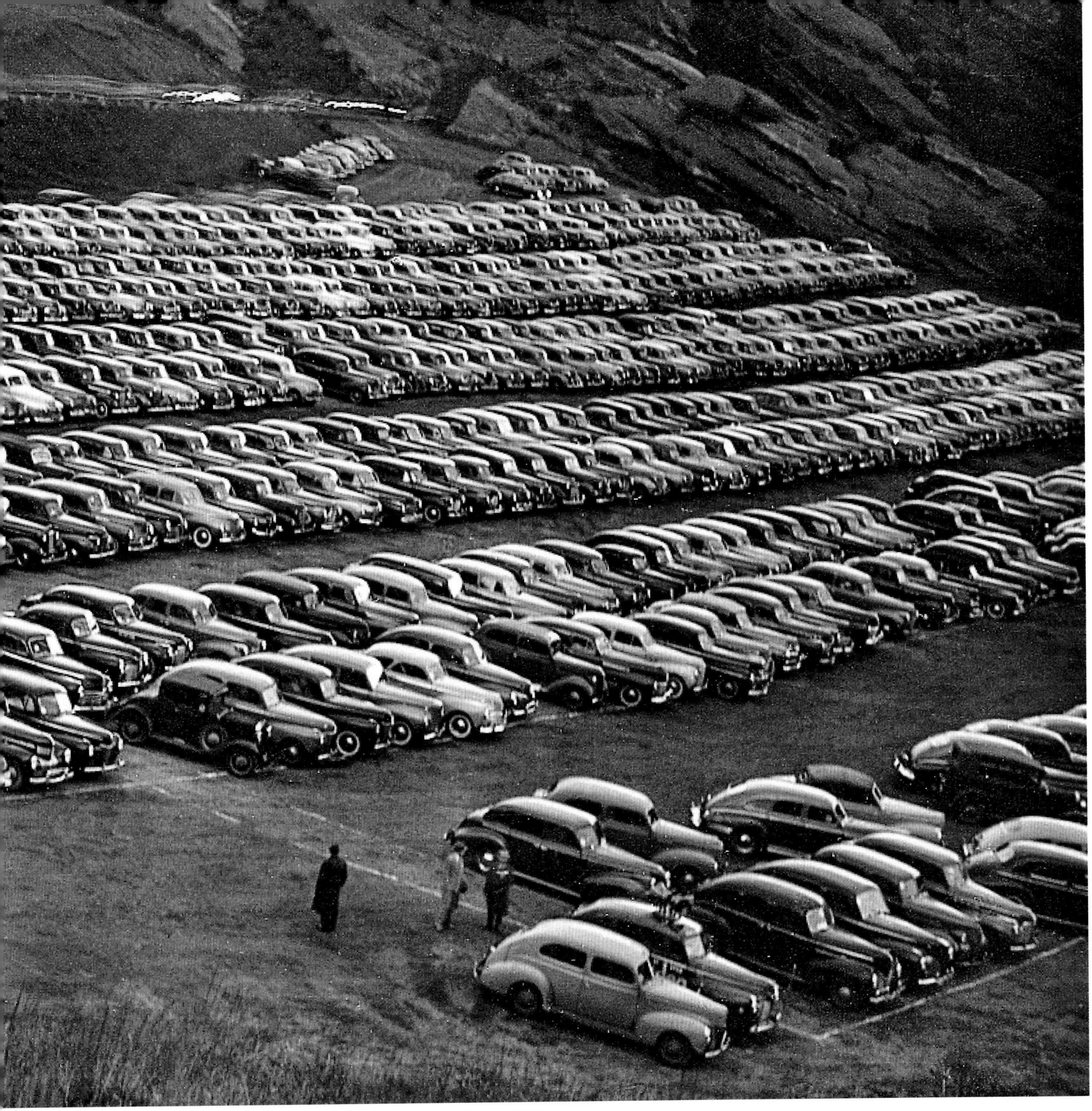

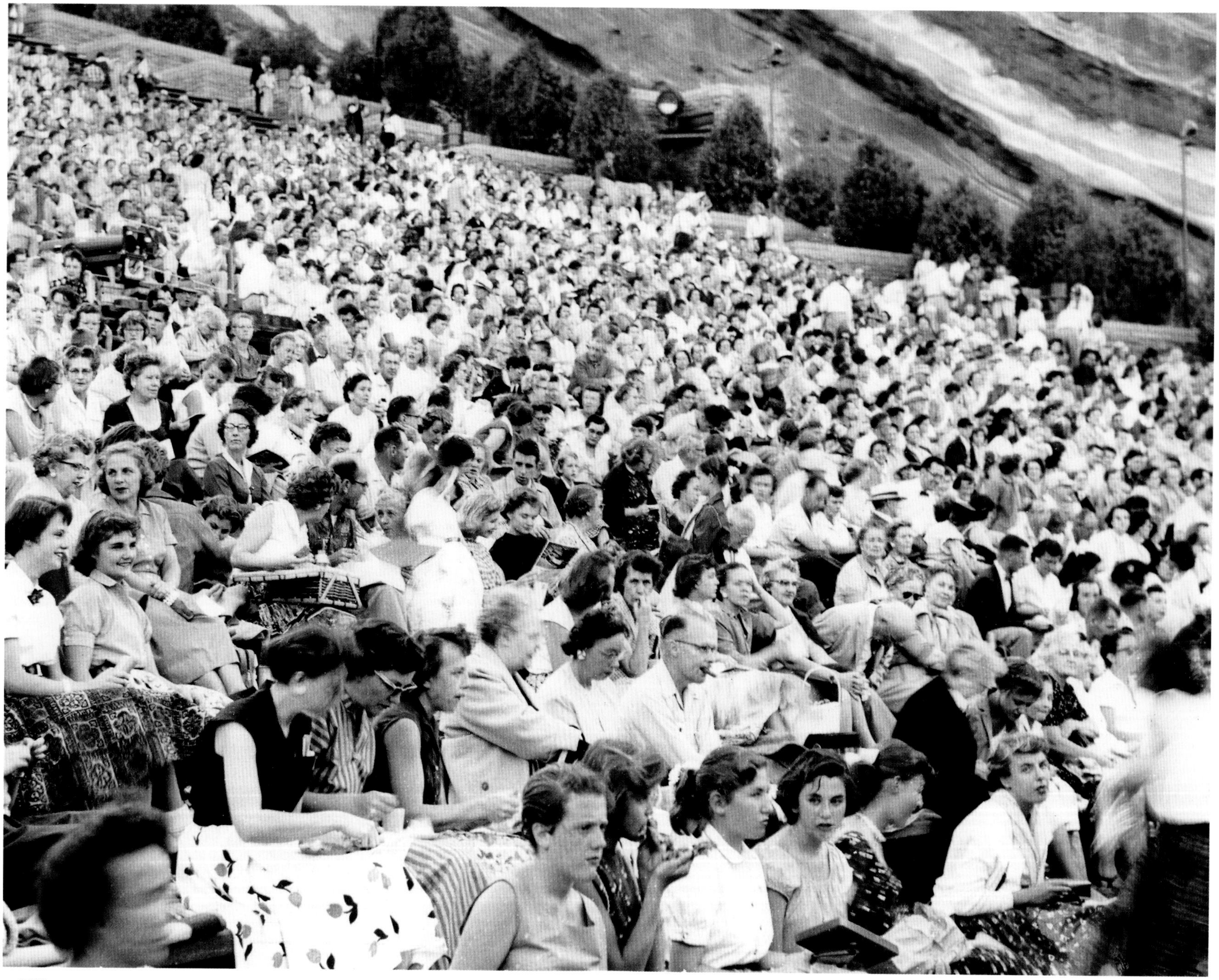

c. 1955

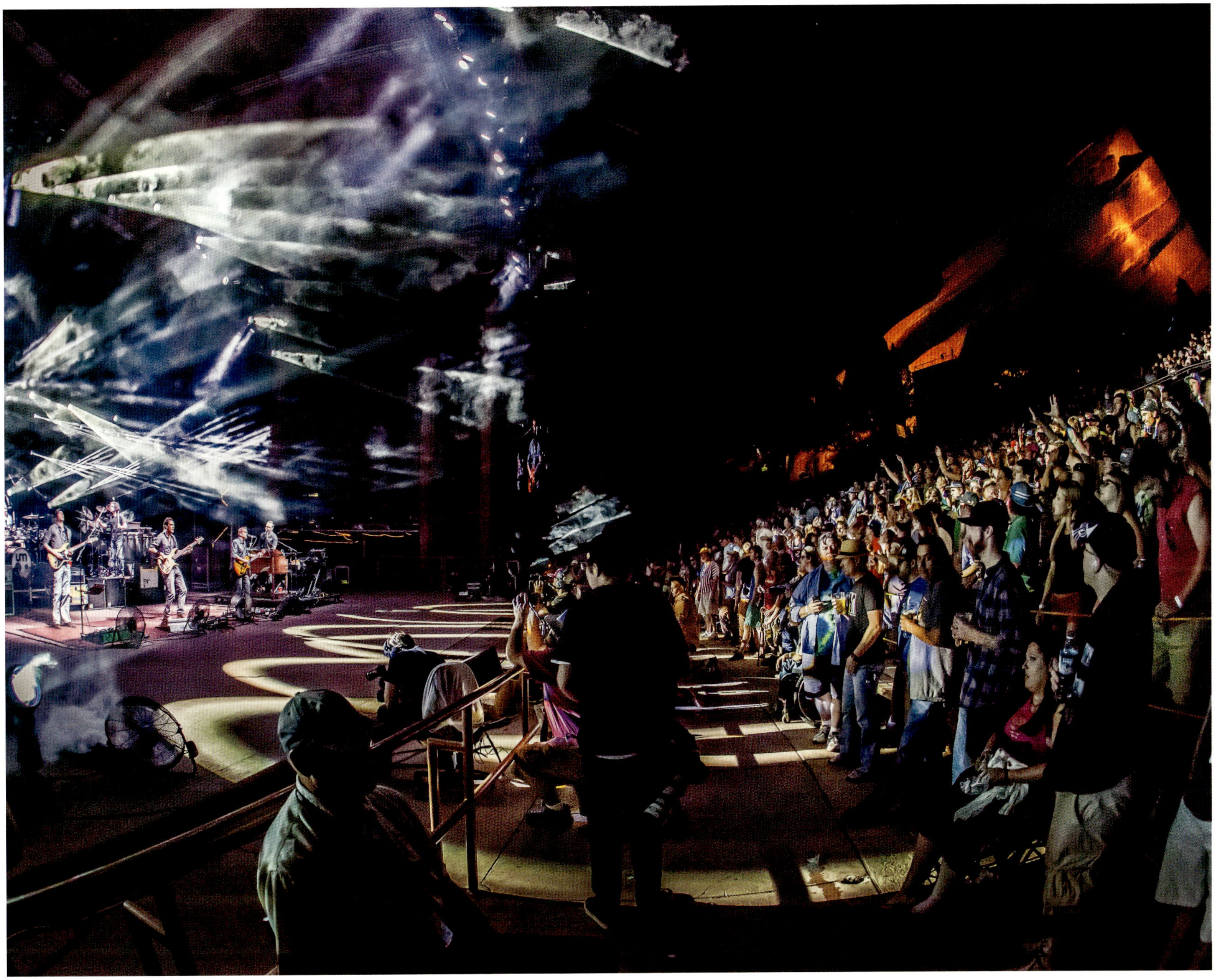

c. 2014

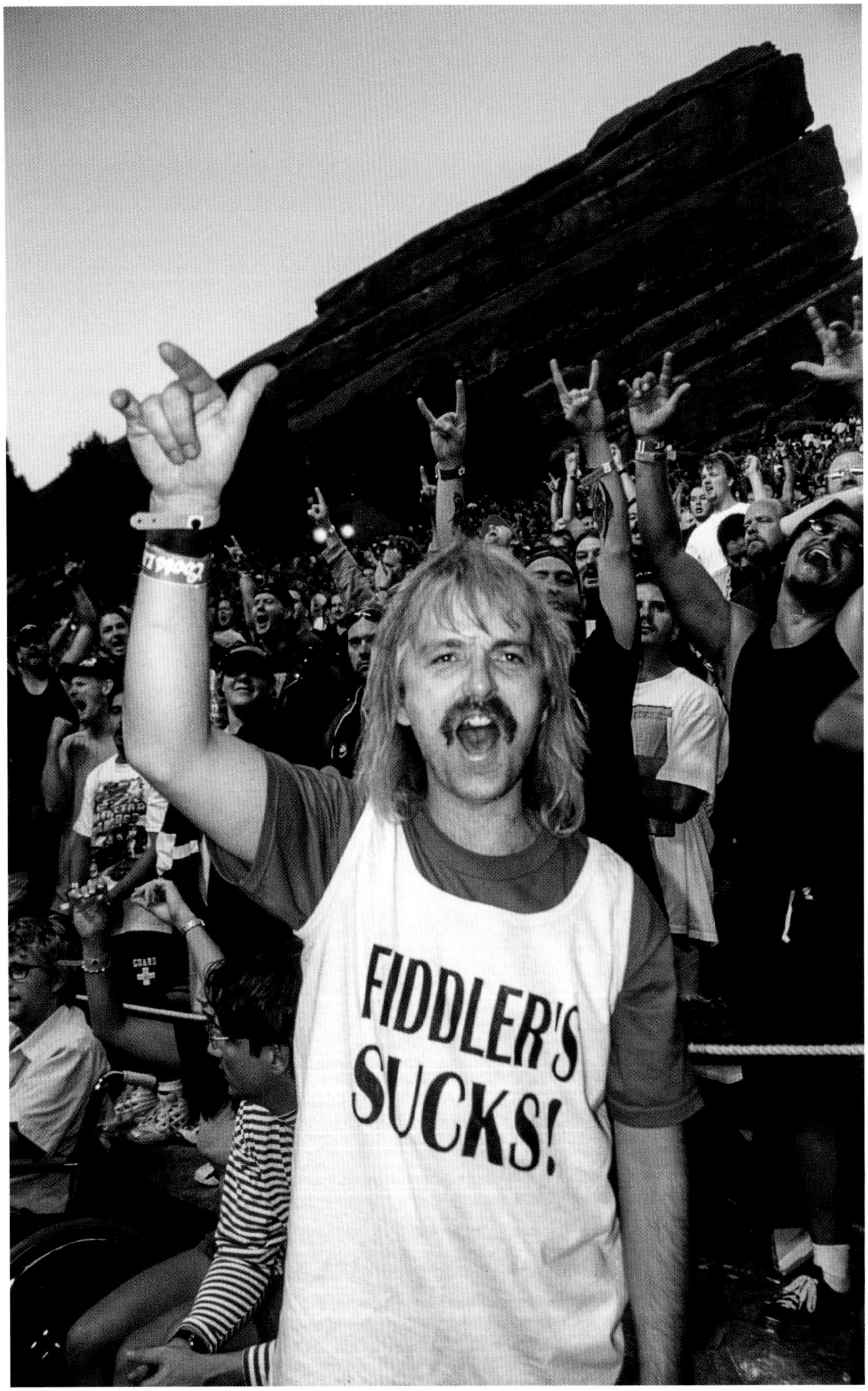

c. 1991

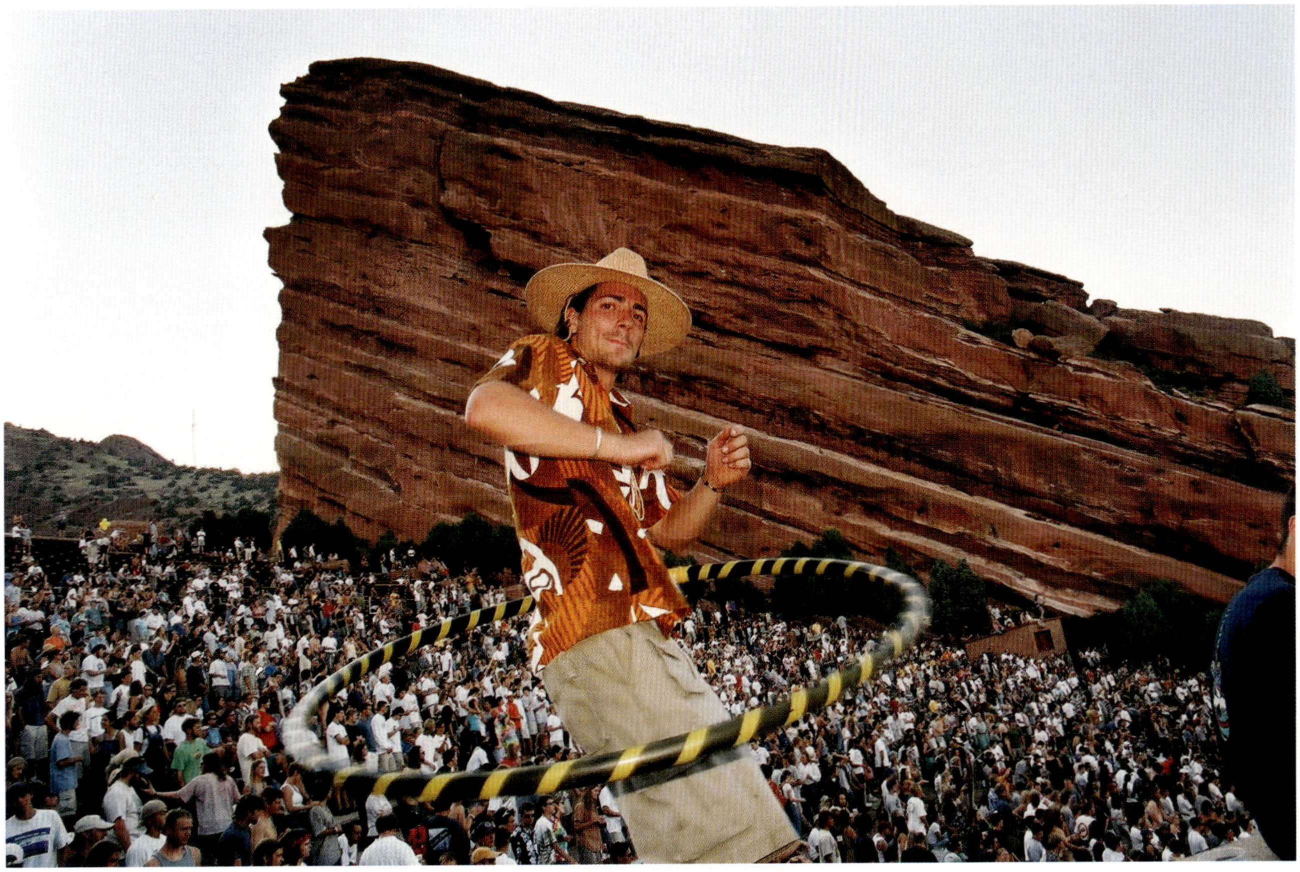

c. 1999

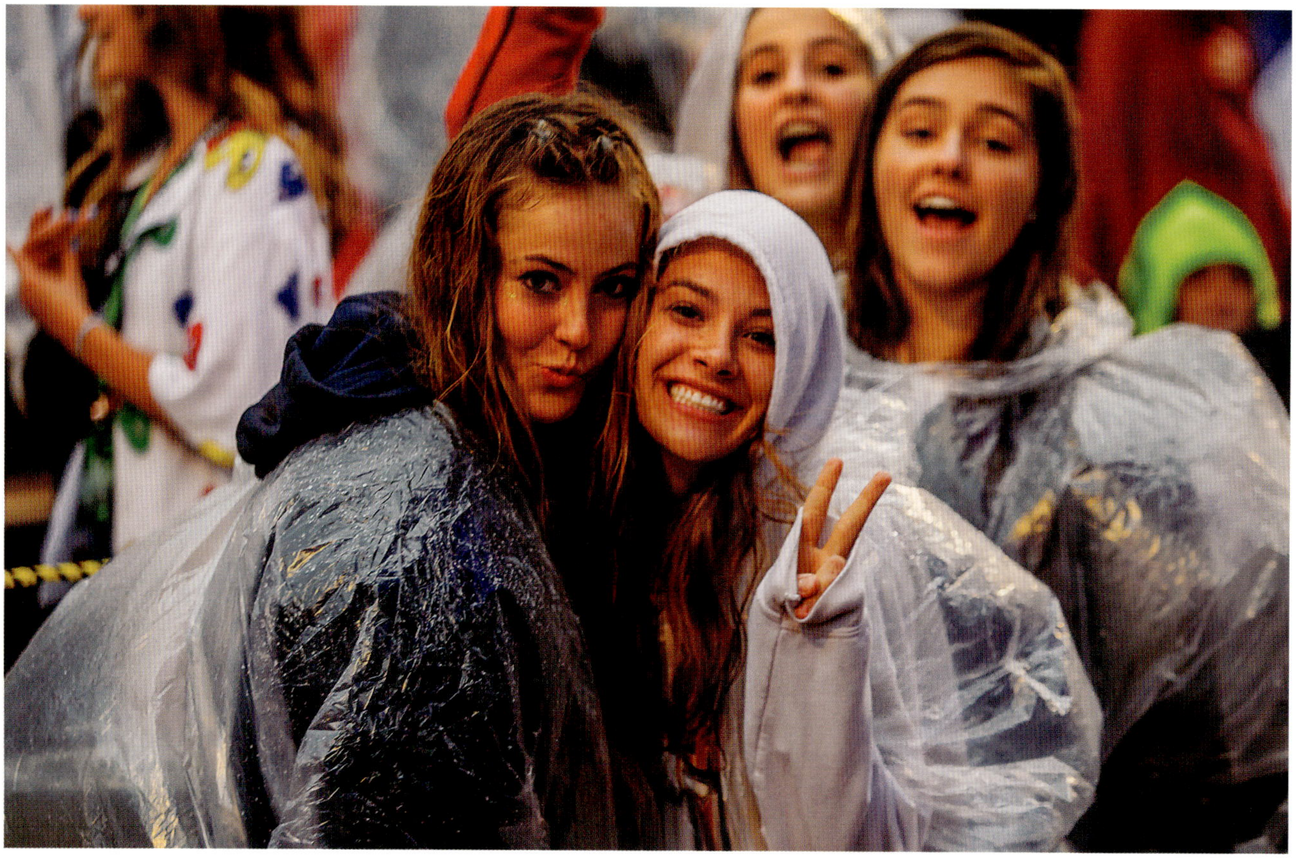

c. 2019

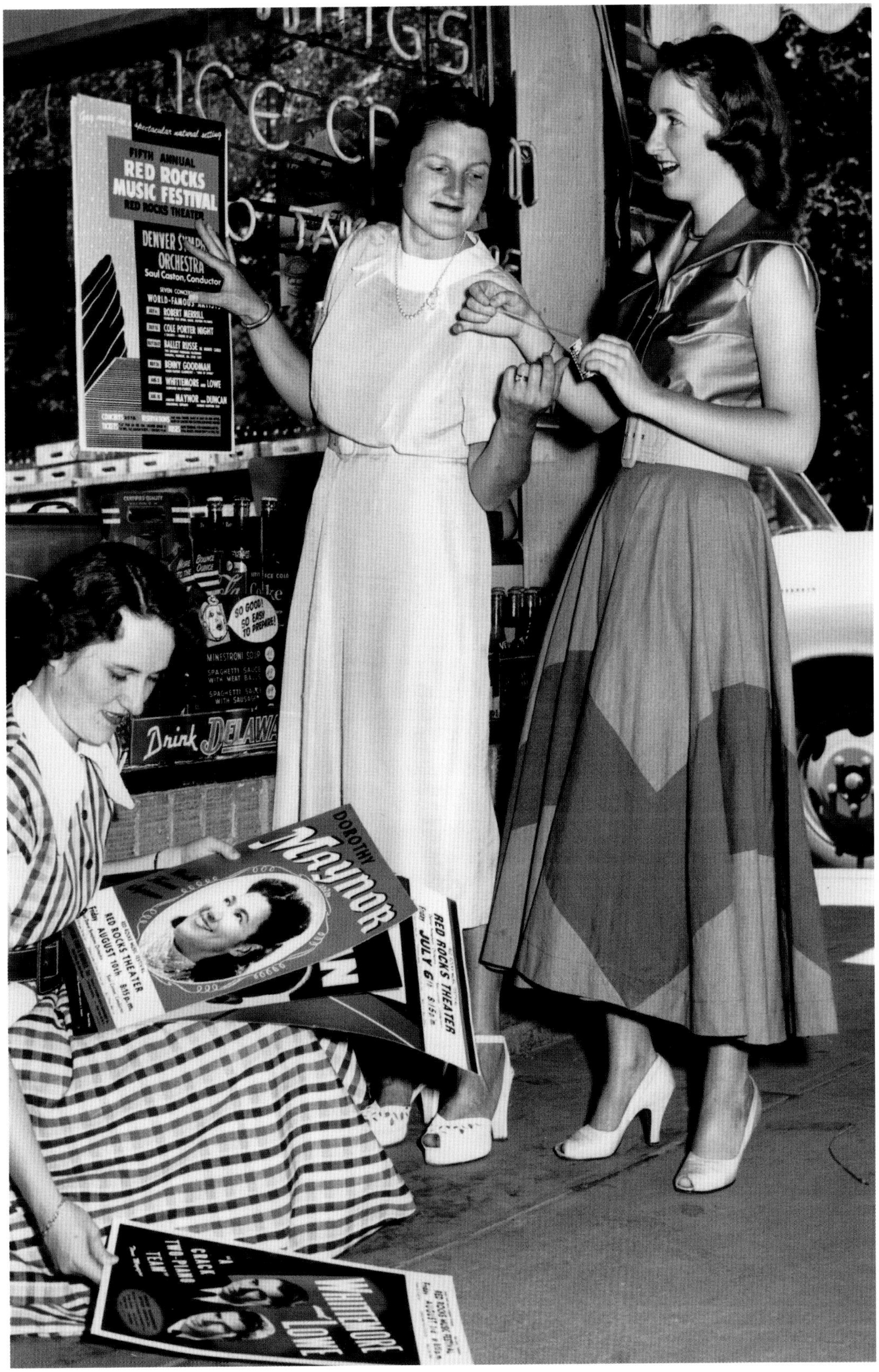
spectacular natural setting
FIFTH ANNUAL
RED ROCKS
MUSIC FESTIVAL
RED ROCKS THEATER
ORCHESTRA
Saul Caston, Conductor
ROBERT MERRILL
COLE PORTER NIGHT
BALLET RUSSE
BENNY GOODMAN
WHITTEMORE LOWE
MAYNOR DUNCAN
SO GOOD! SO EASY TO PREPARE!
MINESTRONI SOUP
Drink
DOROTHY
Maynor
RED ROCKS THEATER
AUGUST 10TH
RED ROCKS THEATER
JULY 6TH
WHITTEMORE LOWE

c. 1951

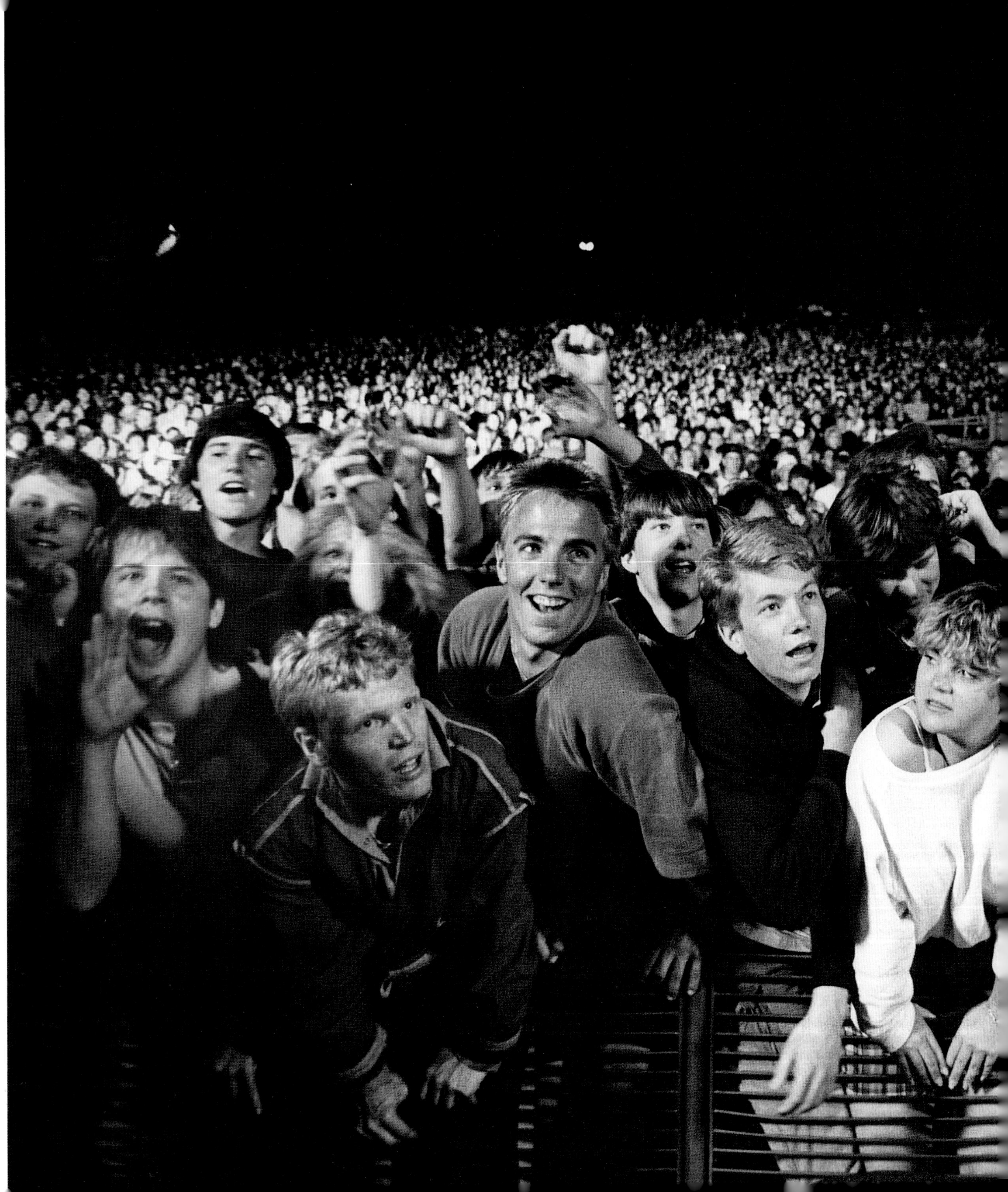

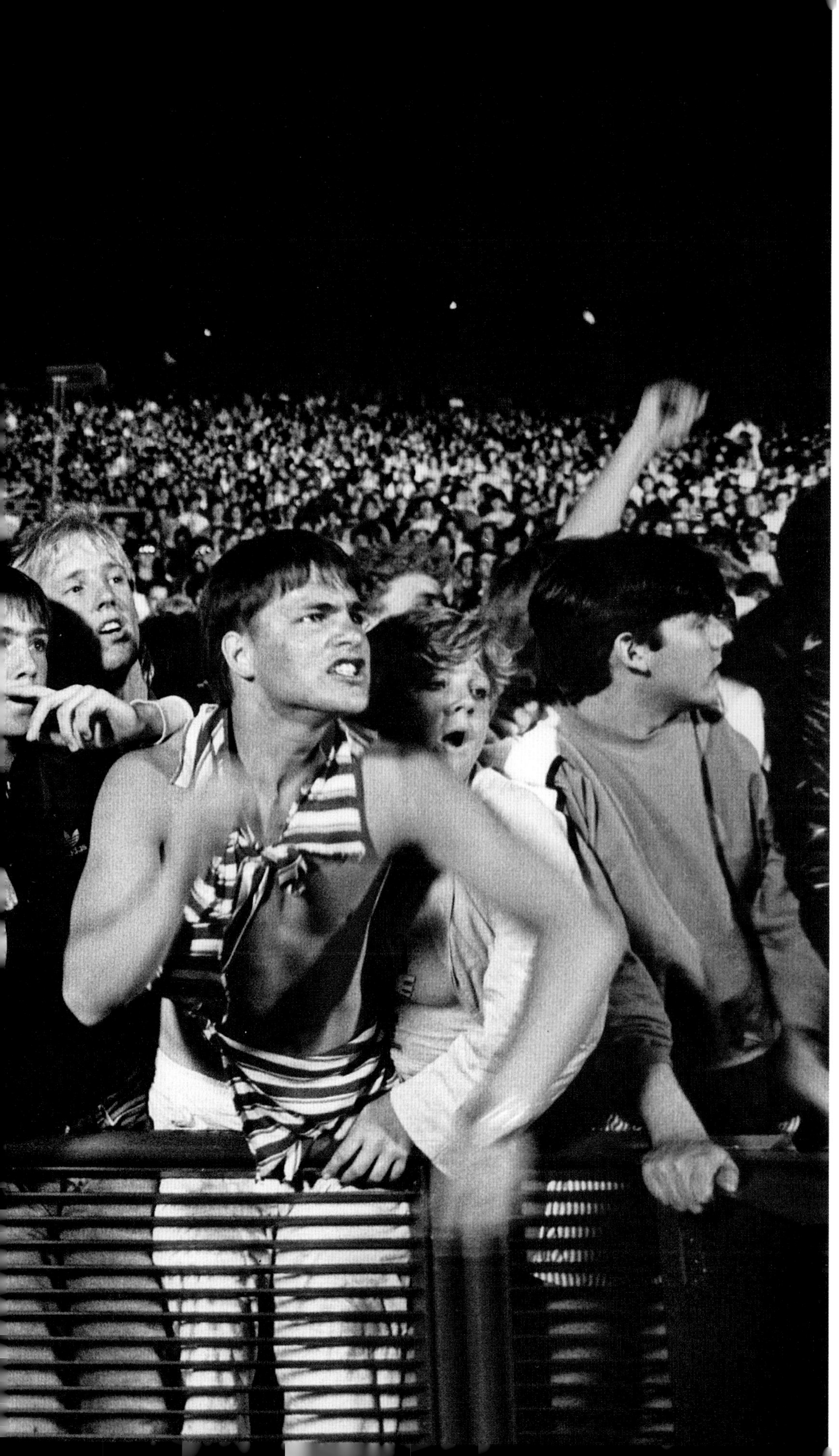

c.1987

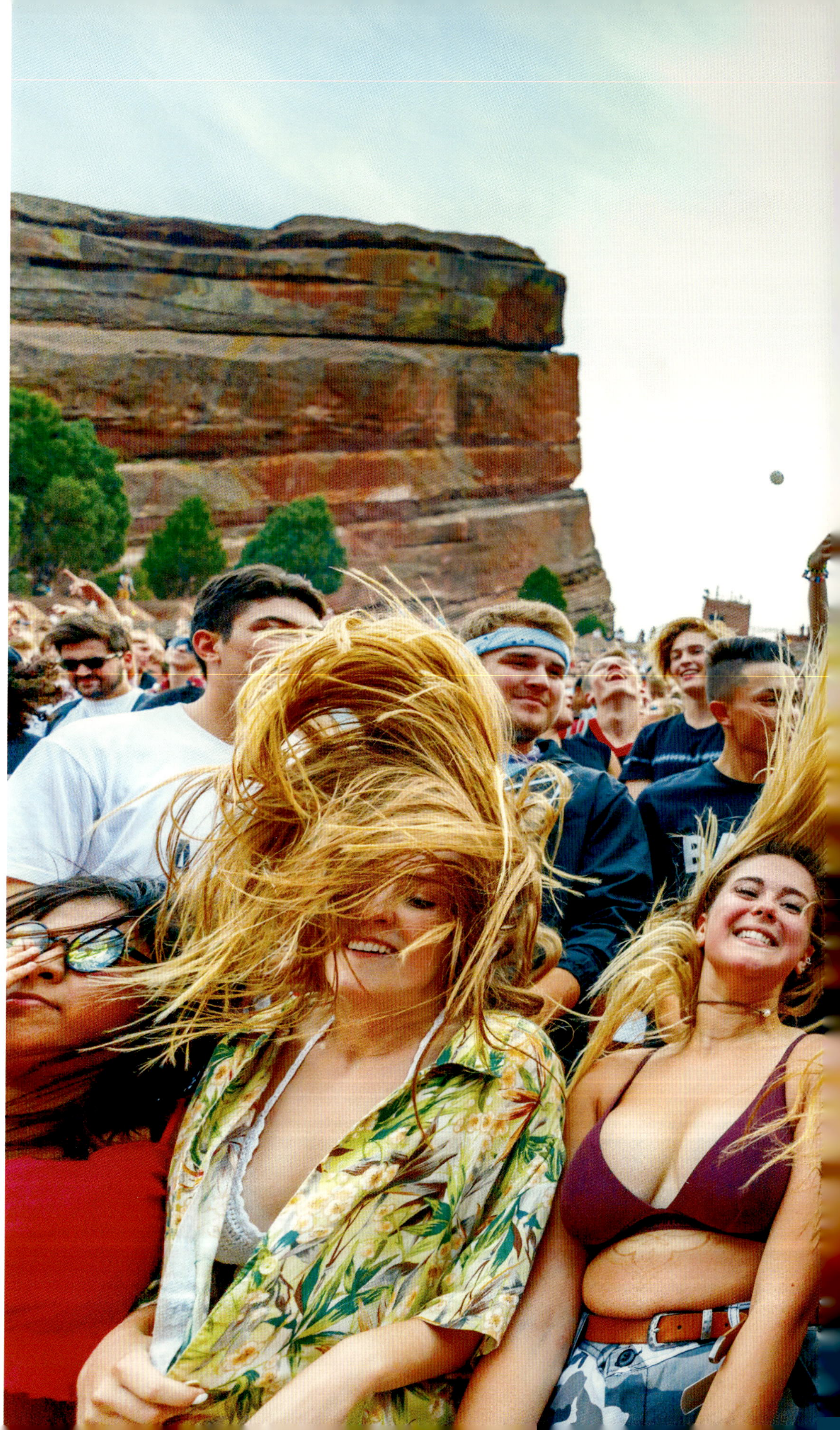

c. 2018

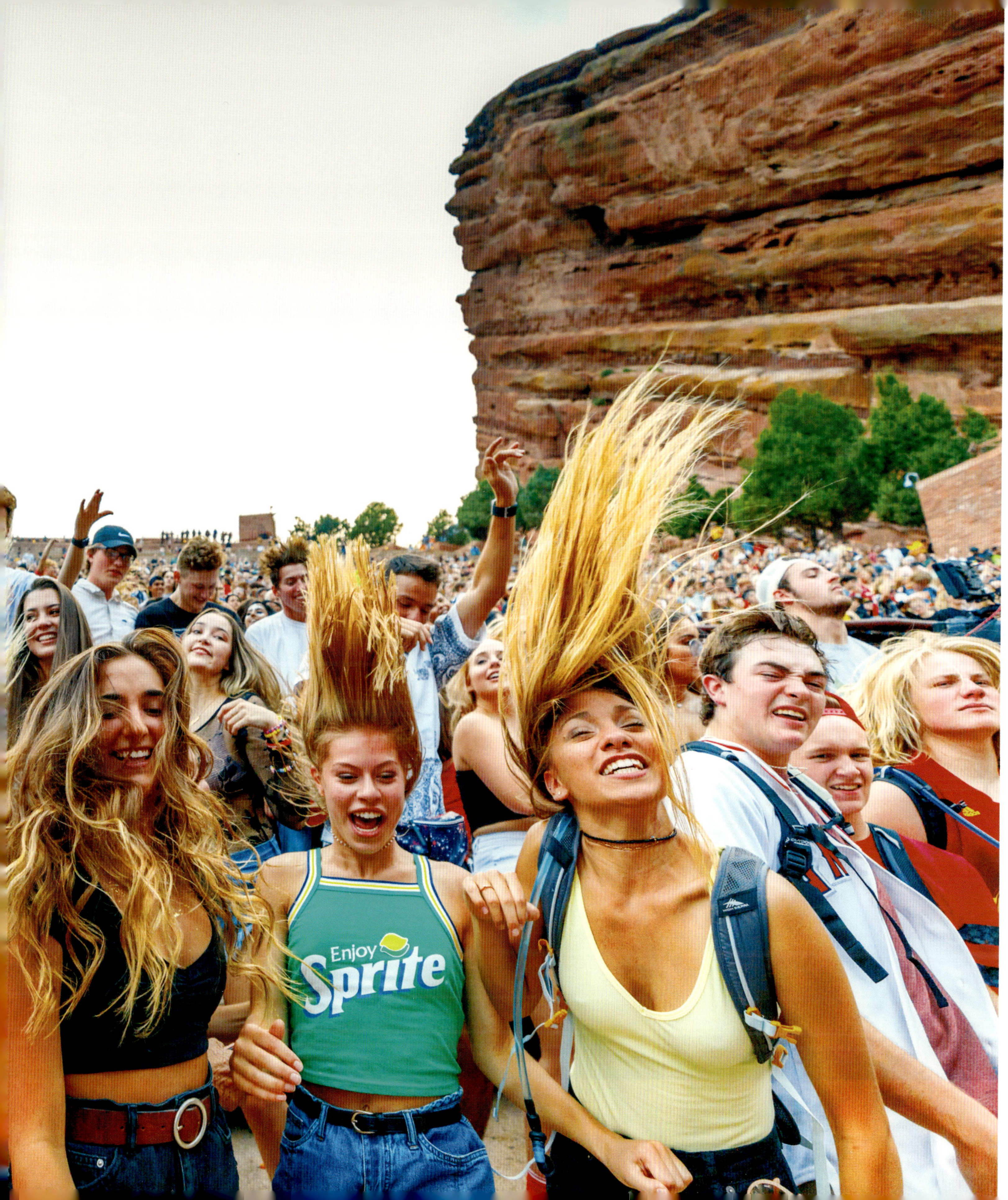
Enjoy
Sprite

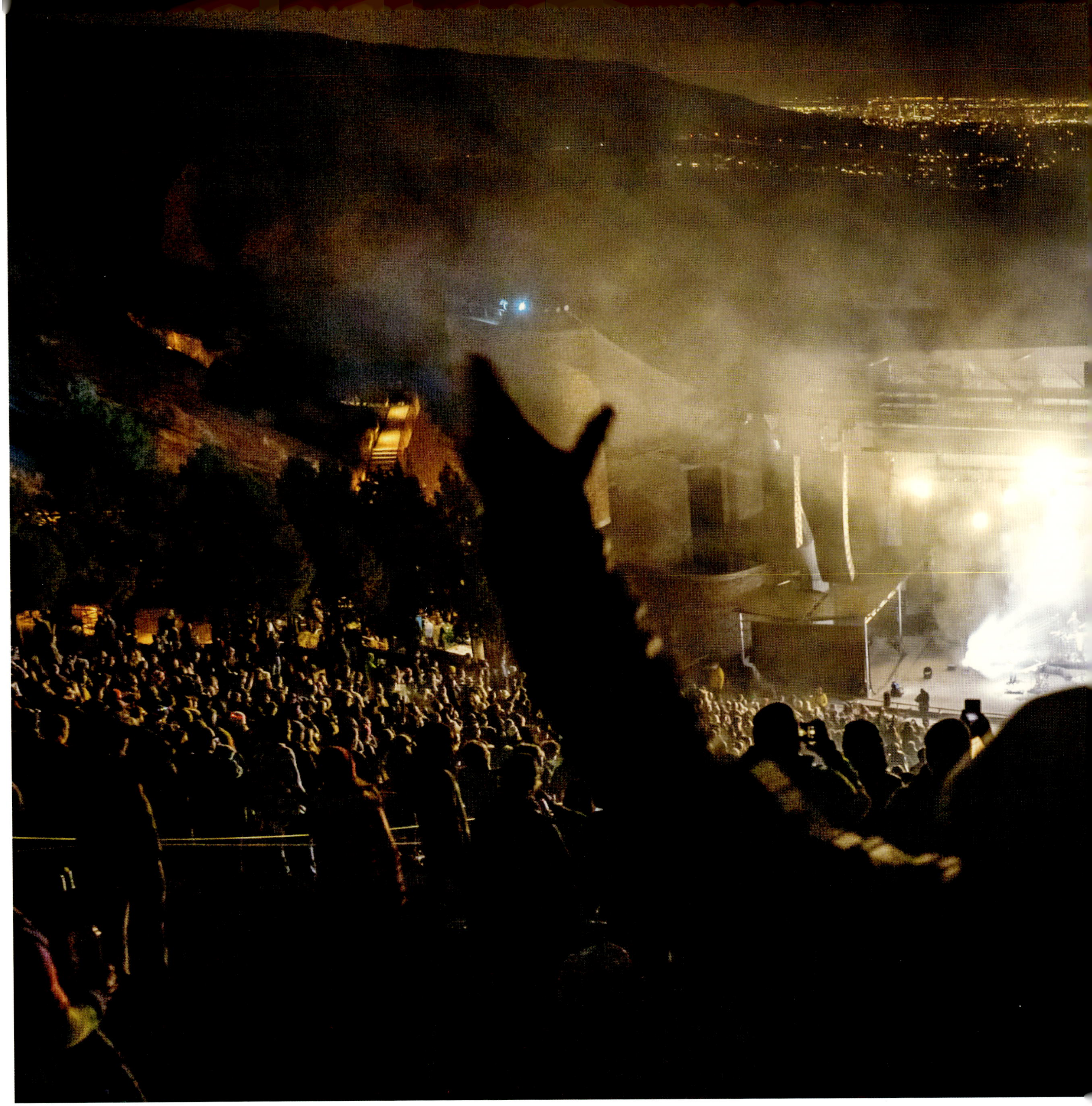

c. 2021

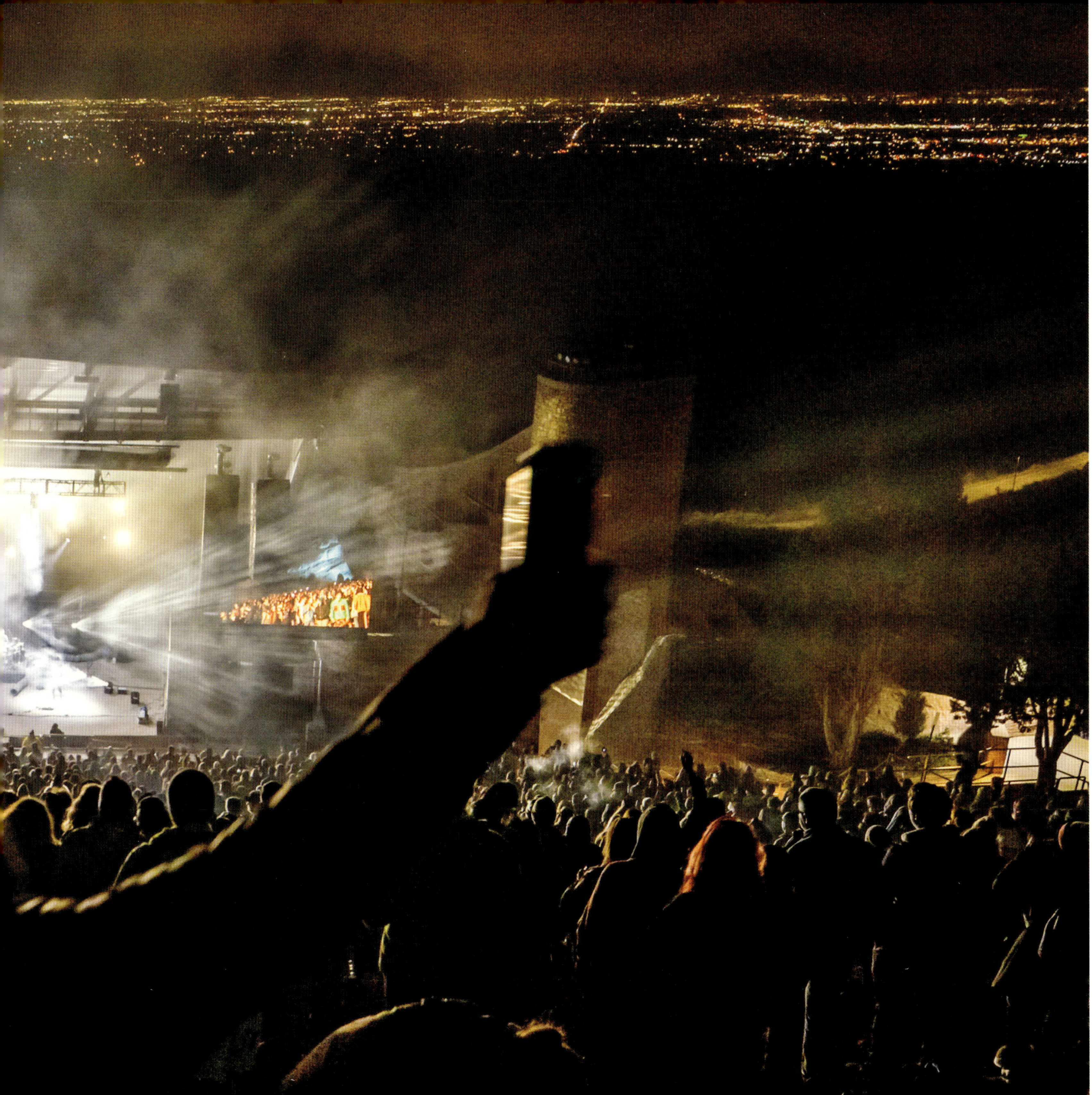

ARCHAEOLOGY

Clockwise from top
U2 VHS tape, 1983; Huey Lewis & the News shirt, 1985; Phish tickets, 1996; Jimi Hendrix/Vanilla Fudge ticket, 1968

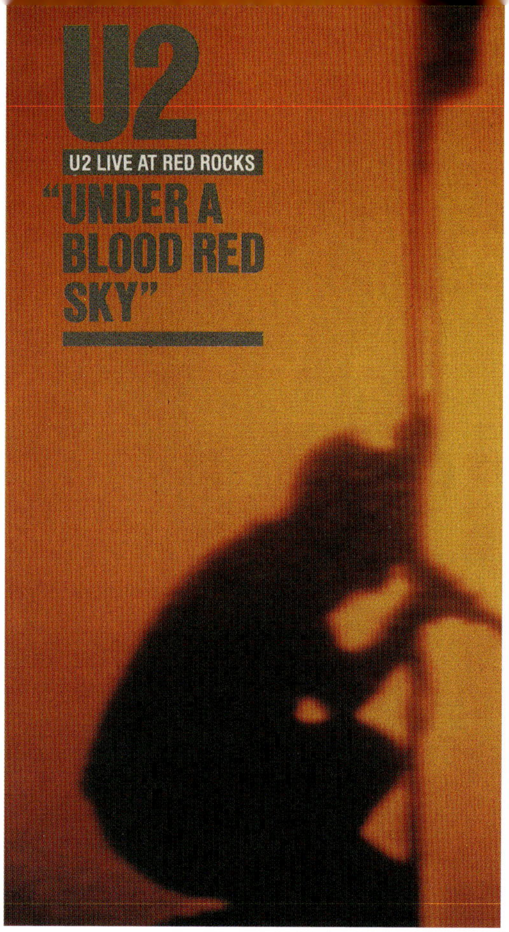

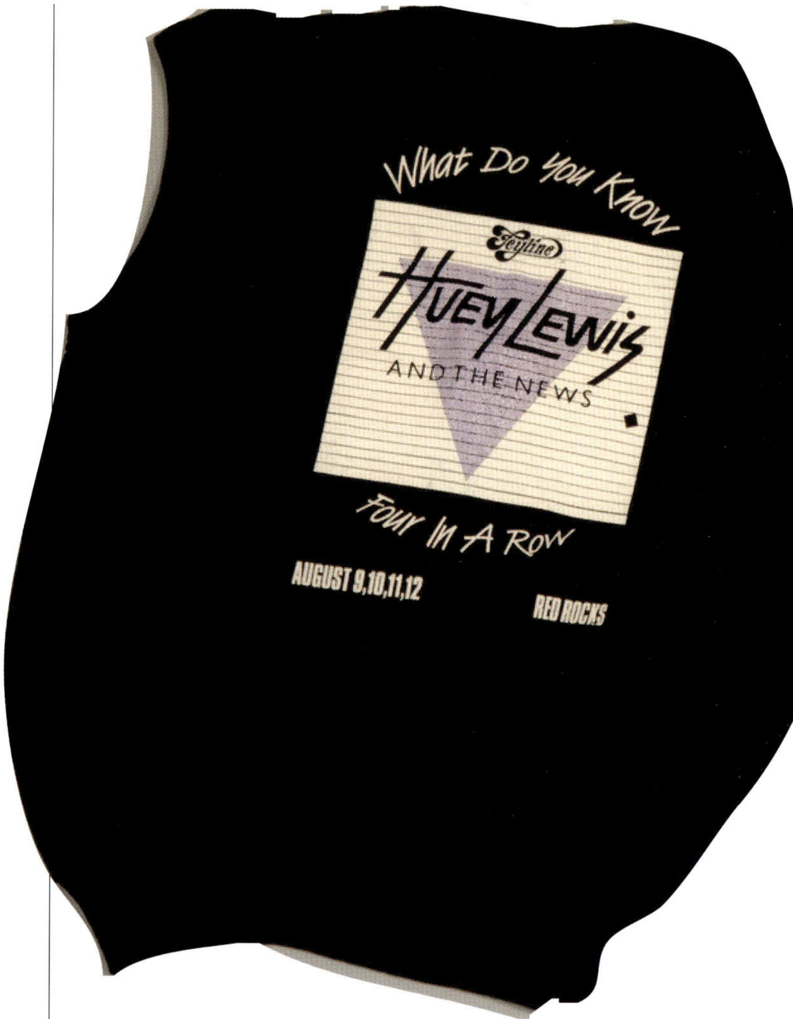

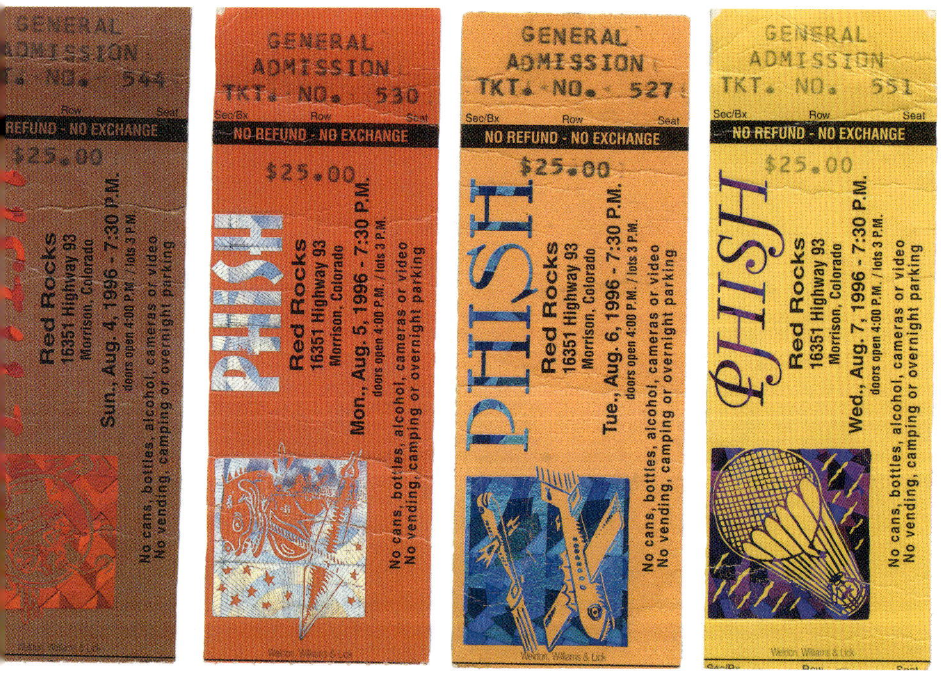

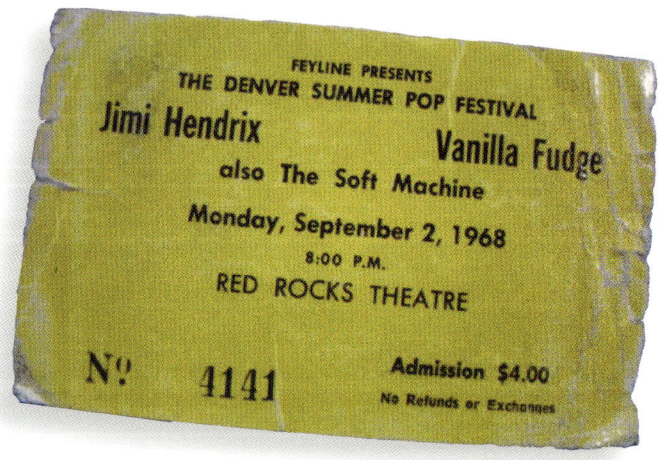

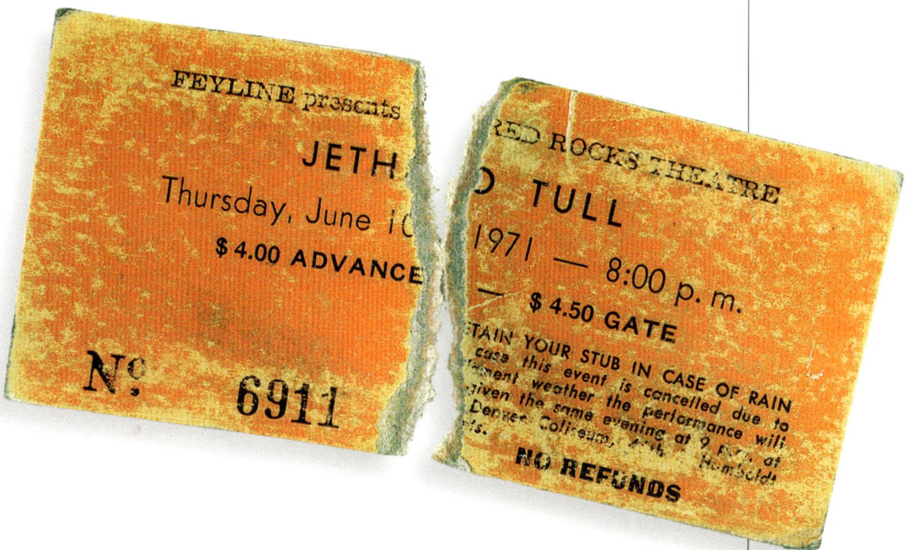

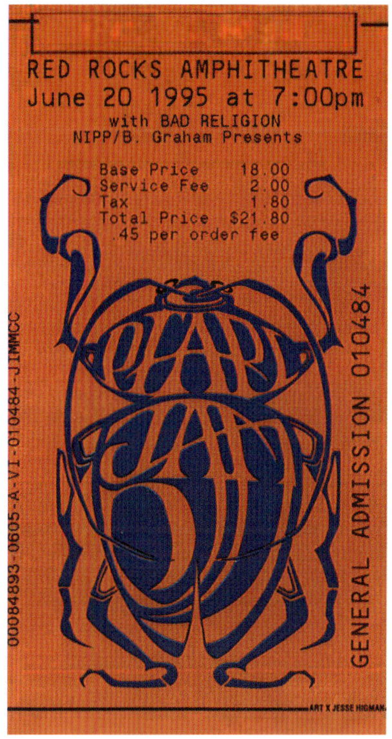

Clockwise from far left

Jethro Tull ticket, 1971; Pearl Jam ticket, 1995; Doobie Brothers t-shirt, 1981; Neil Young DVD, 2000

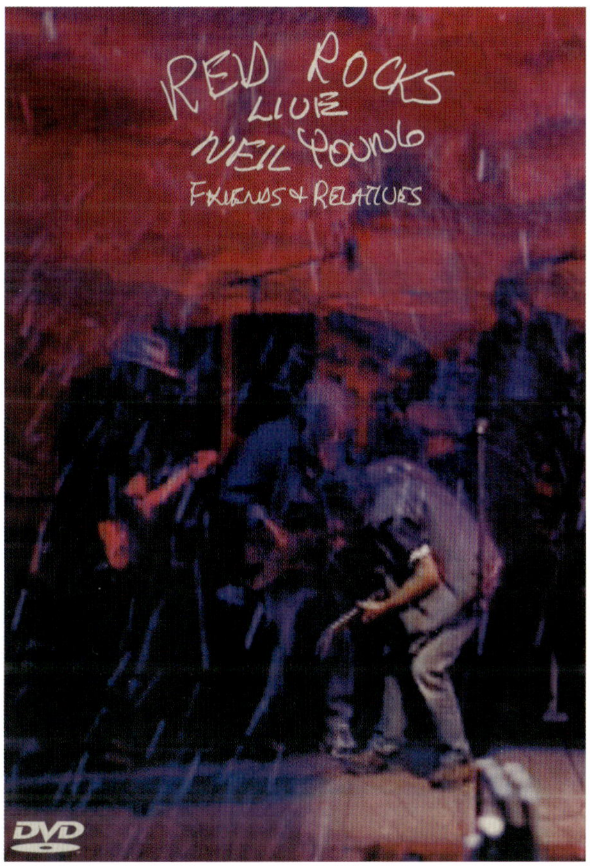

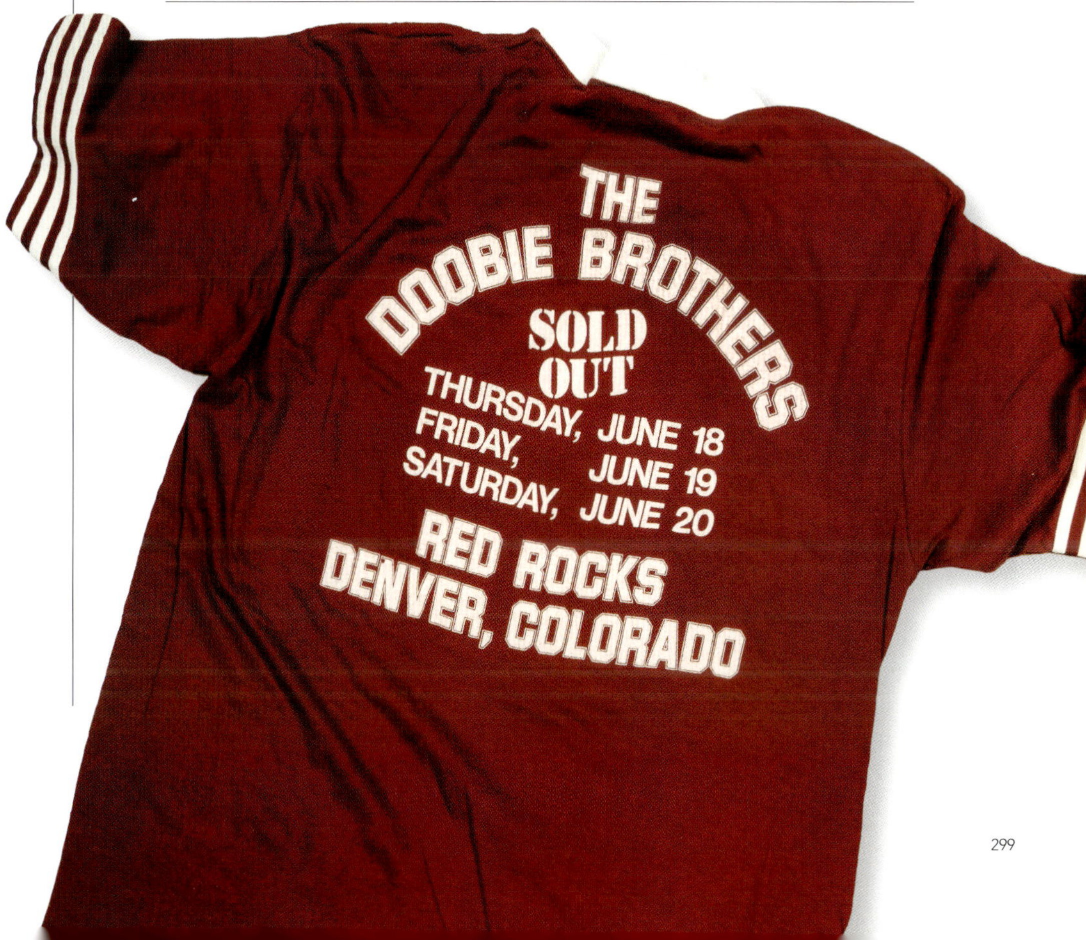

PHOTOGRAPHY INDEX

BIBLIOGRAPHY

BOOKS

Alan, Carter. *U2: The Road to Pop.* Boston: Faber and Faber, Inc. 1992.

Black, Johnny. *Eyewitness Hendrix.* London: Carlton, 1999.

Budnick, Dean. *The Phishing Manual.* New York: Hyperion, 1996.

Eals, Clay. *Steve Goodman: Facing The Music.* Toronto: ECW Press, 2007.

Humphries, Patrick and Hunt, Chris. *Blinded By the Light.* New York: H. Holt, 1986.

Lesh, Phil. *Searching for the Sound.* New York: Little, Brown and Company, 2004.

Martin, George. *All You Need Is Ears.* New York: St. Martin's Press, 1979.

Richmond, Clint. *VH1 Behind The Music: Willie Nelson.* New York: Pocket Books, 2000.

Robins, Wayne. *VH1 Behind The Music: 1968.* New York: Pocket Books, 2000.

MAGAZINES

Allaire, Christian. "Megan Thee Stallion on Getting Back to the Stage, the Success of 'WAP,' and Taking Over TikTok." *Vogue* (September 2020).

Fry, Hap. "Widespread Panic Closes in on 50 Consecutive Sold Out Red Rocks Shows." *Marquee Magazine* (June 1, 2015).

Horst, Blanch. "Red Rocks: An Appreciation." *Higher & Higher* (Winter/Spring 1996).

Humphries, Patrick. "Power To The People." *MOJO Hendrix & The Summer Of Love* (2007).

Joiner, James. "A Rock 'n' Roll Journey to Red Rocks, Colorado." *Esquire* (August 2014).

Jones, Peter. "The Beatles At Red Rocks." *5280 Magazine* (May 2004).

Jornayvaz, Anna. "The Fray Take 2." *Denver Magazine* (November 2008).

NEWSPAPERS

Aguilar, John. *The Denver Post.* "Volume turned up on Red Rocks ruckus as Jeffco enters the fray." April 21, 2014.

Anderson, Allison. *The Denver Post.* "French youths call prelate back for Red Rocks encore." August 12, 1993.

Asmar, Melanie. *Westword.* "Rocks And Roll." May 8-14, 2014.

Baca, Ricardo. *The Denver Post.* "New shows let Panic extend its widespread presence at Red Rocks." June 25, 2010.

Bancroft, Caroline. *The Denver Post.* "To Red Rocks Park by Rail and Burro." August. 9, 1953.

Barrett, Marjorie. *Rocky Mountain News.* "Smothers Brothers Rock Red Rocks." August 25, 1968.

Bernet, Milton. *The Denver Post.* "How Red Rocks came to be." August 4, 1968.

Brown, Mark. *Rocky Mountain News.* "All that matters." July 19, 2005.

Campbell, Jackie. *Rocky Mountain News.* "Elton John rocks Red Rocks." June 14, 1982.

Cardona, Felisa. *The Denver Post.* "Concert a balm for nightmares." September 13, 2005.

Chase, Robert. *Rocky Mountain News.* "Shameful Brawl at Red Rocks." August 24, 1962.

Chester, Britt. *Westword.* "Slug Life." January 26-February 1, 2012.

Clark, Duncan. *Rocky Mountain News.* "Red Rocks Theater Hailed Success By 3,000 After 'Preview Show'." June 9, 1941.

Craig, Betty. *The Denver Post.* "Music In The Mountains." May 24, 1953.

Dittman, Catherine. *Rocky Mountain News.* "Dreams led to Red Rocks Services." April 6, 1982.

Effinger, Cecil. *The Denver Post.* "Red Rocks Concert Premiere Received Warmly By Big Throng." June 28, 1947.

Flynn, Kevin. *Rocky Mountain News.* "Fiddler's Green crimping Red Rocks." July 14, 1988.

Fong, Tillie and Jeter, Alisha. *Rocky Mountain News.* "Rock fans overrun Morrison." August 6, 1966.

Johnson, Vincent. *Rocky Mountain News.* "Red Rocks." May 29, 1938.

Knox, Don. *Rocky Mountain News.* "Clouds over Red Rocks." April 26, 1988.

MacCluskey, Thomas. *Rocky Mountain News.* "Wall-to-Wall Fans at Rock Concert." September 3, 1968.

Marranzino, Pasquale. *Rocky Mountain News.* "Record Traffic Jam at Red Rocks Park." July 9, 1949.

McCoy, Joan. *Rocky Mountain News.* "Supremes at Red Rocks." August 15, 1969.

McGraw, Pat. *The Denver Post.* "Dirt Band friends keep circle unbroken." June 23, 1989.

Melrose, Francis. *Rocky Mountain News.* "Let's Keep Ruffians Out Of Red Rocks." August 26, 1962.

Morrison, Barry. *The Denver Post.* "Beer Can Bombs And The Beatles Just Won't Mix." August 23, 1964.

Murphree, Alex. *The Denver Post.* "Lily Pons Charms Red Rocks Audience." July 4, 1952.

Nakkula, Al. *Rocky Mountain News.* "Beatles Leave Pandemonium In Wake." August 27, 1964.

Nemiro, Guy. *The Denver Post.* "Jethro Tull Pleases Despite Gas at Red Rocks Concert." June 11, 1971.

Nicholson, Kieran. *The Denver Post.* "Gunman fires on vehicle carrying hip hop's Schoolboy Q after Red Rocks show; 3 injured." June 20, 2014.

O'Guin, Becky. *The Denver Post.* "Phish fans confront the police." August 6, 1996.

O'Reilly, Richard and Gerhardt, Gary. *Rocky Mountain News.* "Mayor bans concerts at Red Rocks Amphitheater." June 12, 1971.

Pinney, Greg. *The Denver Post.* "Red Rocks Melee Erupts After Aretha Refuses to Sing." August 5, 1968.

Proctor, Gordon. *Rocky Mountain News.* "Man plunges to death at Red Rocks." August 13, 1979.

Reckler, Joanne. *Rocky Mountain News.* "Joan Baez Thrills Red Rocks Crowd." August 29, 1964.

Reiner, Eric. *The Denver Post.* "An uplifting site." July 30, 1999.

Rogers, Emmy Brady. *Rocky Mountain News.* "Merrill Delights In Red Rocks Final Concert." August 12, 1950.

Rounds, Michael. *Rocky Mountain News.* "7 Hospitalized in Beatles Stampede." August 27, 1964.

Sanders, Mark. *Westword.* "Twenty Fabled moments in Denver Music." May 21, 2012.

Seligson, Paul. *Rocky Mountain News.* "New Role for Music Pleases Kostelanetz." July 13, 1954.

Sinisi, J. Sebastian. *The Denver Post.* "Amphitheater at Red Rocks legacy of CCC." May 5, 1996.

Veatch, Ralph. *Rocky Mountain News.* "Beatles Rock Happy Fans." August 28, 1964.

Zeiger, Dinah. *The Denver Post.* "On-Line Hootie." September 10, 1995.

ACKNOWLEDGMENTS

I cannot express enough thanks to my preeminent publishing team for making this book come to life—Kate Glassner Brainerd for her creativity and patience, and Jon Rizzi for his editorial expertise and advice. Both went beyond the call of duty.

I am deeply beholden to all the photographers whose skill and dedication are reflected in these pages, and I hope that this book does their work justice. This tome would not be possible without research conducted by music historian George Krieger and image preparation by Michael Dickson; I am grateful for their service.

For understanding my long nights at the computer, I bless my wife, Bridget; I also salute family and friends who support and encourage my efforts. Special recognition goes to Eric Pirritt's The Love We Bring Foundation and Mick & Patty Matthews, whose facilitation was essential. The cooperation of the Colorado Music Experience board of directors is also appreciated.

The process of assembling material for a book of this scope requires contributions from many organizations and individuals. Among too many to mention, I must at least recognize Amy Abrams, Gil Asakawa, Ricardo Baca, Larry Baird, Cynthia Bales, Linda Banks, Joe Baran, Chas Barbour, Jock Bartley, Tim Benko, Joel Bernstein, Mark Bliesener, Ron Bostwick, Tad Bowman, Brian Brainerd, Mark Brown, Scramble Campbell, Todd Caudle, John Cerullo, Bill Clarke, Doug Clifton, Kevin Clock, Steve Collector, Paul Conly, Dennis Constantine, Kent Crawford, Chris Daniels, Duane Davis, Joel Davis, David Denny, Nicholas DeSciose, Bob Diddlebock, Sofi Dillof, Mike Drumm, Erik Dyce, Jay Elowsky, Paul Epstein, Brent Fedrizzi, Nate Feld, Bob Ferbrache, Harold Fielden, Kevin Fitzgerald, Rickey Fitzsimmons, Denny Flannigan, Dan Fong, Barbara Forrest, Tony Funches, David Gans, Rich Garcia, Chip Garofalo, Ron Garrison, Michelle Gibson, David Glasser, Deborah Goeken, Michael Goldman, Erika Green, Ed Greene, John Griswold, Garrett Hacking, David Hartley, Butch Hause, Tommy Hauser, John Hayes, Brianna Healy, Richard Hesse, Bruce Hornsby, Larry Hulst, Jeff Humphrey, Michael Jensen, Brandon Johnson, Kathryn Keller, Jerry Kennedy, Steve Knopper, Dick Kreck, Jeff Krump, Gary Lane, David Mackay, Paul Malkoski, Maria Malta, Peter Marcus, Brandon Marshall, Rob Marshall, Jan Martin, Michael Martin, Jim Mason, Nancy May, Soren McCarthy, John McEuen, Bobbi McFarland, Dick Merkle, Steve Mesple, Chris Mickle, Jim Mimna, John Moore, Pam Moore, Ander Murane, Phil Murray, Stan Oliner, Barry Ollman, Scott O'Malley, Bal Patterson, Jim Pagliosotti, Kenny Passarelli, David Plati, Cynthia Procopio-Robitaille, Nancy Rebek, Buzz Reifman, Kent Rice, Scott Roche, Dave Rothstein, Tim Rozner, Leland Rucker, Matt Rue, Jay Ruybal, Jim Salestrom, Mark Samansky, Bret Saunders, Dan Schaarschmidt, Brian Schwartz, Ted Scott, Tom Shahnazarian, Larry Shirkey, Lisa Siciliano, Norm Simmer, Scott Smith, Jennifer Soulé, Tony Spicola, Jeremy Stein, Doug Stewart, Don Strasberg, Anthony Suau, Rod Tanaka, Carol Taylor, Chris Tetzeli, Andy Torri, Brian Trembath, Thom Trunnell, Harry Tuft, Bruce Van Dyke, Kevin Votel, Taylor Wallace, Mark Walsh, Bill Warren, Bill Wedum, Michael Weintrob, LeDia Wesley-Espinoza, Greg Wigler, Tina Wilcox, Sara Williams, Paul Witkovich, Mark Wolf, Mike Wolf, Marty Wolff, Don Woodard, Rick Wurpel, Mark Zaremba and Dave Zobl. —**G. BROWN**

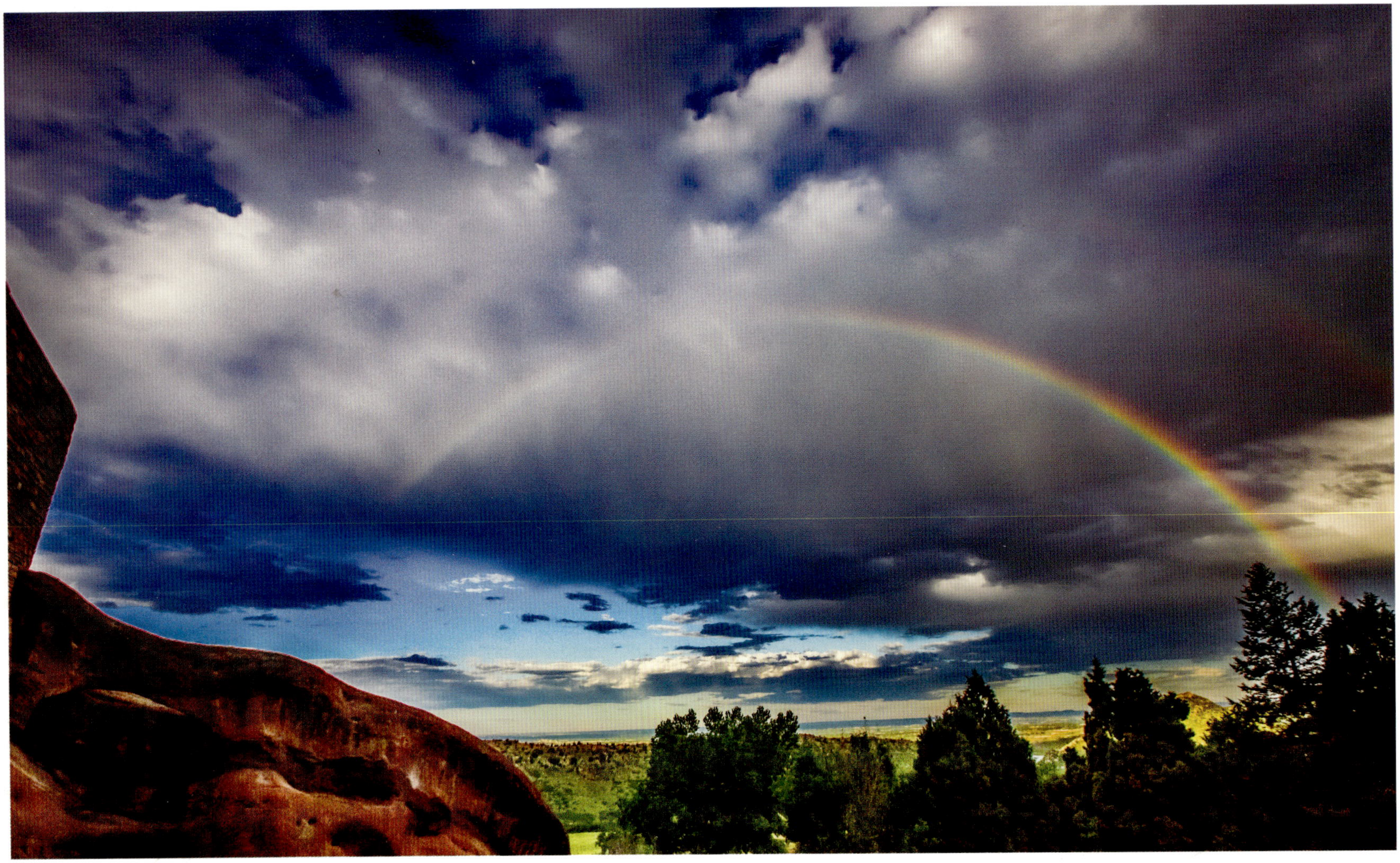